ORGANIZATIONS AND HUMAN BEHAVIOR:
Focus on Schools

ORGANIZATIONS AND HUMAN BEHAVIOR:

Focus on Schools

Edited by

FRED D. CARVER
University of Illinois

THOMAS J. SERGIOVANNI
University of Illinois

McGRAW-HILL BOOK COMPANY

New York   St. Louis   San Francisco   London   Sydney
Toronto   Mexico   Panama

ORGANIZATIONS AND HUMAN BEHAVIOR:
Focus on Schools

Library of Congress Catalog Card Number 69-13215

1 2 3 4 5 6 7 8 9 0   MAMM   7 6 5 4 3 2 1 0 6 9

FOREWORD

The decade around 1950 was a fateful period for educational administration. In this period the profession of educational administration was taking shape. The AASA Committee on the Advancement of School Administration, the Kellogg Foundation–funded Cooperative Project in Educational Administration, the National Conference of Professors of Educational Administration (NCPEA), the University Council for Educational Administration (UCEA), and the Cooperative Research Program of the U.S. Office of Education had their beginnings. School administration felt the impact of widespread school-district reorganization; development and addition of new programs and services; the shifting demography to high urbanization with the concomitant dysfunctional segmentation; high technological development, with its impact on the general society as well as specifically upon the educational world; the mechanization of information presentation and tutorial drill; the confrontation of conflicting interests and values, evidenced by the thrust of racial minorities, the relationship between church and state, the militancy of teachers, and the defiance and alienation of young Americans.

The expertise of a historian, cultural anthropologist, sociologist, or psychologist is needed to treat adequately the counterpart development within the field of educational administration. There was deep concern for the role, responsibility, and value orientation of educational administration. Individuals associated with this field were dismayed by the inadequacy of theory, research, and hard knowledge. They grappled with reorganization of professional preparation programs and the selection of personnel, with interdisciplinary approaches to amalgamate quickly the useful theory and hard knowledge, and with promotion of research beyond the massive slave labor of degree candidates.

Early efforts in restructuring the literature represented hurried attempts at setting up conceptual schema and/or the borrowing-begging-stealing of seemingly pertinent material from other fields. Writers of the textbooks on educational administration either stood pat on tradition (because such books had always sold and would continue to do so); or they modernized by drawing in at every point possible a reference or footnote, if not actual ideas and formulations, from as many related disciplines as they could; or they attempted to be faithful to some particular borrowed approach in their treatment of educational administration. Because adequate courses with this approach had not been developed, most of them tried producing a book for administration courses generally—and thereby failed to serve well any existing or prospective course. One of the current books draws widely and usefully on the behavioral sciences; another abides faithfully by one new approach in surveying and discussing the field of educational administration. Both give evidence of the strain of trying to force the wedding between the borrowed or adapted material and the substance of educational administration.

Organizations and Human Behavior: Focus on Schools avoids these problems. It is directed primarily to advanced graduate seminars in leadership and administrative theory; it presents the basis for initial understanding of one approach and opens the doors to consideration of other related material. It does not purport to grab a little of everything from all the related fields so as to look thoroughly interdisciplinary regardless of the interrelationship of each separate item. Nor does it force the fit of a particular approach upon the treatment of educational administration. The editors have chosen to approach it by moving toward an understanding of organizations and the behavior of people in their organizational interrelationships as a basis from which to consider the field of educational administration and to utilize the relevant content from other pertinent disciplines. Either they might have tried to bring in something from each of the variety of related fields or they might have chosen some related field organizational theory as their base of operations. (They could have selected from such options as administrative personality and behavior, decision making and execution—including bargaining, communications systems, conflict resolution and/or tolerance, the nature and distribution of power, the stimulation and management of innovative change.)

The procedure which the editors chose calls to mind the main lecture of the first teachers' convention ever attended by this writer when he started teaching in 1929. It was entitled "The City Four-Square" and was presented by the curator of the Cleveland Museum. The basic idea was that there were three gates in each of the four walls for which the way was straight and the gate was narrow. The speaker had a logic in assigning the established disciplines to each of these gates and was able to show how, having come through the particular field of study to arrive inside the city of the acculturated, one was able to talk freely and to draw upon the special competence and wisdom of almost all others regardless of the particular gate through which they had entered. It does seem to make more sense to stay with a particular approach until one has arrived and not to try to force the approach on the field of application before one has some functional grasp of it.

In terms of the kinds of literature and the backlog of both study and application which can be marshaled, as well as in terms of the extrapolations providing organization for pertinent materials from other related disciplines, the choice of organizational theory is a wise one. The editors have provided a sufficient array of both classical and current materials with differences in viewpoint so that the reader may develop his own understanding of organizational theory, its usefulness as a base of operation in educational administration, and the value of its structure in helping him assess and appropriate and assimilate materials from other fields. They start with description of the nature and makeup of organizations, move to consideration of theories of organization especially as related to educational administration, incorporate next the interplay between people and organizations, and finally provide leads into the usefulness of a number of related fields as they bear on the specific elements of organizational behavior.

This approach is to be seen as a significant developmental step for the field as well as for the editors. It does provide a very teachable array of materials, whether to the reflective scholar or practitioner who will be self-taught or for use by a professor with a seminar or a study-group leader with a discussion group.

One thinks of the "founding fathers" of the modern regime in educational administration as being those active in studying and writing about the subject around 1950. The first fruits of their modified programs represented a generation which plundered every possible related discipline for treasure to be carted into the field of educational administration, to the high satisfaction and pride of the founding fathers. The first generation also lived up to being the pride and joy of the founding fathers through efforts at inventing schema and models useful for research. Carver and Sergiovanni represent the generation of beloved grandsons of the founding fathers, who have profited from the fruits of the first-generation raids upon other fields for concepts and research design.

Don Carver did his work at Wisconsin, where a strong influence was that of first-generation James Lipham, a product of the Midwest Administration Center at the University of Chicago and of Roald Campbell and associates. At Wisconsin, Carver also came under the influence of Russell Gregg, who, as a strong and active figure in the beginnings of NCPEA and UCEA, was coeditor with Roald Campbell of that bench mark of early materials—*Administrative Behavior in Education*.

Tom Sergiovanni studied in a brand-new program at the University of Rochester, where he profited from the first-generation Robert Howsam, who worked under Ted Reller at the University of California, and first-generation Glen Immegart, who worked under John Ramseyer at Ohio State and also had the stir of interaction as a central staff member of UCEA with Jack Culbertson and others.

It is indeed a pleasure to have been asked to make these prefatory comments and I express my high regard for the editors and their work and my expectation of more to come.

Van Miller,

Professor of Educational
Administration and Supervision,
University of Illinois

PREFACE

Theories of educational administration, to some as amusing as Charlie Brown's flights of philosophy, to others as scholarly as any of the social sciences, comprise an emerging discipline. Moving from prescriptive assertions of "correct" principles of administration, theoreticians began to identify tasks of the school administrator and afterward to place these tasks in their proper social and political context. While this approach offers increasingly sophisticated conceptual lenses with which to observe and analyze the practices of educational administration, it has, we believe, one major limitation. It has not sufficiently considered the organizational context of the school. For while the administrator acts upon and changes the institution, he in turn is acted upon by the internal dynamics of the social organism, the school organization.

Others, to be sure, have perceptively commented on the changing socio-economic milieu, the changing technological milieu, indeed, the changing cultural milieu. On a less macrocosmic level, however, mediating between the larger societal context and the individual administrator, teacher, and student, the school as an organization operates according to its own dynamic. Although affected by shifts in the larger societal setting, the organization can either heighten or diffuse these various pressures from without as it struggles, in somewhat the same way as a living organism, to adapt itself to the changing environment.

Research to date has revealed that human behavior, as a result of organizational life, manifests remarkable similarities as one moves from hospital, to school, to retail store, to welfare agency, and to military unit. Teachers and nurses, for example, react similarly to dysfunctional effects of status hierarchies within their respective organizations. Accountants, middle managers in business and industry, and teachers report remarkably similar orientations to satisfying and dissatisfying factors in their work. Military officers, medical chiefs of staff, hotel managers, police commissioners, school superintendents, and vice-presidents have similar problems and concerns with respect to subordinates who possess more—and often exclusive—technical and professional ability than they. Conflict between line and staff officers occurs in schools in the same manner and probably with same regularity as it does in military, business, and industrial organizations. Thus, while the school administrator is particularly concerned with one kind of formal organization, his vision may very well be improved by studying organizations in general.

The general purpose of this book, then, is to provide the student of educational administration with a series of essays on organizational life, essays not available up to the present under one cover. These readings should complement the more traditional points of view of educational administration. Through exposure to and critical analysis of the montage of concepts presented in these essays, it is hoped that the student of educational administration will be more adequately equipped to think about and come to grips with problems and issues in his field.

For clarity and impact, the essays in this book are organized into four sections. Part 1 is concerned with characteristics of complex organizations, often to the virtual exclusion of individuals. In this section, the organization is treated as a living organism having a composite of characteristics, much as individuals have a variety of personality traits. The emphasis is on those functional and dysfunctional components of organizations which affect the achievement of organizational goals, for organizations, like individuals, need to identify and pursue goals, react to stress, seek homeostasis, adapt, maintain themselves internally, ensure survival, and grow in size, power, and influence if they are to be effective.

Some organizations change haphazardly, by what is described as organizational drift. That is, organizations evolve, adjust, and readjust seemingly unaffected by conscious efforts of their inhabitants. The antithesis of the drift phenomenon is planned change. Here, organizational change takes place as a result of conscious, rational efforts by those individuals who control the organization. Understanding both kinds of organizational change, their characteristics and their interrelationships, should enable a person to combat the harmful side effects of organizational structures and processes.

Part 2 of the book includes some of the better-known theories of administration, prefaced by a statement on the practical art of using theories. None of the theories developed to date possesses the required comprehensiveness to be considered *the* theory of administration, but taken together they offer complementary and thought-provoking tools for administrative analysis and judgment. These administrative theories, however, do not provide prescriptive ingredients for action. Rather, they are attempts to systematize concepts, insights, and propositions into a usable form for increasing understanding of administrative problems and for expanding existing knowledge and thought about behavioral phenomena. Though theory emphasizes analysis and understanding, it is assumed that increased understanding of a problem leads to more effective strategies for identifying and executing acceptable solutions.

Part 3 focuses on the individual as he functions in the organizational milieu. Teachers as professionally oriented members of the organization receive major billing in this section. The essays deal with the problem of providing teachers with an organizational environment which is personally enriching and satisfying and, at the same time, productive for the organization. This section turns its attention to such questions as (1) What do teachers want and need from their job? (2) What keeps them from getting that which they want and need? (3) Are teachers' wants and needs inconsistent with the goals of the organization (the school)? (4) Can existing organizational structures and patterns within the schools provide the necessary level of attainment for teachers' wants and needs? (5) Will schools need to be drastically restructured and repatterned as organizations to accommodate teachers? (6) Will such restructuring result in increased school effectiveness as the school moves toward the achievement of its goal? Although the selections do not deal with each of the questions systematically, they do provide the reader with a view of the organization from the perspective of its inhabitants.

In Part 4, selected aspects of the administrative process, labeled, in the poetic parlance of the sociologist, "the interaction-influence system," are isolated for analysis. (See Figure 1.) Many of these concerns are mentioned in the first three sections as well. Although Part 4 concentrates on administrative action, the emphasis is again on understanding and seeking alternatives rather than on listing rules, regulations, prescriptions, and other instant drugstore remedies for administrative success. Since a book must have some limitations in terms of scope and size, not all areas which might comprise the interaction-influence system are included. Those thought to be at the center of administrative behavior were selected for treatment, such as decision making, leadership style, group processes, and coordination.

Since any healthy organization adapts to changes in the environment and seeks continually to upgrade its performance, administrators must attempt to direct and coordinate the various organizational components and processes toward increasingly effective achievement of organizational goals. The school administrator, then, makes important and difficult decisions, coordinates communications and the flow of activities, and enters into the dynamics of group processes. Further, since the school administrator's world involves people

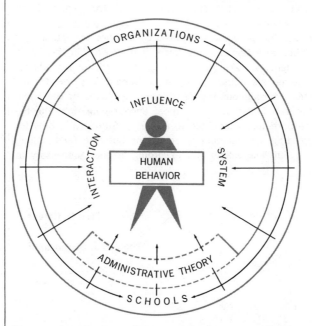

Figure 1. Organizations and human behavior: focus on schools.

primarily, his system of values will guide his behavior. Thus the final selection of Part 4, an essay written especially for this book, relates school administration to humanistic concerns.

Some of the authors may be relatively new to students of educational administration. Among these are Charles Lindblom, Eugen Pusic, Thomas Schelling, and Ralph Smith. The science of educational administration stands to gain, in our view, by attending to the insights of men outside the educational field who have studied the more general aspects of organizational life from the perspectives of political science, business management, sociology, and the humanities. Notable exclusions from this book of readings are Max Weber, Talcott Parsons, and C. E. Bidwell. Many of their ideas, however, are discussed and summarized by authors we have included. We feel that this collection strikes a happy balance between classical authors and more recent contributors to the field.

Although all the selections focus on the general theme, they do not all represent a particular point of view, but rather, intentionally, present a variety of views which are at times opposing. Note the views of Argyris and Sergiovanni in contrast to those expressed by Strauss. Our intent was not to structure a way of thinking about administration, but rather to suggest and stimulate a variety of ways. It is hoped that each article in the book will provoke a sufficient amount of interest for readers so that they will be stimulated to examine and test their own assumptions as well as those of the authors.

The selections in each of the four parts are listed in order of appearance in the Contents. Each also appears a second time under the Topical Contents. This lists the administrative-process concerns which constitute Part 4, and keys into the various subsections of Part 4 appropriate essays from each of the other three sections of the book.

We sincerely appreciate the permission granted by authors and publishers of all previously published selections for inclusion of their work in this book. This book is, after all, theirs. We are grateful to Ralph Smith for his original contribution to this volume. We would like to thank Donald O. Crowe for his suggestions and reactions throughout the developmental stages of the book. Special thanks are due Van Miller, who was most encouraging from the beginning. Finally, we are particularly indebted to Robert J. Starratt not only for his assistance in suggesting and reacting to selections but also for handling many of the important, but less visible and rewarding, aspects necessary to prepare such a book.

Fred D. Carver

Thomas J. Sergiovanni

CONTENTS

Foreword *v*

Preface *ix*

Topical Contents *xvii*

Contributors *xix*

PART ONE
Organizations: Their Nature, Components, and Characteristics

1. The Nature and Types of Formal Organizations
   Peter M. Blau and W. Richard Scott 5

2. Hierarchy, Specialization, and Organizational Conflict
   Victor A. Thompson 19

3. Hierarchical Impediments to Innovation in Educational Organizations
   Max G. Abbott 42

4. Functions and Pathology of Status Systems in Formal Organizations
   Chester I. Barnard 51

5. Dysfunctions in Organizations
   James G. March and Herbert A. Simon 63

6. Formality versus Flexibility in Complex Organizations
   Gerald D. Bell 71

7. Models of Bureaucracy Which Permit Conflict
   Eugene Litwak 82

8. An Axiomatic Theory of Organizations
   Jerald Hage 91

9. Modern Organizational Theory: A Psychological and Sociological Study
   D. S. Pugh 111

PART TWO
Theory in Administration

10. The Practical Art of Using Theory
    Van Miller   133

11. Administration as Decision-making
    Daniel E. Griffiths   138

12. The Human Side of Enterprise
    Douglas McGregor   150

13. Individual Behavior and Group Achievement
    Ralph M. Stogdill   157

14. An Assessment of Two Theoretical Frameworks
    Robert Sweitzer   167

PART THREE
Individuals in Organizations

15. Individual Actualization in Complex Organizations
    Chris Argyris   189

16. The Emergent Role of the Teacher in the
    Authority Structure of the School
    Norman J. Boyan   200

17. Professional Persons in Public Organizations
    Ronald G. Corwin   212

18. Using Professional Talent in a School Organization
    D. A. MacKay   228

19. Relation of Bureaucratization to Sense of Power among Teachers
    Gerald H. Moeller and W. W. Charters   235

20. Factors Which Affect Satisfaction and Dissatisfaction of Teachers
    Thomas J. Sergiovanni   249

21. Some Notes on Power-equalization
    George Strauss   261

22. The Political Community and the Future of Welfare
    (Social Self-management)
    Eugen Pusic   270

PART FOUR
The Interaction—Influence System

23. How Leaders Behave
    Andrew W. Halpin   287

24. Dynamics of Leadership
    Jack R. Gibb   316

25. The Science of Muddling Through
        Charles E. Lindblom   325

26. An Essay on Bargaining
        Thomas C. Schelling   337

27. The Nature of Highly Effective Groups
        Rensis Likert   356

28. Administrative Theory and Change in Organizations
        Daniel E. Griffiths   368

29. Planned Change and Organizational Health:
        Figure and Ground
        Matthew B. Miles   375

30. The Innovative Organization
        Victor A. Thompson   392

31. Human Values, Modern Organizations, and Education
        Ralph A. Smith   404

TOPICAL CONTENTS

LEADERSHIP

23   How Leaders Behave
      Andrew W. Halpin   287

24   Dynamics of Leadership
      Jack R. Gibb   316

12   The Human Side of Enterprise
      Douglas McGregor   150

15   Individual Actualization in Complex Organizations
      Chris Argyris   189

22   The Political Community and the Future of Welfare
(Social Self-management)
      Eugen Pusic   270

DECISION MAKING

25   The Science of Muddling Through
      Charles E. Lindblom   325

26   An Essay on Bargaining
      Thomas C. Schelling   337

2   Hierarchy, Specialization, and Organizational
Conflict
      Victor A. Thompson   19

5   Dysfunctions in Organizations
      James G. March and Herbert A. Simon   63

11   Administration as Decision-making
      Daniel E. Griffiths   138

16   The Emergent Role of the Teacher in the
Authority Structure of the School
      Norman J. Boyan   200

GROUP PROCESSES

27   The Nature of Highly Effective Groups
      Rensis Likert   356

13   Individual Behavior and Group Achievement
      Ralph M. Stogdill   157

14 An Assessment of Two Theoretical Frameworks
Robert Sweitzer 167

17 Professional Persons in Public Organizations
Ronald G. Corwin 212

CHANGE AND INNOVATION

28 Administrative Theory and Change in Organizations
Daniel E. Griffiths 368

29 Planned Change and Organizational Health:
Figure and Ground
Matthew B. Miles 375

30 The Innovative Organization
Victor A. Thompson 392

3 Hierarchical Impediments to Innovation in
Educational Organizations
Max G. Abbott 42

8 An Axiomatic Theory of Organizations
Jerald Hage 91

HUMANITIES AND ADMINISTRATION

31 Human Values, Modern Organizations, and Education
Ralph A. Smith 404

12 The Human Side of Enterprise
Douglas McGregor 150

15 Individual Actualization in Complex Organizations
Chris Argyris 189

21 Some Notes on Power-equalization
George Strauss 261

CONTRIBUTORS

MAX G. ABBOTT
Professor and Director
Center for the Advanced Study of
Educational Administration
University of Oregon

CHRIS ARGYRIS
Professor of Industrial Administration
Yale University

CHESTER I. BARNARD
Late President of New Jersey Bell
Telephone

GERALD D. BELL
Assistant Professor of Business
Administration
Institute for Research in Social Science
University of North Carolina

PETER M. BLAU
Professor of Sociology
University of Chicago

NORMAN J. BOYAN
Acting Associate Commissioner of Research
U.S. Office of Education

W. W. CHARTERS
Professor of Educational Administration
Center for the Advanced Study of
Educational Administration
University of Oregon

RONALD G. CORWIN
Associate Professor of Sociology
Ohio State University

JACK R. GIBB
Western Behavioral Science Institute
La Jolla, California

DANIEL E. GRIFFITHS
Dean, College of Education
New York University

JERALD HAGE
Assistant Professor of Sociology
University of Wisconsin

ANDREW W. HALPIN
Research Professor of Education
University of Georgia

RENSIS LIKERT
Director, Institute for Social Research
Professor of Psychology and Sociology
University of Michigan

CHARLES E. LINDBLOM
Professor of Economics
Yale University

EUGENE LITWAK
Professor of Social Welfare Research
University of Michigan

D. A. MacKAY
Professor of Educational Administration
University of Alberta

JAMES G. MARCH
Dean, School of Social Sciences
University of California, Irvine

DOUGLAS McGREGOR
Late Professor of Industrial Management
Massachusetts Institute of Technology

MATTHEW B. MILES
Professor of Psychology and Education
Columbia University

VAN MILLER
Professor of Educational Administration
University of Illinois

GERALD H. MOELLER
Director, Division of Federal Relations
St. Louis Public Schools

D. S. PUGH
Reader, Industrial Administration
Research Unit
University of Aston in Birmingham,
England

EUGEN PUSIC
Professor of Public Administration
University of Zagreb, Yugoslavia

THOMAS C. SCHELLING
Professor, Center for International
Affairs
Harvard University

W. RICHARD SCOTT
Associate Professor of Sociology
Stanford University

THOMAS J. SERGIOVANNI
Assistant Professor of Educational
Administration
University of Illinois

HERBERT A. SIMON
Associate Dean, Graduate School of
Industrial Administration
Carnegie Institute of Technology

RALPH A. SMITH
Associate Professor of Aesthetic
Education
University of Illinois

RALPH M. STOGDILL
Professor of Business Administration
Bureau of Business Research
Ohio State University

GEORGE STRAUSS
Professor, Institute of Industrial
Relations
University of California, Berkeley

ROBERT SWEITZER
Professor, College of Education
Pennsylvania State University

VICTOR A. THOMPSON
Professor of Political Science
University of Illinois

PART ONE

ORGANIZATIONS: THEIR NATURE, COMPONENTS, AND CHARACTERISTICS

The increased attention given to the study of organizations is not surprising when one considers that individuals spend most of their lives in some form of organizational membership. Schools represent a common denominator for man's experience with organizations in that most members of society have inhabited schools at one time or another. The school's mission is one of forming, freeing, developing, and assimilating its young clients so that they may better function as individual personalities and as sustained contributors to our society. Because of their unique effects on children, the importance of their mission in society, and their common-denominator quality, schools need to become more persistent foci of study for those in the field of organizational theory and organizational behavior.

Under such circumstances, we can afford nothing less than a school climate which is characterized by optimal organizational health. The extent to which we achieve this goal will be reflected in the extent to which school organizations (1) are high performers in terms of achieving meaningful school purposes, (2) are generous in providing organizational members

1

(staff and students alike) with rewards rich in self-fulfillment, and (3) are dynamic, adaptive, and creative in structure, in belief, and in orientation, in order to sustain themselves against uncertainties in the future.

Part 1 takes as its theme the characteristics of organizations as contrasted with characteristics of individuals in organizations. At this level of analysis, it is useful to view organizations (schools) as possessing personalities in and of themselves. Like individuals, organizations are "motivated" to provide for certain basic needs. Three of these can be identified with some agreement: (1) the need to survive, to sustain and grow, (2) the need to eliminate uncertainty, and (3) the need to seek and maintain homeostasis. Much human activity in organizations is motivated by administrative *reaction* to these and other organizational needs. Administrators can behave in a *pro-active* way only within the limits set by these needs. Planning and structuring the growth patterns and directions of schools, developing strategies to overcome uncertainties or developing strengths to live with and accept uncertainties, and establishing the nature and frequency of change (new homeostatic levels) are examples of pro-active administrative behavior.

Schools have traditionally yielded to organizational impulses by providing for organizational needs in a passive and almost docile manner. Administrators, for example, find it easy and comfortable to organize for maintaining schools through efficiency in cost, and for production in terms of number of students processed and low dropout rates. Serious attention is given to follow-up studies, for example, which focus on the number of graduates attending various colleges or holding various jobs. Schools have sought to eliminate uncertainty through heavy reliance on programmed decision making not only in an administrative way as reflected in policy manuals, standardized schedules, and graded classes, but in a supervisory way by introducing "packaged" instruction, homogeneous groups, teaching machines, and the like.

If we value quality outputs for schools, that is, if we are more concerned with the quality of our plumbers than with the number of our plumbers, as a major success criterion for our schools, then we will need to revise drastically our present assumptions regarding organizational prerogatives and organizational behavior. Further, we will need to study more carefully the adequacy of models such as those proposed by Hage (organic) and Litwak (professional) as possible guides for revising organizational patterns in schools.

One of the fallacies of earlier attempts to study organizations was our tendency to view them as rational structures inhabited by rational human beings. We further assumed that the lenses which we used to study organizations were also rational and that rationality would naturally lead to maximization of goals. In the tradition of Cyert, March, and Simon, one needs to exercise caution when viewing schools as maximizing organizations. As man tends not to seek the best needle in a haystack but rather one which satisfies the purpose of the search, so schools tend not to seek maximizing solutions to their problems but rather to accept those solutions which satisfy current needs.

Concepts of formal organizations as viewed by Weber, Simon, and Parsons are presented in Blau and Scott's "The Nature and Types of Formal Organizations." The authors begin their analysis by considering sources of authority which exist in formal organizations. The bureaucratic model, the rational decision-making model, and the general social-systems model are then presented as alternate ways to view organizations. Finally, methods for classifying organizations are explored. Of particular interest is the Blau and Scott *cui bono* formulation, which suggests a taxonomy of organizations based on who benefits from the organization's existence. The authors suggest that the value system or the cultural milieu of organizations may vary substantially depending upon organizational goals and motives as well as clients served.

"Hierarchy, Specialization and Organizational Conflict" by Thompson summarizes in substance several chapters of his book *Modern Organizations*. Thompson continues and extends the themes introduced by Blau and Scott and further explores the dysfunctions of ambiguous and contradictory authority sources in organizations. The gap between authority based on ability and authority based on hierarchy is widening, according to Thompson, as individuals, professions, and businesses become increasingly oriented toward person specialization as opposed to task specialization.

Using change and innovation as a theme, Abbott's "Hierarchical Impediments to Innovation in Educational Organizations" suggests that schools do indeed possess a number of bureaucratic tendencies and that each of these has the potential to retard and frustrate school adaptiveness.

In the next essay, Barnard provides a detailed analysis of the basis for status in organizations and treats those disruptive tendencies which he feels are inherent in status systems. The bureaucratic dysfunction theme is continued as March and Simon use the classic Merton, Selznick, and Gouldner models to illustrate the "unanticipated" consequences of bureaucratically defined organizational acts in their article entitled "Dysfunctions in Organizations."

Bell, in "Formality versus Flexibility in Complex Organizations," suggests that the amount of discretion an employee exercises is directly related to a number of organizational characteristics—rigidity of lines of authority, communications, and productivity, for example. He presents a "discretionary model of organization" in which causes and effects of high and low uses of discretion are depicted and explained.

A more comprehensive view of bureaucratic conflict is presented by Litwak in "Models of Bureaucracy Which Permit Conflict." Professor Litwak describes two revised versions of the Weber model: the human relations model and the professional model. Each of these revisions requires alterations in the direction and intensity of characteristics which constituted the original Weber formulation. As schools approach one or another of the revised models, they will have to reflect this tendency by rearranging their traditional structures.

Hage's "An Axiomatic Theory of Organizations" identifies and relates four key means variables and four key ends variables into a seven-proposition theory of organizations. Hage, relying heavily on the works of Weber, Barnard, and Thompson, then derives from the seven propositions a series of corollaries which together number twenty-nine hypotheses. In summary, Hage develops the "mechanistic" and "organic" models as two ideal types of organizations, each distinguished by the extent to which it values different means variables and seeks to maximize different ends variables.

In "Modern Organizational Theory: A Psychological and Sociological Study," Pugh summarizes and discusses efforts to develop the field of organizational theory. The comprehensiveness of his work is reflected in the 107 citations which support his article. In a very real sense, this piece summarizes Part 1 of the book.

1.

THE NATURE AND TYPES OF FORMAL ORGANIZATIONS

PETER M. BLAU
W. RICHARD SCOTT

To clarify the nature and characteristics of formal organizations, we shall first deal with the major conceptions advanced by organization theorists and then discuss the various forms that such organizations may assume. We begin by presenting Weber's classical theories of authority and of bureaucratic organization. Following a critical analysis of Weber's conception, we shall briefly deal with two other general theoretical treatments of formal organizations. With regard to types of organizations, our main purpose is to suggest some of the dimensions along which classification may occur and to illustrate the utility of one approach for the development of a classificatory scheme.

THEORETICAL CONCEPTS

THE CONCEPT OF AUTHORITY. Max Weber's perceptive and incisive theoretical analysis of the principles of bureaucracy is undoubtedly the most important general statement on formal organization. Since its publication in *Wirtschaft und Gesellschaft* about 40 years ago, it has had a profound influence on almost all subsequent thinking and research in the field. Weber analyzes formal organizations as part of his theory of authority structures, or systems of

From Peter M. Blau and W. Richard Scott, *Formal Organizations: A Comparative Study*, Chandler Publishing Company, San Francisco, 1960, pp. 27–45.

legitimate social control; we shall follow his procedure and begin with a discussion of the concept of authority.

Authority must be distinguished from other forms of social influence—from power, on the one hand, and from persuasion and other kinds of personal influence, on the other. Weber defines power as "the probability that one actor within a social relationship will be in a position to carry out his own will despite resistance."[1] Power, as used by Weber, is a very general and comprehensive concept. It includes control through the use or the threat of physical coercion (as exercised by the stick-up man or by the rapist) and it includes the control of one who can manipulate conditions in such a way that others are forced to act in his interests rather than their own (as exemplified by a monopoly or by the one-company town).

The stick-up man and the monopolist exercise power, but they do not exercise authority, since the essence of the latter is that directives issued by the one in control are *voluntarily* obeyed. Weber defines authority as "the probability that certain specific commands (or all commands) from a given source will be obeyed by a given group of persons."[2] The group willingly obeys because its members consider it legitimate for this source to control them. The source of authority may be a person or it may be an impersonal institution, such as a system of laws. The fact that one individual voluntarily permits another to influence his behavior, however, is not necessarily indicative of an authority relation. There are also other types of personal influence, such as persuasion. In persuasion, one person lets the arguments of another person influence his decisions or actions. Persuasion is distinguished from authority inasmuch as the latter involves an a priori suspension of the first person's judgment, obviating the need for persuasion. In an authority relation the subordinate "holds in abeyance his own critical faculties for choosing between alternatives and uses the formal criterion of the receipt of a command or signal as his basis for choice."[3]

Two criteria of authority, then, are voluntary compliance with legitimate commands and suspension of judgment in advance of command. In concrete situations of social control, however, it is often difficult to determine whether these two criteria are actually met. Take the extreme case of the slave driver whose coercive power rested on his whip. He did not use his whip continually, since the very knowledge of the possibility of its use sufficed to make the slaves obey his orders. While few would classify this case as one of voluntary compliance, it differs only in degree from the case of the employer whose economic dominance over his employees motivates them to carry out official directives; yet, the latter relationship is usually considered to be one of authority. Again, when a person has often persuaded another in the past, his opinion may well carry so much weight that the second person lends a willing ear to his arguments and requires hardly any persuasion to be influenced. Does the first person have authority over the other, or not?

A major reason why there are so many borderline cases is that other forms of social control often develop into authority. For this change to occur, however, another social condition must be met, and this condition provides a final and basic distinguishing criterion for authority. The condition is that a value orientation must arise that defines the exercise of social control as legitimate, and this orientation can arise only in a group context. A single individual forced to comply with the commands of another may seek to adapt to this situation by rationalizing that he really wants to be guided by the other's directives. That this attitude is a mere rationalization would be indicated by the fact that once the coercive power were withdrawn he would not continue to comply. If, however, an entire group finds itself in the same situation, and if its members share the beliefs that it is good and right and, indeed, in their best interest to obey, the rationalizations of individuals become transformed into a common value orientation. For group agreement and approval of what is right constitute a social value that validates the beliefs of individuals and thereby makes them "really" right. Given the development of social norms

that certain orders of superiors ought to be obeyed, the members of the group will enforce compliance with these orders as part of their enforcement of conformity to group norms. The group's demand that orders of the superior be obeyed makes such obedience partly independent of his coercive power or persuasive influence over individual subordinates and thus transforms these other kinds of social control into authority.

A fundamental characteristic of authority, therefore, is that the willingness of subordinates to suspend their own judgment in advance and follow the directives of the superior results largely from social constraints exerted by the collectivity of subordinates and not primarily from the influences the superior himself can bring to bear upon them.[4] Such social constraints are not characteristic of coercive powers, persuasion, or other types of personal influence. If a boy is in love with a girl, for example, he will be eager to do what she wants in order to make his company more attractive to her. Similarly, if a person depends on a colleague for advice, he will feel obligated to accede to this colleague's wishes. In both of these cases, one person's dependence on another for certain rewards motivates him to comply with the other's requests in exchange for obtaining these rewards. But it would not be correct to classify such patterns of personal influence, which are rooted in exchange processes, as authority, even though compliance is voluntary, because there is no social collectivity whose norms require compliance with the directives of the superordinate person in the relation.

Authority relations can develop only in a group or larger collectivity, and not in isolated pairs, because only group values can legitimate the exercise of social control and only group norms can serve as an independent basis for enforcing the pattern of compliance. Once an authority structure has become institutionalized, however, it can find expression in apparently isolated pair relationships. Thus, a father exercises authority over his son, even though there is only one child in the family.

The father's influence does not entirely depend on his superior power, or his success in persuasion, or his willingness to exchange favors for obedience, because culturally defined role expectations obligate the son to obey his father; and members of the community, such as teachers and neighbors, help to enforce these obligations. To be sure, other forms of influence often exist side by side with authority and extend the influence of superiors. Pure authority relationships are analytical abstractions that are found rarely, if at all, in concrete situations, but this rarity makes the analytical distinction between them and other forms of influence no less important.

WEBER'S TYPES OF AUTHORITY. We have seen that authority exists only when a common value orientation in a collectivity legitimates the exercise of control as appropriate and proper. The types of legitimating beliefs that support the exercise of control vary, and Weber uses these differences as the basis for distinguishing three types of authority.[5]

The first type is authority legitimated by the sanctity of tradition. In "traditional" authority, the present social order is viewed as sacred, eternal, and inviolable. The ruling person or group, usually defined by heredity, is thought to have been ordained by supernatural powers to rule over the rest. The subjects are bound to their ruler by traditional feelings of personal loyalty and other cultural beliefs about the social order that reinforce his position, such as the concept of the divine right of kings. Absolute monarchies exemplify traditional authority, as does the patriarchal family or a shop under a paternalistic boss. The ruler's power is great under this system. Although it is limited by the traditions that legitimate it, this restriction is not severe, since a certain amount of arbitrariness on the part of the ruler is often part of the tradition and since a precedent in the past usually can be found to justify his new commands. The need to turn to past traditions for legitimation of present actions, however, sets this type of authority apart from others. In general, traditional authority tends to perpetu-

ate the existing social order and is ill suited for adaptation to social change; indeed, change undermines its very foundation.

The values that legitimate a "charismatic" authority, Weber's second type, define a leader and his mission as being inspired by divine or supernatural powers. The leader, in effect, heads a new social movement, and his followers or disciples are converts to a new cause. There is a sense of being "called" to spread the new gospel, a sense of rejecting the past and heralding the future as symbolized in Christ's words, "It is written . . . , but I say unto you. . . ." Devotion to the leader and a conviction that his actions embody the newly adopted ideals are the source of the group's willing obedience to his commands. Charismatic leaders may appear in almost any arena of social life, as prophets in religion, demagogues in politics, and heroes in battle. Charismatic authority generally functions as a revolutionary force, rejecting the traditional values and rebelling against the established order.

Initially, charismatic movements tend to be anarchistic and eschew even internal organization. Revolutionary ideals and the urgency of the mission make the charismatic leader and his followers contemptuous of anything associated with routines or "business as usual." No confining organization or rigid rules must be allowed to fetter the leader's inspiration, and the devotion to the sacred mission must not be profaned by mundane economic considerations. But it seems axiomatic that the demands of reality—for some routine, some organization, some stable means of economic support—cannot be ignored indefinitely. If it is to persist, the movement must become organized. Accordingly, the members' interest in perpetuating the movement constrains them to overcome their distaste for formal routines and to develop a formal organization. The necessity for organization becomes particularly apparent with the impending death of the charismatic leader. This event confronts the movement with the dangers of collapsing due to lack of inspired guidance or of being torn asunder by struggles over succession unless a regular procedure has been developed for transferring the leader's mantle to a legitimate heir. Charismatic movements are inherently unstable, since they are linked to the life of one man; to endure, they must take on some of the characteristics of that mundane world which initially they arose to combat and change. This process of "the routinization of charisma," as Weber called it, transforms charismatic authority into a different type; it may crystallize into a traditional system or, more often, become bureaucratized into the legal authority of a formal organization.[6]

Weber's third type, "legal" authority, is legitimated by a belief in the supremacy of the law. This type assumes the existence of a formally established body of social norms designed to organize conduct for the national pursuit of specified goals. In such a system obedience is owed not to a person—whether a traditional chief or a charismatic leader—but to a set of impersonal principles. These principles include the requirement to follow directives originating from an office superior to one's own, regardless of who occupies the higher office. All formal organizations—the government, a factory, the army, a welfare agency—are examples of legal authority structures. The epigram for this type might well be: "a government of laws, not of men." Although superior officials command the obedience of their subordinates, they in turn are subject to the authority of the same body of impersonal regulations, and their authority is accordingly limited.

Each of the three types of authority creates an appropriate staff of assistants. Thus, under the traditional form the feudal lord has his vassals and the king his court and retainers; the charismatic prophet has his disciples; and under the legal form, a staff of administrative officials becomes established and rationally organized. The distinctive characteristic of the latter type is that this bureaucratically organized administrative staff is capable of tremendous expansion and often becomes the dominant feature of legal authority systems.

WEBER'S THEORY OF BUREAUCRACY.   Almost all modern administrative organizations (as well as some ancient ones) are bureaucratically organized. Weber enumerates the distinctive characteristics of this type of organization in the following way:[7]

1. Organization tasks are distributed among the various positions as official duties. Implied is a clear-cut division of labor among positions which makes possible a high degree of specialization. Specialization, in turn, promotes expertness among the staff, both directly and by enabling the organization to hire employees on the basis of their technical qualifications.

2. The positions or offices are organized into a hierarchical authority structure. In the usual case this hierarchy takes on the shape of a pyramid wherein each official is responsible for his subordinates' decisions and actions as well as his own to the superior above him in the pyramid and wherein each official has authority over the officials under him. The scope of authority of superiors over subordinates is clearly circumscribed.

3. A formally established system of rules and regulations governs official decisions and actions. In principle, the operations in such administrative organizations involve the application of these general regulations to particular cases. The regulations insure the uniformity of operations and, together with the authority structure, make possible the coordination of the various activities. They also provide for continuity in operations regardless of changes of personnel, thus promoting a stability lacking, as we have seen, in charismatic movements.

4. Officials are expected to assume an impersonal orientation in their contacts with clients and with other officials. Clients are to be treated as cases, the officials being expected to disregard all personal considerations and to maintain complete emotional detachment, and subordinates are to be treated in a similar impersonal fashion. The social distance between hierarchical levels and that between officials and their clients is intended to foster such formality. Imper-

sonal detachment is designed to prevent the personal feelings of officials from distorting their rational judgment in carrying out their duties.

5. Employment by the organization constitutes a career for officials. Typically an official is a full-time employee and looks forward to a lifelong career in the agency. Employment is based on the technical qualifications of the candidate rather than on political, family, or other connections. Usually such qualifications are tested by examination or by certificates that demonstrate the candidate's educational attainment—college degrees for example. Such educational qualifications create a certain amount of class homogeneity among officials, since relatively few persons of working-class origins have college degrees, although their number is increasing. Officials are appointed to positions, not elected, and thus are dependent on superiors in the organization rather than on a body of constituents. After a trial period officials gain tenure of position and are protected against arbitrary dismissal. Remuneration is in the form of a salary, and pensions are provided after retirement. Career advancements are "according to seniority or to achievement, or both."[8]

In Weber's view, these organizing principles maximize rational decision-making and administrative efficiency. Bureaucracy, according to him, is the most efficient form of administrative organization, because experts with much experience are best qualified to make technically correct decisions, and because disciplined performance governed by abstract rules and coordinated by the authority hierarchy fosters a rational and consistent pursuit of organizational objectives.

REFINEMENTS OF WEBER'S CONCEPTIONS. Weber analyzes bureaucratic organizations not empirically but as an ideal type. He does not characterize the "average" administrative organization; rather, he seeks to bring together those characteristics that are distinctive of this type. Just as we can imagine physicians constructing a model of the perfectly healthy man, so Weber

attempts to characterize a perfectly bureaucratized organization. A question which remains to be answered is, what is the criterion of perfection employed by Weber?

Weber's construct of ideal type is an admixture of a conceptual scheme and a set of hypotheses. As a conceptual scheme it defines the phenomenon to be studied. His conception calls attention to what he considers the key elements of bureaucratic organization—those essential for understanding such organizations. Weber provides a definition of the concept of bureaucracy by pointing to these characteristics. He says in effect: bureaucracies are those organizations that exhibit the following combination of characteristics. Such conceptual schemes provide important frameworks for analysis and research, although they themselves are not subject to empirical testing. They are neither correct nor incorrect, only more or less useful in guiding scientific investigations.

But in addition to its conceptual elements, the ideal type contains a series of hypotheses. Weber suggests that many of the characteristics attributed to bureaucracies are interrelated in particular ways; for example, specialization is said to promote expertness, the authority structure and the existence of formal rules are assumed to make vital contributions to the coordination of activities, and detachment is held to increase rationality. Further, Weber states that these characteristics, and, specifically, their combination function to maximize administrative efficiency. A careful reading of Weber indicates that he tends to view elements as "bureaucratic" to the extent that they contribute to administrative efficiency. This contribution to efficiency appears to be the criterion of "perfect" embodied in his ideal type. However, whether or not each of these elements, or their combination, enhances administrative efficiency is not a matter for definition; these are questions of fact—hypotheses subject to empirical testing.

To exploit Weber's insightful theoretical analysis, it is necessary, in our opinion, to discard his misleading concept of the ideal type and to distinguish explicitly between the conceptual scheme and the hypotheses. The latter can then be tested and refined rather than left as mere impressionistic assertions. We can ask, for example: does tenure promote efficiency? Under what conditions does it have this effect, and under what conditions does it not? Only in this way can we hope to progress beyond Weber's insights to the building of systematic theory.

Weber has often been criticized for presenting an idealized conception of bureaucracy. His statements appear to entail an implicit functional scheme; again and again he addresses himself to the problem of how a given element contributes to the strength and effective functioning of the organization. What is missing is a similar systematic attempt to isolate the *dysfunctions* of the various elements discussed[9] and to examine the conflicts that arise between the elements comprising the system. Thus, even if it is true that the hierarchy of authority promotes discipline and makes possible the coordination of activities, does it not also discourage subordinates from accepting responsibility? Or, granted that promotion should be based on objective criteria rather than on personal considerations or family connections, which of the two major criteria is to be selected—seniority or merit? When questions such as these are raised, it is seen that Weber's one-sided concern with the functions of bureaucratic institutions blinds him to some of the most fundamental problems in the study of formal organizations.[10]

Another criticism that has been advanced against Weber's analysis is that he is preoccupied with the formally instituted aspects of bureaucracies and ignores the informal relations and unofficial patterns which develop in formal organizations. Selznick has emphasized that the formal structure is only one aspect of the actual social structure and that organizational members interact as whole persons and not merely in terms of the formal roles they occupy.[11] Many empirical studies demonstrate that friendship patterns, unofficial exchange

systems, and "natural" leaders arise to modify the formal arrangements.[12] Weber's conceptual scheme, by concentrating on the officially instituted aspects of bureaucracies, neglects the ways in which these are modified by informal patterns and thus excludes from analysis the most dynamic aspects of formal organizations.

Finally, Parsons and Gouldner have called attention to an implicit contradiction in Weber's conception of bureaucracy; in Gouldner's words, "On the one side, it was administration based on expertise; while on the other, it was administration based on discipline."[13] By emphasizing both expert judgment resting on technical knowledge and disciplined compliance with directives of superiors as the basis for bureaucratic decisions, Weber implies that there is no conflict between these two principles; that is, he implicitly assumes that in every disagreement between superior and subordinate, the superior's judgment is also the better judgment in terms of technical expertise. This is not a realistic assumption. Executives in complex organizations are not merely occasionally but typically less qualified to make expert technical judgments than their professional subordinates, since they cannot possibly be the leading expert in each of the specialties under their jurisdiction. Often, indeed, they are experts not in any of these specialties but in administration. Administrative considerations, moreover, tend to conflict with technical professional considerations. Hence, the judgment of superiors, who are concerned with administrative problems, will recurrently differ from the judgment of their professional subordinates, who are concerned with technical problems. Generally, one of the central issues in contemporary professional organizations, which will occupy us repeatedly in later chapters, is the conflict between disciplined compliance with administrative procedures and adherence to professional standards in the performance of duties.

Weber's pioneering analysis of bureaucracy has stimulated much further analysis and research on formal organizations, and these studies make it possible critically to review and to refine some of his theoretical concepts. Our criticisms of parts of his discussion on the basis of more recent work in sociology are not intended to disparage the outstanding contribution Weber has made to this field.

OTHER CONCEPTIONS OF FORMAL ORGANIZATIONS. Weber is not the only social scientist who has attempted to develop a theoretical framework for the analysis of formal organizations. The approach of two other students of social organization will be briefly considered here, although our list could easily be extended.

Herbert Simon conceives of administrative organizations primarily as decision-making structures.[14] He has characterized his own focus in the following passage:

> What is a scientifically relevant description of an organization? It is a description that, so far as possible, designates for each person in the organization what decisions that person makes, and the influence to which he is subject in making each of these decisions.[15]

Effective administration, according to Simon, requires rational decision-making; decisions are rational when they select the best alternative for reaching a goal. But administrative decisions are highly complex, and rationality is limited for various reasons: all the consequences that follow from a given course of action cannot be anticipated; the consequences of action lie in the future and thus are difficult to evaluate realistically; and rationality requires a choice among all possible alternatives, but many of these will never even come to mind and so will not be considered. In short, individuals are not capable of making complex decisions rationally. The function of the organization is to limit the scope of the decisions that each member must make; only in this way can rationality be approached.[16] How does the organization accomplish this feat? First, it defines the responsibilities of each official, thus supplying him with goals to guide his decisions. Second, it sets up the mechanisms, such as

formal rules, information channels, and training programs that help to narrow the range of alternatives the official must consider before making his decisions.

This conclusion may be somewhat amplified. Decisions, says Simon, are based on two types of premises. There are factual premises, which are subject to empirical testing in order to ascertain their truth or falsity, and value premises, which are not subject to such tests since they are concerned not with what "is" but with what "ought" to be, what is good or preferable. The former have to do with the choice of means, the latter with the choice of ends. Rational behavior may be viewed as consisting of means-ends chains. Given certain ends, appropriate means are selected for their attainment; but once reached, the ends often become the means for the attainment of further ends, and so forth. For example, a student studies in order to obtain a high mark in a course; he desires a high mark because this will help him attain a high over-all grade average; he desires a high grade average in order to be able to graduate from college; college graduation, in turn, is only a means to the end of getting a desirable job; and so on. The important point about organizational behavior is that the hierarchical structure permits all decisions, except those defining ultimate objectives, to rest on factual rather than on value premises, that is, to be decisions about means rather than ends. Once the objectives of the organization are formally established, the hierarchical organization of responsibilities serves as a framework for means-ends chains—specifying for each official the ends of his tasks and thus confining his duties to the selection of the best means for achieving these ends. To illustrate, the duty of the top manager may be described as finding effective ways for accomplishing the established objectives of the organization; the means he employs for this purpose are work assignments to his department heads. These assignments provide each department with its objectives, which the head seeks to attain by means of assigning responsibilities to the supervisors under him, and so on down the line. The ends of every member of the organization are defined by the directives of his superior, and his responsibility is primarily to decide on the best means for attaining these ends. In other words, each official in the hierarchy has his value premises supplied by his superior; besides, his search for alternative means is narrowed by procedural regulations. The combination of these two limits, according to Simon, permits rational decision-making in an organization.

Simon's suggestive conception of administration as a decision-making structure deals largely with the effects of the formal blueprint on decision-making and does not include a systematic analysis of those interpersonal processes that are not part of the formal structure. Our discussion, in contrast, will be particularly concerned with the significance of these informal interpersonal influences for decision-making. Another limitation of Simon's analysis is that he directs all his efforts to explaining how the various conditions in the organization—the hierarchy, the communication system, training programs—influence rational decision-making and omits consideration of their influence on one another. Such a specific focus on choice behavior as the sole dependent variable makes it impossible systematically to analyze social structure, since it reduces all problems of social structure to sociopsychological problems; that is, all questions of "what produces these characteristics of the organization?" are turned into a concern with "what produces this behavior of the members in the organization?"

Talcott Parsons provides yet another conception of formal organization in the recent application of his general theoretical framework for the study of social systems to such organizations.[17] According to Parson's schema, all social systems must solve four basic problems: (1) adaptation: the accomodation of the system to the reality demands of the environment coupled with the active transformation of the external situation; (2) goal achievement: the defining of objectives and the mobilization of resources to attain them; (3) integration: establishing and organizing a set of relations among the member units of the system that serve to coordinate and unify them into a single entity; and (4) latency: the maintenance over time of the system's motivational and cultural patterns.[18] This scheme has sufficient generality to be applicable to all social systems. For example, if our focus is the society, then the economy may be said to function as the subsystem meeting the problems of adaptation faced by the society. Formal organizations, although they serve different specific functions, are part of the goal attainment subsystem of the larger society. Parsons thus views formal organizations as a major mechanism in modern societies for mobilizing power in the interest of achieving collective objectives.

But each formal organization may also be viewed as a social system in its own right that must possess its own set of subsystems concerned with the solution of the four basic problems. Accordingly, each organization must have structures that enable it to adapt to its environment and mobilize the resources required for its continued functioning. Mechanisms are also required to enable the organization to implement its goals, including structures devoted to specification of objectives, to allocation of resources within the organization, to "production," and to distribution. To solve its integrative problems the organization must find ways to command the loyalties of its members, to motivate their effort, and to coordinate the operations of its various segments. Finally, institutions must be developed to cope with the latency problem, that is, to promote consensus on the values that define and legitimate the organization's goals. All organizations are faced with these problems; however, the particular structures devised to meet them will vary with the type of organization under consideration.

Three major hierarchical levels in formal organizations are distinguished by Parsons. There is first the technical level, where the actual "product" of the organization is manufactured or dispensed; this level is exemplified by workers on assembly lines, doctors in hospitals, and teachers in universities. Above the technical employees is the managerial level, whose primary concern is to mediate between the various parts of the organization and to coordinate their efforts. Finally, the institutional level of the organization connects it with the wider social system; for instance, the function of a board of directors is to oversee the operations of the organization in the light of its position in the larger society. It appears that the first level is chiefly concerned with problems of adaptation and goal attainment, the second with integrative problems, and the third with latency problems.

Parsons suggests that there are clear-cut breaks in the hierarchy of authority and responsibility between these three levels. Only within a level can the superior supervise the work of subordinates and assume responsibility for it, since the differences in function between the levels are too great to make supervision of the lower by the higher possible. Senior professionals, for example, direct the work of junior professionals, but top management does not direct their work in the same sense, since managers do not have the technical qualifications to do so. Indeed, it is not correct even to say that the executive delegates responsibility to professionals. The latter assume full responsibility for technical decisions, and the executive must rely on their expert judgments in discharging his managerial responsibility, which is the area of his special competence. Similarly, the board of directors does not supervise managerial decisions but seeks only to adjust the organization to external conditions by defining general objectives and policies. In matters of internal policy and organizational management, it must permit the independent judgment of executives free scope.

Parsons' analysis of formal organizations is of special interest because it involves the application of the general theory of social systems he has developed to the investigation of this particular institution. A criticism that has been leveled against Parsons' work is that his extremely abstract conceptions yield a theoretical scheme devoid of a system of propositions from which specific hypotheses can be derived; in short, that he has only developed a theoretical framework and not a substantive theory. Cognizant of this criticism, Parsons has recently suggested some theoretical propositions implied by his scheme.[19] But these propositions are again on such a high level of abstraction that it is by no means clear whether empirically testable hypotheses can be derived from them, an essential requirement of scientific theory.

TYPOLOGIES OF FORMAL ORGANIZATIONS

VARIOUS CLASSIFICATIONS. Since formal organizations are complex social objects having diverse characteristics, any one of which may be seized upon as a basis for grouping them in one manner or another, many different classification schemes have been proposed. Some students have emphasized the distinction between private and public ownership as a basic one; some have classified organizations by size; others have concentrated attention on the specific purposes served. Another system of types focuses on the criterion of membership; thus, we may distinguish organizations manned largely by volunteers (the Red Cross), by employees (industrial firms), or by conscripts (citizen armies). Organizations have also been assigned to broad institutional areas on the basis of the function they perform for the larger society; such attempts may provide types like economic, political, religious, and educational organizations.

In contrast to these classifications which stress fairly obvious differences between organizations, there are others that use more analytical criteria of distinction.[20] Thus, Parsons differentiates four types on the basis of which one of the four fundamental problems confronting a society an organization helps to solve. Since this category system is derived from a theoretical scheme, it cuts across traditionally defined institutional areas.[21] Another analytical criterion of distinction is whether the "materials" worked on by the technical personnel of the organization are physical objects or people. The crucial difference between the two resulting types—production and service organizations—is that only the latter are confronted with problems of establishing social relations with the "objects" of their endeavors and of having to motivate them in various ways. The success of a teacher depends on doing this; that of an engineer does not.[22] It should be noted that the term "service organizations" is misleading for the general type, since not all organizations dealing with people provide a service for these same people; it is hardly correct to say that the function of a prison is to furnish services to prisoners.

Hughes provides yet another analytical classification by attempting to describe several basic models of organization found in modern society, which yields five types: (1) the voluntary association of equals, where members freely join for a specific purpose; examples include sects, clubs, and professional associations; (2) the military model, which emphasizes a fixed hierarchy of authority and status; (3) the philanthropic model, consisting of a governing lay board, an itinerant professional staff, and the clients served, as illustrated by hospitals and universities; (4) the corporation model with its stockholders, board of directors, managers, and staff; and (5) the family business in which a group of people related by kin and marriage carry on some enterprise for profit.[23]

A typology, strictly speaking, is a multidimensional classification. If organizations were, for example, divided into large public, small public, large private, and small private ones, this would be a simple typology based on the dimensions of size and ownership. A more complex typology is illustrated by Thompson and Tuden's analysis of the decision-making strategies in organizations.[24] They suggest that the type of decision made depends on two factors: (1) whether there is agreement on objectives; and (2) whether cause-effect relations are known, that is, whether there is agreement on how to bring about given objectives. The combinations of these two factors produce four types of decision-making strategies and four types of organizations considered appropriate for them. First, if there is agreement on both

the objectives and on how to attain them, what Thompson and Tuden call "computational" strategies are possible; that is, decisions can be based on rational calculations. This is the situation for which the rational bureaucracy described by Weber is ideally suited. Second, if there is agreement on objectives but cause-effect relations are not fully known so that insight is needed to decide on the best course of action, a "judgmental" strategy will be used. In this case, a collegium or self-governing body of peers is preferable as an organizational form to bureaucracy. A board of directors illustrates this type, and so does a colleague group of professionals. Third, if there is agreement on how to achieve various objectives but dispute on which objectives have first priority, a "compromise" strategy is required to make collective decisions. The appropriate organization in this case is a representative body, such as the United States Congress. Finally, when there is disagreement on both the objectives and on how to achieve them, "inspirational" strategies are likely to be resorted to. These conditions are usually characterized by the absence of formal organization and by a state of anomie, and would seem to be conducive to the development of charismatic movements.

A CLASSIFICATION BASED ON PRIME BENEFICIARY. Even though the foregoing review of classificatory schemes is only cursory, it suggests that there is no dearth of such schemes in the literature on organizations. In proposing yet another classification, we take upon ourselves the burden of demonstrating the usefulness of our scheme for increasing the understanding of formal organizations. We hope to do so by using it as a basis for discussing several of the recent empirical studies of formal organizations. First, however, we must present the typology.

Four basic categories of persons can be distinguished in relation to any given formal organization: (1) the members or rank-and-file participants; (2) the owners or managers of the organization; (3) the clients or, more generally, the "public-in-contact," which means the people who are technically "outside" the organization yet have regular, direct contact with it, under whatever label—patient, customer, law violator, prisoner, enemy soldier, student; and (4) the public-at-large, that is, the members of the society in which the organization operates.[25] We propose to classify organizations on the basis of *cui bono*—who benefits: Which of these four categories is the prime beneficiary of their operations? It must be emphasized that the prime beneficiary is not the only beneficiary, for each of the various groups who make contributions to an organization does so only in return for certain benefits received. Thus, the owners, the employees, and the customers of a business concern must each receive some recompense for their various contributions; otherwise, they would not provide the investment capital, the labor power, or the purchase price for goods, all of which are necessary for the firm's continued operation. The public-at-large also benefits from the contribution that business concerns make to the "general welfare," specifically, to the production and distribution of desired goods, and this benefit is the reason why the society permits and encourages such firms to operate. But although all parties benefit, the benefits to one party furnish the reason for the organization's existing while the benefits to others are essentially a cost. In the example cited, the prime beneficiary is the owner of the firm. He established it for the purpose of realizing a profit, and he will close it should it operate for very long showing a loss. Indeed, the public expects the owner to operate his business for his own benefit and not as a welfare institution. Contrast this situation with that of organizations whose prime beneficiary is the public. The city is not expected to close its police department or the community hospital because it fails to show a profit, but to operate it in the interest of the public even at a financial loss.[26]

Four types of organizations result from the application of our *cui bono* criterion: (1) "mutual-benefit associations," where the prime beneficiary is the membership; (2) "business concerns," where the owners are prime bene-

ficiary; (3) "service organizations," where the client group is the prime beneficiary; and (4) "commonweal organizations," where the prime beneficiary is the public-at-large. (This classification can be combined with others to yield more refined typologies.) The following discussion of empirical studies illustrating these four types of formal organizations will clarify the distinction and show that special problems are associated with each type. Thus, the crucial problem in mutual-benefit associations is that of maintaining internal democratic processes—providing for participation and control by the membership; the central problem for business concerns is that of maximizing operating efficiency in a competitive situation; the problems associated with the conflict between professional service to clients and administrative procedures are characteristic of service organizations; and the crucial problem posed by commonweal organizations is the development of democratic mechanisms whereby they can be externally controlled by the public.

The significance of the *cui bono* criterion for defining the character of a formal organization is indicated by the fundamental changes that occur when there is a shift in prime beneficiary from one to another of the four categories. Often such changes are strongly disapproved; sometimes they are heralded as revolutionary improvements; in either case, they signify radical alterations in the basic nature of the organization. Thus, unions are mutual-benefit associations, which are expected to serve the interests of the rank and file. If union leaders usurp the role of prime beneficiary and run the union as if they owned it for their personal benefit, the organization is condemned for no longer serving the proper functions of a labor union. The same is true for a union whose membership has been displaced as prime beneficiary by its public-in-contact—the employers or their representatives—as exemplified by company unions or those whose leadership has "sold out" to management.

In the case of business concerns, the owners are expected to be prime beneficiaries. But public corporations transform owners into mere stockholders and vest controlling power in the hands of top-level employees, enabling them to govern the enterprise in their own interests.[27] Moreover, if unions become more powerful than individual employers, a situation illustrated by some segments of the garment industry, the possibility arises that instead of the owners the employees represented by the union become the prime beneficiaries. Government regulations, notably the extreme case of nationalization of industry, might succeed in making the public-at-large the prime beneficiary of a business concern. This change may, of course, be a good thing. Whether such shifts in prime beneficiary are evaluated as advantageous or disadvantageous depends on one's ideological position, but there is no doubt that they would constitute fundamental transformations of business concerns into distinctly different types of organizations.

In service organizations, if the members of the professional staff lose interest in serving clients and become primarily concerned with making their own work easier or furthering their own careers, service will suffer, since the energies and resources devoted to it will no longer be considered as contributing to the prime function of the organization but rather as a necessary cost for obtaining benefits for the staff or some segment of it.

Commonweal organizations, in sharp contrast, are not expected to be oriented to the interests of their "clients," that is, those persons with whom they are in direct contact. A police department, for example, that enters into collusion with racketeers fails to discharge its responsibility to the public-at-large and is no longer the protective organization it is assumed to be. Likewise, if policemen solicit bribes instead of enforcing the law, or if the police commissioner runs the department primarily to further his political ambitions, the public's position as prime beneficiary of the organization suffers.

Note also that the criticism that an organization is "overbureaucratized" means quite different things in the four types of organizations.[28] In the case of mutual-benefit associations, such as unions, overbureaucratization implies centralization of power in the hands of officials. Here it does not refer to inefficiency; indeed, bureaucratized unions are often ruthlessly efficient. But in the case of business concerns overbureaucratization implies an elaboration of rules and procedures that impairs operating efficiency, and here the term is not used in reference to the power of management officials to decide on policies, since such managerial direction is expected and legitimate. Finally, service and commonweal organizations are considered overbureaucratized if in consequence of preoccupation with procedures rigidities develop which impede professional service to clients or effective service of the public interest.

NOTES

[1] Max Weber, *The Theory of Social and Economic Organization*, A. M. Henderson and Talcott Parsons (trans.) and Talcott Parsons (ed.), Glencoe, Ill.: Free Press and Falcon's Wing Press, 1947, p. 152.

[2] *Ibid.*, p. 324.

[3] Herbert A. Simon, *Administrative Behavior* (2d ed.), New York: Macmillan, 1957, pp. 126–127.

[4] The compliance of subordinates in authority relations is voluntary but not independent of social constraints. It is as voluntary as is our custom of wearing shoes on the street.

[5] Weber, *op. cit.*, pp. 324–386. Note the following comment by Bendix: "In Weber's view beliefs in the legitimacy of a system of domination are not merely philosophical matters. They can contribute to the stability of

an authority relationship, and they indicate very real differences between systems of domination." Reinhard Bendix, *Max Weber*, Garden City, N.Y.: Doubleday, 1960, p. 297.

[6] Dostoyevsky's "Grand Inquisitor" graphically deals with the conflict between charisma and organization in the form of a fictional discussion between Christ and a Cardinal of the Church. Fyodor Dostoyevsky, *The Brothers Karamazov*, New York: Random House, 1937, pp. 292–314.

[7] Weber's discussion of these characteristics may be found in H. H. Gerth and C. Wright Mills (trans. and eds.), *From Max Weber: Essays in Sociology*, New York: Oxford University Press, 1946, pp. 196–204; and in Weber, *op. cit.*, pp. 329–336.

[8] *Ibid.*, p. 334.

[9] Merton has called for this balanced approach in his paradigm for functional analysis. Robert K. Merton, *Social Theory and Social Structure* (2d ed.), Glencoe, Ill.: Free Press, pp. 50–54.

[10] Defenders of Weber will argue that he did note certain conflicts or dilemmas inherent in bureaucratic structures. The point here is, however, that he did not subject these dysfunctions to the same kind of systematic analysis that he furnished for the functions of various characteristics for bureaucratic efficiency.

[11] Philip Selznick, "Foundations of the Theory of Organization," *American Sociological Review*, 13 (1948), pp. 25–35.

[12] See, for example, Charles H. Page, "Bureaucracy's Other Face," *Social Forces*, 25 (1946), pp. 88–94, and Ralph H. Turner, "The Navy Disbursing Officer as a Bureaucrat," *American Sociological Review*, 12 (1947), pp. 342–348.

[13] Alvin W. Gouldner, *Patterns of Industrial Bureaucracy*, Glencoe, Ill.: Free Press, 1954, p. 22. See also Talcott Parsons' "Introduction," in Weber, *op. cit.*, pp. 58–60, footnote 4.

[14] See Simon, *op. cit.*, pp. 1–11, 45–78, *et passim.*

[15] *Ibid.*, p. 37.

[16] Rationality is always only approached, never achieved. The organization member must be willing to forgo a search for the best of all possible alternatives and be content with finding a satisfactory one; in Simon's language, administrators must "satisfice [sic] because they have not the wits to maximize." *Ibid.*, p. xxiv; see also James G. March and Herbert A. Simon, *Organizations*, New York: Wiley, 1958, pp. 140–141, 169.

[17] Talcott Parsons, *Structure and Process in Modern Societies*, Glencoe, Ill.: Free Press, 1960, pp. 16–96.

[18] See Talcott Parsons *et al.*, *Working Papers in the Theory of Action*, Glencoe, Ill.: Free Press, 1953, pp. 183–186.

[19] Talcott Parsons, "Pattern Variables Revisited," *American Sociological Review*, 25 (1960), pp. 481–482.

[20] For examples, see Robin M. Williams, Jr., *American Society* (2d ed.), New York: Knopf, 1960, pp. 488–489.

[21] Banks and credit agencies, for instance, are assigned to the political sphere rather than to the economic. Parsons, *Structure and Process in Modern Societies*, op. cit., pp. 44–47.

[22] See *ibid.*, pp. 20–21. Parsons mentions, as a third type, organizations that deal with cultural objects; for example, research firms which add to knowledge. For an analysis of the ways in which people are similar to as well as different from physical objects as material to be worked with by organizations, see Erving Goffman, "Characteristics of Total Institutions,"

Walter Reed Army Institute of Research, *Symposium on Preventive and Social Psychiatry*, Washington, D.C.: U.S. Government Printing Office, 1957, pp. 66–69.

23 Everett C. Hughes, "Memorandum on Going Concerns," unpublished paper read before the Society for Applied Anthropology, 1952.

24 James D. Thompson and Arthur Tuden, "Strategies, Structures, and Processes of Organizational Decision," James D. Thompson *et al.* (eds.), *Comparative Studies in Administration*, Pittsburgh: University of Pittsburgh Press, 1959, pp. 195–216.

25 The first three of our four types are similar to those used by Simon in his discussion of the economic firm. See Simon, *op. cit.*, pp. 16–17.

26 The reader will note that our typology is not as unequivocal on this point as it might be. In the case of a police department, is not the public also the owner, and is not therefore the owner, as in the case of the business concern, the prime beneficiary? Technically speaking, of course, the public is the owner and prime beneficiary. However, it appeared to us that there were such major differences separating the two types—public organizations and privately owned ones—that more would be lost than gained by combining them into a single type.

27 See Adolf A. Berle and Gardner C. Means, *The Modern Corporation and Private Property*, New York: Macmillan, 1932.

28 For a discussion of the conditions that lead to overbureaucratization and its opposite, see S. N. Eisenstadt, "Bureaucracy, Bureaucratization, and Debureaucratization," *Administrative Science Quarterly*, 4(1959), pp. 302–320.

2.

HIERARCHY, SPECIALIZATION, AND ORGANIZATIONAL CONFLICT

VICTOR A. THOMPSON

Many elements undoubtedly combine to make up that particular ordering of human behavior which we call bureaucratic organization, but two are of rather obvious and particular importance. These are the social process of specialization and the cultural institution of hierarchy. A great deal of insight into these organizations can be gained by tracing out the relations between specialization and hierarchy. Particularly, many underlying tensions or conflicts can be illuminated in this fashion.

Modern bureaucracy attempts to accommodate specialization within an hierarchical framework. A hierarchy is a system of roles—the roles of subordination and superordination—arranged in a chain so that role 1 is subordinate to role 2; 2 is superordinate to 1 but subordinate to 3; and so forth until a role is reached that is subordinate to no other role (but perhaps to a group of people, such as a board of directors or an electorate).

A role is an organized pattern of behavior in accordance with the expectations of others. Social scientists often refer to the pattern of expectations as a person's social position—his rights and duties in a particular interactional situation—and his role as behavior appropriate to his position.

Roles are cultural items and are learned. The roles of subordinate and superior (i.e., man-boss roles) are likewise learned cultural patterns of behavior transmitted from genera-

From Victor A. Thompson, "Hierarchy, Specialization, and Organizational Conflict," *Administrative Science Quarterly*, 5:485–521, 1961. Reprinted by permission.

tion to generation. We will refer to these roles in shorthand fashion as hierarchical roles.

Defining position as a system of rights and duties in a situation of interaction, and role as behavior appropriate to a position, we will first turn our attention to a discussion of the rights and duties associated with hierarchical roles.

First let us consider the role of a "superior"—the superordinate role. When a person is designated as the "boss," what does this mean? In the first place, it means that he has a right to veto or affirm the organizationally directed proposals of his subordinates, subject to no appeal. Furthermore, the superior's rights include a near-absolute power over the organizational ambitions and careers of subordinates, such as raises or promotions. Although there are many promotional arrangements, nearly all depend heavily and ultimately on the kind word from the "boss."[2]

Hierarchical relations overemphasize the veto and underemphasize approval of innovation. Since there is no appeal from the superior's decision, a veto usually ends the matter. An approval, however, will often have to go to the next higher level where it is again subject to a veto. Thus, an hierarchical system always favors the *status quo*. In a collegiate body, individual members have a free constituency to which they can appeal and get a hearing. However, even in collegiate bodies (e.g., legislatures) there is some hierarchy, and so the *status quo* is also favored in these bodies. The advantage is on the side of those who oppose innovations (e.g., new legislation); the advantage is on the side of the veto. (Here we do not refer to collegiate bodies which are hierarchical creations such as a Russian Soviet).

The superior is generally considered to have the right to expect obedience and loyalty from his subordinates.[3] Although Weber thought that the separation of public (i.e., organizational) from private (i.e., personal) rights and duties was one of the hallmarks of modern bureaucracy, bureaucratic demands upon subordinates extend to many aspects of their personal lives.[4] The right to obedience is only another aspect of the right to command. It should be noted that this is the right to command autocratically and arbitrarily, as Weber indicated. Although there are many superiors who do not supervise autocratically and arbitrarily, they nevertheless have the right to do so.

The superior has the right to monopolize communication, both official communication between the unit and the outside world and communication between the members of the unit. The right to monopolize outgoing communication is often expressed by the insistence upon "going through channels" and bitter resistance to the use of specialist, nonhierarchical channels. The right to dominate internal communication is less often pressed. In autocratically supervised units, however, communication often comes close to a one-way, star-shaped pattern—a restriction of communication to the superior-subordinate relationship only.

The superior has the right to deference from his subordinates, the right to be treated with extra care and respect. What makes this right significant is that it is one-way. The superior has a right to be somewhat insensitive as to subordinates' personal needs.[5] The ranking of roles with regard to the amount of deference due them is what we mean by the "status system." Although specialties are also status ranked, by far the most visible and virile ranking in organization is ranking according to hierarchical position. Thus, the status system of an organization corresponds very closely to the hierarchy of superior-subordinate roles. It will be discussed below.

From these primary rights of the superior flow, logically, certain secondary rights—the right to determine the personnel of the unit and its organizational form; the right to initiate activities (set the unit's goal) and to assign them (confer jurisdiction); the right to settle conflicts (make decisions). His power of command makes it possible for him to create nonhierarchical authority by ordering his subordinates to submit to the influence of persons other than himself in various specialized areas —the delegation of authority. In this way the propriety of specialist influence can be assured.

The rights associated with hierarchical positions are cultural givens. Actual behavior associated with these positions will be modified by personality, any one person being more or less authoritarian than another. Actual behavior may also be modified by the social process within the groups of people which compose the organization. Thus a superior may form strong affective attachments to his subordinates; he may identify with them. Having become their friend, so to speak, he will find he has assumed the duties of friendship, most of which are at war with his hierarchical rights and usually with his duties to his superior. In extreme cases of this kind, a specific individual may engage in almost no behavior appropriate to his hierarchical position; he may not enact his hierarchical role. It is not unusual in such a situation for a person so entrapped to be considered useless by the hierarchy and to be replaced. Perhaps most people in hierarchical positions find their roles compromised in this fashion to a greater or lesser degree.

Above what might be considered a market minimum, the good things, the satisfactions which the organization has to offer, are distributed according to hierarchical rank, hence status rank. These goods, in addition to money, include deference, power, interesting activities and associations, inside knowledge, conveniences, and the like. Because these goods are distributed according to status rank, and access to any rank is controlled by hierarchical position, these positions acquire great power even over those who might not recognize all the rights of the position as they have been outlined above. Likewise, these positions become great personal prizes as means to personal (as opposed to organizational) ends, and as such are the objects of a constant struggle.[6]

The superordinate role is chiefly characterized by rights. If it has duties, they constitute the correlatives of subordinate rights. On the other hand, the subordinate role is chiefly characterized by duties—all those duties which constitute the correlatives of the superordinate's rights. They are the duties of obedience, of loyalty, of deference; the duty to accept a superior's veto without attempting to appeal around him (is anything more organizationally immoral than attempting to "go around" a superior?); and so on. In our modern democratic culture there are demands for rights of subordinates—rights to personal dignity, to be treated on the basis of merit, to extraorganizational freedom from organizational superiors. All of these "rights" are ambiguous because they conflict with superordinate rights, and this conflict has not yet been worked out in our culture. That is to say, the doctrines of democracy and liberalism which underlie our state have made almost no impact upon our bureaucratic organizations. The only nonlabor-union movement in this direction has been the attempt by some personnel people to introduce rudimentary elements of procedural due process into the bureaucracy; but because of the persistence of the old role definitions and the actual power of hierachies the assurance of procedural due process is problematical in any particular organization and more or less dependent upon the personalities or connections of the people involved.

Since a large part of the role behavior associated with hierarchical positions is concerned with deference or prestige, it would be well to take a closer look at the status system. Prestige has been defined as the invidious value of a role.[7] We have defined the "status system" as a hierarchy of deference ranks and seen that it corresponds to the hierarchy of subordinate-superordinate roles. Although positions can be differentiated without ranking, they are usually ranked.[8]

Since a person's hierarchical position is a matter of definition, of defined rights and duties, it should be clear at the outset that any special deference paid to the incumbent may constitute a confusion of person and role. That is to say, a person may be entitled to deference by virtue of one or more of his qualities, but his role is not one of his qualities. A person is perceived by others, however, through his roles, his public or perceived personality being the sum of his various roles.[9]

The confusion of office (role) and person is a very old phenomenon; it was part of the charismatic pattern. In fact, status can be regarded as the continuation of charismatic attitudes and practices. It has often been noted that people impute superior abilities to persons of higher status.[10] Furthermore, this imputed superior ability is generalized into a halo of general superiority. Thus, persons of very high status are called upon to help solve problems of every conceivable kind—problems about which they could have no knowledge whatsoever. In public affairs, this halo effect of status requires high-status persons to speak out on all sorts of matters from a position of almost complete ignorance. They are, therefore, forced to develop plausible-sounding jargons and propositions which come to constitute pseudo technologies in terms of which many of our public problems must be publicly analyzed and discussed.[11] If, with this handicap, real solutions are found to these problems, they must be found by unsung "staff" specialists who must perforce solve the problems in ways which do not jolt the pseudo technologies too profoundly.

It has already been pointed out that status has a dominant position in the distributive system. Studies with small groups show that high-status persons get the most satisfactions from such groups.[12] Studies of military behavior suggest that high-status persons are more interested in preserving the system of status ranking than are low-status persons.[13] Above a certain level it would seem that salaries are to some, rather large, extent a function of status—the higher the status, the higher the salary. In fact, it would seem that salaries operate chiefly as symbols of status rank.[14] That the perquisites and conveniences of the work situation are distributed according to status rather than organizational need is common knowledge, and it has been argued that they are distributed in inverse ratio to need.[15] These perquisites also act as symbols and, along with other symbols such as salaries, methods of payment, clothing, insignia, titles, and the like, help to maintain the status system by increasing its visibility.[16] The amount of deference a person receives is made manifest by the good things others give him, and so, in one sense, the status system *is* the distributive system.

We have said that a hierarchical position carried with it rights to a certain amount of deference. But the system of deference ranking, the status system, while it corresponds to the hierarchical system, is much more than a hierarchy of deference rights. These rights are owed by a group of subordinates, but a person's status spreads its influence over a much broader area. Furthermore, the amount of prestige attached to hierarchical positions increases as we go up the hierarchy at what would appear to be an "abnormal" rate. The status system appears to have a "quasi-neurotic" character.[17] This element of exaggeration in status systems has both structural and psychological determinants.

Cognitive stability is promoted if one's superior by definition is perceived as one's superior in abilities.[18] The subordinate's self-image is protected by the same mechanism.[19] The superordinate position and the person who occupies it are perceptually merged.

The superior's restriction of the subordinate's freedom and his power to frustrate the subordinate's ambitions result in hostilities. The hostilities are not compatible with acts of submission, and they create guilt. Consequently, according to Erich Fromm, they are suppressed and replaced by admiration.[20] My superior is wonderful, and I neither need to be ashamed of submission to him nor need I try to be equal to him in any way. If Fromm is correct, hierarchical status may be partly a result of "reaction formation."

Furthermore, the person as perceived by others is the result of his many roles. His prestige relates to the perception of his roles. Prestige is more easily maintained when there is considerable vagueness about a person's roles—about what he actually does. On the other hand, a person whose prestige is based on what he actually can do must constantly struggle to maintain it.[21] That is to say, charis-

matic status rank is both more sure and more general than status rank based upon a specialty. Incumbents of high office are held in awe because they are in touch with the mysteries and magic of such office; they are "on the inside,"[22] have "inside information", and so forth. Since one knows less and less about the activities of superordinates the farther away on the hierarchy they are, the more the awe in which he holds them and consequently the greater their prestige or status. Thus it is difficult for workers to impute superior qualities to their foremen because they know fairly well what the foremen do, both at work and away from work. The same is not true for men higher up.[23] In this sense, status rank is a function of ignorance. The hierarchy is a highly restricted system of communication with much information coming in to each position, but the amount sent out to subordinates is subject to the control of the incumbent and always limited, for stragetic reasons or otherwise. There results an increasing vagueness as to the activities at each level as one mounts the hierarchy, and this vagueness supports the prestige ranking which we call the status system.

Experimental studies with small groups indicate that stratification (invidious ranking) in such groups is positively correlated with leader dominance behavior and negatively correlated with leader membership behavior.[24] Hierarchical roles are simply institutionalized dominance. The status system is thus seen as inseparable from the hierarchy. Furthermore, groups seem to have a process or mechanism similar to homeostasis in biology. If one member of the group engages in tension-producing behavior, the others act so as to reduce tension.[25] Thus if the rights of deference are pushed by a group's superior (if he "pulls rank"), tension may be reduced by acceding to the superior's demands. Communication blockages between the superior and the group reduce its influence over him so that the group must usually adjust to the superior rather than the reverse. Supporting this deference-building process is the cultural norm in our society that a person's presentation of himself should be taken at face value.[26] Thus, the role relations between superior and subordinates create a situation where there is almost no limit to the expansion of the superior's prestige except the prestige rank of the superior at the next level.

People vary greatly in their needs for dominance and for status. One would expect a sort of natural selection to bring into hierarchies persons with great dominance and status needs. Persons whose dominance needs are satisfied by mastery over materials rather than people will probably become specialists of some kind. Others may satisfy their dominance needs by identifying with their organization superior, thereby reinforcing his drive to dominance and status. Whereas specialists are always subordinate, a hierarchical position always includes a superordinate role and hence a chance to dominate people.[27] Given the group adjustment mechanism of homeostasis and the natural selection by the hierarchy of people with great status and dominance needs, the exaggerated character of the status system becomes intelligible, since people with great status needs can get just about as much deference as they demand if they occupy hierarchical positions.

It has often been noted that there are few operational performance standards for hierarchical positions.[28] Incumbents can never be sure "how well they are doing." This insecurity increases as one goes up the hierarchy. Furthermore, as one mounts the hierarchy, his activities have less and less specialist content and become more and more purely hierarchical role playing.[29] What specialist content remains at very high levels relates only to the particular organization he is in and has to do mostly with its history, its organization and methods, and the idiosyncracies of some of its personnel, clients, or suppliers. Thus, as one goes up the hierarchy, he has less and less value for other organizations.[30] The result of these two conditions—lack of operational performance standards and lack of opportunities in other organizations—make for great anxiety. This anxiety

is most likely to express itself in conformism—which means conformism to the wishes of the boss. The resulting neurotic overemphasis on pleasing the boss further inflates the deference system and modifies upwards the boss' self-evaluation and consequent demands for deference.

Prolonged enactment of a role reacts upon the personality.[31] People become what they do. Thus the deference accorded a person who performs a hierarchical role gradually modifies his self-characterization and hence his self-projection. He comes to feel that the deference is due him by right, that he truly is a superior person, and the deference system is further inflated.

The inflation at the upper end of the status system results in a deflation at lower levels. Since the status system controls distribution, the organization gives a great deal at the top and very little at the bottom.[32] It has often been observed that at the middle and lower-middle reaches of the hierarchy, concern with status and the symbols of status reaches an almost pathological intensity.[33] At these points people with great dominance and status needs find less than enough to satisfy their needs because so much has been allocated to the positions above. The status system skews the distribution system.

We have shown that hierarchical roles, as culturally defined, have strong charismatic elements connected with them. Current conceptions of organization are clearly based upon charismatic assumptions concerning these roles. It will be recalled that current formulations of bureaucratic organization (which we have called "monistic" and Weber "monocratic") conceptualize organization entirely in terms of hierarchy, as follows:

1. The person in each hierarchical position is told what to do by the person in the hierarchical position above him, and by no one else. He in turn, and he alone, tells his subordinates what to do. They, and they alone, do the same for their subordinates. These instructions establish the division of work,

namely the organization. The authority to do anything is cascaded down in this way, and only in this way, by the process of delegation.

2. Each subordinate is guided (supervised or directed) in carrying out these instructions by his superior and no one else, who, in turn, is guided in this guiding by his superior and no one else, etc.

3. Each superior "controls" his subordinates in carrying out the instructions by holding them responsible for compliance with the instructions or with performance standards associated with them. The subordinates are responsible to their superior, and no one else; he, in turn, is responsible to his superior and no one else; etc. Thus all authority comes from the top and is cascaded down by progressive delegations, while responsibility comes from the bottom and is owed to the next superior and to no one else.[34]

This monistic formulation is based upon charismatic assumptions at various points. It is assumed that the superior, at any point in the hierarchy, is able to tell his subordinates what to do, and to guide them in doing it. That is, it is assumed that he is more capable in all of his unit's activities than any of his subordinate specialists who perform them. The concept of responsibility for results assumes the ability or capacity to determine the results (or else the responsibility is merely ritualistic). The concept of unity of command or influence denies the relevance of the nonhierarchical expertise within the organization; the hierarchy of subordinate-superior roles, the "line of command," is sufficient. When these assumptions of superordinate ability are viewed against the background of the increasing range of activities subordinate to hierarchical positions at successively higher stages in modern bureaucracy, the assumptions clearly leave the realm of objective reality and become charismatic.

The monistic concept has other weaknesses. It is unable to account for specialization. More specifically, it cannot account for the delegation of nonhierarchical authority. The existence of such authority is consequently denied or hidden by fictions (e.g., "staff only advises; it does not command"). Furthermore, the monistic concept asserts that hierarchical authority is created by delegation from above, whereas, as we have seen, it is a cultural item, compounded from the culturally derived roles of the superior and the subordinate.

The monistic concept, since it is based entirely upon the institution of hierarchy and completely ignores the fact of specialization, naturally confuses rights with abilities—for example, the right to make decisions with the ability to do so. This confusion of rights with abilities results in the popular journalistic presentation of the actions of organizations, including states, as the actions of their top officials. It also encourages elitist interpretations of society.

Hierarchical roles began to develop at times and under conditions when it was credible to think of the chief as the most capable person. Under these circumstances, vast rights became associated with the role. The belief in unusual powers of persons who perform such roles—charisma—has continued in the form of the status system. Although specialization has enormously changed the circumstances of organized action, modern organization theory, and to a considerable extent practice, is fixated on the system of hierarchical roles. The fact and implications of specialization are hardly recognized.

In modern bureaucracy specialization is incorporated into the older hierarchical framework. Consequently, our problem is to describe and explain the interactions between specialist and hierarchical roles and the kind of order resulting therefrom.

The behavior of people in organizations is purposive in two senses. First, this behavior must be minimally oriented to a common (organizational) purpose or it would not be meaningful to speak of an organization. Second, behavior within organizations is oriented to personal goals. Consequently, we are interested in role interaction in the promotion of organizational goals and in the pursuit of personal goals. The first interest stresses capacities (abilities, powers), while the second stresses tastes, i.e., motivation.

Activities and relations oriented to the objective, externalized goals of the organization stress instrumental considerations. These activities and relations reflect an institutional framework characterized by specificity of function and the norms of rationalism and universalism. They grow out of specialization and out of advancing science and technology. On the other hand, the relations most closely associated with personal goals in bureaucratic structures stress rights or authority rather than instrumental considerations. These relations are characterized by diffuseness of function (in relation to personal goals) and particularism. They are the relations of hierarchy. The subordinate's obligations to his superior which rise out of his dependence upon the superior for the satisfaction of his personal goals (needs, satisfactions, motivations, and so on) are diffuse and ill-defined; and since objective standards governing the relationship tend to be absent (e.g., bills of rights) particularistic norms appear in their place (who one knows, mannerisms, appearance, out-of-office behavior, and so on).[35] The institutional pattern of functional diffuseness and particularism associated with our hierarchical relations is older than the pattern of functional specificity and universalism associated with specialization. Bureaucracy is thus seen to be compounded of the old and the new, of hierarchy and specialization.

We have defined a specialist as a person skilled in a number of programs—fairly complex sets of organized activities of a practical nature. As problem-solving mechanisms, organizations can be viewed as a breakdown (factoring) of a general problem (accomplishing the organizational goal) into simpler and more specific sets of organized activities until actual programs are reached. New problems for an existing organization are likewise factored. If this factoring is done in defiance of existing specialties (hence programs), new and usually unacceptable specialties are created with all their implicit problems of tension, co-operation,

and coordination. Such factoring would not be freely undertaken by specialists and could thus be only an act of authority. For these reasons, problem factoring, hence the definition of organization structure, is being forced into specialist hands (though note; the hierarchical role includes the right to do this job and it is almost universally claimed as an "executive function" by writers). The overwhelming need for co-ordinated (hence co-operative) activities among specialists makes this development inevitable.

Associated with the factoring of the organization's goal is the delegation of jurisdictions (i.e., the creation of nonhierarchical authority relations). Previously we emphasized the principal system of authority in organizations—the hierarchy. The authority relations of hierarchy are the relations of a superior to a subordinate. The superior's right to command, however, makes it possible for him to create (delegate) nonhierarchical authority relations. He can command his subordinates to accede to the influence of another person in some defined area or specialty. He can therefore centralize activities or create interdependencies.[36] Since this power of a superior is not necessarily restricted by any formula or operational standard, it is essentially political power—the personal power to confer favors. To the extent that this power is exercised in accordance with the needs of specialization, it constitutes a *pro forma* legitimizing of a technical reality, an official promulgation of a technically existing interdependence.

Although the making of assignments—the setting of goals or purposes—is almost universally designated an "executive function," programs are for the most part activated by received information or the proceduralized flow of work, unless new programs (innovations) are called for. Although approval (legitimizing) of innovations is a superordinate right, innovation is actually a specialist function. Innovation is a specialist function not only because new programs come from specialist organizations and educational curricula, but also because they are suggested by the interpretation of incoming raw data, an activity which of necessity is specialist. (Particular executive positions often combine specialist and superordinate roles.) The *approval* of innovations must, of necessity (i.e., if organization goals are to be achieved), be determined by confidence in the sources of innovation and the order of their appearance.[37] If the approval is based upon the technical adequacy of the proposal, necessarily a specialist determination, the right of approval becomes a formality only.

The adequacy of problem solving within organizations depends upon the adequacy of communication as well as upon the skills available. We have already pointed out that the interdependence of specialists is made more tolerable if communication between them is adequate, and this fact exerts pressure for developing specialized languages and useful shorthand categories for classifying large amounts of information. The relation between adequate and reliable communication and the tolerance of interdependence also exerts pressures for the creation of specialist communication channels beyond the formal channel of the hierarchy. Not only has specialization resulted in an intolerable overloading of the formal channels, but they are no longer technically adequate for much of the communication. Furthermore, these channels are notoriously unreliable because of opportunities and motives for suppression and censorship at each communication station (hierarchical position). Most problem-solving communication, consequently, takes place through specialist communication channels. These communication channels are generally not officially recognized and legitimatized by organization hierarchies, so that most problem-solving communication is either "illegal" and surreptitious or its existence repressed from official consciousness (i.e., notice) by means of myths and fictions.

Since problem solving in organizations is a specialist activity, it is a group rather than an individual activity. A decision by a group of specialists must be almost unanimous, and

modern organizations try to make decisions about organization goals by unanimous groups.[38] In matters involving the personal goals or ambitions of employees, however, autocratic hierarchical decision is still the rule. Although group decision is an inevitable result of specialization (hence interdependence), it is also a result of the perceived need for group decision. Thus, there may be and probably usually is more group consultation in modern bureaucratic organizations than the objective facts of interdependence warrant.[39] This overworking of group processes, the exaggeration of interdependence, appears to result from conditions within the hierarchy rather than from specialization.[40] Since the hierarchy, by definition, is an allocation of rights rather than abilities, this emphasis on the right to be consulted, the right of review, is understandable. The relation of the hierarchical role to the decisional process is a relation of right (competency or jurisdiction). "Has everyone with a legitimate interest been consulted?" Furthermore, the more joint decision is engaged in, the more the immediate superior will be called upon to settle differences, and hence the greater his influence will be. When only single recommendations can reach him, he becomes largely a captive of his organization. It is not surprising, therefore, that the superior will see the need for joint decision whether it exists or not and that he may be tempted to create technically unnecessary interdependence by delegating authority in defiance of the criteria of specialization. However, in addition to the right to be consulted, and desire for enhanced influence, excessive insistence upon joint decision reflects insecurity growing from dependence upon specialists, which increases both in time and with elevation in the hierarchy.

Although, in general, group decision can be greatly superior to individual decision as a problem-solving device,[41] bureaucratic structure severely limits the effectiveness of the group process. For the small-group-thinking process to be most effective, a substantial degree of group cohesion is required. This cohesion greatly increases the ability of the group members to accept and back up affectively one another's analyses and suggestions.[42] It minimizes autocratic procedures and behavior which create tensions, dry up spontaneity and creativity, and attack co-operativeness.[43] Although many spontaneous, nonhierarchical, informal group discussions constantly take place in organizations, the decisions which commit the organization, the official ones, take place in hierarchically structured situations including hierarchically structured groups. Although attempts are often made to hide the hierarchical structure in the formal group-decision process, to pretend that it is not there,[44] the hierarchy is *in fact* present and all group participants know it. Consequently, because of hierarchical control over personal goals, everything said and done in the group situation must be evaluated from the standpoint not only of its relation to the organization's goals but also of its relation to personal goals. In bureaucracy, ideas do not stand on their merits alone.[45] It is not only an opinion or an idea that wins but also a man. The situation is inherently competitive rather than co-operative, and, as Kurt Lewin has pointed out, competition attacks group solidarity and consequently the ability of the group to employ specialization in pursuit of the group goal.[46]

An organizational decision-making group is ostensibly a small problem-solving group and so all the experimental data concerning the latter are relevant to the former. These data roughly indicate that the problem-solving process goes through three stages[47]—orientation (the statement of the problem, definitions, and the like), evaluation (setting up the relevant values and norms), and control (attempts to influence decision or solution). It is necessary to get agreement at each phase before a joint decision at the control end can be achieved. One of the prerogatives of the superior position in hierarchically structured groups is to monopolize the orientation phase—to define the problem ("we are meeting here for the following purpose"). If the problem is thus hierarchically defined, the resulting decision cannot be called a group decision. Although in specific

cases particular superiors may forego the exercise of this right, common experience indicates that the right is frequently claimed. Such a hierarchical statement of the problem will almost certainly have inarticulate premises relating to personal goals (or informal group goals), and this fact contributes to the difficulty of obtaining an effective solution.

In a nonstratified group, positive and negative responses of other members act as controls over participants both in the direction of goal accomplishments and of eventual consensus (true group decision). In the stratified (hierarchical) group, high status or prestige protects a person from group influence but increases the power of his own positive and negative reactions as controls over others in the group. The group must therefore yield to him.

It has been observed in experimental groups that the perception of leadership (who is the leader?) is related to the quantity of activity rather than its quality.[48] Furthermore, as groups increase in size, a larger and larger proportion of the activity is addressed to the perceived leader, and he addresses himself more and more to the group as a whole. The process tends to become one of informal lecture with questions and answers (with the familiar rimless wagon-wheel or star pattern of communication). In the formal organizational group, the position of "leader" is predefined— he is the person with the highest hierarchical position.[49] Thus, even apart from the *rights* of his position there is a strong tendency for him to dominate the group process.

In a group with considerable cohesion, "questions provide a means of turning the process into the instrumental-adaptive direction of movement, with a low probability of provoking an affective reaction, and are an extremely effective way of turning the initiative over to the other."[50] Questions, however, prevent the asker from improving his status because the initiative is given to another and so are much less likely to be used in a competitive, stratified group.

In the experimental group without formal

structure, the idea man is most disruptive of group equilibrium and hence is most likely to arouse hostility. He is also most likely to be perceived as the group leader. In the formally structured group, the idea man is doubly dangerous. He endangers the established distribution of power and status, and he is a competitive threat to his peers. Consequently, he tends to be suppressed.[51]

These potential weaknesses in the group thinking process in formally structured groups raise the question of how effective organization decisions are made in our modern bureaucracies. Four possible answers suggest themselves, all of which are no doubt true to some extent. First, the problems taken up for formal group decision may not usually have a high degree of importance to the organization's success, and a de facto delegation of important decisions to specialist, informal group processes actually takes place. Secondly, it is likely that a considerable degree of self-restraint in the exercise of hierarchical decisional rights must be and usually is practiced.[52] In the third place, it is possible that formal bureaucratic decisions are not as effective as they could be.[53] And, finally, much of the effective decisional process in organization is camouflaged by myths and fictions to give it an apparent consistency with the culturally sanctioned rights of hierarchy.

Durkheim said that specialization as an adjustment to achieve a more satisfactory life involves not only a function which reduces competition but also one suited to a person's constitution or tastes.[54] Thus the organization must be capable of satisfying personal goals. It is not only a distribution of powers (capacities and rights) designed to promote an official system of values but also a means toward personal goals.[55]

The ability of an organization to satisfy the personal needs and motives of all its participants is compromised by the definitions of hierarchical roles. Job satisfaction depends upon the degree of skill involved, the variety of activities, the degree of autonomy, the consistency of the job with the individual's self image, and the predictability of work relations. These elements of job satisfaction may come into conflict with hierarchical rights to assign activities and to supervise them. The right of arbitrary command may conflict with cultural norms of independence, and the right to unusual deference, with norms of equality and dignity. Thus, the self-images of subordinates are endangered.[56]

Within the hierarchy, the opportunities for job satisfactions other than the exercise of authority are particularly scarce, and increasingly so as one mounts the hierarchy, since the specialist element in such jobs becomes increasingly attenuated. Consequently, hierarchical positions are more instrumental to other goals such as power, money, and prestige. With the decline in specialist content goes the possibility of operational performance standards. Since the distribution of the more formal and obvious personal rewards of power, money, and prestige is the prerogative of a superior, the satisfaction of such personal goals requires conformity to a superior's demands whatever they may be. Thus "brownnosing," hypocrisy, "false personalization,"[57] are endemic in modern bureaucracies and especially in those areas where the instrumental satisfactions of work (skill satisfactions) are not so available, namely the upper reaches of the hierarchy. Anxiety generated by the nonoperational demands of superiors and the actual dependence upon subordinates often expresses itself in a preference for "bureaucratic" practices—excessive formalism and impersonality, strict compliance with rules and regulations, close supervision.[58]

The full exercise of hierarchical rights results in autocratic rule, or "bureaucratic" supervision as the term "bureaucratic" was used in the previous paragraph. Whereas a person in a hierarchical position can be expected to dislike the insecurity of his own position and the application of autocratic practices to himself, he may be less sensitive to his subordinates' reactions to such practices, may even need to impose autocratic discipline as an outlet for aggressions necessarily repressed in his role as subordinate.[59] Many studies testify to the deleterious effect which autocratic supervision has on the satisfactions (personal goals) of participants.[60]

The superior's right to monopolize official communication can be particularly damaging to personal satisfactions or goals. As Lewin has pointed out, denial of pertinent information to participants prevents a cognitive structuring of the situation and results in emotionalism, lack of direction, alienation, and conflict.[61] Furthermore, the denial of information, by concealing the relation between activities and the larger group objectives, denies the satisfactions of knowing one is part of a larger, important, co-operative effort. Although the hierarchical role does not *require* the withholding of information, it does condone a certain insensitivity to subordinate needs. Furthermore, the strategic considerations surrounding hierarchical competition and the need to protect the legitimacy of the positions[62] counsel caution in the distribution of information, both to subordinates and to others.

We pointed out above that the currently prevalent concept of organization, the monistic concept, was essentially a formalization of the institution of hierarchy. The monistic concept gives rise to practices and relationships that duplicate childhood to a considerable extent. In monistic theory and somewhat less in practice, each individual in the organization (except the top man) is subordinate to a parentlike figure who instructs, reviews, admonishes, reproves, praises, criticizes, evaluates, supports, rewards, and punishes, thereby duplicating much of the experience of childhood. This denial of adulthood is surely one of the more painful aspects of modern organization.[63] Furthermore, we suspect that performing the role of the parentlike figure would be equally painful for mature, sensitive adults. It may not usually be performed very faithfully.

The most serious impact of the hierarchical system upon the achievement of personal goals within organizations results from its appropriation of the definition of success in our culture. Since the time of the Reformation, success in Western civilization has been interpreted in competitive and individualistic terms of relative social prestige or status.[64] Wealth has long been a dominant symbol of status. As we have shown above, status or social prestige, with all its symbols, including income, has become largely a monopoly of the hierarchy in modern bureaucracy. Bureaucratic hierarchy has inherited the rights and privileges of the early charismatic leader and his retainers, the traditionalistic king and his nobility, and the entrepreneurial owner-manager and his familial protégés. Consequently, to be socially defined as "successful" in our culture, one must proceed up some hierarchy. To have public recognition and esteem, hence self-esteem, one must succeed hierarchically. This situation is painful for the specialist. Even if he is the kind of person who can satisfy his dominance needs by mastering a skill rather than people, he will be denied "success" unless he gives up his specialty and enters hierarchical competition.[65] The converse of the hierarchical appropriation of success is the derogation of intellect, imagination, and skill so prevalent in modern bureaucracy.[66]

As pointed out above, the status system, which apportions prestige largely according to hierarchical position, skews the distribution of personal satisfactions other than those related to work—such satisfactions as power, income, deference, interesting opportunities and associations. This tendency is reinforced by the fact that persons in hierarchical positions have greater opportunities to manipulate the organization in the interest of personal goals.[67] These opportunities result from the superior's strategic power to satisfy or frustrate the personal goals of others in the organization unit, from his ability to control the flow of official communication, from his hierarchical rights *in re* subordinates (for example, the institutionalized plagiarism involved in the obligation to use the boss' signature); and from the fact that superiors cannot practically be subjected to very close supervision by *their* superiors. The resulting maldistribution causes a sense of injustice within organizations and suspicion of the upper hierarchy (the "management").[68] This general sense of injustice reduces the willingness and ability to co-operate, thereby sabotaging the promise of specialization.

This damage to co-operativeness is increased by the hierarchical appropriation of success. Employees of our modern organizations are culturally conditioned to expect promotions for good work. With some exceptions in professional specializations (e.g., junior chemist to chemist to senior chemist), promotions are defined as improvement in hierarchical rank. But the number of hierarchical positions decreases rapidly, and so opportunities for promotions, so defined, are extremely limited. Furthermore, above a very low level of actual operations, "merit" becomes an essentially subjective judgment of superiors, despite the attempted quantification of formal performance-rating schemes.[69] Furthermore, above very low hierarchical levels, the admission of new persons into the hierarchy is best described as sponsorship and co-optation. The crucial questions are not merit and ability in the ordinary sense, but the compatibility and loyalty of the newcomers from the standpoint of the existing "management team" ("is he our kind?").[70] The result of these various considerations is that many persons of great merit according to one set of criteria will nevertheless be "failures" in our society. Since they have been led to expect promotion for good work, they will interpret their nonpromotion as rejection by superiors and the organization as a whole. As March and Simon point out, this feeling of rejection is less painful if the persons involved do not identify with the organization.[71] Thus, the definitions and structures of modern bureaucratic organizations are not compatible with a high degree of organization identification and resulting co-operativeness, further sabotaging the promise of modern specialization.

The foregoing discussion of the relations between specialist and hierarchical roles in the accomplishment of organizational and personal goals provides a basis for the analysis of conflict in modern organizations. Concerning conflict in industrial bureaucracy, Melville Dalton has said: "Approached sociologically, relations among members of management in the plants could be viewed as a general conflict system caused and perpetuated chiefly by (1) power struggles . . . from competition between departments . . . ; (2) drives . . . to increase . . . status; (3) conflict between union and management; and (4) the staff-line friction."[72] Without in any way disagreeing with Dalton we view the pattern of intraorganizational conflict as arising from the interactions between the principal behavior systems in these organizations—the system of rights (authority), the system of deference (status), the system of specialization (the distribution of abilities) which governs the pattern of technical interdependence, and the system of communicative interaction which governs the pattern of identifications. We will discuss conflict under three general organizing topics: (1) conflict due to the violation of role expectations; (2) conflict concerning the reality of interdependence; and (3) conflict arising from blocks to spontaneous communication.

The newer specialties in organizations are usually lumped together conceptually under the name "staff specialist." A number of upsetting relations arise from these new specialties. In the first place, they threaten older specialties with the loss of functions or the addition of new unwanted ones. Especially is this so if the centralizations involved in the new specialties result from the exercise of the hierarchical prerogative to assign duties (create jobs) rather than from the social advance of specialization.[73] Apart from such acts of power, however, the new specialty must achieve social accreditation before it is accepted.

Advancing specialization upsets status expectations as well as vested interests in functions. Specialization, by giving a function to everyone, brings persons of low and high status into interdependent relations, thereby violating the status expectations of the latter.[74]

The "staff" threat to function and status is

particularly acute with regard to hierarchical positions low enough down to contain specialist content.[75] In fact, the conflict arising from these new specialties is usually designated as the line (hierarchy) versus staff conflict. Since specialties eventually win legitimacy one way or another, they acquire authority of a non-hierarchical kind which invades the domain of hierarchical authority. In this way there arises a growing discrepancy between expected authority and actual authority which lies at the heart of the line-staff conflict. Mechanisms of hierarchical protection against this threat of specialization are many, but here we wish only to call attention to the universally adopted devices of derogating staff importance ("line is more important than staff") and of attempting to suppress recognition of the unpalatable features of the relation by the use of fictions ("staff only advises; it does not command").

Much conflict in organizations concerns the reality of interdependence (or the need for joint decision). As we pointed out above, part of this conflict is due to differing perceptions of reality between persons in specialist and hierarchical positions. The need for the new special, hence the new interdependence, may also be questioned by existing specialists because of fear of loss of function. More important from the standpoint of conflict in organizations is disagreement as to the need for new interdependence which arises when rights (competencies) are allocated in disregard of technical criteria. As pointed out above, one of the rights of heirarchical positions is the right to delegate rights (authority). Thus, it is possible for rights (e.g., the right to review or be consulted) to be distributed in a manner inconsistent with the distribution of ability. It is possible for competencies to be defined in defiance of the needs of specialization.

The existence of the authority to defy the needs of specialization, the possibility of pure acts of political power, creates the possibility for interpersonal and intergroup competition for authority (e.g., jurisdiction). An ambitious person may bring more activities, hence people, under his jurisdiction and thereby increase his power and status by two methods. He may contrive to get himself promoted to a higher hierarchical position, or he may get rights reallocated so as to increase his jurisdiction. The first method, being more legitimate, is less likely to arouse conflict, but, as we have seen, promotional opportunities are inherently scarce in relation to demand and may not in any case be available to a particular person because of the sponsorship system prevailing in the organization. Thus the second method, that of expanding jurisdiction, may be the only one practically available. Furthermore, if a given group of subordinates seeks status vicariously through identification with its superior and organizational unit, its influence will be in the direction of expansion of jurisdiction. Once again, as pointed out above, since the hierarchy is more impressed by the need for joint decision than are others in the organization, its defenses against attempts to expand jurisdiction are weakened, resulting in much unnecessary interdependence in bureaucracy. Since expansion of one jurisdiction often means the diminution of another, this method of increasing status produces conflict.

It is likely that newer specialties are more expansionist than old ones, deprived as they are of the full measure of their expected status and function because of lack of full acceptance.[76] If the new centralization (specialization) is an act of hierarchical power rather than a result of the advance of specialization, expansionism probably reflects an attempt to allay the inevitable insecurity associated with an imbalance between authority and ability (the right to be consulted versus the ability to make a contribution). However, expansionism may also reflect simply the attempt by a newer specialty to realize a full measure of function consistent with its technical promise. In this latter case, free interaction between the new and the old will eventually cure the cause of conflict, allowing the new to demonstrate its validity and hence the need for the new interdependence.[77] However, conflict arising from resistance to the interdependence resulting from pure power plays can only be eliminated by a redefinition of jurisdictions to the actual needs of specialization, or by defeatist acceptance of the new jurisdictions. In the latter case, any change in the distribution of political power in the organization (power which comes from the personal support of persons with power) will likely be followed by more or less intense activity seeking to reallocate rights of jurisdiction. In this way, an allocation of rights by arbitrary authority creates an unstable and potentially explosive situation.

A common form of the conflict concerning the reality or need for interdependence is that which sometimes arises over the joint use of means. When centralization is undertaken to allow full employment of the latest specializations in skills or equipment, the minor conflicts from joint use which arise because of some inevitable degree of scarcity are not important and are easily resolved without destroying co-operation. The amount of denial and frustration involved can be shown to be necessary and thus acceptable. When the centralization of means is an act of power, however, frustrations arising from the interdependence cannot be made acceptable because they cannot be demonstrated to be necessary. Attempts to ameliorate the conflict by the permanent, full-time assignment of subunits of means to each client cannot remove the instability in the situation, disclosing as it does the fact that the centralization in question is purely a matter of right, of authority, with none of the requirements of specialization involved. Whenever it is technically possible permanently to assign subunits of means, it is technically possible to decentralize.

To illustrate our point, suppose Miss Brown is the subordinate of Mr. Jones and that she is his stenographer. The organization then decides to centralize stenography by creating a stenographic pool. Miss Brown is transferred to the pool but, to avoid conflict over the joint use of means, she is permanently assigned to Mr. Jones. Her technical relation to Mr. Jones is the same; she is his stenographer. Her authority relationship, however, has been changed. She is now the subordinate of Mrs. Smith, the pool chief, rather than Mr. Jones. The centralization was a pure act of authority. Only authority relations were involved.

We should point out that part of the difficulties which arise from centralization can be traced back to the monocratic character of the hierarchical institution. We have said that activities are frequently centralized to assure full employment of the latest specialization in skills or equipment by concentrating demand for them. If the new specialist could be a member of several organization units instead of one, this centralization of activities would not be necessary. It is held that such multiple membership would violate the principle of "unity of command" and must hence be avoided. The reason it is avoided is that it is incompatible with the institution of hierarchy. It would place the specialist in the subordinate relationship with more than one superior. He would have more than one *boss*. While a person can be placed in a subordinate relation to several nonhierarchical authority positions, and always is so placed in modern bureaucracy, he cannot be placed in a subordinate relationship to more than one boss. The rights of the superordinate role preclude more than one boss. The hierarchical institution is monocratic. Among the many suggestions which Frederick Taylor made, his suggestion for several "functional foremen" for each operator was never taken seriously by management. Such an arrangement would attack the very heart of the institution of hierarchy.

Apart from conflicts due to role invasion and the reality of interdependence, the system of communicative interaction also affects the amount and kind of conflict. A great deal of communication works toward a common conception of reality and the sharing of goals. Conversely, blocks to such interaction result in differentiation of reality perception and of goals.[78] The pattern of the distribution of these blocks in modern bureaucracy produces a pattern of groups—clusters of people who, by virtue of frequent and free interaction, share goals and reality perceptions.

The pattern of interaction is determined by the principal behavior systems in organizations. Involved are the systems of authority, status, and specialization (the system of technically necessary interdependence in regard to the organization's goal). The pyramidal distribution of hierarchical rights tends strongly to create groups composed of subordinates and a superior with a wagon-wheel pattern of communication.[79] The hierarchical control of official communication tends to divide the organization into management (hierarchy) and employees (labor). The status system, with its blocks to interaction between strata, reinforces this division and both together alienate the group—"employees"—from the organization as a whole. Shared goals and reality perceptions do not easily extend across this barrier.

Hierarchical control of official communication in conjunction with the status system subdivides the whole organization into status strata. Although there are status strata among purely specialist positions (e.g., junior classification analyst, analyst, and senior analyst), and general status divisions between clerical and professional and blue-collar and white-collar, the heavily emphasized status divisions correspond to hierarchical rank. Status blocks to interaction between strata prevent the development of common goals and perceptions of reality, creating some degree of alienation from the organization, strata by strata, diminishing as one goes up the hierarchy of strata. This alienation within the hierarchy is reduced by two factors. First, mobile individuals, expecting to climb to high positions, try to adopt, or appear to adopt, the values and reality perceptions of higher levels.[80] Second, through the practice of sponsorship, certain likely individuals at lower levels are chosen early and "groomed" for high management positions.[81] By virtue of these various forces and mechanisms, the "management group" is actually much smaller than everyone in supervisory positions, and, in fact, it is customary these days to speak of a still smaller "inner cabinet" or "top management" composed of the head of the organization and his immediate subordinates.

The system of specialization requires the interaction of persons whose specialties must be harmonized in order to achieve the organization goal. This interaction is restricted both by the distribution of authority, hierarchical and delegated, and by the groupings formed by the official communication system. The superior's right to be the sole source of influence over subordinates ("unity of command"), his right to be fully appraised of what is going on (supervision), his right to monopolize communication, his right to the loyalty of his subordinates, all restrict free interaction between subordinate specialists of one organization unit and those of another. Reinforcing these restrictions are the demands of the individual's immediate work group (fellow subordinates and possibly his superior) that he share and give effect to their values and perceptions of reality. Although his status grouping may also interfere with communication with a lower-level specialist, it is our belief that this factor is not serious in purely specialist interaction.[82]

Despite these blocks, interaction is technically necessary. And since no formal-unit work group or status strata could contain all the relevant specialties, specialist interaction must take place across formal-unit and status-strata lines. As mentioned above, this necessary interaction carves out specialist channels of communication, and hence channels of influence, of a semi-illegal nature. More important, it leads to the sharing of values and reality perceptions between the specialists—to multiple group membership—and hence, perhaps to divided loyalties, doubts, and guilts. Interunit conflict becomes internalized in the individual. All these effects are likely to be reinforced by the specialist's dependence upon specialist lines and channels for personal satisfactions of status and function, unless he is willing to forego his specialty and enter hierarchical competition. Finally, we should point out that the dimensions of the dilemma of specialist interaction are qualified by the importance of the interdependence, by whether the interdependence involves functional necessities or only working convenience (e.g., the clearance of proposed new programs versus the installation of an additional telephone extension).[83]

The bases of intraorganizational conflict can be summarized in a few general propositions, as follows:[84]

1. Conflict is a function of disagreement over the reality of interdependence.
    1.1. Lack of agreement about the reality of interdependence arises from lack of acceptance of specialties.
    Lack of acceptance of specialties results from lack of accreditation of specialties, which, in turn, is a function of
        1.1.1. their newness, or
        1.1.2. the creation of specialties by acts of authority in defiance of technical criteria.
    1.2 Lack of agreement about the reality of interdependence is also a function of differing perceptions of reality. These differing perceptions are a function of position in
        1.2.1. the authority system,
        1.2.2. the status system, and
        1.2.3. the system of person-to-person communication (the group system).
2. Conflict is a function of the degree of disparity between authority (the right to be consulted) and the ability to contribute to goals. This disparity arises from
    2.1. Growing dependence upon specialists (a function of the process of specialization) while hierarchical role definitions change more slowly; and
    2.2. The allocation of rights (delegation) in disregard of the needs of specialization (acts of sheer authority).
3. Conflict is a function of the degree of status violation involved in interaction.
    3.1. Status violation results from advancing specialization and consequent growing interdependence of high- and low-status positions—from positional claims to deference, on the one hand, and the fact of dependence upon specialists, on the other.
4. Conflict is made more or less intense by the relative importance of the interdependence to the success of the organization.
5. Finally, conflict is a function of the lack of shared values and reality perceptions (identifications), which are, in addition to personalities,
    5.1. A function of the lack of spontaneity and freedom in communicative interaction, which is
        5.1.1. a function of the resistance to penetration from without of the principal behavior systems—the authority system, the status system, and the technical system (specialization).

In short, conflict arises from growing inconsistencies between specialist and hierarchical roles. Whereas there are other bases for conflict, it is likely that they could be easily managed under a regime of specialist solidarity based upon the mutual recognition of the need for interdependence.

The conflict between specialist and hierarchical roles has generated mechanisms of role defense. From the standpoint of the hierarchical role, defense involves the securing and maintenance of the legitimacy of the role. Here we only wish to set forth briefly some of the mechanisms of specialist role defense.

We have already mentioned that in order to claim "success," as culturally defined, the specialist must give up his specialty and enter hierarchical competition. A person who chooses this course of action must adopt the values of the managerial group to which he aspires. This "anticipatory socialization" enables such a person to avoid the worst consequences of specialist-hierarchical conflict.[85] Merton has pointed out that a specialist not wishing to follow this path may adopt a sort of schizoid separation of his roles, maintaining his own values privately and relating himself to the organization solely in his specialist or technical capacity. Thus he refuses to take any responsibility for the use or nonspecialist consequences of his advice, regarding such matters as "policy questions" to be handled by the "administrative people." Much specialist training, especially of engineers, contains a liberal amount of preparation for such a subaltern status.[86]

We have also pointed out that specialists engaged in organization problem solving consistently evade official prescriptions in order to get the job done, especially in the matter of communication. This evasion of official prescriptions also takes place in the lower levels of the hierarchy where hierarchical positions contain a good deal of specialist content, perhaps mostly specialist content.[87]

An increasingly used device of specialist role protection is the fromation of local, state, and national associations of specialists. These associations compensate to some extent for lack of rights of appeal from hierarchical vetoes by providing a "free constituency" to which vetoed items may be presented.[88] Although some professional associations may function as devices of managerial control of specialists (perhaps some engineering associations have so functioned in the past), it would seem that most of them severely limit managerial control by specifying just how their members may be employed in organizations.[89] In short, they are devices for protecting specialist status and function.

Where a particular skill is concentrated under one or a few employers (that is, in a specific organization), efforts of the skill group to protect its status and function are more effective, resulting in distinctive career groups and peculiar "problems of personnel administration." Examples of such career groups in government organization are: the Forest Service, the Geological Survey, social workers, police, firemen, school teachers, public health workers. Protective activities of such groups result in strong attachments to the careers and the organizations through which they are pursued, emphasis upon objective or proceduralized distribution of recognition (status), life commitments to the careers, a long-range program for the whole career, and the like.[90]

Finally, we should mention that pressures for "due process" proceduralized protection of organization employees have specialist rather than hierarchical origins. They originate both in the new specialties of personnel administration and in the employee associations (whether they be called unions or professional societies).

— The resolution of conflict in modern organization is made difficult by the fact that conflict is not formally recognized, hence legitimated. To legitimate conflict would be inconsistent with the monocratic nature of hierarchy. It would require formal bargaining procedures. Modern organizations, through the formal hierarchy of authority, seek an "administered consensus."[91] Conflict resolution, therefore, must occur informally by surreptitious and somewhat illegal means. Or else it must be repressed, creating a phony atmosphere of good feeling and superficial harmony.

NOTES

[1] This article is condensed from chs. iii and iv of *Modern Organization* (New York: Alfred A. Knopf, Inc., 1961).

[2] See Norman Powell, *Personnel Administration in Government* (Englewood Cliffs, 1956), pp. 395–398; also see Harold J. Leavitt, *Managerial Psychology* (Chicago, 1958), pp. 259–262; Wilbert E. Moore, *Industrial Relations and the Social Order* (2d, ed.; New York, 1951), p. 143.

[3] Note the widespread reaction against the late Senator McCarthy's assertion that public officials owe their first loyalty to the United States,

not to their bureaucratic superiors. For the same reasons there has been considerable criticism of the Nuremberg trials of war criminals because the command of a superior officer was not accepted as a defense.

4 See William H. Whyte, Jr., *The Organization Man* (New York, 1957).

5 Moore, *op. cit.*, pp. 183–184, says this insensitivity of superiors in regard to needs of subordinates is the cause of much trouble in organizations. Harold Leavitt says superiors generally resist the introduction of objective performance standards because they interfere with the superiors' right to dominate the situation, to command respect, to rule the roost (*ibid.*, p. 261).

6 For a discussion of the various psychological "goods" or advantages enjoyed by the person with superior power in a relationship, see John W. Thibaut and Harold H. Kelley, *The Social Psychology of Groups* (New York, 1959), pp. 116–119.

7 Kingsley Davis, A Conceptual Analysis of Stratification, *American Sociological Review*, 7 (1942), 309–321.

8 Robert K. Merton, *Social Theory and Social Structure* (rev. ed.; Glencoe, 1957), p. 315.

9 G. H. Mead, *Mind, Self, and Society* (Chicago, 1934); Theodore R. Sarbin, "Role Theory," in Gardner Lindzey, ed., *Handbook of Social Psychology* (Cambridge, Mass., 1954); Davis, *op. cit.*

10 See Chester I. Barnard, "Functions and Pathology of Status Systems in Formal Organizations," in William Foote Whyte, ed., *Industry and Society* (New York, 1946).

11 See Cecil A. Gibb, "Leadership," in Lindzey, *op. cit.*, p. 905. See also R. T. LaPiere and P. R. Farnsworth, *Social Psychology* (New York, 1936), pp. 308–309; and Norton E. Long, The Local Community as an Ecology of Games, *American Journal of Sociology*, 64(1958), 251–261. The pressure upon high-status people to speak out plausibly on a great range of subjects has given rise to a new and highly paid profession—the ghost writers. See Daniel M. Burham, Corporate Ghosts, *Wall Street Journal*, Jan. 4, 1960, p. 1.

12 Robert F. Bales, "The Equilibrium Problem in Small Groups," in Talcott Parsons, Robert F. Bales, and Edward A. Shills, *Working Papers in the Theory of Action* (Glencoe, 1953).

13 Samuel Stouffer *et al.*, *The American Soldier*, I (Princeton, N.J., 1949), pp. 391 ff.

14 See Moore, *op. cit.*, p. 125. Washington and Rothschild do an effective job of refuting arguments that the existing pattern of executive compensation has a purely utilitarian function in relation to organization goals. *Compensating the Corporation Executive* (New York, 1951).

15 Fritz Roethlesberger, *Management and Morale* (Cambridge, Mass., 1941), p. 77; Victor A. Thompson, *The Regulatory Process in OPA Rationing* (New York, 1950), p. 323.

16 See Barnard, *op. cit.* See also Thibaut and Kelley, *op. cit.*, ch. xii. They equate the status system with the distributive system.

17 With regard to the military status system, Ralph H. Turner says: "However, through their charisma officers are generally held in far greater awe than their actual powers or inclinations warrant, and a lesser officer is often afraid even to suggest to a superior that his request is not in keeping with regulations" (The Navy Disbursing Officer, *American Sociological Review*, 12 [1947], 342–348).

[18] See works by F. Heider, for example, Social Perception and Phenomenal Causality, *Psychological Review,* 51 (1944), 358–374.

[19] Barnard, *op. cit.* The difficulties encountered when orders must be taken from persons perceived as having lower status are well illustrated by interpersonal problems of chefs and waitresses. See William Foote Whyte, *Human Relations in the Restaurant Industry* (New York, 1948).

[20] *Escape from Freedom,* pp. 165–166. On the ambivalence generated by the authority relationship, see also G. Murphy, *Personality* (New York, 1947), pp. 845–846; and Krech and Crutchfield, *Theory and Problems of Social Psychology* (New York, 1948), p. 421.

[21] See Norman Miller, "The Jewish Leadership of Lakeport," in Gouldner, ed., *op. cit.,* pp. 206–207.

[22] Philip Selznick, An Approach to a Theory of Bureaucracy, *American Sociological Review,* 8 (1943), 323.

[23] See Henri de Man, *Joy in Work* (London, 1929), pp. 200–204.

[24] Gibb, *op. cit.,* p. 899.

[25] *Ibid.,* p. 901.

[26] See Erving Goffman, *The Presentation of Self in Everyday Life* (Garden City, 1959).

[27] According to Eric Fromm, this fact contributed much to the Nazi's success in Germany, *op. cit.,* ch. vi, esp. pp. 236–247. The elaborate Nazi hierarchy provided opportunities for domination and submission for many authoritarian personalities with their combination of sadistic and masochistic characteristics.

[28] Moore, *op. cit.,* p. 143; also James G. March and Herbert A. Simon, *Organizations* (New York, 1958), p. 63. Of course, a particular office may include specialist as well as hierarchical activities, and operational performance standards for the former may be available.

[29] This loss of functions to specialists has been noted by many writers. See for example, Leavitt, *op. cit.,* pp. 266, 269, 238; Moore, *op. cit.,* p. 76; and Reinhard Bendix, *Work and Authority in Industry* (New York, 1956), pp. 226 ff.

[30] See March and Simon, *op. cit.,* p. 102.

[31] Merton, *op. cit.,* ch. vi, "Bureaucratic Structure and Personality." See also Willard Waller, *The Sociology of Teaching* (New York, 1932).

[32] See Barnard, *op. cit.*

[33] Moore, *op. cit.;* Carl Dreyfuss, *Occupation and Ideology of the Salaried Employee,* tr. by Eva Abramovitch (New York, 1938).

[34] For examples of this monistic concept in organization theory see: Mary Cushing Howard Niles, *Middle Management* (New York, 1941); Marshall E. Dimock, *The Executive in Action* (New York, 1945); L. C. Marshall, *Business Administration* (Chicago, 1921); Paul E. Holden, Lounsberry S. Fish, and Hubert L. Smith, *Top Management Organization and Control* (Stanford, 1941); first Hoover Commission Report (Washington, D.C., 1949).

[35] See Peter B. Hammond, "The Functions of Indirection in Communication," in *Comparative Studies in Administration,* ed. by staff of the Administrative Science Center, University of Pittsburgh, Pittsburgh, 1959.

[36] Nonhierarchial authority differs from hierarchical authority in the following ways: (1) it is more specific; (2) it relates to organizational rather than personal goals; (3) it can be withdrawn without destroying the position; (4) it is always subject to formal appeal; and (5) it is

organizationally rather than culturally defined (i. e., it is peculiar to the organization rather than the culture).

37 See March and Simon, *op. cit.*, p. 188; also Thompson, *op. cit.*, pp. 303 ff.

38 See Moore, *op. cit.*, p. 124, n. 14; March and Simon, *op. cit.*, p. 118; Gordon, *Business Leadership in the Large Corporation* (Washington, D. C., 1945), pp. 99 ff.; W. H. Whyte, *op. cit.* Consultants are probably brought in because unanimity cannot be obtained (Moore, *op. cit.*, p. 124).

39 Note W. H. Whyte's complaints on this score.

40 March and Simon say that the felt need for joint decision increases as one goes up the hierarchy. They feel that since the chief legitimation of hierarchy is co-ordination, the hierarchy is likely to see the need for co-ordination whether or not it exists (*op. cit.*, p. 124).

41 See E. L. Thorndyke, The Effect of Discussion upon the Correctness of Group Decisions when the Factor of Majority Influence is Allowed For, *Journal of Social Psychology*, 9 (1938), 342–362; and Thibaut and Kelley, "Experimental Studies of Group Problem Solving Process," in Lindzey, ed., *op. cit.*

42 For example, see M. Deutsch, An Experimental Study of the Effects of Cooperation and Competition upon Group Processes, *Human Relations*, 2 (1949), 199–232; K. Back, The Exertion of Influence through Social Communication, *Journal of Abnormal Psychology*, 46 (1951), 9–23; S. Schachter, Deviation, Rejection and Communication, *Journal of Abnormal Psychology*, 46 (1951), 190–207.

43 See Kurt Lewin, *Resolving Social Conflict* (New York, 1948); L. Cock and J. R. P. French, Jr., Overcoming Resistance to Change, *Human Relations*, 1 (1948), 512–532; D. McGregor, Conditions of Effective Leadership in the Industrial Organization, *Journal of Consulting Psychologists*, 8 (1944), 55–63; and R. Lippitt and R. K. White, "The Social Climate of Children's Groups," in R. G. Barker, J. S. Kounin, and H. F. Wright, eds., *Child Behavior and Development* (New York, 1943), pp. 485–508.

44 For example, "brainstorming," or the Harwold Group Thinkometer which allows each participant to press a button for "yes," "no," or "maybe," thus not endangering his position in the organization with open discussion.

45 See Lyman Bryson, Notes on a Theory of Advice, *Political Science Quarterly*, 66 (1951), 321–329. On the problem-solving superiority of groups low in self-oriented need, see N. T. Fouriezos, M. L. Hutt, and H. Guetzkow, Measurement of Self-Oriented Needs in Discussion Groups, *Journal of Abnormal Social Psychology*, 45 (1950), 682–690.

46 *Resolving Social Conflicts.*

47 See Robert F. Bales, "The Equilibrium Problem in Small Groups," in *op. cit.*, pp. 111–163.

48 *Ibid.*

49 See W. H. Crockett, Emergent Leadership in Small, Decision-Making Groups, *Journal of Abnormal Psychology*, 51 (1955), 378–383.

50 Bales, *op. cit.*, p. 127.

51 Note the growing antipathy to idea men, to brillance, that pervades our bureaucracies. The average person who will *get along* with others and *go along* with the system is preferred. See W.H. Whyte, *op. cit.*, pp. 143 ff.

52 See Chester I. Barnard, *The Function of the Executive* (Cambridge, Mass., 1938), pp. 193–194. He says the "fine art" of executive decisional ability is knowing when *not* to decide.

53 Note March and Simon's contention that satisficing rather than maxi-

mizing norms are usually applied to organization decisions, and that the approval of proposals is as much a function of their source and timing as of their utility (*op. cit.*, pp. 140–141, 188).

[54] *The Division of Labor in Society* (Glencoe, 1947), pp. 374–375.

[55] On this point are especially the works of Chris Argyris, for example, The Individual and Organization: Some Problems of Mutual Adjustment, *Administrative Science Quarterly* 2 (1957) 1–22, and "Understanding Human Behavior in Organizations: One Viewpoint," in Mason Haire, ed., *Modern Organization Theory* (New York, 1959), pp. 115–154.

[56] March and Simon summarize the observed bases of job satisfaction (*op. cit.*, pp. 76–77, 94–97). Expectations of independence, equality, and dignity, being cultural, will vary from country to country. Their impact upon organization will, hence, also vary. See Stephan A. Richardson, Organizational Contrasts on British and American Ships, *Administrative Science Quarterly* (1956).

[57] The term is from *The Lonely Crowd* (New Haven, 1950), by David Riesman, Nathan Glazer, and Reuel Denney; see pp. 303–305. See also Harold Leavitt, *op. cit.*, p. 264, and Moore, *op. cit.*, pp. 142–145.

[58] Anxiety has been defined as a vague, nonspecific fear resulting from threats to values basic to the integrity of the personality (Rollo May, *The Meaning of Anxiety* [New York, 1950], p. 191). The values in question in our society are those related to social prestige or status. Status in our society is largely a function of hierarchical position; but so is *loss* of status. Consequently, acute anxiety is a normal condition within the bureaucratic hierarchy.

[59] See Fromm, *op. cit.*

[60] This statement applies to a society where expectations of democratic treatment predominate. Where people have been brought up to expect autocratic supervision, it would probably not apply. See Gibb, *op. cit.*, pp. 910–912.

[61] *Ibid.*

[62] Leavitt says that equalitarian, multichannel communication nets are best but are seldom used because they conflict with hierarchical prerogatives (*op. cit.*, p. 204).

[63] See Leavitt, *op. cit.*, pp. 264–265, and Argyris, *op. cit.*, pp. 18–21.

[64] See May, *op. cit.*, pp. 215 ff.; also Abram Kardiner, *The Psychological Frontiers of Society* (New York, 1945). Since the dominant symbol of status has been money, "success" in America is usually equated with "making money." See Irvin Gordon Wyllie, *The Self-Made Man in America* (New Brunswick, 1954); Kenneth S. Lynn, *The Dream of Success* (Boston, 1955); Richard D. Moiser, *Making the American Mind* (New York, 1947).

[65] See Moore, *op. cit.*, ch. vi; Riesman, *op. cit.*, pp. 154–155; and Alvin W. Gouldner, *Patterns of Industrial Bureaucracy* (Glencoe, 1954), p. 226.

[66] See W. H. Whyte, *op. cit.*, ch. x and *passim.*

[67] See Philip Selznick, An Approach to a Theory of Bureaucracy, *American Sociological Review.*, 8 (1943). The office, because of its advantages, comes to be regarded as an end rather than a means. For this process in labor unions, see A. J. Muste, "Factional Fights in Trade Unions," in J. B. S. Hardman, ed., *American Labor Dynamics* (New York, 1928).

[68] Many people report this general sense of injustice resulting from the hierarchically skewed distribution system. See, for example, Barnard, "The Functions and Pathology of Status Systems in Formal Organizations," in *op. cit.*; Moore, *op. cit.*, p. 184; Roethlesberger, *op. cit.*, p. 77; Peter Drucker,

The New Society: The Anatomy of the Industrial Order (New York, 1950), pp. 92–95.

[69] See Norman J. Powell, *op. cit.*, chs. xi and xvi; Moore, *op. cit.*, p. 143; and Leavitt, *op. cit.*, pp. 259–262.

[70] See note 80, below; also C. Wright Mills, *The Power Elite* (New York, 1957), ch. vi. Since the operationality of performance standards declines as we go up the hierarchy (see Moore, *op. cit.*, pp. 140–143, and March and Simon, *op. cit.*, p. 63), the superior's rights with relation to the subordinate's ambitions or personal needs become more and more analogous to political power; the process of climbing the hierarchy or "getting ahead" becomes more and more a political process; and the kind of person who can succeed at this game becomes more and more like the political type. On this point generally, see Harold Lasswell, *Politics: Who Gets What, When, How* (New York, 1936).

[71] *Op. cit.* p. 74. See also R. C. Stone, Mobility Factors as they Affect Workers' Attitudes and Conduct toward Incentive Systems, *American Sociological Review*, 17 (1952), 58–64.

[72] Conflicts between Line and Staff Managerial Officers, *American Sociological Review*, 15 (1950), 342–351. He points out that the intensity of the conflict was exaggerated because recognition of the conflict had to be repressed.

In the following discussion we do not wish to leave the impression that we believe conflict, per se, is bad.

[73] Dalton's study showed only 50 per cent of staff people doing work related to their college training, thereby casting doubt on the validity of some of the specializations.

[74] In Dalton's study, staff specialties were the new ones, and these specialists were much younger than others in the organization on the average. "Line" resistance was especially pronounced.

[75] Dalton, *op. cit.*; Moore, *op. cit.*, ch. vi.

[76] Dalton says that staff people have less chance of hierarchical advance and hence must engage in empire building activities.

[77] It should be noted that specialist organizations may block this free interaction and thus slow up the integration of the new with the old and the adjustment of the old to the new for considerable periods of time. The activities of building trades unions are notorious examples of this process, but the same elements are at work, for example, in medical resistance to a redefinition of nurses' roles. See Harvey L. Smith, Contingencies of Professional Differentiation, *American Journal of Sociology*, 63 (1958), 410–414.

[78] See March and Simon, *op. cit.*, pp. 124–129.

[79] Under strictly autocratic practices, the pattern of communication would be star-shaped; little group identification would result. As the group composed of supervisor and subordinates becomes more cohesive, the structure of the communication pattern changes until it is difficult to tell who is the formal head and, in fact, most communication may eventually be directed to a person other than the appointed head—to an "informal leader." When this development occurs, the formal head has accepted the obligations of group membership and has rejected his hierarchical duties and forfeited his hierarchical rights.

[80] See Merton, *op. cit.*, ch. ix, "Continuities in the Theory of Reference Groups and Social Structure."

[81] See Mills, *op. cit.*, ch. vi; Everett C. Hughes, Queries concerning In-

dustry and Society Growing Out of Study of Ethnic Relations in Industry, *American Sociological Review*, 14 (1949), 218–220; Orvis Collins, Ethnic Behavior in Industry: Sponsorship and Rejection in a New England Factory, *American Journal of Sociology*, 51 (1946), 293–298; Joseph W. Eaton, Is Scientific Leadership Selection Possible? *American Journal of Sociology*, 52 (1947), 523–535. E. L. Thorndike, *Human Nature and the Social Order* (New York, 1940); W. R. Kornhauser, The Negro Union Official: A Study of Sponsorship and Control, *American Journal of Sociology*, 57 (1952), 443–452; Melville Dalton, Informal Factors in Career Achievements, *American Journal of Sociology*, 56 (1951), 407–415.

[82] We are arguing, for example, that a senior economist will have little difficulty dealing with a junior statistician in another unit who can actually perform some service that an economist requires. For the chief of the economics section to deal with the same junior statistician would be more painful.

[83] It should be noted, however, that trivia may have great symbolical significance. Much of the conflict in organizations has a trivial origin.

[84] We should emphasize again that we are discussing *only* organizationally generated phenomena. Conflict also results from extraorganizational influences such as the general social conditioning that shapes personality, conflicting group affiliations, racial and religious attitudes, and the like.

[85] See Merton, *op. cit.*, pp. 265–271. Conscious, opportunistic adoption of managerial values is likely to involve the specialist in difficulties with his peers who will regard him as "pushy," a "climber," a person "bucking for a promotion," an "upstart," and even a "renegade" (Merton, *ibid.*).

[86] *Ibid.*, chs. vii, xvii. Others have pointed out that technical specialists are generally easy for power seekers to manipulate. See Hans H. Gerth and C. Wright Mills, A Marx for the Managers, *Ethics*, 3 (1941–1942), 200–215. The specialized training acts as a blinder to other aspects of experience. Veblen referred to this phenomenon as "trained incapacity."

[87] See Melville Dalton, Unofficial Union-Management Relations, *American Sociological Review*, 15 (1950), 611–619. This study shows that lower-level management officials and lower-level union officials both evade the prescriptions of their respective hierarchies in order to solve their mutual problems. See also Charles Hunt Page, Bureaucracy's Other Face, *Social Forces*, 25 (Oct. 1946), 88–94.

[88] On this point see Bryson, *op. cit.*; Selznick, *TVA and the Grass Roots* (Berkeley, 1949), esp. pp. 145–147; and David Truman, *The Governmental Process* (New York, 1951), *passim*. Because ideas are not considered on their merits alone in bureaucratic organizations, it would seem reasonable to argue that these "free constituencies" are a necessary condition of organization success in the long run.

[89] Note, for example, how the Group for the Advancement of Psychiatry seeks to determine the activities of the various specialists in mental institutions. The role of the social worker is defined in the GAP Report Number 16; the role of the "Consultant Psychiatrist in a Family Service or Welfare Agency," in GAP Letter Number 259; and so on.

[90] See Wallace S. Sayre and Frederick C. Mosher, *An Agenda for Research in Public Personnel Administration* (Washington, D.C., 1959), pp. 37–42.

[91] The term was suggested to me by Robert V. Presthus.

3.

HIERARCHICAL IMPEDIMENTS TO INNOVATION IN EDUCATIONAL ORGANIZATIONS

MAX G. ABBOTT

A discussion of the topic of change would not be complete without a serious examination of the nature of the organization in which change was expected to occur. That is, it seems obvious that the structure of the organization has important implications for the way in which that organization will function.

As I proceeded with the preparation of this paper, however, it became equally obvious that it would be necessary to limit my attention to only a few of the many structural elements which might be considered. Since, in my view, the appropriation of hierarchical prerogatives to enhance the personal status of administrative officials represents a most serious obstacle to the introduction of meaningful innovations in the educational organization, I decided to concentrate my attention on this aspect of organizational structure. Thus, the choice of the term "hierarchical impediments" rather than the term "structural impediments" as a focus for this focus for this paper has been deliberate.

During recent years, it has become respectable, or, perhaps to be more accurate, it has become popular to talk about change and innovation in education. At times one is led to the conclusion that change has become the new "royal road" to respectability for educa-

From Max G. Abbot & John T. Lovell, eds., *Change Perspectives in Educational Administration*, School of Education, Auburn University, Auburn, Ala., 1965, pp. 40–53. Reprinted by permission.

tors. During the past ten years, particularly, we have witnessed the introduction of numerous "new" practices in the schools: new math and science curricula, team teaching, large- and small-group instruction, and programmed learning, to mention only a few. Yet, not all of these practices represent genuine innovations, and of those which do, not all have been adopted and applied in such a way as to assure progress. As Professor Thelen has commented:

> In the face of all these changes . . . the schools' society and culture seems largely undisturbed. Comparing classrooms now with the classrooms of 40 years ago, one notes that at both times there were numbers of students not much interested in what was being done; the typical teacher still presents material and quizzes the kids to see if they understand it; the amount of creativity and excitement is probably no greater now than then. The development of new materials and techniques has enabled us to spin our wheels in one place, to conduct business as usual in the face of dramatic changes in the society and in the clientele of the school. The operation of the educational enterprise has encountered what can only be thought of by the traditional teacher as a very large number of increasingly serious obstacles and the new devices sustain the forlorn hope of protecting and maintaining, rather than changing, the old orthodoxy in the face of the most important revolutions in the history of mankind.[1]

Thelen suggests that the changes which have occurred have gone through three distinct phases: (1) *enthusiasm*, (2) *vulgarization* and *spread*, and (3) *institutionalization*. That is, each new idea has been introduced with a flurry of activity, accompanied by widespread excitement, and followed by a period of rationalization, during which traditional practices have been redefined to make them fit the rubrics of the innovations. Thus, to cite an example, an administrator who is confronted with a lack of classroom space will combine two groups of students under the direction of two teachers, house the newly formed group in an auditorium or a cafeteria, and refer to the new arrangement as an experiment in team teaching.

How are we to account for this widespread unwillingness to deal realistically with new ideas, new practices, and new demands? How can we explain such resistance to meaningful innovation? It is neither accurate nor helpful to attribute such behavior to mere perversity on the part of teachers and other school personnel. Any formal organization is constantly subject to competing sets of forces: those that represent inertia, or the maintenance of the status quo, on the one hand, and those that represent change, or innovation, on the other.

Much of the inertia in formal organizations occurs as a result of the "sunk costs" of those organizations; in the educational enterprise, these "sunk costs" consist of a substantial investment in training and experience, and of a psychological commitment to particular ways of programming activities. Conversely, the forces for change represent some sort of dissatisfaction with the status quo.

As long as the forces for maintaining the status quo are equal to or greater than the forces to change, the organization is said to be in a state of equilibrium. As March and Simon have stated the case:

> Individuals and organizations give preferred treatment to alternatives that represent continuation of programs over those that represent change. . . . Presistence comes about primarily because the individual or organization does not search for or consider alternatives to the present course of action unless that present course is in some sense "unsatisfactory."[2]

Disequilibrium occurs when the forces to change become greater than the forces to maintain the status quo. Such disequilibrium represents an occasion for innovation. Thus, we would define innovation as the adaptive response which an organization makes to a situation in which a program of action, which has been regarded as satisfying certain criteria, no longer does so.

When we employ this type of a definition, we do not attribute persistence of behavior to perversity or to a particular "resistance to change"; rather, such persistence is explained more adequately in terms of a lack of dissatisfaction with the present state of affairs and, thus, with a lack of search for new alternatives. Since change for its own sake has apparently become a valued goal in education, as it frequently does in an immature profession, school people have shown a strong inclination to board bandwagon movements, not because of dissatisfaction with present programs, but because it is fashionable to be "progressive." It is hardly surprising, therefore, that new curricula and new procedures have frequently been viewed as gimmicks, adopted and applied with little enthusiasm and even less understanding.

Assuming that meaningful innovations are necessary if the schools are to meet the challenges of the social and technological revolution that is taking place in the world today, the problem confronting us is to identify those elements in the school organization which inhibit and impede such innovations. Thus, I am led to ask two fundamental questions: (1) Are there forces in the school organization that make it difficult to determine the point at which previously satisfactory programs are no longer satisfactory? (2) Do present organizational arrangements and relationships inhibit the implementation of new programs of action when old ones have been demonstrated to be unsatisfactory?

As a prelude to a more thorough discussion of these two questions, I propose to examine briefly the school organization as it now exists. This can probably best be done by referring to the bureaucratic paradigm which Weber developed with such keen insight a number of years ago.

Weber viewed bureaucracy as the ideal type of structural arrangement for accomplishing large-scale administrative tasks. "The decisive reason for the advance of bureaucratic organization," he wrote, "has always been its purely technical superiority over any other form of organization. The fully developed bureaucratic mechanism compares with other forms exactly as does the machine with non-mechanical modes of production."[3]

For Weber, the essential and distinctive characteristics of a bureaucracy were somewhat as follows:

1. The regular activities required for the purposes of the organization are distributed in fixed ways as official duties. Since the tasks of an organization are too complex to be performed by a single individual, or by a group of individuals possessing a single set of skills, efficiency will be promoted by dividing those tasks into activities which can be assigned to specific offices or positions. This division of labor makes possible a high degree of specialization which, in turn, promotes improved performance in two ways. First, it enables the organization to employ personnel on the basis of technical qualifications; second, it enables employees to improve their skills by limiting their attention to a relatively narrow range of activities.

2. The positions in an organization are arranged on the principle of office hierarchy and of levels of graded authority. This means that there is a firmly ordered system of superordination and subordination in which the lower offices are supervised by the higher ones. Although specialization makes possible the efficient performance of specific tasks, specialization also creates problems of coordination. To achieve the required coordination, it is necessary to grant to each official the requisite authority to control the activities of his subordinates.

3. The management of activities is controlled by general rules which are more or less stable, more or less exhaustive, and which can be learned. These rules are general and abstract, and they constitute standards which assure reasonable uniformity in the performance of tasks. They preclude the issuance of directives based on whim or caprice, but require the application of general principles to particular cases. Together with the hierarchical authority structure, rules provide for the coordination of organizational activities and for

continuity of operations, regardless of changes in personnel.

4. Bureaucracy develops the more perfectly the more completely it suceeds in eliminating from official business love, hatred, and all purely personal, irrational, and emotional elements which escape calculation. The essence of bureaucratic arrangements is rationality. A spirit of formalistic impersonality is necessary to separate organizational rights and duties from the private lives of employees. Only by performing impersonally can officials assure rationality in decision making, and only thus can they assure equitable treatment for all subordinates.

5. Employment in a bureaucracy is based upon technical competence and constitutes a career. Promotions are to be determined by seniority, or achievement, or both; tenure is to be assured; and fixed compensation and retirement provisions are to be made. Since individuals with specialized skills are employed to perform specialized activities, they must be protected from arbitrary dismissal or denial of promotion on purely personal grounds.

The American schools have been particularly receptive to the bureaucratic ideology, albeit perhaps unwittingly. Bureaucratic principles have been incorporated into the organizational practices of the educational enterprise in at least the following respects:

First, the school organization has clearly been influenced by the need for specialization and the factoring of tasks. The division of the school into elementary and secondary units; the establishment of science, mathematics, music, and other departments within a school; the introduction of guidance programs and psychological services; indeed, the separation of the administrative function from the teaching function, all represent responses to this need.

Second, the school organization has developed a clearly defined and rigid hierarchy of authority. Although the term "hierarchy" is seldom used in the lexicon of the educational administrator, the practices to which it refers are commonly prevalent. The typical organization chart is intended specifically to clarify lines of authority and channels of communication. Even in the absence of such a chart, school employees have a clear conception of the nature of the hierarchy in their school systems. In fact, rigid adherence to hierarchical principles has been stressed to the point that failure to adhere to recognized lines of authority is viewed as the epitome of immoral organizational behavior.

Third, the school organization has leaned heavily upon the use of general rules to control the behavior of members of the organization and to develop standards which would assure reasonable uniformity in the performance of tasks. Whether they have taken the form of policy manuals, rules and regulations, staff handbooks, or some other type of document, general rules have been used extensively to provide for the orderly induction of new employees into the organization and to eliminate capricious behavior on the part of all school personnel, including administrators and members of boards of education.

Fourth, despite frequent proclamations regarding togetherness and democracy, the school organization has made extensive application of Weber's principle of impersonality in organizational relationships. Authority has been established on the basis of rational considerations rather than charismatic qualities or traditional imperatives; interpersonal interactions have tended to be functionally specific rather than functionally diffuse; and official relationships have been governed largely by universalistic as contrasted with particularistic considerations. Thus, by operating in a spirit of "formalistic impersonality," the typical school system has succeeded, in part, in separating organizational rights and obligations from the private lives of individual employees.

Fifth, employment in the educational organization has been based upon technical competence and has constituted for most members a professional career. Promotions have been determined by seniority and by achievement; tenure has been provided; and fixed compensa-

tion and retirement benefits have been assured.

The school organization as we know it today, then, can accurately be described as a highly developed bureaucracy. As such, it exhibits many of the characteristics and employs many of the strategies of the military, industrial, and governmental agencies with which it might be compared.

In many respects, this organizational pattern has served us well. It has provided the means by which reasonable control might be exercised over the behavior of members of the organization, and by which the activities of individuals and groups of individuals with diverse interests and responsibilities might be coordinated. At the same time, as Moeller has demonstrated through empirical research,[4] rational bureaucratic structure has in many respects increased, rather than diminished, the teachers' sense of personal power in the organization.

Having made this point, however, I will proceed to argue that our present organizational arrangements and practices produce some seriously dysfunctional consequences in respect to the need for innovative activities in the educational establishment. The remainder of this paper, then, will be devoted to an analysis of some of these dysfunctional consequences.

Earlier, I pointed out that Weber emphasized the importance of arranging positions on the principle of office hierarchy and of levels of graded authority; that is, he viewed a firmly ordered system of superordination and subordination as a necessary condition in large organizations. The acceptance and implementation of this principle has resulted in a monistic formulation, which is based upon a number of charismatic assumptions. Thompson has pointed out, for example, that under the monistic formulation:

It is assumed that the superior, at any point in the hierarchy is *able* to tell his subordinates what to do, and to guide them in doing it. That is, it is assumed that he is more capable in all of his unit's activities than any of his subordinate specialists who perform them.[5]

This statement seems to capture neatly the ideology which exists in the educational establishment; yet, despite the ideology, candid observation belies the myth underlying the assumption. The concept of unity of command, which denies the relevance of non-hierarchical expertise within the organization, is applicable only in an organization where specialization refers to tasks, where activities are divided into simple, repetitive routines. In this kind of a situation, people are interchangeable in much the same way that parts of a machine are interchangeable. The foreman or supervisor, who has generally advanced through the ranks, is frequently more capable in performing his unit's activities than are his subordinates.

In the school organization, however, specialization refers not to tasks, but to people. Through education and specialized training, teachers have been adapted or changed. They have developed the competence to perform socially valued functions which other people cannot perform. When the assumption of superordinate ability is considered in apposition to this type of specialization, the assumption takes on an aura of charisma.

Yet, charisma is an insufficient and unacceptable basis for the exercise of authority in a supposedly rationally ordered system. Therefore, educational administrators and students of educational administration have been faced with the necessity of rationalizing the charismatic assumptions which undergird the monistic formulation of authority. This rationalization has led to a general acceptance of the largely nonsensical notion that authority can be delegated to subordinates in the organization, but that responsibility rests with those in superordinate roles.

When the concept of responsibility is used in this way, it readily becomes translated into blamability; that is, the administrator who feels that he must be responsible for the decisions of his subordinates must also accept the blame for their errors. For self-preservation, therefore, he must retain the ultimate power to make decisions or to veto the decisions of subordinates. In doing so, he fails to provide for any effective delegation of authority, and he perpetuates the monistic conception of hierarchical role definitions.

Since the right to innovate represents a potent source of power in the organization, and since the monistic formulation demands that power be concentrated in superordinate roles, innovation from below is difficult to achieve in an organization which adopts the monistic formulation. This is true for at least two reasons. First, ideas that originate at the lower levels in the hierarchy encounter difficulty in receiving an adequate hearing. Second, any individual in a subordinate position, who takes the lead in introducing new programs of action, runs the risk of having sanctions imposed by his superordinate to allow that superordinate to escape the blamability which is inherent in the monistic system. It is not uncommon, for example, for a subordinate to be fired in order to protect the position of his superior.

A second major dysfunctional consequence of structuring the schools bureaucratically, and in my view a major deterrent to meaningful innovation, grows out of the hierarchical definition of roles. Although roles in general are defined in terms of both rights and obligations, there is a tendency in bureaucraticies, including the educational bureaucracy, to emphasize rights when referring to superordinate roles and to emphasize obligations when referring to subordinate roles. In analyzing this distinction, let us first consider the superordinate role. The office of "superior" in the typical bureaucracy is characterized primarily by the rights which are associated with that role. Whatever obligations exist are usually correlatives of the few rights which are guaranteed to subordinates.

RIGHT TO VETO OR AFFIRM. One of the "rights" of the superordinate role is the right to veto or to affirm the organizationally relevant proposals of subordinates. This right applies not only to decisions which govern the organization in general, but also to decisions which govern the personal goals of individuals. Consider, for example, the difficulty a teacher encounters in obtaining a new position without a supporting recommendation from former administrative superiors.

Moreover, hierarchical relationships tend to over-emphasize the right to veto and to under-emphasize the right to affirm. Frequently, there is no organizationally legitimate means for appealing a superior's decision to veto a proposal, whereas a decision to approve will often be subject to confirmation by higher officials. In one large university, for example, a proposal to introduce a new course, or to revise an existing one, must run the gauntlet of bureaucratic machinery which contains five decision points. At any one of these points, the proposal may be vetoed; however, final approval can be given only at the top of the hierarchy. Under these conditions it is remarkable that any revision of the curriculum occurs.

Such a system obviously favors the status quo and inhibits innovation from below. Yet, in an organization which consists largely of professionals, as is the case in an educational institution, meaningful and workable innovations almost necessarily originate at the lower levels of the hierarchy.

RIGHT TO CONTROL COMMUNICATIONS. The superordinate in the hierarchy has the "right" to control communications, both those internal to the organization and those external to the organization. There is a strong emphasis on following "channels" in attempts to communicate, particularly when the communication is upward.

The strict exercise of this right may have at least two deleterious effects on innovation. First, subordinates may be prevented from obtaining sufficient information to enable them to determine accurately the relevance of their immediate activities for achieving the terminal goals of the organization. Second, superordinates may be prevented from obtaining sufficiently accurate feedback from their activities to enable them to assess realistically the effects of their decisions.

RIGHT TO DEFERENCE. By tradition, the hierarchical superior has the right to deference from subordinates. The ranking of roles in terms of the amount of deference due them is what is generally meant by the "status system" in an organization. In this regard, the superintendent or the principal of a school need not apologize for interrupting a teacher in her classroom, either to observe her work or to transmit routine business. Such an interruption is considered to be part of the administrator's job, a right associated with his position. Yet, the same teacher may interrupt the administrator only for "good cause," and the administrator's office frequently is guarded by a secretary who considers it her mission to see that he is not disturbed.

OTHER RIGHTS. A number of other rights grows out of the rights which I have just discussed. Thus, the superordinate has the right to decide the form of the organization, to determine the personnel to be employed, *to initiate activities*, to set the goals for sub-units, to assign activities, to confer jurisdictions, to determine the agenda for meetings, and to settle conflicts.

RIGHTS OF SUBORDINATES. The subordinate role is generally defined in terms of obligations, not rights. Since each of the rights defined for the superordinate role is accompanied by an obligation for the subordinate role, subordinates have an obligation to follow channels of communication, to be deferent in the presence of superordinates, and to await official approval before engaging in innovative activity. There is, at the present time, a general trend toward clarifying some of the rights of subordinates, including such things as the right to a hearing in the case of a recommendation for dismissal, the right to access to grievance machinery, and the right to academic freedom. But, such rights as do exist have been secured through collective efforts and hard bargaining, and they are granted only subject to the approval of the administrator. We have barely begun to accept the notion of rights as basic to the definition of the subordinate role.

It is true, of course, that not all occupants of superordinate positions insist on exercising fully the rights which are associated with their roles. Actual behavior may be modified by the personality of the administrator or by the social relationships which exist among the members of the organization. This fact does not alter the way in which roles are culturally defined, however, as evidenced by the observation that subordinates are pleased and grateful when a superordinate exercises his rights with humanitarian restraint.

The power of the hierarchy, and of the rights associated with superordinate roles, can be illustrated by describing what Victor Thompson has called hierarchical dramaturgy. For purely arbitrary reasons, I tend to prefer the term "status charades." To quote Thompson:

> What are the impressions fostered by hierarchical dramaturgy? As would be expected, they are the heroic and charismatic qualities—the same ones that leadership-trait studies have been seeking. The impression is fostered that occupants of hierarchical positions are, of all people in the organization, the ablest, the most industrious, the most indispensable, the most loyal, the most reliable, the most self-controlled, the most ethical, which is to say, the most honest, fair, and impartial.[6]

Successful performance of status charades requires the solidarity of the performing team. Since impressions are all important, and since the control of impressions requires the discreet withholding and editing of the available information, all members of the administrative team must be trustworthy and discreet. Thus, hierarchical positions tend to be filled, not on the basis of technical competence alone, but also on the basis of the ability to create the right impressions, those of busyness, loyalty, sound judgment, and so on.

To assure adequate control, therefore, such positions tend to be filled by the sponsorship system. Promising young people with administrative timbre, that is, those who appear to be "our kind," are carefully groomed to fill positions in the hierarchy. During the grooming period, recruits for the hierarchy are made

aware of the fact that they are being observed, and that if they make the team it will be because someone above trusted them. Such trust tends to be earned by those who demonstrate their ability, and willingness, to conform to established procedures.

Subordinates follow the rules of this game of charades by creating the impression that they are awed by their superiors, that the performance of the superiors has gone off well, and by creating the impression that they *need* to be told what to do and how to do it. Since the official impression is that the administrator is the busiest man in the organization, subordinates reinforce this impression by seeking conferences with him infrequently and apologetically, and by making such conferences brief.

In most school organizations, the game is played with dispatch and sincerity. The performers frequently believe that the rules represent reality. The status system aids impression management by isolating the behavior which might discredit the official impressions.

In an institution, such as the school, where superior performance occurs when superior technical competence is found at the base of the hierarchy, among the teachers, and where changes must be implemented by those who possess this superior competence, status charades are more of a tragedy than a comedy. The tendency to attach status to hierarchical positions, and the tendency to impute superior abilities to persons who occupy status positions, encourages the perpetuation of the status quo. Under these conditions, we will continue to encounter the situation which was described by Thelen in the quotation at the beginning of this paper.

A final dysfunctional consequence of adhering to rigid bureaucratic structure in the school organization, one that has important implications for innovation, relates to the extent to which such structure impedes the professional development of the teaching role.

Although the professional form of occupational life shares many of the characteristics of bureaucratic employment, there are some important respects in which professionalism is unique. In particular, the professions are characterized by a distinctive control structure which is fundamentally different from the hierarchical control of a bureaucracy. As Blau and Scott have pointed out, the control of professionals is accomplished through two sources:

> First, as a result of the long period of training undergone by the practitioner, he is expected to have acquired a body of expert knowledge and to have internalized a code of ethics which governs his professional conduct. Second, this self control is supported by the external surveillance of his conduct by his peers, who are in a position to see his work, and who have the skills to judge his performance, and who, since they have a personal stake in the reputation of their profession, are motivated to exercise the necessary sanctions.[7]

This control structure differs greatly from that employed in the typical school organization. The source of discipline in the bureaucratically organized school system is not the colleague group, but the authority vested in the hierarchy. Administrators establish regulations governing such factors as working hours, acceptable teaching procedures, criteria to be employed in determining promotions, and others. Even when such regulations are developed cooperatively, they are subject to the ratification of administrators and boards of education.

It might be argued that teachers are neither able nor willing to accept and discharge the responsibility for exercising professional control over their colleagues. Whether or not this is the case, and I seriously doubt that it is, it is highly unlikely that innovation will become common among members of the teaching force as long as teachers are subject to rigid hierarchical controls and as long as promotions consist of moving into the hierarchy and are determined by an individual's demonstrated capacity to conform.

I am not suggesting that the granting of self control would necessarily be accompanied by a flurry of innovative activity. The pressures for uniformity which groups exert upon their members are too well known for any such naive assumption. I am suggesting, however, that the freedom which could accompany professional control is a necessary condition to meaningful innovation at the point where it must occur, in the classroom.

In essence, I have argued that it is unreasonable to expect any radical departure from traditional educational practices so long as we insist on placing undue emphasis upon hierarchical status. If we are to break out of the strait jacket in which we now find ourselves, we must examine our ideology with rigor and with candor. We must be willing to admit that we do not necessarily live in the best of all possible organizational worlds. And we must display creativity in devising some type of organizational arrangement which will serve more adequately the type of institution in which we work.

I must admit that I do not now visualize very clearly what type of an organization that will be. I do suspect, however, that the educational administrator of the future will be more like the hospital administrator and less like the industrial tycoon, who appears to be our model today.

I also suspect that in the educational organization of the future, teachers will be viewed as true professionals, and they will be able to gain reasonable status while continuing to teach. Performance in this organization will be controlled by self-imposed standards of knowledge and ethics and by peer-group surveillance, rather than by directives from administrative officials. It is my contention that the greatest obstacle to achieving this type of control structure in the public schools rests not with the inability or unwillingness of teachers to behave responsibly, but with the bureaucratic ideology which permeates the educational enterprise, particularly that part of the ideology which supports and encourages the appropriation of hierarchical prerogatives to enhance the personal status of those in administrative positions.

NOTES

[1] Herbert A. Thelen, "New Practices on the Firing Line," *Administrator's Notebook,* Vol. XII, No. 5 (January, 1964).

[2] James G. March and Herbert A. Simon, *Organizations* (New York: John Wiley & Sons, Inc., 1959), p. 173.

[3] Max Weber, "Bureaucracy," in Joseph A. Litterer (ed.), *Organizations: Structure and Behavior* (New York: John Wiley & Sons, Inc., 1963), p. 45.

[4] Gerald H. Moeller, "Bureaucracy and Teachers' Sense of Power," *The School Review,* Vol. 72, No. 2 (Summer, 1964), pp. 137–57.

[5] Victor A. Thompson, *Modern Organizations* (New York: Alfred A. Knopf and Company, 1961), p. 75.

[6] *Ibid.,* p. 143.

[7] Peter M. Blau and W. Richard Scott, *Formal Organizations* (San Francisco: Chandler Publishing Co., 1962), p. 63.

4.

FUNCTIONS AND PATHOLOGY OF STATUS SYSTEMS IN FORMAL ORGANIZATIONS

CHESTER I. BARNARD

The following is a report of a preliminary inquiry into the nature and functions of systems of status in formal organizations. So far as I am aware, this subject has not been given extensive consideration by students of organization. This neglect appears not to be due to failure to recognize the importance of problems of status in organizations but rather to failure to recognize that status is systematic and that systems of status have a considerable degree of independence of other structural aspects of organization. Status systems are very closely related, for example, to systems of specialization, to systems of organization communication, and to systems of authority, so that differences of status have appeared to be incidental to these other structural aspects of organization and not to constitute a separate system. This view appears to be inadequate.

Formal organizations are not independent societies but are rather limited forms of social behavior growing out of the more general societies of which they are part. This observation is especially pertinent to systems of status, particularly as respects their function of providing incentives, which largely depends upon the general conception of status obtaining in society as a whole. Thus the nature of the status system in any formal organization

Abridged from William F. Whyte (ed.), *Industry and Society*, McGraw-Hill Book Company, New York, 1946, pp. 46–47; 52–62; 71–83. Copyright © 1946. Used by permission of McGraw-Hill Book Company.

is largely determined by the notions of class and caste governing the needs and desires of those whose behavior constitutes the formal organization. Hence, a comprehensive treatment of the subject would logically begin with the study of status in the general social system. Some of this background has been provided in the preceding chapter. The present inquiry is restricted to the relatively simple study of the general facts about status systems in formal organizations, and the functions that such systems serve in such organizations.

The analysis to be presented herein is based upon experience and observation of the kind commonly understood by those who have organizing and executive experience, but it does not purport to express a consensus of opinion. It sets forth that systems of status in formal organizations are necessary as a matter of need of individuals, and as imposed by the characteristics of cooperative systems, especially with respect to the techniques of communication essential to coordination. But it also appears that systems of status generate uncontrolled and even uncontrollable tendencies to rigidity, hypertrophy, and unbalance that often lead to destruction of organization.

THE FUNCTIONS OF SYSTEMS OF STATUS WITH RESPECT TO INDIVIDUALS

Systems of status of different kinds and of various degrees of elaborateness and complexity are found in most if not all formal organizations. The establishing of a nucleus of such a system is one of the very first steps in creating an organization.[1] Are these facts merely reflections of habitual attitudes and needs transferred from general society and coming down from antiquity? The view to be developed here is that systems of status, though they may be affected in degrees and in details by habitual attitudes and needs projected from the customary beliefs of people, are fundamentally determined by the necessities associated with the needs and interests of individuals as biological and social units; and upon the requirements arising from the physical and social limitations inherent in systems of cooperation. In the present section we shall deal with the relation of status systems to the needs of individuals.

It may be asserted first of all that systems of status arise from the differential needs, interests, and capacities of individuals. I shall discuss these in five topical divisions, as follows:

1. The differences in the *abilities* of individuals.
2. The differences in the *difficulties* of doing various kinds of work.
3. The differences in the *importance* of various kinds of work.
4. The desire for formal status as a social or organizational tool.
5. The need for protection of the integrity of the person.

1

Differences of ability with respect to any kind of effort in which there is social interest obviously lead to a recognition of difference of status of individuals in respect to that kind of effort. This does not necessarily imply superiority or inferiority in general, although, in fact, usually the lack of capacity of individuals for most kinds of effort or even for any valued effort whatsoever does inescapably establish for them a general position of at least technical or productive inferiority.

Differences of ability among individuals arise from a variety of conditions. The most obvious and possibly the most important are physiological or anatomical conditions, either inherent in the constitution of the individual from birth or imposed later by accident or disease. Cases of extreme physical or mental incapacity or even partial incapacity require no comment.[2] There are also some very important differences such as lethargic constitution, slowness of reactions, and lack of curiosity as contrasted with vigor, alertness, quickness of reaction, natural accuracy of physical coordination, and active curiosity. The latter characteristics or their lack when manifested in early years are especially important as affecting the capacity to receive instruction and other social conditioning and to acquire experience. Differences that are small or deemed unimportant in early years thus may cumulate to be substantial at maturity or at the end of the most active learning period.

Other differences of capacity so obviously depend upon education and specialized training that little need be said on this subject. Broadly considered, it includes the social conditioning attendant upon living in a social milieu. Differences in education come from differences in ability to receive instruction and from differences in interest; hence, from differences in willingness to accept the discipline and sacrifices involved; from differences in economic and social resources; and from differences in the educational resources available.

Finally, differences of individual ability arise from differences of experience. Physical, social, and intellectual skills develop through practice. There appears to be a considerable degree of chance in the distribution of opportunities for experience. There is also wide variation in the disposition to adhere to a long course of experience, to "stick to one job." Again, there is considerable variation in the capacity to learn from experience, *i.e.*, in the faculty of self-education.

Such differences among individuals as are here outlined do not prove the necessity of formal systems of status; nor that, if they imply such formal systems in some respects, they involve a formal qualification or disqualification in all respects. They do suggest that the first base upon which status systems rest is the undeniable differences, whatever their origins, between the physical, mental, and social capacities and interests of individuals. It will be recognized that these are fundamental conditions of immediate practical and inescapable significance, e.g., to the teacher, the military officer, or the employer.

2

Differences in the capacities of individuals undoubtedly lead to differences of informal status quite aside from the requirements of formal organizations. For example, some groups tend to form on the basis of educational level, or physical strength, or endurance, etc. But the important significance of differences of ability stems from differences in the nature of various kinds of activities. Many kinds of work, unskilled labor, for example, usually require only sound health and normal physiological abilities. Other work, say that of a laboratory chemist, may require unusual delicacy of physiological reaction in the use of laboratory equipment, long arduous technical education, powers of imagination, thorough experience, and a willingness to work persistently without supervision or instruction. The work requires an exceptional combination of powers, some of which may need to be developed to an exceptional degree. Recognition of the status of being exceptional is forced upon such a man by his own experience. He is made aware of it by the difficulty of finding those competent to carry on his work or to assist him. He is also elevated to exceptional status by those who wish his work to be done and who find that there are few competent to do it. Those whose interests are narrowly concentrated in one field for this reason often regard exceptional ability in that field as indicating not only special but general superiority. The banker finding few who can function effectively in his field, whatever their condition of education and experience, may be led to believe that those who can do so are of status generally superior to all others. A broader view, of course, recognizes that great superiority in one field does not imply general superiority.

Thus the second base for status is, as contrasted with personal ability, the relative difficulty of things to be done. The difficulties will usually be appraised on judgment based on general experience and observation; or, more objectively, on the basis of the numbers or proportions of individuals who can or cannot do well the various tasks.

3

The exceptional ability to do things that are exceptionally difficult, while it is a sufficient basis for establishing differences of status in the general estimation, is not sufficient to establish a *system* of status involving authority or responsibility. Superiority in formal organizations depends upon exceptional ability for exceptionally difficult work of exceptional *importance*. "Importance" in this context includes more than economic importance. High status is not accorded to superior ability to do unusually difficult things of trivial character, except perhaps in very restricted circles. On the contrary, if an activity is regarded as exceptionally important, even though not very difficult, superior status is nevertheless likely to be accorded to superior ability with respect to it. This is probably most evident in the economic world, but it is readily seen in other spheres, e.g., in military organization.

The importance of the work, then, establishes the importance of the position that "seeks" those of exceptional ability. Relative difficulty is a factor but is usually of minor importance except when importance is approximately equal. Status becomes systematic because activities regarded as important are systematized and organized.

4

The next basis for status is pragmatic. Insignia and titles of status have the effect of credentials. They create a presumption with respect to the character, ability, and specific skills or functions of individuals. They are not conclusive, of course, but as preliminaries, as introductions, they save time and prevent awkwardness and embarrassment. The general's stars indicate at a glance the nature of his responsibilities and the probable relative reliability of his utterances in certain fields. The title "M.D." creates a presumption that the holder of that degree may usefully be approached without reticence about bodily ills. The degree of "Ph.D." may be granted to a fool, but very generally it is a sign of the possession of a considerable intellectual experience, scholarly or scientific skill, and mental discipline. "Vice-president" of a corporation indicates one who probably understands business language and organization. "Foreman" indicates the man through whom the most effective approach may probably be had respecting the group under him and the work they are doing. "Bishop" is the title of one whom the communicant may accept as having certain ecclesiastical responsibilities and authority and as being able to perform certain spiritual functions, though the communicant may never before have seen him or been told about him.

Generally, the possession of title and of other indicia of rank certifies that those in the best position to have responsible judgment acknowledge and publish the status indicated, which all whom it may concern may accept at least tentatively. The convenience and efficiency of the status system is such that men seek status as a necessary tool in their work; and for the same reasons it is imposed upon them by those responsible for their work. It is to be noted that this applies as much to functional status as it does to scalar status.

5

Insofar as systems of status are imposed "from the top" they are expressions of the requirements of coordination rather than of the ambitions of the most able and powerful acting on the basis of personal motives. The personal motivation of most profound effect, applying equally to those of superior and to those of inferior status, is the need for protecting the integrity of the person in a social environment. This leads some to seek superior formal status, but it also leads others to refuse superior status and even to seek inferior status, depending upon the individual and the

circumstances. This may be demonstrated sufficiently by presenting four modes in which the need for status is expressed: (a) The need of integrating personal history by the conferring of status; (b) the need of imputing superior status to those from whom commands are to be received; (c) the need of imputing superior status as a means of symbolizing possession of personal value in participating in an organization; and (d) the need of status as a protection against excessive claims against the individual.

a. The need of integrating one's personal history into one's personality by the attainment of improved status and by the conferring of status publicly is exceptionally important to those who by deliberate effort or sacrifice condition themselves to the possession of superior knowledge, skill, or experience. The need is for an endorsement of the individual's past history as a creditable element in his existing personality. The granting and attainment of improved or different status here is not reward but anointment. it serves a ceremonial function of announcement, of proclamation, that an approved course has been followed by this person. Without such endorsement the effort often appears to the individual to have been in vain. A sense of frustration, sometimes devastating, may follow. Even when the individual is one of extraordinary self-sufficiency, the attainment of recognized distinction of status may be desired to maintain standing with relatives and supporting and cooperating friends. No one who watches the contemporary parade of diplomas, degrees, public honors, and the award of innumerable insignia of achievement and distinction, and who observes the reaction of individuals, of families, of organizations, and of the public to them can doubt the importance of these recognitions in nearly every field of individual and social activity. If such distinctions, often of ephemeral value, are an important element in individual behavior, it is evident that permanent position of status is even more so. It may be thought that the need of status here discussed is merely a reflection of the effect of attitudes, inculcated by mores and institutions that no doubt do reinforce the need; but the response of small children to status and the use made of status in instruction and discipline of the very young suggest that the need is more primitive and is individual.

b. The need of imputing higher status to those from whom commands come is rather certain though it is not often obvious. It is apparent to nearly everyone on the basis of even simple and limited experience that the coordination of effort necessary for effective cooperation can be practically secured only by specializing the function of command. It is obvious that everybody cannot give orders to everybody else at the same time and for the same activity. But except at times of great danger, to receive orders from a nondescript "some-other" is felt to be an injury to the self-respect, to the integrity, of the person. This can be avoided or alleviated only if it is felt that command is exercised by "right" either conferred by supernatural authority; or, more generally in our present society, conferred by superior ability; or by the burden of superior responsibility. Men are eager to be "bossed" by superior ability, but they resent being bossed by men of no greater ability than they themselves have. So strong is this need of assigning superior status to those in positions of command that, unless the obvious facts preclude it, men will impute abilities they cannot recognize or judge. They want to believe that those of higher authority "know what they are doing" when they appoint someone over them. Since men in the ranks are not capable of judging or are not in a position in advance to judge the competence of men in posts of command remote from them by two or more grades or even of those in immediate command if special technical abilities are required (e.g., the surgeon in the operating room or the navigator of a ship), this desire for the justification of subordination leads often to profuse rationalization about status and even to mythological and mystical explanations of it; but the ways in which a need is manifested ought not

to be permitted to obscure its nature or the function of the means that satisfy it.

What has just been said as respects the need of imputing higher scalar status to those from whom commands are received applies somewhat less definitely and more subtly to differences in functional status where authoritative advice rather than formal authority is involved. Thus the advice or even the directions of one having the status of an expert in a particular field will be accepted against that of someone recognized as being equally expert but not having status. The subjective factor involved may be that of a diffuse feeling of public authorization to transfer responsibility to one having functional status. Though there is wide variation in the competence of those having the same status and reliance upon mere formal status is subject to much error and abuse, nevertheless there can be little doubt that the system of functional status affords great relief to nearly everybody in practical everyday social behavior.

c. The need felt by those of subordinate rank for imputing personal superiority to those in command, i.e., the need of protecting the integrity of the person, is also expressed in sentiments of valuation of an organization as a whole. To be a member of a good organization is a personal asset. It is among the claims to distinction of most men. To be ejected from an organization is a serious, sometimes a catastrophic, injury to the integrity of the person. "Patriotism," "sense of communion," "loyalty," "esprit de corps" are common expressions of this attitude. Few, if any, with experience of command will doubt this, and those who observe behavior of men in military organizations in war know how powerful and indispensable this sentiment is, though perhaps not many would express the facts in terms of personal integrity.

One of the effects of this need is to sustain the system of status. For if it is not practicable for all to command, and command, i.e., coordination, is essential to organization, then a system of status is indispensable. Office becomes symbolic of the organization. The commander in chief not only occupies the supreme position of command, but he speaks for the army and in his person symbolizes it.

d. Individuals of superior ability and those of inferior ability can comfortably work together only on a basis of physical or social segregation. If no formal segregation is established, either friction and noncooperation occur or there is spontaneous informal segregation, "natural" leaders leading "natural" groups, without being adequately integrated into the system of formal command. The necessity for differentiation from the standpoint of those of inferior ability is that without it they are constantly in a position of disadvantage, under pressure to exceed their capacities, perpetually losing in a race in which no handicaps are recognized, never able to attain expected goals so long as they are treated as the equals of those who are in fact superior; therefore they are always in a position of never securing respect for what they do contribute, of always incurring disrespect for what they cannot do. Men cannot stand this kind of inferiority and its frustrations. The inferiors will group themselves and command respect by various means if they are not protected by being assigned a formal status, which, though inferior, recognizes their position as being more or less indispensable and participating even though individually less important. The practice of labor unions of restraining the production of the more able workers of an undifferentiated craft to a level approximating that of the poorer workers, though in practice doubtless of complex motivation, seems clearly in accordance with the human needs of the situation.

Concordantly, the abler individuals press for segregation corresponding to the observed differences in abilities and in contributions. To be lumped in with inferiors in ability seems an unjust withholding of recognition, an injury to the integrity of the person. Their escape from this position will probably be more individualistic than that of those of inferior abilities who must more often resort to group solidarity. One escape or attempt to escape for the supe-

rior individual is to try to organize the group, to adopt a function of leadership, or to dominate without authority. Another is to leave the group for various alternative activities—found a new sect, start a new business, establish a party, and so on.

Much experience demonstrates that those who are unequal cannot work well for long as equals. But experience also demonstrates that where differences of status are recognized formally, men of very unequal abilities and importance can and do work together well for long periods.

This discussion of the relationship of integrity of the person to systems of status is not exhaustive or comprehensive, but it is enough to suggest that personal need of status system is one of their foundations.

DISRUPTIVE TENDENCIES INHERENT IN STATUS SYSTEMS

The concern of executives is not only with the organizing functions of systems of status, but with their disruptive tendencies; for, paradoxically, such systems operate like principles of growth, necessary to attain maturity, but without a self-regulative control that prevents disproportionate development of parts, unbalance, and maladaptation to the environment. Thus, the executive who promotes by positive means an improved system of status, however essential to immediate purposes, thereby generates disorganizing forces, the neutralizing of which is the more difficult in that the executive himself is a central part of the system of status. Thus the effort to detect and correct hypertrophy and abuse of the status system is somewhat akin to correcting psychopathic difficulties by introspection. Nevertheless, some executives, being individuals as well as officials, are undoubtedly able to project themselves mentally to a position outside their organizations and to view it with detachment. They then can recognize that a system of status presents a persistent dilemma.

The pathological aspects of systems of status to which these remarks refer have not been adequately investigated. We shall focus our consideration of the subject on the following topics:

1. The status system tends in time to distorted evaluation of individuals.
2. It restricts unduly the "circulation of the elite."
3. It distorts the system of distributive justice.
4. It exaggerates administration to the detriment of leadership and morale.
5. It exalts the symbolic function beyond the level of sustainment.
6. It limits the adaptability of an organization.

1

As set forth hereinbefore, the system of status is founded on and made necessary by the following four factors, in addition to others, relevant to the present topic: (a) differences in the abilities of individuals, (b) differences in the difficulties of various kinds of work, (c) differences in the importance of various kinds of work, and (d) the needs of the system of communication.

The first of these factors is strictly personal and individual. This does not mean, of course, that the capacities of the individual may not have been largely determined socially, but that at any given time they are the personal possession of the individual and that the application or nonapplication of these capacities at any given time or period is taken to be a matter of personal choice or will. To the extent that status depends upon individual ability and willingness to employ it, it may be said to be individual and not social. Personal status may to this extent be said to be correlative with personal merit. Undoubtedly, evaluation from this point of view is widely conceived as just. If this were the only basis of status, it seems probable that differences of status would be accepted as proper and necessary even where material distribution could be conceived as properly made on the basis of "to each according to need."

As we ascend to the other bases of status, more and more qualification of the conception of individual merit is required. Thus the differences in the difficulties of tasks are in some degree merely matters of the nature of the physical world and of the capacities of individuals; but where acquired skills and technologies are involved, being almost entirely of social origin, relative difficulties indirectly are socially determined. Further, almost every task in a formal society involves adaptation of behavior to and utilization of the social system itself. What is rated as easy or difficult behavior is socially evaluated. Hence, individual merit in performing the difficult often lies in capacity and willingness to resign personal preferences. The qualification on account of the social element in "difficult" is not important. "Difficult" reflects a social standard of measurement of abilities; the standard and the abilities together are a basis for status.

Variations in the *importance* of work as a basis for status are quite another matter. "Importance" is almost entirely determined socially in the same sense, though not necessarily in the same way, that economic value is determined by demand and supply as socially expressed, *i.e.*, in exchange. To the extent that the individual accepts the social valuation and does that which is regarded as important, there is personal merit. Whether the status accorded is inferior or superior, however, will depend upon whether those able and willing are relatively numerous or not. Thus, low status frequently accompanies work of primary importance in the aggregate, e.g., wheat growing, in which numerous individuals are employed; high status often accompanies work which *in the aggregate* is relatively unimportant, but scarce, hence valuable, e.g., silversmithing.

The rating of the individual by the importance of his work, a social evaluation, may be necessary to effective and efficient allocation of ability in the social system, and it may therefore be essential to the adaptation of the society as a whole to its environment. However, status so determined tends, as experience shows, to be imputed to the individual *as such* rather than to a particular socially valued *role* of the individual. When inferior status is assigned on this basis, it is transferred to the individual generally, and similarly when superior status is assigned. Thus exaggeration of personal inferiority and superiority results. The effect upon the characteristics of the individual contributors to an organization is deleterious—depressing and limiting those of inferior status, stimulating and sometimes intoxicating those of superior status. Restoring or creating morale in the one, restraining the other, then becomes a major problem of organization.

The system of communication by means of which coordination is secured in cooperation is a strictly social phenomenon. Being indispensable to purposeful cooperation, the necessities of the system of communication become prime, being secondary only to the prior existence of an organization whose members are willing to cooperate. Now, undoubtedly the capacity of individuals to function in a system of communications depends upon natural abilities, general knowledge and experience, facility in general and special languages, technical and other special abilities; but though often indispensable, such general capacities and potentialities are secondary to the abilities directly associated with a particular communication position and with immediate concrete knowledge. One cannot function as or in a communication center if one is not at that center; nor, if at that center, without knowledge of the immediately available means of communication and of the immediately precedent communication materials, *i.e.*, what has just transpired, what further communication is called for, to whom and where further communication should be made, from whom and where communication should be elicited. Neither general nor special abilities suffice to meet the requirements if this local and concrete knowledge is not available.

Thus the primary specific abilities required in communication are those of *position*—of being at the place where communication may effectively be had and where immediate concrete knowledge may be obtained. The manning of posts of communication by those possessing the requisite abilities of position is so indispensable to cooperation that a system assuring such manning and hence of the acquirement of such abilities has precedence over all other considerations in an organization, for the breakdown of communication means immediate failure of coordination and disintegration of organization. It should not be understood from this that the general capacities and abilities of individuals are not important. If positions of communication are not manned by those of requisite general and special abilities, other than ability of position, disintegration of organization occurs slowly through failure to accomplish the aims of cooperation in ways that permit the satisfaction of the motives of the contributing individuals of an organization. The analogy is that of starvation by malnutrition as against death by trauma, such as the severing of an essential nerve. The logical is well as the instinctively acceptable choice is to avoid fatal accident even at the expense of serious and dangerous limitations; for fatal injury admits of no recovery, whereas the tendency toward dissolution even when regarded as probably certain, admits of the possibility of reversal.

It may be seen from the foregoing that schemes ensuring continuity of ordered communication are of primary importance in the adaptation of a society to its environment as well as to the attainment of ends transcending mere biological adaptation. In the past, schemes for the manning of communication posts of society have been based upon heredity (feudal systems), heredity and marriage (kinship systems), systems of property rights, systems of commission and appointment, and systems of election. All of them create differential status essential to ordered communication. The failure of any of them prior to the acceptance of a substitute system disrupts communication, and hence leads to prompt disorganization.

The indispensability of systematic communication in organization thus leads to imputing a value to the individual that relates to the role he plays and to the exaggeration of the importance of immediate local ability in communication as against more general and more personal ability.

The dilemma involved may be brought out in terms of a practical organization problem. It will ordinarily be the experience of the general executive that there are able men available for appointment to positions occupied by men recognized to be of inferior ability, but who are immediately superior with respect to local knowledge and experience in their posts, and also superior in the sense that they are accepted in their posts by others. It may be clear that in the long run, provided immediate breakdown is not involved, it would be better to replace the inferior with the superior man. Nevertheless, to do so may involve costs in terms of immediate organizational disadvantages so substantial that the net effect even for the long run might be adverse. These disadvantages are: (a) If replacement is made, there will be ineptitude of functioning for a longer or shorter period. Insofar as this occurs because of lack of local knowledge, it will correct itself in time, which in general will be shorter the greater the general ability of the replacing individual. The less difference there is in ability, the more doubtful is the utility of change. (b) Communication involves mutual relationships and habitual responsive reactions. A new man entirely aside from his intrinsic abilities in the position, is new to others in the immediate communication network. *Their* capacity to function is disturbed by change. (c) The operation of the system depends in considerable degree upon mutual confidence of the communicators. Change decreases this confidence. This is ordinarily not important as related to single changes not frequently occurring. Its importance increases at an accelerating pace as either the number or the frequency of replacements increases.

2

Thus, although systems of status are based upon individual abilities and propensities as related to tasks socially evaluated and upon

the requirements of the system of communication in organizations, we find that the rating of the individual by the role he occupies and emphasis upon the importance to the organization of immediate local abilities of position leads to under- and overvaluation of individuals artificially, *i.e.*, in terms of status as an end instead of as an intermediate means.

Whatever the system or principle by which posts of communication are filled, in general, errors occur, with the result that some men of inferior abilities are placed in relatively superior positions. Moreover, even if men at a given time were all placed with ideal correctness, they change so that some become inferior to their positions, and others become more than adequate for them. Further, changes in the conditions or the purposes of cooperation may make obsolete the capacities of individuals in particular positions for which they were initially well adapted. Finally, individuals will develop or mature whose abilities are superior to those of persons who have preferred status, even though the latter have not changed and at the time of selection were the best available. The effects of aging, of physical, moral, and intellectual deterioration, of changing conditions and purposes, all call for continual readjustment and replacement in the status system. The process of readjustment and replacement is well known as the "circulation of the elite." Ideally the circulation of the elite should be so free that the status of all should at any given time be in accordance with their relative capacities and the importance of their functions. It is rather obvious that failure of this circulation to the extent that generally those of inferior capacity occupy positions of superior status will so reduce the efficiency of cooperation that survival of organization is doubtful, and that the dangers of rebellion and revolution will be so great that even for the short run such a stoppage of circulation may be fatal.

Nevertheless, even a rough approach to the ideal condition of free circulation is not possible. This is due to three essential factors: (a) A considerable degree of stability of status is necessary if improvement of status is to serve as an incentive. The more uncertain the retention of achieved status is, the fewer to whom the achievement of status will appeal. (b) The resistance to loss of status is in general stronger than desire to achieve higher status, so that it is often probable that the disruptive effects of demotion made to attain a more perfect assignment of capacities more than offset the advantages. (c) Good communication depends to a great extent upon accuracy of interpretation largely associated with habitual personal relationships. These are broken down if changes are frequent.

3

Without a system of status, as has already been stated, injustice results to those who are the less capable, by failure to protect them against overburden. If an adequate system of status is employed, it may involve injustice when the higher emoluments of higher status are greater than warranted in the sense that they are greater than necessary. It is not intended to discuss here the problem of distributive justice generally involved in differential emoluments. We shall assume that a differential system is necessary and just. What concerns us now is the distortions of justice arising from the restrictions upon freedom of promotion and demotion. The injustices arising are of two sorts: (a) The aggregate of emoluments of higher status are excessive in the sense that they do not secure the degree of service that the capacities ideally available make possible. The "social dividend" in the broadest sense is less than it should be, and the failure is a loss to those of inferior status generally. (b) Individuals capable of filling positions of higher status better than those occupying such positions are unjustly deprived of the emoluments that they are often encouraged to seek. I am using emoluments in a most general sense, including not only remuneration, but also recognition, prestige, the satisfaction of exercising one's abilities, and, for those of philanthropic motivation, the satisfactions of the largest service of which they are capable.

These injustices inherent in the practical operations of systems of status are not hidden. Men are aware of them in general and sometimes exaggerate them; and they are also aware of them specifically as affecting them individually in many circumstances. The effect of the sense of injustice involved depends partly upon the degree to which the status system is sluggish or congealed. When status is fixed by birth or limited by race or religion the extreme of disorganization may follow. When the status of individuals corresponds well with their abilities some loss of *esprit de corps* and of cooperative efficiency only may be involved.

Nevertheless, the effects of the injustices inherent in status systems are sufficiently great to require positive balancing considerations and sentiments. The consideration of most importance is that, except as to those of the lowest status (and at least in some conditions probably also to them), conservatism is protective of individuals. Even though the retention of someone in a position of higher status may be felt to be specifically unjust to one of lower status, the situation may be duplicated with respect to the latter and someone of still lower status. In some degree recognition of a right to retain status is therefore felt to be generally just even though in particular cases the effect may be thought not so.

The sentiments supporting conservatism with respect to status are developed and maintained by rationalizations, ceremonies, and symbolism. They have for their broad purpose the inculcation of the doctrine that the primary interest of the individual is dependent upon the maintenance of the whole organization and its effective operation as a whole, and that whatever is necessary to this end, even though it adversely affects the individual, is offset even to him by the larger advantage accruing from it.

4

An effective system of communications requires not only the stable filling of specific positions of different status, but also habitual practices and technical procedures. Failure to follow these procedures with routine persistence in general leads to confusion, lack of coordination, and inefficiency or breakdown of the system. The lines of communication, the system of status, and the associated procedures, though by no means constituting "administration," are essential tools of administration and are the most "visible" general parts of it. Being the tangible machinery of administration and indispensable to it, the protection both of status and of procedure come to be viewed quite sincerely as the *sine qua non* of the organization.

The overvaluation of the apparatus of communication and administration is opposed to leadership and the development of leaders. It opposes leadership whose function is to promote appropriate adjustment of ends and means to new environmental conditions, because it opposes change either of status in general or of established procedures and habitual routine. This overvaluation also discourages the development of leaders by retarding the progress of the abler men and by putting an excessive premium on routine qualities.

5

Among the phenomena connected with the status system are symbols of office or of class or trade. In many cases these are not conspicuous, and may be only evident in matters of behavior, such as deference; in others, e.g., military organizations, they are conspicuous. The investment of office with symbols is, moreover, often preceded by ceremonies of graduation, promotion, consecration, induction, installation, and inauguration, in which the organization and its purpose are dramatized and glorified by symbolic means. Much of this symbolic practice related to office in the abstract is transferred to the person of the individual filling the office, and in this way the individual himself by reason of his status becomes a symbol of the organization and of its purposes. This is so true that although it is usually not difficult to distinguish between personal and official acts *per se*, it is not acceptable in general to distinguish personal and official behavior of officials or for them to tolerate contumelious behavior of others toward them when wearing insignia of office or otherwise publicly known to hold office. Thus the rule is general that the private conduct of officials at least in public must not be "unbecoming a gentleman," though the rule is expressed in different manners and enforced in different degrees and in different ways. Conversely, an insult to an officer or person of other status publicly known as an officer or member of an organization is regarded as an injury to the organization itself, and especially so when committed by a member of the same organization.

This is rather evident and commonplace as respects clergymen, military personnel (in uniform), officers of the law, and judges when in courts. It is less obvious but nonetheless real in business, academic, and many other organizations where the symbols of office and status are primarily utilitarian, such as large office quarters, automobiles, guarded privacy, and special privileges.

One effect of the symbolic function of office and its associated status is to retard the circulation of the elite. The removal of an official to whom symbolic attributes have become attached, whether for incompetence or for other more reprehensible causes, unless they are very grave and publicly known, is widely felt to be derogatory to the office and to be an injury to the organization both internally and often externally as respects its prestige. Thus in one city some years ago it was said that it was practically impossible to discharge the presidents of banks except for flagrant, publicly known derelictions. Also it is often, not without ground, suspected that men are "kicked upstairs" to avoid the effects of crass degradation; and usually care and decorum is used. These considerations also in some cases explain and justify the provisions of pensions for officers under compulsory retirement rules.

Thus it comes about that the symbolism involved in office and status in the aggregate outruns the capacities of the men who have become symbols of organization.

6

From what has been presented it is perhaps evident that in sum the effect of the status system, though essential to coherence, coordination, and *esprit de corps*, is to reduce flexibility and adaptability. When the external conditions to which an organization must be adapted are stable, the importance of flexibility and adaptability is much less than under rapidly changing conditions, and the importance of coherence and refinement of coordination, in terms of efficiency, is much greater. Were it possible to forecast for a long period what the conditions will be, the problem in principle would be merely to establish an optimum system of status, a mean between extremes minimizing disadvantages and dangers, but reasonably conserving the advantages and certainly adequate to the minimum necessities. It would hardly be appropriate to call such a problem a dilemma. The dilemma lies in the fact that future conditions cannot be forecast correctly. Hence for current purposes it is necessary to employ and often to elaborate a system of status whose inherent tendency is to become unbalanced, rigid, and unjust.

We have seen that both functional and scalar systems of status are necessary to formal organizations of scalar type but that interests are generated by or within them forcing them to rigidity, lack of correspondence to real merits and real needs, and to hypertrophy, especially in their symbolic functions. As these

matters are reflected on and as the technical apparatus of organization is studied, no doubt corrective measures can be known. They can be applied, however, only with great difficulty from within an organization, for even the chief executive is the chief of the status system and dependent on it. It therefore requires endless persistence, extraordinary ability, and great moral courage to control the dangerous developments in them. Probably, the principal needs can be summarized as three: to ensure that there is correspondence between status and ability by free movement; to prevent the systems of status from being ends or even primary means; and to see that the emoluments of office and of trade or profession are proportionate to the necessary level of incentives and morale. Some devices, e.g., retirement rules, are known that facilitate these controls; but this is not the place to discuss them.

Insofar as we are concerned only with subordinate organizations, the correction of the pathologies of status systems in relatively "free" societies is largely accomplished by competition, regulation, and the pressure of public opinion, attended by the disintegration of organizations that cannot correct conditions. This does not usually involve catastrophic effects except for a few individuals, or sometimes for small communities. When the organization is that of a highly centralized state, however, it is doubtful whether there is as yet any means of correcting extreme investment of interests in the system of status, except by revolution or by military defeat.

NOTES

[1] In the case of corporations, corporation law provides at least often for both boards of directors and for two or more general officers. Bylaws almost always provide for additional general officers. In the case of individually owned businesses and partnerships the nucleus of the status system rests initially directly upon property ownership. Similarly with noncommercial organizations, the first steps in organizing are likely to be to create an initial governing board and a set of officers.

[2] The importance of such limitations in a population is commonly disregarded. Among adults probably not less than 1 in 20, or 5 per cent, is to be so classified.

5.

DYSFUNCTIONS IN ORGANIZATIONS

JAMES G. MARCH
HERBERT A. SIMON

Modern studies of "bureaucracies" date from Weber[1] as to both time and acknowledged intellectual debt. But, in a sense, Weber belongs more to the preceding chapter than he does to the present one. His major interests in the study of organizations appear to have been four: (1) to identify the characteristics of an entity he labeled "bureaucracy"; (2) to describe its growth and the reasons for its growth; (3) to isolate the concomitant social changes; (4) to discover the consequences of bureaucratic organization for the achievement of bureaucratic goals (primarily the goals of a political authority). It is in the last-named interest that Weber most clearly differentiates himself from the other writers who will be considered here. Weber wishes to show to what extent bureaucratic organization is a rational solution to the complexities of modern problems. More specifically, he wishes to show in what ways bureaucratic organization overcomes the decision-making or "computational" limits of individuals or alternative forms of organization (i.e., through specialization, division of labor, etc.).

Consequently, Weber appears to have more in common with Urwick, Gulick, and others than he does with those who regard themselves as his successors. To be sure, Weber goes beyond the "machine" model in significant ways. In particular, he analyzes in some detail the relation between an official and his

From James G. March and Herbert A. Simon, *Organizations*, John Wiley & Sons, Inc., New York, 1958, pp. 36–46. Reprinted by permission.

office. But, in general, Weber perceives bureaucracy as an adaptive device for using specialized skills, and he is not exceptionally attentive to the character of the human organism.

When we turn from Weber to the more recent students of bureaucracy, however, we find them paying increasing attention to the "unanticipated" responses of the organization members.[2] Without denying Weber's essential proposition that bureaucracies are more efficient (with respect to the goals of the formal hierarchy) than are alternative forms of organization, the research and analyses of Merton,[3] Selznick,[4] and Gouldner[5] have suggested important dysfunctional consequences of bureaucratic organization. In addition—explicitly in the case of Gouldner and implicitly in the other two authors—they have hypothesized that the unintended consequences of treating individuals as machines actually encourage a continued use of the "machine" model.

The general structure of the theoretical systems of all three writers is remarkably similar. They use as the basic independent variable some form of organization or organizational procedure designed to control the activities of the organization members. These procedures are based primarily on what we have called the "machine" model of human behavior. They are shown to have the consequences anticipated by the organizational leaders, but also to have other, unanticipated, consequences. In turn, these consequences reinforce the tendency to use the control device. Thus, the systems may be depicted as in Figure 5–1.

The several systems examined here posit different sets of variables and theoretical relations. However, their structures are sufficiently similar to suggest that these studies in "bureaucracy" belong to a single class of theories.

THE MERTON MODEL

Merton[6] is concerned with dysfunctional organiational learning: organization members generalize a response from situations where the response is appropriate to similar situations

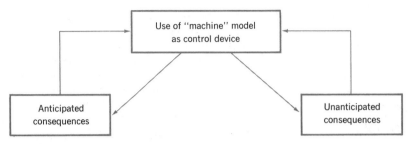

Figure 5–1. The General Bureaucracy Model.

where it results in consequences unanticipated and undesired by the organization. Merton asserts that changes in the personality of individual members of the organization stem from factors in the organizational structure. Here personality refers to any fairly reliable connection between certain stimuli and the characteristic responses to them. The label "personality" is attached to such a response pattern when the pattern does not change easily or rapidly.

Merton's system of propositions begins with a *demand for control* made on the organization by the top hierarchy. This demand takes the form of an increased *emphasis on the reliability of behavior* within the organization. From the point of view of the top hierarchy, this represents a need for accountability and predictability of behavior. The techniques used to secure reliability draw upon what has been called here the "machine" model of human behavior. Standard operating procedures are instituted, and control consists largely in checking to ensure that these procedures are, in fact, followed.

Three consequences follow from this emphasis on reliability in behavior and the techniques used to install it:

1. There is a reduction in the *amount of personalized relationships*. The bureaucracy is a set of relationships between offices, or roles. The official reacts to other members of the organization not as more or less unique individuals but as representatives of positions that have specified rights and duties. Competi-

tion within the organization occurs within closely defined limits; evaluation and promotion are relatively independent of individual achievement (e.g., promotion by seniority).

2. *Internalization of the rules of the organization* by the participants is increased. Rules originally devised to achieve organizational goals assume a positive value that is independent of the organizational goals. However, it is important to distinguish two phenomena, both of which have been called the "displacement of goals." In one case, a given stimulus evokes an activity perceived as leading to a preferred state of affairs. In a series of such situations, the repeated choice of the acceptable alternative causes a gradual transfer of the preference from the final state of affairs to the instrumental activity. In the other case, the choice of a desired alternative reveals additional desirable consequences not originally anticipated. The instrumental activity has, therefore, positively valued consequences even when it does not have the originally anticipated outcomes. It is this latter phenomenon (secondary reinforcement) that is operating in the present situation: the organizational setting brings about new personal or subunit consequences through participation in organizationally motivated actions.

3. There is increased *use of categorization as a decision-making technique*. To be sure, categorizing is a basic part of thinking in any situation. The special feature involved here is a tendency to restrict the categories used to a relatively small number and to enforce the first formally applicable category rather than

search for the possible categories that might be applied and choose among them. An increase in the use of categorization for decision-making decreases the *amount of search for alternatives*.

The reduction in personalized relationships, the increased internalization of rules, and the decreased search for alternatives combine to make the behavior of members of the organization highly predictable; i.e., they result in an increase in the *rigidity of behavior* of participants. At the same time, the reduction in personalized relationships (particularly with respect to internal competition) facilitates the development of an *esprit de corps*, i.e., increases the *extent to which goals are perceived as shared among members of the group*. Such a sense of commonness of purpose, interests, and character increases the *propensity of organization members to defend each other against outside pressures*. This, in turn, solidifies the tendency toward rigid behavior.

The rigidity of behavior has three major consequences. First, it substantially satisfies the original demands for reliability. Thus, it meets an important maintenance need of the system. Further needs of this sort are met by strengthening in-group identification, as previously mentioned. Second, it increases the *defensibility of individual action*. Simple categories rigorously applied to individual cases without regard for personal features can only be challenged at a higher level of the hierarchy. Third, the rigidity of behavior increases the *amount of difficulty with clients* of the organization and complicates the achievement of client satisfaction—a near-universal organizational goal. Difficulty with clients is further increased by an increase in the *extent of use of trappings of authority* by subordinates in the organization, a procedure that is encouraged by the in-group's defensiveness.

The maintenance of part of the system by the techniques previously outlined produces a continuing pressure to maintain these techniques, as would be anticipated. It is somewhat more difficult to explain why the organiza-

tion would continue to apply the same techniques in the face of client dissatisfaction. Why do organizational members fail to behave in each case in a manner appropriate to the situation? For the answer one must extend Merton's explicit statements by providing at least one, and perhaps two, additional feedback loops in the system. (It is not enough to say that such behavior becomes a part of the "personality." One must offer some explanation of why this apparently maladaptive learning takes place.)

The second major consequence of rigidity in behavior mentioned above (increased defensibility of individual action) is a deterrent to discrimination that reinforces the emphasis on reliability of behavior. In addition, client dissatisfaction may in itself reinforce rigidity. On the one hand, client pressure at lower levels in the hierarchy tends to increase the *felt need for the defensibility of individual action*. On the other hand, remedial action demanded by clients from higher officials in the hierarchy may be misdirected. To the extent to which clients perceive themselves as being victims of discrimination (a perception that is facilitated in American culture by the importance attached to "equal treatment"), the proposals of clients or of the officials to whom they complain will probably strengthen the emphasis on reliability of behavior. This conflict between "service" and "impartiality" as goals for public organizations seems to lie behind a good deal of the literature on public bureaucracies.

We see that Merton's model is a rather complex set of relations among a relatively large number of variables. A simplified version of the model, designed to illustrate its major features, is provided in Figure 5–2.

THE SELZNICK MODEL

Where Merton emphasizes rules as a response to the demand for control, Selznick[7] emphasizes the delegation of authority. Like Merton, however, Selznick wishes to show how the use of a control technique (i.e., delegation) brings about a series of unanticipated consequences.

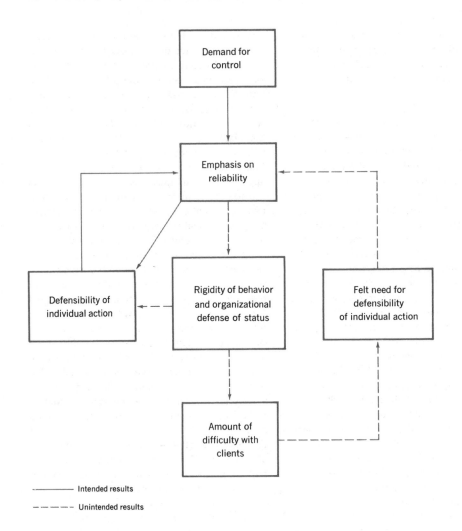

Figure 5–2. The Simplified Merton Model.

Also, like Merton, Selznick shows how these consequences stem from the problems of maintaining highly interrelated systems of interpersonal relations.

Selznick's model starts with the demand for control made by the top hierarchy. As a result of this demand, an increased *delegation of authority* is instituted.

Delegation, however, has several immediate consequences. As intended, it increases the *amount of training in specialized competences.*

Restriction of attention to a relatively small number of problems increases experience within these limited areas and improves the employee's ability to deal with these problems. Operating through this mechanism, delegation tends to decrease the *difference between organizational goals and achievement,* and thus to stimulate more delegation. At the same time, however, delegation results in departmentalization and an increase in the *bifurcation of interests* among the subunits in the organization.

The maintenance needs of the subunits dictate a commitment to the subunit goals over and above their contribution to the total organizational program. Many individual needs depend on the continued success and even expansion of the subunit. As in the previous example, the activities originally evaluated in terms of the organization goals are seen to have additional important ramifications for the subunits.

Bifurcation of interests is also stimulated by the specialized training that delegation (intendedly) produces. Training results in increased competence and, therefore, in increased *costs of changing personnel* and this results, in turn, in further differentiation of subunit goals.

The bifurcation within the organization leads to increased *conflict among organizational subunits*. As a consequence, the *content of decisions* made within the organization depends increasingly upon considerations of internal strategy, particularly if there is little *internalization of organizational goals by participants*. As a result there is an increase in the difference between organizational goals and achievement and this results in an increase in delegation.

This effect on daily decisions is accentuated by two other mechanisms in Selznick's system. The struggle for internal control not only affects directly the content of decisions, but also causes greater *elaboration of subunit ideologies*. Each subunit seeks success by fitting its policy into the official doctrine of the large organization to legitimize its demands. Such a tactic increases the *internalization of subgoals by participants* within subunits.

At the same time, the internalization of subgoals is reinforced by a feedback from the daily decisions it influences. The necessity for making daily decisions creates a system of precedents. Decisions depend primarily on the operational criteria provided by the organization, and, among these criteria, subunit goals are of considerable importance. Precedents tend to become habitual responses to the situations for which they are defined as relevant and thus to reinforce the internalization of subunit goals. Obviously, internalization of subgoals is partially dependent on the *operationality of organizational goals*. By operationality of goals, we mean the extent to which it is possible to observe and test how well goals are being achieved. Variations in the operationality of organizational goals affect the content of daily decisions and thus the extent of subunit goal internalization.

From this it is clear that delegation has both functional and dysfunctional consequences for the achievement of organizational goals. It contributes both to their realization and to their deflection. Surprisingly, the theory postulates that both increases and decreases in goal achievement cause an increase in delegation. Why does not normal learning occur here? The answer seems to be that when goals are not achieved, delegation is—within the framework of the "machine" model—the correct response, and the model does not consider alternatives to simple delegation. On the other hand, the model offers explicitly at least two "dampers" that limit the operation of the dysfunctional mechanisms. As is indicated in Figure 5–3, where the skeleton of the Selznick model is outlined, there are two (not entirely independent) variables treated as independent but potentially amenable to organizational control, each of which restrains the runaway features of daily decision-making. By suitable changes in the extent to which organizational goals are operational or in the internalization of organizational goals by participants, some of the dysfunctional effects of delegation can be reduced. (To be sure, this ignores the possible effect of such procedures on the maintenance problems of the subunits and the consequent results for the larger organizations, but these are problems we are not prepared to attack at the moment.)

THE GOULDNER MODEL

In terms of number of variables and relations, Gouldner's model[8] is the simplest of the three presented here; but it exhibits the major fea-

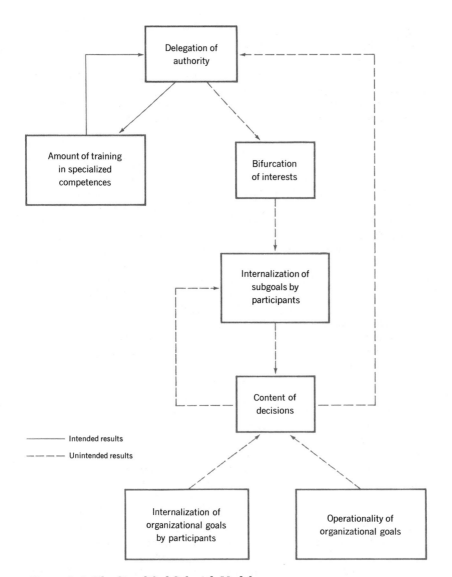

Figure 5–3. The Simplified Selznick Model.

tures of the two previous systems. Like Merton, Gouldner is concerned with the consequences of bureaucratic rules for the maintenance of organization structure. Like both Merton and Selznick, he attempts to show how a control technique designed to maintain the equilibrium of a subsystem disturbs the equilib-

rium of a larger system, with a subsequent feedback on the subsystem.

In Gouldner's system, the *use of general and impersonal rules* regulating work procedures is part of the response to the demand for control from the top hierarchy. One consequence of such rules is to decrease the *visibility of power relations* within the group. The visibility of authority differences within the work group interacts with the *extent to which equality norms are held* to affect the *legitimacy of the supervisory role*. This, in turn, affects the *level of interpersonal tension* in the work group. In the American culture of egalitarian norms, decreases in power visibility increase the legitimacy of the supervisory position and therefore decrease tension within the group.

Gouldner argues that these anticipated con-

sequences of rule-making do occur, that the survival of the work group as an operating unit is substantially furthered by the creation of general rules, and that consequently the use of such rules is reinforced.

At the same time, however, work rules provide cues for organizational members beyond those intended by the authority figures in the organization. Specifically, by defining unacceptable behavior, they increase *knowledge about minimum acceptable behavior*. In conjunction

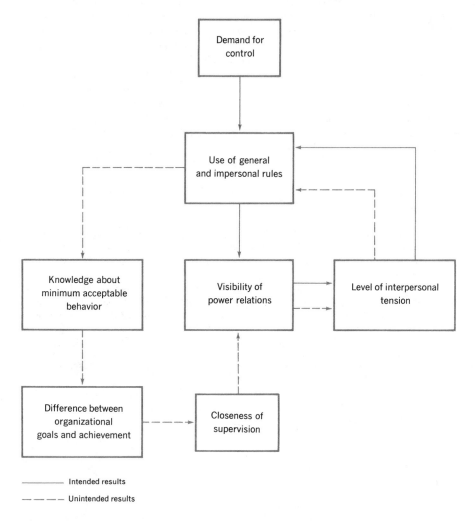

Figure 5–4. The Simplified Gouldner Model.

with a low level of internalization of organizational goals, specifying a minimum level of permissible behavior increases the disparity between organization goals and achievement by depressing behavior to the minimum level.

Performance at the minimum level is perceived by hierarchical superiors as a failure. In short, the internal stabilizing effects of the rules are matched by the unbalance they produce in the larger organization. The response to the unbalance is an increase in the *closeness of supervision* over the work group. This response is based on the "machine" model of human behavior: low performance indicates a need for more detailed inspection and control over the operation of the "machine."

In turn, however, close supervision increases the visibility of power relations within the organization, raises the tension level in the work group, and thereby upsets the equilibrium originally based on the institution of rules. The broad outline of the model is shown in Figure 5–4.

Gouldner's model leaves some puzzles unexplained. In particular, why is increased supervision the supervisory response to low performance? It seems reasonable that the tendency to make such a response is affected both by role perceptions and by a third equilibrating process in the system—the individual needs of the supervisors. Thus, the intensity of supervision is a function of the *authoritarianism* of supervisors and a function of the *punitivity of supervisory role perception*.

As in the Selznick model, the existence of "dampers" on the system poses the question of their treatment as external variables. Appropriate manipulation of equality norms, perceived commonality of interest, and the needs of supervisors will restrict the operation of the dysfunctional features of the system. The failure of top management to use such techniques of control suggests that the system may be incompletely defined.

NOTES

[1] Max Weber, *From Max Weber, Essays in Sociology*, Gerth and Mills, trans. (New York: Oxford University Press, 1946); *The Theory of Social and Economic Organization*, Henderson and Parsons, trans. (New York: Oxford University Press, 1947).

[2] Robert K. Merton, "The Unanticipated Consequences of Purposive Social Action," *American Sociological Review*, (vol. 1, 1936), 894–904; A. W. Gouldner, "Theoretical Requirements of the Applied Social Sciences," *American Sociological Review* (vol. 22, 1957), 91–102.

[3] Robert K. Merton, "Bureaucratic Structure and Personality," *Social Forces*, (vol. 18, 1940), 560–568.

[4] P. Selznick, *TVA and the Grass Roots* (Berkeley: University of California Press, 1949).

[5] A. W. Gouldner, *Patterns of Industrial Bureaucracy* (Glencoe, Ill.: The Free Press of Glencoe, 1954).

[6] Merton, *op. cit.*

[7] Selznick, *op. cit.*

[8] Gouldner, *op. cit.*

6.

FORMALITY VERSUS FLEXIBILITY IN COMPLEX ORGANIZATIONS

GERALD D. BELL

Although there has been much research on organization in the past decade, for the most part it is segmented and loosely interrelated. There is an absence of theoretical formulations which tie current findings into a systematic framework. The stage has been attained, therefore, at which a middle-range theory might be beneficial in gaining a perspective on where our findings have brought us and in which direction we might aim.[1] As Robert V. Presthus comments, "An explicit systhesis between conceptual theory and empirical field research" is required at the present time in the study of organizations.[2]

We attempt here to formulate strategic, interrelated sets of hypotheses based on current research. Our attention is directed toward one, if not the most, significant topic with which recent investigations have been concerned. This is the problem of formal versus flexible patterns of organization.

We will analyze why contemporary research suggests that flexible, loosely structured enterprises are more efficient for given situations than more formally arranged systems. We first review early "formalistic investigations" to ascertain productive factors which are assumed to cause efficiency in work performance. Then, we compare these causal assumptions to those reported in recent "flexible studies." Following

From Gerald D. Bell (ed.), *Organizations and Human Behavior: A Book of Readings*, Prentice-Hall, Inc., Englewood Cliffs, N.J., 1967, pp. 97–106. © 1967. Reprinted by permission of Prentice-Hall, Inc., Englewood Cliffs, New Jersey.

this analysis we attempt to trace consequences of these productive variables upon specific aspects of organization.

Formalized structures and processes refer to the degree to which role expectations and behavior are explicitly established and regulated by the administrative apparatus. An organization is formally structured when there is extensive regulation and control of behavior. Flexible structures and processes characterize those institutions in which the majority of tasks are not governed by explicitly stated regulations and policies and in which employees are not strictly governed by a rigid, clearly specified authority structure.

Theoretical foundations

Early research viewed industrial research and service enterprises as formally and rationally structured units. Production activities were assumed to be clearly defined, well coordinated, and performed in a rigid, impersonal manner.[3] The "formalized theories" were given their most elaborate development, of course, in Max Weber's organizational precepts.[4]

We find evidence of widespread influence of these doctrines in the fact that much research in the past several decades has clustered around three problems arising from formal theories. First, the "human-relations school" attacked assumptions of formalized theories concerning workers' psychological dispositions and motivational orientations.[5] Second, researchers have been concerned with dysfunctional aspects of formalized modes of organization.[6] Finally, and of most significance for the present study, recent investigations have been in the direction of "structural alterations or qualifications" of the formalistic model.[7] For the most part these efforts, which we have tentatively labeled the "flexible school," suggest that in many cases organizations with structures opposite to those prescribed by Weber exist and are conducive to a high degree of efficiency.

Examples of "flexible studies" are Alvin Gouldner's research on the subsurface division of a Gypsum plant,[8] Morris Janowitz's investigation of the changing structures of the military,[9] James Thompson and Arthur Tuden's analysis of formal and flexible tendencies which result from the extent of agreement that exists on decisions concerning both causative issues and preferences among alternatives,[10] Arthur Stinchcombe's formulations on "craft bureaucracies,"[11] and, finally, in Eugene Litwak's research on "human-relations" types of organization.[12] In general, these investigations suggest that authority structures are at a minimum, interaction is on a personal basis, and there is little rule usage.

Although the points of departure and variables considered are somewhat different, the flexible studies have proposed quite divergent patterns of organization than those expounded in the formalistic design; however, the causes for these differences are by no means clear. Let us attempt to explain, then, the causal assumptions upon which these two divergent theories stand.

Lack of discretion in the formal theories

The causal notions of formalistic theorists— as exemplified by F. W. Taylor, Luther Gulick, and Max Weber—are revealed in their special emphasis upon subdivision of tasks, strict delimitation of duties, and reliability and calculability of behavior. These notions imply that duties to be performed by an individual are susceptible to easy specification and preplanning. They hold the idea, furthermore, that work demands performed in the productive system are highly predictable and repetitive. And finally, they make the all-important assumption that workers carry out their tasks by exercising only a small degree of discretion or decision-making effort.

Presence of discretion in the flexible theories

Flexible investigations have been based upon notions quite contrary to the causal assumptions of formal theorists. Flexible studies have

assumed, although somewhat implicitly, that the work environment is relatively nonpredictable and encourages much discretion on the part of the workers. And, a careful analysis of the assumptions implied in the "flexible theories" suggests that the amount of discretion workers exercise is a key feature which is causally related to the degree of formality of organizational structures. It is not, as is suggested in the flexible studies, improvisation, lack of rule usage, lack of close supervision, variation in work load, professionalization, or social skills *per se* which directly cause differences in organizational design. More precisely (1) we hypothesize that several of these variables are *important causes of the discretion a worker exercises in performing his tasks, and* (2) *discretion, in turn, has a significant influence on the flexibility of formalistic tendencies of organizational structure.* We will now direct our attention to these two postulates in their respective order.

DISCRETION

For each task a worker performs he is confronted with the opportunity or sometimes the necessity to exert a certain degree of discretion—that is, judgment, choice, or selection among alternatives in order to carry out his tasks. Furthermore, the total amount of discretion he exercises is directed toward one or some combinations of three main aspects of task performance—(1) *which tasks* he performs during a given period of time, (2) *how or by which methods,* and (3) *in which sequence* he performs his tasks.

DETERMINANTS OF DISCRETION

Discretion on the part of the employee is brought into play when the character of the work itself and the routines governing how the work is done do not automatically determine for the employee doing the job the best way to do it in every respect. Discretion and judgment are necessary when there are more ways than one to go about doing a task. When causes of a problem are not clearly defined and when the solution is lacking acceptable alternatives, the final answer must rely on judgment.[13] And when there are many such situations, it is likely that an individual will learn to exercise his discretion, since there is a certain point at which it is uneconomical for the supervisor to make decisions for him. Beyond this point, the supervisor might as well be doing the job himself. An analysis of the flexible studies previously mentioned suggests that discretion taken as the dependent variable is caused by the following independent variables: (a) predictability of work demands, (b) management control, and (c) professionalization.

Predictability

Predictability of work demands refers to the extent to which unexpected events confront an individual while he is performing his job. Stinchcombe's "unstable work situations,"[14] Litwak's "nonuniform tasks,"[15] and Janowitz's "changing elements of battle technology"[16] all seem to cluster around the predictability category.

When situational demands are unpredictable, they present the worker with novel events toward which he has the opportunity to utilize his judgment in completing his tasks. When a surgeon, for example, opens a patient's stomach and finds an unexpected object inside he will be encouraged, presumably, to alter his activities (or to utilize his discretion) to meet the exigencies of the situation. In the same manner if a stockbroker meets a new customer and begins his sales talk by presenting a "front region" of an intellectual and then perceives that he is presenting the wrong front because the customer sympathizes with anti-intellectuals, he will be encouraged to change his behavior, that is, to use his judgment in order to come up with a new "self" which will enable him to carry out his tasks more effectively. This assumes, of course, that the worker is motivated to perform his tasks adequately.[17]

In addition to the direct effect of predictabil-

ity upon discretion, predictability also indirectly influences discretion via two intervening variables. These are the degree of closeness of supervision and, in turn, rule usage, both taken as components of management control.

Management control and discretion

Management has the opportunity and ability to determine the exact degree of discretion a worker exercises regardless of the extent of predictability of job demands. For example, a supervisor of a research department (a fairly unpredictable unit) might normally expect that he would have much opportunity to exert his judgment in completing his tasks; however, if management decided, for whatever reason, to establish a very rigid, encompassing set of rules for this supervisor to follow, then he would not exert high discretion even though he still was faced with many unpredictable events on his job. New problems would continue to arise, new solutions would appear; however, the supervisor would not exert his judgment in meeting these unexpected events, rather he would follow management's directives.

The point to be made here is that even though predictability might significantly affect discretion, discretion can also be influenced by management's control. But we hypothesize that management will perceive that if they control very tightly the tasks of workers who are faced with unpredictable work situations, then the rate of efficiency will be decreased. Consequently, we expect management to encourage workers who have unpredictable jobs to utilize their discretion.[18] Hence, in this case predictability is an independent variable influencing management control, and management control is an intervening variable causally related to workers' discretion.

Professionalization

Professionalization here means that workers have received a technical training to achieve a recognized occupational competence. The more professional training an employee has acquired, the more he will possess and demand skills which require discretion. In Stinchcombe's terms, craft administration differs from mass-production administration ". . . by substituting professional training of manual workers for detailed centralized planning of work."[19] In a similar light, Thompson and F. L. Bates rehearse the idea that the university must allow its personnel to exercise much discretion, since "knowledge" is given recognition as the basis of authority.[20] Simon Marcson also suggests that discretion and flexibility are important aspects of professional ranks of scientific research firms.[21]

Professional training improves technical competence; in a sense it creates technical and discretionary skills and at the same time produces expectations of freedom from supervisory control in the work setting. We hypothesize, then, that the higher the professional training, the higher the discretion. Correspondingly, professionalization indirectly affects discretion through the intervening variable of management control. In this latter instance the higher the professional training, the lower will be the degree of management control over a worker's behavior, and thus the higher will be an individual's discretion.

In summary, predictability, management control, and professionalization act as important determinants of employees' discretion.

Problem in past assumptions

There are several problems associated with past theories which state that some of the above variables which we assume to affect discretion act independently to cause flexible or formalistic characteristics of work arrangement.

For example, in one of the first illuminating approaches to the general flexibility-formalistic dilemma, Litwak offered a provacative first step in attempting to explain why organizations had quite varying structures. He concluded, following Weber, that jobs (1) which stress uniform situations, that is, " . . . the task to be dealt with is recurrent (in time as well as among many people) and important, exemplified in such occupations as that of research scientist or developmental engineer, as opposed to supervisor of an assembly line;"[22] and (2) which stress traditional areas of knowledge, such as knowledge of engineering, chemistry, economics, law, company rules, and the like, are those which bring about a rational, Weberian type of organization. On the other hand nonuniform jobs and those which require social skills tend to create organizations which stress primary relations and organizational goals.[23]

Litwak, indeed, has made a major contribution to the solution of the dilemma of formalistic-flexibilistic work patterns; however, we must carry his analysis further, and this necessitates some modifications in his causal assumptions. It is possible, for example, that such categories as social skills and traditional areas of knowledge can be somewhat misleading if, as has been proposed in this paper, the degree of discretion initiated by the worker is one of the key dimensions producing varying patterns of organization; for it is possible that jobs which require social skills (Litwak suggests jobs such as salesmen's, psychiatric social workers', and politicians') due to various circumstances may in fact allow the job incumbent only a small degree of discretion and, therefore, tend to produce a formalistic work structure, which is opposite to that expected in Litwak's interpretation. Similarly, jobs which stress traditional areas of knowledge (economics, law), contrary to what is implied by Litwak, might be nonpredictable and require a very high degree of discretion. Again, in this latter case, we would have quite different consequences for traditional, yet high-discretion, jobs than are proposed by Litwak. Work would tend toward flexible patterns of organization rather than toward the Weberian model as Litwak proposed.

Furthermore, Litwak's concept of uniform work tasks evidently refers to the activities *actually performed* by the employee, whereas predictability as developed here refers to the work demands which confront an individual. These are two distinct variables. A worker might be confronted by many unique and unexpected situations while carrying out his job; however, he might meet these unique events by performing tasks in a very repetitive, routine, or—in Litwak's terms—uniform way. In this situation unexpected events would continue to occur, but the worker would in a sense ignore these situational demands and perform his tasks in a routine manner. And in this case he would be making few decisions in performing his job. Consequently, his job would fit rather easily into a formalistic work structure.

It would appear that the general categories mentioned by Litwak and others might profitably be modified by considering predictability of work demands and discretion. What Litwak and several of the other "flexible theorists" were exploring, in essence, was something similar to these two variables, but their causal assumptions were too broad to be able to generalize to precise causal relationships concerning organizational structure. Let us view now how discretion influences organizational design.

THE DISCRETIONARY MODEL OF ORGANIZATION

It is hypothesized that the relationships portrayed in the following chart will prevail in organizations in which the productive systems are high on discretion. If these hypotheses are valid, then high discretion units may be characterized as having more flexible structures and processes. On the other hand, in the less discretionary units the direction of each of the hypotheses will be reversed, and, therefore,

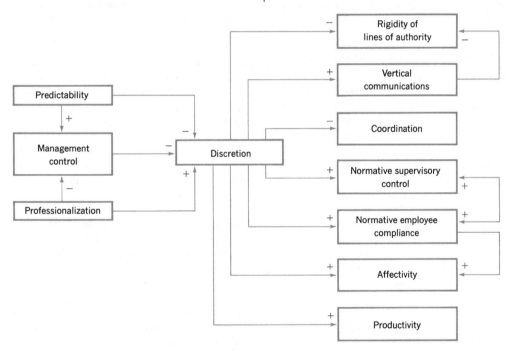

Figure 6–1. The Discretionary Model of Organization. The arrowed lines in the chart indicate the assumed causal direction of the relationships; and the plus and minus signs represent positive and negative associations, respectively. For example, when predictability is high, discretion is low.

there firms will be more formal and rigid in their patterns of work arrangement. In other words, the more predictable the work demands and the fewer the decisions which must be made in the productive process to attain organization goals, the more formalized will be the patterns of administrative activities, communication, and coordination; and more flexible patterns of organization will result from unpredictable and highly discretionary productive processes.

The following set of hypotheses is in no way purported to be exhaustive, rather it is a first attempt to build organizational theory from existing research. Limits must be placed upon each of these propositions, since there are many factors in addition to discretion which enter into the predicted relationships. The notation of "other things being equal" should be placed behind each hypothesis. We will begin our analysis by discussing relationships between discretion and the authority structure.

Discretion and the authority structure

We are concerned here with the extent to which lines of authority are clearly defined and rigidly adhered to. When tasks are unpredictable and encourage employees to make decisions frequently, lines of authority will be very ambiguous and flexible. Subordinates will not be expected to report to a specific superior for each action they take, rather they will tend to scatter their consultations among several different combinations of supervisors. Similarly, since demands placed upon workers' efforts are assumed to encourage them to utilize their abilities in solving work problems and to call forth fairly unique solutions to their tasks, it would not appear likely that a rigid, carefully delineated authority system would be created in unpredictable, high-discretion systems.

On the contrary, in low-judgmental units employees' tasks will be easily specified and controlled, since work demands are highly predictable and require little decision-making effort. Correspondingly, superiors will be able to plan for and to establish rigid lines of authority

more easily, and the predictability of situational demands will enable subordinate-superior relationships to be handled adequately through formalized channels. As Thompson and Bates have said, since standardization is high, deviations can be measured readily and thus responsibility accurately assigned to specific individuals.[24]

Vertical communication

A survey of literature relevant to this variable suggests a rather interesting pattern between predictability, discretion, and vertical communications. There appears to be a positive relationship between vertical communications (any verbal, written, or symbolic exchange of information between members of different levels of authority) and discretion and, thus, predictability.[25]

In high-predictability–low-discretion organizations, administrators are able to determine fairly accurately the tasks, methods, and sequence in which employees are to perform their tasks, and employees make few decisions. This enables managers to coordinate and train employees easily in their routine decision-making activities and consequently requires less control of their performance.[26] Furthermore, since communication and training partially substitute for each other, the better trained a person is for a job, the less becomes the need to communicate with him about his work.[27]

On the other hand, in high-discretion units, there will be much vertical communication. But instead of work demands being so predictable and involving so few decisions that close supervision and training are facilitated, work demands are unpredictable, and employees are highly skilled and competent . . . exercising much discretion. These factors encourage supervisors and subordinates to communicate frequently about work-related problems. The uniqueness and complexities involved in unpredictable and high-discretion demanding activities create a great need for exchange of ideas and information between workers and superiors concerning the solution of unique events.[28] The content of supervision in the latter case will be more on an equal "give-and-take" basis than on one in which supervisors closely regulate subordinates' activities. It would be a two-way, rather than merely a downward, communication as in the former case. Topics of exchange would in both cases probably be concerned with work activities—the solution of task-related problems, grievances, and so forth. However, the type of communication in the latter case might differ in being somewhat more complex, unique, and abstract than in the former.

Coordination of activities

There is less need to coordinate activities between departments which involve unpredictable demands and high discretion than between those with high predictability and low discretion. Departments in which decision-making ability has been decentralized appear to be more self-contained than are less discretionary units. For instance, one might compare the amount of coordination which takes place between two divisions on an assembly line in an automated production plant with two departments, such as history and sociology, in the relatively discretionary organization—the university. The reason for differences in coordination is that high-discretion units are arranged in parallel department specialization, whereas low-discretion units are more functionally interdependent in Peter M. Blau and W. Richard Scott's terms.[29] In parallel specialization, work activities of one department are different from but not highly dependent on actions of others. In contrast, interdependent specialization exists when the activities of one unit are dependent upon the performance of tasks in other departments. The latter case makes coordination a fundamental managerial problem.

Why are nonpredictable, high-discretion departments specialized in a parallel manner, and why are predictable, low-discretion units interdependently specialized? The answer appears to be that when work demands are predictable

and routine they can be subdivided and controlled fairly easily. Thus, more specialization can be obtained. And the more that tasks can be subdivided, the more they can be effectively planned for and coordinated by management's efforts. And thus, the more likely it is that they will be interdependently specialized.

Normative supervisory control

When an employee's superior attempts to motivate him to work by appealing to service norms and professional ideologies as opposed to such monetary rewards as pay, bonuses, or promotions, the supervisor, in Etzioni's terms, is using normative control attempts.[30] In departments in which tasks, methods, and sequence of performance are not clearly specified, and thus in which responsibility for the performance of each task is not clearly definable, administrators cannot easily direct the completion of each task. Correspondingly, rewards and responsibility cannot easily be assigned to tasks which are nonpredictable and which involve a high degree of discretion.

In these cases normative control attempts will provide incentives for members to perform necessary tasks on their own, since manipulation of pay does not lead to internationalization of values but produces only superficial, expedient, and overt commitment.[31] In this connection Marcson points out that in large scientific organizations there is a necessity for a shift to less arbitrary, less direct, and less dominating control practices. In research organizations the utilization of direct and calculative control not only evokes resentment but also resistance to such control attempts.[32] Thus, we theorize that when work demands are nonpredictable and involve much discretion, normative and/or somewhat more informal constraints will appear.

Employee compliance structure

Employees meet and adjust to control attempts by management in particular patterns and intensities of compliance. Job incumbents in high-discretion and unpredictable organizations will be oriented toward administrative control more in terms of normative and ideological commitment to work than by monetary or calculative involvement. Employees will make many decisions, have a relatively high degree of self-investment and responsibility, and consequently will be highly involved in their work. When an individual exercises his judgment and initiative in solving problems, he invests a good portion of his "self" in their outcome. Research scientists, for example, often indicate a need for an authority system based on persuasion and normative encouragements.[33]

Furthermore, the coterminous presence of professionalization of jobs and normative control attempts by supervisors directed toward discretionary jobs exerts important pressures toward a congruent normative control-normative compliance structure. The internalization by workers of professional ideologies and codes of conduct partially eliminates administrators' needs to motivate and to control employees. Professional-technical socialization acts as an arm of management in the sense that it "builds" motivation into workers and at the same time acts as a continuing motivational reference group for them.

In predictable, low-discretion jobs, however, a worker invests little of his "self" in the outcome of his productive efforts. In fact, he seldom sees how his activities contribute to the final product on which he is working. Similarly, responsibilities and rewards can be more clearly assigned. Therefore, managers can revert more easily to monetary and manipulative control attempts. In turn, employees will possess a calculative orientation toward their work and the organization.

Donald I. Warren has reported tentative evidence which indirectly supports these notions. He also introduces another dimension into the relationship between predictability, discretion, and normative involvement. He points out, following Rose Coser, that when visibility of formal authority agents is low (as is presumably the case in nonpredictable, high-discretion units) then attitudinal commitment

to one's work and informal constraints are more likely to be conducive to effectiveness.[34]

Affectivity in interpersonal relations

In high-discretion and unpredictable organizations workers are considered to not only have a high degree of responsibility and investment of "self" in their work, but they also are thought to have more freedom in expressing their opinions and beliefs. They are given more leeway and encouragement to display their emotions, and thus there is a high degree of affectivity in the relationships between workers in these organizations. In his pioneering study of the operating room (a high-discretion unit) in the hospital setting, Wilson reports that doctors and nurses frequently maintain close personal relationships and share many experiences.[35] Similarly, Blau suggests that in a government unemployment agency the counseling role which employees performed was often carried out with highly affective personal relationships.[36]

Productivity

Finally, in enterprises which entail highly discretionary productive units if the above variables take on the directions predicted, we assume they will obtain optimum levels of efficiency. That is, if departments in which jobs are unpredictable and involve much discretion on the part of workers are (1) left relatively unattended by members in authority, (2) entail high vertical communications, (3) have a low degree of coordination with other departments, (4) are sanctioned and rewarded by normative control attempts, (5) and, correspondingly, normatively committted to on the part of the employees, and (6) are associated with affectivity in interpersonal work relationships, then we expect this type of flexible work arrangement to be conducive to an (7) optimum level of efficiency.

Similarly, if the hypotheses are reversed for nondiscretionary firms, efficiency will also be at a high level. In other words, we are maintaining that efficiency can best be reached by two separate patterns of organization for the two ideal extremes of the discretionary predictability productive systems. On the one extreme, Weber's rational model appears to be efficient for those enterprises which encompass non-discretionary productive tasks. On the opposite pole, more flexible patterns of work arrangement are considered to be most conducive to efficiency when productive tasks are nonpredictable and high on discretion demands.

SUMMARY AND CONCLUSIONS

We have attempted to formulate tentative hypotheses which partially explain why contemporary research has reported quite varying findings from Weber's early formulations. It is assumed that in organizations in which employees exert a high degree of discretion there will be: (1) less rigid lines of authority, (2) high vertical communications, (3) low coordination, (4) high normative control by supervisors, (5) high normative commitment by employees, (6) high affectivity in interpersonal relationships, and, finally (7) relatively high productivity.

It is further theorized that discretion is determined by predictability, management control, and extent of professionalization of jobs. These postulates are tentative and, of course, assume that "other things are held equal." Hopefully, this "discretionary model" will offer suggestions to some of the provocative questions concerning formal and flexible patterns of work arrangement raised in recent works and will suggest new avenues of research.

NOTES

[1] Alvin Gouldner, "Organizational Analysis," in *Sociology Today*, Robert Merton *et. al.*, eds. (New York: Basic Books, Inc., Publishers, 1959), p. 404; James D. Thompson *et. al.*, *Comparative Studies in Administration* (Pittsburgh: University of Pittsburgh Press, 1959), p. 200; Amitai Etzioni, *A Comparative Analysis of Complex Organizations* (New York: Free Press of Glencoe, Inc., 1960), p. xiii; Simon Marcson, *The Scientist in American Industry* (Princeton, N.J.: Princeton University Press, 1960), p. 122; M. D. Field, "Information and Authority: The Structure of Military Organization," *American Sociological Review*, 24 (February, 1959), p. 17; Stanley H. Udy, Jr., *Organization of Work* (New Haven, Connecticut: Human Relations Area Files Press), 1959.

[2] Robert V. Presthus, "Behavior and Bureaucracy in Many Cultures," *Public Administration Review*, 19 (1959), p. 25; See also, James March and Herbert Simon, *Organizations* (New York: John Wiley & Sons, Inc., 1958), p. 17–26, especially their discussion of Merton, Selznick, and Gouldner; Chris Argyris, "The Fusion of an Individual with the Organization," *American Sociological Review*, 14 (June, 1954), p. 272; Peter M. Blau and W. Richard Scott, *Formal Organizations* (San Francisco: Chandler Publishing Company, 1962), p. 35.

[3] March and Simon, *op. cit.*, p. 13. The flexible model, it should be pointed out, is rational in the sense that ends are related to the means in possibly the most appropriate method available. F. W. Taylor, *Shop Management* (New York: Harper & Row, Publishers, Inc., 1912); Luther Gulick and L. Urwick, eds. *Papers on the Science of Administration* (New York: Institute of Public Administration, 1937).

[4] Hans Gerth and C. Wright Mills, trans. and eds., *From Max Weber:*

Essays in Sociology (New York: Oxford University Press, Inc., 1946), p. 214.

⁵ See William F. Whyte, *Man and Organization: Three Problems in Human Relations in Industry* (Homewood, Illinois: Richard D. Irwin, Inc., 1959).

⁶ For an excellent review of these studies see March and Simon, *op. cit.*, pp. 26–47.

⁷ We are using "model" to refer to a general theory. Included in this category are Gouldner, *op. cit.*; Arthur Stinchcombe, "Bureaucratic and Craft Administration of Production: A Comparative Study," *Administrative Science Quarterly* 4 (September, 1959); Morris Janowitz, "Changing Patterns of Organizational Authority: The Military Establishment," *Administrative Science Quarterly,* 3 (March, 1959), pp. 473–493; Eugene Litwak, "Models of Bureaucracy Which Permit Conflict," *American Journal of Sociology,* 67 (September, 1961), pp. 177–184.

⁸ Gouldner, *op. cit.*; James D. Thompson and F. L. Bates, "Technology, Organization and Administration," *Administrative Science Quarterly,* 11 (December, 1957), pp. 325–343.

⁹ Janowitz, *op. cit.*, p. 481.

¹⁰ James D. Thompson and Arthur Tuden, "Strategies, Structures, and Processes of Organizational Decision," in James D. Thompson *et al., op. cit.*, pp. 195–213.

¹¹ Stinchcombe, *op. cit.*

¹² Litwak, *op. cit.*, pp. 177–184.

¹³ Elliot, Jaques, *The Measurement of Responsibility* (Cambridge: Harvard University Press, 1956), p. 86; Thompson and Tuden, *op. cit.*, p. 199.

¹⁴ Stinchcombe, *op. cit.*

¹⁵ Litwak, *op. cit.*

¹⁶ Janowitz, *op. cit.*

¹⁷ Finally, there is a fascinating sidelight which should be mentioned in this connection. This is the fact that if unpredictable situational demands take the form of a threat to the organization, it is possible that the hypothesized association between predictability and discretion will be reversed. Several studies have indicated that outside threats tend to cause centralization of decision-making. (Janowitz, *op. cit.*)

¹⁸ It should also be pointed out here that it is possible that management's control might, in turn, affect the degree of predictability of an employee's job.

¹⁹ Stinchcombe, *op. cit.*, p. 175.

²⁰ Thompson and Bates, *op. cit.*, p. 333.

²¹ Marcson, *op. cit.*, p. 44.

²² Litwak, *op. cit.*, p. 178.

²³ *Ibid.*, p. 170. Social skills refer to the actual capacity to communicate with others, to motivate them to work, to cooperate with others, and to internalize the values of the organization.

²⁴ Thompson and Bates, *op. cit.*, p. 334.

²⁵ On this point see Richard L. Simpson, "Vertical and Horizontal Communication in Formal Organizations," *Administrative Science Quarterly,* 4 (September, 1959), p. 196. Although the predicted directions differ from those reviewed in Simpson's research, it does not appear that the problem lies in the theory as much as it does in the difficulty of ascertaining what actually is a high level of discretion, or mechanization. This appears to be

an important point for scholars of administration to consider in future research.

26 Edward Gross, "Some Functional Consequences of Primary Controls," *American Sociological Review,*" 18 (August, 1953), p. 379.

27 Etzioni, *op. cit.,* p. 138.

28 When specific vertical communication exchange networks are used repeatedly and therefore become relatively patterned and accepted paths for exchange of information, communication channels are said to exist. In high-discretion organizations, since there will be many and varied decisions which must be made at a variety of times and in numerous situations, it is possible that there will be less opportunity for vertical communications to become patterned, and workers will presumably be required to consult with many different supervisors in inconsistent and sporadic patterns. Stinchcombe's analysis of communication files is consistent with this notion. (Stinchcombe, *op. cit.*)

29 Blau and Scott, *op. cit.,* p. 183.

30 Etzioni, *op. cit.,* p. xv.

31 *Ibid.;* see also Andrew F. Henry and Edgar Borgatta, "A Comparison of Attitudes of Enlisted and Commissioned Air Force Personnel," *American Sociological Review,* 18 (December, 1953), p. 670.

32 Marcson, *op. cit.*

33 *Ibid.*

34 Donald I. Warren, "The Role of Professional Peer Relations in a Formal Organization Setting: Some Correlates of Administrative Style" (unpublished paper presented at the Annual Meeting of the American Sociological Association, Montreal, Canada, September, 1964).

35 Robert N. Wilson, "Teamwork in the Operating Room," *Human Organization,* 12 (1954).

36 Blau and Scott, *op. cit.*

7.

MODELS OF BUREAURCRACY WHICH PERMIT CONFLICT

EUGENE LITWAK

In the present paper an attempt will be made to suggest some conditions for polar models[1] of bureaucracy. This will in turn permit some specifications of an intermediate model of bureaucracy which may more clearly fit contemporary urban society.

The two models of bureaucracy to be contrasted are that which stresses secondary relations and organizational rules (i.e., as Weber's), and that which stresses primary-group relations and organizational goals[2] (as in the "human-relations" approach). Weber's model is most efficient when the organization deals primarily with uniform events and with occupations stressing traditional areas of knowledge rather than social skills. The human-relations model will be most efficient for dealing with events which are not uniform (research, medical treatment, graduate training, designing) and with occupations emphasizing social skills as technical aspects of the job (as that of psychiatric social worker, salesman if there is little differentiation in the products, and politician).

However, for most organizations in our society a theoretical model of bureaucratic organization must be developed that combines the central and conflicting features from both types. Since they are conflicting, what characterizes this third model and distinguishes it from the other two is a need for "mechanisms of segregation." These permit mutually antagonistic social forms to exist side by side in the same organization without ruinous friction.

From Eugene Litwak, "Models of Bureaucracy which Permit Conflict," *American Journal of Sociology,* 67:177–184, 1961. Reprinted by permission of The University of Chicago Press.

THE UNIFORM AND THE NON-UNIFORM

Weber's model of bureaucracy[3] can be characterized by: impersonal social relations, appointment and promotion on the basis of merit, authority and obligations which are specified a priori and adhere to the job rather than the individual (i.e., separation of work from private life), authority organized on a hierarchical basis, separation of policy and administrative positions, the members of the bureaucracy being concerned with administrative decisions, general rules for governing all behavior not specified by the above, and, finally, specialization. If the organization is large and structured by these ideal conditions, it will be more efficient[4] than any other kind of organization. Weber's theoretical model assumes that the organization will be dealing with uniform situations.

By "uniform" two things are meant: The task to be dealt with is recurrent (in time as well as among many people) and important, exemplified in such occupations as that of: research scientist or developmental engineer, as opposed to supervisor of an assembly line; doctor or surgeon providing treatment in areas of medicine where little is known (neurosurgeon), as opposed to one dealing with standardized problems; soldier in combat, as opposed to in peacetime; administrator of a large organization producing a rapidly changing product (e.g., chemicals, electronic apparatus, pharmaceuticals, or missiles), as opposed to one dealing with standardized procedures, such as a public utility or a large governmental agency administering well-established regulations.

The importance of distinguishing between the uniform and the non-uniform as well as noting Weber's assumption of uniformity can best be seen if the criticisms of his model are reviewed.[5] The critics point out that the larger the organization, the more likely is it to encompass diverse social situations and people. If a general rule is developed for each situation, the rules would be so numerous as to defy learning. If rules are not developed, then either the administrator will apply rules which are not appropriate or substitute for them his private system of values. In all cases there is likely to be a drop in efficiency when general rules are used and the task is not uniform.

The same point can be made with regard to the hierarchy of authority and delimitation of duties and privileges of the office, for both are only special cases of general rules. Thus, for maximum efficiency, a hirerarchy or delimitation of jobs should be based on merit. Setting up a hierarchy based on merit is a relatively simple matter when dealing with one uniform event. However, if the event is relatively unique, it is difficult for any one hierarchy to suffice for all tasks in the organization. Yet this is the assumption which must be made in all cases where Weber's specifications are applied to organizations dealing with the nonuniform. Since this is too heroic, the individuals concerned might do better to internalize the values of the organization and reach *ad hoc* rather than a priori decisions as to job hierarchy and boundaries.

In his pioneering work, Pelz investigated a large industrial concern whose parts were classified into several groups: those dealing with non-uniform events (i.e., scientists and engineers) and those working with relatively uniform events (central staff and manufacturing).[6] He found that among those in the occupations dealing with nonuniform tasks there was a higher correlation between their motivation to work and productivity when they were free to make their own decisions. In contrast, among those working on uniform tasks there was a higher correlation between motivation and productivity when they were restricted in making decisions. Permitting each individual to control decisions on the job indicates a trend toward a colleague rather than a hierarchical relationship. Pelz's study supports the point of

view advocated here, that is, there are differential efficiencies in organizational structure depending on whether the task is uniform or not.

Somewhat the same analysis holds with regard to specialization, which is efficient where there are relatively constant problems. Where there are many problem areas and where they change rapidly, the demand for specialization may lead to premature organizational closure and great inflexibility in deciding, as in the armed forces where a rapidly changing technology has made traditional specialties obsolete. Many argue that the clinging to the traditional specialties has led to a dangerous lag in military preparedness as well as wasteful conflict between specialties.[7]

Weber's demand for impersonality also assumes uniform events. Individuals faced with non-uniform events which are not clearly covered by rules are insecure. In such situations, they must be able to call on colleagues in whom they put great trust[8] if they are to perform efficiently. In other words, in the ambiguous situation brought about by non-uniform events, frequently personal primary group relations conduce to more efficiency than would impersonal ones.

Finally, it can be argued that the separation of policy and administrative decisions is inefficient when the organization is confronted with non-uniform situations. Such separation implies that general rules can be laid down a priori to guide administrative decisions along common lines of policy. As suggested above, such general rules become impossibly complex when the organization faces non-uniform situations. Internalizing organizational policy and localizing discretion (combining administrative and policy decisions) would then be more efficient.

In short, where organizations deal with non-uniform events, a model of bureaucracy may be more efficient which differs in degree from Weber's in at least six characteristics: horizontal patterns of authority, minimal specialization, mixture of decisions on policy and on administration, little a priori limitation of duty and privileges to a given office, personal rather than impersonal relations, and a minimum of general rules. This form of organization generally characterizes the "human-relations" model described as ideal by many contemporary industrial psychologists.

SOCIAL AND TRADITIONAL JOB SKILLS

Weber also implicitly assumes in his discussion of bureaucracy that occupations stressing traditional areas of knowledge (as compared to social skills) dominate the organization. By traditional areas of knowledge is meant, say, knowledge of engineering, of chemistry, of economics, of the law, of company rules, and the like. By social skills or abilities is meant the actual capacity to communicate with others, to motivate them to work, to co-operate with others, and to internalize the values of the organization.

Granted Weber's assumptions about traditional areas of knowledge, his model of bureaucracy does not necessarily lead to efficiency when the job requirements stress social skills.

PERSONAL AND IMPERSONAL. Weber's strictures concerning the importance of impersonal social relations are far from self-evident when social abilities rather than traditional knowledge are at issue. The capacity to motivate others to work, to co-operate and to communicate with others, to internalize the norms of the organization, might well increase, not decrease, as a consequence of positive emotional involvement. Thus, studies of psychiatric wards, involving professions whose chief technical tools are social, suggest that greatest efficiency requires some positive emotional involvement.[9] Weber's analysis tends to overlook the virtues of close personal relations, concentrating on negative features. Since in an advanced bureaucratic society these latter are minimized,[10] many of Weber's objections to close personal relations are not so important.

STRICT DELIMITATION OF OBLIGATION AND DUTIES TO THE OFFICE. Weber's view that in an efficient organization there should be a strict delimitation of obligations and duties to a specified office assumes that the work can be shut off from private life (e.g., the family). This assumption has considerable validity when one is dealing with the traditional areas of knowledge. However, it is questionable when the chief technical demand of the job is for social skills. This is so because family and friends are major sources for the development of social skills. Therefore, experience in primary groups is likely to enter into one's life at work.[11] More generally, where it is difficult to separate work from other situations, such as family life, the organization must seek to control the latter for the sake of efficiency. The development in large organizations, such as the DuPont Corporation, of family counseling services can be understood in this light.

SEPARATION OF POLICY AND ADMINISTRATIVE DECISIONS. The inability to isolate work from other situations also makes it difficult, if not impossible, to keep decisions on policy and administration separate. To do so would require that administrative decisions have a code of ethics of their own. Thus an engineer working on a bomb, a dam, or an automobile can say how good an engineer he is in terms of common engineering standards and somewhat independently of organizational policy. By contrast, the psychiatric social worker, because her major technical tool is social skills, finds such distinctions hard to maintain: is participation of the client or the avoidance of physical punishment an administrative technic or the agency's policy? When such distinctions are hard to make, it is more efficient to inculcate policy and give the professional discretion with regard to "administrative" decisions.

SPECIALIZATION AND GENERALIZATION. In part, Weber's assumptions regarding efficiency of specialization would not hold where social skills are the technique required for the job.

The ability to communicate with others is general in every area of work and is the same for the engineering administrator, the accounting administrator, and every other administrator. The need to train "generalists" for administration is seen in the systematic efforts to move promising executives to a variety of departments in the company.[12] It can also be noted that the most recent recommendation concerning the curriculum in schools of social work (dealing with occupations whose chief technical tool is social abilities) was to drop the specialties and train all students in the basic social skills.[13]

Thus, in some technical fields there has been increasing specialization, while in the fields characterized by administration and by the demand for social skills there has been increasing generalization; and the total picture may indeed suggest the growth of both specialization and generalization.

Hierarchical and horizontal relations. Hierarchical relations may well lead to efficiency when the job is defined by traditional areas of knowledge. However, there is some evidence that participation in making decisions is crucial where it is necessary to motivate people to identify themselves with organizational goals, to co-operate in their social relations, and to communicate.[14] Since these involve social skills, participation in making decisions is important where jobs are chiefly defined by those abilities. Put differently, jobs characterized by social skills might be carried out most efficiently under a horizontal structure of authority, that permits all individuals to participate equally in decisions.[15]

SPECIFICATIONS FOR A THIRD MODEL OF BUREAUCRACY

To point out the weaknesses of Weber's model is not to suggest its elimination. Quite the contrary; this paper argues that there are several models of organization with differential efficiencies depending on the nature of the work and the types of tasks to be performed. In this regard, at least three types have been suggested: Weber's, that found in "human relations," and what may be called the "professional bureaucracy."[16] The third model, not discussed as yet, is characterized by the degree to which the organization must deal with events both uniform and not uniform, or by the need to have jobs requiring great social skills as well as jobs requiring traditional areas of knowledge. Perhaps the outstanding illustrations of the third type would be a large hospital, a graduate school, or a research organization. To more systematically highlight the difference between the three models, Table 7–1 has been presented.

It can be seen from Table 7–1 that the chief distinguishing characteristic of the professional model is its inclusion of contradictory forms of social relations. This model is particularly relevant to contemporary society where most large-scale organizations have to deal with uniform and non-uniform tasks[17] or with occupations that demand traditional knowledge as well as social skills.[18]

Granted this assertion, one of the key theoretical and empirical problems facing the student of complex organizations is the study of "Mechanisms of Segregation"—the procedures by which potentially contradictory social relations are co-ordinated in some common organizational goals.[19] That this central issue might be clearly seen as well as to suggest possible paths of inquiry, four mechanisms of segregation will be discussed in greater detail.

1. *Role separation as a mechanism of segregation.*—One way of co-ordinating contradictory forms of behavior is to restrict primary group behavior to one set of individuals and formal relations to another.[20] This is a well-known procedure, in part recognized in Parsons' analysis of current occupational structure.[21] One particularly relevant illustration of role segregation comes from Blau's analysis of bureaucracy.[22] Using the analogy of the civil service, he suggests that all hiring and firing

TABLE 7–1   CHARACTERISTICS OF THREE MODELS OF BUREAUCRACY

Characteristic	Weber's model*	Human relations†	Professional model‡
Impersonal relations	Extensive	Minimal	One part extensive One part minimal
Appointment on merit	Extensive	Extensive	Extensive
A priori specification of job authority	Extensive	Minimal	One part extensive One part minimal
Hierarchical authority	Extensive	Minimal	One part extensive One part minimal
Separation of policy and administrative decisions	Extensive	Minimal	One part extensive One part minimal
General rules to govern relations not specified by above dimensions	Extensive	Minimal	One part extensive One part minimal
Specialization	Extensive	Minimal	One part extensive One part minimal

* This model would be most efficient where tasks are uniform and involve traditional areas of knowledge, such as: governmental agencies given little discretion by law—police force, enforcing traffic and criminal law, the army during peacetime, processing most income tax returns; and private concerns with constant products and technologies—public utilities such as gas, water, and electricity.

† This model would be most efficient where tasks are relatively not uniform or involve social skills; to illustrate: situations which are so non-uniform that government cannot lay down highly specified laws but rather sets up commissions with broad discretionary powers—National Institutes of Mental Health, National Labor Relations Board, etc.; and situations involving the selling of undifferentiated products—large advertising firms.

‡ This model would be most efficient where the job requires dealing with both uniform and non-uniform events or with social skills as well as traditional areas of knowledge; e.g., situations requiring standardized administrative tasks and great professional autonomy—large hospitals, large graduate schools, large research organizations—and situations requiring both knowledge of administrative details as well as high interpersonal skills—large social work agencies or psychiatric hospitals.

functions be handled by a special group which has no responsibilities for production or administration. In this way, the potential contradiction between positive affect and objectivity can be minimized, while the virtues are maximized.

Another principle of segregation by role is illustrated by Melman in his study of a large auto concern organized into several large gangs, with each being given a production goal.[23] The management paid individuals on the basis of their gang's endeavor. Within the gang the management made little effort to deal with the non-uniform everyday problems of man-to-man supervision. This was left to the gang, with its own mechanisms of supervision.

However, the setting-up of gangs and the over-all policy of expansion and contraction of goals of production (relatively uniform problems dealing with traditional areas of knowledge) were based on a hierarchy of authority.

Thus, within the same organization there were two kinds of decision systems. On the one hand, there was a centralized hierarchy of authority and, on the other hand, local discretion. There was little conflict between the two systems because management and workers had agreed in advance that interaction between one set of roles was to be handled by local discretion, but between another set of roles by centralized authority. Since the roles were clearly differentiated, it was possible to do this with minimal friction.

2. *Physical distance as a mechanism of segregation.* A mechanism of segregation suitable only in limited cases is physical separation. Perhaps the most dramatic use of this procedure is illustrated by recent developments in research departments in business concerns.[24] The purer the research, that is, the more non-uniform the event, the more likely will physical distance be put between the departments of research and production. The Bell Laboratories, a subsidiary of American Telegraph and Telephone Company, which is a case in point, tends to fit the "human-relations" model of bureaucracy,[25] while the part of it dealing with the production of telephones and the installation of telephones is, comparatively speaking, more likely to follow Weber's model. Conflict between the two systems is minimized by their being kept physically apart.

Though the mechanism of physical separation permits a solution, it is inadequate because, as studies of larger organizations indicate, there are within the same job or closely interrelated jobs both uniform and non-uniform events, or there is within the same job the demand both for knowledge and for social skills. In such cases, mechanisms of physical separation are, by definition, inappropriate.

3. *Transferral occupations as mechanisms of segregation.* Where the organization is based on technological innovation, such as the modern industrial concern, the advances of science might transform an event from non-uniform to uniform, or vice versa. This means that there must be certain occupations whose major function is to switch areas of work from one set of social relations to another without contaminating the atmospheres of either. For instance, the engineer must frequently be in a position to take the pure scientist's work and put it on the production line. This means that he must move between the world of science, with its colleague relationships, to the world of production, with its formal hierarchical relations, without permitting the attitudes to mix.[26]

Transferral occupations have unique problems and become central when the assumption is made that organizations consist of potentially conflicting modes of behavior working harmoniously toward some over-all goal. As such, transferral occupations deserve considerable attention on the part of those interested in elaborating bureaucratic theory.

4. *Evaluation procedures as mechanisms of segregation.* Highly related to the transferral occupations are the procedures of evaluation. If the organization contains contradictory social relations and, at the same time, is subject to constant changes, then there must be some procedure for determining points at which one kind of social relations should be replaced by another. Melman indicates that management has set up occupations for evaluating all new machines for eventual incorporation into the organization.[27] In an analogous manner, the organizations containing conflicting social relations will operate more efficiently if they have procedures for deciding at what point there should be a shift from one form of social relation to another. This is in contrast to the common assumption that the structure is permanent. Focusing on evaluation will be a major concern of future research if the model of bureaucracy geared to organizational change suggested here is to be effected.

This now sums up consideration of some possible mechanisms of segregation. It also indicates why a key area for advancing the theory of complex organizations is the study of ways by which contradictory forms of organizational structure exist side by side without ruinous friction.

NOTES

[1] The term "model" is not being used in a rigorous sense: all that is meant is that a given organization may have unique dimensions, no rules being specified to predict the interrelations between the dimensions.

[2] *From Max Weber: Essays in Sociology,* trans. and ed., H. H. Gerth and C. Wright Mills (New York: Oxford University Press, 1946), pp. 196–203. Similarly, James G. March and Herbert A. Simon differentiate between process and purpose theories of organization (*Organizations* [New York: John Wiley & Sons, 1958], p. 29).

[3] These do not exactly duplicate Weber's statement, but they are sufficiently close to do no violence to it (see Weber, *op. cit.,* pp. 196 ff.).

[4] The terms "efficiency" and "productivity" are deliberately left undefined since many well-known problems of value would require extensive consideration of a formal definition were attempted. But it is here assumed that efficiency is defined in terms of some central set of liberal social values which have dominated our society within the last two hundred years; and that when the value problems revolving around the definition of efficiency are more fully solved they will not be inconsistent with this usage.

[5] Julian Franklin, *Man in Society* (New York: Columbia University Press, 1955), I, 941–42; Peter M. Blau, *Bureaucracy in Modern Society* (New York: Random House, 1956), pp. 58, 62; Robert K. Merton, "Bureaucratic Structure and Personality," in *Reader in Bureaucracy,* ed. R. K. Merton, A. P. Gray, B. Hockey, and H. C. Selvin (Glencoe, Ill.: Free Press, 1952), p. 364; Philip Selznick, "A Theory of Organizational Commitment," in *Reader in Bureaucracy,* pp. 194–202.

[6] D. C. Pelz, "Conditional Effects in the Relationship of Autonomy and Motivation to Performance," (August, 1960) (mimeographed). The development of colleague relations among scientists and members of graduate departments of universities would also provide evidence on the point.

[7] It is frequently said that, because of their commitment to a specialty, members of the armed services tend to overlook the general problem of defense in favor of their own immediate tasks, with a consequent loss for the basic goals of defense (see H. L. Wilensky and C. N. Lebeaux, *Industrial Society and Social Welfare* [New York: Russell Sage Foundation, 1958], pp. 235–65).

[8] Blau, *op. cit.,* pp. 63–64. This point is buttressed by the studies of combat troops or miners engaged in dangerous operations, both cases involving great uncertainty and severe risk where, apparently, strong primary group relations are effective (see E. A. Shils and M. Janowitz, "Cohesion and Disintegration in the *Wehrmacht* in World War II," in *Public Opinion and Propaganda* [New York: Dryden Press, 1954], pp. 91–108).

[9] D. A. Hamburg, "Therapeutic Aspects of Communication and Administrative Policy in the Psychiatric Section of a General Hospital," in *The Patient and the Mental Hospital,* ed. M. Greenblatt, D. S. Levinson, and R. H. Williams (Glencoe, Ill.: Free Press, 1959), pp. 91–107, and P. Barrabee, "The Community, the Mental Hospital and the Aged Psychotic," *ibid.,* pp. 530–35. For a general statement relating primary group relations to communication, see E. Katz and P. F. Lazarsfeld, *Personal Influence* (Glencoe, Ill.: Free Press, 1955), pp. 15–30.

[10] E. Litwak, "The Use of Extended Family Groups in the Achievement of Social Goals," *Social Problems,* VII (Winter, 1959–60), 184–85.

[11] This point is clearly illustrated in Jules Henry's analysis of an institution for child treatment which provides twenty-four-hour care on the assumption that successful treatment concerns every aspect of life. He notes how much the therapist's own life becomes involved with that of the patient ("Types of Institutional Structures," *The Patient and the Mental Hospital,* pp. 73–91).

[12] M. Janowitz, *The Professional Soldier* (Glencoe, Ill.: Free Press, 1960), pp. 166–71.

[13] The stress toward generalization can also be noted among ward personnel in psychiatric wards (R. A. Cohen, "Some Relations between Staff Tensions and the Psychotherapeutic Process," *The Patient and the Mental Hospital,* pp. 307–8).

[14] For a review of the literature see March and Simon, *op. cit.,* p. 81.

[15] Hamburg (*op. cit.,* pp. 95–96) points out that where nurses, ward attendants, and patients are permitted to participate in decision-making— among other things—the efficiency of the ward goes up, there is a smaller labor turnover, fewer aggressive actions of the patients, etc. This is not to rule out the importance of vertical relations but only to suggest that they are least likely to lead to efficiency in bureaucratic organizations where jobs require social skills.

[16] See Robert Vinter, "Notes on Professions and Bureaucracy" (unpublished manuscript, September, 1960).

[17] One assumption which should be made explicit is that non-uniform events will constitute a major factor in organizational analysis in the foreseeable future. This assumption rests on the following considerations: (*a*) scientific advance not only reduces prior areas of ignorance to known uniformities but reveals new areas; (*b*) as Talcott Parsons suggests (*The Social Systems* [Glencoe, Ill.: Free Press, 1951], pp. 44–45), the processes of socialization are inevitably imperfect, and as a consequence one must always assume the idiosyncratic to be part of any model of human behavior; and (*c*) a society committed to technological advance must be prepared for constant social change, and for dealing with phenomena for which it has no prior uniform modes of interaction.

[18] The assumption is made that jobs calling for social abilities will constitute a significant proportion of all jobs in the foreseeable future. This assumption is based on investigations such as were made by Nelson N. Foote and Paul K. Hatt who in their paper, "Social Mobility and Economic Advancement" (*American Economic Review,* XLIII [May, 1953], 364–67), suggest a shift from the primary extractive and secondary manufacturing industries to the tertiary, quaternary, and quinary industries consisting largely of human services. It also rests on analyses such as made by Reinhard Bendix (*Work and Authority in Industry* [New York: John Wiley & Sons, 1956], pp. 216 ff.), who points out that as the organization becomes larger, personal relations become important as technical features of the job.

[19] To stress mechanisms which permit the coordination of potentially conflicting relations is not to deny that there are certain relations which can never be reconciled. Thus, one important aspect of organizational analysis (the resolution of conflict rather than its co-ordination), not included in this discussion, would have involved an analysis of physical violence, strikes, arbitration, propaganda, etc.

[20] Robert K. Merton, in "The Role-Set: Problems in Sociological Theory" (*British Journal of Sociology,* VIII [June, 1957], 106–20), suggests by

analogy several additional mechanisms of segregation which will not be discussed here.

[21] Parsons points out the need to keep the family separated from the occupational life, one of the major devices being to keep the family physically isolated by a division of labor by sex ("The Social Structure of the Family," *The Family: Its Function and Destiny,* ed. Ruth N. Anshen [New York: Harper & Bros., 1949]).

[22] Blau, *op. cit.,* pp. 64–66.

[23] Seymour Melman, *Decision Making and Productivity* (Oxford: Basil Blackwell, 1958), pp. 92–135; also see Blau, *op. cit.,* p. 66, and Ralph J. Gardiner, *New Frontiers for Professional Managers* (New York: McGraw-Hill Book Co., 1956), pp. 40–80.

[24] Between 1953 and 1956 there was an estimated 67 per cent increase in the total amount of money spent for research in America ($5.4 billion to $9 billion). Business concerns whose major purpose was not research increased their expenditures almost 50 per cent (from $3.7 billion to $6.5 billion) (see *Reviews of Data on Research and Development* [National Science Foundation, No. 10, NSF-58–10, May, 1958], pp. 1–2). There seem to be no estimates of business expenditures or research which go past 1953; however, estimates of federal expenditures for research, which might be correlated with business expenditures, are that between 1940 and 1958 the federal government expanded its research budget almost three times (*Proceedings of a Conference on Research and Development and Its Impact on the Economy* [National Science Foundation, NSF-58–36, 1958]).

[25] The Bell Laboratories will frequently hire scientists with the explicit provision that they are free to work on the problems they like and in the manner, within reason, they choose, with the restriction that any resulting product belongs to the company. As a consequence, social relations within the laboratory may be like a university's colleague relationship—non-hierarchical, personal, informal, face to face, with few a priori rules on duties and obligations.

[26] The same phenomena can be seen in the mass media if the analysis of Katz and Lazarsfeld and Inkeles can be taken as a given. These men see two elements in the mass media: (*a*) the formal organization which broadcasts messages, and (*b*) the small primary groups which receive and interpret them. Katz and Lazarsfeld suggest that these two diverse and somewhat antithetical worlds are breached by the opinion leader, and Inkeles argues (to a lesser extent) that they are breached by the agitator. Like the engineer, the opinion leader and the agitator move between the two worlds without contaminating either (see Elihu Katz and Paul F. Lazarsfeld, *Personal Influence* [Glencoe, Ill.: Free Press, 1955], pp. 162–208; Alex Inkeles, *Public Opinion in Soviet Russia* [Cambridge, Mass.: Harvard University Press, 1951], pp. 38–135).

[27] Melman, *op. cit.*

8.

AN AXIOMATIC THEORY OF ORGANIZATIONS

JERALD HAGE

The major purpose of this paper is to suggest a theory of organizations in an axiomatic format.[1] Eight variables are related to each other in seven simple, two-variable propositions. These seven propositions are then used to derive twenty-one corollaries. An eighth proposition, which sets limits on these propositions and corollaries, completes the theory. It defines two ideal types of organizations. The propositions and corollaries provide twenty-nine hypotheses, which are used to codify a number of research studies and to analyze the problems of organizational change.

The eight variables are formal characteristics of organizations: four of the variables represent organizational means, and four represent organizational ends. Many writers have used the distinction between means and ends in sociology, and Weber suggested that this was the essence of the sociological approach.[2] The distinction leads to questions such as whether a particular social means is most appropriate for a particular social end; for example, does the degree of centralization have any consequences for the amount of production.[3] The axiomatic theory attempts to provide at least a partial answer to this and similar questions.[4]

THE EIGHT VARIABLES

A major consideration in the choice of the variables was that they be general enough so

From Jerald Hage, "An Axiomatic Theory of Organizations," *Administrative Science Quarterly*, 10:289–320, 1965. Reprinted by permission.

that they could be applied to any kind of organization. As Nadel has noted, formal characteristics are on a high level of abstraction and allow a much greater generality than content categories.[5] For example, Simmel's discussion of the number of individuals in a group indicates how size is a formal characteristic of groups independent of the specific individuals and content involved.[6] Production can be measured to include such diverse content as patient care, sales, welfare services, victories, and so on. Although content is important, if a general theory of organizations is to be constructed, the variables will have to be formal characteristics.[7]

The first obvious advantage of formal characteristics is that they can both differentiate between organizations with similar objectives and also indicate similarities between organizations with different objectives. One welfare agency might have the same degree of complexity (that is, the number of occupational specialties), as a retail store, while another welfare agency might be much more complex than either of these two organizations, and may be as complex as a hospital. Two furniture manufacturing companies might vary considerably in their method of decision making, that is, one being autocratic and one being democratic. The second advantage is that formal characteristics are not time specific or culturally bounded. Complexity is a variable that can be equally well applied to an Australian hunting organization, a Roman galley ship, a Chinese bureaucracy, or an American manufacturer. A third advantage is that because formal characteristics are independent of time and culture, they are useful in studying organizational evolution. It becomes possible to say, for example, that organizations are becoming steadily more complex.

Although the original variables were selected on an *ad hoc* basis, they have some theoretical justification. The four ends were suggested by the work of Parsons, Bales, and their associates[8] on the four functional problems of a social system (although they might disagree with the author's interpretation[9]). Production is equivalent to their goal achievement; efficiency is equivalent to their integration; job satisfaction is equivalent to their tension management; and adaptiveness is equivalent to their adaptation. The four means are major characteristics of organizations: complexity is a measure of how many specialties are utilized, centralization is a measure of how power is distributed, formalization is a measure of how many rules are used, and stratification is a measure of how rewards are distributed. Table 8–1 lists these eight variables and the indicators by which they can be measured.

The four organizational ends

The environment changes: competition increases, technology alters, new needs are recognized. Adaptations to changes in the environment by organizations are reflected in the adoption of new programs or techniques; for example, the therapeutic milieu in a mental hospital, a computer inventory control system in a retail store, a vocational training program for the mentally retarded in a welfare agency, and an atomic cannon in an army unit. The *adaptiveness*, or flexibility, of an organization is measured by the number of new programs and techniques adopted in a year; the higher the rate of changes, the more adaptive the organization.

All organizations accomplish specific objectives, but they differ in the relative importance attached to production.[10] Some organizations not only handle a large number of clients or produce a high volume of products, but also attempt to increase their production each year; that is, either the number of clients or the number of products. Some organizations are less concerned with the quantity of production and its growth and more concerned with the quality of service or products, and attempt to improve quality each year. These organizations are likely to keep their volume of production low as the decision makers allocate their resources to the improvements of quality instead of expanding production. The *production*, or effectiveness, of an organization is measured by the number of units produced and the rate of increase in these per year. The higher the volume of production and increase in volume, the more productive the organization.

Since resources are scarce, organizations are forced to conserve them. This is especially true of funds, although human resources are equally important. The *efficiency*, or cost, of an organization is measured by computing the amount of money used to produce a single unit of production and the amount of idle resources. The lower the cost, the more efficient the organization.

Organizations must maintain a certain level of satisfaction among their members. Some organizations emphasize good working conditions, while other organizations are less concerned about the welfare of their employees. *Job satisfaction*, or morale, is measured by standard attitude batteries and the amount of turnover. The higher the morale and lower the turnover, the higher the job satisfaction in the organization.

The four organizational means

Organizations must divide work into jobs in order to achieve their specific objectives. Some organizations hire individuals in specific occupations, such as the professions or the crafts, which require long periods of training, i.e., person specialization; some organizations divide work into specific tasks that require little education or skill, i.e., task specialization.[11] The *complexity*, or specialization, in an organization is measured by the number of occupational specialties included and the length of training required by each. The greater the number of occupations and the longer the period of training required, the more complex the organization.[12]

Organizations must make decisions about the addition of new programs or techniques, the hiring of personnel, the allocation of resources, and so on. Some organizations allocate power to only a few jobs, an elite, whereas other organizations allow much wider participation in decision making. *Centralization*, or

TABLE 8–1   THE EIGHT VARIABLES

Variable	Indicators*
Organizational means:	
Complexity (specialization)	Number of occupational specialties. Level of training required.
Centralization (hierarchy of authority)	Proportion of jobs that participate in decision making. Number of areas in which decisions are made by decision makers.
Formalization (standardization)	Proportion of jobs that are codified. Range of variation allowed within jobs.
Stratification (status system)	Differences in income and prestige among jobs. Rate of mobility between low- and high-ranking jobs or status levels.
Organizational ends:	
Adaptiveness (flexibility)	Number of new programs in a year.† Number of new techniques in a year.
Production (effectiveness)	Number of units produced per year. Rate of increase in units produced per year.
Efficiency (cost)	Cost per unit of output per year. Amount of idle resources per year.
Job satisfaction (morale)	Satisfaction with working conditions. Rate of turnover in job occupants per year.

Two indicators are used for each variable because of the possibility of errors in measurement. In general, the first indicator should be the stronger one, with the second accounting for exceptions.

†*The time unit of a year is used to level out random variation resulting from specific and idiosyncratic organizational events. This time period also has the advantage of corresponding to one which is used by many organizations in the compilation of their records.*

hierarchy of authority, is measured by the proportion of occupations or jobs whose occupants participate in decision making and the number of areas in which they participate. The lower the proportion of occupations or jobs whose occupants participate and the fewer the decision areas in which they participate, the more centralized the organization.

Organizations learn from past experience and employ rules as a repository of that experience. Some organizations carefully codify each job, describing the specific details, and then ensure conformity to the job prescription. Other organizations have loosely defined jobs and do not carefully control work behavior. *Formalization*, or standardization, is measured by the proportion of codified jobs and the range of variation that is tolerated within the rules defining the jobs. The higher the proportion of codified jobs and the less the range of variation allowed, the more formalized the organization.

All organizations distribute rewards, whether salary or prestige, or both. Some organizations maintain great status differences while other organizations are more equalitarian. Some organizations allow occupants of low-ranking jobs to reach the top levels of the hierarchy; others have barriers to particular status levels, (Caplow's status schisms[13]). The *stratification*, or status system, is measured by determining the difference in rewards between jobs and the relative rates of mobility between them. Although the relative rate of mobility is called the amount of openness, the author suggests that it is also an indicator of the degree of stratification; that is, the more open the status system, the less stratified it is. The greater the disparity in rewards between the top and bottom status levels and the lower the rates of mobility between them, the more stratified the organization.

The four organizational means and the four organizational ends should represent what the organization actually does, not public goals or organizational policy. Organizational policy may indicate a democratic style of decision making with equalitarian rewards, whereas organizational practice may show centralization and stratification. The public goals of the organization may emphasize low volume, high-quality production, and high morale; whereas the private goals may reflect an emphasis on high-volume, low-quality production, and little concern with the satisfaction of the members.

THE AXIOMATIC THEORY

Central to the theory are seven propositions, which have been drawn from the writings of Weber, Barnard, and Thompson.[14] The first three propositions summarize much of Weber's model of bureaucracy, while the second three are extracted from Barnard's discussion of the functions of status systems. A seventh proposition is obtained from Thompson's work. Combining the seven propositions makes it possible to derive twenty-one corollaries. In some instances, these corollaries are discussed in one or more of the writings of these three organizational theorists, but many of the corollaries are not mentioned. Some of the derived corollaries appear to represent entirely new hypotheses, indicating areas for future research.

The major theme running through this axiomatic theory is the idea of functional strains, as discussed in the writings of Parsons, Bales, and their associates, or the concept of organizational dilemma, as it is called by Blau and

Scott.[15] This means that an increase in one variable results in a decrease in another variable, or that the maximization of one social means results in the minimization of another. Although this dependence of one variable on another is an old idea, the problem is to specify which variables are in opposition, and perhaps more important, why they are. This is exactly what the theory attempts to do.

The seven propositions

The essence of Weber's model of bureaucracy is a hierarchy of offices where the duties are clearly codified by rules and regulations.[16] Although he was describing the administrative staff, his principles can be applied to other areas of the organization, such as production, as illustrated by the production of the Ford Model T. Weber felt that the bureaucratic arrangement was superior to other forms because it had more precision and speed, and reduced both material and personal costs.[17] Part of his reasoning for the efficacy of bureaucracy was its superior discipline and control of role performance,[18] for he specifically stated that if officials were elected instead of appointed, discipline and control would be weakened.[19] The high formalization of offices or jobs results in the development of expertise in a limited area and therefore greater efficiency in performance with fewer errors being made. The combination of centralization and formalization is nothing more than coordination.[20] There are individuals who supervise and who have rules or standards by which to evaluate the performance of their subordinates, which not only results in more uniformity of behavior but in a higher volume of production as well. Weber's model can be formulated into the following three propositions:

I. The higher the centralization, the higher the production.
II. The higher the formalization, the higher the efficiency.
III. The higher the centralization, the higher the formalization.

Barnard was concerned with the consequences of status systems.[21] He viewed stratification as a method for ensuring the incentive to work hard because it not only provided an objective, promotion, but also specified a clear line of advancement, an idea very similar to Weber's concept of bureaucratic career.[22] While Barnard believed the motivation to work hard resulted in increased production because of greater effort, he saw some dysfunctional consequences as well. Stratification satisfies the man at the top, but not the men at the bottom. It builds in failure because there are a limited number of jobs at the top. Barnard also noted that status systems tended to reduce mobility or circulation of elites, the second indicator used to measure stratification; this in turn lowered job satisfaction, and in fact, resulted in injustices.[23] Blau and Scott have noted that status differences result in the reduction of informal relationships, and the lessening of emotional support, thereby producing dissatisfaction.[24]

Barnard also noted that stratification reduced adaptiveness. Thompson suggests that status systems encourage the *status quo*. In part, the elites remain unaware of the need for change, and in part, with their right to veto, they discourage suggestions for change. Status systems diminish communications that are critical of the system and that bypass it. Blau and Scott suggest that stratification reduces adaptiveness because changes are likely to have upsetting consequences for the status system, and therefore, those who have the most to lose are likely to oppose changes.[25] This is, of course, Veblen's concept of vested interests. All of these ideas can be expressed in three propositions:

IV.   The higher the stratification, the higher the production.
V.   The higher the stratification, the lower the job satisfaction.
VI.   The higher the stratification, the lower the adaptiveness.

In sum, Barnard pinpointed a crucial organizational paradox. Stratification makes employees work harder, but they do not like it, and it tends to turn them into organizational men, who will not criticize superiors for fear of loss of advancement.

Thompson noted that a proliferation of occupational specialties, particularly those requiring long periods of training, results in an undermining of hierarchical authority.[26] In part, this dilemma stems from the increasing difficulty of a person in an authority position having the requisite knowledge in all the areas of specialization found in complex organizations. To make decisions, he must consult the job occupants of the appropriate specialities, thus sharing the decision making with the specialist. The specialist has access to information, and by giving or withholding information, he has a source of power over the decision maker. He has channels of communication, usually informal, that cut across hierarchical lines of authority. Specialists need information from different areas of the organization, and they are consulted by job occupants in different areas. Consequently the elites lose some control. Gouldner has discussed a motivational assumption that tends to encourage these processes, which he calls the functional strain towards autonomy.[27] He assumes that specialties or occupations strive for the right to make their own decisions and this results in decentralization of the organization. Blau and Scott have called this phenomenon the dilemma of managerial coordination and individual initiative.[28] These ideas can be summarized as proposition VII.

VII.   The higher the complexity, the lower the centralization.

The corollaries

On the assumption that the eight variables form a closed system of interrelated variables, it is possible to derive additional hypotheses by applying the simple rules of the syllogism; for example:

The higher the centralization, the higher the production.

(Prop. I)

The higher the stratification, the higher the production.

(Prop. V)

The higher the centralization, the higher the stratification.

(Corol. 19)

In other words, combining propositions I and V gives a corollary that is essentially Michel's iron law of oligarchy.

In the same way, a total of twenty additional corollaries are derived. Table 8–2 lists the propositions and corollaries of the theory. The corollaries are numbered in the sequence in which they were derived. Table 8–3 presents a schemata of the association between each of the eight variables along with the number of the proposition or corollary that describes the relationship. It should be noted that each corollary can be obtained in several different ways depending upon the sequence in which they are derived. Together, the seven major propositions and the twenty-one corollaries represent all the possible two-variable relationships, when order does not make a difference. The resulting twenty-eight hypotheses explicate all the interrelationships of this organizational system of eight variables, making research easier.

TABLE 8–2   MAJOR PROPOSITIONS AND COROLLARIES OF THE THEORY

Major Propositions

- I. The higher the centralization, the higher the production.
- II. The higher the formalization, the higher the efficiency.
- III. The higher the centralization, the higher the formalization.
- IV. The higher the stratification, the lower the job satisfaction.
- V. The higher the stratification, the higher the production.
- VI. The higher the stratification, the lower the adaptiveness.
- VII. The higher the complexity, the lower the centralization.

Derived Corollaries

1. The higher the formalization, the higher the production.
2. The higher the centralization, the higher the efficiency.
3. The lower the job satisfaction, the higher the production.
4. The lower the job satisfaction, the lower the adaptiveness.
5. The higher the production, the lower the adaptiveness.
6. The higher the complexity, the lower the production.
7. The higher the complexity, the lower the formalization.
8. The higher the production, the higher the efficiency.
9. The higher the stratification, the higher the formalization.
10. The higher the efficiency, the lower the complexity.
11. The higher the centralization, the lower the job satisfaction.
12. The higher the centralization, the lower the adaptiveness.
13. The higher the stratification, the lower the complexity.
14. The higher the complexity, the higher the job satisfaction.
15. The lower the complexity, the lower the adaptiveness.
16. The higher the stratification, the higher the efficiency.
17. The higher the efficiency, the lower the job satisfaction.
18. The higher the efficiency, the lower the adaptiveness.
19. The higher the centralization, the higher the stratification.
20. The higher the formalization, the lower the job satisfaction.
21. The higher the formalization, the lower the adaptiveness.

Limits Proposition

- VIII. Production imposes limits on complexity, centralization, formalization, stratification, adaptiveness, efficiency, and job satisfaction.

TABLE 8–3   THE INTERRELATIONSHIPS BETWEEN ORGANIZATIONAL
MEANS AND ORGANIZATIONAL ENDS *

	Organizational means				Organizational ends			
	Com- plexity	Cen- tral- ization	Formal- ization	Strati- fication	Adap- tiveness	Pro- duc- tion	Effi- ciency	Job satis- faction
Organizational means:								
		−	−	−	+	−	−	+
Complexity		(VII)	(7)	(13)	(15)	(6)	(10)	(14)
			+	+	−	+	+	−
Centralization			(III)	(19)	(12)	(I)	(2)	(11)
				+	−	+	+	−
Formalization				(9)	(21)	(1)	(II)	(20)
					−	+	+	−
Stratification					(VI)	(V)	(16)	(IV)
Organizational ends:								
						−	−	+
Adaptiveness						(5)	(18)	(4)
							+	−
Production							(8)	(3)
								−
Efficiency								(17)
Job satisfaction								

* The Roman numerals refer to the seven basic propositions, and the arabic numerals refer to the corollaries that are derived from these propositions. A plus sign means a positive association between the two variables; a minus sign means a negative association between the two variables.

Some corollaries merely specify ideas already contained in the writings of the organizational theorists: corollaries 1, 2, and 8 are found in Weber's discussion of bureaucracy; corollaries 15 and 21 have been suggested by Thompson. Some corollaries are found in different areas. Corollary 4, which relates job satisfaction and adaptiveness, is found in the human relations writings, where the idea that dissatisfied workers will resist change is a principle of research. Corollaries 11, 14, and 20 along with proposition IV represent three of the organizational conditions that produce alienation, as suggested by Seeman, a point discussed below.[29] Some corollaries are new hypotheses that deserve study. Corollaries 5, 12, and 18 relate to the problem of organizational adaptiveness, a relatively unexplored area. Thus the axiomatic theory, by making explicit all the implicit hypotheses, makes it possible to integrate previously isolated schools of thought as well as suggesting new avenues of thought.

If job satisfaction is taken as an indicator of alienation from the organization and its work activities, the axiomatic theory not only includes many of the ideas suggested in the literature on alienation but provides new hypotheses. The following relationships between job satisfaction and the other seven variables are indicated:

The higher the stratification, the lower the job satisfaction.

(Prop. IV)

The higher the production, the lower the job satisfaction.

(Corol. 3)

The lower the adaptiveness, the lower the job satisfaction.

(Corol. 4)

The higher the centralization, the lower the job satisfaction.

(Corol. 11)

The higher the complexity, the higher the job satisfaction.

(Corol. 14)

The higher the efficiency, the lower the job satisfaction.

(Corol. 17)

The higher the formalization, the lower the job satisfaction.

(Corol. 20)

Proposition IV is a restatement of the idea of estrangement, while corollary 11 describes the condition of powerlessness. Corollary 14 is the condition of meaningfulness: when person specialization is practiced, the work is much more meaningful, and job satisfaction is correspondingly higher. The condition of normlessness (which is indicated by no formalization), is not represented in the theory, nor is the condition of social integration. The theory indicates that too many norms or high formalization leads to alienation as represented by lower job satisfaction.

High efficiency, indicated by lower wages and salaries and lower fringe benefits, lowers job satisfaction. On the other hand, high production is associated with low satisfaction because high volume indicates an emphasis on speed, as indicated by Blauner's study of the automobile industry.[30]

Similarly, we can examine the hypotheses that relate complexity with the other seven variables. Two of the seven logical possibilities, proposition VII and corollary 14, have already been discussed. The remaining five are:

The higher the complexity, the lower the production.

(Corol. 6)

The higher the complexity, the lower the formalization.

(Corol. 7)

The higher the complexity, the lower the efficiency.

(Corol. 10)

The lower the complexity, the higher the stratification.

(Corol. 13)

The lower the complexity, the lower the adaptiveness.

(Corol. 15)

Corollary 15 is a summary of some of Durkheim's ideas.[31] Although society was Durkheim's unit of analysis, the corollary is equally applicable to organizations. It might be added that specialists have access to channels of information, both internal and external to the organization, which makes them more aware of the need for innovations, whether the innovations represent a response to internal or external strains. From the organizational viewpoint, the more occupational specialties that organizations have, the more closely organizations are linked by communication networks with other organizations. As has already been discussed, specialists establish internal informal channels of communication, which not only tend to undermine the hierarchy of authority but also the status system.

Corollaries 6, 7, and 10 appear to be more provocative and have not received as much discussion in the literature as the other corollaries. In an organization with high complexity, there is apt to be less efficiency or lower productivity because of higher cost for the specialists' salaries and because of lower formalization, which itself decreases efficiency. The strain between complexity and formalization has been called the dilemma of the professional and the bureaucracy by Blau and Scott, and by others.[32] These vary inversely with each other, as Thompson has also hypothesized. The lower volume of production is, as a consequence of high complexity, likely to result from an organizational emphasis on the quality of product or service being produced. The differences between craft and mass-production industries are examples of this phenomenon of low-volume, high-quality production versus high-volume, low-quality production.

Two ideal types

It is possible to examine each of the eight variables as job satisfaction and complexity have been examined, but another way of examining the theory is to consider the two extreme types of organizations that it suggests (see Table 8–4). Some of the same characteristics of the two types are described by Burns and Stalker.[33] The mechanistic model is described as "the precise definition of rights and obligations and technical methods attached to each functional role" (high formalization), "hierarchic structure of control, authority and communication" (high centralization). The organic model is characterized by "the adjustment and continual redefinition of individual tasks" (low formalization), "a network structure of control, authority and communication" (low centralization). Burns and Stalker also suggest other differentiating characteristics, which are not among the eight variables given here.[34] The content of communication in the organic model is information and advice; in the mechanical model it is instruction and orders. The mechanical model requires loyalty to the organization and emphasizes local knowledge; the organic model requires commitment to the tasks of the organization and emphasizes expertise.

Burns and Stalker suggest that the emphasis on adaptiveness, and, correspondingly, on organic or mechanistic structural arrangement, is directly related to the rate of change in technical or market conditions. Several factors other than production can affect the relative emphasis on adaptiveness as the dominant organizational end. The nature of the output of the organization has an effect. When the outputs are services to clients rather than manufacturing products, the organization is apt to show more adaptiveness, because there is less opportunity for standardization of tasks. If the organization is competing with another firm that has a particular social means, for example, high centralization, then it is likely to adopt a similar means. Under conditions of extreme threat, the organization is likely to move toward high centralization. Some organizations, such as military units, are more likely to have this environmental condition than others.[35] The dominant value patterns in the society may favor high centralization in government, and this will tend to be reflected in other kinds of organizations. Similarly, the society may consider one social end more important than another, resulting in the adoption of certain means to maximize the desired ends. In fact, most ideological disputes about organizations can be translated into an argument over the relative importance of the volume of production and efficiency *versus* job satisfaction and adaptiveness.[36]

Pugh *et al.* have suggested a number of variables, which they call contextual variables, that can be used to predict the social means and ends that an organization is likely to maximize.[37] Besides technology, they have hypothesized that ownership, size, charter, location, and resources will affect organiza-

TABLE 8–4   TWO IDEAL TYPES OF ORGANIZATIONS PREDICTED BY THE AXIOMATIC THEORY

Organic model (emphasis on adaptiveness)	Mechanistic model (emphasis on production)
High complexity	Low complexity
Low centralization	High centralization
Low formalization	High formalization
Low stratification	High stratification
High adaptiveness	Low adaptiveness
Low production	High production
Low efficiency	High efficiency
High job satisfaction	Low job satisfaction

tional means and ends. The intention here is not to introduce additional variables into the theory, but to specify the two ideal types for purposes of contrast. Most organizations will be between these two extremes. In fact, there is no single best organizational solution to the problem of survival; each ideal type has its advantages and disadvantages. As environmental conditions change, an organization is also likely to change. The difficulty for organizations is that, regardless of which ideal type the decision makers choose, performance is inadequate. In an adaptive organization, production is a problem, and it will be difficult to conserve resources, especially monetary ones. In a production organization, the problem is adaptiveness, and the problem will be maintaining morale.

The limits proposition

Although each ideal type has advantages and disadvantages, there is a limit to how much the decision makers can emphasize one organizational end over another. If there is no codification of jobs, then a condition of normlessness prevails, and there is likely to be low job satisfaction. If new programs and techniques are not adopted, the organization is apt to fail in the face of an everchanging environment. On the other hand, too high a rate of change in new programs and techniques is likely to have the same consequence because of spiraling costs. There are limits on each of the eight variables, beyond which an organization dare not move. This idea can be expressed in the following proposition:

> VIII. Production imposes limits on complexity, centralization, formalization, stratification, adaptiveness, efficiency, and job satisfaction.

The determination of the actual limits requires a considerable amount of research; yet, this would appear to be a strategic area for study. By examining the consequences of extreme scores, a better understanding of organizational dynamics is achieved. The limits proposition provides the basis for explaining the failure of organizations, because it suggests that extremes in any variable results in the loss of production, even in an organization that has the means that maximize this end.

The logical consequences of the limits proposition are complex. One consequence is that all of the relationships specified in the previous propositions are curvilinear ones. If centralization becomes too high, production will fall; if stratification becomes too low, job satisfaction will drop. Exceeding the limits then results in a reversal of the hypothesized relationships. Another consequence is that the reversal of these relationships would manifest itself first in declining production figures. These represent important qualifications to the axiomatic theory.

AVAILABLE EVIDENCE

The findings reported here represent a variety of methodologies and even variations in definitions; therefore some interpretation is necessary. The research cited includes voluntary associations, hospitals, colleges, schools, prisons, corporations, and others. Many of the studies involve only a single organization, and a few represent multiple organizations or units within organizations. Although the author attempted to review a large number of studies, the review was hardly exhaustive, if only because there are so many.[38] In general, research reviews have been relied upon, because they usually attempt some exhaustive search in particular areas and because they usually provide bibliographies of pertinent studies.

The findings reported below are organized around three variables, each of which corresponds to an organizational problem: (1) adaptiveness or the problem of organizational change, (2) centralization or the problem of organizational democracy, and (3) job satisfaction or the problem of organizational morale. The last two problems have been frequently discussed, whereas the first problem is seldom mentioned. Since the variables are interrelated, there is some obvious overlap in the discussion of the research findings; for example, adaptiveness, as stipulated by the theory, is associated with low centralization and high job satisfaction. At the same time, this organization of findings around three key organizational problems helps clarify what the theory says about them, thereby making its practical import easier to understand.

Adaptiveness

In a series of studies of adaptiveness, Mort and his associates developed a scale of 176 innovations in school techniques and programs.[39] In a study of 43 school systems, Buley, using Mort's scale, found that adaptiveness correlated positively with complexity, as measured by professional training and experience of the teachers; but correlated negatively with the efficiency of the school system, as measured by expenditures per pupil (corol. 10, 15, 18).[40] Georgopoulos and Tannenbaum used two attitudinal questions to measure adaptiveness in 32 organizational units of a business organization.[41] They found adaptiveness highly correlated with the lack of strain between supervisor and employees, but the correlation with volume of production was much lower. If the lack of strain is considered to be one of the elements of job satisfaction, then the findings support corollaries 3, 4, and 5. The study also lends support for the necessity of proposition VIII; there must be some job satisfaction in order to have production at all.

Several case studies have examined the organizational consequences of increases in adaptiveness, whether the addition of new techniques or the addition of new programs. In a study of the military, Janowitz disclosed that the increasing technology of warfare was leading to increased complexity and resulting in a decentralization of decision making.[42] In a case study of a community hospital, the introduction of a new department of medical education led to decentralization of decision making and increased costs (corol. 10, prop. VII).[43] Introducing the changes was easiest in those departments of the hospital that had the highest degree of specialization and a history of adaptiveness (corol. 15). The department that resisted change the most not only had little history of adaptiveness, but was also low in specialization and higher in stratification (prop. VI, corol. 13).[44]

Blau and Scott reviewed the literature relating stratification and adaptiveness and concluded that status differences tended to reduce criticism of the ideas of those superior in power and prestige.[45] Ronken and Lawrence in a case study of change found that status differences severely restricted communications, lowered job satisfaction, and as a result, retarded the addition of an assembly line for the manufacturing of a new electrical tube (prop. IV, VI).[46] The well-known French and Coch study suggested that low job satisfaction, created by piece rates, led to resistance to change, implying low adaptiveness.[47] This was successfully overcome by decreasing centralization and allowing the workers to discuss changes. The workers made suggestions in their group discussions with management that resulted in even more changes being made. This study provides partial support for the hypothesized relationship between high satisfaction, low centralization, and high adaptiveness (corol. 4, 12); it also represents some negative findings about the relationship between adaptiveness and production (corol. 5). As a consequence of the increased worker satisfaction, production was higher than it had ever gone before. The only explanation that can be provided for this negative finding is that job satisfaction was so low that it had exceeded the minimal limit suggested by proposition VIII, having negative consequences for production.

Cillié, using Mort's scale, contrasted the degree of adaptiveness in 16 decentralized and 16 centralized schools in districts which were matched in socio-economic characteristics.[48] (All 16 centralized schools were part of one system.) He found that the decentralized schools had adopted more of the 176 items on the list than the centralized schools; significantly, they were more likely to have adopted techniques and programs that increased their capacity for change. The changes allowed for greater individual attention to the pupil, a greater scope of instructional services, and for the teachers to participate more in decision making. In contrast, the centralized schools were more likely to have adopted practices that increased efficiency (*corol. 2, 12*).

Centralization

In an experiment conducted by Morse and Reimer, centralization was increased in one department and lowered in another.[49] At the end of a year the centralized department had a higher rate of production but a lower rate of job satisfaction (*prop. I, corol. 3*). A similar finding was obtained in the communication studies of Bavelas and his associates.[50] The centralized nets had higher production and fewer errors (an indication of efficiency), but lower job satisfaction among the members in the occupants of peripheral positions. The centralized nets tended very quickly to develop a formalized procedure for passing messages, whereas the decentralized nets did not standardize their work. Although these were experiments conducted in a laboratory, they suggest that centralization increases production, efficiency, and formalization, while lowering job satisfaction among the lower-ranking members (*prop. I, III, and corol. 2, 11*).

If the number of levels in an organization is accepted as a rough indication of centralization, then Udy's study of organizations in non-industrial societies provides cross-cultural evidence for some of the hypotheses.[51] He found that the more centralized organizations, which he called bureaucracies, were more likely to have task specialization, i.e., low complexity, and to distribute rewards on the basis of office, i.e., high stratification (*prop. VII, corol. 19*). Michel's iron law of oligarchy (*corol. 19*) has received partial support in the Lipset, Trow, and Coleman study.[52] They suggest that the International Typographical Union had a lower level of centralization because of a number of factors that tended to limit stratification

in the union. There were fewer status differences between the leaders and members, more specialization per person and less task specialization on the job, and an occupational community apart from the organizations involved.

Hall developed a series of scales to measure several dimensions of Weber's model, which he called hierarchy of authority, division of labor, system of rules, and system of procedures.[53] The hierarchy of authority had high correlation with a system of rules and procedures and lower correlation with division of labor, which in turn had almost no correlation with the use of rules. Centralization and formalization, as defined by Hall, are highly correlated (*prop. III*). The studies of assembly-line work, as reported by Blau and Scott, showed that the routinization of tasks (high formalization) was associated with high centralization, higher production, higher productivity (efficiency), but lower job satisfaction and higher levels of turnover.[54] These studies support Weber's theory applied to areas other than administration; they also reinforce the Bavelas findings (*prop. II, III, corol. 1, 20*).

Blau and Scott also discussed the reverse relation, noting that group decision making (low centralization) is slow and highly inefficient.[55] Harrison's study of the Baptist Church is a single example of low centralization of decision making being associated with the absence of rules and regulations.[56] An independent management-consulting firm rated the effectiveness of the organization and found it to be low, but there is no report of what criteria were used. The same firm rated the Roman Catholic Church and found its effectiveness to be high. The two religious organizations represent an example of two ideal types, with the Baptist Church approximating the adaptive organization and the Catholic Church approximating the productive organization.

Thompson's basic hypothesis of increasing complexity leading to a decentralization of decision making has support in several different research studies. The studies of staff-line conflict reflect how complexity undermines hierarchical authority.[57] In a study of five correctional institutions, Zald found that the control structure was much more decentralized in treatment organizations, where specialization of persons was much higher and more individual attention was given to the inmates.[58] The more decentralized organizations had a higher inmate-staff ratio as well, suggesting lower efficiency (*corol. 10, prop. VII*). Becker's case study of teachers in schools suggests some of the mechanisms that they use to decrease supervision and authority over their work, that is, centralization.[59] Another revealing case study made by Lipset explores how centralized and formalized bureaucracies reduce adaptiveness (*corol. 12*).[60] Hage, in a study of 142 hospitals, observed that those with more highly specialized staffs of physicians tended to have more decentralized authority structures.[61]

Although the decision-making study of the American Association of University Professors did not relate the increased complexity of universities to its findings of increased decentralization, this seems a highly plausible interpretation, since most of the universities in their sample did add many new occupations in the period covered.[62] Lazarsfeld and Thielens found in a study of 70 colleges that the faculty had more influence in high-quality schools, where quality was measured by an index composed of the proportion of faculty having a Ph.D. (a measure of technical skill), the cost per student (efficiency), and the number (production) of students awarded a Ph.D. degree. Although this measure mixes several variables, it does seem that low centralization is related to high complexity and low efficiency.[63]

Job satisfaction

March and Simon reviewed the factors that affect job satisfaction and reported that it was higher when there was a high level of skill, i.e., high complexity; many programs, i.e., low formalization; and autonomy in decision making, i.e., low centralization (*corol. 11, 14, 20*).[64] Two case studies of changes in the degree of formalization, as measured by the number of rules and their enforcement, sug-

gest that there are very definite limits to the relationships between job satisfaction and formalization. In Gouldner's study of a gypsum plant, increases in formalization led to decreases in satisfaction. But Guests's study of an automobile plant disclosed that relaxing bureaucratic rules and especially their enforcement led to increases in satisfaction and increases in both production and productivity.[65] Therefore, increases or decreases in the scores of variables should be viewed in terms of proposition VIII, because a limit, whether maximum or minimum, may have been exceeded. There is some suggestion of this in Guests's work. Tsouderos's study of voluntary associations disclosed that increases in formalization resulted in raising larger amounts of funds (high production) and lower costs, but that memberships dropped.[66] Although voluntary associations are different from businesses, Tsouderos's findings support many of the hypotheses in the theory.

This brings us to what is probably the most controversial hypothesis in the theory: corollary 3. There have been many studies of morale and volume of production, but the results have been conflicting.[67] About one-half of them report a small positive correlation between high morale and high production, contrary to the hypothesis. Another third of the studies indicate that there is no relationship. The studies use a variety of definitions, of course, and the definition of high morale varies.

There is some support for a number of the hypotheses, and even though the evidence for specific hypotheses is not strong, there is considerable support for the theory. As Zetterberg has suggested, it is easier to prove a theory than specific hypotheses.[68] Most of the studies involve only two or three of the hypotheses of the theory. Some of them, such as corollaries 6, 7, 9, and 16, do not appear to have been examined by researchers. Some of them have both supporting and negative evidence. Certainly, the relationships between job satisfaction and volume of production, and between either complexity or adaptiveness and volume of production are not completely clear.

Two explanations are possible for the negative evidence. One explanation is that when the limits of a variable are exceeded, there is a reversal of the usual hypothesized relationship. Proposition VIII stipulates both minimum and maximum levels, which must be maintained before the predicted relationships can hold. Another explanation is that the contradictory studies are using different levels of the same variables or even different definitions. But one must also be cautious about accepting the positive evidence. Perhaps the major qualification that must be made is that the scales that have been employed in the various organizations are not the same.

ORGANIZATIONAL CHANGE

If the theory is a general one, it should be able to explain, at least within a narrow scope, the problem of organizational change. There are two aspects to this problem: the Parsonian distinction between change within the system and change of the system of variables.[69] The former aspect is the variable of adaptiveness defined as the rate of change in new programs and techniques; the latter aspect is the consequence of a change in one variable as related to the other seven variables, which effects a change in the entire system of variables. Decision making becomes decentralized or status differences decrease. The axiomatic theory indicates how the scores on the other variables should change as a consequence.

Several of the studies reported in the previous section, e.g., Morse-Reimer, Bavelas, Tsouderos, were longitudinal ones. They indicate how changing one variable affected the scores on other variables. Although the number of longitudinal studies of organizations is small, they are extremely useful because by examining whether a change in one variable leads to changes in the other variables, a more exacting test of the hypotheses is possible. Longitudinal experiments also allow a test of the validity of proposition VIII.

One study that investigated societies over a very long span of time, 125 years, is Ben-David's study of medical research in France, Great Britain, Germany, and the U. S.[70] It indicates that for a period of time, the countries with centralized medical research had much higher production but also higher stratification, as indicated by slow rates of mobility among medical researchers. The countries with decentralized medical research kept adding new specialties and new techniques and programs, as well as research laboratories. The lack of adaptiveness by the centralized organizations for a long period of time gradually resulted in a reduction in production. This study suggests the importance of the limits hypothesis, proposition VIII. Without at least some adaptiveness in the organization, production drops and the advantages of centralization are lost.

The reverse problem is represented in a case study of the General Dynamics Corporation, which kept adding new programs and services in its various divisions at a very rapid rate. This resulted in a high adaptiveness score, but procedures for coordination were not set up and the organization suffered staggering losses until centralization and formalization were increased.[71] The same point is made in Sloan's reminiscences of General Motors during the days of Durant.[72] Durant kept adding new programs and services, but made no attempt to effect some centralization of decision making and formalization of procedures. The consequence was loss of efficiency and the near-bankruptcy of the company. In contrast, Ford used the policy of one product under rigid control with high production and high productivity, but, in the long run, the company's lack of adaptiveness resulted in a loss of sales to General Motors, which was pioneering new techniques, until Ford itself became much more adaptive.

All of these studies indicate that the continued emphasis on one organization end to the neglect of another gradually results in the exceeding of the limits, as suggested by proposition VIII. It should be noted that both a maximum limit and minimum limit are exceeded simultaneously. In the Ben-David studies of Great Britain and France, the maximum of centralization and stratification is exceeded while the minimum level of adaptiveness is not reached. The General Motors study suggests that the maximum of adaptiveness was exceeded while the minimum of efficiency was not reached. In contrast, Ford Motor Company illustrates an exceeding of the maximum on centralization and formalization along with a failure to reach the minimum of adaptiveness. Thus, these case studies document not only the interrelationships between the variables, but how they can articulate as a system.

As is well known from a number of studies of changes in organization, the introduction of a new program or a new technique is known to lower satisfaction temporarily during the implementation. Increases in complexity and adaptiveness can produce temporary conflicts between groups, but the theory attempts to predict permanent changes in variables, rather than these temporary consequences. An illustration is the McCleery study of a prison.[73] Before the introduction of a rehabilitation program, which resulted in the addition of new occupations and new techniques, the prison was described as having high stratification, high centralization, and high formalization. The rehabilitation program resulted in temporary conflicts and considerable job dissatisfaction among the guards. The permanent consequences were reduced stratification, centralization, and formalization. These findings are supported by another study of a prison, reported by Grusky.[74] The adoption of the therapeutic technique in handling prisoners reduced status differences between guards and prisoners, increased interaction between them and the staff, resulted in a decentralization of authority, and a reduction in the use of bureaucratic procedures (lower formalization).

It should be noted that these case studies do not provide measures of the amount of change in adaptiveness or centralization or other variables. Consequently it becomes impossible to state how much of an increase in adaptiveness is necessary for a reduction of a given unit in centralization or how much increased formalization is necessary for an increase of one unit of efficiency. Such statements require the development of metrics such as the coefficients of the variables, the power values of the variables, and the limits suggested by proposition VIII.[75] Metrics are the necessary first step before precise prediction can be made. Once this is done, then a much more exacting test of the hypotheses is possible.

SUMMARY

Four organizational ends and means have been defined in this paper. Each variable is a formal characteristic of organizations and refers to a major issue in organizational life. The variables have been interrelated in an axiomatic theory, specifying how means and ends influence each other. Thus the theory provides a basis for making an improvement in organizational performances. If greater efficiency is desired, the theory suggests increasing the formalization of rules; if greater job satisfaction is desired, the theory suggests decreasing the stratification of rewards.

While several theoretical justifications for the choice of these particular variables have been given, perhaps the best justification is that each has proved useful in a large variety of research studies.

Seven major propositions have been presented. Each proposition is a familiar one and can be found in the writings of Weber, Barnard, or Thompson. The propositions have been interrelated in an axiomatic theory, integrating different organizational perspectives. The twenty-one derived corollaries represent such diverse writings as Durkheim, Michel, and the literature on human relations and alienation.

In order to derive corollaries it was necessary to assume that the eight variables formed a relatively closed system. There is some support for this assumption, since the major organizational theorists have used approximately the same concepts and in some instances have hypothesized the same relationships. It seems plausible that they are describing the same closed system, but looking at different parts of it. The argument becomes more compelling when it is remembered that the derived corollaries reflect hypotheses found in previously isolated writings. Still the assumption of a relatively closed system of variables must remain only an assumption, for it is difficult to prove.

Although a large number of research studies have been codified by the axiomatic theory, several qualifications must be made. The major qualification is that the definition of the variables used in the wide diversity of organizational types is not the same. The evidence for some of the hypotheses is negative; this may be a definitional problem or a limits problem. Since there are no metrics, a precise test of the hypotheses in the axiomatic theory is not possible; predictions cannot be made and then either verified or denied. At the same time, there is enough supporting evidence to indicate that the development of metrics and the consideration of definitions is a worth-while undertaking. It would appear that this axiomatic theory is pointing in the right direction toward the understanding of organizations.

NOTES

[1] For a discussion of the various kinds of axiomatic theory, see Hans Zetterberg, *On Theory and Verification in Sociology* (Totowa, New Jersey: The Bedminster Press, 1963), ch. iii.

[2] For a similar distinction see Basil Georgopoulos and Arnold Tannenbaum, A Study of Organizational Effectiveness, *American Sociological Review*, 22 (October, 1957), p. 536; Pugh *et al.*, A Scheme for Organizational Analysis, *Administrative Science Quarterly*, 8 (December, 1963), who define means as structure and ends as performance. Talcott Parsons made this means-ends distinction the basis of his review of early sociological writers; see his *Structure of Social Action* (New York: McGraw-Hill, 1938), ch. ii.

[3] This axiomatic theory and the distinction between means and ends makes it possible to clarify much of the conceptual confusion involved in structural-functional analysis. With the hypotheses in the theory, it is possible to provide precise definitions and illustrations of such concepts as structural incompatibility, functional and dysfunctional, equilibrium, etc. Limitations of space prevent a detailed discussion of how the present theory is an example of structural-functional analysis and of how the many terminological pitfalls in this mode of analysis can be resolved.

[4] The author is grateful for support as a post-doctoral trainee at the University of Wisconsin under the sponsorship of the National Institutes of Health, U.S.P.H.S., Grant No. 5T1 MH-7413-03, which allowed for the preparation of this paper.

[5] S. F. Nadel, *The Theory of Social Structure* (Glencoe, Illinois: The Free Press, 1957, pp.7–17. See Ernst Cassirer, *Substance and Function* (Chicago, Ill.: Dover, 1955, ch. i, for a general discussion of these two kinds of concepts and their epistemological consequences.

[6] Kurt Wolff (ed.), *The Sociology of Georg Simmel* (Glencoe, Illinois: The Free Press, 1950).

[7] A more detailed discussion of this point is presented in Jerald Hage and Gerald Marwell, "Research Towards the Development of Role Theory—A New Approach," paper read at the American Sociological Association, 60th annual meeting, August, 1965.

8 Talcott Parsons, Robert Bales, and Edward Shils, *The Working Papers in the Theory of Action* (Glencoe, Illinois: The Free Press, 1958). Perhaps the most serious source of disagreement would be the interpretation of efficiency as an indicator of integration. The author believes that the better the integration of personnel, machines, and other resources, the greater the efficiency. The sociological emphasis on social integration has ignored the importance of other resources. The use of volume of production as an indicator of goal achievement, rate of change as an indicator of adaptiveness, and satisfaction as a parameter of tension-management are probably less subject to argument.

9 In order to test propositions it is necessary to have measurable variables. While the properties of the four social ends used in this paper are measurable and appear to represent indicators of the four functional prerequisites, they may not include the totality of meaning intended by Parsons and Bales. Nevertheless it was their work that suggested the social ends used in this paper.

10 See Allen Barton, *Organizational Measurement* (New York College Entrance Examination Board, 1961), pp. 11–19, for a discussion of some of the problems involved in measuring outputs. The determination of units produced is difficult in organizations such as army units or police departments. In these organizations it might be better to count the number of operations performed in the course of a year, such as the number of military maneuvers or the number of crimes investigated.

11 Victor Thompson, *Modern Organization* (New York: Alfred Knopf, 1961), ch. iii. A similar distinction is found in Pugh *et al.*, *op. cit.*

12 These two indicators of complexity can be combined into an index of complexity. A similar procedure can be used for each of the other organizational means.

13 Theodore Caplow, *Principles of Organizations* (New York: Harcourt, Brace, 1964), p. 60.

14 The specific works are: Max Weber, *The Theory of Social and Economic Organization*, trans. by M. Henderson and T. Parsons (Glencoe, Illinois: The Free Press, 1947), pp. 324–340; Hans Gerth and C. Wright Mills, *From Max Weber: Essays in Sociology* (New York: Oxford University Press, 1958), pp. 196–244; Chester Barnard, "Functions and Pathology of Status Systems in Formal Organizations," in William Foote Whyte (ed.), *Industry and Society* (New York: McGraw-Hill, 1964), pp. 46–83; and Victor Thompson, *op. cit.*, pp. 3–113.

15 Parsons, Bales, and Shils, *op. cit.*, pp. 64, 88–90, 180–185. Bales discussed this problem in his "Adaptive and Integrative Changes as Sources of Strain in Social Systems," in A. Paul Hare, Edgar F. Borgatta, and Robert F. Bales (eds.), *Small Groups* (New York: Alfred Knopf, 1955), pp. 127–131. Peter Blau and W. Richard Scott, *Formal Organizations* (San Francisco: Chandler, 1962).

16 Weber, *op. cit.*, pp. 330–331.

17 Gerth and Mills, *op. cit.*, p. 214.

18 *Ibid.*, p. 197, and Weber, *op. cit.*, p. 334.

19 Weber, *op. cit.*, p. 335.

20 Blau and Scott, *op. cit.*, p. 32.

21 For a comparison of Weber and Barnard's conceptualization of organizations, see Terence Hopkins, "Bureaucratic Authority: The Convergence of Weber and Barnard," in A. Etzioni (ed.) *Complex Organizations* (New York: Holt, Rinehart, and Winston, 1961), pp. 82–98.

[22] Barnard, *op. cit.*, p. 68; Weber, *op. cit.*, p. 334.

[23] *Op. cit.*, pp. 71–83.

[24] *Op. cit.*, p. 122.

[25] *Ibid.*, p. 100.

[26] *Op. cit.*, pp. 83–100. This proposition is in direct confrontation of the idea expressed in Weber, that technical competence is always found in the authority position or office; see *op. cit.*, pp. 333–335. This assumption has been much criticized; see Blau and Scott, *op. cit.*, pp. 35–36. For a more detailed discussion, see Robert Peabody, Perceptions of Organizational Authority, *Administrative Science Quarterly*, 6 (March, 1962), 463–482.

[27] Alvin Gouldner, "Organizational Analysis," in R. K. Merton, L. Brown, and L. S. Cottrell (eds.), *Sociology Today* (New York: Basic Books, 1959), pp. 400–428.

[28] *Op. cit.*, pp. 247–250.

[29] Melvin Seeman, On the Meaning of Alienation, *American Sociological Review*, 24 (December 1959), 783–791.

[30] Robert Blauner, *Alienation and Freedom* (Chicago: University of Chicago, 1964), ch. v.

[31] Emile Durkheim, *Division of Labor in Society*, trans. by George Simpson (Glencoe, Ill.: The Free Press, 1947).

[32] *Op. cit.*, pp. 244–247.

[33] Tom Burns and G. M. Stalker, *The Management of Innovation* (London: Tavistock Publications, 1961), pp. 119–125.

[34] The eight variables of the theory, however, appear to be useful for predicting these and other variables. They can be utilized to explain the basis of conflict and cooperation, the periodicity of conflict, styles and content of communication, patterns of integration, and even the stages in the process of change. In other words, the eight variables appear to be fundamental ones, which allow the researcher and theorist to examine a large number of organizational problems.

[35] See Bernard Berelson and Gary Steiner, *Human Behavior* (New York: Harcourt, Brace and World, 1964), p. 370.

[36] Most ideological disputes can be reduced to an argument about the relative importance of one or two social ends. For other discussions of this aspect of organizational analysis, see A. Etzioni, *op. cit.*: James Thompson and William McEwen, "Organizational Goals and Environment," pp. 177–186; S. N. Eisenstadt, "Bureaucracy, Bureaucratization and Debureaucratization," pp. 268–276; Peter Rossi, "The Organizational Structure of an American Community," pp. 301–311. See also Blau and Scott, *op. cit.*, ch. viii.

[37] *Op. cit.* The use of these contextual variables allows for the development of three variable relationships. It is one method for expanding the scope of the theory.

[38] Although the author has attempted to find negative evidence, he freely admits the danger of selective bias. The number of findings reduces this danger, but does not eliminate it.

[39] For a review of these studies, see Donald Ross (ed.), *Administration for Adaptability* (New York: Institute of Administrative Research, Teachers College, Columbia University, 1958).

[40] Hilton Buley, "Personnel Characteristics and Staff Patterns Associated with the Quality of Education," (Unpublished Ed.D. Project, Teachers College, Columbia University, 1947).

[41] *Op. cit.*

[42] Morris Janowitz, Changing Patterns of Organizational Authority, *Administrative Science Quarterly*, 3 (1959); also "Hierarchy and Authority in the Military Establishment," in A. Etzioni, *op. cit.*, pp. 198–212.

[43] See Jerald Hage, "Organizational Response to Innovation: A Case Study of Community Hospitals," (Unpublished Ph.D. dissertation, Columbia University, 1963), ch. xi.

[44] *Ibid.*, ch. xii.

[45] *Op. cit.*, pp. 122–125.

[46] Harriet Ronken and Paul Lawrence, *Administering Changes* (Cambridge: Harvard Graduate School of Business, 1955).

[47] Lester Coch and John French, Jr., Overcoming Resistance to Change, *Human Relations*, 1 (1948), 512–532.

[48] See Francois Cillié, *Centralization or Decentralization* (New York: Teachers College, Columbia University, 1940), especially p. 96.

[49] Nancy Morse and Everett Reimer, The Experimental Change of a Major Organizational Variable, *Journal of Abnormal and Social Psychology*, 52 (1955), 120–129.

[50] See Alex Bavelas, "Communication Patterns in Task-oriented Groups," in Dorwin Cartwright and Alvin Zander (eds.), *Group Dynamics* (Evanston, Ill.: Row, Peterson, 1960), pp. 669–682; Harold Leavitt, "Some Effects of Certain Communication Patterns on Group Performances," in Eleanor E. Maccoby, Theodore M. Newcomb, and Eugene L. Hartley, *Readings in Social Psychology* (New York: Henry Holt, 1958), 546–563; and the replications under various circumstances of Arthur Cohen, Changing Small-Group Communication Networks, *Administrative Science Quarterly*, 6 (March 1962), 443–462.

[51] Stanley Udy, Jr., *Organization of Work* (New Haven: Taplinger Press, 1959), pp. 36–40. It might be noted in passing that Udy suggests that specialization encourages the development of hierarchy, but he is discussing task specialization, not person specialization. Blau and Scott (*op. cit.*, p. 210) take exception to Udy's interpretation but again they do not make this distinction.

[52] Seymour Lipset, Martin Trow, and James Coleman, *Union Democracy* (Glencoe, Ill.: The Free Press, 1956), ch. ii.

[53] Richard H. Hall, The Concept of Bureaucracy: An Empirical Assessment, *American Journal of Sociology*, 69 (July 1963), 32–40.

[54] *Op. cit.*, pp. 211, 251.

[55] *Ibid.*, p. 48.

[56] Paul Harrison, *Authority and Power in the Free Church Tradition* (Princeton: Princeton University, 1959).

[57] Blau and Scott, *op. cit.*, p. 172; Melville Dalton, Conflicts Between Staff and Line Managerial Officers, *American Sociological Review*, 15 (June 1950), 342–351.

[58] See Mayer Zald, Organizational Control Structures in Five Correctional Institutions, *American Journal of Sociology*, 68 (November 1962), 335–345.

[59] Howard S. Becker, "The Teacher in the Authority System of the Public School," in A. Etzioni, *op. cit.*, pp. 243–251.

[60] Seymour Lipset, *Agrarian Reform* (Berkeley: University of California, 1950), ch. xii.

[61] Jerald Hage, "Centralization, Specialization, Effectiveness, and Efficiency in Professional Organizations," (Unpublished manuscript, University of Wisconsin).

62 American Association of University Professors, The Place and Function of Faculties in College and University Government," *American Association of University Professors Bulletin*, 41 (1955), 62–81.

63 Paul Lazarsfeld and Wagner Thielens, Jr., *The Academic Mind* (Glencoe, Ill.: The Free Press, 1958), ch. vii.

64 James March and Herbert Simon, *Organizations* (New York: John Wiley, 1958), ch. iv.

65 See Blau and Scott, *op. cit.*, pp. 239–240.

66 John Tsouderos, Organizational Change in Terms of a Series of Selected Variables, *American Sociological Review*, 20 (1955), 206–210.

67 See Berelson and Steiner, *op. cit.*, pp. 409–411.

68 *Op. cit.*, ch. vi.

69 Talcott Parsons, *The Social System* (Glencoe, Ill.: The Free Press, 1951), ch. xii.

70 Joseph Ben-David, "Scientific Productivity and Academic Organization in Nineteenth-Century Medicine," in Bernard Barber and Walter Hirsch (eds.), *The Sociology of Science* (New York: Free Press of Glencoe, 1962), pp. 305–328.

71 Richard Smith, "How a Great Corporation Got Out of Control," *Fortune*, 65 (January 1962), p. 64; 65 (February 1962), p. 120.

72 Alfred P. Sloan, Jr., "My Years with General Motors—Part I," *Fortune*, 68 (September, 1963), 135.

73 Richard McCleery, "Policy Change in Prison Management," in A. Etzioni, *op. cit.*, pp. 376–399.

74 Oscar Grusky, Role Conflict in Organizations, *Administrative Science Quarterly*, 3 (1959), 452–472.

75 When this is done, it will be possible to treat the problem of organizational evolution precisely. If the coefficients of the variables in the theory are not the same, or there is a difference in other metrics, which seems a likely assumption, then movement toward one or the other ideal types of configuration is favored. There is some evidence to suggest that over very long periods of time many organizations, not only in the United States but in other societies as well, are moving towards an adaptive ideal type, that is, high complexity, low centralization, low formalization, low stratification, and so on. This is partially a consequence of the exponential growth in occupational specialties, especially the trend toward professionalism. The parallel growth in knowledge is accelerating the rate of change in new programs and techniques, that is, adaptiveness. But the available evidence also suggests that the negative consequences of increasing complexity and adaptiveness for production and efficiency are not as great as the reverse relationship, therefore there should be little concern about the organizational world moving towards inefficiency and lower production.

9.

MODERN ORGANIZATIONAL THEORY: A PSYCHOLOGICAL AND SOCIOLOGICAL STUDY

D. S. PUGH

"Organization theory" is the study of the structure and functioning of organizations and the behavior of groups and individuals within them. It is an emerging interdisciplinary quasi-independent science, drawing primarily on the disciplines of sociology and psychology, but also on economics and, to a lesser extent, on production engineering. The purpose of this paper is to discuss the lines of development which compose this subdiscipline (some of which may be relatively little known to psychologists) and to present an overview of attempts to develop a unified science of man in organizations.

The importance of developing such a science cannot be overemphasized. Most people spend a considerable portion of their time in formal organizations. Preschool children, nonworking wives, and old people are the only sizable groups not necessarily so involved as members, and even they are affected as patients, clients, customers, or citizens. The bureaucratic organization, and the individual operating within it, is one of the dominant institutions of our time. Of course organizations do not exist in a vacuum, they have to respond to the pressures impinging on them from the society in which they exist. The demands of a market economy, political decisions, legal re-

From D. S. Pugh, "Modern Organizational Theory: A Psychological and Sociological Study," *Psychological Bulletin*, 66:235–251, 1966. © 1966 by the American Psychological Association, and reproduced by permission.

strictions, technological requirements, etc., all affect organizational operations. But just as the O is coming back into the S-R bond in contemporary psychology, so the "O," in this case the organization, is the mediating organism between the "S" (Society) and the "R" (the Resultant achievement of goals, the higher standard of living, the longer expectation of life, etc.). Highly colored exaggerations of this situation, such as Burnham's (1941) *The Managerial Revolution* and Whyte's (1956) *The Organization Man*, only serve to underline the organization's important place in society.

There is a second reason for the importance of organization theory which is of particular interest to those psychologists who believe that the proper study of mankind is man *outside* the laboratory. Those of us who are concerned with the empirical study of man *in situ* cannot fail to be impressed with the achievements of the laboratory method in other sciences, even though we are more uncertain of its usefulness in our own. But the fact that we substitute the statistical method for the laboratory one in our experiments and use statistics to control our independent variables rather than laboratory simulation only serves to emphasize that we are working within the same basic underlying experimental "model." The study of men in organizations can offer possibilities of direct comparisons between individuals approximating to a laboratory investigation, but without its artificiality. For example, a factory can have a row of people sitting at a bench doing the same *real* job. This makes the achievement of experimental control outside the laboratory much easier. Studies of factors affecting the motivation to perform, the effects of personality on role behavior, the transmission of information along communication channels—all these can benefit from study in a real situation which has in it many of the advantages of the artificial laboratory situation, such as repeatability on large numbers, specificity of process studied, etc.

One may ask why it is considered less artificial to study men getting paid for standing on the assembly line at a motor factory screwing on car-door handles than to study men getting paid for taking part in a laboratory ergograph experiment. The answer is that it is not so much the actual laboratory task itself that is artificial—although there are difficulties here (Rolfe & Corkindale, 1964)—as the social situation in which it is performed. The social role of mass production operator is far removed from that of laboratory subject. The enormous disparity in the duration of role occupancy is sufficient to ensure differences in sanctions and motivations, with consequent divergence in performance.

DEFINITION OF THE SUBJECT

Defining a new subject carries with it a built-in dilemma. One can either use the technical terms of the established disciplines to indicate the area of interest (this has the advantage of containing verbal stimuli which produce recognition responses in potential recruits in relevant fields, and might therefore be called a "political" definition) or one can create new terms which define exactly what is meant in terms of the new discipline (this has the obvious advantage of precision, and might thus be called a "scientific" definition). The disadvantage of the political definition is that the established terms may carry with them connotations and overtones, to overcome which may be the precise purpose of setting up the new discipline. The disadvantage of the scientific definition is that it conveys little to the uninitiated, which is a limitation in encouraging potential interest.

The definition of organization theory given above is clearly a political one. It indicates in general terms the areas of interest, using established social science terminology: structure, functioning, organization, behavior, groups, individuals. It seems to form a nice balance between sociological and psychological "clang" words and thus to interest practitioners in both fields. But it suffers from the disadvantage of a political definition in that there may be read into it the implication that

the structure and functioning of organizations is the province of the sociologist, the behavior of individuals is dealt with by the psychologist, while groups are left to a peculiar man in the middle, the social psychologist. He appears to be so peculiar that one writer (Smith, 1954) has suggested that he could be divided up and a distinction made between the "sociological social psychologist" and the "psychological social psychologist."

It is precisely because this compartmentalization is unhelpful that we wish to break away from the traditional division of the ground, and have used the concept of organization theory as a way of integrating these disciplines (and some others) into a unified science of individual, group, and organizational behavior. The behavior itself at these three levels is intimately interrelated, and so, therefore, should be the study of it. It is our contention that sociologists and psychologists can jointly make contributions to all problems of organization theory.

Let us take two examples: a considerable limitation on all major sociological theories of organizational functioning is an extremely naïve treatment of human motivation combined with a neglect of individual differences which are characteristically devalued into "personal idiosyncrasies." An organization is a system of functioning human beings who are different, and if the sociologist neglects these differences he is not leaving them *out of account*, he is saying that for the processes with which he is concerned, these differences are of *no account*—that is, they are equal to zero. This is a most important psychological statement which may very well be true—or not, as the case may be—but which requires empirical investigation rather than a priori assertion. Similarly, psychological studies of leadership patterns in relation to personality and social skill training imply a very naïve view of the relationship between personality and role behavior, combined with a neglect of structural differences in organizational positions. Again the psychologist cannot say that he is not concerned with differences in organization structure since he is only discovering the best leadership style to suit the particular personality. Leadership is exercised within different organizational structures, and if he neglects these differences the psychologist is not leaving them *out of account*, he is maintaining that for the processes with which he is concerned they are of *no account*. This is a very important sociological statement, which may very well be true—or not—but which again requires empirical investigation.

It was considerations such as these which led us to conceptualize our work as the attempt to develop an interdisciplinary unified study of organization theory. It would be impossible to describe all the lines of development which affect a new study even if one were aware of them. We can only briefly and summarily give here a number of main strands which have been particularly formative. Pugh, Hickson, and Hinings (1964) summarized in greater detail the work of many of these writers. They are not given here in any order of importance, overt or implied. Indeed, we would wish explicitly to disavow the primacy of any particular approach and to maintain that an integrated unified orientation, drawing on all these approaches and interrelating them (and, most importantly, *rejecting* something of all of them), offers the best promise for future development.

MANAGEMENT THEORISTS

Managers, administrators, and government officials have always had an interest in describing their experiences with more or less insight, but the first manager whose theoretical analysis of organizational functioning has had a lasting impact was a Frenchman—Henri Fayol (1949), who was writing about 50 years ago. His "General Principles of Management" have little in the way of systematic evidence to support them, but most managers find that they square with experience. As empirical scientists, we are right to be wary of such "proverbs" as these, but not to dismiss them out of hand.

They include such tenets as "authority must equal responsibility," "one man, one boss," and so on. A whole series of managers (and others) have developed these practical insights. "Specialization increases efficiency" is a favorite one. "The span of control of a manager, that is, the number reporting directly to him, should never be more than six," is another. The almost completely descriptive writings of political scientists and industrial relations experts belong here too (Dahl, 1959; Drucker, 1955; Goldstein, 1952).

From the scientific point of view, there are two main difficulties in this approach. There is first the very considerable prescriptive content. Very much more is said about how organizations should be run than about how they are run—not unnaturally since these are guides to the manager on what he ought to do. The contemporary British manager Wilfred Brown (1960) illustrated this attitude very well. He noted that wherever there is an authority system (i.e., a situation in which some people are in a position to make decisions, give orders, allocate work, etc., to others) there are also developed ways of letting those in authority know what the people underneath them think and feel about these decisions, even if in only the most rudimentary and unsystematic way. Since this will happen anyway, it is clearly bad management to allow it to happen inefficiently. Brown therefore maintained that wherever there is an executive authority system, there must be set up feedback channels of equivalent formality and complexity (which he called a "Representative System") if communication is to improve and the organization to function efficiently. Brown's own firm has a highly complex system of representative committees formally elected by all levels of employees. It will be seen that Brown represents a considerable increase in sociological and psychological sophistication from the common sense analyses of Fayol, but the normative orientation is still very much to the fore.

The second difficulty with the management theorists, particularly the common sense ones, is that not being scientists, their statements do not usually have sufficient precision to enable crucial experiments to be undertaken to test their validity. This is their attraction for the layman, since the proverbs appear to be wise and true for all occasions. But scientific statements are precisely *not* true for *all* occasions, and it is an integral part of the process of science to look for occasions for which they are not true. A scientific hypothesis is essentially a falsifiable statement. When the statements of the management theorists are subject to the same scrutiny, and attempts made to operationalize them, it is usually found that they do not stand up to such analysis very well (Simon, 1957).

For example, consider the principle already mentioned: "specialization increases efficiency," which spelled out would presumably mean "increased specialization will lead to greater efficiency." Does this mean that *any* increase in specialization will increase efficiency? Take the case of a firm with three factories: Factory A makes washing machines, Factory B makes refrigerators, and Factory C makes vacuum cleaners—in each case complete. How do we increase efficiency by increasing specialization? Could we let Factory A make the electric motors which are required for all three products; Factory B do the machine shop work for all three; and Factory C do the assembly and finishing work for all three? Would this be an increase in specialization? As soon as the problem is stated in these concrete terms, it is clear that the proverb is no help in making the decision. It does not define what is an "increase in specialization" as distinct from a change in specialization except in terms of an increase in efficiency. Specialization is an inevitable concomitant of organization (efficient or inefficient), and the problem is not "how to specialize" but "how to specialize efficiently." The operational translation of the principle would be: Efficiency is increased by such specialization as will lead to increased efficiency!

In fact, the specialization problem is an absolutely fundamental one, having its ramifications throughout the whole of organization theory, at the organization, group, and individual levels. At the organization level, it is the "assignment" problem. Given an overall set of tasks which can be partitioned in a number of ways and a total set of resources which can be partitioned in a number of ways, what partitioning of the resources assigned to what partitioning of the tasks will yield the maximum efficiency? There are three sets of decisions here; the partitioning of the tasks, the partitioning of the resources, and the assignment; and the difficulty lies in the fact that the efficiencies are nonadditive. For example, the man-hours required for 100 jobs if 10 men each do 10 jobs may be more than or less than, but it is unlikely to be equal to, the man-hours required for 1 man to do all the 100 jobs or for 100 men to do 1 job each. Since the factors which affect efficiency range from machine set-up costs through operator skills and restriction of output to technological know-how and administrative flexibility, it is not surprising that no underlying principles for tackling this problem have emerged. The only available solution is a "brute force" one, involving testing all the possible partitions of the resources assigned to all the possible partitions of the task. This is normally an unrealistic undertaking, and although with computer techniques there are methods of reducing the magnitude of the computational task involved (Kuhn, 1955), no general propositions about optimal assignment have emerged, only methods of obtaining the best solution in a particular case.

In the face of this major unsolved problem of operations research, the management principle "specialization increases efficiency" does no more than serve to point out the existence of the problem. Management theory has great interest for the social scientist, for the problems with which it deals nearly always point to topics with which he is concerned. But it has great dangers too, for if the social scientist allows outsiders to set the topics on which he works, his contribution to the development of the discipline (which should be his main concern) is much hampered.

STRUCTURAL THEORISTS

All organizations have to make provision for continuing activities directed towards the achievement of given aims. Regularities in such activities as task allocation, the exercise of authority, and coordination of functions are developed. Such regularities constitute the organization's structure, and sociologists have studied systematic differences in structure related to variations in such factors as the objectives of the organization, its size, ownership, geographical location, and technology of manufacture, which produce the characteristic differences in structure of a bank, a hospital, a mass production factory or a local government department.

The concept of bureaucracy as described by the German sociologist Max Weber (1947) is central to this approach. In popular discussion, bureaucracy is synonymous with inefficient administration, pettifogging legalism, and red tape, and yet the bureaucratic form of organization has become the dominant one in all modern societies. Weber drew critical attention to the strengths of the bureaucratic structure of organization. He noted that characteristically in a bureaucracy, authority is exercised by means of a system of rules and procedures through the official position which an individual occupies. These positions are arranged in a hierarchy, each successive step embracing in authority all those beneath it. Rules and procedures are drawn up for every theoretically possible contingency. There is a "bureau" for the safekeeping of all written records and files—it being an important part of the rationality of the system that information is written down. Particularly important is the stress on the appointment of experts who are specialists with formal qualifications for their positions. The system thus aims to develop the most efficient methods for achieving its goals by depersonalizing the whole administrative process. Written rulebooks, standardized procedures, and formal training and qualification for appointment all act to minimize capricious differences in the treatment of the same prob-

lem, eliminate nepotism in promotion, and set and maintain high standards of efficiency in working. In modern computer jargon, a bureaucracy is an organization which is completely programmed.

The major development of this approach has been to compare the organization's structure and functioning with Weber's description of bureaucracy and to point out that he was incomplete and inadequate in his formulations of bureaucratic action. These are the classic studies of bureaucratic dysfunction of Merton (1940), Dubin (1949), and Gouldner (1955), among others. They underline that Weber gave only a description of the formal (i.e., intended) characteristics of bureaucracy and left out the unintended consequences which may have very important disrupting effects upon the organization. Crucial significance must be given to the attitudes, values, and goals of specialist subunits and individuals and the way in which these continuously modify the organization's formal structure.

Selznick (1949), for example, on the basis of a study of the Tennessee Valley Authority, showed that Weber's formal description of an efficient bureaucracy left out the dysfunctions which must occur when the top administrators in a large organization inevitably delegate some of their authority. They do so differentially, and this has several consequences. As intended, it increases the specialized competences of the various groups which now have authority over the different parts of the organization's functioning. But at the same time, it also has the unintended effect of increasing departmentalization and underlining the differences of interest between the department and the organization as a whole. Each department soon develops its own goals and values, and conflict between departments ensues with consequent greater identification of the individual with his own department and smaller identification with the organization. A man's career comes to appear to be best served by conforming to his department's ideology, rather than by optimizing his contribution to the whole organization if this involves flouting his department. This is the problem of specialization again, at the group level. Specialist competence can certainly increase efficiency, but the price has to be paid in increased division of interest. The problem is: At what point does the price become too high?

Burns and Stalker (1961) have developed a consideration of these dysfunctions into a postulated continuum of organizations in terms of their flexibility of structure. The mechanistic type of organization is adapted to relatively stable conditions. In it, the problems and tasks of management are broken down into specialisms within which each individual carries out his assigned, precisely defined task. There is a clear hierarchy of control and responsibility for overall knowledge, and coordination rests exclusively at the top. The organic type (later called "organismic," Burns, 1963) is adapted to unstable conditions when new and unfamiliar problems continually arise which cannot be broken down and distributed among the existing specialist role. There is therefore a continual adjustment and redefinition of individual tasks; interaction and communication (information and advice rather than orders) occur across any level as required and reliance on the normal hierarchical processes is rejected in favor of going out and getting things done. A much higher degree of commitment to the success of the organization is generated, presumably at a greater cost in ulcers and coronaries.

Burns and Stalker studied the attempts of traditional, mechanistic Scottish firms to absorb electronics research and development engineers into their organizations. The almost complete failure of these attempts led them to doubt whether a mechanistic firm can consciously change into an organismic one. This is because the individual in a mechanistic organization is not only committed to the organization as a whole, he is also a member of a group or department with a stable career structure and with sectional interests in conflict with those of other groups. Thus there develop power struggles between established sections to obtain control of the new functions

and resources. These divert the organization from purposive adaptation and allow out-of-date mechanistic structures to be perpetuated and "pathological" systems to develop.

The first major limitation of structural theory is that it involves what one might call "Hebb's fallacy." Hebb (1949) wished to explain psychological behavior in terms of physiological intervening variables, but his data was solely psychological. His physiology was purely speculative—reverberating neural feedback mechanisms, etc. Structural organization theorists deal with sociological phenomena and use psychological concepts as explanatory intervening variables—such concepts as "the process of sanctification of the rules of the organization" (meaning the internalization of rules by bureaucrats), "the development of esprit de corps," and "the resort to categorization" in decision-making. But the data are purely sociological; the psychology is only speculative—or perhaps it would be better to say "common sense." Merton's (1940) famous paper criticizing Weber was entitled "Bureaucratic Structure and Personality" and it used the three concepts just mentioned, but a psychologist reading it for signs of a link between structural theory and personality theory can only have the same feelings of exasperation as a physiologist reading Hebb. There is a continual use of lower order concepts as intervening variables and yet no attempt to devise ways of operationalizing them in order to carry out direct empirical tests of their validity. The use of a concept such as "sanctification of rules" must surely imply consideration of individual differences in such sanctification. The difficulty is that sociologists consider that they know enough speculative psychology for their purposes, just as psychologists think they know enough speculative physiology for theirs. But speculative "common sense" explanations, if they are not used as a spur to direct empirical investigation, are the enemy of scientific ones.

The second major limitation of structural theory is that it has been subject to what a sociologist (Wrong, 1961) has characterized as "the oversocialized conception of man in modern sociology." It is implicit in the structural approach that conformity to social expectations is the only effective motivation. Any more complex motivations are ignored. In addition, consideration is given only to the effects of the organization's demands and the expectations of other members in their roles, on the behavior and personality of the individual. These are assumed to be all-pervading. Merton's (1940) paper, referred to above, listed a number of problems for research such as: To what extent are particular personality types selected by various bureaucracies? Does holding bureaucratic office increase ascendancy traits of personality? What are the mechanisms for obtaining emotional commitment to the correct enforcement of the rules? Typically, they are all concerned with the effects of the organization on the individual. The most that an individual can do, it appears, if he does not conform, is to leave the job.

The structural approach gives no reciprocal account of the possible effects of the individual and his personality on the organization. For those of us who want a balanced understanding of integrated individual and organizational functioning, this is too limiting. What is required is a conceptual frame of reference which admits the equal validity of the demands of both the organizational structure *and* the individual personality; which looks for the way in which the structure determines the role behavior, but also notes that many role demands are permissive rather than mandatory so that the individual's behavior within the role may legitimately vary according to his personality—and that these variations may act *to change the structure.*

GROUP THEORISTS

This approach stems from Elton Mayo (1933) and Kurt Lewin (1943), and their "discovery" of the influence of the immediate informal group on motivation and behavior. Some of the findings of those who have developed this line of approach are: the amount of work carried out by a worker is determined not by his physical capacity but by his social capacity; noneconomic rewards are most important in the motivation and satisfaction of workers, who react to their work situations as groups and not as individuals; the leader is not necessarily the person appointed to be in charge, informal leaders can develop who have more power; the effective supervisor is "employee-centered" and not "job-centered," that is, he regards his job as dealing with human beings rather than with the work; communication and participation in decision making are some of the most significant rewards which can be offered to obtain the commitment of the individual. The prewar Hawthorne and leadership studies (Lewin, Lippit, & White, 1939; Roethlisberger & Dickson, 1939), the postwar studies of groups in the restaurant, pajama, and ball-bearing industries (Coch & French, 1948; Jaques, 1951; Whyte, 1948), and in the Army (Shils, 1950); Homans' (1951) survey of "The Human Group," Cartwright and Zander's (1953) of *Group Dynamics,* Likert's (1961) *New Patterns of Management* all add up to an impressive body of data.

The first limitation of the group theorists is that they have restricted their sights to too narrow a range of variables. Most of their studies are industrial ones, yet they have had little, if anything, to say about the political, social, and industrial power relationships that form the setting for work behavior. It may well be true that in the Hawthorne interviewing program—which was completed by 1932—not one worker spontaneously mentioned a trade union (as Landsberger, 1958, has confirmed), yet that would hardly be the case today. Having discovered the informal group and its importance, investigators in this tradition seem loath to allow other institutions some importance too. Even the formal executive organization seems to be looked upon as a sort of necessary evil. Many of the structural theorists, reacting against Weber and management theory, also seem to have this implicit bias against the formal organization.

Cartwright (1953) took up another aspect

of this same criticism when he accused group psychology of being "soft on power." Concepts such as leadership, authoritarianism, and influence have been well-investigated in social psychology, but not factors such as power or control. Partly as a result of Cartwright's observations, what might be thought of as the "second generation" Michigan investigators have recently begun to make good this deficiency (French, 1956; Kahn, 1964; Tannenbaum, 1962). In view of the long tradition in group theory that it is "psychological participation"—the *feeling* that one is participating in decision-making, not the actual participation itself—which matters, a study by Tannenbaum and Smith (1964) must be regarded as something of a breakthrough. They showed that in a voluntary organization with a large number of local groups, when individual perception of ability to influence decisions is held constant, there remains a significant relationship between the groups' average perception of influence and the level of loyalty and activity. Thus, members' participation was not just a function of subjective perceptions, although this factor was present. The average perceptions—which reflect the actual power exerted —must also be regarded as a causative factor. The emerging acceptance of the structured social relationship as real is an important stage in the development of group theory and is the innovation which best warrants the use of the new term "organizational psychology" (Bass, 1965; Schein, 1965). The studies of Porter and his associates (Porter & Henry, 1964; Porter & Lawler, 1964, 1965) have also contributed to this development by linking attitudes and job satisfaction firmly to positions in the formal organization structure.

The second limitation of the group theorists is theoretically more important though ideologically not so dramatic. It applies with equal force to both the structural and management theorists, but is dealt with here because it does not apply to the remaining approaches to be considered. There have been few attempts so far to relate organizational functioning and group behavior in any systematic

way. This is not surprising, as a striking characteristic of all these approaches is that the analysis has been primarily processual as opposed to factorial, as Komarovsky (1957) would put it, or clinical as opposed to statistical, using Meehl's (1954) terms. These writers have discussed the administrative process or the processes of group interaction, and their work has led to the development of management control systems and techniques in human relations. There has been almost no systematic statistical exploration of the causal connection between contextual factors and certain administrative systems rather than others, or certain group and individual behavior rather than others. The method of dealing with the problems has been the adumbration of broad generalizations based either on the experience and insights of the writer, or on the intensive one-case study of the empirical researcher. Because the problems have been conceived entirely in processual-clinical terms, the fact that the one-case study is of a particular work group, in a particular factory, in a particular firm, in a particular industry, in a particular country, or at a particular time has not prevented the development of generalizations that claim to apply to all individuals and all groups in all organizations and in all contexts. The inadequacies of this noncomparative approach are apparent. It may postulate that the designation of the correct mode of functional specialization is a vital part of the task of administration, but, as we have seen, it will give no systematic leads as to why a particular form of specialization exists in a particular organization. It may discover that some supervisory practices lead to a decrease in conflict, but it will not explain why particular industries (e.g., the chemical industry), which certainly do not have a monopoly of these practices, nevertheless have consistently less conflict than others (Kerr & Fisher, 1957).

The concept that the processual-clinical and the factorial-statistical approaches to analysis are in conflict has rightly been labelled by Komarovsky (1957) as a "pseudo-issue" in social science. Both approaches are vital. But processual analysis must take place in relation to the contextual framework provided by factorial analysis, not in neglect of it. The present study of work organization and behavior can no longer be content with a priori postulations or a continuing succession of one-case studies.

INDIVIDUAL THEORISTS

The investigation of psychological factors affecting a worker's performance on the job has a long tradition stemming from the Health of Munition Workers Report and the Industrial Fatigue Research Board during World War I. Since then, a considerable series of studies has developed designed to achieve the task of the applied psychologist, which is as Rodger (1950) put it "to fit the man to the job, and to fit the job to the man."

In many ways, this approach, concerned as it is with such concrete problems as counselling, selection, training, human engineering, conditions of work, and methods of payment, is the one where the psychologist can demonstrate that he has made a real contribution. Using his complementary twin objectives of, in Heron's (1954) neat formulation, "job satisfaction" and "job satisfactoriness," he has been able to concentrate his efforts on the mechanics of the work situation to the exclusion of wider factors such as group dynamics, social norms and values, and institutional conflict. But the growing body of data which indicates that satisfaction and productivity are not necessarily complementary (Brayfield & Crockett, 1955; Kahn, 1960) and that job satisfaction itself is by no means a unitary concept (Hertzberg, Mausner, & Snyderman, 1959) suggests that this approach too, as that of the group theorists, is embarking on a new stage of development.

The great contribution of the individual theorists has been in terms of methods. The management approach and the structural approach have relied on "intensive" rather than "systematic" methods of data collecting. The group approach has used Likert-type questionnaires.

But if we wish to seek any more sophisticated or potent techniques, then we must go to the individual theorists. If we wish to have tests of demonstrated reliability, or attitude questionnaires which have more than face validity; if we wish to use activity sampling or the critical incident technique—for all of these we must go to the individual theorists. Their overwhelming limitation is that almost without exception, they have defined their work in terms of management problems not psychological ones, and this has turned them from scientists into applied scientists or technologists. (This is also true to a considerable, but much less, extent of the group theorists.) It is no criticism to be an applied scientist if there is some science to apply. But applied psychology is a contradiction in terms because there is yet no coherent body of acceptable theory and data which can be drawn upon and applied once we get beyond the level of learning of perceptual and motor skills in ergonomics. There are some empirical techniques (e.g., intelligence testing, selection procedures), but no corpus of theory.

The choice of management problems for study rather than scientific ones imposes a considerable limitation. The whole of the work on industrial selection, for example, has contributed little more to the understanding of human behavior than a series of (usually modest) validity coefficients. This does not detract from the individual theorists' achievement in being the only ones who have tackled the problem of validity of data at all. But their concentration on the factorial-statistical approach to the almost complete exclusion of processual-clinical studies has buttressed the theoretical aridity of their formulation, although Fleishman's (1953) study of the International Harvester Company's supervisory training scheme is a notable exception. Such other processual studies of the effects of selection and training have drawn on the group and structural approaches (Sykes, 1962; Wilson, 1959).

The one example there has been of the wholesale application of a body of psychological theory—that of psychoanalysis—has not been very encouraging. Consideration is given only to the effects of the individual's personality structure and mechanisms on his behavior. These are assumed to be all-pervading and no systematic account is given of the effects of the organization and his role in it. Since the development of psychoanalysis relies so much on clinical insights obtained when the people concerned are not in their normal roles (i.e., they are patients, clients, interviewees; not managers, teachers, clerks), it is the subjective aspects of reality which receive major emphasis. Reality is out there, pressing, often hostile, but basically unstructured, so that it is an individual's personality dynamics which cause him to carve out for himself his role in life. A man's projection of his relationship to his father assumes more importance than the actual behavior of his boss (Cohen & Cohen, 1954; Holt & Salverson, 1960).

There has been one recent study in Britain, by Rogers (1963), in this tradition. He studied firms in the domestic appliance market and related their success to a psychoanalytic discussion of the motivation of their sales executives. He maintained that the successful executives had more dominant mothers and thus were able to identify better with the housewife to whom they were trying to sell their products. Unfortunately, his thesis was maintained by reference to a small number of case studies of individuals, which are notoriously unreliable. We are nowhere near the stage where we can apply established theories. A discussion of the motivation to undertake a sales rather than manufacturing career which goes into great detail about the subject's identification with his mother but says nothing about his mechanical intelligence or level of technical ability leaves much to be desired. A much wider range of psychological variables than Rogers took account of must be considered. As was suggested at the beginning of this paper, the study of the individual in the organization is just as much a theoretical adventure and has potentially just as much to contribute to the development of psychology as any other part of the discipline.

But this will only happen if the individual theorists widen their sights and choose the problems that they wish to study in terms of the development of the discipline.

There has already been one monumental effort in this direction—March and Simon's (1958) book, *Organizations*. The title may be a bit misleading for those who do not think of organization theory as a unified discipline, since March and Simon are very much in the individual theorist's approach. They viewed an organization as a system of decision-making individuals, and they were concerned with discovering the factors which affect the individual in making his decisions. They were insistent that it is the individual organism which mediates decision making and behavior (in contrast to the group theorists), and their variables were put in subjective terms: "the perceived consequences of evoked alternatives," "the expected value of reward," "the visibility of the organization." These are the "plans" of Miller, Galanter, and Pribram (1960); the "personal constructs" of Kelly (1955); and the March and Simon book is just as important to the present development of theoretical psychology as those two.

TECHNOLOGY THEORISTS

The techniques involved in achieving the goals of an organization, and, in industry, particularly the technology of manufacture, have generally been regarded as an important factor in organizational functioning. But there are some theorists who give it considerably greater emphasis than this, regarding it as the preemptive determinant of structure, functioning, and behavior. This approach is very much more heterogeneous than the others that have been considered, since its protagonists range from production engineers to political scientists and there are few signs that the members are aware of each others' work. Each of them has many affinities with one or other of the previous approaches, but they can be usefully classified together because their general impact on organization theory has been to underline the causal importance of technology.

At the societal level, it is the process of industrialization. This is considered by some political scientists and economic sociologists (Hoselitz, 1952) to be *the* major contemporary phenomenon. The modern world is divided into countries which are industrial and those in the process of becoming so: everything else is overshadowed by this distinction. The Soviet revolution was an instrument for industrializing Russia in one generation instead of five, and revolution is presumably serving the same purpose in China today. But when industrialization has been achieved, Communist industrial man, as he serves and is served by the same technology of manufacture, is no different from his Western capitalist counterpart.

This is an extremely global theory which is the subject of considerable dispute (Halmos, 1964). Such psychological evidence as there is (e.g., Harbison & Myers, 1960) suggests that it is a considerable oversimplification. Organizational functioning appears to be as much a product of cultural tradition as of technological level. Attitudes of managers in a highly industrialized Catholic country such as France appear to have more in common with those in a relatively poorly industrialized Catholic country like Spain than with their counterparts in the equally industrialized, but Protestant, Sweden (Haire, Ghiselli, & Porter, 1963).

At the other extreme of the individual and physiological levels, there is the whole of the tradition which has developed from the work of F. W. Taylor: time-study, work-study, industrial engineering, and ergonomics. Taylor was a production engineer who functioned in the early years of the century when mass production techniques with their consequent need for the specification and control of the process and the product were just coming to the fore. The technology also required specification and control of the human operator as well as the machine, and Taylor (1911) devised methods to achieve this. His ideas led to bitter controversy at the time over the alleged inhumanity of his system which was said to reduce men

to the level of machines, and his activities and those of his successors have remained a subject for argument. His importance for organization theory, as distinct from management techniques, is that from him has flowed the demonstration that given the right selection and training, and a suitable incentive scheme, it certainly is possible for men's working behavior to be narrowly restricted and specialized, as determined by the demands of the machine and technology. Not completely, of course; there are strikes, there is "restriction of output," there are "fiddles" on the bonus scheme. But these are relatively minor compared with the basic determinism which allowed the mass-production revolution to happen and to bring with it the consumer society. When Taylor's latest successor, the modern ergonomist, talks about man-machine systems he can do so in the knowledge that the control of the man by the machine is merely the reciprocal of the control of the machine by the man.

This is the problem of specialization at the individual level. The continual narrowing down and deskilling of man's job—the transfer of intelligence from the shop floor, as an early advocate, Elbourne (1934), called it—has been regarded as the cause of much of the malaise in modern industry and indeed in modern society (Argyris, 1960; Friedman, 1955). The advocates of "job enlargement" (Walker & Guest, 1952) are saying that the human costs of tailoring jobs completely to the demands of the machine are too high a price to pay.

At the structural level, the work of Woodward (1958, 1965) has had the most impact. As a result of a survey of manufacturing firms, she developed a scale of the technical complexity of the production systems used, running from unit production through batch and mass to process production, and found systematic relationships between a firm's technology and its pattern of organization. This led her to criticize the management theorists very strongly. Their "principles of management" have no general validity, she maintained. Even as intuitive rules of thumb, they have relevance mainly for mass-production firms: unit production firms and process firms have quite different organization structures.

By far the most sophisticated use of the concept of technology has been at the group level in the work of Trist and his colleagues at the Tavistock Institute (Trist & Bamforth, 1951; Trist, Higgin, Murray, & Pollock, 1963). From a study of the changeover from the shortwall to the longwall method of coal mining (which may be thought of roughly as being the change from the "individual craftsman" miner to the "mass-production operator" miner), Trist developed the conception of the working group as being neither a social system (as viewed by the group theorists) nor a technical system (as viewed by the engineers) but an interdependent "socio-technical" system. From this point of view, it makes as little sense to regard social relationships at work as being determined by the technology as it does to regard the manner in which a job is performed as being determined by the social psychological characteristics of the workers. The social and technical requirements are mutually interactive.

The Tavistock work has also been the most consistent in applying the systems approach in organization theory. The organization and the group have come to be regarded in the light of the cybernetic concept of an "open system" (von Bertalanffy, 1950). The systems are regarded as having inputs (resources such as raw materials, people, information), on which they operate a conversion process to produce outputs (such as products, services). Both the inputs and the outputs must take account of the environmental opportunities and demands (Rice, 1963; Emery & Trist, 1965). The systems theory approach has great potential for organization theory, particularly with its emphasis that the organization is a self-maintaining "organism" rather than a "mechanism" which can be designed and redesigned to achieve given ends. But it is the "political" impact (using the term as defined at the beginning of this paper) which is most impressive. Any concept which can be used by mathematicians (Weiner, 1948), biologists

(Ashby, 1954), physiologists (Walter, 1953), engineers (Tustin, 1953), economists (Boulding, 1956), experimental psychologists (George, 1956), social psychologists (Herbst, 1954), sociologists (Etzioni, 1960), managers (Vickers, 1957), and operational researchers (Beer, 1959), to give only one example of each, must command respect by that very fact. Saying this still allows us to keep an open mind on the wisdom of attempting to develop a general systems theory to encompass all knowledge or the usefulness of writing on the "comparative physiology of the enterprise" (Lombard, 1960).

One limitation of the technology theorists is that the concept has been systematically applied only in respect of manufacturing and extractive industry. Technology in its widest sense of techniques to achieve the purposes of the organization is clearly applicable to a much wider range. Work is beginning to extend the concept as in Thompson and Bates (1957) who compared a mine, a manufacturing plant, a hospital, and a university. But technology must be treated as one of a number of causative variables, and the main limitation of the technology theorists is their comparative devaluation of other factors. With the acceptance of multiple causation and the availability of multivariate analysis, this is a considerable lack. Even the nondeterministic approach of the Tavistock group is still highly biased in this respect. In the long run, we shall come to regard the attempt to interpret all organization functioning and behavior in relation to the technology of the means of production in the same light as we now regard the Marxist attempt to relate it all to the ownership of the means of production.

ECONOMIC THEORISTS

The traditional economic theory of the firm (Marshall, 1890) assumed that the firm was an entrepreneur operating to maximize profits in a perfectly competitive market. This "personalization" of the firm meant that problems of internal organization did not arise, and the focus was on the market viewed in terms of marginal analysis. This emphasis remained when the theory was made more complex to cover imperfect competition (Robinson, 1934) although, as Boulding (1960) has pointed out, in the imperfect situation the way in which information is obtained and processed for decision making becomes crucial. The behavior of the firm itself is now regarded as an active participator in economic decisions, rather than as a passive resultant of market forces; and this change of focus has led economists to study the problems of decision making under conditions of uncertainty.

The development of econometrics, linear programming, and game theory are formal attempts of economists to tackle this problem in mathematical terms. Their interest in organization theory also comes from its attempt to deal with psychological and sociological factors affecting decision making, and has led to the "behavioral theory of the firm" (Cyert & March, 1963), and the theory of "managerial capitalism" (Marris, 1964). The more specifically structural aspects have been discussed by Leibenstein (1960).

The interest of economists in organization theory is a very fruitful source of development. The main traffic at the moment is from social science to economics—Cyert and March, for example, may be regarded as, roughly, applied March and Simon. To an empirically oriented science like organization theory, the development of formal models derived from simulation has less impact than empirical studies of actual decisions being taken; economics has always been light on data at this level of empiricism. But this situation can be expected to change and the potential contribution of economics to organization theory is considerable. The facts that all organizations operate in an economic environment and the success or failure of many is judged on economic terms mean that the study of the context and the performance of organizations must rely primarily on economic concepts. The intriguing analysis by Goode (1960) of the phenomenon of

role conflict in organizations in terms of marginal utility theory illustrates what potential there is for cross-fertilization of ideas.

CONCLUSIONS

What lessons can be drawn for organization theory from this brief survey? There are two important ones. Organization theory must be left free to find its own problems and develop its own formulations (a) unrestricted by the need to choose managerial problems for study rather than scientific ones and (b) unfettered by artificial boundaries between established disciplines.

The need to develop by choosing scientific problems for study is basic to the establishment of any discipline. Management problems always give interesting pointers and often insightly analytic concepts for hypotheses. But these have to be tested out in systematically designed investigations if we are to carry forward the scientific process of developing new theories to cover the known facts and discovering new facts to upset the known theories. Science is essentially a theoretical venture, and in the face of outside demands a scientist should never forget that he is wedded to Lewin's dictum: "There is nothing so practical as a good theory." A continual diet of management oriented problems (selection, morale, restriction of output, resistance to change, overcentralization, productivity, etc.) with their almost inevitably ex post facto design, at best distorts, and at worst frustrates, development.

For example, the translation of the management problem of "restriction of output" into psychological terms, as "social factors affecting motivation [Hickson, 1961]," or into sociological terms, as "the development of norms in a social system [Lupton, 1963]," is not simply an unnecessary change of jargon. It is a way of bringing to bear a whole new range of variables on a much wider topic. Lupton found in a comparative study that restrictive norms prevailed in a large factory employing mainly men, whereas no restrictions were found in a small factory employing mainly women. In an effort to tease out these and other relevant factors, he then directed a study of the production norms of a large factory employing mainly women. This is the only study known to the present author, in the whole history of the investigation of this phenomenon from the Hawthorne Bank Wiring Observation Room onwards, where the investigators did not happen to come across worker restriction of output and then try to explain it *ex post facto*, but where they chose the site and the group of subjects to be studied in the light of the need to test out their own hypotheses. This is an infinitely more efficient way of developing a valid body of knowledge, and now at least we do know that size of firm is as relevant a factor as sex of operative, since girls in this large factory developed restrictive norms although not to the same extent as the men (Lupton & Cunnison, 1965).[1]

The need to develop by abolishing artificial boundaries between disciplines is vital. We have already seen how managers provide many useful insights which have to be operationalized and tested out by social scientists. One of the most common views held by practicing managers is that the structure of an organization is a reflection of the personality of its chief executive. The author knows of no evidence bearing on this hypothesis because it cannot be tackled in terms of the separate disciplines of psychology and sociology.

The sociologist, with his conceptual limitation against accepting that an individual can more than marginally affect an organization, tends to regard the hypothesis as naïve; while the psychologist's conceptual limitations make him regard the notion of organization structure with suspicion as being unreal since it cannot be reduced to behavior. But to anyone who has not had the benefit of a specifically sociological or specifically psychological training, it seems an eminently reasonable hypothesis and well worth further study. But this can only be done by people who are equally at home in the structural and individual traditions and who are therefore prepared to develop a balanced

model of the relationship between the two. Argyris (1957) and Bennis (1959) are two writers who attempted this, but there are not many as yet. An essay of the present author's on T-group training (Pugh, 1965) may be cited as an attempt to examine a topic in organization theory from a consciously interdisciplinary point of view.

Many other examples can be given of how fruitful development depends upon an interdisciplinary approach. The work of Likert (1961) on the effectiveness of employee-centered leadership contrasts strongly with the work of Fiedler (1960), who has evidence to show that the effective leader needs to be "psychologically distant" from his subordinates. That is, he must be able and prepared to evaluate his subordinates, rejecting some as being less efficient than others rather than playing down the differences between the best and the worst because "we are all members of a team together." Within a psychological frame of reference, there does not seem to be a way in which these contradictory findings can be reconciled. It was Daniel (1965) who noted that Fiedler's groups tended to be in fairly well-structured tasks—bomber and tank crews, open hearth steel gangs, baseball teams—whereas Likert, running a consultancy organization, tends to be called in to study organizations under conditions of change and stress. Daniel suggested that if we combine the study of leadership style with organization structure we might find that employee-centeredness is linked with success in organismic organizations (Burns, 1963), whereas psychological distance is linked with success in mechanistic ones. He thus opened out a fruitful line of, inevitably interdisciplinary, study.

The contribution of the individual theorists in terms of methods cannot be overestimated. Role theory, which at one time was hailed as a basic interlocking explanatory concept for all the social sciences, has in fact proved to be relatively sterile as a heuristic device (Levinson, 1959). This has to a large extent been due to its holistic use. The term has been used in a blanket way and not enough attention has been given to separating expectations from behavior and legitimate from illegitimate expectations; consensus on role definition has been assumed among groups and even in society-at-large and thus not subjected to verification. In the past few years, this picture has been completely altered by the appearance of two major studies which have applied the methods of the individual theorists to this field (Gross, Mason, & McEachern, 1958; Kahn, Wolfe, Quinn, Snoek, & Rosenthal, 1964). The concepts involved have been operationally defined and not just described, the information has been collected systematically and reliably and not just impressionistically, the data have been subjected to statistical analysis and not just discussed, and so on. As a result, role theory has again become one of the growing points of social science, and, particularly in organization theory, its explanatory power at all three levels of organization, group, and individual, is beginning to be explored.

Organization theory itself is a growth point at the present time in the social sciences. In particular, the attempt to draw from all the approaches here mentioned, and interrelate them, is proving to have considerable potential. Attempts are being made to generalize and develop the study of work organization into a consideration of the interdependence of three conceptually distinct levels of analysis of behavior in organizations: (a) organizational structure and functioning, (b) group composition and interaction, and (c) individual personality and behavior. It thus becomes possible to study a particular level of analysis, say group composition and interaction, systematically in relation to particular organizational structures, not, as so often in the past, in neglect of them (Argyris, 1964; Kahn et al., 1964; Pugh, Hickson, Hinings, MacDonald, Turner, & Lupton, 1963).

Kahn et al. (1964) concluded their important study with the view that

knowledge can best be advanced by research which attempts to deal simultaneously with data at different levels of abstraction—individual, group, and organization. This is a difficult task, and the out-come is not uniformly satisfactory. It is, nevertheless, a core requirement for understanding human organizations. Organizations are reducible to individual human acts; yet they are lawful and in part understandable only at the level of collective behaviour. This duality of level, which is the essence of human organization as it is of social psychology, we have attempted to recognize in our theoretical model and in our research design. Our hope is that the effort and its product may contribute to the understanding of organized human behaviour. We know of no more urgent problem [pp. 397–398.]

Organization theorists can only concur, grateful in the knowledge that the *Zeitgeist* is with us.

NOTE

[1] T. Lupton and S. Cunnison, personal communication, 1965. This study is at present being analyzed and prepared for publication.

REFERENCES

Argyris, C. *Personality and organization.* New York: Harper, 1957.

Argyris, C. *Understanding organizational behavior.* London: Tavistock, 1960.

Argyris, C. *Integrating the individual and the organization.* New York: Wiley, 1964.

Ashby, W. R. *Design for a brain.* London: Chapman & Hall, 1954.

Bass, B. M. *Organizational psychology.* Boston: Allyn & Bacon, 1965.

Beer, S. *Cybernetics and management.* London: English Universities Press, 1959.

Bennis, W. G. Leadership theory and administrative behavior: The problem of authority. *Administrative Science Quarterly,* 1959, 4, 259–301.

Boulding, K. E. General systems theory—A skeleton of a science. *Management Science,* 1956, **2**, 197–208.

Boulding, K. E. The present position of the theory of the firm. In K. E. Boulding & W. A. Spivey, *Linear programming and the theory of the firm.* New York: Macmillan, 1960. Pp. 1–17.

Brayfield, A. H., & Crockett, W. H. Employee attitudes and employee performance. *Psychological Bulletin,* 1955, **52**, 396–424.

Brown, W. *Exploration in management.* London: Heinemann, 1960.

Burnham, J. *The managerial revolution.* New York: Day, 1941.

Burns, T. Industry in a new age. *New Society,* 1963, No. 18, 17–20.

Burns, T., & Stalker, G. M. *The management of innovation.* London: Tavistock, 1961.

Cartwright, D. Toward a social psychology of groups. Address to the Annual Meeting of the Society for the Psychological Study of Social Issues, 1953. Quoted in R. L. Kahn & E. Boulding (Eds.), *Power and conflict in organizations.* London: Tavistock, 1964.

Cartwright, D., & Zander, A. *Group dynamics.* Evanston: Row, Peterson, 1953.

Coch, L., & French, J. P. R., Jr. Overcoming resistance to change. *Human Relations,* 1948, 1, 512–532.

Cohen, M., & Cohen, R. A. Personality as a factor in administrative decisions. *Psychiatry,* 1954, 14, 47–53.

Cyert, R., & March, J. G. *A behavioural theory of the firm.* London: Prentice-Hall, 1963.

Dahl, R. A. Business and politics: A critical appraisal of political science. In R. A. Dahl, M. Haire, & P. F. Lazarsfeld, *Social science research on business: Product and potential.* New York: Columbia University Press, 1959. Pp. 3–44.

Daniel, W. W. How close should a manager be? *New Society,* 1965, No. 158, 6–9.

Drucker, P. F. *The practice of management.* London: Heinemann, 1955.

Dubin, R. Decision-making by management in industrial relations. *American Journal of Sociology,* 1949, 54, 292–297.

Elbourne, E. *Fundamentals of industrial administration.* London: Macdonald & Evans, 1934.

Emery, F. E., & Trist, E. L. The causal texture of organizational environments. *Human Relations,* 1965, **18**, 21–32.

Etzioni, A. Two approaches to organizational analysis: A critique and a suggestion. *Administrative Science Quarterly,* 1960, 5, 257–278.

Fayol, H. *General and industrial management.* London: Pitman, 1949.

Fiedler, F. E. The leader's psychological distance and group effectiveness. In D. Cartwright & A. Zander (Eds.), *Group dynamics.* (2nd ed.) Evanston: Row, Peterson, 1960. Pp. 586–606.

Fleishman, E. A. Leadership climate, human relations training, and supervisory behavior. *Personnel Psychology,* 1953, **6**, 205–222.

French, J. R. P., Jr. A formal theory of social power. *Psychological Review,* 1956, **63**, 181–194.

Friedmann, G. *Industrial society: The emergence of human problems of automation.* Glencoe: Free Press, 1955.

George, F. H. Logical networks and behavior. *Bulletin of Mathematical Biophysics*, 1956, **18**, 337–348.

Goldstein, J. *The government of British trade unions.* London: Allen & Unwin, 1952.

Goode, W. J. A theory of role strain. *American Sociological Review*, 1960, **25**, 483–496.

Gouldner, A. W. *Patterns of industrial bureaucracy.* London: Routledge & Kegan Paul, 1955.

Gross, N., Mason, W. S., & McEachern, A. W. *Explorations in role analysis.* New York: Wiley, 1958.

Haire, M., Ghiselli, E. E., & Porter, L. W. Cultural patterns in the role of the manager. *Industrial Relations*, 1963, **2**, 95–117.

Halmos, P. (Ed.) *The development of industrial societies.* (The Sociological Review Monograph No. 8) Keele: University of Keele Press, 1964.

Harbison, F., & Myers, C. *Management in the industrial world.* New York: McGraw-Hill, 1960.

Hebb, D. O. *The organization of behavior.* New York: Wiley, 1949.

Herbst, P. G. The analysis of social flow systems. *Human Relations*, 1954, **1**, 327–353.

Heron, A. Satisfaction and satisfactoriness: Complementary aspects of occupational adjustment. *Occupational Psychology*, 1954, **28**, 140–153.

Herzberg, F., Mausner, B., & Snyderman, B. *The motivation to work.* (2nd ed.) New York: Wiley, 1959.

Hickson, D. J. Motivation of work people who restrict their output. *Occupational Psychology*, 1961, **35**, 111–121.

Holt, H., & Salverson, M. E. Psychoanalytic processes in management. In C. W. Churchman & M. Verhulst (Eds.), *Management sciences: Models and techniques.* Vol. 2. Oxford: Pergamon Press, 1960. Pp. 45–66.

Homans, G. *The human group.* London: Routledge & Kegan Paul, 1951.

Hoselitz, B. F. (Ed.) *The progress of underdeveloped areas.* Chicago: University of Chicago Press, 1952.

Jaques, E. *The changing culture of a factory.* London: Tavistock, 1951.

Kahn, R. L. Productivity and job satisfaction. *Personnel Phychology*, 1960, **13**, 275–287.

Kahn, R. L. Field studies of power in organizations. In R. L. Kahn & E. Boulding, *Power and conflict in organizations.* London: Tavistock, 1964. Pp. 52–66.

Kahn, R. L., Wolfe, D., Quinn, R., Snoek, J. D., & Rosenthal, R. A. *Organizational stress.* New York: Wiley, 1964.

Kelly, G. A. *The psychology of personal constructs.* New York: Norton, 1955.

Kerr, C., & Fisher, L. H. Plant sociology: The elite and the aborigines. In M. Komarovsky (Ed.), *Common frontiers of the social sciences.* Glencoe: Free Press, 1957. Pp. 281–309.

Komarovsky, M. (Ed.) *Common frontiers of the social sciences.* Glencoe: Free Press, 1957.

Kuhn, H. W. The Hungarian method for the assignment problem. *Naval Research Logistics Quarterly*, 1955, **1**, 83–97.

Landsberger, H. A. *Hawthorne revisited.* New York: Cornell University Press, 1958.

Leibenstein, H. *Economic theory and organizational analysis.* New York: Harper, 1960.

Levinson, D. J. Role, personality and the social structure in the organizational setting. *Journal of Abnormal and Social Psychology*, 1959, **58**, 170–181.

Lewin, K. Forces behind food habits and methods of change. *Bulletin of the National Research Council*, 1943, **108**, 35–65.

Lewin, K., Lippit, R., & White, R. K. Patterns of aggressive behavior in experimentally created "social climates." *Journal of Social Psychology*, 1939, **10**, 271–299.

Likert, R. *New patterns of management.* New York: McGraw-Hill, 1961.

Lombard, R. *La Physiologie Comparée de L'Entreprise.* Paris: Editions d'Organization, 1960.

Layton, T. *On the shop floor.* Oxford. Pergamon Press, 1963.

March, J. G., & Simon, H. A. *Organizations.* New York: Wiley, 1958.

Marris, R. *The economic theory of "managerial" capitalism.* London: Macmillan, 1964.

Marshall, A. *Principles of economics.* London: Macmillan, 1890. (8th ed. 1920, reprinted 1947)

Mayo, E. *The human problems of industrial civilization.* New York: Macmillan, 1933.

Meehl, P. E. *Clinical versus statistical prediction.* Minneapolis: University of Minnesota Press, 1954.

Merton, R. K. Bureaucratic structure and personality. *Social Forces,* 1940, **18**, 560–568.

Miller, G. A., Galanter, E., & Pribram, K. H. *Plans and the structure of behavior.* New York: Holt, 1960.

Porter, L. W., & Henry, M. M. Job attitudes in management: Perceptions of the input of certain personality traits as a function of job level. *Journal of Applied Psychology*, 1964, **48**, 31–36.

Porter, L. W., & Lawler, E. E. The effects of "tall" versus "flat" organization structures on managerial job satisfaction. *Personnel Psychology*, 1964, **17**, 135–148.

Porter, L. W., & Lawler, E. E. Properties of organizational structure in relation to job attitudes and job behavior. *Psychological Bulletin*, 1965, **64**, 23–51.

Pugh, D. S. T-group training from the point of view of organization theory. In G. Whitaker (Ed.), *T-group training: Group dynamics in management education.* (A.T.M. Occasional Paper No. 2) Oxford: Blackwell, 1965. Pp. 44–50.

Pugh, D. S., Hickson, D. J., & Hinings, C. R. *Writers on organizations.* London: Hutchinson, 1964.

Pugh, D. S., Hickson, D. J., Hinings, C. R., MacDonald, K. M., Turner, C., & Lupton, T. A conceptual scheme for organizational analysis. *Administrative Science Quarterly*, 1963, **6**, 289–315.

Robinson, J. *The economics of imperfect competition.* London: Macmillan, 1934.

Roethlisberger, F. J., & Dickson, W. J. *Management and the worker.* Massachusetts: Harvard University Press, 1939.

Rodger, A. Industrial psychology. In, *Chambers Encyclopaedia.* Vol. 7. London: Newnes, 1950. Pp. 542–548.

Rogers, K. *Managers—Personality and performance.* London: Tavistock, 1963.

Rolfe, J. M., & Corkindale, K. G. The influence of the excluded variable. *Bulletin of the British Psychological Society*, 1964, **17**, 31–38.

Rice, A. K. *The enterprise and its environment.* London: Tavistock, 1963.

Schein, E. H. *Organizational psychology.* Englewood Cliffs, N. J.: Prentice-Hall, 1965.

Selznick, P. *TVA and the grass roots.* Berkeley: University of California Press, 1949.

Shils, E. A. Primary groups in the American army. In R. K. Merton & P. F. Lazarsfeld (Eds.), *Continuities in social research.* Glencoe: Free Press, 1950. Pp. 16–39.

Simon, H. A. *Administrative behavior.* (2nd ed.) New York: Macmillan, 1957.

Smith, M. B. Anthropology and psychology. In J. Gillin (Ed.), *For a science of social man.* New York: Macmillan, 1954. Pp. 19–23.

Sykes, A. J. M. The effect of a supervisory training course in changing supervisor's perceptions and expectations of the role of management. *Human Relations,* 1962, **15,** 227–243.

Tannenbaum, A. S. Control in organizations: Individual adjustment and organizational performance. *Administrative Science Quarterly,* 1962, **7,** 236–257.

Tannenbaum, A. S., & Smith, C. G. Effects of member influence in an organization: Phenomenology versus organization structure. *Journal of Abnormal and Social Psychology,* 1964, **69,** 401–410.

Taylor, F. W. *Principles of scientific management.* New York: Harper, 1911. (Reprinted: In F. W. Taylor, *Scientific management.* New York: Harper, 1947. Pp. 5–143.)

Thompson, J. D., & Bates, F. L. Technology, organization and administration. *Administrative Science Quarterly,* 1957, **2,** 325–343.

Trist, E. L., & Bamforth, K. W. Some social and psychological consequences of the longwall method of coal-getting. *Human Relations,* 1951, **4,** 3–38.

Trist, E. L., Higgin, G. W., Murray, H., & Pollock, A. B. *Organization choice.* London: Tavistock, 1963.

Tustin, A. *The mechanism of economic systems.* London: Heinemann, 1953.

Vickers, Sir G. Control, stability and choice. *General Systems,* 1957, **2,** 1–8.

von Bertanlanffy, L. The theory of open systems in physics and biology. *Science,* 1950, **111,** 23–29.

Walker, C. R., & Guest, R. *The man on the assembly line.* Cambridge, Mass.: Harvard University Press, 1952.

Walter, W. G. *The living brain.* London: Duckworth, 1953.

Weber, M. *The theory of social and economic organization.* Glencoe: Free Press, 1947.

Weiner, N. *Cybernetics.* New York: Wiley, 1948.

Whyte, W. F. *Human relations in the restaurant industry.* New York: McGraw-Hill, 1948.

Whyte, W. H. *The organization man.* New York: Simon & Schuster, 1956.

Wilson, S. A sociological case-study of operator training. *Occupational Psychology,* 1959, **3,** 166–172, 244–254.

Woodward, J. *Management and technology.* London: Her Majesty's Stationery Office, 1958.

Woodward, J. *Industrial organization: Theory and practice.* Oxford: Oxford University Press, 1965.

Wrong, D. The oversocialized conception of man in modern sociology. *American Sociological Review,* 1961, **26,** 183–193.

PART
TWO

THEORY
IN
ADMINISTRATION

Each theory presented in this section offers a powerful, albeit unique, means for increased understanding of administrative behavior and its subsequent organizational response. Yet none possesses the comprehensiveness to be considered *the* theory of administration. As Halpin has suggested, "there is more than one gate to the kingdom of knowledge. Each gate opens upon a different vista, but no one exhausts the realm of reality—whatever that might be."[1] That the editors subscribe to this suggestion is evident from the diversity of selections included in this section.

Fully developed, theories of administration encompass but are not limited to organization theory. Organization theory is concerned with the organization qua organization often without regard to the individual. Further the focus of organization theory tends to be on what is—although Hage's axiomatic theory (in Part 1) suggests future-time effects of changes in structural variables as well as provides a useful framework for understanding past- and present-time differences. To the "organization" and "is" perspectives, administrative theory has potential for adding variables associated with the behavioral and value dimensions implicit in administrative organization.

To date, the theory literature in administration is marked by a vast range of ideas moving on a continuum from statements of simple relationships to complex axiomatic propositions each possessing delimiting qualifications. The range of theory usage is equally as broad. The conceptually oriented practitioner's use of theory, for example, differs markedly from that of the

[1] Andrew W. Halpin, "Ways of Knowing," in Roald F. Campbell and James M. Lipham (eds.), *Administrative Theory as a Guide to Action*, Midwest Administration Center, University of Chicago, Chicago, 1960, p. 3.

theoretician who seeks to create new knowledge. A third, appropriate but again different, usage of administrative theory is its application by the empirical researcher. Implicitly, the practitioner is assumed to be utilizing theory at a lower level than either the researcher or the theoretician. A more apt assumption, which we suggest, is that the varied usages of theory are parallel and complementary. Each requires different but nonetheless complex skills. The viability of conceptual practice, theoretically based empirical research, and continued theory development depends, to a large extent, on their interdependence.

The value of conceptual theory to the practitioner is lucidly portrayed by Miller as he addresses school administrators. Students of educational administration will find "The Practical Art of Using Theory" a useful bridge between their own intuitive approaches to administrative problems and the more systematic approaches which follow in this section.

"Administration as Decision-making" by Griffiths presents an overview of theory development in education and suggests a definition of "good theory." The Griffiths article then presents a theory of administration which uses decision making as a focus for analysis. Griffiths' pioneering work in the development of educational theory and his resultant development of a decision-making theory are bench marks against which subsequent theory is measured.

McGregor's "The Human Side of Enterprise" portays his classic theory X and theory Y formulations as alternative approaches to management. Mc-Gregor's two approaches are based on different assumptions managers hold about their subordinates. He maintains that theory X assumptions lead to theory X management behavior and to theory X subordinate responses. A change in management behavior or subordinate response from theory X to theory Y requires a commensurate change in managerial assumptions. McGregor's theory and its self-fulfilling prophecy have much to merit one's attention. Of particular interest is his reliance on Maslow's theory of human need.

The articles remaining compose a package which presents and critiques two theories of administration. The first paper, Stogdill's "Individual Behavior and Group Achievement," represents a summary of his book of the same title. Stogdill utilizes a systems framework of inputs, throughputs, and outputs as he views the group as a focal point in his development of a "middle-range theory" of administration.

The second paper, Sweitzer's "Assessment of Two Theoretical Frameworks," builds an assessment schema for evaluating administrative theory, applies the schema to the middle-range Stogdill theory and to the Getzels and Guba social-systems formulation, and suggests questions and propositions for further study.

Sweitzer's summary and presentation of the Getzels and Guba formulation is particularly noteworthy in that this theory has received the most acclaim and broadest usage in educational administration.

10.

THE PRACTICAL ART OF USING THEORY

VAN MILLER

The difference between the "practical" and the "theoretical" in school administration and the relationship between the two is up for renewed discussion. This kind of argument used to be pretty much localized to exchanges between professors and their students. When they left the campus, many students felt they had escaped the ivory tower of theory to enter the "real" world of practice.

This is no longer the case.

Interest in practical theory and in sound theoretical practice has been widely stirred within the past few years. The studies and conferences of the Cooperative Project on Educational Administration has related practitioners and professors directly and in great number. This relationship promises to continue as the Committee for the Advancement of School Administration extends consideration of what is good practice and what is sound theory throughout the profession nationally. Impetus to this renewed discussion was provided through development of *Administrative Behavior in Education*, a book sponsored by the National Conference of Professors of Educational Administration.

Just how does theory relate to the work of the practicing school administrator?

THEORY IN CONTEXT

The directional title of this article is intended to provide a basis for keeping the consideration of theory in proper context. Note that it

From Van Miller, "The Practical Art of Using Theory," *The School Executive*, 77:60–63, 1958. Used by permission of the Buttenheim Press.

starts with practice and returns to practice; in this form it is a continuing process since the arrows can lead through the cycle over and over. Practice is real and tangible. Of the items in the title only practice can actually be seen or experienced; the rest are verbalisms and must be thought about or they have no existence.

This title might have been written in a number of ways, each of which would represent relationships existing somewhere in educational administration.

It might have been written simply: PRACTICES→ PRACTICE. (Some one will paraphrase this as "monkey see—monkey do!") Practice spreads just because it exists. School is held five days a week because other schools hold school five days a week. The band gets uniforms because the school band in the next town has uniforms. Program and procedures are added because other schools do it that way. Frequently a proposal for some change or addition is challenged simply by "where else is this being done?" This is a blind-leading-the-blind kind of school administration.

It might have been written: PRACTICES→ HUNCH→ PRACTICE. Such an arrangement indicates that various practices are considered and then some hunch is followed in selecting one which will best suit the situation. If it fails the next best hunch is tried.

It might have been written: PRACTICES→ HUNCHES→ PRINCIPLES→ PRACTICE. The addition of principles implies that hunches and experience have been reviewed and abstracted to establish some guides or rules to use in the selection of the most appropriate hunch to follow. This stage is a step beyond trial and error. By drawing up principles to guide action the chance of a wrong choice is reduced and the inefficiency of merely trying one practice after another is avoided. Administration is making better use of its experience.

When it is written: PRACTICES→ HUNCHES→ THEORY→ PRINCIPLES→ PRACTICE, a new step in efficiency is reached. Theory provides a rational and systematic view of the situation and serves as a guide in the selection of principles. But it is the hunches and the principles which are tested through practice. The results of practice either support or question the theory. Theories about the nature of electrical energy or light or the causes of disease have had to be modified from time to time or even replaced, but each theory was useful in the establishment of principles upon which to base practice. An acquaintance who knows the physical sciences well has said that theory is not the truth but is a rational scaffolding from which men can work with the truth. He pointed out that this scaffolding needs repair from time to time.

The directional title might have been written in still other ways. Some would leave out the formulation of principles. Some would include experimenting as a step in the process. If it starts with practice and returns to practice the verbal-mental activity will be considered in context.

IDEAS VIA WORDS

It may pay to digress for a moment to consider the use of language not only in communication but as the means by which we think. Through the use of words the human mind can consider ideas. As words become more abstract they are symbols embracing more experience and are therefore more efficient (unless they become so remote from reality that they have lost their meaning for the user). There is a corresponding progression from practice to theory. Einsteinian theory may be too remote for most of us to understand, but for those who do it provides an efficient way to think of physical force and the variety of interactions within physical science.

The process represented in the directional title may be carried all the way through by a good practicing school administrator individually. Or by a scholar working in cooperation with practicing administrators. Or parts of the process may be done by individuals. Some may practice; some may observe and state their hunches about practice; some may state principles of administration based on hunches and/or derived from theory; some may theorize. By whatever arrangement the process is carried out, the usefulness of those who formulate principles or who theorize is dependent upon their relationship to and their communication with those who practice.

You can administer without using theory, e.g.:

practices——▶ practice

> This is monkey-see-monkey-do operation. Your practices are rooted in custom. When something new is proposed, you ask, ''Where else is it being done?''

practices——▶ hunch——▶ practice

> The addition of a hunch shows at least that you're thinking.

practices——▶ hunches——▶ principles——▶ practice

> Here you use experience to form guides in selecting the most appropriate hunch. This takes you a step beyond trial and error.

practices——▶ hunches——▶ theory——▶ principles——▶ practice

> **but...**
> With theory, you've reached a new step in efficiency. It provides you with a rational view of the situation and serves as a guide in the selection of principles. (This article suggests some of the practical uses of theory that can help you as a practicing school administrator.)

USEFULNESS OF THEORIZING

In a graduate seminar on administrative leadership one of the members complained of the "impractical level" of much of the group discussion. When pressed for practical content he would describe a situation encountered in his teaching experience that he had already acted upon. The group found, however, that merely discussing a problem already solved or disposed of was impractical; that unless they theorized on the basis of the elements in the problem they would have only an already-used answer of no further value unless the identical situation should recur. But by theorizing they could have some means of coping with tomorrow's problem when it did come up. They convinced their colleague that nothing was as practical as good theory.

Theorizing as urged by the members of this class is more inclusive than the delineation of pure theory. It represents the common garden variety of thoughtful mental consideration of administration which should be characteristic of all concerned with it. It includes all the words between the two "practices" in the directional title. Theory in this broad sense is what concerns us here.

UNIFYING ASPECT OF THEORIZING

Because of the diversity of personalities and circumstances, discussions of what was done or should be done can be divisive. But the discussion of these experiences in terms of theory or the direct discussion of theory can be unifying. When talk is only at the level of practice, the critic is likely to judge in terms of similarity or dissimilarity to his own behavior. He may say to himself that he could never get by with that in his situation and throw away a bit of experience shared which would have been useful in considering the validity of a hunch or principle or theory.

Talk only at the level of practice tends therefore to establish a divisive atmosphere with each privately thinking himself right and others wrong so that each individual might be expected to grow even more stubborn in his own behavior.

When the attempt in discussion is to generalize upon experiences reported as a means of sharing them to build theory, each can then draw upon the theory in terms of understanding better and improving his own performance in the specific situations in which he is responsible. Such an approach to professional communication is unifying for it has use for the variety of experiences each brings into the discussion.

Professional discussion at the level of theory leaves room for—in fact, it must take into account—the individual differences of those involved. This is unifying. It calls for understanding and accepting rather than for judging and rejecting. Standard organization and procedures derived only from practice may use only fragments of people. Sound theory of human behavior or of school administration leaves room for individual freedom.

FOCUSING ASPECT OF THEORY

When professional exchange is only at the level of practice or at the level of hunches about practices, administrators may be so busy doing all of the chores that have become their lot that they have no time nor basis for thinking about whether they should even be *doing* such tasks at all. Frequently the choice depends upon time available, and in administrative staffing frequently a new position is added only

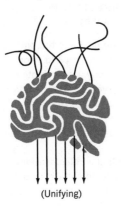

(Unifying)

because the array of chores and routine have become more than present staff can handle.

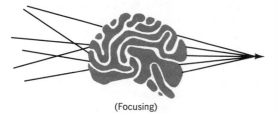

(Focusing)

Some studies report administrators acting in response to a variety of pressures. A theory of educational administration would provide the basis for some organization of these chores and pressures. As the priorities in administration and the interrelationship of tasks are developed through theorizing, relief will be provided from many present tensions and uncertainties.

Two potential outcomes of such theorizing may already be discerned. Articles, studies and reports have appeared on the role of the school administrator. These are different from the earlier lists of duties of school principals or responsibilities of school superintendents. They combine experience and thinking to give focus to the position so that the holder is not confronted by an unending array of seemingly unrelated and sometimes conflicting chores and obligations. Rather he has formulated a view of his job or task and can use this as the basis for determining which chores he shall do and with what priority.

Theorizing about administration has also provided more consideration of the inter-relationship among staff members so that a team approach to administration is possible. This is more unifying and provides a basis for communication which coordinates activities in contrast to the earlier lists of duties which served as job descriptions of each specific position and thus separated activities.

EXTENDING ASPECT OF THEORY

The manner in which a cooperatively developed theory of educational administration would ex-tend knowledge in the field, and extend the participation of scholars in studying administration, should also be noted. As theory provided a table of chemical elements, gaps were exposed which directed research into areas where new knowledge was needed. As theory of astro-physics advanced, new stars were located. As germ theory of disease developed it opened new possibilities for study and identification. As a theory of educational administration develops we should find value in a systematic arrangement both of what we do know and what we need to know.

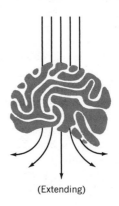

(Extending)

This kind of systematization will also serve as an open invitation to scholars from related disciplines to bring their competence and insights to bear upon educational administration.

THEORY IS DIFFERENT IN BEHAVIORAL SCIENCES

In this technological age the pattern for "good" theory is frequently cited from the physical sciences. The physical scientist is always an external observer and the material under investigation does not understand the experiment. This represents two major differences for theory development in the behavioral sciences.

The individual subjects under consideration are automotive and self-determining in responding to the experiment or to the circumstances of the investigation. The investigator, a human like the subjects of his investigation, will find detachment for the sake of objectivity difficult to obtain—and frequently, if such detachment is approached, the investigator fails to get the inside view necessary to really interpret and apply the results of the investigation.

This latter difference is likely to be a real advantage in the behavioral sciences and the shibboleth of objectivity so urgent in the *physical* sciences may call for reinterpretation.

The development of theory, rather than the standardization of roles and procedures, is necessary for the development of professional school administration. Standardization of roles and procedures puts the administrator in the position of doing what he must do; adequate theory gives him a basis for contemplating what he can do and how he can do it more effectively. Standardization of roles and procedures invites scape-goating or concern for who or what is to blame. Adequate theory will encourage seeing what can be done and how it can be done better.

We do not have the question of how we can put theory into practice, but rather the question of how we can use theory to better understand and thereby improve practice.

11.

ADMINISTRATION AS DECISION-MAKING

DANIEL E. GRIFFITHS

[The remainder of Griffiths book] is devoted to a presentation and discussion of a theory of administration. There is, of course, no intention of creating the impression that this is a story in its final form; rather, it is a statement which is offered for criticism and improvement. Theories are made to be superseded, and this one is no exception.

With this in mind, the purpose of [this reading] is to state assumptions which constitute the theory, develop certain relevant concepts, and present a set of propositions. [The next chapter in Griffiths' book] is devoted to an elaboration of certain aspects of the theory and the implications of the theory.

STATEMENT OF A THEORY OF ADMINISTRATION

[It has been stated] that the use of the term *theory* would be restricted to that meaning assigned to it by Feigl, namely: "a set of assumptions from which can be derived by purely logico-mathematical procedures a larger set of empirical laws." The assumptions should be of such a character as to explain fully and completely the nature of the pheonomenon under consideration, in this case, administration. The exposition of this theory takes the form of a declarative statement of each assumption followed by a brief explanation.

From Daniel E. Griffths, *Administrative Theory*, Appleton-Century-Crofts, Inc., New York, 1959, pp. 71–91. Copyright © 1959 by Appleton-Century-Crofts, Inc. Reprinted by permission of Appleton-Century-Crofts, Division of Meredith Corporation.

1. *Administration is a generalized type of behavior to be found in all human organizations.* Administration is a term used to describe an aspect of life in a social organization. Since there is no aspect of living unrelated to a social organization, administration is an integral part of all human life. A logical deduction from this assumption is that the adjectival varieties of administration are more alike than different. This means that there must be a departure from the over-concern in the field of educational administration with the adjective. Not only have we been concerned almost exclusively with the adjective *educational*, but we have been spending our time looking at, for instance, the field of secondary school administration and saying that it differs substantially from elementary school administration. This is carried even farther in that a separation is created within secondary education. For example, it is not at all uncommon to separate the teaching of the administration of health and physical education programs from that of other high school departments, such as English or mathematics, to say nothing of the complete separation of vocational administrators from all other educators. If the difference between educational and public administration, for instance, can be termed *adjectival*, then the difference between secondary and elementary educational administration can be called *subadjectival*. When one starts to compare the content of these various areas of administration, one finds almost complete duplication. In a study carried out at a large university, the dean reported that there were ten different departments teaching various varieties of educational administration, and they duplicated each others' offerings to the extent of 90 per cent. In all probability the same situation exists at most other universities.

No strong case can be made for the *exclusive* study of adjectival administration, and no cast at all can be made for the exclusive study of subadjectival administration! With this assumption we shall proceed to talk about administration using particular fields for illustrative purposes. There will, however, be no attempt made to indicate that any particular thesis is drawn exclusively from any one adjectival area of administration.

2. Administration is the process of directing and controlling life in a social organization. This assumption means that administration is the implementation of the purposes for which an organization is designed through such procedures as establishing criteria for the performance of individuals as they live in the organization and establishing controls to make certain that performance agrees with plans. Administration is not an artificial function superimposed on the normal activities of human beings; it is rather the process (cycle of events) engaged in by the members of a social organization in order to control and direct the activities of the members within the organization. Administration occurs whenever the life processes of an organization are being controlled. In contrast to this, it can be said that administration is not the production of the organization. Barnard indicated this quite clearly when he said, "Executive work is not that of the organization, but the specialized work of *maintaining* the organization in operation."[1] This leads into the next assumption.

3. The specific function of administration is to develop and regulate the decision-making process in the most effective manner possible. It is sometimes assumed that the function of the chief executive officer is to *make* decisions, generally by himself because others are incompetent. This is not the basic assumption of this theory; rather it is the assumption that it is the function of the executive to see to it that the decision process proceeds in an effective manner. (An effective manner is one which results in the accomplishment of a stated objective.) In fact, the executive is called upon to make decisions only when the organization fails to make its own decisions. To put this into other words, if the executive is personally making decisions this means that there exists malfunctioning in the decision process. The executive then needs to correct the malfunctioning. Barnard was referring to this point

when he said:[2] "It is the organization, not the executive, which does the work on the external environment. The executive is primarily concerned with decisions which facilitate or hinder in the effective or efficient operation of the organization."

4. The administrator works with groups or with individuals with a group referent, not with individuals as such. An administrator interacts with others in the organization primarily in terms of the *group* to which others belong. The school administrator's perception of X is of a member of a teaching group, rather than Miss X as a unique individual. The same is true of his perception of other administrators in the organization. Subordinates rebel against this perception of the administrator, and the rebellion has taken the form of strong unions in industry and the strengthening of teachers' organizations in education. The interesting point is that the worker joins the union to develop "self" but rather quickly finds that he is perceived the same way in the union as he is in industry. This, no doubt, is one of the major reasons why unions are now having the same organizational problems that management is having.

The administrator perceives others in the same way; for instance, he regards board members as members of the board of education rather than as individuals. Officers of the Parent-Teacher Association change each year; yet the perception of the officers remains much the same from year to year. In other words, administrators are oriented to groups, not individuals.

CONCEPT DEVELOPMENT

In order to work with the assumptions stated above, it is necessary to have a set of working tools or concepts. The concepts must be relevant to the theory, must be stated clearly, must be used wherever the same idea is being discussed, and must be operational. Their meanings must correspond to empirically observable facts or situations. The concepts actually provide the building blocks of the theory, and the theory can be no stronger than its concepts.

Decision-making

The key concept in this discussion is that of directing and controlling the decision-making process. It is not only central in the sense that it is more important than other functions, as some writers have indicated; it is also central in that *all* other functions of administration can best be interpreted in terms of the decision-making process. Decision-making is becoming generally recognized as the heart of organization and the process of administration. Mc-Cammy states this clearly and concisely: "The making of decisions is at the very center of the process of administration, and the discussion of administration will be more systematic if we accept a framework for the analysis of decision-making."[3] Simon caps his argument on this line by stating: "A general theory of administration must include principles of organization that will insure correct decision-making, just as it must include principles that will insure effective action."[4] Livingston, using the term *management as administration* is used in this paper, states:[5]

If we expand the concept of decision-making to include, on the one hand, the process by which the decision is arrived at, and on the other hand, to include the process by which we implement or make the decision "work," and if we further recognize that this is a continuing, dynamic process rather than an occasional event, then decisioning means something quite different than heretofore and becomes the basis of all managerial action.

Such a statement calls for an explanation of the concept of decision and a clarification of the extent and content of the decision-making process.

One approach to a definition is to employ the one used by the dictionary. In this case we have: "A settling or terminating, as of a controversy, by giving judgment on the matter; also, a conclusion arrived at after consideration." It can be seen that a decision is essentially a judicial proceeding—that is, a state of affairs is present, and a judgment is made concerning it. The judgment is such as to influence action which results from the decision. Action is implicit in a decision. The judgment is made so that a course of action will be influenced.

Decisions are closely interrelated with action. A decision may alter the present course of such action, that is, change the direction of action to a noticeable degree. A decision may adjust a present course of action, merely correct it; or a decision may be made to permit the present course of action to continue.

Decisions are totally pragmatic in nature—that is, the value of a decision is dependent upon the success of the action which follows it. Since all rational action is in terms of goals, the value of a decision is related to the degree to which the goals are attained.

In the dictionary definition above there is the implication that a decision is a time consuming matter. It is explicit that a decision follows a period of consideration. It is possible for the period of time to be minimal and consideration to be of a fleeting nature. A decision does not, by its nature, have to be a long and painful process. In fact, if a state of affairs is judged very quickly and with little deliberate thought, what would it then be called? The term *decision* is to be applied to all *judgments which affect a course of action.*

The concept *decision-making process* is therefore construed to mean not only the decision but also the acts necessary to put the decision into operation and so actually affect the course of action of an enterprise.

SEQUENTIAL DECISIONS. Practically every decision is one of a series. That is to say, practically every decision is one of a *sequence*. It is almost impossible to determine which decision on a certain state of affairs was the original decision. Furthermore, it is almost impossible to determine which decision of all those made is a unique one. Each decision made appears to tie into another decision

reached previously. From this we note the sequential and interrelated nature of decision. This is a deviation from the dictionary or commonly accepted definition in that a decision rarely terminates or settles a controversy; it alters, changes its direction, or sometimes prolongs it.

Probably the clearest illustration of sequential decision-making is found in the law. The essence of the judicial process is found in the *precedent*. Each decision is based upon one or more previous decisions. Only the introduction of new knowledge of tremendous impact will cause a change in the direction which the sequence of decisions takes. The sequence of judicial decisions is of such a pronounced nature as to warrant being characterized as the "seamless web of the law."

All organization is built around a system of sequential decisions. Those who effect the decisions are functioning as administrators.

Organization

All administration takes place within the context of an organization. In the discussion of administration, organization is subsumed. It is a vitally important subtopic under the subject of administration as administration is concerned with the control and direction of living in a social organization. What is meant by organization? First, we shall recognize that we are concerned primarily with two types of organization, the *formal* and the *informal*, and incidentally with a third type which is neither.

Formal organization is construed to mean an ensemble of individuals who perform distinct but interrelated and coordinated functions in order that one or more tasks can be completed. Thus, we have the business organization, the governmental bureau, the hospital, the public school. In each type of organization the task is more or less clearly understood by the general public. It is obvious that organizations result, in part at least, as a consequence of division of labor in society. It then follows that any *one* organization functions as part of a larger social system. The task of the organization must have value for the larger social system if that system is to tolerate the organization's development.

Why is it that organizations take the form they do? Why do separate organizations have so much in common? Why, on the other hand, are there differences among organizations? Parsons gives us the insight which might answer these questions:[6]

> In its internal reference, the primacy of goal-attainment among the functions of a social system gives priority to those processes most directly involved with the success or failure of goal oriented endeavors. *This means essentially the decision-making process* [italics are the author's], which controls the utilization of the resources of the system as a whole in the interest of the goal, and the processes by which those responsible for such decisions can count on the mobilization of those resources in the interest of a goal. These mechanisms of mobilization constitute what we ordinarily think of as the development of power in a political sense.

Organizations take their common form from the decision-making process, and their differences occur in the modifications of the process as required by their task and the way in which the public perceives the task. As one example, the monolithic nature of the military organization is determined by the narrow task and the absolute necessity for unidimensional decision-making. There is no time for argument in the heat of battle. In hospitals we observe two lines of decision-making, one professional through the doctors, the other semiprofessional through the hospital administrator or manager. The *need* for two types of decisions gives form to the kind of hospital organization which we now have. In the public schools the decision-making process is almost wholly prescribed by state legislatures and arises largely out of prudential considerations. A business organization does not differ *primarily* from a school organization in that one is a profit-making organization and the other is not; the difference resides in dissimilarities in the decision-mak-

ing process. This is a difference of *substance*, not *form*.

Let us note how the issues in organization can be resolved on the basis of a decision-centered theory. For instance, should an organization be tall or flat? This issue should be decided on the basis of what one believes concerning decision-making. If one wants decisions made on a decentralized basis, made by those close to the problems, then a flat organization is built. If one wants decisions made on a highly centralized basis then a tall organization is imperative.

The span of control issue can be resolved in much the same fashion. Instead of asking the question, "How many persons should report to the administrator?" we should ask, "Who is responsible for what kind of decisions?" Structure should be related to the decision-making process, not to the number of human relationships which a mathematician believes an administrator can remember.[7] A small span of control is no doubt necessary in the military where the general staff makes decisions of a far-reaching nature affecting the actions of all in its command. The general himself needs greater control over the decisions made by subordinates in order to mobilize all of the organization's resources toward a narrow objective. In a university, the professor makes many decisions for himself which in the military would be made for him. The soldier is told what type of uniform is to be worn during each hour of the day. If, for instance, it appears to the soldier that it might rain, he does not have to decide whether to wear a raincoat—he merely waits until he hears the uniform of the day announced over the loud speaker. On the other hand, the professor makes practically all decisions as regards his clothing, hours of work (outside assigned teaching hours), and similar concerns. He also decides by himself what references to use, what to teach, and how to teach it. The soldier has no choice as to what he does—the professor, almost complete choice. This difference in choice is reflected in the organization of each institution. Many more professors report

to a dean than soldiers report to a military officer because of the difference in the nature and number of decisions made by each administrator in controlling the decisions made by others.

A rather obvious use of the concept that organizations are built in terms of the way in which decisions are to be made is in determining the degree of decentralization existing in an institution. In discussing this point Dale says:[8]

We may say that the degree of managerial decentralization in a company is the greater:

1. The greater the number of decisions made lower down the management hierarchy.
2. The more important the decisions made down the management hierarchy. For example, the greater the sum of capital expenditure that can be approved by the plant manager without consulting anyone else, the greater the degree of decentralization in this field.
3. The more functions affected by decisions made at lower levels. Thus companies which permit only operational decisions to be made at separate branch plants are less decentralized than those which also permit financial and personal decisions at branch plants.
4. The less checking required on the decision. Decentralization is greatest when no check at all must be made; less when superiors have to be informed of the decision after it has been made; still less if superiors have to be consulted *before* the decision is made. The fewer people to be consulted, and the lower they are on the management heirarchy, the greater the degree of decentralization.

This is a clear example of the use of decision-making in the analysis of an organization after it has been in existence. The organization could be built in accordance with convictions as to how decisions should be made, and no doubt, many are built in just this manner, as witness General Electric, General Motors, and Sears, Roebuck.

An understanding of the decision-making

process in a particular enterprise is the key to its organizational structure.

An *informal organization* is present in every formal organization and is the system of interpersonal relations which forms to affect decisions made in the formal organization. This informal system is omitted from the formal scheme or is in opposition to it. The informal organization is a dynamic structure composed of special interest groups. In the past, the concept has been that of constant change—the informal structure being subject to continual revision as new decisions face the formal organization. For example, Barnard states:[9]

informal organization is indefinite and rather structureless, and has not definite subdivision. It may be regarded as a shapeless mass of quite varied densities, the variation in density being a result of external factors affecting the closeness of people geographically or of formal purposes which bring them specially into contact for conscious joint accomplishments. These areas of special density, I call informal organizations, as distinguished from societal or general organizations in their informal aspects. Thus there is an informal organization of a community, of a state. For our purposes, its is important that there are informal organizations related to formal organizations everywhere.

Much the same pattern of informal groupings has been found in the political scene and has been described by Ernest S. Griffith:[10]

One cannot live in Washington for long without being conscious that it has there whirlpools or centers of activity focusing on particular problems. . . . There is nothing really mysterious about this sort of government. It is essentially "of men" and these men behave very naturally. "Who says what to whom and what is the reaction?" This question, if we could obtain enough answers, would capture the spirit, the genius of our own or any other government. It is my opinion that ordinarily the relationship among these men—legislators, administrators, lobbyists, scholars—who are interested in a common problem—is a much more real

relationship than the relationship between congressmen generally or between administrators generally. In other words, he who would understand the prevailing pattern of our present government behavior instead of studying the formal institutions or even generalizations is the relationships between these institutions or organs, important though all these are, may possibly obtain a better picture of the way things really happen if he would study these "whirlpools" of special social interest and problems.

One can think of these areas of "density" or the "whirlpools" as being in constant change as in the nebulae. The decisions constitute the external force which brings the change.

Two recent studies in different types of schools systems would lead us to believe that the informal structure has more permanency than Barnard suggests.[11] It now appears that there are groupings among teachers which maintain themselves over a long period of time. They have typical characteristics of small groups and generally form with at least one strong bond.[12] Thus far, it has been found that the dominant variables in the formation of groups are those of propinquity of teaching station, age, and length of service. A minor variable is that of religion. It appears that the informal groups may be either of a passing nature or of a permanent nature. *They all have in common, however, the altering of the decision-making process of the formal organization.*[13]

There are, in all formal organizations, groups which are formed for reasons other than affecting decisions. These are *ad hoc* coffee groups and other types of groups whose purpose is singly social. These social groups, however, contain the material from which informal groups sometimes develop. Since this set of groups does not concern itself with the purposes of the organization, it will not be discussed further.

Perception

Observation of administrators functioning in concrete situations leads one to speculate concerning what they "see" in these situations and in the world around them. Perception is defined in the dictionary as "awareness of objects; consciousness" and is generally concerned with that which interests us. However, there is more to perception than mere awareness. We find it helpful to consider perception from the frame of reference of a recent study which uses what is called the *transactional approach*.[14]

In working toward a definition of perception, this study presents the major characteristics of perception, the central problem and ways of studying the phenomena. According to Ittelson and Cantril the three major characteristics of human perception are:

1. Perception can be studied only in terms of *transactions*, that is concrete individuals dealing with concrete situations.
2. Perception comes into the transaction from the unique *personal behavioral center* of the perceiver.
3. Preception occurs as the perceiver creates his own psychological environment by identifying certain aspects of his own experience to an environment which he believes exists independent of his own experience. This is called *externalization*.

Since the concept most difficult to understand is that of *transaction*, it would be well to consider it for a moment. Ordinarily the term *interaction* is used to describe what goes on between an individual and his environment. We say, "Man interacts with his environment and brings about a desired change." This assumes that "man" and his "environment" exist as independent entities and that when they interact they do so without affecting their own identities. The concept of *transaction* uses the content of the interaction as the subject matter to be discussed.[15] Ittelson and Cantril state:[16]

Neither a perception nor an object-as-perceived exists independent of the total life situation of which both perception and object are a part. It is meaningless to speak of either as existing apart from the situation in which it is encountered. The word *trans-*

action is used to label such a situation. For the word transaction carries the double implication, (1) that all parts of the situation enter into it as active participants, and (2) that they owe their very existence as encountered in the situation to this fact of active participation and do not appear as already existing entities merely interacting with each other without affecting their own identity.

The concept of the *personal behavior center* has as its meaning the fact that the person enters into a transaction from his own unique position. He is somewhat different from all others in the transaction. We say, then, that each person enters a transaction from his own unique personal behavior center. To the extent that his perception is common with others we have social activity.

The concept of externalization is of recent historical origin. Early studies in perception were concerned with what the environment did to the individual. The Greeks started this chain of thought by formulating the concept that objects emitted small replicas of themselves which were received by the perceiver. The fact that different viewers received different replicas did not bother them to any great extent. Recently, there has been interest in what the organism does when it perceives. The concept of externalization describes, but does not explain, how we perceive. It states that when we perceive anything, we consider it as external to ourselves. As Ittelson and Cantril say, "When we perceive, we externalize certain aspects of our experience and thereby create for ourselves our own world of things and people, of sights and sounds, of tastes and touches."[17]

The concept of transaction is basic to the concepts of the personal behavior center and externalization. It can be seen readily that each situation will be perceived differently by different individuals and that each individual will assume to be real that which he perceives. He then acts accordingly. This has been neatly summarized as follows:[18]

The three major characteristics of perception can be summarized by saying that perceiving is that part of the process of living by which each one of us, from his own particular point of view, creates for himself the world within which he has his life's experiences and through which he strives to gain his satisfcations.

Communication

A close relationship exists between communication and perception in that perception sets the limits within which communication is possible. Each of us creates the world within which we live. By so doing we (with the help of others) set up the conditions under which it is possible to communicate with others, or to have others communicate with us. A recent study by Cherry gives new insights to the administrative theoretician. In an introductory essay entitled "Communication and Organization" he points out:[19]

When "members" or "elements" are in communication with one another, they are associating, cooperating, forming an "organization," or sometimes an "organism." Communication is a social function. That old cliche, "a whole is more than the sum of its parts," expresses a truth; the whole, the organization or organism, possesses a structure which is describable as a set of *rules*, and this structure, the rules, may remain unchanged as the individual members or elements are changed. By the possession of this structure the whole organization may be better adapted or better fitted for some goal-seeking activity. Communication means *sharing* of elements of behavior, or modes of life, by the existence of set of rules.

The elements of behavior or modes of life can only be shared by those who can perceive common stimuli in a common manner. In order, then, for communication to exist in an organization and between the organization and the outside, common perceptual bases must be established; that is, there must exist the set of rules referred to by Cherry. It is clear that, if decisions are to be made and put into operation, there must be cooperation and coordination of the activities of many individuals. Com-

munication is the process by which cooperation and coordination take place.

Power

As people live within the framework of an organization, it is observed that their lives are ordered in various ways. They are moved to behave in one manner or another, and it is necessary to explain the various resultant types of behavior. Certainly one promising lead is offered by the way in which one perceives the situation in which he is placed, but there are others. The first of these is the concept of *power*. To many, the concept of power holds first place in a theory of organization. For instance, Parsons states: "Subject to the over-all control of an institutionalized value system in the society and its subsystems, the central phenomenon of organization is the mobilization of *power* for the attainment of the goals of the organization.[20]

The concept of power helps to account for the control which an organization holds over those who are within it. We note that society has an ordered procedure for teaching its young. The relationship between the teacher and the young is an ordered one; it is institutionalized. Underlying the ordering of these interactions of teacher and student is power. Bierstadt states this idea of power very well: "Power supports the fundamental order of society and the social organization within it, wherever there is order. Power stands behind every association and sustains its structure. Without power there is no organization, and without power there is no order."[21]

In a definition of power which has had general acceptance, Hunter states: "Power is a word that will be used to describe the acts of men going about the business of moving other men to act in relation to themselves or in relation to organic or inorganic things."[22] We do not regard power as the central concept in a theory of administration in that there appears to be a question as to *why* power is exercised. While there appears to be some evidence that power is sought for the sake of power[23] there appears to be a more rational answer. Power is sought in order to control the decision-making process in the organization. This is clearly apparent in the business and political world, but it is less apparent in the public school or the university. It is, however, no less present.

It would appear that power can be operationally defined only in terms of the decisions which a power-holder actually makes. Thus power is a function of *decisions made* and can be operationally defined as:

$$P = f(D)$$

A person, therefore, has power to the extent that he makes decisions which:

1. Affect the course of action of an enterprise to a greater degree than do decisions made by others in the enterprise.
2. Influence other decisions.

Thus it can be seen that the one who exercises most control over the decision-making process in an organization has the most power.

In studying an organization the power distribution can be determined by counting the number of decisions made, by noting the extent to which the decisions affect the course of action of the enterprise, and by noting the effect of any one decision on subsequent decisions. Control of the decision-making process is in turn the key to greater power—that is, control means the right to make decisions which provide the criteria for those who make the other decisions in the sequential process.

Authority

In continuing our analysis of administration to determine relevant concepts, we find that a consideration of power leads us to the concept of *authority*. Although many writers use the terms *power* and *authority* interchangeably, there is a distinct difference between the terms. Simon has used the definition of authority which states that *authority* may be defined as the power to make decisions which guide the actions of others.[24] In discussing this concept,

he points out that in every authority situation there is a superior and subordinate. The superior frames decisions and anticipates that they will be followed. "The subordinate expects such decisions, and his conduct is determined by them."[25] A formal operational definition of the concept is that of Simon, "a subordinate may be said to accept authority whenever he permits his behavior to be guided by a decision reached by another, irrespective of his own judgment as to the merits of that decision."[26]

The crucial point here is that authority is the willingness of some to accept the power of another. That is, members of the organization acknowledge the legitimacy of the decisions made by some to control the decisions of others. When this concept is put into practice it helps to clean the fuzziness out of some of the concepts currently in use. Take for example, line and staff. It is generally understood that the line gives "orders" and the staff gives "advice" as Thompson puts it so well:[27]

> Now we all know the difference between orders and advice. Or do we? When a staff assistant to my boss indicates that I am doing something inefficiently, have I received advice or an order? In many cases, I am convinced, advice has been given (or intended), but orders have been received (or perceived). The line-staff distinction is common sense to a great many administrators, but, in my opinion, it has seriously interfered with the development of administrative theory.

The vital process in an organization is the making of decisions, not the giving of orders or advice. If A perceives B as one who may legitimately make decisions which establish the criteria for the decisions which A makes, then B has authority over A regardless of whether he is called "line" or "staff."

A SET OF PROPOSITIONS

The most fruitful consequences of theory building are the testable propositions which result. What are the propositions which can be derived from the assumptions and concepts of the theory described in this chapter? Below is a set of propositions, some designated as major, with subpropositions called minor, others called converse. It is presumed that this section will indicate some of the research needed in administration as well as the direction the research should take. Some of this research is now under way. One of the major studies which is concerned in part with the following propositions is the Development of Criteria of Success in School Administration, a major research effort financed by the U.S. Office of Education Cooperative Research Program and sponsored by the University Council for Educational Administration and the Educational Testing Service.

Major proposition. The structure of an organization is determined by the nature of its decision-making process. The issues of organizational structure such as "span of control" can be resolved if viewed as the outgrowth of a particular type of decision-making process.

Minor proposition. An individual's rank in an organizational structure is directly related to the degree of control he exerts over the decision process. Another way of saying this is that the individual who makes the decisions which establish the criteria by which others make decisions has highest rank in an organization.

Minor proposition. The effectiveness of a chief executive is inversely proportional to the number of decisions which he must personally make concerning the affairs of the organization. It is not the function of the chief executive to make decisions; it is his function to monitor the decision-making process to make certain that it performs at the optimum level.

This proposition may be expressed mathematically as follows:

$$E(t) = \frac{1}{\Sigma D(t)}$$

In this formula E is effectiveness in achieving the stated objectives of the orga-

nization; t is a specific time interval; and ΣD is the sum total of the number of decisions made in t, the specific time interval.

Minor proposition. Differences in the organizational structure of military, industrial, educational, business, and public administration institutions are related to differences in decision-making processes rather than such conventional concepts as private enterprise.

Major proposition. If the formal and informal organization approach congruency, then the total organization will approach maximum achievement. By "approaching congruency" is meant that the formal and informal organizations must perceive the task of the organization as being the same for both, and both must behave in much the same way to carry out the task. In all probability congruency could never be attained; in fact, it would be undesirable if it ever were attained since there would then exist a state of balance in which there would be no progress.

Converse proposition. If the total organization is not approaching maximum achievement, then, in all probability, the formal and informal organizations are divergent. This proposition suggests that the major reason for failure to achieve at a maximum level is the divergency of perceptions and resultant behaviors between the formal and informal organizations.

Minor proposition. There exists an optimum divergency between the formal and informal structures. This proposition suggests that in organizations which produce at a maximum level there is a difference in how each structure perceives the task of the total organization and in resultant behavior. In other words, the two cannot be so far apart in their perceptions as to be striving for different goals, nor so close together that there is no conflict in perception.

Minor proposition. If there is no conflict between formal and informal structures in the perception of the task of the organization, the organization will not achieve at a maximum level. This proposition takes into account the fact that both structures exist to achieve legitimate purposes for their members and that, if the task is perceived without conflict, the purposes of the two structures are imperfectly formulated.

Major proposition. If the administrator confines his behavior to making decisions on the decision-making process rather than making terminal decisions for the organization, his behavior will be more acceptable to his subordinates.

Major proposition. If the administrator perceives himself as the controller of the decision-making process, rather than the maker of the organization's decisions, the decisions will be more effective.

SUMMARY

Four basic assumptions of a theory of administration as decision-making are presented: (1) Administration is a generalized type of behavior to be found in all human organizations. (2) Administration is the process of directing and controlling life in a social organization. (3) The specific function of administration is to develop and regulate the decision-making process in the most effective manner possible. (4) The administrator works with groups or with individuals with a group referent, not with individuals as such.

A set of concepts is presented and includes decision-making, organization, perception, communication, power, and authority. The chapter concludes with a set of propositions.

NOTES

[1] Chester I. Barnard, *The Functions of the Executive* (Cambridge, Mass., Harvard University Press, 1938), p. 215.

[2] *Ibid.*, p. 211.

[3] James L. McCammy, "Analysis of the Process of Decision Making," *Public Administration Review*, Vol. 7, No. 1 (1947), p. 41.

[4] Herbert A. Simon, *Administrative Behavior* (New York, Macmillan, 1950), p. 1.

[5] Robert Teviot Livingston, "The Theory of Organization and Management," *Transactions of the ASME* (May, 1953), p. 659.

[6] Talcott Parsons, "Suggestions for a Sociological Approach to the Theory of Organizations—I," *Administrative Science Quarterly*, Vol. 1, No. 1 (June, 1956), p. 66.

[7] V. A. Graicunas, "Relationship in Organization," in Luther Gulick and Lyndall Urwick, eds., *Papers on the Science of Administration* (New York, Institute of Public Administration, 1937), pp. 183–187.

[8] Ernest Dale, *Planning and Developing the Company Organization Structure* (New York, American Management Association, 1952), p. 107.

[9] Reprinted by permission of the publishers from Chester I. Barnard, *The Functions of the Executive* (Cambridge, Mass., Harvard University Press, copyright, 1938, by The President and Fellows of Harvard College), p. 115.

[10] Ernest S. Griffith, *The Impasse of Democracy* (New York, Harrison-Hilton, 1939), p. 182.

[11] Reported in Daniel E. Griffiths, David L. Clark, D. Richard Wynn, and Laurence Iannaccone, *Modern Organizational Theory and Practice* (Danville, Ill., Interstate, in press), Part IV.

[12] For a further discussion of the structure of groups see Daniel E.

Griffiths, *Human Relations in School Administration* (New York, Appleton-Century-Crofts, 1956), Chapter 8.

[13] For a thorough discussion of the theoretical justification for this statement see Conrad M. Arensberg, "Behavior and Organization; Industrial Studies," in John H. Rohrer and Muzafer Sherif, eds., *Social Psychology at the Crossroads* (New York, Harper, 1951), Chapter XIV.

[14] William H. Ittelson and Hadley Cantril, *Perception* (New York, Random House, 1954).

[15] A more complete discussion of this concept is to be found in John Dewey and Arthur F. Bentley, *Knowing and the Known* (Boston, Beacon Press, 1949).

[16] Ittelson and Cantril, *op. cit.*, p. 3.

[17] *Ibid.*, p. 5.

[18] *Ibid.*, p. 5. For a detailed discussion of perception and its relation to administration see Daniel E. Griffiths, *Human Relations in School Administration, op. cit.*, Chapter 3.

[19] Colin Cherry, *On Human Communication* (published jointly by John Wiley & Sons, Inc., and the Technology Press, copyrighted, 1957, by the Massachusetts Institute of Technology), p. 6.

[20] Talcott Parsons, "Suggestions for a Sociological Approach to the Theory of Organizations—II," *Administrative Science Quarterly*, Vol. 1, No. 2 (September, 1956), p. 225.

[21] Robert Bierstadt, "An Analysis of Social Power," *American Sociological Review*, Vol. 15 (December, 1950), pp. 730–736.

[22] Floyd Hunter, *Community Power Structure* (Chapel Hill, University of North Carolina Press, 1953), pp. 2–3.

[23] Alfred McClung Lee, "Power-Seekers," in Alvin W. Gouldner, ed., *Studies in Leadership* (New York, Harper, 1950), pp. 667–678.

[24] Simon, *op. cit.*, p. 125.

[25] *Ibid.*, p. 125.

[26] *Ibid.*, p. 22.

[27] James D. Thompson, "Modern Approaches to Theory in Administration," in Andrew W. Halpin, ed., *Administrative Theory in Education* (Chicago, Midwest Administration Center, 1958), p. 30.

12.

THE HUMAN SIDE OF ENTERPRISE

DOUGLAS McGREGOR

It has become trite to say that industry has the fundamental know-how to utilize physical science and technology for the material benefit of mankind, and that we must now learn how to utilize the social sciences to make our human organizations truly effective.

To a degree, the social sciences today are in a position like that of the physical sciences with respect to atomic energy in the thirties. We know that past conceptions of the nature of man are inadequate and, in many ways, incorrect. We are becoming quite certain that, under proper conditions, unimagined resources of creative human energy could become available within the organizational setting.

We cannot tell industrial management how to apply this new knowledge in simple, economic ways. We know it will require years of exploration, much costly development research, and a substantial amount of creative imagination on the part of management to discover how to apply this growing knowledge to the organization of human effort in industry.

MANAGEMENT'S TASK: THE CONVENTIONAL VIEW

The conventional conception of management's task in harnessing human energy to organizational requirements can be stated broadly in terms of three propositions. In order to avoid

From Douglas McGregor, "The Human Side of Enterprise," *The Management Review*, 46:22–28; 88–92, 1957. Reprinted by permission.

the complications introduced by a label, let us call this set of propositions "Theory X":

1. Management is responsible for organizing the elements of productive enterprise—money, materials, equipment, people—in the interest of economic ends.
2. With respect to people, this is a process of directing their efforts, motivating them, controlling their actions, modifying their behavior to fit the needs of the organization.
3. Without this active intervention by management, people would be passive—even resistant—to organizational needs. They must therefore be persuaded, rewarded, punished, controlled—their activities must be directed. This is management's task. We often sum it up by saying that management consists of getting things done through other people.

Behind this conventional theory there are several additional beliefs—less explicit, but widespread:

4. The average man is by nature indolent— he works as little as possible.
5. He lacks ambition, dislikes responsibility, prefers to be led.
6. He is inherently self-centered, indifferent to organizational needs.
7. He is by nature resistant to change.
8. He is gullible, not very bright, the ready dupe of the charlatan and the demagogue.

The human side of economic enterprise today is fashioned from propositions and beliefs such as these. Conventional organization structures and managerial policies, practices, and programs reflect these assumptions.

In accomplishing its task—with these assumptions as guides—management has conceived of a range of possibilities.

At one extreme, management can be "hard" or "strong." The methods for directing behavior involve coercion and threat (usually disguised), close supervision, tight controls over behavior. At the other extreme, management can be "soft" or "weak." The methods for directing behavior involve being permissive, satisfying people's demands, achieving harmony. Then they will be tractable, accept direction.

This range has been fairly completely explored during the past half century, and management has learned some things from the exploration. There are difficulties in the "hard" approach. Force breeds counter-forces: restriction of output, antagonism, militant unionism, subtle but effective sabotage of management objectives. This "hard" approach is especially difficult during times of full employment.

There are also difficulties in the "soft" approach. It leads frequently to the abdication of management—to harmony, perhaps, but to indifferent performance. People take advantage of the soft approach. They continually expect more, but they give less and less.

Currently, the popular theme is "firm but fair." This is an attempt to gain the advantages of both the hard and the soft approaches. It is reminiscent of Teddy Roosevelt's "speak softly and carry a big stick."

IS THE CONVENTIONAL VIEW CORRECT?

The findings which are beginning to emerge from the social sciences challenge this whole set of beliefs about man and human nature and about the task of management. The evidence is far from conclusive, certainly, but it is suggestive. It comes from the laboratory, the clinic, the schoolroom, the home, and even to a limited extent from industry itself.

The social scientist does not deny that human behavior in industrial organization today is approximately what management perceives it to be. He has, in fact, observed it and studied it fairly extensively. But he is pretty sure that this behavior is *not* a consequence of man's inherent nature. It is a consequence rather of the nature of industrial organizations, of management philosophy, policy, and practice. The conventional approach of Theory X is based on mistaken notions of what is cause and what is effect.

Perhaps the best way to indicate why the conventional approach of management is inadequate is to consider the subject of motivation.

PHYSIOLOGICAL NEEDS

Man is a wanting animal—as soon as one of his needs is satisfied, another appears in its place. This process is unending. It continues from birth to death.

Man's needs are organized in a series of levels—a hierarchy of importance. At the lowest level, but pre-eminent in importance when they are thwarted, are his *physiological needs*. Man lives for bread alone, when there is no bread. Unless the circumstances are unusual, his needs for love, for status, for recognition are inoperative when his stomach has been empty for a while. But when he eats regularly and adequately, hunger ceases to be an important motivation. The same is true of the other physiological needs of man—for rest, exercise, shelter, protection from the elements.

A satisfied need is not a motivator of behavior! This is a fact of profound significance that is regularly ignored in the conventional approach to the management of people. Consider your own need for air: Except as you are deprived of it, it has no appreciable motivating effect upon your behavior.

SAFETY NEEDS

When the physiological needs are reasonably satisfied, needs at the next higher level begin to dominate man's behavior—to motivate him. These are called *safety needs*. They are needs for protection against danger, threat, deprivation. Some people mistakenly refer to these as needs for security. However, unless man is in a dependent relationship where he fears arbitrary deprivation, he does not demand security. The need is for the "fairest possible break." When he is confident of this, he is more than willing to take risks. But when he feels threatened or dependent, his greatest need is for guarantees, for protection, for security.

The fact needs little emphasis that, since every industrial employee is in a dependent relationship, safety needs may assume considerable importance. Arbitrary management actions, behavior which arouses uncertainty with respect to continued employment or which reflects favoritism or discrimination, unpredictable administration of policy—these can be powerful motivators of the safety needs in the employment relationship *at every level,* from worker to vice president.

SOCIAL NEEDS

When man's physiological needs are satisfied and he is no longer fearful about his physical welfare, his *social needs* become important motivators of his behavior—needs for belonging, for association, for acceptance by his fellows, for giving and receiving friendship and love.

Management knows today of the existence of these needs, but it often assumes quite wrongly that they represent a threat to the organization. Many studies have demonstrated that the tightly knit, cohesive work group may, under proper conditions, be far more effective than an equal number of separate individuals in achieving organizational goals.

Yet management, fearing group hostility to its own objectives, often goes to considerable lengths to control and direct human efforts in ways that are inimical to the natural "groupiness" of human beings. When man's social needs—and perhaps his safety needs, too— are thus thwarted, he behaves in ways which tend to defeat organizational objectives. He becomes resistant, antagonistic, uncooperative. But this behavior is a consequence, not a cause.

EGO NEEDS

Above the social needs—in the sense that they do not become motivators until lower levels are reasonably satisfied—are the needs of greatest significance to management and to man himself. They are the *egoistic needs,* and they are of two kinds:

1. Those needs that relate to one's self-esteem—needs for self-confidence, for independence, for achievement, for competence, for knowledge.
2. Those needs that relate to one's reputation—needs for status, for recognition, for appreciation, for the deserved respect of one's fellows.

Unlike the lower needs, these are rarely satisfied; man seeks indefinitely for more satisfaction of these needs once they have become important to him. But they do not appear in any significant way until physiological, safety, and social needs are all reasonably satisfied.

The typical industrial organization offers few opportunities for the satisfaction of these egoistic needs to people at lower levels in the hierarchy. The conventional methods of organizing work, particularly in mass-production industries, give little heed to these aspects of human motivation. If the practices of scientific management were deliberately calculated to thwart these needs, they could hardly accomplish this purpose better than they do.

SELF-FULFILLMENT NEEDS

Finally—a capstone, as it were, on the hierarchy of man's needs—there are what we may call the *needs for self-fulfillment.* These are the needs for realizing one's own potentialities, for continued self-development, for being creative in the broadest sense of that term.

It is clear that the conditions of modern life give only limited opportunity for these relatively weak needs to obtain expression. The deprivation most people experience with respect to other lower-level needs diverts their energies into the struggle to satisfy *those* needs, and the needs for self-fulfillment remain dormant.

MANAGEMENT AND MOTIVATION

We recognize readily enough that a man suffering from a severe dietary deficiency is sick. The deprivation of physiological needs has behavioral consequences. The same is true—although less well recognized—of deprivation of higher-level needs. The man whose needs for safety, association, independence, or status are thwarted is sick just as surely as the man who has rickets. And his sickness will have behavioral consequences. We will be mistaken if we attribute his resultant passivity, his hostility, his refusal to accept responsibility to his inherent "human nature." These forms of behavior are *symptoms* of illness—of deprivation of his social and egoistic needs.

The man whose lower-level needs are satisfied is not motivated to satisfy those needs any longer. For practical purposes they exist no longer. Management often asks, "Why aren't people more productive? We pay good wages, provide good working conditions, have excellent fringe benefits and steady employment. Yet people do not seem to be willing to put forth more than minimum effort."

The fact that management has provided for these physiological and safety needs has shifted the motivational emphasis to the social and perhaps to the egoistic needs. Unless there are opportunities *at work* to satisfy these higher-level needs, people will be deprived; and their behavior will reflect this deprivation. Under such conditions, if management continues to focus its attention on physiological needs, its efforts are bound to be ineffective.

People *will* make insistent demands for more money under these conditions. It becomes more important than ever to buy the material goods and services which can provide limited satisfaction of the thwarted needs. Although money has only limited value in satisfying many higher-level needs, it can become the focus of interest if it is the *only* means available.

THE CARROT-AND-STICK APPROACH

The carrot-and-stick theory of motivation (like Newtonian physical theory) works reasonably well under certain circumstances. The *means* for satisfying man's physiological and (within limits) his safety needs can be provided or withheld by management. Employment itself is such a means, and so are wages, working conditions, and benefits. By these means the individual can be controlled so long as he is struggling for subsistence.

But the carrot-and-stick theory does not work at all once man has reached an adequate subsistence level and is motivated primarily by higher needs. Management cannot provide a man with self-respect, or with the respect of his fellows, or with the satisfaction of needs for self-fulfillment. It can create such conditions that he is encouraged and enabled to seek such satisfactions for *himself*, or it can thwart him by failing to create those conditions.

But this creation of conditions is not "control." It is not a good device for directing behavior. And so management finds itself in an odd position. The high standard of living created by our modern technological know-how provides quite adequately for the satisfaction of physiological and safety needs. The only significant exception is where management practices have not created confidence in a "fair break"—and thus where safety needs are thwarted. But by making possible the satisfaction of low-level needs, management has deprived itself of the ability to use as motivators the devices on which conventional theory has taught it to rely—rewards, promises, incentives, or threats and other coercive devices.

The philosophy of management by direction and control—*regardless of whether it is hard or soft*—is inadequate to motivate because the human needs on which this approach relies are today unimportant motivators of behavior. Direction and control are essentially useless in motivating people whose important needs are social and egoistic. Both the hard and the soft approach fail today because they are simply irrelevant to the situation.

People, deprived of opportunities to satisfy at work the needs which are now important to them, behave exactly as we might predict—with indolence, passivity, resistance to change, lack of responsibility, willingness to follow the demagogue, unreasonable demands for economic benefits. It would seem that we are caught in a web of our own weaving.

A NEW THEORY OF MANAGEMENT

For these and many other reasons, we require a different theory of the task of managing people based on more adequate assumptions about human nature and human motivation. I am going to be so bold as to suggest the broad dimensions of such a theory. Call it "Theory Y," if you will.

1. Management is responsible for organizing the elements of productive enterprise—money, materials, equipment, people—in the interest of economic ends.
2. People are *not* by nature passive or resistant to organizational needs. They have become so as a result of experience in organizations.
3. The motivation, the potential for development, the capacity for assuming responsibility, the readiness to direct behavior toward organizational goals are all present in people. Management does not put them there. It is a responsibility of management to make it possible for people to recognize and develop these human characteristics for themselves.
4. The essential task of management is to arrange organizational conditions and methods of operation so that people can achieve their own goals *best* by directing *their own* efforts toward organizational objectives.

This is a process primarily of creating opportunities, releasing potential, removing obstacles, encouraging growth, providing guidance. It is what Peter Drucker has called "management by objectives" in contrast to "management by control." It does *not* involve the abdication of management, the absence of leadership, the lowering of standards, or the other characteristics usually associated with the "soft" approach under Theory X.

SOME DIFFICULTIES

It is no more possible to create an organization today which will be a full, effective application of this theory than it was to build an atomic power plant in 1945. There are many formidable obstacles to overcome.

The conditions imposed by conventional organization theory and by the approach of scientific management for the past half century have tied men to limited jobs which do not utilize their capabilities, have discouraged the acceptance of responsibility, have encouraged passivity, have eliminated meaning from work. Man's habits, attitudes, expectations—his whole conception of membership in an industrial organization—have been conditioned by his experience under these circumstances.

People today are accustomed to being directed, manipulated, controlled in industrial organizations and to finding satisfaction for their social, egoistic, and self-fulfillment needs away from the job. This is true of much of management as well as of workers. Genuine "industrial citizenship"—to borrow again a term from Drucker—is a remote and unrealistic idea, the meaning of which has not even been considered by most members of industrial organizations.

Another way of saying this is that Theory X places exclusive reliance upon external control of human behavior, while Theory Y relies heavily on self-control and self-direction. It is worth noting that this difference is the difference between treating people as children and treating them as mature adults. After generations of the former, we cannot expect to shift to the latter overnight.

STEPS IN THE RIGHT DIRECTION

Before we are overwhelmed by the obstacles, let us remember that the application of theory is always slow. Progress is usually achieved in small steps. Some innovative ideas which are entirely consistent with Theory Y are today being applied with some success.

Decentralization and delegation

These are ways of freeing people from the too-close control of conventional organization, giving them a degree of freedom to direct their own activities, to assume responsibility, and, importantly, to satisfy their egoistic needs. In this connection, the flat organization of Sears, Roebuck and Company provides an interesting example. It forces "management by objectives," since it enlarges the number of people reporting to a manager until he cannot direct and control them in the conventional manner.

Job enlargement

This concept, pioneered by I.B.M. and Detroit Edison, is quite consistent with Theory Y. It encourages the acceptance of responsibility at the bottom of the organization; it provides opportunities for satisfying social and egoistic needs. In fact, the reorganization of work at the factory level offers one of the more challenging opportunities for innovation consistent with Theory Y.

Participation and consultative management

Under proper conditions, participation and consultative management provide encouragement to people to direct their creative energies toward organizational objectives, give them some voice in decisions that affect them, provide significant opportunities for the satisfaction of social and egoistic needs. The Scanlon Plan is the outstanding embodiment of these ideas in practice.

Performance appraisal

Even a cursory examination of conventional programs of performance appraisal within the ranks of management will reveal how completely consistent they are with Theory X. In fact, most such programs tend to treat the individual as though he were a product under inspection on the assembly line.

A few companies—among them General Mills, Ansul Chemical, and General Electric—have been experimenting with approaches which involve the individual in setting "targets" or objectives for himself and in a self-evaluation of performance semiannually or annually. Of course, the superior plays an important leadership role in this process—one, in fact, which demands substantially more competence than the conventional approach. The role is, however, considerably more congenial to many managers than the role of "judge" or "inspector" which is usually forced upon them. Above all, the individual is encouraged to take a greater responsibility for planning and appraising his own contribution to organizational objectives; and the accompanying effects on egoistic and self-fulfillment needs are substantial.

APPLYING THE IDEAS

The not infrequent failure of such ideas as these to work as well as expected is often attributable to the fact that a management has "bought the idea" but applied it within the framework of Theory X and its assumptions.

Delegation is not an effective way of exercising management by control. Participation becomes a farce when it is applied as a sales gimmick or a device for kidding people into thinking they are important. Only the management that has confidence in human capacities and is itself directed toward organizational objectives rather than toward the preservation of personal power can grasp the implications of this emerging theory. Such management will find and apply successfully other innovative ideas as we move slowly toward the full implementation of a theory like Y.

THE HUMAN SIDE OF ENTERPRISE

It is quite possible for us to realize substantial improvements in the effectiveness of industrial organizations during the next decade or two.

The social sciences can contribute much to such developments; we are only beginning to grasp the implications of the growing body of knowledge in these fields. But if this conviction is to become a reality instead of a pious hope, we will need to view the process much as we view the process of releasing the energy of the atom for constructive human ends—as a slow, costly, sometimes discouraging approach toward a goal which would seem to many to be quite unrealistic.

The ingenuity and the perseverance of industrial management in the pursuit of economic ends have changed many scientific and technological dreams into commonplace realities. It is now becoming clear that the application of these same talents to the human side of enterprise will not only enhance substantially these materialistic achievements, but will bring us one step closer to "the good society."

13.

INDIVIDUAL BEHAVIOR AND GROUP ACHIEVEMENT

RALPH M. STOGDILL

A rather exacting and laborious procedure has been followed in developing a theory of group achievement and examining it in reference to the pertinent experimental data. In order to construct a satisfactory system, it has been necessary to start with concepts that are firmly anchored in the scientific literature, to define them strictly, to examine the interrelationships among them, and to trace in systematic detail the effects generated by their interactions upon each other.

A group is regarded as an input-output system. The inputs are the performances, expectations, and interactions of the group members. These variables in combination account for the development of group structure and for the initiation and maintenance of group operations. The input behaviors, transformed into group structure and operations, result in outcomes which describe the achievement of the group. The logical development of the system has required that group achievement be analyzed in terms of productivity, integration, and morale. A group may be examined at any stage in its operations to evaluate its status in respect to these three aspects of achievement.

Various concepts used in the system are reviewed in the following sections.

From Ralph M. Stogdill, *Individual Behavior and Group Achievement: A Theory: The Experimental Evidence*, Oxford University Press, Fair Lawn, N.J., 1959, pp. 273–290. Copyright © 1959 by Oxford University Press, Inc. Reprinted by permission.

CHARACTERISTICS OF INDIVIDUALS AND OF GROUPS

Performance and expectation are characteristics of individuals. Interaction is an interpersonal form of behavior. A group by definition involves interactions and performances (actions and reactions). A group also involves expectations. The structuring of positions in a group tends to confirm differential expectations relative to the predictable initiative of certain members and the predictable reactions of other members. In addition, the members tend to confirm for each other a normative set of values relative to the group purpose and member behavior affecting the group purpose. Not only do the members in interaction develop norms which define expected behavior, but they exert strong pressures upon each other to conform with the norms of the group. Purpose and norms represent mutually confirmed sets of expectations which must be regarded as characteristics of groups. Structure and operations are also characteristic of groups.

THE INPUT BEHAVIORS

The concepts *performance, interaction,* and *expectation* must be regarded as abstractions which refer to observed or inferred aspects of behavior that are recognized in general conversation as well as in the scientific literature. The concepts have been defined in the scientific literature by a variety of research operations. For this reason, we know more about the concepts and the behaviors to which they refer than we do about various other concepts that might have been used for the theory. The fact that several concepts have been redefined according to the demands of the theory and in order to bring them into closer conformity with research findings requires us to keep in mind the scientific rather than the cultural meanings of the terms.

Interaction is defined as an action-reaction sequence in which the reactions of each participant in the sequence are responses to actions initiated by other participants. A *group* is defined as an interaction system. It must be regarded as an open system because it gains and loses members, and exchanges values with its environment. The structure of a group is determined by the actions and reactions of its members. A position in a group is defined as a predictable sequence of actions by a member which elicits predictable reactions from other members of the system. Successive interactions and the gain or loss of members do not change the identity of the system. Although interaction is not self-perpetuating, the continuance of interaction, at least intermittently, is necessary to maintain the identity of the system. The degree of structure of a system determines the freedom of action permitted its members. The concept of interaction, as here developed, enables us to account for group structure, identity, and freedom of action, which are important concepts in a theory of groups.

Performance is defined as any action exhibited by an individual which identifies him as a member of a group. A performance may be an action initiated by a member or a reaction to the action of another member. Each action and each reaction is a performance. The nature or content of an interaction sequence is described in terms of the performances (actions and reactions) involved. The performances of the members, singly or in interaction, accomplish the work of the group and describe the operations of the group. The concept of performance increases our ability to explain group identity. It enables us to describe the nature of interaction. It provides a means of explaining group operations, or group task performance.

Expectation is defined as readiness for reinforcement. It is regarded in this theory as a function of drive, the estimated level of desirability of a possible outcome, and the estimated probability of the outcome. A reinforcing outcome confirms or disconfirms desirability estimates and probability estimates. A reinforcing outcome usually, but not always,

reduces drive temporarily. Successive reinforcements increase expectation, but add progressively smaller increments of strength. Inconsistent schedules of reinforcement reduce freedom of action in that they mobilize drive and maintain the organism in a state of constant readiness for the reinforcement of a dominant expectation.

Motivation is regarded as a function of drive and confirmed desirability estimates. The confirmation of desirability estimates determines the value of an outcome in relation to a scale of value or previously confirmed desirability estimate. Secondary reinforcement and generalization account for the development of value systems, which may be regarded as sets of desirability estimates whose confirmation is not dependent upon the confirmation of probability estimates. Value systems provide the individual with stable reference scales for the evaluation and direction of behavior in an environment that exhibits a high degree of uncertainty and unpredictability. The concept of expectation enables us to account for the goal direction and continuity of behavior, as well as for prediction and value.

GROUP STRUCTURE AND OPERATIONS

Variance among the members in the initiation of behavior and in response to the initiative of others results in the differentiation of a structure of positions in a group. The mutual confirmation of expectation among the members that comes about in the process of establishing the structure of positions tends to define the contribution of each position to the accomplishment of the group purpose. These expectations, when mutually acknowledged and confirmed, define the function and status of each position in the system. Since function and status are defined in relation to the group purpose, they tend to remain unchanged even though a succession of different persons may occupy a given position.

In order to accomplish the group purpose, it is necessary for the members to act and interact in carrying out the tasks assigned to each position. These performances and interactions describe the operations of the group. Because of the impact of environmental pressures and changing operational requirements, and because of differences between individuals, function and status cannot define in detail the manner in which a member is expected to behave in a group. Successive occupants of the same position are not expected to act alike. The members in interaction develop mutually confirmed expectations relative to the role that each is expected to play as a participant in the changing group operations. A member's role defines the responsibility and authority he is expected to exercise by virtue of the functions and status of his position, the demands made upon him by changing group operations, and the kind of person he is perceived to be. The mutual acknowledgement and confirmation of positions and roles tends to legitimize these systems and to insure their stability. Both role definition and group norms tend to specify a set of sanctions which reward conformity and penalize nonconformity. The continued legitimation of a role depends on the correspondence between the behavior of a member and the specifications and norms pertaining to his role. A member may act in such a manner as to undermine the legitimacy of his role without affecting the legitimacy of the function and status defined for his position. Role conflict occurs when contradictory expectations are made upon the occupant of a position.

Groups are found to develop structures of positions and roles as means of subdividing the group task, controlling group operations, and insuring unity of goal direction. The provision for operations control gives some members greater access to power than is available to others. Conflict within groups tends to center around the legitimation of the uses of power. Power is defined as the differential right to control the reinforcement of expectation.

It is found that the concepts of performance, interaction, and expectation, when used in combination, are able to account for group structure and operations. They are also able to account for group achievement.

GROUP ACHIEVEMENT

Achievement is defined as the group outcome resulting from the member inputs, mediated through group structure and operations. The achievement of a group at any stage of its operations may be analyzed in terms of its productivity, morale, and integration. Productivity is defined as the degree of change in expectancy values resulting from group operations. Integration is a measure of capacity to maintain structure and function under stress. Morale is defined as freedom from restraint in action toward a group goal.

The three aspects of achievement are necessarily defined in terms of group capacity. The standards of reference for measuring group achievement involve time and capacity. Productivity measures the extent to which operational capability has been utilized with past performance as a standard of reference. Morale is a measure of the degree to which a group actually utilizes its potentiality for freedom of action at the time of observation. Integration has a future reference, in that it is a measure of capacity to maintain structure and function under conditions of stress.

Because of the fact that the achievement of a group is valued differently by different members as well as by observers who are not members, it is difficult to establish any absolute standards for evaluating different aspects of achievement. Nevertheless, both members and outside observers make evaluative judgments of group achievement and tend to accept such appraisals as valid.

An increase or decrease in inputs permits an increase or decrease in productivity, morale, and integration simultaneously. However, with inputs constant, an increase in productivity is accomplished at some expense to integration. An increase in integration involves some decrease in productivity. Morale is usually, but not always, related positively to productivity. Morale tends to be higher under medium degrees of integration than under extremely high or low degrees of integration.

BALANCE AND COUNTERBALANCE

Membership provides a means for the accomplishment of individual goals while aiding in the achievement of group goals. An organization is usually interested in the creation of specific productivity values which are defined in its declaration of purpose. The end values created by the performances of the members and the operations of the group are accomplished at a cost to the members and to the group. The cost to the members is reckoned in terms of the time and effort they devote to the group, the dues they pay, the illnesses and accidents they suffer in the performance of their duties, the frustrations and disappointments they experience, the freedom of self-determination they surrender, and the subordination of personal loyalties and goals to the welfare of the group. Such factors as these are costs to the members, even though they cannot all be measured in dollars and cents.

The group also must pay a cost of one sort or another for the participation of the members. It must create for the members such values as are necessary to reinforce their expectations. Groups, as collectivities of individuals, generally expect the contributions of the members to be related to the productive purpose of the group. In turn, they expect the members to be content with rewards that may be derived from the accomplishment of the group purpose. If it is the purpose of the group to produce material values, the members are expected to be satisfied with material rewards. In athletic groups the return to the members may be the fun of playing the game or of watching others play it. In religious groups it may be the reinforcement of personal value systems and perhaps the rendering of humanitarian services. In business groups it may be the financial reward for the effort and responsibility invested in task performance. In a social group it may be the pleasure of interaction, mutual stimulation, and emotional support. However, these primary values are not the only ones that the members expect to derive from a group. Some members value the pride that comes with membership in a high prestige organization. Others value the opportunity provided by a group to exercise responsibility and authority and to experience a sense of achievement. Some members value the sense of security provided by a group, while others derive satisfaction from the opportunity for innovation, advancement in status, and the exercise of power. The members of a group may differ widely among themselves depending upon differences in social background, training, and reference group identifications. The meeting of these various expectations takes time and effort which the group might otherwise devote to task performance, and thus represents a cost to the group.

All that is a cost to a member represents an input for the group. Some of the input may not be highly valued, but it will exert an effect someplace in the group. Although inputs that have a high positive or negative value are often recognized, groups as organized entities appear to exhibit little awareness of the total costs paid by their members. Thus, there is usually more invested in a group than is recognized as constituting individual and collective input. Correspondingly, the group creates outputs, such as integration and morale, which are seldom recognized as aspects of achievement.

Performance is regulated to a high degree by operational demands and subgroup norms which may bear no close relationship to the amount, nature, or relevance of the rewards for performance. Group structures, on the other hand, exhibit numerous mechanisms for their mutual reinforcement. Value systems are highly reinforcible. Although work decrement in response to dissatisfaction is to be observed, productive effectiveness may be maintained at high levels despite a state of extreme dissatisfaction among the members. Griping, hostility, absenteeism, accidents, separations, malco-ordination, and other evidences of low group integration are observed instead. It is the structural-functional integrity of the group that is most vulnerable to inadequate or inappropriate reinforcement.

A member tends to judge the outcomes he experiences as satisfying or unsatisfying in reference to his own expectations and in comparison with the outcomes he perceives other members to be experiencing in the group. If he perceives some members to be receiving excessive rewards, he sees the group as potentially able to increase his own rewards as well.

When the members permit the group to accumulate a surplus of values, they realize that this surplus gives the group a degree of power that the members could not exert individually if the surplus were divided equally among them. Therefore, all the members, except perhaps a few who are antagonistic to certain of its goals, are interested in seeing that the group has a sufficient reserve to insure its power to operate and to fulfill its purpose. The greater the extent to which their own welfare is perceived to be dependent upon, and served by, the activities of the group, the greater the interest of the members in the adequate reserve power of the group.

The decision by a group to play a game or perform a task involves much more than the accomplishment of the stated objective. It involves also the differentiation of function and status, a process which places different values on the contributions of the various members. Thus, the basic process of organizing creates a situation which is likely to reward certain members but to disappoint the expectations of certain others. Although this outcome may not be avoidable, the integration of the group may depend upon the extent to which the group sensitizes itself to the expectations of its members and succeeds in satisfying or else restructuring them.

Organization seeks to establish stable structures of expectations relative to interaction, performance, and outcomes. However, the model structure can never anticipate nor represent all the demands that the organization will be required to fulfill. Therefore, it is confronted by two extreme alternatives with a wide range of values in between. It can spend all its energy on the reinforcement of structural integrity, or it can devote all its energies to task achievement. The former solution represents little advantage over the primal group, for it merely formalizes the original struggle for structure in the form of a non-productive ritualism. The latter solution may be expected eventually to jeopardize integration and morale. Therefore, a realistic concern for the survival of the group demands a solution that lies between these two extremes.

In times of crisis, the members may sacrifice most, if not all, of their personal goals for the benefit of the organization. The internal problems of the group are likely to be simplified under these circumstances because it can devote most of its attention to maximizing productive effectiveness. Nevertheless, many groups that do not live under continued crisis, persist in operating under routine conditions as if crisis were ever present. Under continued pressure for productivity when no crisis exists, the members are likely to become wearied and disillusioned. When this occurs, the time has passed for the group to have sensitized itself to the expectations of its members and to its structural integrity and morale.

The real test of the integrity of a group is whether its members will support it in time of crisis. A member's loyalty to a gorup appears to be determined by some ratio between the personal cost he has to pay to support the group and the magnitude of the discrepancy between his expectations and the outcomes he experiences in the group. When this ratio becomes so unbalanced that the member feels cheaply valued or that his interests are betrayed, he may also feel inclined to let the organization suffer whatever reverses may be in store for it.

The formal organization does, or should, structure the expectations of the members. Correspondingly, it is the responsibility of the formal structure to fulfill the relevant expectations of the members. The integration of a group is founded on its formal structure and on the correspondence between individual goals and group goals. This mutual support is brought about by the clear definition of roles, by the careful structuring of expectations, and by the reinforcement of those expectations.

Not only the group as a system, but the members as individuals, are interested in the primary purpose of the group, its productive achievement. However, the necessity of maintaining operational balance, and the setting of limits upon the personal reward that can be achieved for increased effort tend to counteract the attempts by the group to increase productivity through the use of various motivating measures. In addition, the subgroups tend to demand uniformity of performance and rewards, and the solution of problems by formula. For example, they may expect promotions to be based on seniority, technical ability, or some other standard formula. A group can hardly hope to devise a formula which will satisfy all the members. It is difficult for the group, even when it realizes the desirability of doing so, to sensitize itself to the expectations of the individual members with the aim of satisfying each in a maximum degree. In fact, the primary concern of the group is for the welfare and accomplishment of the group as a whole rather than for the satisfaction of the individual members, and it tends to reject those members who cannot conform to this concern.

High status members are found to experience a greater degree of personal freedom in the group, to enlarge the area of freedom of other members, and to be more tolerant and supportive to the deviate. Thus, there are some functions which neither the group as a whole nor the various subgroups can perform, but which the members will permit high status members to perform. It now becomes clear why group productivity is related to supervisory leadership rather than to satisfaction with the job or the group as a whole. The group is conservative by nature and necessity. It must maintain balance and control if it is to survive. Productivity among the various subgroups must be equalized in order to prevent a wastage of group resources, and the rewards to peers in the same subgroup must be equalized in order to prevent dissension. The members tend to produce more when they are given freedom to perform and interact in conformity with the demands of their tasks and roles. Excessive degrees of freedom are observed to result in indecision, confusion, and malco-ordination. The desirability of balancing responsibility and authority is more than a trite saying. It is a requirement for effective performance. The high status member provides freedom of action, definition of structure, and co-ordination control.

There are many balancing and counterbalancing factors at work in an organized group. An excess in any one factor may be accomplished at the cost of a deficiency in others. The exercise of a high degree of control over performance and interaction reduces satisfaction and productivity. Granting an optimum degree of freedom of action increases productivity and satisfaction but weakens co-ordination control. Under a maximum degree of freedom, co-ordination breaks down, production is reduced, and satisfaction is lowered. If disproportionate amounts of time and effort are devoted to the structuring and reinforcement of expectations, satisfaction tends to increase, but productivity suffers. On the other hand, if the member expectations relative to status and function, responsibility and authority, recognition and reward are disregarded, satisfaction and loyalty to the organization are depressed.

The subgroups develop norms which tend to regulate performance. On the other hand, the subgroups may exert pressures which induce conformity to the group standards. The subgroups may also provide support which enables members to resist the attempts of internal and external agents to alienate them from the group. It is equally true that an alienated subgroup may make life very difficult for a member who is loyal to the group. In the interests of survival, it is important for the group to structure and satisfy the legitimate expectations of its members. The development of structural integrity under normal operating conditions, even at the expense of productive effectiveness, strengthens the group for times of crisis.

If responsibility and authority are too rigidly structured and controlled, the members suffer a reduction in their freedom of action. Thus, a too rigid role structure may incapacitate the organization for coping with changing environmental demands. However, if roles are not clearly defined, the members may not know what they are expected to do in the way of task performance or interaction with other members. As a result, initiative is lowered, operations become disorganized, and dissatisfaction increases.

In order for an organization to cope with changing conditions, it is necessary that initiative and freedom of decision be permitted at the operative levels where technical problems are encountered first hand. This is true, not only for combat troops in the field, but for civilian organizations as well. Even when the technical details of task performance are strictly prescribed and controlled, there are always situations arising which demand technical knowledge and action on the spot. Lacking freedom to decide and act within his defined area of responsibility, the individual feels frustrated and distrusted in the performance of his task. Given too much freedom, the member may feel confused and inhibited lest he overstep his authority or make decisions which conflict with those made by other members.

Group productivity, as well as morale and integration, are dependent upon structure and control. All aspects of achievement are frustrated when structure is not firmly controlled. All are inhibited when structure is too rigid and operations control is too firm. The maintenance of an optimum balance among the different elements of group achievement requires insightful attention to the problems involved in group structure and operations.

An organized group may be regarded as a complex system of overlapping and interacting input values, structures, operations, and output values. The various elements and subsystems of elements are in constant balance, change, and counterbalance. The theory that we have developed outlines the structure and functioning of a group as a generally conceptualized operating system. Although the theory cannot describe in detail the many specific variations to be found in different groups, it should be of value in specifying the important variables to be considered in analyzing the problems of groups in general.

CHANGE AND SURVIVAL

The survival of a group may depend upon the manner in which it responds to the demand for change. The problems created by the demand for change and those resulting from the requirement for stability are not identical. Neither are they entirely contradictory.

We have observed that function and status define the stable relationship of a position to the group purpose. The formal acknowledgment of function and status provides the formal structure of positions with a high degree of legitimation in the expectations of the members. This legitimation is attached to the position and is independent of the behaviors of different occupants of the position. The formal system tends to exhibit a profound degree of stability as long as group purpose remains unchanged.

Whereas function and status are defined in general terms, responsibility and authority are given flexible, detailed definitions which provide for a high degree of adaptation to changing operational demands. The role that a member can play in a group is determined not only by the extent to which his responsibility and authority are acknowledged by himself and others but also by the extent to which others knowingly or unknowingly exercise responsibilities and authority defined for his role or permit him to invade the boundaries of their roles. It is more difficult for a member to establish the legitimacy of his role behavior in a group than it is to establish the legitimacy of his position. A member in a high status position may be granted an enlarged or a restricted role in initiating and controlling group operations, depending on the contribution he is perceived to make to group productivity, morale, and integration. Role performance is expected to change as operations change and as the environment imposes forces which demand adaptation or resistance in order to cope with the problem of change.

An organized group contains structures which are well designed to preserve its stability and other structures which enable it to cope with change. The continued power of a group depends upon its ability to maintain the legitimation of these structures, to utilize them continuously, and to keep them in balance.

Continued change in a group is dependent upon a structure that exhibits stability. A structure that disintegrates under the influence of change cannot continue to change because it no longer exists. At the opposite extreme, a completely rigid structure may collapse under the impact of internal or external stresses. There appears to be a median range within which flexibility and stability optimize the capacity for survival.

Numerous factors operate to complicate the problem of change. The overlapping structures of a group are not easy to perceive. The more clearly defined the structures of a group, the greater the utility of the structures for rational decision and action on the part of all the group members. However, individuals differ in the extent to which they will acknowledge the legitimacy of structure not controlled by themselves or by refrence groups with which they identify themselves. Group members also differ in the extent to which they value stability and change. Many persons feel threatened by change. Others appear highly motivated to promote group improvement and growth. Still others seem to thrive on turmoil and confusion. When active proponents of these differing ideologies begin operating in a group, both the group and its individual members have much at stake.

Reactions to proposals for change are likely to differ, depending on the part of the organization affected. Change in the formal structure of a group is likely to be accepted by the members if they perceive the change to be instrumental to more effective group achievement. They are likely to resist change in the formal structure when such change is perceived as a device for reinforcing the power available to individuals who seek to exploit the group. Members are also likely to resist change which results in lowering the status of their positions. A member feels devalued when he loses status in a legitimized status structure.

Changes in the role structure may affect a member's responsibility and authority directly, or indirectly by enlarging or restricting the responsibility and authority of associated roles. A member may welcome a change in role if it gives him a valued responsibility or relieves him of an unwanted burden. He may oppose role change if it takes away a valued responsibility or burdens him with a "dirty job." A member's reactions to marked changes in group operations and operational technologies are likely to be determined by his perception of the impact of the changes on his role.

Members in different status levels tend to react differently to the same proposal for change. Those in low status positions tend to be affected most seriously by change in operational technologies. Those in high status positions are more directly affected by change in formal structure. Changes in the occupancy of high status positions may affect all the members.

The readiness of individuals and subgroups to accept change may depend upon the origin of the proposal. Changes proposed by superiors, peers, subordinates, and outsiders are not viewed alike. Whether or not a proposal is regarded as potentially beneficial to the group or to its members as individuals tends to be determined by the members' perceptions of the motive behind the proposal. Both individuals and subgroups are likely to oppose a change which challenges the legitimacy of their roles, dislodges them from their positions, reduces the value of the outcomes they can experience in the group, imposes unnecessary hardships, or places them at a comparative disadvantage in relation to other individuals or subgroups.

Any effective disparagement of the formal system and the goal values it supports is most damaging to a group. Such action tends to undermine the legitimacy of the organization in the eyes of its members and reduces their capacity to support it as vigorously as they might otherwise do. Actions on the part of a member which cause others to challenge the legitimacy of his role, and power struggles between individuals or factions, are likely to be perceived by most members as threatening to the survival of a group. The direction in which the members throw their support may or may not be related to the objective merits of the issue being contested. Any action they take is likely to be determined by the extent to which the group has served as an effective medium for the reinforcement of their expectations.

We have observed that groups contain within themselves the structures necessary to preserve their stability and to cope with change. Granted a formal structure that is adequate to serve the group purpose, a group can best insure its survival by a continuously sensitive regard for the definition and utilization of its role system in conformity with the norm systems of the group. In concrete terms, this means that each member is permitted to perform near the outer bounds of his role as clearly defined by his responsibility and authority, and in conformity with the norms pertaining to his role. The more responsibly a member is engaged in the solution of operational problems defined for his role, the greater his opportunity to perceive the need for useful change. The more effectively he is involved in the planning and initiation of change, the greater his acceptance of it. The more adequate the authority of a member to carry out the responsibilities in which he is effectively involved, the greater his support of the role system which provides him with these satisfying outcomes. It must be admitted that these observations apply most directly to organizations that start out "right" and keep going that

way. They are not necessarily invalid when applied to organizations with a less fortunate history, but they are certainly more difficult to put into effect.

APPLICATIONS

A theory need not define an applied technology. However, a useful theory may stimulate the development of a variety of technologies. Although a theory provides a set of concepts and hypotheses that may be used for analytical purposes, neither the theory nor the technologies derived from it can yield a solution to a problem until analytical operations have been performed. This fact is generally understood in regard to the physical sciences. However, a theory in the behavior sciences tends to be regarded as useful only if it provides answers and solutions to practical problems without the necessity of diagnosis and analysis. This misconception of the nature of theory in the social sciences has at times resulted in considerable disillusionment relative to the value of the sciences. In order to avoid the disappointment of expectation, it is necessary to regard a theory, both in the physical and the social sciences, as a systematic method for increasing our understanding rather than as a given solution to all problems that may arise.

The theory presented in this book is based upon, and incorporates, a variety of sub-theories, the validities of which are well documented. The integration accomplished by this system defines related sets of problems for the scientist and for the practitioner. For the scientist, is has shown the need for more clearly defined research on expectation, particularly in regard to the relationships between drive, desirability estimates, and probability estimates. It has suggested a new approach to the design of research on group achievement. It points out the strong need that exists for refinement of methods for measuring morale and integration. The current methods of measuring productivity are far from satisfactory. The set of hypotheses relative to the relationships between productivity, integration, and morale should be subjected to rigorous experimental testing. There is need for research in a wide variety of operating organizations to determine the exact conditions under which various remedial measures may be applied effectively.

Despite its research orientation, the theory here proposed has generated a number of hypotheses which are relevant to the administration of organized groups. These hypotheses challenge the viewpoint that productive effectiveness is the only value with which managerial leadership need concern itself. Group integration and morale are here shown to be achievement values which are equal in importance with productivity. If this theory is confirmed by the results of further systematic research, it will necessitate a new formulation of the basic responsibilities of managerial leadership.

The theory presented does not suggest any ready-made solutions to group problems. However, it defines a set of concepts that may be useful for the diagnosis of problems. Although the theory cannot relieve the members or the leadership of a group from the responsibility for continued analysis of their concrete situations, it can be counted a gain if it sensitizes them to the important factors that need to be considered in their efforts to understand the problems of organization structure, operations, and achievement.

14.

AN ASSESSMENT OF TWO THEORETICAL FRAMEWORKS

ROBERT SWEITZER

One of the questions involved in trying to relate theory and research in educational administration is that suggested by a phrase of Peter F. Drucker:[1] the "organization of ignorance." Organizing our ignorance requires a systematic review of what must be learned, developed, and tested if we are to understand, use, and improve research in educational administration. This is no small task. It requires that we come to know what we "know" and try to discover what we don't know. It demands that we identify some of the things we need to know and do. Perhaps during the process of working on this never completed task, we shall come to learn more about what "knowing" means. The fact that there has been a recent outpouring of theories of organizational behavior, with an accompanying increase in investigations using a variety of pieces of these theories, tends to increase the importance and complexity of asking meaningful questions, of organizing our ignorance, and of our coming to know.

One approach to organizing our ignorance in educational administration is that of assessing one or more theories of administration and describing the implications this assessment has for research. Egon Guba has suggested that one of the problems of research is that of identifying and describing operationally the "information" or experimental variables, while at the same time preventing the operation of

From Stephen Hencley and Jack Culbertson (eds.), *Educational Research: New Perspectives*, The Interstate Press, Danville, Ill., 1963, pp. 199–200; 206–232. Copyright © 1963. Reprinted by permission of The Interstate Press, Danville, Illinois.

non-relevant, noisy, and confounding factors. The same problem exists in attempting to assess and understand a theory of administration: What is included and what is excluded, and why?

Two conceptual frameworks or theories of administration will be examined in this paper. Ralph Stogdill's "middle range theory"[2] and the Getzels-Guba "nomothetic-idiographic" theory[3] are both concerned with the internal social system of an organization. Both theories conceive of this social system as an open system that interacts with and is influenced by the larger social environment. Both theories employ a socio-psychological approach using as their reference points both intra-individual and inter-individual processes or variables. These two theoretical frameworks will be examined to illustrate some of the relationships between the theories and to point up some implications for the conduct of research in educational administration.

The concepts or elements that will be used as points of departure are not original with the writer. They are contained in a paper written by Egon G. Guba[4] which previews much of the more recent expansions and refinements of the original nomothetic-idiographic model.

The concepts or elements selected are: (1) behaviors, (2) formal institutional structure, (3) role structure, (4) morale, (5) conflict, (6) effectiveness-efficiency, (7) adjustment-integration, and (8) administration-leadership. This order, you will notice, corresponds to the left-to-right development that is characteristic of the structural arrangement of both frameworks, and the topics tend to move from single concepts to relationships between and among concepts.

GENERAL STRUCTURAL CHARACTERISTICS

First, let us look at some of the general characteristics of the Getzels-Guba nomothetic-idiographic "model" and of Stogdill's input-output "middle range theory." Getzels and Guba developed a theory of the social system through a hypothetico-deductive analysis of

Talcott Parsons' suggestion that the structure of an organization may be analyzed from the point of view of the sub-organizations or roles which participate in the functioning of the total organization. They perceived that their social system theory was isomorphic to administration. Thus, their theory can be used as a model for thinking about and analyzing administration. In Willower's terms, this conceptual development reflects analogical reasoning and polarization.

This theory of Getzels and Guba conceives the social system (the organization/administration) as composed of two classes of phenomena which are, simultaneously, independent conceptually as well as phenomenally interactive. The first class of phenomena is the *institutions* made up of expectations and roles aimed at meeting the goals of the system. The second class of phenomena is the *individuals*, each having certain personalities and needs-dispositions, and whose interactions make up group behavior. Thus, the first class of phenomena reflects a sociological analysis aimed at understanding group behavior in terms of the normative dimension of activity, namely, the elements of institution, role, and expectation. This dimension is referred to as *nomothetic*. The second class of phenomena reflects a psychological analysis aimed at understanding group behavior in terms of the personal dimension of activity, namely, the elements of individual, personality, and needs-disposition. This dimension is referred to as *idiographic*.

Since both the institutional (nomothetic) and the individual (idiographic) dimensions interpenetrate one another, an intermediate dimension is included in the theory. This *transactional* dimension is a "blend" of the other two dimensions and is composed of the elements of group, climate, and intentions. The term was used to communicate the assumption that the processes within a social system may be seen as a dynamic transaction between roles and personality, and that the phenomenon of behavior includes both the socialization of personality and the personalization of roles. Thus, nomothetic and idiographic are relative rather than absolute dimensions. It seems that in these terms, transactional implies "situation-oriented" rather than "institution-oriented" (nomothetic) or "personality-oriented" (idiographic).

The institution operates within and interacts with a larger environment. So does the individual. This external or larger environment is made up of three elements: ethos, mores, and values.

Each element on each dimension serves as the analytic unit for the element preceding it; *e.g.*, the social system is defined by its institutions, each institution by its constituent roles, and each role by the expectations attaching to it. Thus, on the following diagram of the theory, the primary direction of effects between the elements of each dimension is from left to right.

Stogdill's "middle range theory" was derived

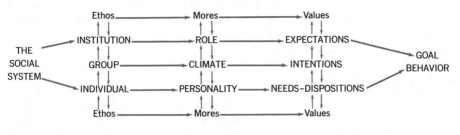

Nomothetic Dimension

Idiographic Dimension

Figure 14–1.

from his analysis of previous theories of administration and his review of research. He discovered that previous theories placed an overemphasis on certain elements and ignored other elements, especially group purposes and norms, expectations as an input variable, and group achievement. His framework attempts to relate psychological and sociological approaches to group achievement in an institutional setting. In Willower's terms, this conceptual development reflects the analysis of empirical generalizations.

The theory attempts to explain how member roles emerge in the social group and the respects in which the behavior of the members exerts effects upon the group. One assumption of the theory is that the structure and operations of a group can be described in terms of the behaviors of members in interaction. A second assumption is that "the different aspects of group achievement represent transformations of member behavior into forms of value which differ from the input behaviors of the individuals who comprise the membership of the group."[5] Three major complex aspects of behavior, each exclusive of the other, are performances, interactions, and expectations. A social group, Stogdill believes, can be at least partially described in terms of these three complex aspects of behavior. Human beings act, sense, perceive, feel, and learn, and these experiences help influence their behavior in relation to other persons. External to the group is a social order that influences the behavior of individual group members as well as the groups that are formed in the institutional group. Thus, the nature of a group is determined by the kinds of people who make up the group as well as the social environment of the group.

Stogdill regards an organized group as an input-output system that is an open system (exchanges members and values with its environment) in unstable balance. It is not assumed that an absolute equality exists between input and output, but a high degree of equivalence is assumed since in order to increase output above a standard level, some increase in input energy or values seems necessary. The structure of his theoretical system is diagrammed by Stogdill in Figure 14–2.

At the risk of oversimplification, the structure of the theory may be summarized briefly. Performances and expectations, two of the input variables, are aspects of individual behavior. The third input variable, interactions, concerns interpersonal behavior. The effects of these three input behavior variables in combination are evidenced in the form of role differentiation and role performance, or in group structure and operations. The interrelated performances, interactions, and expectations of group members tend to result in role structure and group operations. Group achievement, the end effect of these interpersonal and personal behaviors, is mediated through group structure and operations. The different aspects of group achievement are productivity, morale, and integration.

Schematically, the primary direction of effects between the four sets of variables (behaviors, formal structure, role structure, and achievement) is from left to right. However, the specific variables in each of these four sets

MEMBER INPUTS	MEDIATING VARIABLES		GROUP OUTPUTS
Behaviors	*Formal Structure*	*Role Structure*	*Achievement*
Performances	Function	Responsibility	Productivity
Interactions	Status	Authority	Morale
Expectations	(Purpose, norms)	(Operations)	Integration
GROUP STRUCTURE AND OPERATIONS			*EFFECTS*

Figure 14–2.

of variables interact and exert forward and backward effects upon the specific variables in each of the other sets of variables. The mediating sets of variables (formal structure and role structure) are conceived as the structuring and patterning of member input variables which result in group outputs.

In a more recent discussion of his theory,[6] Stogdill has pointed out that his theory has the characteristics of a paradigm. It suggests a basis for the classification and analysis of present knowledge and research on administration in terms of a systematic terminology. As a paradigm, Stogdill has diagrammed his conceptual framework[7] as indicated in Figures 14–3 and 14–4.

Elements on the left tend to influence elements on the right, and elements at the top of the diagram tend to influence elements on lower levels. Thus, "movement" tends to be from left to right and from top to bottom resulting in a "downward-to-the-right" movement from "Performance" to "Achievements."

Figure 14–4 shows the Intergroup Outputs resulting from the Intragroup Inputs of Group A and the Intragroup Inputs of Group B. In this case the "movement" is from the outside to the inside and from top to bottom, then moving from the outside at the bottom to the outside at the top. The result is a kind of "overlapping, circular movement."

From this brief and oversimplified description of the general structural characteristics of the Getzels-Guba and Stogdill conceptual frameworks, certain broad complementarity emerges. Both frameworks are assumed to be open systems; *i.e.*, the organized group interacts with its larger environment. Both frameworks assume that the organized group is in a dynamic condition of unstable balance and is self-regulating. The matter of relationships between variables is a question of degree, not of kind; the view is relative, rather than absolute. (This means that the analyses of data obtained through research that uses these two frameworks should employ non-parametric statistical concepts and techniques.) The basic emphasis of both frameworks is on role expectations which are viewed as stemming simultaneously from the transaction between institutional and individual roots.

BEHAVIORS

In the Getzels-Guba theory both dimensions, the institution and the individual, interpenetrate. It is necessary to know both the role expectations and needs-dispositions in order to understand the behavior and interaction of specific role incumbents in a given institution. Motives for behavior may be thought of as needs and expectations, the needs deriving from personalistic sets and propensities and

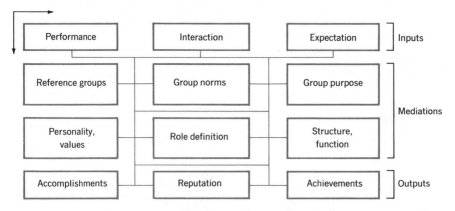

Figure 14–3. Conceptual structure for a person-interperson system.

Intragroup A (Inputs)	Intergroup (Outputs)	Intragroup B (Inputs)

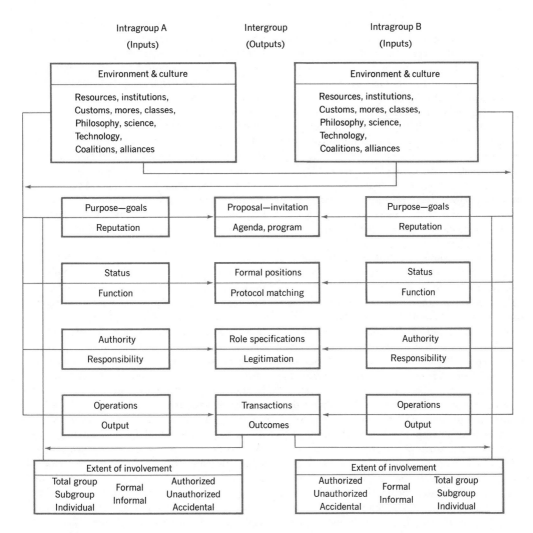

Figure 14–4. Conceptual structure for an intragroup-intergroup system.

the expectations deriving from institutional obligations and requirements.

In the Getzels-Guba theory a given act is thought of as deriving simultaneously from both the nomothetic and idiographic dimensions. The social behavior of an individual results as he attempts to cope with an environment made up of patterns of expectations for his behavior in ways that are consistent with his own independent pattern of needs. Thus,

behavior is defined by the general equation $B = f (R\ P)$, where B is observed behavior, R is a given institutional role defined by the expectations attaching to it, and P is the personality of the particular role incumbent defined by his needs-dispositions. A role incumbent's behavior may be described along a continuum ranging from primary emphasis on role-relevant performance (nomothetic) to primary emphasis on personality-relevant performance (idiographic). The transactional mode of behavior is not just a compromise between nomothetic and idiographic dimensions. It describes a deliberate attempt to be thoroughly aware of the limits and resources of both individual and institution and to apply the two as a particular problem may demand. Thus, in the equation B = f (R P), in transactional behavior R and P are maximized or minimized as the situation requires.

In Stogdill's conceptual framework three variables are conceived as major elements in behaviors: interaction, performance, and expectation. Interaction consists of an action-reaction sequence in which the reactions of each participant in the sequence are responses to actions initiated by other participants. Thus, in a system composed of two members, X reacts to Y and Y reacts to X in such a way that the response of each is a reaction to the behavior of the other. Performance is conceived as a response which may be identified as one of the actions or reactions that make up the operations of an interaction system. Expectation is defined as a readiness for reinforcement. It is conceived as a function of drive, the estimated level of desirability of a possible outcome, and the estimated probability of the outcome. The estimated probability of the occurrence of an outcome is an individual's prediction, judgment, or guess relative to the likelihood that a given event will occur. The estimated desirability of an outcome is an individual's judgment relative to the satisfying of, need for, demand for, appropriateness of, or pleasantness or unpleasantness of a possible outcome. The interrelationship among these three variables of behavior was illustrated in Figure 14–3.

From this cryptic and somewhat distorted summary of the framework of Getzels-Guba and of Stogdill, it is apparent that there is an overlapping as well as a difference in these two frameworks regarding "behavior." The concepts used in each framework, however, contribute to a more complete understanding of the corresponding concepts of behavior used in the other framework. Stogdill uses the more global or molar concept of behavior whose three component parts (performance, interaction, and expectations) are operationally defined. The Getzels-Guba model emphasizes both the institutional and individual dimensions of the interaction and expectation components. Both frameworks place a strong emphasis on the importance of expectations, with Stogdill pointing out that his elaborated concept of expectation (a complex function of drive, estimated probability of occurrence, and the estimated desirability of occurence of an outcome) enables us to account for the direction and continuity of behavior as well as accounting for prediction and value. Both frameworks explicitly and impilictly conceive of behavior as having an institutional as well as an individual base. Both limit behavior to the institutional setting, while at the same time realizing the effect of external events on institutional behaviors.

At least one contribution to research in administration that each framework makes could be stated as follows: Stogdill provides a broad framework or concept of behavior and relates this input variable with other variables and combinations of variables (mediating variables, group structure and operations, and group outputs) in his total classification system. The result is a rather tight, inclusive conceptual sub-system composed of interpenetrating but somewhat discrete variables. Getzels and Guba provide us with a simpler but equally compact and interrelated framework that suggests useful dimensions of the expectation variable suggested by Stogdill and which could be used for research purposes. Both frameworks are extremely heuristic regarding the concept of "behaviors."

FORMAL INSTITUTIONAL STRUCTURE

The Getzels-Guba theory conceives of administration structurally as a hierarchy of subordinate-superordinate relationships within a social system, and functionally as a hierarchy of relationships that serves as the locus for allocating and coordinating roles and facilities. All societies (social systems) have certain imperative functions that are to be carried out in certain established ways. Functions such as governing, educating, or policing within a society tend to become "institutionalized," and the agencies carrying out these institutionalized functions for the society are referred to as "institutions." Institutions share the common values of the larger society of which they are a part. Institutions are structural because carrying out a specific purpose or function requires an organization, and organization implies component parts and some rules about how these parts should be interrelated. The institutional functions, of course, are carried out by human agents.

Formal structure is conceived by Stogdill as relating to at least five elements: the function of a position, status of a position, group purpose, group norms, and formal organization. The function of a position defines the general nature of the contribution that the position incumbent is expected to make toward the accomplishment of the group purpose. The status of a position is, in essence, the degree of freedom granted the position incumbent in initiating and maintaining the goal direction and structure of the system in which his position is located. It is defined contextually in relation to the status and function of all other positions in the system. The group purpose consists of a set of mutually confirmed desirability estimates relative to and appropriate for valued outcomes that may obtain as a result of group structure and operations.

Group norms and goals are to the group what value systems are to the individual. They represent sets of values that are used to evaluate alternative outcomes and to compare the norms and purposes of other groups. The norms tend to induce conformity in belief, conduct, and performance when perceived as pertinent to group purpose and operations. In this sense norms—along with goals, rules, traditions, and rituals—represent mutually reinforced sets of expectations.

Formal organization represents the stability and legitimacy of the system of structured positions. It can be conceived as a set of expectations which the group has defined on the basis of rational considerations of suitability, legitimacy, and stability. It acknowledges the mutual obligations among the positions regarding the manner and form of initiation and response to initiation of behavior.

Stogdill suggests that a number of sub-systems interact to describe the structure and operations of a large organized group. Among these sub-systems are the following: (1) the structure of positions which is given formal definition and sanction by the differentiation of function and status; (2) the operative role system which is defined by the different degrees of responsibility, authority, and delegation exhibited by position incumbents; (3) the formal interaction system which is influenced by deviation in response to changing demands for co-ordination of behavior and subgroup operations; (4) the norm system of sanctions and prescriptions which defines acceptable behavior; (5) the system of member performances which describes group operations and changes in response to variations in the group task; (6) the system of informal interactions which relates the group on the basis of propinquity, mutual liking, and similarity of interests; and (7) the system of covert interactions which may bring together persons who challenge the legitimacy of the operative role structure and its associated sanctions.

If differences occur between the frameworks of Getzels-Guba and Stogdill, they seem to be those of inclusiveness, emphasis, and degree of delineation. Getzels and Guba tend to relate both status and position with role, viewing status as an outgrowth derived from role expectations which they classify as being on the institutional dimensions (having a base more in institutional purposes and related tasks than in individual personality and needs). Stogdill, by differentiating between—as well as relating—structure and operations, tends to suggest that structure as defined by Getzels and Guba may carry too great a burden. His inclusion of the concepts "authority" and "responsibility" as aspects of role structure, while being correlative with the Getzels-Guba concept of "role," tends to add additional meaning to the interplay between formal structure and role structure. This is an excellent example of the need to understand each "theory" within its own structure of concepts. Both frameworks seem to be taking into consideration the same phenomena, but the variables of the conceptual system indicate how these phenomena are described and "fit into" the structure of the entire conceptual system.

Examples of the "kinds" of questions generated by one or both of these frameworks are:

Do individuals in higher status positions have a greater degree of freedom than do occupants in lower status positions?

Does the survival of an organization require both the reinforcement of structural integrity and the achievement of tasks?

Does the basic process of organizing itself create a situation that rewards certain group members and at the same time disappoints the expectations of other group members?

If the formal operations of an organization do not sufficiently structure and fulfill the expectations of the members of the organization, will there result insufficient organizational cohesion, stability, and morale to accomplish institutional purposes?

ROLE STRUCTURE

In the Getzels-Guba conceptual framework, the most important analytic unit of the institution is the role. Roles are viewed not only as the dynamic aspects of the offices, statuses, and positions within an institution, but also as the definition of the behavior of role incumbents. When a role incumbent puts into effect the privileges, obligations, responsibilities, and powers of the role, he is said to be performing his role. Roles are defined in terms of role expectations which define for the actor what

he should or should not do so long as he is the incumbent of the particular role. Institutional tasks are organized into roles which serve as norms for the behavior of the role incumbent.

Roles are seen by Getzels and Guba as interdependent, since each role derives its meaning from the other related roles in the institution. Thus a role prescribes not only what is expected of a given role incumbent but also implies what is expected of the incumbents of other roles within the institution and for related roles outside the institution. The resulting fusing of two of more roles into a coherent, interactive unit produces the structure characteristic of a given institution.

Getzels and Guba recognize that roles have an individual as well as an institutional dimension. The needs-dispositions of a role incumbent govern his unique reactions to the environment and to the expectations in the environment. These needs-dispositions influence individual tendencies to orient and act with respect to tasks and persons in certain manners and to expect certain consequences from these actions.

Stogdill conceives the role system of an institution as a set of expectations arrived at through the mutual interaction of group members. A group member's role defines the responsibility and authority he is expected to exercise by virtue of the status and functions of the position he occupies, the demands made upon him by changes in group operation, and the kind of person he is perceived to be by other group members. Thus, Stogdill views expectations as an input variable and conceives of the role structure of an institution as being composed of three variables: responsibility, authority, and group operations.

Responsibility is defined by Stogdill as the specific set or range of performances (behavior) that a member is expected to exhibit by virtue of the operational demands made upon his position in a formally acknowledged structure. Organizational authority consists of the degree of freedom a position incumbent is expected to exercise in initiating performance and interaction within this formally acknowledged group structure. Group operations consist of all the actions and interactions which maintain the structure and accomplish the purpose of the group.

Both frameworks make a distinction between role and the status and function of a position. Both frameworks reflect the influence of Talcott Parsons: the status of a position is viewed as being more "universalistic" while the role of an incumbent of a position is viewed as being more "particularistic." Stogdill's linking of "status" with "enduring operations" and "role" with "changing operational demands" tends to suggest considerations that might possibly be incorporated into the Getzels-Guba model without distorting the structure of the model. The difficulty for Getzels and Guba in attempting to do this would not be in deciding whether status and enduring operations are *implicit* in the nomothetic dimension, but in deciding whether role (now on the nomothetic dimension) and changing operational demands could be placed on the nomothetic dimension, *i.e.*, whether these changing demands can originate from individual sources as well as from institutional sources (job definitions, policy shifts, and so on).

MORALE

Morale is one of the "most researched" phenomena and still one of the least understood. Confusion of satisfaction and morale, definitional disagreements concerning morale as an input or output variable or both, and resulting inconsistent research findings about the relationship between morale and productivity abound in the literature. Morale has been defined for research purposes according to the conceptual predilections of the researchers. The two theories being examined try to clarify these problems in different ways.

Guba has pointed out[8] that morale is related to the extra amount of energy output required to carry out institutional tasks. When there is conflict and antagonism, disharmony

between the individual and the institution, greater energy is required to produce a given outcome. Satisfaction is related to the compatibility between "wants" and "gets." Guba suggests that there is a need for an optimum degree of satisfaction prior to situations that call for greater and extended periods of extra effort. Thus, satisfaction should precede, and is a necessary prior condition for, obtaining an optimum level of morale.

Two components are contained in most definitions of morale: a communality of goals and a feeling of belongingness. Using the nomothetic-idiographic framework, Guba has suggested three dimensions of morale which arise from the congruence in the relationships among needs-dispositions, role expectations, and institutional goals.[9] Commitment is used to refer to the congruence between needs-dispositions and goals; belongingness is the congruence between needs-dispositions and role expectations; and rationality is the congruence between role expectations and goals. In other words, the morale of role incumbents may be said to depend on how well they can integrate the goals of the institution with their own needs (their sense of commitment); how much they can anticipate satisfying role expectations and personal needs-dispositions simultaneously (their sense of belongingness); and how clearly they perceive the logical appropriateness of their role expectations with the goals of the institution (their sense of rationality). Thus, morale is suggested in Figure 14–5 as being a function of the relationships among commitment, belongingness, and rationality, $M = f$ (C R B).

Stogdill conceives of morale as the degree of freedom from restraint exhibited by a group in working toward a goal objective. Morale is

Figure 14–5.

seen as being related to motivation in that an individual or group may be highly motivated to act but unable to do so. Given freedom to act, the degree or level of morale may be highly related to the strength of motivation. Thus, morale may be viewed as evidence of the motivation exhibited in overt action toward a goal, motivation providing potential for morale.

Stogdill sees morale as only one of three group outputs, the other two being group productivity and group integration. Productivity is used to refer to those outcomes that are designed to satisfy the expectations of the group as a whole. It measures the values created by the members for the group. Productivity is achieved at a cost to the members, while the satisfaction of the individual values of group members is seen as representing a cost to the group. Group integration represents the extent to which the structure and operations of the group are capable of being maintained under stress. The intensity of individual and group goals, satisfaction with the group and with the individual's role, a feeling of acceptance, mutual liking among members, satisfaction or expectations, support of group leadership, and subgroup support of goals are elements contributing to group integration. The result is a stable and clearly differentiated role structure that enables group members to know what they are expected to do and with whom they are expected to co-ordinate in times of emergency or crisis.

It seems sufficient to say that both frameworks define morale more explicitly than has been evident in many previous theories. Morale in these two conceptual frameworks is conceived as an effect related to expectations, group operations, and individual needs. However, the old problem of macroscopic versus microscopic is still unresolved. If morale is conceived as a general group (macroscopic) phenomenon, then how can one "measure" it except through obtaining information from individuals (microscopic)? Is the whole equal to, or greater or less than, the sum of its parts? This is a methodological question which is not

resolved nor even suggested by either framework.

The questions generated by these frameworks are of a number sufficient to keep groups of researchers busy for several years. Some of these questions include the following:

If there is no group structure, does there result little or no freedom of action?

If optimum group structure can increase group output, does maximum structuring of group operations tend to affect adversely group output?

—Does increasing the structure of a group tend to increase its freedom of action to a point beyond which further increases in structure result in decreases in freedom of action?

Does optimum group structuring become increasingly more critical in less stabilized situations and during periods of transition or conflict?

Since persons in higher status positions have a relatively large degree of freedom, is there a greater probability that they achieve an optimum level of morale more often and readily than do persons in lower status positions?

Does "group leadership," which determines group structure and operations, have a direct influence on the level of group morale?

Do applications of pressure and persuasion as a means of motivating individuals and groups tend to result in an unacceptable level of morale, especially when such persuasion may be needed in times of crisis?

Under what conditions is morale closely related to group integration and group productivity?

Is a desirable level of morale dependent upon the presence of the optimum or the maximum level of *all* of the following factors?

—congruity between institutional values and goals and individual values and goals.

—probability of the individual meeting his

own needs within the organizational structure.

—a rational relationship between individual role and institutional goals and policy.

CONFLICT

Getzels and Guba have noted four types of conflict: conflict between the cultural values of the larger environment and institutional expectations and individual needs-dispositions, conflict between the pattern of expectations attached to a given role and the pattern of needs-dispositions of the particular incumbent of that role, role conflict, and personality conflict. The latter two types of conflict need further amplification.

Role conflict occurs, according to Getzels and Guba, when a particular role incumbent is required to conform simultaneously to a number of expectations which are mutually exclusive, contradictory, or inconsistent, so that it is virtually impossible to meet one set of expectations or requirements and at the same time adjust to another set of requirements. They suggest three kinds of role conflict. One is the disagreement that arises among the members of the same referent group in defining a given role. Second, disagreement may also occur among several referent groups, each having a legitimate right to define expectations for the same role, but defining these expectations in significantly different ways. The third kind of role conflict is evidenced when there are contradictions in the expectations of two or more roles which the occupant of a given position is occupying at the same time (e.g., a superintendent who is also a parent, local taxpayer, member of the local Catholic church, spokesman for the profession, and executive officer of the school board).

Personality conflict occurs when there exist opposing and contradictory needs and dispositions within the personality of a given role incumbent. This conflict may be due to un-resolved discrepancies among needs, goals, and potentialities.

Stogdill suggests that role conflict occurs when a subgroup member discovers that he has acquired a role that differs somewhat from his role as defined by the larger institutional group, or when he defines his role in terms of personal values and preconceptions that have little reference to the purposes or norm structure of the group. Role conflict also occurs when contradictory expectations are made upon a position incumbent.

The conditions leading to role conflict are also discussed by Stogdill. Role confusion and role conflict tend to be created by at least three conditions: Roles may not be clearly defined; various persons and subgroups may entertain different and incompatible expectations relative to the same role; and the role may be perceived differently by the position incumbent and by others. But Stogdill also points out that although the group situation creates conditions which stimulate role conflict, such conflict is an attribute of individuals —their perception of discrepancies and their reaction to it—not of the stimulus situation. He suggests that conformity to the group norms tends to reduce uncertainty and role conflict. Conflict can also be resolved by overt action, the support provided by the formal definition of status and functions, and by perception of the legitimacy of others holding contradictory expectations and exercising differing sanctions.

Both conceptual frameworks define conflict as essentially growing out of differences within or between (1) institutional requirements, role structure, and goals, and (2) personal needs and expectations. It is rather surprising that neither framework includes "cognitive dissonance"[10] as one kind or source of conflict, especially when the concept of rationality is included as an element related to perception. Other kinds or sources of conflict that can be identified by one or both frameworks are notable by their absence, e.g., the conflict generated by a discrepancy between (1) the expectations a role incumbent perceives that others hold regarding his role, and (2) the expectations for his role that others actually hold; or between (3) the expectations a role incumbent thinks a group should hold regarding his role, and (4) the expectations he perceives that the group actually holds for his role. Yet both frameworks do suggest an adequate number of propositions and hypotheses for even the most ambitious researcher to explore. In these terms, both frameworks are extremely heuristic.

EFFECTIVENESS-EFFICIENCY

We shall now take a look at three problems that are often discussed in most theories of organizational behavior. The first of these is concerned with evaluating or describing institutional outcomes. Most of the literature indicates that when institutional purposes and objectives are met satisfactorily, group operations may be considered as being effective. When the individual needs of group members are met through tasks that contribute to the accomplishment of institutional goals, group operations may be considered as being efficient.

Both the Getzels-Guba and Stogdill frameworks point out the importance of separating the institutional (purpose) and individual (needs) elements when discussing organizational outcomes or achievements. They suggest that a single measure of outcome is insufficient to describe or discover what actually obtains from organizational operations. They underline the fact that multiple effects may result from a single act. They also suggest that the importance attached to (1) institutional outcomes (goal achievement or productivity) and (2) the meeting of individual and group needs may tend to shift from time to time and from one kind of task to another. The frameworks point out the need for more intensive and longitudinal studies that obtain a variety of measures of multiple organizational outcomes regarding a variety of tasks under a variety of conditions. More intensive studies of this kind in carefully selected institutions need to be undertaken.

The Getzels-Guba conceptual framework illustrates how these theories deal with the effectiveness-efficiency problem. Effectiveness is viewed as a function of the relationship between behavior and role expectations. The greater the compatibility, the higher the degree of effectiveness. Efficiency is viewed as a function of the relationship between behavior and individual needs-dispositions. Thus, effectiveness is concerned with the relationship between behavior and the institutional (nomothetic) dimension of the theory while efficiency is concerned with the relationship between behavior and the individual (idiographic) dimension.

Examples of questions that may be derived from these two conceptual frameworks are those generated by the Getzels-Guba model regarding the knotty problem of selecting capable administrators:

> Since effectiveness is germane only at the institutional level and not at the individual level, are tests of personality poor predictors of an individual's institutional effectiveness?
>
> How can efficiency be measured only in terms of the particular needs structure of the individual concerned when he may not be conscious of or able to express his needs structure?
>
> Can the institutional effectiveness of an administrator (or of an organization) be measured only in a specific situation and in regard to specific tasks at specified times under specified conditions?

ADJUSTMENT-INTEGRATION

A second problem that deals with the effects of group operation upon individuals is that of adjustment and integration. Getzels and Guba relate adjustment to the institutional dimension of their theory and integration to the individual dimension. A person is adjusted when his behavior is compatible with the expectations held regarding his role; he is integrated when his behavior is compatible with his needs-dispositions. However, the expectations held by others regarding a role and the institutional prescriptions of the role are perceived by the role incumbent in an idiosyncratic manner in terms of his needs-dispositions and goals. When role expectations and needs-dispositions are incompatible, at least as perceived by the role incumbent, he may be torn between attempting to become adjusted or becoming (or remaining) integrated. He may deal with this problem in at least two ways: he may adapt his idiographic needs-dispositions to nomothetic role expectations (socialization of personality), or adapt nomothetic role expectations to idiographic needs-dispositions (personalization of role).

Stogdill views integration as a group phenomenon that is based upon the adjustment of the individual to the organizational structure and operations. This is usually achieved through such means as the identification of individual and group goals, satisfying role expectations, and the like (previously listed under the discussion on morale).

Although the specific terminology differs in these two conceptual frameworks and the referents used vary slightly, they seem to produce overlapping if not identical conclusions. The dilemma of macroscopic versus microscopic elements (discussed previously under "morale") appears to be a major question raised by an examination of these two frameworks. For example, can there be such a thing as group integration without individual integration? Stogdill, using his set of terms, seems to say "yes," and the Getzels-Guba model seems to say both "no" and "yes." Can evidence of group integration be obtained in a manner that does not require that such information be obtained from individuals? Stogdill, as he defines integration, seems to imply "yes" while the Getzels-Guba model implies a "no" response. While each framework addresses itself to the term "integration," each framework conceives of and uses the term differently. The frameworks thus pose a most difficult problem for research technicians and experts in research methodology as well as for the theory builders.

A few questions suggested by the Getzels-Guba framework include the following:

Do most role incumbents seek a compromise between conforming to institutional expectations and conforming to individual needs?

—Does the "transactional" dimension represent a natural condition? If so, could deviation from this "norm" by individuals and organizations be used to describe the profile of an institution?

If the degree of congruence between expectations and needs is small, does over-adjustment (over-socialization) to the role result in personality problems that may be of a rather severe nature? Is a person likely to reject those portions of his personality which are least consistent with institutionalized role expectations and develop mal-integration or a psychoneurotic condition? (One cannot help but note the possibility that this problem may account for the growing popularity of various philosophies, such as Zen, that were previously not perceived as appropriate for Western civilization.)

If the degree of congruence between expectations and needs is small, does over-integration (over-personalization) to the role result in a role incumbent becoming "socially delinquent" or an institutional deviant or trouble-maker?

If social demands are generally seen as more imperative than individual ones (at least within the institution), does *socialization* usually take precedence—in terms of order and quality—over *personalization* in meeting perceived incongruity between expectations and needs?

ADMINISTRATION-LEADERSHIP

The literature abounds with discussion of administration and leadership, often using the terms interchangeably. It is interesting to note how the two theories we have been examining tend to look at administration and leadership.

Guba[11] suggests that administration is affiliated more with the institutional dimension, while leadership is more closely allied with the individual dimension. Administration is defined as beng concerned primarily with the implementation of policy "as it is" (goal-attaining), while leadership is seen as being concerned with the process of examining and improving existing goals (goal-setting). The difference is basically one of the purpose of the role incumbent, not his style of behavior or the position he might hold. For example, an administrator's concern for personnel development would be primarily that of improving the competencies and attitudes of group members so they might accomplish existing goals more effectively and efficiently. The leader's concern for personnel development would be primarily to facilitate the altering of goals as the purposes of the institution may come to take on new meaning to more competent group members. Administration is seen as being primarily "present oriented" and concerned with the perfection of means or operations that are directed toward present goals. Leadership is seen as being more "present-future oriented" and concerned more with processes of change for redefining present directions as well as for improving operations.

A few miscellaneous comments by Stogdill reflect his approach to administration and leadership. The higher a member's status, the greater will be the area of freedom granted him to initiate group operations. High status members experience a greater degree of personal freedom in the group, tend to try to enlarge the area of freedom of other members, and tend to be more tolerant and supportive of the group deviate. The group as a whole and its various subgroups permit members in high status positions to carry out functions the groups themselves cannot perform. Thus, Stogdill sees group productivity as being related to supervisory leadership, rather than to satisfaction with the job or with the group as

a whole. He characterizes the group as being conservative by nature and by necessity since it must maintain balance and control if it is to survive. To prevent the waste of group resources, productivity among subgroups must be equalized; to prevent dissension, rewards to all subgroup members must be equalized. He points out that although group productivity increases when members are given freedom to perform and interact according to task and role demands, excessive freedom tends to result in group indecision, confusion, and mal-coordination. In order to achieve effective group performance, the high status member must provide the necessary degree of freedom of action, definition of structure, and co-ordination of control to obtain a desirable institutional balance between responsibility and authority. The hear of the problem is to discover what is the optimum degree of freedom, structure, and control. An excess in any one factor may be accomplished at the cost of a deficiency in one or more necessary group outputs.

The structure of each of the two conceptual frameworks being examined creates difficulty in identifying their complementarity. Both frameworks move from the common emphasis on the power of a status position to a more contextual, interaction concept. Each framework, while recognizing hiearchical arrangements and differentiations, views role expectations as the major factor related to the ability of a role incumbent to influence others. Both frameworks suggest that administration, regardless of the particular style of behavior used or the task involved, is oriented toward achievement of existing institutional goals and probably should be primarily nomothetic in concern, nature, and emphasis.

These two frameworks would suggest that the results of the Development of Criteria of Success in School Administration project,[12] which show that elementary school principals do not exhibit "leadership behavior" or "consideration" behavior so much as they show concern for "group maintenance" and exhibit "initiating structure" behaviors, should come as no surprise. Both theories suggest that the investigation of the nature of the behavior of persons occupying various status positions in institutions should probably include an examination of this administration-leadership problem.

SOME QUESTIONS GENERATED BY THE ASSESSMENT

These miscellaneous descriptions and comments illustrate only one of the ways that might be used in making an assessment of two or more theories of administration. Admittedly, these are incomplete and somewhat distorted illustrations (e.g., they do not raise the question about the applicability of these two general frameworks of organizational behavior to educational institutions). However, I hope that this exercise does suggest some of the advantages—as well as the difficulties and dangers—of attempting to seek out the complementarity of two or more theories. In addition to providing a better understanding of each theory, such an examination can also produce a chain of questions of a different kind and level than often results from the examination of only one theory of administration.

Some examples of questions which derive from a look at both conceptual frameworks are:

1. Are expectations an individual (idiographic) input variable as suggested by Stogdill, or are they an institutional (nomothetic) input or mediating variable as suggested by the Getzels-Guba model?

2. Is the status of *both* an administrator and a leader defined by (or derived from) institutional prescription or by performance and interaction?

3. Is the style of administration (nomothetic, idiographic, transactional) defined in terms of the concepts and values held by the *subject* regarding his *own* role, or is it defined in terms of the expectations held by the subject regarding the role of *others* (the object of the expectations) and regarding the institutional task concerned?

4. Is "transactional behavior" defined in terms of average performance, interaction, and/or expectations; or is it defined in terms of the value given consistently to specified norms and sanctions by a given group or role incumbent; or is it defined in terms of a particular pattern of consistent performance, interaction, and expectations?

5. What effects on productivity, morale, and integration result from role conflict, personality conflict, and role-personality conflict within and between alter-groups and referent groups? Are these effects greater or less than similar conflicts between an administrator and these groups or between administrator and administrator?

6. What differences really exist between:
   a. Stogdill's "integration" and "morale" and the Getzels-Guba "belongingness" and "identification"?
   b. Stogdill's "productivity" and the Getzels-Guba "rationality"?

7. What outputs other than "rationality," "identification," and "belongingness" are conceived as relating to the "goals" of the Getzels-Guba model? Are these three variables seen as mediating or output variables?

8. Is the "degree of freedom" concept as described in both frameworks sufficient to describe the difference between two positions on different levels of the hierarchy? How is the concept "degree of freedom" related to the administrator-leader dilemma?

In regard to this last question, the two frameworks examined seem to suggest the following propositions:

Major proposition

The degree of freedom of a role incumbent is a function of the relationship between (a) the clarity of the size or range of the field of behavior that is defined as legitimate, and (b) the number of considerations that sanctions and expectations indicate the role incumbent should take into consideration in the decision-making process.

Minor propositions:

a. The higher the status and the clearer and greater the range of legitimate behavior, *but* the greater the number and importance of considerations that must be examined—the greater the difficulty a role incumbent has in exercising individual freedom of independence in decision-making (a definition of the administrator?).

b. The lower the status and the smaller the range of clearly defined legitimate behavior, *but* the fewer the number and the less the importance of the considerations that must be examined—the easier it is to exercise limited individual freedom of independence in decision-making (a definition of a leader on lower levels of the hierarchy?).

c. The lower the status and the less the clarity and range of legitimate behavior, *but* the greater the number and importance of the considerations that must be examined—the greater the difficulty in exercising individual freedom of independence in decision-making. (This may define the problem of school teachers and university faculty members.)

a + b Establishes a condition suitable for change by combining administration and leadership on differentiated levels of the hierarchy and for clear delegation of a balance between responsibility and authority regarding specified functions and operations.

a + c Describes a condition that lacks potential for change since only administration is possible under delimited conditions and when conflict is present. (This may describe many educational institutions.)

SUMMARY

In this chapter we have looked at the problem of assessing theories of administration, some ways in which a theory or theories may be assessed, and we have looked at some selected characteristics as well as the complementarity of two conceptual frameworks. We have highlighted the need to understand the structure of a theory of administration in a context larger than the framework of a single theory, no matter how "complete" or "good" that theory may be, especially if we are to use a particular theory in carrying out research.

As a departing thought, let me quote from Sir Frederick Bartlett:[13]

Sir Henry Head used to say that there are two sorts of young scientists. One can be led into what seems like a forest, and left alone. He will find for himself a path and follow it, though not without winding; and after a while he will get himself out on to a broad highway. The other can be set upon a well-marked track, and left alone, and he will pursue some by-path and go on and on and eventually he will end "up a tree."

Today with the numerous theories concerning organizational achievement and administrative behavior available to the aspiring researcher, we must be careful that we do not end "up a tree" in our enthusiastic attempts to promote theory development and refinement, as well as research, in educational administration. I am suggesting that one way which might help prevent such an unfortunate result is to assess two or more theories in one or more of the ways suggested earlier as a means of identifying some areas or aspects of complementarity of these theories. Not only will we then be able to identify the important concepts and questions that need to be investigated regarding *each* theory, but a higher level of question for research purposes may be identified that contributes to an understanding of *both* conceptual frameworks. We may even perceive better how we "learn to know" about educational administration. Such efforts and outcomes might result in a further and more rapid nibbling away by research and theory at the perimeters of our present limited knowledge about educational administration.

NOTES

[1] Peter F. Drucker, *Landmarks of Tomorrow* (New York: Harper & Brothers, 1959).

[2] Ralph M. Stogdill, *Individual Behavior and Group Achievement* (New York: Oxford University Press, 1959).

[3] J. W. Getzels, "Administration as a Social Process," in Andrew W. Halpin (ed.), *Administrative Theory in Education* (Chicago: Midwest Administration Center, University of Chicago, 1958), pp. 150–165; and Egon G. Guba, *Role, Personality, and Social Behavior,* Bureau of Educational Research and Service, The Ohio State University, September, 1958. (Mimeographed.)

[4] Guba, *Role, Personality, and Social Behavior, op. cit.*

[5] Stogdill, *Individual Behavior and Group Achievement, op. cit.*, Preface, v.

[6] Ralph M. Stogdill, a paper presented at a seminar on social psychology, sponsored by Muzafer Sherif, University of Oklahoma, April, 1961.

[7] *Ibid.*

[8] Egon G. Guba, "Morale and Satisfaction: A Study in Past-Future Time Perspective," *Administrative Science Quarterly*, September, 1958.

[9] Guba, *Role, Personality, and Social Behavior, op. cit.*

[10] Leon Festinger, *A Theory of Cognitive Dissonance* (White Plains, N.Y.: Row, Peterson & Company, 1957). See also Irwin A. Berg and Bernard M. Bass (eds.), *Conformity and Deviation* (New York: Harper & Brothers, 1961).

[11] Guba, *Role, Personality, and Social Behavior, op. cit.*

[12] John Hemphill, Daniel Griffiths, Norman Frederiksen. *Administrative Performance and Personality* (Bureau of Publications, Teachers College, Columbia University, 1962).

[13] Sir Frederick Bartlett, *Thinking: An Experimental and Social Study* (New York: Basic Books, Inc., 1958), p. 151.

PART THREE

INDIVIDUALS IN ORGANIZATIONS

The world of work has enormous potential to provide individuals with enrichment, enjoyment, challenge, and self-development. This is particularly true in such professionally oriented occupations as teaching. If one accepts the premise that all individuals seek meaningful satisfactions from work and wish to view themselves as competent, significant, and worthwhile contributors to society, then it is easy to understand why individuals who confront work environments characterized by distrust, arbitrariness, passivity, conformity, and paternalism often look to recreation, hobbies, and fraternal or social groups for sources of meaningful satisfaction. Some, on the other hand, seek more militant alternatives as they attempt to increase their control over the reward-granting structures of the organization. Still another group chooses to play the "organizational game" in hopes that they may be promoted to positions which afford more potential for satisfaction.

The relationship between morale-satisfaction and productivity or improved performance remains a subject of controversy in the literature. A careful analysis of this literature suggests that the two sets of variables are generally not related unless sources of morale-satisfaction are indeed dependent upon production or improved performance. By the same token, if morale-satisfaction is linked to dysfunctional individual or group activity, then poorer performance, at least from the organization's viewpoint, may result. Since morale is generally considered as a form of group sentiment, commitment on the part of the teacher group to the goals of the school is necessary for effective educational programs. The returns from individual satisfaction will depend upon the extent to which the rewards one seeks are linked to activities and behaviors which the organization judges to be directed toward achievement of its goals.

Teachers face at least two levels of decisions in the course of their organizational lives. At the first level, a teacher decides to become and remain a member of a given school. This requires that he display at least minimum loyalty, abide by the rules, and do what is asked of him in a satisfactory manner. In exchange for this service, he receives a salary, fringe benefits, a sense of belonging, security, and a commendation upon retirement. A decision at the second level, however, requires an exchange of services and rewards which, although more subtle and more difficult, are much more potent for the school and the teacher. At the second level, a teacher decides to increase his commitment beyond that which is necessary simply to maintain satisfactory organizational membership to strive for excellence and high-quality professional performance of his job. This second-level decision requires in exchange such rewards as recognition of competency, autonomy, and opportunities for assuming responsibility, for participating in decision making, and for experiencing success.

Deficiencies in the rewards associated with decisions of the first level result in, at best, marginal membership. Deficiencies in the rewards associated with decisions of the second level frequently result in a gradual decline in job performance, a condition which often goes unnoticed. This phenomenon seems to be explained by our tendency to be concerned with performance which is less than satisfactory rather than performance which is less than extraordinary. The extent of the commitment teachers make is dependent partly upon the nature of the school environment, and partly upon the expectations, values, and behavior of the school administration. Ultimately, the quality of the school is largely determined by the decision level for which most teachers opt.

Part 3 is concerned with the world of work as perceived by those who live and work in organizations. Although the focus of this section is on teachers, the essays seem to apply to administrators and students as well. Argyris, in "Individual Actualization in Complex Organizations," rehearses the theme of the inconsistency between the needs of healthy individuals and the demands of formal organizations, and thus sets the tone for the subsequent essays. In his study of high-skill and low-skill employees, the author demonstrates the prevailing need for self-actualization in man and dramatizes the dysfunctional effects—both personal and organizational—of the frustration of self-fulfillment processes by organizational life.

Included in Boyan's "The Emergent Role of the Teacher in the Authority Structure of the School" is an analysis of the teacher militancy movement and the subsequent development of collective negotiations and strengthened teacher organizations. Besides reviewing recent studies, Boyan penetrates beyond the usual treatment of symptoms of these phenomena to the underlying conflict between the aspirant professional in public bureau-cracies and the traditional authority structure of school organizations.

"Professional Persons in Public Organizations" by Corwin suggests limitations in the individual-versus-organization hypothesis developed by Argyris. Corwin proposes a framework which posits conflict in organizations between the bureaucratically and professionally oriented employees in schools. MacKay examines and extends the Corwin theory in his article "Using Professional Talent in a School Organization."

"Relation of Bureaucratization to Sense of Power among Teachers" by Moeller and Charters reports a study which presents a comprehensive examination of teacher reactions to bureaucratic tendencies of schools. The authors' finding that sense of power of teachers is greater in highly bureaucratic than in less bureaucratic schools is of particular interest since it is contrary to general expectations.

In the next article Sergiovanni uses the Herzberg motivation-hygiene theory as a framework for studying "Factors Which Affect Satisfaction and Dissatisfaction of Teachers." This paper tends not to support the popu-lar assumption that satisfaction and dissatisfaction factors are arranged on a conceptual continuum. The conception of man as a self-actualizing orga-nism is heavily emphasized in this section. Autonomy, influence, profes-sional and personal development, and the redistribution of authority based on ability are the suggested roads to self-actualization. Although the argu-ment is persuasive, not everyone is without reservations about the uni-versality of this position. One unconvinced scholar is Strauss, who critically explores the need for self-actualization and the arguments of its proponents in "Some Notes on Power-equalization."

In the final article Eugen Pusic sees traditional leadership patterns which rely on hierarchical control and extensions of these patterns which rely on hierarchical coordination as being self-consuming. He contends that coordinating functions in organizations are growing rapidly as a result of increased professionalization of employees. Further, each index of growth reduces the amount and kind of resources available for other organizational needs. "The Political Community and the Future of Welfare" (Social Self-management) discusses coordination by self-direction as opposed to hier-archical coordination as a means for conserving organizational resources while increasing organizational performance and individual satisfaction.

15.

INDIVIDUAL ACTUALIZATION IN COMPLEX ORGANIZATIONS

CHRIS ARGYRIS

Recently the writer completed the first phase of a research project having two objectives. The first is to provide knowledge concerning mental health problems in industrial organizations; more specifically, with understanding the difficulties the individual faces and the opportunities he has for self-actualization in complex organizations. The second objective is to test parts of a theoretical framework about human problems of complex organizations and is reported in detail elsewhere.[1] The purpose of this paper is to present some recent results which may alter some commonly accepted notions of individual self-actualization in complex organizations.

Although the research to be discussed is being conducted in an industrial organization, the theory and the results are believed to apply to other kinds of complex organizations (for instance, hospitals, schools, banks, government agencies). Therefore, although the terms "management" and "employee" will be used, it is assumed that the results apply to any (genotypically) similiar relationship between any administrator and employees.

THEORETICAL FRAMEWORK

Since discussions of the theoretical framework and the many studies from which it is evolved are available in other publications[2]

From Chris Argyris, "Individual Actualization in Complex Organizations," *Mental Hygiene*, 44:226–237, 1960. Reprinted by permission.

only some of the main propositi[o] fined in order to give the reader a ance with the theoretical foundations of the research. The most relevant propositions follow:

Personality is conceptualized as a) being an organization of parts in which the parts maintain the whole and the whole maintains the parts; b) seeking internal balance (usually called adjustment) and external balance (usually called adaptation); c) being propelled by psychological as well as physical energy; d) located in the need systems; and e) expressed through the abilities. f) The personality organization may be called "the self" which g) acts to color all the individual's experiences, thereby causing him to live in "private worlds," and which h) is capable of defending or maintaining itself against threats of all types.

The development of the human personality can be hypothesized to follow the directions and dimensions outlined in the following model. It is assumed that human beings in our culture:

a) Tend to develop from a state of passivity as infants to a state of increasing activity as adults. (This is what Erikson[3] has called self-initiative and Bronfenbrenner[4] has called self-determination.)

b) Tend to develop from a state of dependence upon others as infants to a state of relative independence as adults. Relative independence is the ability to "stand on one's own two feet" and simultaneously to acknowledge healthy dependencies.[5] It is characterized by the liberation of the individual from his childhood determiners of behavior (for example, his family) and his development of his own set of behavioral determiners. The mature individual does not tend to react to others (for example, the boss) in terms of patterns learned during childhood.[6]

c) Tend to develop from being capable of behaving only in a few ways as an infant to being capable of behaving in many different ways as an adult.[7]

d) Tend to develop from having erratic, casual, shallow, quickly-dropped interests as an infant to having deeper interests as an adult. The mature state is characterized by an endless series of challenges; and the reward comes from doing something for its own sake. The tendency is to analyze and study phenomena in their full-blown wholeness, complexity and depth.[8]

e) Tend to develop from having a short time perspective (that is, one in which the present largely determines behavior) as an infant, to a much longer time perspective as an adult (that is, one in which the behavior is more affected by the past and the future[9]). Bakke cogently describes the importance of time perspective in the lives of workers and their families and the variety of foresight practices by means of which they seek to secure the future.[10]

f) Tend to develop from being in a subordinate position in the family and society as an infant to aspiring to occupy an equal and/or superordinate position relative to their peers.

g) Tend to develop from a lack of awareness of self as an infant to an awareness of and control over self as an adult. The adult who tends to experience adequate and successful control over his own behavior tends to develop a sense of integrity (Erikson)[11] and feelings of self-worth.[12] Bakke,[13] shows that one of the most important needs of workers is to enlarge those areas of their lives in which their own decisions determine the outcome of their efforts.

Most human problems in organizations arise because relatively healthy people in our culture are asked to participate in work situations which coerce them to be dependent, subordinate, submissive, to use few of their more than *skin-surface* abilities.

There are three major sets of variables which cause the dependence and subordination. The formal organization structure is the first variable. (This includes the technology.) Directive leadership is the second, and managerial control (budget, incentive systems, quality control, motion and time studies) is the third.

The degree of dependence and subordination that these three variables cause tends to increase as one goes down the chain of command, and the lower echelons of the organization take on the characteristics of mass production.

Healthy human beings (in our culture) tend to find dependence, subordination and submissiveness frustrating. They would prefer to be relatively independent, to be active, to use many of their deeper abilities; and they aspire to positions equal with or higher than their peers. Frustration leads to regression, aggression, and tension. These in turn lead to conflict. (The individual prefers to leave but fears doing so.) Moreover, it can be shown that under these conditions, the individual will tend to experience psychological failure and short time perspective.

Individuals will adapt to the frustration, conflict, failure, and short time perspective by creating any one or a combination of the following *informal* activities.

a) Leave the situation (absenteeism and turnover).

b) Climb the organizational ladder.

c) Become defensive (daydream, become aggressive, nurture grievances, regress, project, feel a low sense of self-worth).

d) Become apathetic, disinterested, non-ego involved in the organization and its formal goals.

e) Create informal groups to sanction the defense reactions in c) and d).

f) Formalize the informal groups in the form of the trade unions.

g) De-emphasize in their own minds the importance of self-growth and creativity, and emphasize the importance of money and other material rewards.

h) Accept the above described ways of behaving as being proper for their lives outside the organization.

Management will tend to increase the employees' dependence, subordination, submissiveness, which in turn will increase their frustration, and sense of failure, which in turn will increase the informal activities. Management will react to the increase in the informal activities by the formal structure, directive leadership and managerial controls. This closes the circuit and one has a circular process in seemingly perpetual motion.

THE FOCUS OF THE STUDY
AND THE SAMPLE

The objective of the research, conducted in a multi-story manufacturing plant, is to study the mental health of highly skilled as compared to low-skilled employees. Our hypothesis is that since highly skilled employees tend to have a greater opportunity to express more mature behavior (be creative, use many abilities, be challenged in their work, and so on), they will tend to have a healthier work world. This in turn should lead to the highly skilled employees' behaving in more mature ways (as defined by our model above). For example, the high-skill employees (Department A) should express less indifference, apathy, dependence and submissiveness than the low-skill employees (Department B). Also the high-skill employees should express greater sense of self-worth, self-satisfaction, and develop more lasting friendships than the low-skill employees.

Thirty-four employees from Department A and 90 employees from Department B constitute the sample. The schedules of the questions used are semi-structured. They outline specific areas which ought to be covered but leave the interviewer free to decide upon the sequence of the questions.[14]

The interviews were held in the plant, on company time. Notes were taken during the interview and recorded immediately at the end of the day. Interviews were held on different days of the week for a period of seven months.[15]

EVIDENCE THAT THE
EXPERIMENTAL CONDITIONS
EXIST FOR THE EMPLOYEES

The design of the study calls for a priori predictions about employee behavior in Departments A and B. The differences, if any are found, are to be attributed to the differential characteristics assumed to exist in the technology of Departments A and B. (For example, A gives employees much more opportunity for varied, creative work than does B.) Before the hypotheses can be tested, however, we must show some evidence that the employees perceive the differences between A and B as we assume they do. The researcher's assumption of differences are based upon management's job-classification structure. It is one thing for management to classify the jobs in Department A as skilled and Department B as nonskilled and to pay the employees according to these classifications; it is quite another for the employees to perceive these differences.

Evidence that the employees experience the experimental conditions as the researchers assume can be obtained from a number of sources. Ninety-four percent of the employees in Department A (high-skilled) report that they have jobs in which they experience "plenty of variety," "as much variety as they can handle or more." Eighty-seven percent of the employees in Department B report that they have jobs which are "completely routine," "dull," monotonous," "with little if any variety."

Further evidence is obtained by analyzing the data related to "perceived personal satisfaction" about their jobs. Eighty-five percent of Department B (low skill) report that they obtain "no satisfactions from their work excepting good wages." Eighty-three percent of the employees in Department A report that they gain "much personal satisfaction because they have challenging and creative work."

A few qualitative examples to illustrate the differential feelings are:

> Department A: "I think the satisfaction I get is to know that I have done a job well. I like to do a perfect job; I like to feel something's done really good; it's really perfect. When I take a look at a piece that I can tell has been made well, I get a real sense of satisfaction."

> Department B: 1. "If the work is all right, then I make money, and that's my biggest satisfaction. If I don't, I get pissed off. What else is there to be satisfied about? I learned long ago the only thing you can get out of a good job is good pay."

> 2. "The only reason I work is to make money. No other reason. Some guys (damn few) say they work for pleasure. They must be bats. How the hell am I supposed to get satisfaction from this job? I'd just as soon get out and dig holes, at least I'd be in the fresh air."

A second assumption made by the research design is that the degree of dependence and subordination required of the employees by the leadership and the managerial controls will not vary significantly between Departments A and B. These assumptions must also be verified as representing reality from the employees' point of view.

Seventy-five percent of the employees in B and 84% in A view the leadership as "excellent because they hardly ever bother us, because they continually try to help us earn good wages and have secure jobs." In discussing the contacts that they have with management, 63% in B and 68% in A view the management as being "friendly," "down-to-earth," "interested in the employees," and "continually striving to make the employees feel they are not simple machines."

Turning to controls, we find that almost no employees in either department describe the budgets as pressuring them. One explanation of this may be that the budget system is only a few months old and has not had an opportunity to be felt by the employees. Turning to

the incentive system, 67% in Department B and 62% in Department A view the piece rates as "being fair," "some rates tough, some easy, but the overall average is fair," and "wish they were slightly higher, but this is not a complaint."

In response to a question on the freedom the employees feel, reflecting on the leadership and the controls together, 83% in Department B and 100% in Department A report they have "as much, or almost as much, freedom as they desire." Finally, in an over-all indication of the degree of pressure the employees feel, 91% in Department B and 100% in Department A say that they "never, or hardly ever, experience pressure."

It seems reasonable to assume that the degree of dependence and subordination required of the employees in Departments A and B does not vary significantly between the departments. This says nothing about the amount of dependence and submissiveness *perceived* by the employees. We are simply saying that whatever the amount is it is about equal in both departments.

SOME DIFFERENCES BETWEEN HIGH SKILL AND LOW SKILL EMPLOYEES

A method has been developed to infer the predispositions that individuals manifest *while at work*, plus their potency (in the Lewinian sense of the term).[16]

A word about our use of the concept "predisposition." For the sake of consistency and simplicity the personality aspects upon which we focus are all categorized as "predisposition." A predisposition is defined as a tendency to act in a particular situation. The predispositions are inferred from the interview data. The analyst combs the interview for any themes from which he can infer the desires that the participant wishes to satisfy while at work.[17] An analysis of these data show that statistically the high-skill (HS) employees differ significantly from the low-skill (LS) employees as follows.

TABLE 15-1

High skill	Statistical significance[11]	Low skill
1. Express a high sense of self-worth and self-regard related to their technological capabilities.	.001	1. Express a very low sense of self-worth and self-regard.
2. Express need to be active.	.001	2. Express need to be passive.
3. Express need to work with others.	.001	3. Express need to be alone.
4. Express need for variety and challenge in their work world.	.001	4. Express need for routine, non-challenging work.
5. Express need to have some close friendships while at work.	.01	5. Express desire not to make close friendships while at work.
6. Express need to produce quality work.	.001	6. Express need to produce adequate (quantitative) work to make a fair day's pay.
7. Express almost no need to overemphasize the importance of material rewards.	.01	7. Overemphasize the importance of material rewards.
8. Express need to learn more about other kinds of work within the same job family.	.001	8. Express almost no need to learn other kinds of work.
9. Participate in activities outside their workplace judged by the researcher to be creative.	.01	9. Participate in activities outside their workplace judged by the researcher to be non-creative.

These data confirm the hypothesis that the technology has an impact upon the predispositions and activities of human beings. Further analysis, however, raises the question of how significant this impact is if one is focusing on mental health problems.

THE DEGREE OF SELF-ACTUALIZATION OF HS AND LS EMPLOYEES

The answer to this question becomes evident when we note that the self-actualization scores of the LS and HS employees do *not* differ significantly. Both sets of employees have equally high scores. These scores purport to quantify (in a primitive manner) the degree to which an individual actualizes himself while in the organization.

In other words, even though the LS and HS employees differ significantly in terms of the characteristics listed above, their degree of self-actualization is the same. *Thus, in this case, the often-quoted generalization by mental*

TABLE 15-2 **FREQUENCY DISTRIBUTION OF SELF-ACTUALIZATION SCORES IN HIGH SKILLED AND LOW SKILLED EMPLOYEES**

	HS, %	LS, %
0–49.5	..	..
50–54.5	2.9	1.1
55–59.5	2.9	1.1
60–64.5	..	3.3
65–69.5	5.9	8.9
70–74.5	5.9	16.7
75–79.5	8.8	11.1
80–84.5	23.6	16.7
85–89.5	20.6	21.1
90–94.5	14.7	10.0
95–100	8.8	10.0

health practitioners that low skill employees will tend to have a lower degree of self-actualization than high skill employees is not upheld.

SIMILARITIES BETWEEN HS AND LS EMPLOYEES

If the HS and LS employees do not differ significantly in self-actualization, then it must be that in addition to the dissimilar predispositions, they must have similar ones which are of higher potency and which are being expressed. The data confirm this hypothesis. The four predispositions with the highest potency are similar for both groups of employees. They are:

	Frequency of choice	
	HS, %	LS, %
1. To be left alone by management	97.0	89.0
2. To be non-involved, indifferent and apathetic about the formal goals and problems of the organization	96.0	86.0
3. The experience skin-surface interpersonal relationships	96.0	90.0
4. To earn fair wages and to have secure jobs	92.0	89.0

From the first two predispositions we may infer the employees desire to be left alone by the formal authorities and not to be required to become ego-involved in the objectives of the company. Apparently the employees have withdrawn psychologically from the organization. They may be said to be in a state of apathy.

Apathy also seems to characterize the employees' predispositions with regard to their interpersonal relationships with others. We note that they desire few interactions and those to be mere skin-surface relationships. This apathy toward human relationships (as differentiated from apathy toward nonhuman relationships) may be defined as *alienation.* Employees who are alienated are therefore defined as those who do not tend to desire the rich interpersonal activity usually assumed by some personality theorists to be a basic characteristic of man.[18] In short, alienated people are willing to separate themselves from human relationships.

From the employees' point of view (especially those on low-skill jobs) alienation may be a sensible way to adapt to their working world. Why, they reason, should they become ego-involved in a world that will not permit them to express mature aspirations and to gain satisfaction of their adult needs?

At this point, the data simply permit us to hypothesize that the primitive state of interpersonal relationship inferred to exist inside the plant also seems to exist in the activities the employees engage in during their nonworking hours.[19] Thus the employee may be hurting his "long-range self" without realizing it.

Here is an important area for research. What precisely are the mental health implications of prolonged experiences of apathy and alienation? Can prolonged apathy and alienation lead to mental illness? If so, by what processes and toward what types of illnesses?

Returning to the data, one may further hypothesize that the alienation (apathy towards others and towards one's self) will tend to lead the employees in *both* groups to express a low degree of competence in their relationships with people. At the same time, recalling the job differences between the LS and HS employees, we may hypothesize further that only the latter will tend to express a high degree of competence in their dealing with "things." These hypotheses are confirmed. LS and HS employees' sense of competence and regard for their competence in interpersonal relationships is low and about the same for both groups. On the other hand, we have seen (Table 15–2) that only the HS employees report a high degree of competence in their dealing with "things."

SOME COMMENTS ON THE "HUMAN CLIMATE" OF THE ORGANIZATION

Let us now look briefly at the environmental culture of the organization in which these results are being obtained.

An analysis of the data shows that management believes, *and the employees agree*, that the organization is *not* pressure-oriented. (In fact, in the writer's experience, this is the least pressure-oriented plant he has ever studied.) The leadership consciously refrains from pressure tactics. As to managerial controls, they are just being established. One of the highest officials remarks that if controls upset people, the controls will go!

The employees in both groups report they appreciate the lack of pressure. They are very loyal to the organization, produce an amount that is appreciated by all levels of management, have continually voted down a union, and have a long record of low absenteeism, low turnover, and low grievance rates.

OVERSIMPLIFIED THEORIES OF INDIVIDUAL-ORGANIZATIONAL HEALTH

From the above, it is not difficult to see why both management and employees are quite content with each other and with the organization. Each group feels it is getting what it desires.

On the other hand, the employees report that they desire a world in which 1) they are not required to become ego-involved and made (partially) responsible for the organization's health, 2) they are permitted to be alienated and 3) they are paid well (from their point of view) and guaranteed a secure job. It must be stressed again that no adequate evidence exists to help the mental health practitioner decide how mentally unhealthy or healthy is this state of affairs. (As far as the writer is aware, not even a reliable and valid concept of mental health exists.) It may be that the situation herein described is not unhealthy for individuals and will not lead to mental health problems. On the other hand, there is enough evidence to hold with equal vigor the hypothesis that, as Fromm implies, alienation can lead us to become a sick society.[20] I tend to believe Fromm has made an important point. However, much research is needed really to test the hypothesis.

The other side of the argument that must be kept in mind is that mental health of the individual is a product of his total life situation. It may be that an individual can endure a significant amount of deficiency in actualization within the plant and make up for it in activities outside the plant. What little evidence I have seen seems to suggest that there is a correlation between the in-plant actualization and outside activities. People with low actualization within the plant do not seem to make up for it as judged by the kind of community activities in which they participate.[21] Recent, and as yet unpublished, research by the writer reinforces the above conclusion. For example, most of the employees (low- and high-skill) do not participate in "outside" organizations in the community. However, systematic research is lacking and no definite conclusions may be drawn at this time.

On the other hand, we find that the managers' concept of organizational health is equally obscure if not invalid. Management is using a set of criteria about organizational health which leads the executives to diagnose the health of the organization as high. For example, they see that absenteeism, turnover, grievance rates are low and that the production and loyalty are high, and on the basis of their theory, judge that all is well. The problem is that their theory about organizational health is oversimplified and internally inconsistent. It is oversimplified because it does not include the health of the individuals working for the organization. It is inconsistent because it has two inconsistent and independent sets of criteria for organizational health rather than one unified set. For example, management assumes that an organization with low absentee-ism, low turnover, low grievance, will also tend to have employees who are productive and who desire to be identified with the company, to participate in all decisions that directly influence them, to worry about making the company more effective, to feel some responsibility for the over-all health of the company, and to develop close relationships with management and each other so that such phrases as "one happy family," and "we're a close company," mirror reality.

Our data show that the above theory is not as integrated as management assumes. For example, the plant has a very low rate of absenteeism, turnover, and grievances. The employees are productive. Up to this point, management's theory holds. The same employees, however, also express little identification with the company, little desire to feel some responsibility for its over-all health, little desire to win promotions as foremen, little desire to have close friendships with management or with each other. Nor do they express strong needs to belong to cohesive groups.

This does not mean, however, that the plant isn't "one happy family." The employees, according to our measures, are very loyal to the organization because they need to be in situations where they are simply asked to produce and not required to become identified with, or deeply involved in, the company. As one employee puts it, "I love this company; it's a wonderful place. They pay excellent wages, give good benefits and they leave you alone. There's a relaxed friendly feeling here. You don't feel the constant pressure as you do in Company Y. No sir, I wouldn't leave this company even if someone wanted to pay me more." Thus, strong loyalty is not necessarily built upon an active, interested, healthy employee group. On the contrary, the opportunity to be apathetic, disinterested, non-involved, could generate strong loyalties within the employees as long as wages and job security remain high.

The most crucial needs HS and LS employees report are wages, job security, job control, non-involvement and togetherness, following that order. Does this mean that money is most important? Are we back to the economists' theory of rational man? The answer to the first question is, "Yes," and to the second, "No." If money is important, it is not because man is the inherently rational being pictured by some economists. The employee is still a complex organism with inner strivings to grow, to develop, to have a sense of inner worth. It is precisely because he is not permitted truly to actualize his potential that he makes a decision to "simplify" his personality, making money and other material factors most important. It is as if the employee says to himself, "I want to be a healthy creative human being; I cannot be, and still produce what I am required to produce. Therefore, I will say, 'To hell with my total personality,' and place the major emphasis on money."[22]

Such a decision is not a rational one. It is a *deep, emotional, human one.* Nevertheless, it makes money and job security very important to the employee. If this is valid, then administrators of complex organizations are faced with one of the most difficult human problems ever to challenge them. On the one hand, it becomes easy for both the administrator and the employees to deemphasize human values and to operate on a *quid pro quo* basis of money, job security, and benefits. As long as a minimum standard of human relationships is maintained, the "rational man relationship" could well flourish. But, as the data point out, such a theory will produce and reward apathy, indifference, alienation, and non-involvement.

RELATING INDIVIDUAL HEALTH TO ORGANIZATIONAL EFFECTIVENESS

If the above is valid, clearly individual and organizational "health" are so interrelated that it may be impossible to consider one without considering the other. Men like Lewin and Harry Stack Sullivan showed years ago that man cannot be separated from his environment. In studying the problems of industrial mental health, it may be that man may not be separated from the organization. The unit becomes the individual-organization.

In stating this position, are we making a value judgment that it is good for organizations to exist? The answer must be provided on two levels. First, as far as the researcher is concerned, organizational survival is not a matter of value. Organizations must exist for the researcher as do leaves for the botanist, human bodies for the biologist, and birds for the ornithologist. Without organizations, the researcher on organizations would have nothing to study.

Turning to the value problem from the mental health practitioner's point of view, the following may be said. Most students agree that, basically, organizations are created by man to fulfill needs that require the collective efforts of human beings. These needs are essential if man is to survive. Thus, stating that organizations must survive is simply affirming the most basic needs of mankind. *It is precisely because human survival and health are crucial that organization effectiveness is emphasized.* Without organizational effectiveness, man could lose his individual health.

This position is openly acknowledged by the employees. Interviews with the employees show quite clearly that they *feel* responsible for keeping the organization alive. The problem, from a mental health point of view, is that they too have internalized management's inadequate standards of organizational effectiveness. Consequently, they too, feel that low absenteeism, turnover, grievance rates and high production imply a healthy organization. They report a high degree of satisfaction with their mental health. In fact, our data lead us to predict that over 90% of the employees and 100% of the management in this plant would resist or even reject a mental health program that attempts to emphasize individual health "vs" or "over" the requirements of the organization. The employees report themselves to be "too realistic" to see such a program as in their interest.

Difficult as the situation may sound, there is at least one possible direction to consider. These feelings of responsibility for organizational effectiveness could become the foundations for the building of an effective *preventive* mental health program in industry. Is it not a sign of some health when an individual is willing to see himself in a realistic perspective in his relationship with his society? To be willing to give of one's self without feeling one is giving up one's self may be an important building block for a healthy society.

The argument is not being made that an overemphasis on organization could not lead to the ideal of an "organization man" who submits his uniqueness and his health to the demands of the organization. This possibility is admitted and must be avoided. It is the contention of the writer that, in the final analysis, the existence of organization man is symptomatic of sick organizations. Organizations are tools which help man to survive. They are created by man. Man can change them to facilitate individual growth.

Changing organizations today, however, is a very difficult task and the major barrier is that there exists no theory or empirical knowledge that tells us in which direction changes ought to be made. As mentioned above, the traditional management theories are inadequate, but the new human relations theories may be equally inadequate. One must conclude from this study that the informal employee system, assumed by many social scientists to be one answer to the problem, does not offer a solution. *The informal employee system in this plant sanctions and protects employees' apathy, indifference, and alienation.*

Herein lies the challenge of the future for preventive mental health. Much thinking needs to be done on developing dimensions of organizational effectiveness.[23] Much research needs to be conducted on how to maximize individual-organization health. In the organization studied only such a theory would appeal to both the employees and the management, who express a deep desire that the plant must survive, even, if necessary, at their psychological "expense."

NOTES

[1] Chris Argyris, "Individual-Organizational Actualization," *Administrative Science Quarterly* (September, 1959).

[2] *Ibid.*; see also Chris Argyris, *Personality and Organization* (New York: Harper & Row, Publishers, Inc., 1957).

[3] See E. H. Erikson, *Childhood and Society* (New York: W. W. Norton & Company, Inc., 1950); see also R. Kotinsky, *Personality in the Making* (New York: Harper & Row Publishers, Inc., 1952), pp. 8–25.

[4] Urie Bronfenbrenner, "Toward an Integrated Theory of Personality," in Robert R. Blake and Glen B. Ramsey, eds., *Perception* (Chicago: G. P. Putnam's Sons, 1953).

[5] This is similar to Erikson's "sense of autonomy" and Bronfenbrenner's "state of creative interdependence."

[6] Robert W. White, *Lives in Progress* (New York: Dryden Press, 1952).

[7] Lewin and Kounin believe that as the individual develops needs and abilities the boundaries between them become more rigid. This explains why an adult is better able than a child to be frustrated in one activity and still behave constructively in another. See Kurt Lewin, *A Dynamic Theory of Personality* (New York: McGraw-Hill Book Company, 1935); and Jacob S. Kounin, "Intellectual Development and Rigidity," in R. Barker, J. Kounin, and H. R. Wright, eds., *Child Behavior and Development* (New York: McGraw-Hill Book Company, 1943), pp. 179–198.

[8] White, *op. cit.*, pp. 347 ff.

[9] Lewin also cites the billions of dollars that are invested in insurance policies. See Kurt Lewin, "Time Perspective and Morale," in *Resolving Social Conflicts* (New York: Harper & Row, Publishers, Inc., 1958), p. 105.

[10] See E. W. Bakke, *The Unemployed Worker* (New Haven: Yale University Press, 1940).

[11] Erikson, *op. cit.*

[12] Carl R. Rogers, *Client-centered Therapy* (Boston: Houghton Mifflin Company, 1951).

[13] Bakke, *op. cit.*, pp. 29, 247.

[14] For a more detailed discussion see Chris Argyris, *Human Problems in a Large Hospital* (New Haven: Labor and Management Center, Yale University, 1956).

[15] A monograph being written provides detailed discussion of the research methods and analysis of the organization as a social system. This work is tentatively entitled "Theory and Method of Diagnosing Organizational Behavior."

[16] Lewin, *op. cit.*

[17] A predisposition is not assumed to be as basic as the "needs" or "need system" postulated by many psychologists. The psychologist's concept of "need" usually refers to those predispositions (to use our terms for the moment) that are more genotypic (that is, they are manifested in many different types of situations). Our predispositions are limited to the organizational context being studied.

[18] See Lewin, *A Dynamic Theory of Personality*; Erich Fromm, *The Sane Society* (New York: Holt, Rinehart & Winston, Inc., 1955); Harry Stack Sullivan, *Conceptions of Modern Psychiatry* (William Alanson White Psychiatric Foundation, 1947); Rogers, *op. cit.*

[19] Argyris, *Personality and Organization*.

[20] Fromm, *op. cit.*, p. 275.

[21] Argyris, *Personality and Organization.*

[22] Two points worth noting are: It is not only industry which forces the employee to simplify his personality. The family, schools, churches, etc., may all have similar impacts. Second, the employee is willing to simplify his personality up to a point. This does not mean he will accept money to be treated in an inhuman manner.

[23] For some preliminary dimensions of organizational health, see the author's "Organizational Leadership," ONR Conference (March, 1959), in a book to be edited by Luigi Petrullo.

16.

THE EMERGENT ROLE OF THE TEACHER IN THE AUTHORITY STRUCTURE OF THE SCHOOL

NORMAN J. BOYAN

The aspirations of teachers as professionals in public bureaucracies and the militant behavior of teachers as members of extra-school organizations have brought them into sharp confrontation with the traditional authority structure of the school. Teacher-administrator relationships in the authority structure have received little systematic attention from students of school organization. Role analysis represents a more established research tradition in education than structural analysis. As a result, investigators of teacher-administrator relationships have produced a more extensive literature on the congruence of role expectations, and on the congruence of organizational needs with personal needs, than on the distribution of organizational authority.

The differences between role analysis and structural analysis as modes of inquiry emerge neatly in a comparison of "The Social Background of Teaching" by Charters[1] with "The School as a Formal Organization" by Bidwell.[2] Charters reviews in depth the theoretical literature and empirical investigations which have drawn on role analysis as their intellectual source. The place of the teacher in the authority structure of the school receives only passing attention. Bidwell also notes the contributions which the role analysts have made to the description of the school as a formal orga-

From R. Allen and J. Schmid (eds.), *Collective Negotiations and Educational Administration*, University of Arkansas Press, Fayetteville, Ark., 1967, pp. 1–21. Reprinted by permission.

nization. However, he concludes that the conceptual and methodological tools of role analysts have produced only a meagre empirical literature on the place of the teacher in the authority structure of the school. Bidwell argues that understanding of the authority structure is crucial to understanding the behavior of teachers as professionals in public bureaucracies. It is also crucial to understanding the implications of the militant behavior of teachers as members of extra-school organizations.

FACTORS INFLUENCING THE EMERGENT ROLES OF TEACHERS

Changes in teachers as individuals, changes affecting teachers as members of school organizations, changes in the external environment, and changes in the posture of extra-school organizations have all contributed to a new level of teacher confrontation with the authority structure of the school.

Two personal characteristics of today's teachers are salient. First, teachers bring to their work increased levels of preparation and expertise. The availability of new and enlarged public and private resources has spurred them to pursue continuous upgrading of their professional preparation. The opportunities to do so, especially in the national curriculum development programs and supporting institutes, have encouraged many teachers to turn outward from their school systems and to develop a stronger cosmopolitan, colleague-group orientation which feeds professional aspirations. Second, the ratio of the sexes in the teaching force has shifted dramatically. Men now constitute more than half the total number of all secondary-school teachers. They generally express themselves more vigorously than women on career and employment issues.

Reduction in the number of local school districts and the pupil population explosion have led to the growth of larger and more complex school systems. Size and organizational complexity tend to generate bureaucratic tendencies. Meanwhile, teachers have developed growing distaste for and have demonstrated growing disenchantment with authoritarian and paternalistic administration. Teachers, too, have heard the message on broadening the base of staff participation in educational decision-making and they have liked what they have heard. In addition, the introduction of structural rearrangements in school organization, such as term teaching and the employment of para-professionals, has encouraged some teachers to assume expanded responsibilities for decision-making and most teachers to seek initial or additional relief from non-instructional tasks and activities.

Teachers have also felt the impact of powerful extraorganizational forces. The public at all levels has demonstrated its acceptance of the crucial role of education as an instrument of national policy. The new climate of public opinion has encouraged teachers to feel more confident that their work is important, to feel more justified in demanding greater recognition for their services, and to seek a more central seat at the educational decision-making table.

As members of extra-school organizations (both "professional association" and "union"), the behavior of teachers has shifted from relative docility to aggressive militancy. The contributing factors reside in themselves, in the school systems in which they work, and in the larger society in which they live. Part of their more militant behavior derives from personal desire and associational press to act more like professionals and to aspire to professional-level social and economic rewards. Part derives from the intense competition between professional association and union for membership and for exclusive recognition as bargaining or negotiating representative. Part, it is suspected, derives from the larger proportion of men who have entered teaching as a career and who are determined that they shall enjoy a rewarding career. Part, it is hypothesized, derives from a reaction to protect themselves from the militancy of attacks on schools and teachers from both the "hard right" and the "new left."

The cumulative effect of personal, intra-organizational, and extra-organizational factors has stimulated large numbers of teachers to seek, through extra-school organizations, an expanded role in the government and governance of schools.[3] It is the search for this expanded role which has brought teachers into direct confrontation with the existing authority structure of schools. It is in this search that reside the critical implications for teacher-administrator relationships.

THE TEACHER IN THE AUTHORITY STRUCTURE OF THE SCHOOL

Weber, the father of modern organizational analysis, defines authority as legitimated power. Legitimation refers to acceptability by subordinates of the exercise of power by super-ordinates, in particular the exercise of influence over organizational behavior. Contemporary students of formal organizations generally follow Weber's lead in their discussions of authority. Etzioni,[4] for example, relates the distribution of authority to the organizational need for control of behavior.[5] Katz and Kahn[6] speak of the authority structure as directly derivative of the inescapable organizational need to monitor the performance of members. Dornbusch and his associates,[7] in similar vein, locate evaluation as central to the distribution of authority. In the literature on educational organizations, Griffiths[8] implies that the authority structure reflects the distribution of control over decision-making.

In the "ideal-type" bureaucracy, as described and advocated by Weber, the authority of position and the authority of competence coincide. Contemporary organizational analysts have noted, however, the potential for conflict between the authority of position and the authority of competence when the organizational "subordinate" performs complex, technical tasks. For example, Parsons[9] observed that the articulation between managerial and technical levels in organizations suffers as the expertise of the technical personnel increases.

The more expert (that is, professional) the technical personnel become, the more restive they become about managerial decisions concerning technical activities and about the competence of the managerial personnel to supervise technical performance.

Parsons has neatly identified the source of conflict between conventional bureaucratic authority and professional authority. Bureaucratic authority presumes a rational distribution of power over a hierarchy of positions in which incumbents of superordinate positions possess authority over subordinates. Professional authority, on the other hand, presumes a collegial, rather than a hierarchical, relationship in which the distribution of authority rests on demonstrated knowledge or competence.

> The source of discipline within a bureaucracy is not the colleague group but the hierarchy of authority. Performance is controlled by directives received from one's superiors rather than by self-imposed standards and peer-group surveillance, as is the case among professionals. This difference in social control, which is related to that between expertness and discipline . . . constitutes the basic distinguishing feature between professional and bureaucratic institutions, which have otherwise many similar characteristics. The significance of this difference is brought into sharp relief if one examines people who are subject to both forms of social control; that is, professionals in a bureaucracy.[10]

Teachers as aspirant professionals in public bureaucracies

The traditional authority structure of the school includes a unique mix of administrative and supervisory dimensions of authority. Administrative authority, here, refers to the distribution of legitimated power to promulgate rules and regulations which govern the organizational behavior of members in general. Supervisory authority refers to the distribution of legitimated power to define and to assess the specific task performance of members of the organization. In schools, administrative officers have traditionally exercised both the administrative and the supervisory dimensions of authority. The administrative dimension of authority, however, rests on the social control of organizational discipline. The supervisory dimension of authority rests, presumably and hopefully, on the social control of expertness.

It is exactly at the points of difference between the social control of discipline and the social control of expertness that the emergent role of the teacher *as an aspirant professional* thrusts him into confrontation with the traditional authority structure of the school. The traditional structure assumes a differential in technical expertness between teachers and administrators that justifies merger of the authority of position and the authority of competence at the managerial level. When teachers perceive that the assumed differential narrows, vanishes, or reverses itself, they tend to challenge vigorously one of the foundations of the existing authority structure.

The challenge itself is not new (Lieberman[11]). Becker[12] reported that teachers recognized and desired to confirm (legitimate) the difference between administrative authority and supervisory authority. The Chicago public school teachers whom he interviewed strongly preferred the principal to work with them on a collegial basis in matters of curriculum and instruction. At the same time, they wanted him to exercise his administrative authority to control pupil behavior and to regulate parental "interference." Other empirical studies of teacher-administrator relationships provide support for the distinction between administrative and supervisory dimensions of authority (Bidwell,[13] Bush,[14] Chase,[15] Moyer,[16] Sharma[17]).

The sparse research literature on the teacher as a professional in a public bureaucracy supplies complementary evidence. Washburne[18] concluded that the administrator either ignores or punishes professional behavior by the teacher. He also prophetically anticipated the development of teacher militancy arising from the lack of machinery for resolving the conflict of bureaucratic and professional authority.

Corwin,[19] almost a decade later, observed that increased teacher professionalism tends to provoke teacher militancy because the demands for enlarged autonomy stimulate strong resistance from lay boards of education and administrators. He found that initiative-prone teachers were more professionally and less bureaucratically oriented than compliant teachers. They also exhibited consistently higher rates of conflict with the administrative authority structure of the school.

Moeller's[20] report of the relationship between bureaucracy and teacher sense of power prompts the need for guarded generalization from the few studies available on the place of the teacher in the authority structure. He did not find support for his central hypothesis that extent of bureaucracy varies inversely with teacher sense of power to affect policies and procedures. Contrary to his expectations, teachers in "high" bureaucracies reported higher sense of power over their own behavior than teachers in "low" bureaucracies. In addition, he found that teachers in "low" bureaucracies reported that they received closer supervision, which he attributed in part to a lower administrator-teacher ratio and in part to more active community interest in the schools.

Bidwell's[21] extensive analysis of the school as a public bureaucracy confirms the need for sharper definition and more refined analysis of the teacher as an aspirant professional. He has identified the conditions in school systems which contribute to the development of bureaucratic orientations among administrators and which perpetuate a strain toward autonomy among teachers. Administrators must assume responsibility for coordinating the tasks and activities of personnel to insure the movement of cohorts of pupils through the public schools at a relatively uniform pace. Responsibility for coordination tends to produce bureaucratic orientations and behavior, such as reliance on general, impersonal directives from superordinates to subordinates. On the other hand, the "structural looseness" of school systems, derivative of the geographical decentralization of school units and isolated classrooms, tends to generate a pattern of relatively unsupervised teacher behavior, which supports and draws support from a professional norm in favor of teacher autonomy.

Mixed into the conditions which contribute to both bureaucratic reality and professional potentiality exists a common teacher orientation to develop affectively loaded rather than affectively neutral relationships with pupils. Bidwell[22] attributes this tendency to personal, training, and experience biases among teachers which contradict both classical bureaucratic and classical professional norms. In sum, organizational purposes and personal characteristics of members create three distinct sets of orientations among school personnel: bureaucratic, near-professional, and excessively client-centered.

There exists a rough parallel between these orientations and the characteristics of teacher types proposed by Griffiths and his associates[23] in their interview study of 1,000 New York City public school teachers. The investigators identified four categories: administrative aspirants (colloquially designated as GASers); pupil-oriented teachers; subject-oriented teachers; and benefits-oriented teachers.

Whether the Bidwell and Griffiths typologies will stand the test of empirical replication remains moot. However, they prompt properly cautious acceptance of the assumptions that *all* teachers are aspirant professionals or that there is a neat dichotomy between bureaucratic and professional orientations. It is more defensible to assume that teachers vary over a wide range in their commitment to professional norms (classically defined) and in their reactions to the exercise of administrative and supervisory authority. These assumptions, in turn, require specific identification of the points where the sub-group of aspirant professionals confronts the traditional authority structure of the school. To date, the confrontation has focussed on achieving two aspirations. The first is establishing an acceptable or collegial base of participation in decision-making on education as an expert endeavor. This aspiration directs itself to construction and legitimation of a pattern of school government in which teachers participate as *equal* partners with administrators and governing boards on the basis of their technical expertness. The second aspiration springs from challenge to the competence of administrators to assess teaching performance. Here, the level and direction of aspiration represents an attack on the status quo more than a proposal for reconstruction. Classical professional orientations include not only a preference for collegial participation in reaching decisions on technical activities. They also include a willingness and a determination to achieve self-control through strong voluntary associations *and* external surveillance by "peers who are in a position to see his (the practitioner's) work, who have the skills to judge his performance, and who, since they have a personal stake in the reputation of their profession, are motivated to exercise the necessary sanctions."[24]

Teachers have rarely proposed that self-regulation of performance be substituted for hierarchical assessment of performance. They have traditionally preferred substitution of the principle of seniority, tied to years of teaching experience and level of preparation, to any system of relating rewards to qualitative assessment of performance. The principle of seniority does not, however, meet the test of classical professional criteria.

The ambivalence of teachers on the issue of self-regulation threatens to slow, if not undermine, the drive toward professional status represented by aggressive claims for greater economic rewards, social prestige, and participation in school government. The same ambivalence casts its shadow on acceptable reconstruction of the supervisory dimension of the school's authority structure. Despite the strain toward autonomy and relatively unsupervised teacher behavior which has characterized schools, governing boards and administrators will resist formal discontinuation of hierarchical supervision unless a viable alternative is substituted. The discontinuity between teachers' professional aspirations for enlarged partici-

pation in decision-making on education as an expert endeavor and their reluctance to assume greater responsibility for self-regulation as professionals generates continuous tension in teacher-administrator relationships.

Teachers as members of militant extra-school organizations

Teachers as employees share a number of beliefs with teachers as aspirant professionals. First, they express concern about the wisdom of administrators in the exercise of administrative authority. Their aspirations on this score center on restricting through contractual agreement the arbitrary exercise of administrative authority. They also appear determined to monitor administrator behavior through provision for public processing of grievances.

Second, teachers in general express their restiveness about the competence of administrators to exercise supervisory authority. Their aspirations on this score center on restricting the rights of and opportunities for administrators to assess teaching performance and to make decisions on teacher assignments which are related to qualitative assessment. These aspirations are typically complemented by searching behavior designed to expand the boundaries of teacher autonomy and/or to expand the base of collegial participation in decisions on educational policies and procedures.

Teachers in general also share aspirations for relief from non-instructional chores, ranging from yard and lunch duty to clerical work, and for establishing equitable bases to determine load and assignments. They also share restiveness over their ability to improve their status *in* the organization through conventional organizational machinery.

In addition, teachers want greater economic rewards for their services. They want the higher social status and prestige which come with higher salary. They wish to protect the "in-group" from outside attack, to which the educational establishment has been submitted in the last two decades. They also desire to protect their rights to seek the most favorable conditions of work, including opportunities for mobility and transfer to more "desirable" teaching locations.

Teachers have expressed their aspirations most militantly through their membership in extra-school organizations. Their collective action through extra-school organizations has also challenged the traditional authority structure of schools, in both its administrative and supervisory dimensions. The challenge poses questions not only for teacher-administrator relationships but also for the tripartite relationships of governing boards, administrative officers, and teachers. As members of militant extra-school organizations teachers question the wisdom of administrator exercise of administrative authority and administrator competence to exercise supervisory authority. They also question the whole of the existing authority structure and its limitations on their opportunities to influence decisions on *all* organizational matters, not just decisions on educational program. Their aspirations as employees are more diffuse and global than their aspirations as professionals. The diffuseness and the universal extent of their goals, and the methods of collective action which they have chosen to achieve these goals, represent strategic advantages in their confrontation with the traditional authority structure of the school. Governing boards and administrators appear confused about what teachers really want and appear even more confused by the power play which the militant teacher organizations have initiated.

Teacher militancy and "power equalization"

The collective, militant action of teachers as employees in public bureaucracies represents their search to achieve "power equalization" in schools and school systems. Leavitt[25] provides a provocative and enlightening treatment of power-equalization in his analysis of the sources of organizational change. He identifies the influence of technology, of structural reorganization, and the "people-changers" on the introduction of changes in organizational tasks. The people changers fall into two groups: the manipulators and the power-equalizers. Leavitt describes at length the position, strategies, and tactics of the advocates of power-equalization, such as McGregor. However, he also notes the possibility of introducing power-equalization in organizations through involuntary as well as voluntary means. The collective action of unions, he suggests, represents one "involuntary" way of achieving power-equalization in industry and business.

The drive of teacher organizations to establish agreements with local boards for collective bargaining or professional negotiations fits the characteristics of involuntary power-equalization. Central to the achievement of power-equalization through collective action is securing the right, *as a right*, for greater participation by teachers in organizational decision-making which has traditionally been the preserve of the administration and governing board. The drive for greater participation in decision-making, moreover, goes beyond the boundaries of education as an expert endeavor. It encompasses employment conditions which are not unique to education.

The primary intellectual and philosophical tool available to governing boards and school administrators for extending voluntary power-equalization is the classical participation hypothesis (Golembiewski; Leavitt[26,27]). It is misleading, however, to equate classical participation with the kind and degree of participation which teacher organizations seek through collective bargaining or professional negotiations. Collective bargaining agreements pursued by teacher unions and "Level III" agreements advocated by the N.E.A. contain two singular extensions beyond the boundaries encompassed in conventionally-based participation.

First, teacher organizations seek to establish participation in organizational decision-making as a *right*, supported in law, as distinct from a permissive opportunity extended by governing boards and/or administrators. Second, and more significant, teacher organizations seek to establish provision for third-party involvement when their elected representatives and the legally constituted officials of the organization reach an impasse. Classical advocacy of teacher participation in school government makes no provision for the possibility of impasse. The more conventional approach envisions the participation of the professional staff and board in policy *development*, the *enactment* of policy by the board, and the *execution* of policy by the board's executive and professional staff. Both collective bargaining and professional negotiations anticipate a blurring of the usually sharp demarcation between the development and enactment of policy. For example, should the elected representatives of the teacher organization and board negotiators reach an impasse on salary, the right of the board to make a final decision would be restricted by referral to a third-party.

Referral of policy decisions to external third-parties threatens to encroach significantly on the power traditionally vested in local boards of education. It also threatens the balance of power previously held by the administrative staff, which has often constituted the third-party in consultations between teachers and boards of education.

Generally, militant teacher organizations prefer to negotiate directly with boards of education, to by-pass the administrative hierarchy. The reason is simple enough. Representatives of teacher organizations desire to negotiate with representatives of boards who possess the authority to make agreements. The determination of teachers to reach the board directly may, in turn, drive the administrative hierarchy into a more clearly defined "managerial" and executive posture. Teachers' unions, on the whole, seem to care little about such a consequence. Professional associations, on the other hand, reveal greater ambivalence on this score. Their ambivalence exposes itself in typical preambles which stipulate the "identity of interest" which teacher and administrators "as professional educators" share with each other.

"Power equalization" and the teacher in the school authority structure

The search for power-equalization touches the administrative dimension of authority where teacher organizations seek greater control over the rules and regulations which govern their behavior as employees, over working conditions, and over salary. There is some question as to whether increase in teacher power will automatically result in less power for governing boards and their administrative officers (Ohm and Monahan).[28] Tannenbaum,[29] for example, suggests that the "power-pie" is variable, not fixed. He argues that the power of both managers and workers in industry has expanded as a result of collective bargaining agreements.

It is too early in the history of collective action by teachers to support or reject the Tannenbaum thesis. It is not too early, however, to observe that the collective action of teachers aims to alter the conventional authority structure of schools through increased teacher participation in determining the rules and regulations which govern their organizational behavior.

Equally important to teachers acting in concert is securing the right to monitor the administration of these rules and regulations at the level of the individual school unit, as well as at the level of the school system. Contracts, or written agreements, typically provide for grievance procedures and machinery which permit a teacher to expose publicly the performance of an administrator who violates, in the teacher's judgment, the intent or the letter of the agreement.

It is at the point of participating in determining rules and regulations and in monitoring administrative performance that the teacher confronts the traditional authority of the school principal. The principal anticipates no relaxation of the level of responsibility set for him by his superordinates. Yet, he sees teachers' gaining and exercising the right to participate in determining the rules and regulations which he is expected to administer. He also sees their gaining and exercising the right to monitor and to expose his administrative performance while his right to monitor their performance threatens to evaporate. That principals are vexed and perplexed is not surprising. They are, more than ever, "men in the middle." They have reacted by signalling their own intention to gain, by collective action if necessary, a more central place in determining the rules and regulations which they must administer. The collective action of principals, stimulate and supported by the collective action of teachers, represents another alteration of the traditional authority of schools brought on by the emergent roles of teachers.

The relationship of power-equalization to the supervisory dimension of authority is more complex than its relationship to the administrative dimension of authority. Here, the critical elements are establishment of stronger collegial relationships in determination of the educational program and reconstruction of the system for regulation and assessment of teacher performance. The crucial question is whether or not the posture of teacher-employee on power equalization will completely overwhelm the posture of teacher-professional. Teacher-employee and teacher-professional agree on the need for redefining the authority structure of the school and teacher-administrator relationships. However, their agreement masks the need for adopting different strategies to reconstruct the administrative dimension of authority and the supervisory dimension of authority. Militant, collective action may well be required to initiate change in both dimensions. Once the change is initiated, the opportunity must be available to pursue uniquely professional aspirations through compatible organizational structure and machinery. The point may be illustrated through re-examination of the issue of self-regulation and assessment of performance.

The more extreme posture of teacher organizations is that teaching is so complex a set of technical behaviors that it resists objective assessment, especially by generalist administrators and supervisors. Therefore, a straightforward seniority system is preferable to any system which attempts to relate material or status rewards to judged performance. Indeed, the group norm on this score is so strong that administrators and supervisors generally support the position of teacher organizations. The only exception is agreement among teachers and administrators that the latter will, and must, assume responsibility for decisions on retention or dismissal of teachers during the probationary period and on advancement to tenure.

However, the strong sentiment for the institutionalization of seniority as the central measure of teacher differentiation threatens in the long run to blunt the edge of teacher aspirations for professional status. One of the major tenets of professionalism, mentioned earlier, is peer regulation of technical performance. Substitution of a seniority principle for hierarchically-based supervision on the grounds that the authority of competence rarely coincides with the authority of position does not represent a professionally viable alternative.

A strong collegial supervisory structure, unequivocally based on the authority of the competence of senior colleagues rather than the authority of administrative position, represents a preferred alternative. It also represents an alternative which can contribute to the amelioration of conflict between teachers and administrators on the issue of assessment of performance. The structural specifics include extension into an interstitial level, between the technical and managerial levels, of senior teacher colleagues whose expertise is accepted by their peers.[30]

Surrender for less by governing boards, administrators, and *teachers themselves* threatens to undermine the future of teaching as a mature profession and of teachers as responsible professionals. For their responsibility, in the supervisory dimension of authority, goes beyond gaining and exercising the right to participate on a collegial basis with administrators in decisions on curriculum and instruction. Their responsibility includes, eventually, acceptance of the basic professional criterion of self-regulation of technical performance. Their collective action, as employees outside the organization, must provide for this alternative *within* the structure of the organization if they are to achieve their professional aspirations.

Separation of teacher participation in the administrative and supervisory dimensions of authority

Wildman[31] has observed that the search for power-equalization in schools through standard patterns of collective negotiations may lead to institutionalization of conflict between teachers on the one hand and governing boards and administrators on the other hand. Collective bargaining assumes that the parties involved are adversaries, that there exist inherent conflicts between managers and employees, and that struggle for power characterizes the relationship. In addition, each party must possess sufficient power to inflict injury on the other if it is to press its demands with effect.[32]

Griffiths (in press)[33] has proposed that one way to divert the institutionalization of conflict is to separate the decision areas of working conditions and salary from the decision area of educational program development. The separation he advocates would permit administrators to serve as executives of governing boards when negotiating with teachers on matters of salary and conditions of work, in the extrinsic sense, and at the same time would encourage preservation of professional identity in deciding on matters of curriculum and instruction.

In essence, Griffiths[34] proposes the establishment of unique patterns of teacher-administrator participation in the administrative and supervisory dimensions of authority. In the administrative dimension the administrator would unequivocally assume a position differentiated by hierarchical authority. In the supervisory authority structure, the administrator would attempt to establish a collegial leadership role based on the authority of competence.

The need for two separate structures for teacher participation in school government is compelling. The first would encompass the participation of teachers as members of extra-school associations in the development of organizational policy on salaries and extrinsic conditions of work. The second would encompass the participation of teachers as professional colleagues, *in* the organization, on organizational decision-making in education as an expert domain. The first would permit teacher involvement via a bargaining or negotiations model in the development of organizational legislation addressed to general employment conditions. The second would extend the classical participatory model to include the *right, as a right,* of teachers to participate in organizational decisions on educational programs.

The relevance of the separation becomes especially critical at the point of third-party involvement. If there is only one structure of school government, if this structure rests on the base of conventional industrial bargaining, if third-party involvement is provided for the resolution of impasse as an alternative to withholding of services (strike), then it follows that third parties who themselves may not possess the authority of educational competence will make educational, as well as employment, decisions. Only by separating decision-making on educational policy from decision-making on employment conditions can this intolerable consequence be avoided.

"Conditions of employment" cuts into both the spheres of participation in organizational legislation by teachers as employees and teachers as professional colleagues. The assignment of a particular condition to one domain or the other may be moot. However, the very possibility that discussion on a given condition of employment may be referred to the bargaining table promises to encourage full "voluntary" review and consideration. At the same time, initial assignment of problematical conditions of employment to the "voluntary" sector promises to permit for flexibility of discussion and freer application of technical expertise.

In his analysis of the need for separating the administrative and the supervisory dimensions of authority, Griffiths explicitly cites the hospital analogy. The university analog is also apt. In the university, the administrator and the professor appear able to separate their administrative and their supervisory relationships. Furthermore, professors appear able to participate at various levels of militancy in local and national AAUP drives for improved salaries and working conditions while they participate as independent professionals in local faculty senates or academic councils.

Unfortunately, the past history of teacher participation in school government and governance has produced neither the ideology nor the machinery for separating decision-making on the administrative and supervisory dimensions of authority. Whether it is too late to establish a new historical tradition in the public schools which enables teachers to participate as members of militant extra-organizational associations in negotiating on salary and working conditions and to participate as professional partners in the determination of educational programs depends not only on what course teachers themselves choose, but also on what alternatives administrators and board members offer. Therefore, governing boards and administrators should take the lead in establishing and maintaining two separate structures for teachers to participate in school government. Without such an alternative teachers may turn increasingly to extra-school organizations to press for participation in school government and governance through bargaining or negotiating agreements based on the experience of private industry. In this connection, action by associations of governing boards and administrators, as well as teachers, at the state level is also critical. Unless legislators recognize the need for the two separate structures of school

government, each restricted to its unique sphere of organizational policy, they may indiscriminately project the machinery and procedures of private sector bargaining into education. If they do so, they may well contribute irreversibly to the institutionalization of conflict between teachers on one hand and governing boards and administrators on the other. It is this potential conflict which constitutes the overriding implication for teacher-administrator relations of the emergent roles of teachers.

SUMMARY

The implications for teacher-administrator relations of the emergent roles of teachers center on the authority structure of the school. Teachers as individuals, and the teaching force as a group, have become more expert. Teachers are, in general, better educated than they were in previous years. They have found new strength in their local teacher organizations, a phenomenon related in part to the intra-fraternity competition between the A.F.T. and N.E.A. for membership and exclusive representation. They have been encouraged by new patterns of public and private support for continuous technical upgrading to look more to their colleague groups than to their hierarchical superordinates as relevant reference groups. They have also begun to take seriously the exhortation of students of school administration to participate more vigorously in local educational decision-making. Because as individuals and as members of increasingly powerful organizations they are no longer the same, they have launched the search for a new pattern of teacher-administrator relations.

The aspirations of teachers have prompted them to search for a new level of involvement in the government and governance of schools. In the former instance, their aspirations include the establishment of the right rather than the sufferance to participate in decisions concerning the allocation of public resources to education and also in decisions concerning the distribution of resources within the school system.

In the latter instance, they are attempting to place publicly-exposed boundary conditions on the legitimated power of administrative personnel. In both instances, they have projected demands for involuntary power-equalization; involuntary, in the sense that governing boards and the administrative heirarchy have generally not assumed the initiative in extending the right for teachers to do so.

The flexing of new-found muscle will bring aggravation both to governing boards and to school administrators. In addition, the intra-fraternity struggle between the A.F.T. and the N.E.A. will prompt the introduction of issues which the leaders of the respective organizations see as functional to their competition for membership and exclusive representation. Here, even the best-intentioned boards of education and administrators will find themselves in extremely difficult circumstances.

Furthermore, the usual excess associated with early revolutionary activities will develop. Boards of education and administrators will ask teachers as individuals and as members of organizations when and how they propose to assume the self-regulatory responsibility which goes with the new place which they will seek, and win, in the authority structure of the school. Teachers will tend to be impatient with questions of this order, however crucial the questions may be to achievement of full professional status.

As for the administrator, he must take the lead in establishing new structures of school government which separate participation in the administrative authority structure from the supervisory authority structure. It is here that he can make his unique contribution to the resolution of hardening of conflict in teacher-administrator relations.

NOTES

[1] W. W. Charters, Jr., "The Social Background of Teaching," *Handbook of Research on Teaching*, ed. N. L. Gage (Chicago: Rand McNally & Company, 1963), pp. 715–813.

[2] C. E. Bidwell, "The School as a Formal Organization," *Handbook of Organizations*, ed. J. G. March (Chicago: Rand McNally & Company, 1965), pp. 972–1022.

[3] The author is indebted to W. H. Cowley, David Jacks Professor of Higher Education, Emeritus, Stanford University, for his insight into the distinction between educational government and governance.

[4] A. Etzioni, *Modern Organizations* (Englewood Cliffs, N.J.: Prentice-Hall, Inc., 1964).

[5] A. Etzioni, "Organizational Control Structure," *Handbook of Organizations*, ed. J. G. March (Chicago: Rand McNally & Company, 1965), pp. 650–77.

[6] D. Katz and R. L. Kahn, *The Social Psychology of Organizations* (New York: John Wiley and Sons, Inc., 1966).

[7] S. M. Dornbusch et al., "Evaluation and Authority" (Unpublished paper, Laboratory for Social Research, Stanford University, 1965).

[8] D. E. Griffiths, *Administrative Theory* (New York: Appleton-Century-Crofts, 1959). Not all students of formal organizations tie the distribution of authority directly to the need for control over behavior. See Barnard and Hopkins.

[9] Talcott Parsons in P. M. Blau and W. R. Scott, *Formal Organizations* (San Francisco: Chandler Publishing Co., 1962).

[10] *Ibid.*, p. 63.

[11] M. Lieberman, *Education as a Profession* (Englewood Cliffs, N.J.: Prentice-Hall, Inc., 1956).

[12] H. S. Becker, "The Teacher in the Authority System of the Public School," *Journal of Educational Sociology*, XXVII (1953), pp. 128–41.

[13] C. E. Bidwell, "Administration and Teacher Satisfaction," *Phi Delta Kappan*, XXXVII (1956), pp. 285–88.

[14] R. N. Bush, "Teaching and Administrative Roles" (Unpublished manuscript, Stanford University, 1962).

[15] F. S. Chase, "The Teacher and Policy Making," *Administrator's Notebook*, I (1952).

[16] D. C. Moyer, "Leadership That Teachers Want," *Administrator's Notebook*, VII (1955).

[17] G. L. Sharma, "Who Should Make What Decisions?," *Administrator's Notebook*, VIII (1955).

[18] S. Washburne, "Teacher in the Authority System," *Journal of Educational Sociology*, XXX (1957), pp. 390–94.

[19] R. G. Corwin, "Militant Professionalism, Initiative and Compliance in Public Education," *Sociology of Education*, XXXVIII (1965), pp. 310–31.

[20] G. Moeller, "Bureaucracy and Teachers' Sense of Power," *Administrator's Notebook*, III (1962). (See Neal Gross, 1965, pp. 162–63, for a treatment of professionals in the public school bureaucracy from the "executive" perspective).

[21] Bidwell, *op. cit.*

[22] *Ibid.*

[23] D. E. Griffiths et al., *Teacher Mobility in New York City* (New York: School of Education, New York University, 1963).

[24] Blau and Scott, *op. cit.*

[25] H. J. Leavitt, "Applied Organizational Change in Industry: Structural, Technological, and Humanistic Approaches," *Handbook of Organizations*, ed. J. G. March (Chicago: Rand McNally & Company, 1965), pp. 1144–70.

[26] R. T. Golembiewski, "Small Groups and Large Organizations," *Handbook of Organizations*, ed. J. G. March (Chicago: Rand McNally & Company, 1965), pp. 87–141.

[27] Leavitt, *op. cit.*

[28] R. E. Ohm and W. G. Monahan, "Power and Stress in Organizational Response to Collective Action," *Negotiations in the Schools*, ed. R. E. Ohm and O. D. Johns (Norman, Oklahoma: College of Education, University of Oklahoma, 1965), pp. 71–76.

[29] A. S. Tannenbaum, "Unions," *Handbook of Organizations*, ed. J. G. March (Chicago: Rand McNally & Company, 1965), pp. 710–63.

[30] Bidwell, *op. cit.*

[31] W. A. Wildman, "Teacher Collective Action in the United States," *Negotiations in the Schools*, ed. R. E. Ohm and O. D. Johns (Norman, Oklahoma: College of Education, University of Oklahoma, 1965), pp. 20–34.

[32] Tannenbaum, *op. cit.*

[33] D. E. Griffiths, "Viable Alternatives to the Status Quo," *The Struggle for Power in Education*, ed. F. W. Lutz and J. Azzarelli (Englewood Cliffs, N.J.: Prentice-Hall, Inc., in press).

[34] *Ibid.*

17.

PROFESSIONAL PERSONS IN PUBLIC ORGANIZATIONS
RONALD G. CORWIN

Advances toward a better comprehension of man's role in society await the discovery of fruitful questions to ask. The development of sound methods and validated knowledge, for which there is much demand currently, hinges directly on this more fundamental problem.

CONCEPTUALIZING ORGANIZATIONAL CONFLICT

The individual versus the organization

A perennial question which philosophers and social scientists alike have asked in one way or another concerns the individual's conflict with society. Hobbs stated the question bluntly in terms of individuals versus other individuals: "How is society possible in a state of war of all against all?" Since such frightful issues were first raised, social scientists have become sophisticated enough to realize that man is basically a group-centered creature and hardly in a constant state of warfare with his fellows. On the contrary, critics complain of the opposite, an "organization man" with little independent will of his own.[2] With this prospect of conformity in view, contemporary scholars have posed the issue in a slightly different form—the individual versus the organization.

Contemporary literary and social critics have been aware of the apparent problems that or-

From Ronald Corwin, "Professional Persons in Public Organizations," *Educational Administration Quarterly*, 1:1–22, 1965. Reprinted by permission of University Council for Educational Administration.

ganizations have posed for individuals. The influence of this issue is quite apparent in American literature. Plots of many current novels analyzed by Friedsam center around the fact the hero is a bureaucrat.[3] The dilemma posed in such novels as Wouk's *The Caine Mutiny* is that, while the employee ought to be able to afford the luxury of his own integrity, bureaucracy increasingly erodes his intellectual responsibility and compromises his moral integrity. Social scientists also have formulated the issue in a similar way. Argyris' work, for example, is based on a presumed conflict between the needs of "mature" individuals for independence, variety, and challenge and the demands of organizations for dependent and submissive employees.[4]

Toward an organizational conception of organizational problems

Such statements of the problem pit the individual against the organization. There are, however, serious disadvantages in this way of formulating the problem. One disadvantage stems from the component of "the individual" in the equation; it prompts analysts to explain what are essentially *organizational* problems in individualistic terms. This approach deflects the focus of attention from the central problem of organization to philosophical speculation on the nature of individuals, which is a residual problem from the standpoint of organization theory. Given this formulation, the person in trouble is defined either as a hero or a maladjusted personality, depending on one's point of view. But personality seems to be significant precisely *because* a given way of organizing is taken for granted; if a specific organization is assumed to be legitimate, then nonconformity will, by definition, appear as a personal "maladjustment."

Still other problems are associated with conceptions of organization that seem implicit in this way of formulating the issue (individual versus organization). The organization is portrayed as an overbearing entity, a unified set of values and goals which are in opposition to personal values and needs. This unitary conception of organization is fostered by two common implicit preconceptions of organization held by those who study organizations: (1) institutional favoritism and (2) organizational bias.[5] Institutional favoritism refers to the exaggerated attention that customarily is given to legitimate institutional ideals embodied in an organization. For example, theorists tend to focus almost exclusively on educational values in schools, religious values in churches, or efficiency in businesses. Correspondingly, with a few exceptions, value conflicts within each of these settings have been neglected.[6]

This institutional perspective tends to emphasize the static image implicit in the very concept of organization. Not only does the study of structure tend to be preferred over process, but structure itself is conceived statically; earlier formulations of structure as a set of "positions" (of teachers, administrators, etc.) obscured the role conflicts or tensions built into each position. Subsequent developments in role theory have helped to correct the impression that structure is necessarily consistent, but the almost exclusive attention to the normative quality implicit in the concept of role (or expectations) has continued to distract attention from the perplexing discrepancies that exist between role conceptions and actual behavior. Finally, little attention has been given to longitudinal studies of the outcomes of role conflicts; consequently little is yet known about the forces within organizational structure itself that produce systematic changes in roles.

The term organizational bias refers to the related prominence given to a presumed set of overriding organizational goals. If it is assumed that it is "normal" for all personnel to work toward a set of organizational goals, then conformity to a rational decision-making model is also "normal"; and, conversely, nonrational behavior can only be attributed to "abnormal" sources. Hence, given these assumptions, any behavior which does not conform to the organizational logic—i.e. the logical means for ful-

filling the organization's official objectives—is difficult to explain except in terms of "problems" and personal deviations. Consequently, all forms of behavior which do not "fit" the assumed logical structure are usually grouped into a *residual* category—that is, a category consisting of elements which have little in common except the fact that they don't correspond to the logic. Whenever behavior cannot be explained in organizational terms, it is explained in such residual categories as accident, circumstance, personality, or that amorphous creature bred for the purpose, "informal organization."

To summarize, when the logic of organization is taken for granted, behavior unsuitable to the organization in question tends to be explained in individualistic rather than organizational terms. The problem is that organizational tension, despite its prevalence, cannot be incorporated into existing models of organization in other than a residual way.[7]

Professional versus employee principles of organization

There is another alternative. Using a different line of reasoning, behavior that is deviant in one form of organization may be seen as conformity in another. It is well known, of course, that the bureaucratization of American society is one of the fundamental developments of this century and that bureaucracy presently represents a dominant form of organization. Drucker, in fact, has termed this an "employee" society; that is, one in which the rights and obligations between employers and employees (i.e. those who work for another for wages) determine the character of the society.[8] As individual employers have disappeared, these relationships increasingly have been defined by impersonal administrative principles.

However, it is equally true that the social forces which have produced this bureaucratic society have also created alternative forms of organization. Professional principles constitute a prominent but competing way of organizing an employee society.[9] In a professional-employee society, the fundamental tension is not between the individual and the system, but between parts of the system—between the professional and the bureaucratic principles of organization.[10]

Dual professional and bureaucratic principles have been evolving in teaching for some time. The employee status of teachers has been reinforced, first by a strong tradition of local, lay control over educators, and then by the subsequent growth of complex school systems, which have required more administrative control to maintain coordination.

At the same time, the growth of systematic knowledge in teaching and a firm sense of responsibility for students' welfare supports teachers' claims to an exclusive monopoly over certain aspects of teaching, which is the basis of a *professional image* that points teaching in quite another direction. Behind professionalization is a "drive for status," or the efforts of members of a vocation to gain more control over their work—not only more responsibility, but more authority.[11] For decades teachers have subscribed to the idea that they have professional obligations (such as staying late to work with students); now they are demanding professional rights as well (such as the right to select their own teaching materials and methods).

Professional associations were, of course, originally formed in order to free vocations from lay control; and the efforts of teachers to professionalize are no exception. The process of professionalizing publicly-supported vocations, then, is likely to be militant. It represents a challenge to the traditional ideologies of control by laymen and their administrative representatives. The professionalization of any vocation (including school administration) will involve boundary disputes among laymen, the professionals, and public administrators. These boundary disputes, it should be noted, also infect the vocation itself, breaking it into segments or coalitions which compete among themselves: one, a small but active militant leadership group, spearheads the movement, while other coalitions constitute small groups of supporters and the opposition. Each segment then attempts to control the conditions of work in terms of its own definitions.

In teaching, the immediate issues concern the amount of autonomy which teachers should have over the selection of textbooks, over methods, and over curriculum development. But the underlying issues are not peculiar to teaching. One issue concerns the appropriate role of professional-employees in complex organizations. A second involves the place of experts in a democracy. In a sense, this conflict between expertise and democratic principles has already been waged by administrators of public organizations. In these struggles, on the one hand, the growth of knowledge has almost forced laymen to forego their right to make many technical decisions; but on the other hand, many people feel that ultimately only public control will safeguard public interests. Militant professionalism, then, is intended to compromise both the control that administrators have gained over public education and the control traditionally exercised by the lay public.

Despite the efforts of many occupations to professionalize, the characteristics of complex organizations do not uniformly support professional behavior. In fact, there is evidence from a variety of settings that inconsistencies between professional and employee principles are responsible for tensions. As one example, the professional roles of physicians in the military have been found incompatible with the bureaucracy in which they operate.[12] The professional person's self-conception as an individual capable of critical ability and capacity for original thought could be only superficially followed in the structure of the military organization, according to McEwan, who believes that the bureaucratic principles on which the military is organized—such as standardization of positions and superordination-subordination by rank—are, in practice, incongruent with the need for creative thinking and peer relations that prevail among professionals.[13] The principle of delegating authority seems inconsistent especially with the idea that professional authority is independent of the sanctions applied by a particular organization.[14]

Professional-employee role conflicts

Bureaucratic principles can serve as a point of departure for conceptualizing organizational role conflicts.[15] These principles include: (1) specialization of jobs, (2) standardization of work, and (3) centralization of authority. Each may be visualized as a separate continuum, ranging from more to less bureaucratic (see table 17–1). The configuration of these variables influences the opportunity that members of an organization have to act professionally in their relations with clients, colleagues, the administration, and the public, and the amount of pressure that is exerted on them to behave as bureaucratic employees in these relationships.[16] For example, group practice of medicine is characterized by a highly specialized but uncentralized form of bureaucracy. On the other hand, school systems probably do not differ from factories in degree of centralization, or even of standardization, but they differ fundamentally in level of specialization of their personnel. Therefore, because of these different configurations of bureaucratic principles, different types of tensions would be expected in schools, medical centers, and factories.

As professionals, teachers are expected to defend the welfare of students, even against *organizational* practices that are likely to be detrimental; so professional teachers will be disposed toward supporting school consolidation and toward defending the right of students to read significant American authors such as Steinbeck or Faulkner, and they will adjust their teaching to the unique capacities of their students. As bureaucratic employees, however, they will be expected to subscribe to the expectations of the administration and the community. Hence, it is possible for a teacher to be successful as an employee while failing to fulfill professional obligations, or vice versa.

Some of the tensions arising from these bureaucratic principles are illustrated in the case of *specialization*. As Gouldner observes, much organizational tension can be attributed to the fact that administrators frequently supervise and evaluate professional subordinates who are more competent in their work than they.[17] This situation, in turn, raises such questions as whether the criteria for promotion should be seniority and loyalty to the organization or professional skill and competence, which is difficult for non-specialized administrators to evaluate. The problem of evaluation is compounded by the fact that the reputations of professionals are based on the opinions of their colleagues outside the organization. Blau and Scott report that of the social welfare workers they studied, those who were most closely oriented to their profession were also less attached to the welfare agency, more critical of its operation, and less confined by its administrative procedures.[18] On the one hand, the expert is expected to be loyal to the organization, and on the other hand, his primary identification often is with groups on the outside. (However, there also exist locally oriented professionals who are primarily concerned with the opinions of their peers in the organization.)

Similar tension exists between the professional and his client, for while professionals are obliged to serve the best interests of their clients and to provide them with needed services regardless of other considerations, they are not obliged to accept their advice; professionals develop ways of rationalizing their clients' evaluations of them. This indifference to clients' opinions poses a problem in public organizations like public schools where neither the professional nor the client has much choice in entering the relationship.[19]

Second, *standardization* presents another problem, not because it is incompatible with individualism, but because it probably discourages creative and original thought, which is so necessary if organizations are to adapt to changing environments. Watson concludes, for example, that team work is a substitute for creativity, and is responsible for much mediocrity in academic institutions.[20] From the short-

TABLE 17-1 CONTRASTS IN THE BUREAUCRATIC- AND PROFESSIONAL-EMPLOYEE PRINCIPLES OF ORGANIZATION

Organizational characteristics	Bureaucratic-employee expectations	Professional-employee expectations
Standardization:		
Routine of work	Stress on uniformity of clients' problems	Stress on uniqueness of clients' problems
Continuity of procedure	Stress on records and files	Stress on research and change
Specificity of rules	Rules stated as universals; and specific	Rules stated as alternatives; and diffuse
Specialization:		
Basis of division of labor	Stress on efficiency of techniques; task orientation	Stress on achievement of goals; client orientation
Basis of skill	Skill based primarily on practice	Skill based primarily on monopoly of knowledge
Authority:		
Responsibility for decision-making	Decisions concerning application of rules to routine problems	Decisions concerning policy in professional matters and unique problems
Basis of authority	Rules sanctioned by the public	Rules sanctioned by legally sanctioned professions
	Loyalty to the organization and to superiors	Loyalty to professional associations and clients
	Authority from office (position)	Authority from personal competence

run perspective in which administrators and workers see their daily problems, predictability and consistency often appear more convenient than change and the risk of applying new ideas. (It is interesting, for example, that usually it is not sufficient to demonstrate that a proposed change will be no *worse* than the existing situation; change is avoided when possible.)

However, despite the complaints of professionals, standardized procedures do have advantages for them. From his examination of school systems of varying degrees of bureaucratization, Moeller concludes that, contrary to his expectations, standardized systems can provide teachers with a sense of power that does not exist in systems where there is a lack of policy; for policy reduces particularism and increases predictability. Hence teachers demand rules, especially in dealing with other groups such as students.[21] What the professional employee resists is the imposition by outsiders of rules which do not support him; even then, rules are preferred to their absence unless the group has such power that it can maintain its interests without them. The major difference between professional- and bureaucratic-employees in this respect is the established ideology which grants professionals the right to make the rules, and which sanctions the diffuseness of the rules that are made.

In considering the procedures by which rules are established, the third bureaucratic dimension, *centralized authority*, has been introduced. The problems of centralized authority, however, are more extensive than the mere question of the organizational level at which rules are made. For the very basis of authority in complex organizations is involved: bureaucratic and professional principles provide different ways of legitimating authority.[22] In bureaucratic organization, one derives his authority primarily from the position that he holds. He may be competent in the profession, but the amount of deference that is due him is based directly on his rank rather than on, or at least in addition to, his personal or technical competence. In bureaucracies, a superior

has the right to the last word because he *is* the superior.

The notion of heirarchical authority, on the other hand, is not central to professional organizations; the last word presumably goes to the person with greater knowledge or the more convincing logic. In other words, the professional employee, in comparison with the bureaucratic employee, distinguishes between his obligations to accomplish his work and his obligations to obey; the bureaucratic employee is hired to "do what he is told," while the professional already knows what he is to do and how to do it. Thus, the professional's loyalties are split between the organization and the profession according to these competing bases of authority.

In this connection, when Peabody compared school employees, police officers, and welfare workers on the degree to which each group stressed each basis of authority, he found that the most striking contrast among the three groups was in the relative importance that the elementary school teachers attached to the professional basis of their authority.[23] Yet, their typical reaction to conflict was acquiescence to the authority of position, particularly among the less experienced members of the sample.

However, this presumed tension between professional and bureaucratic principles of organization will vary systematically with different types of organizations. Two variables are especially important: the *complexity* of the organization, and the degree of *technical* specialization that employees have achieved. Specialization gives employees power; the more specialized they are, the less competent are administrators and laymen to supervise and evaluate them. On the other hand, the more complex the organization, the greater the need for internal coordination, which enhances the power of administrators whose primary internal function is coordination. Lay control is challenged simultaneously by the development of both conditions; and at the same time the concurrent development of specialization and complexity has fertilized the soil for conflict between administrators and professional employees.

The implication is that if a particular organization is structured around several, often divergent but legitimate principles, then the personnel in it can legitimately disagree on the appropriateness of each principle.

SOME PRELIMINARY RESEARCH FINDINGS

In view of some of these considerations, a research project was outlined to explore some of the implications of possible tensions among professional-employees in the public schools.[24] The general working hypothesis was that professionalization in bureaucratic organizations is a militant process.

Methodology

In the conceptual model, the teaching position was visualized as a product of the teacher's role expectations concerning students, the public, administrators, and colleagues. Professional and bureaucratic (or employee) role conception scales containing items pertaining to each of these role expectations were constructed and administered to 284 teachers who represented seven secondary schools of varying sizes (from 9 to 120 teachers) located in Ohio and Michigan. Each scale consisted of Likert-type pretested items derived from the focal concepts: centralization, standardization, and specialization. The professional orientation scale contained sixteen items and the employee orientation scale consisted of twenty-nine items, selected from among those judged by a panel of sociologists to be relevant to the several dimensions of each concept. These dimensions were referred to as "subscales."[25] Possible responses weighted on a five point scale ranged from "strongly agree" to "strongly disagree." Using critical ratio tests and scale value difference ratios, the final set of items proved to be internally consistent, in the sense that they discriminated between groups of respondents whose total scale scores were in the extreme quartiles.[26]

Each major scale also discriminated between respondents who exemplified logical extremes (high versus low) of professional and of employee conduct. Criteria found to be associated with the extreme professional groups included a combination of levels of education, time devoted to reading journals and number of journals subscribed to, number of articles published, and professional activities; extremes of the employee groups were identified from a combination of loyalty to the administration as rated by principals, expression of agreement and disagreement with criticisms toward the organization and administration, and absenteeism. Also, a group of university high school teachers, who technically are members of the university faculty, and whose professional orientation is reputedly high, scored at the expected extremes of each scale. The employee scale differentiated among the means of the set of seven schools in the sample, and the professional scale differentiated between the means of the two extreme schools.

Total professional scale scores of the sample were not significantly correlated with total employee scale scores, which bears out the conceptual model hypothesizing professional and employee expectations as part of independent systems. The absence of correlation between the two major scales suggests that analysis of the way respondents organize their professional and employee conceptions is of promising importance for studying role conflicts. A significant difference was found in the proportion of the faculties at each school who were simultaneously highly committed to both conceptions, simultaneously low on both, or simultaneously high on one and low on the other.

In addition to the scale analysis, 143 teachers were randomly selected for open-ended interviews and were asked to describe friction incidents involving themselves or other staff members. Respondents identified 326 separate incidents, which were then classified by methods of content analysis as to the openness of the conflicts, the type of issue, and the parties involved.[27]

There was general consensus within schools on the frequency with which different types of problems have created incidents, although not all incidents described were specifically corroborated by a second respondent. Many of the incidents which were not directly corroborated were mentioned by "reliable" respondents, i.e., those who did report at least one corroborated incident; nearly half of the incidents are either corroborated or reported by reliable respondents. The frequency with which corroborated, reliable, and non-corroborated types of incidents were mentioned is not significantly different, as tested by chi square.

It was found that the number of conflicts reported in a school increased directly with the number of the staff interviewed, but this was not related to either the size of the school staff or to the proportion of the staff interviewed. Therefore, in order to avoid a measure of conflict rates which is a simple function of the number of interviews, the number of incidents reported per interview is the index of organization conflict rates that was used.

This method of computing the rate of conflict was compared to a "global tension" measure in the questionnaire which asked "how much tension" exists between each of thirteen types of role partners in each school (e.g., teacher-administrative role, teacher-teacher role, etc.). The alternatives ranged from severe to none. There was a direct Spearman rank order correlation of .82 between the total number of incidents reported per interview and this global measure of tension. The rank order correlation between this global measure and the rate of "open or heated discussions or major incidents" reported per interview was even higher: .93. Also respondents were asked to indicate "how much tension exists" between them and each other member of the faculty. When schools were ranked only on the basis of the proportion of faculty mentioning "severe" tension, the rank order correlation with the number of "open or heated discussions or major incidents" per interview was .86, and with rate of "open or heated discussions or major incidents per interview" that specifically involved teachers and administrators it was .89.

The rates of conflict computed from interviews also correlated with other independent measures of conflict, such as the frequency with which respondents reported that their contacts with the principal have involved disputes, the proportion of teachers checking at least one negative statement about their principal, and the proportion of teachers who mentioned that compliance impresses their principal.

Types of Conflict

Approximately forty-five per cent of all the incidents involved teachers in opposition to members of the administration; about one-fifth of these disputes were "open" discussions involving direct confrontations of parties in an argument or "heated" discussions (as judged by content analysis), or "major incidents" including a third party in addition to those teachers and administrators initially involved; this is a larger number of open conflicts than reported among teachers themselves. About one-half of all incidents involved *groups* of teachers (teacher's organizations in seven per cent of the cases).

Twenty-four per cent of all conflict incidents fell in the categories of classroom control, curriculum management, and authority in the school; these incidents embraced such issues as the use of proper teaching techniques and procedures, changing the curriculum and selection of textbooks. About half of these involved administrators. (Table 17–2). Of the 159 incidents that were in the open, about one-fourth were with the administration over these issues of authority.

Professional Militancy

There was a significant rank order correlation ($r_s = .91$) between the mean professional orientation of the seven schools and their rates of conflict per interview. The seven schools also were grouped into three categories on the basis of their rank on mean professional orientation (2-high, 3-middle, and 2-low schools) (Table 17–3). The two high ranked schools (combined) reported a rate of open or heated discussions or major incidents per interview

TABLE 17–2 FREQUENCY OF OCCURRENCE OF INCIDENTS
INVOLVING AUTHORITY, THE DISTRIBUTION OF SCARCE REWARDS,
AND VALUES, BY LEVEL OF INTENSITY

Type of issue involved	Number of open or heated discussions or major incidents	Proportion of all incidents*
I. Authority, total	81	48.7
A. Over the classroom		
1. with respect to superiors (curriculum management and authority over classroom)	35	17.4
2. with respect to subordinates (student discipline and problems)	23	15.6
B. Within the school		
1. with respect to superiors (authority over school)	7	6.8
2. with respect to public (school-community realtions)	2	1.8
3. with respect to peers (disputes among teachers' organizations)	14	7.1
II. Distribution of scarce rewards, total	48	25.2
A. Teachers economic and job status (salary problems, distribution of physical facilities and job status)	23	13.1
B. Scheduling problems	21	10.4
C. Economic status of the educational program (school finances)	4	1.5
III. Value conflicts, total	26	22.1
A. Moral, ideological and interpersonal issues	9	8.6
B. Educational philosophy	3	4.9
C. School policy	14	8.6
VI. Unclassifiable (insufficient information)	4	3.9
Total number	159	

* Based on total number of incidents of all types, including complaints and impersonal competition. $N = 326$.

several times as great as that of the low-ranked schools (.4 compared to 1.9 per interview). There was a parallel ranking on such incidents that specifically involved the administration. The reverse also tended to be true; schools with higher rates of conflict had higher mean professional scores than schools with lower professional orientations.

Finally, persons who held simultaneously high-professional and low-employee orientations had higher rates of conflict than persons who held low-professional and high-employee

TABLE 17–3   RATES OF CONFLICT IN SCHOOLS WHOSE FACULTY HAVE HIGH, MIDDLE, AND LOW PROFESSIONAL ORIENTATIONS

Level of professional orientation	Rate of incidents per interview			Rate of open, heated discussions or major incidents per interview			Rate of open, heated discussions or major incidents per interview involving teachers and administrators		
	Number			Number			Number		
	Conflicts	Interviewed	Rate	Conflicts	Interviewed	Rate	Conflicts	Interviewed	Rate
High: Schools 3 and 7 $\overline{X} = 58.69$	93	27	3.44	50	27	1.85	24	27	0.88
Middle: Schools 1, 5, and 6 $\overline{X} = 57.17$	131	83	1.58	94	83	1.13	38	83	0.46
Low: Schools 2 and 4 $\overline{X} = 56.76$	102	36	2.83	15	36	0.42	4	36	0.11
Total	326	146	2.23	159	146	1.08	66	146	0.45

orientations, or any of the other possible role combinations (Table 17–4). Nearly half of the group with combined high-professional and low-employee orientations were involved in one or more incidents, and about one-fourth of them were involved in two or more incidents. This finding illustrates that it is as important to ascertain what a group is *against* (low-employee orientation) as to determine what it is for (high-professional orientation).

The weight of evidence from this very limited sample suggests that there is a consistent pattern of conflict between teachers and administrators over the control of work, and that professionalization is a militant process. In future phases of the study, larger samples will be collected. Also, more intensive analysis of concomitant variations between professionalism and organizational variables eventually will help to assess the relative significance of each type of variable in relation to conflict.

IMPLICATIONS

Complex authority systems

It seems likely that if the sources of organizational tension are structural, then potential solutions to organizational problems also will be found at that level. Hence, use by administrators of more benevolent methods in working with teachers will not necessarily solve the problems unless these administrative practices are supplemented with structural changes. Many school boards and administrators today are talking about "allowing" teachers to participate more in the decision process. However, teachers appear to want the authority to make certain types of decisions, not merely the opportunity to become involved with some stages of decision-making at the discretion of the administration. The problem with so-called "democratic" administration is that the participation of subordinates usually continues to be at the discretion of the administration. As an uncertain privilege, the opportunity to participate may be withdrawn or withheld in practice. Lefton, Dinitz and their associates, for example, found that when wards in a hospital were operated according to so-called "democratic" principles of administration, the actual result was far from democratic;[28] moreover, professionals working in this situation, where only an illusion of democracy was perpetuated, were more frustrated and negative than those working on wards that were admittedly less democratic. Hence, those who regard the problem simply as one of creating "good administration," ignore the very condition that professionalization is designed to remedy that, under benevolent authoritarian administration, the status of the teacher's authority still depends on the discretion of the administration.

When the problem is viewed as one of organization, it becomes apparent that the teacher's professional authority will be in jeopardy until it is supported by the structure of the

TABLE 17–4   ORGANIZATION OF STATUS CONCEPTIONS AND RATES OF CONFLICT

Status organization	N	No. of conflicts per person	Per cent involved	
			1 or more	2 or more
High professional— high employee	67	0.61	.34	.16
High professional— low employee	60	1.27	.47	.28
Low professional— high employee	59	0.56	.29	.14
Low professional— low employee	71	0.89	.31	.17

organization itself. For example, in one study dual lines of authority which developed between physicians and administrators in a hospital helped to minimize professional-employee conflicts.[29] On the one hand, the hospital administration maintained the right to make certain administrative decisions, such as scheduling and chart review, and the right to give advice. However, physicians reserved the right to accept or reject administrative suggestions about patient care. It was up to the physician actually attending the patient to make the final decision. Physicians interpreted the official right of the administrator to supervise as the right to "advise" rather than to make the decisions. This consulting relationship was even more acceptable because respected physicians held the administrative positions. Whether or not physicians accepted advice with which they disagreed depended on whether they considered the sphere of authority in question to be administrative or professional in nature. Although following administrative regulations was not very important to physicians when these regulations conflicted with their professional tasks of taking care of patients, they did otherwise comply with them; for, by complying in strictly administrative spheres, physicians gained freedom from administrative responsibility, which they considered to be onerous.

Goss, the author of the study, concludes that although the hierarchical organization of the hospital in which professionals work might appear to conflict with the essence of professional autonomy, in fact the hospital avoided this conflict by using this kind of separation of spheres of authority.

In thinking of organizations, administrators often seem to have had in mind a stereotype implicitly based on the military bureaucracy, which they have attempted to apply wholesale to virtually every type of organization, under the myth that a central office must have authority over every decision throughout the organization. This myth can bridle professionals, who have first hand acquaintance of their client's problems and who have specialized *training* for dealing with them, but who have

insufficient *authority* over the way clients are treated. Conversely, those who are most removed from the operating level are put in the impossible position of being held *responsible* for the decisions that must be made there. Moreover, these discrepancies among authority, competence, and responsibilty have more significance for professional-employee organizations than, for example, for factories or prisons.

Perhaps more than any other factor, the myth that a central office must stand responsible for every decision throughout an organization is now deterring administrators from considering alternative designs by which organizations could be adapted to accommodate the fact of professionalization.

Administrative training programs and conflict

The prospect of growing conflict among professionals within school systems also is likely to transform traditional leadership functions of the school administrator. Increasingly, his functions will involve mediation between groups; his job will be less that of "directing" the organization, as legal theory stipulates, and more one of just holding it together sufficiently to enable the professionals to improve their own effectiveness. His influence will be felt, but less directly than formerly, by the support that he gives to, or withholds from, the innovations that his subordinates suggest.

If conflict is a routine and normal occurrence within the administrative process, then administrative training programs should address themselves systematically to the proper role of conflict—its positive as well as its negative functions. Yet, to the extent that conflict has been fully recognized, it probably has not been considered with the intent of redefining administrative roles in terms of these conflict functions. Training programs seem to have focused on ways of limiting and managing conflict by screening people on the basis of their backgrounds or personality tests or teaching-group dynamics in hope of establishing cooperative and harmonious relationships among people on the job. However, in the first place, the disadvantages of such harmony have not been thoroughly explored; nor have the boundaries within which conflict can fruitfully occur been established. And secondly, it is possible that even the most peaceable, reticent person will become militant when he is operating under certain pressures. Perhaps it is these pressures that school administrators, especially, need to understand.

Evaluating professional employees

Finally, many administrators lack a coherent philosophy for evaluating their professional employees and for guiding their own conduct with respect to professional employee conflicts. The principal fact is that the teachers who are the most loyal employees, and the ones who make the administrator's job easier, are not always the most professional teachers. Conversely, those professionally oriented teachers who also want to be good employees are likely to receive little recognition, but endure much blame, for the moral responsibility that they do demonstrate when they are forced by an administrative regulation or by public fiat to compromise one set of principles in the interests of their school's or their students' welfare. What is to be the fate of a teacher who is guilty of "insubordination" while attempting to protect his students from a textbook or a curriculum guide which he believes would be ineffective, or detrimental, to students? How will an otherwise competent teacher who leaves the building early be treated? The same issues, of course, apply to administrators. Will a superintendent who has been requested by a school board to violate a professional ethic (e.g., fire a competent teacher for prejudicial reasons) dare to be insubordinate?

The answers to these questions depend upon the relative merits of professional and employee norms. The question of merit is in part a value judgment, but it is also partly an empirical question. Are professionally oriented teachers more effective? The answer, of course, depends on the criteria used to assess effectiveness. Are professionally oriented teachers bet-

ter liked by students and parents? Do they have a better grasp of subject matter, and do they communicate more effectively? Perhaps professionally oriented teachers are not superior in all these respects. But, one hypothesis does merit further consideration. That is, professionally oriented teachers, in comparison with less professional ones, can be expected to protect the interests of clients against both bureaucratization and the special interests of laymen. For example, because classroom teachers interact daily with slum-school children, they are probably under greater direct pressures than the central city administration to adapt the organization to the problems of this unique clientele and environment; increased professional autonomy for these teachers might tend to alleviate those discriminatory practices otherwise fostered by standardization.

Professional norms also can counteract community pressures to maintain an outmoded curriculum or to censor the literary works of major American authors. More generally, because many professionals have less reason than administrators to be committed to a particular form of institutional structure, with the support of a strong organization they would be in a more opportune position than the administration to exercise leadership in changing the structure. Also in this regard, if more autonomy were granted to professionals (especially the younger ones trained recently), who may be partially insulated by the administration and their own professional organizations from outside pressures, the diffusion of those educational innovations most in harmony with professional values might be accelerated; and, conversely, teachers would be in a better position than administrators to resist adverse outside pressures.[30] If so, then the preference of administrators for loyal, compliant employees may be in conflict with their responsibilities as professional educators.

Conclusions

In conclusion, while individual personalities do become involved in conflicts, the individual-versus-the-organization hypothesis has obscured some potential contributions that studies of conflict can make to organization theory. A more fruitful approach to the problem focuses on the contrasting organizational principles which individuals uphold. From this perspective, one function of conflict is to defend conflicting but valued principles and to effect creative compromises between them. Group conflicts, in other words, function as "checks and balances."

Yet, although traditional theory has been concerned with divisions of labor, and more recently some attention has been given to distinctions between formal and informal organization, the conflicts among other largely ignored structural divisions, such as professional and employee modes of organization, have been relatively neglected. Moreover, to the extent that organizational structure has been recognized as a potential source of conflict, it often has been with the intent of showing only that the known principles of organization have not been applied, as in the case where illogical work flows have been discovered.

Behind the current interest in professional-employee organization is the idea of process, the simultaneous professionalization and bureaucratization of American society. It is not possible to consider the problem of organization without considering the possibilities and probabilities of organizational change. In considering potential reorganization of large scale systems, administrators will have to take into account one of the most powerful phenomena of our times—the professional organization of employees.

NOTES

[1] This is a revision of a paper written for a conference on "Developments in Professional Staff Relationships: Research and Practices," sponsored by the U. S. Office of Education, Washington, D.C., May 27–28, 1964. I wish to thank Russell Dynes, Willard Lane, and Robert Howsam for their thoughtful comments on an earlier version of this paper.

[2] William H. Whyte, *The Organization Man* (New York: Simon and Schuster, 1956).

[3] Hiram J. Friedsam, "Bureaucrats as Heroes," *Social Forces*, XXXII (March, 1954), 269–74.

[4] Chris Argyris, *Personality and Organization* (New York: Harper and Brothers, 1957), pp. 50–51.

[5] Cf. Willard Lane and Ronald G. Corwin, *Foundations of Educational Administration: The School as a Complex Organization* (New York: The Macmillan Company, forthcoming).

[6] Callahan's study, which analyzes the effects of business principles on education, is a notable exception. See Raymond E. Callahan, *Education and the Cult of Efficiency* (Chicago: University of Chicago Press, 1962).

[7] For criticisms of social scientists' neglect of conflict models, see: Ralf Daerendorf, "Out of Utopia: Toward a Reorientation of Sociological Analysis," *American Journal of Sociology*, LXIV (September, 1958), 115–27; Jessie Barnard, "Where Is the Modern Sociology of Conflict?," *American Journal of Sociology*, LVI (July, 1950), 11–16; also, Dennis H. Wrong, "The Oversocialized Conception of Man," *American Sociological Review*, XXVI (April, 1961), 183–93.

[8] Peter F. Drucker, "The Employee Society," *American Journal of Sociology*, LVIII (January, 1952), 352–63.

[9] Cf., Ronald G. Corwin, "The Professional Employee: A Study of Conflict of Nursing Roles," *American Journal of Sociology*, LXVI (May, 1961), 604–15.

[10] Parsons has warned of the dangers in analyzing occupational be-

havior on the basis of individual motives. See Talcott Parsons, "The Professions and the Social Structure," *Social Forces*, XVII (May, 1939), 457–67.

[11] The term profession is conventionally applied to a set of structural characteristics (i.e., an organized occupational group with a legal monopoly over recruitment and knowledge); but most of what might be called professional behavior is in fact the striving of a group to achieve the right to claim the title of a profession. In other words, to study professions is to study process. See also Howard S. Becker, "The Nature of a Profession," *Education for the Professions*, Sixty-first Yearbook of the National Society for the Study of Education, Part II (Chicago: University of Chicago Press, 1962).

[12] William J. McEwan, "Position Conflict and Professional Orientation in a Research Organization," *Administrative Science Quarterly*, I (September, 1956), 208–24.

[13] There is also a hierarchy among professionals, but it has a different basis of authority; and communications between ranks of professionals are more nearly reciprocal.

[14] Walter I. Wordwell, "Social Integration, Bureaucratization and Professions," *Social Forces*, XXXIII (May, 1955), 356–59.

[15] Of course, there are many similarities between professional and bureaucratic expectations, but the differences will be the focus of this discussion.

[16] For an empirical study showing low inter-correlation among these variables, see Richard H. Hall, "The Concept of Bureaucracy: An Empirical Assessment," *American Journal of Sociology*, LXIX (July, 1963), 32–40.

[17] Alvin W. Gouldner, "Organizational Tensions," *Sociology Today*, ed. Robert Merton *et al.* (New York: Basic Books, 1959), pp. 400–28.

[18] Peter Blau and W. Richard Scott, *Formal Organization* (San Francisco: Chandler Publishing Company, 1962), p. 244.

[19] The factor of choice is an important control mechanism for both clients (who can boycott professionals from whom they receive little benefit) and for professionals (who can do a more effective job with clients who have faith in them). Private practice, however, overcompensates for the first problem, because of the professional's dependence on private fees; and bureaucratic employment accentuates the second problem. The fact that teachers are arbitrarily assigned students who are compelled to accept the service is a serious strain in the teacher-student relationship.

[20] Goodwin Watson, "The Problem of Bureaucracy, a Summary," *Journal of Social Issues* (December, 1945), 69–72.

[21] Gerald H. Moeller, "Relationship Between Bureaucracy in School Systems and Teachers' Sense of Power" (Unpublished Ph.D. dissertation, Washington University, 1962). Centralized authority systems support professional autonomy by resisting outsiders (as when principals defend teachers against interfering parents) and by refusing the use of essential facilities to competing groups.

[22] Gouldner, *op. cit.*

[23] Robert L. Peabody, "Perceptions of Organizational Authority," *Administrative Science Quarterly*, VI. (March, 1962), 463–82.

[24] Ronald G. Corwin, *The Development of an Instrument for Examining Staff Conflicts in The Public Schools*, U. S. Office of Education Cooperative Research Project No. 1934, Department of Sociology and Anthro-

pology, The Ohio State University, 1964. The research reported here was supported through the Cooperative Research Program of the Office of Education, U. S. Department of Health, Education, and Welfare in cooperation with The Ohio State University.

[25] *Employee Orientation "Subscales"*: Administrative orientation, loyalty to the organization, competence based on experience, interchangeability of personnel and standardization of work, stress on rules and procedures, and public orientation. *Professional Orientation "Subscales"*: Client orientation, orientation to the profession and professional colleagues, competence based on monopoly of knowledge, decision-making authority, and control over work.

[26] The corrected split-half reliability of the employee and professional scales is .85 and .70, respectively.

[27] An "incident" is defined as a description of a discrete episode in which a verbal complaint or attack was made against a person or group. A single episode was considered to be one incident regardless of the number of teachers involved or the number of times it was reported.

[28] Mark Lefton, Simon Dinitz, and Benjamin Pasamonick, "Decision-Making in a Mental Hospital: Real, Perceived, and Ideal," *American Sociological Review*, XXIV (December, 1959), 822–29.

[29] Mary E. W. Goss, "Influence and Authority Among Physicians," *American Sociological Review*, XXVI (February, 1961), 39–50.

[30] At the same time, of course, while professional autonomy can protect clients, professions in a status struggle also can jeopardize the interests of clients because of their own self interests, special viewpoints, and status hierarchies. For example, most professions seem to give preferential treatment to clients with more power. Similarly, in our study of conflicts between teachers, reported below, it was clear that teachers were competing with each other for students for their extra curricular activities in order to enhance their own positions, and apparently at the expense of the students' welfare in some cases.

18.

USING PROFESSIONAL TALENT IN A SCHOOL ORGANIZATION

D. A. MacKAY

INTRODUCTION

This paper is intended to do four things: (1) suggest a way of defining professionalism, (2) illustrate some relationships between organizational requirements and professional norms, (3) outline some strategies for resolving conflict, and (4) relate administrator behavior to these strategies.

The notion underlying this approach to the topic is that before an administrator can use the professional talent available in his school organization he must be more cognizant of certain aspects of organizational life as it affects the professional staff member. One should stress at this point that there will be no universally sound solution to problems; each principal or central office supervisor can examine his own situation and attempt to modify the organization, the individuals, and especially his own behavior. Analysis, of the type to be attempted in this presentation, must precede any prescriptive remedies. The hope is that some of the ideas contained in this paper may provide administrators with some useful frames of reference as they consider their own school organizations and the individual professionals who staff them.

A DEFINITION OF PROFESSIONALISM

It goes without saying that attempts to define a profession or "professionalism" have been

From D. A. MacKay, "Using Professional Talent in a School Organization," *Canadian Education and Research Digest*, 6:342–352, 1966. Reprinted by permission.

numerous in the literature of education and the social sciences. The typical approach has been to list several characteristics of a "profession" and to use these as criteria in testing any given occupational group for professionalism. Thus, one speaks of such characteristics as long years of specialized education, legal control over entrance to the occupation, adherence to a strong organization with an enforceable code of ethics, a spirit of dedicated service, and so on. One then examines a particular occupational group in order to assess the degree to which one or more of the characteristics is present. This approach has of course certain limitations. For one thing, it is premised on an ideal typology of professionalism and is therefore subject to the weaknesses of any such conceptualization. Secondly, empirical measurement of the characteristics of the profession is usually difficult, if not impossible. For example, the question as to what constitutes a long or an adequate period of professional education is a difficult one to answer. It may be that institutions engaged in the preparation of professionals have extended their period of training well beyond the time required for acquiring the necessary knowledge and skills. There is every reason to believe that the image makers of some of the emerging professions see the long period of training as one of the useful promotional devices in selling the "profession" to the public.

The kind of questions underlying just this one so-called professional characteristic point out the problems involved in applying an idealized model to a set of individuals, organizational standards, personal attitudes, and public opinions. What might be more useful is a recognition of the limitations in this approach coupled with an approach which is more in keeping with what social scientists know about human behavior.

One attempt which more or less recognizes this limitation has been made by an American sociologist, Ronald Corwin.[1] His approach, while not completely unique, does have the strength of stressing the importance of the attitudes held by members of an occupational group. As with any analysis of attitudes, Corwin's description of what he calls the "professional orientations" of individuals does not take account of actual behavior, of legal controls, of actual skills and competencies, and the like. However, it deals with an area of human behavior in which social psychologists have been able to provide at least tentative conclusions. For this reason, the limitations in the scope of Corwin's formulation are compensated for by its methodological and theoretical strengths.

According to Corwin[2], the professional person may be characterized by his orientation or attitude towards: (1) the client, (2) his colleagues, (3) participation in decision-making, and (4) his monopoly of skill and knowledge. The extent to which an individual possesses certain attitudes towards these aspects of occupational life is regarded, by Corwin, as a measure of his professionalism. One can therefore talk about a "highly professional" person or a "non-professional" person. When one looks at a collection of individuals in an organization or in an occupational group, one can describe the organization as being staffed by highly professional persons, non-professionals, a mixture of the two extreme types, etc. The often used notion of a "professional staff" may then become rather meaningful, at least in the limited attitudinal way in which Corwin defines professionalism.

In a school setting one can therefore describe the teaching staff members in terms of their attitudes towards pupils and towards their colleagues, their view of the monopoly of skill and knowledge required for teaching, and their attitude towards decision-making. It would be useful at this point to move away from Corwin's basic formulation and to attempt to translate what he says into a set of professional-employee expectations. He provided a useful lead in this direction when, in a recent article, he described nine expectations for behavior of professionals. These are simply more operational statements of the behavior one would expect of a person who holds positive attitudes towards clients, colleagues, etc.

Professional-employee expectations

1. Stress on uniqueness of client's problems
2. Stress on research and change
3. Rules stated as alternatives
4. Stress on achievement of goals; client orientation
5. Skill based primarily on monopoly of knowledge
6. Decisions concerning policy in professional matters and unique problems
7. Rules sanctioned by legally sanctioned professions
8. Loyalty to professional associations and clients
9. Authority from professional competence

This framework may prove useful in examining the staff of school organization in order to assess the extent to which it is professional. At least two research studies currently underway in the University of Alberta are designed to test the applicability of these expectations to teachers and other staff members in school organizations.[3] The first phases of data analysis have indicated that Corwin's criteria do make good sense, and do discriminate among individual teachers and groups of teachers.

ORGANIZATIONAL-PROFESSIONAL CONFLICT

If the criteria listed above constitute valid reference points for the description of professional attitudes it would seem to be useful to suggest a parallel analysis of organizational structure. Then, by considering the organizational requirements and professional attitudes side by side, one may be able to identify points of contact between the two. Of course, as points of contact are recognized, areas of possible conflict will also become apparent. By identifying these potential conflicts and considering their nature and origin, it may become possible to understand where and why conflict occurs and to suggest some strategies for their solution.

Again, the approach used to describe organizational structure flows from an ideal typology. In this case the classic bureaucratic model stemming from the writings of Max Weber may provide a useful, analytical framework. The long tradition of speculative writing about the nature of formal organizations has been supplemented in recent years by a growing body of research evidence. In fact, sociologists have gathered substantial proof as to the usefulness of the classic bureaucratic model in describing and explaining some functional aspects of organization and the unanticipated dysfunctions which characterize so much of organizational life. Primarily, the research up to the past few years has been centered in business, government, and industrial organization. However, there has been an increased interest in using the bureaucratic model in the analysis of school organizations in both Canada and the United States. One part of Corwin's research treated this question. Also, a study of Alberta school organizations was completed in 1964,[4] and at least three similar studies are currently underway in Alberta, Ontario, and New York State.[5] The point here is that there is good reason to argue that the school, in spite of what many people like to say about it, is in fact, a more or less bureaucratic organization. As a bureaucratic organization, it possesses certain characteristics which can be empirically identified and at least tentatively measured. The set of characteristics which describes a bureaucratic organization is as follows:[6]

Bureaucratic Dimensions

1. authority–position
2. division of labor
3. specified behavior
4. defined procedures
5. impersonality
6. competency

In order to indicate possible relationships between these organizational characteristics and the professional attitudes mentioned earlier, the set of nine operational statements developed by Corwin has been reduced to six characteristics which more or less run parallel to the bureaucratic dimensions.

A more useful way of examining the relationships between the two sets of criteria would be to place them in a broader frame of reference. Here, one may think of certain organizational "needs" which elicit responses from organizational planners on one hand, and professional staff members on the other. To do other than to recognize the logical basis for demanding certain responses by the organization would be to suppose that all organization is in some way unnecessary, that rules, procedures and authority are but the arbitrary creations of whimsical administrators. The logical approach is then to delineate some of the reasons why organizations are the way that they are, and to suggest typical responses from the organizational planner and the professional staff member.

Presented in these specific terms, the response patterns clearly indicate at least potential conflict areas between the organization and the professional person. If one applies these notions to school organizations at either the system or school staff level, some rather interesting speculations may emerge.

For instance, it may be that whatever conflict exists is of a fundamental nature. That is, the logicality of organizational needs may run

TABLE 18–1   PROFESSIONAL—ORGANIZATIONAL CONFLICT

The organization	The professional
1. Authority–position	Skill–knowledge
2. Division of labor	The individual pupil
3. Specified behavior	Behavioral alternatives
4. Defined procedures	Adaptability
5. Impersonality	Interpersonal relations
6. Competency	Competency

TABLE 18–2   PATTERNS OF RESPONSE TO ORGANIZATIONAL NEEDS

Administrator activities	Logical basis for demand	Organizational response	Professional response
1. Makes decisions	Accountability	Hierarchical authority	Skill-knowledge
2. Allocates personnel	Development of special subject fields	Division of labor	Integrated treatment
3. Controls and predicts	Human error	Specified behavior	Behavioral alternatives
4. Conserves resources	Efficiency	Defined procedures	Adaptability
5. Structures inter-personal relations	Equity	Impersonality	Stress on individual person
6. Evaluates	Performance criteria	Competency	Competency

directly counter to the professional response patterns. That there is the possibility of such a basic, inherent conflict is apparent in the view of some professionals who behave as if any level of organizational or administrative requirement constitutes an unwarranted imposition upon them. At the opposite pole is the administrator who lives a worried, threatened existence as head of an organization peopled by what he would call "prima donnas," "eggheads," "impractical academics," and so on. In either case, the assumption seems to be that professionalism in an organizational setting is in some way unreal, that to be truly professional in behavior there must be no organizational framework surrounding and delimiting professional activities. At the same time, there is the implied notion that the professional will probably be a maverick, that at best he will be insolently passive to administrative requirements, at worst openly rebellious. This rather fatalistic assumption that there is an enmity between formal organization and individual professionalism is, in part, verifiable by the empirical evidence which is now being accumulated. However, one ought to seriously question whether the assumption is entirely supportable on either a logical or empirical basis. Unless the assumption is questioned, any solutions to conflict situations will have to consist of short-range compensations rather than effective long-term remedies.

STRATEGIES FOR RESOLUTION OF CONFLICT

At this point, as it becomes useful to point to various strategies for resolving conflict in school organizations, it is necessary to give close consideration to the assumption that conflict is inevitable. In fact, whatever validity there is in talking about different strategies is based on the idea that different interpretations may be placed on the assumption. These interpretations or levels of acceptance of the assumption are as follows:

Basic assumptions

1. Conflict is inherent.
2. Conflict is more semantic than real.
3. There is some very real conflict; but there *are* points of agreement.

As one or another of these viewpoints is accepted, different basic approaches or strategies seem to emerge as possibilities.

THE PURE CONFLICT ASSUMPTION. If conflict is inherent, the rather obvious solution is to build into the organization some compensatory mechanisms which will maintain the organization in a viable state, while reducing the overt resistance of professional staff members. This is, of course, a cold war strategy which accepts the inevitability of conflict while avoiding outright war.

A wide spectrum of organizational, administrator, and individual behaviors may fit into this overall strategy of compensatory adjustments. For example, the incentive and rewards system designed by the organizational policymakers may buy the uneasy peace. Again, both administrators and professional staff members may reinterpret the situation by creating a distinction between administrative decisions and professional decisions. In this approach, there will be much talk about delegating authority while retaining responsibility or "blame-ability". This strategy may result in a functional specialization of the administration so that one has two distinct groups, the "administration" with its clearly delineated sphere of operations, and the professionals with their special areas. Neither party infringes upon the other's territory, or so the mythology would suggest.

THE SEMANTIC ASSUMPTION. In effect, if one says that the conflict is more semantic than real, one is saying that there is no conflict at all. These sets of criteria which purport to describe some aspects of professionalism and the central dimensions of formal organization become, in this view, mere verbalizations which are in no way related to the real world. The strategic decision flowing from this assumption would be, of course, not to worry at all about problems. In fact, most problems become logistic problems of obtaining scarce resources and allocating them in the most effective way. The problems that cannot be solved in economic terms can usually, according to this viewpoint, be classified as "personality problems" and treated as such. In a school organization, this would mean that careful selection of the "right kind" of staff member and administrator, and carefully planned socialization procedures will mitigate, if not entirely eliminate, the conflict problem.

THE MODIFIED CONFLICT ASSUMPTION. The third level of acceptance of the assumption regards the situation as a dynamic, fluctuating one. In this view, there are areas of contention which cannot be removed by the organizational planners. However, in certain important areas, the organizational needs and the professional attitudes tend to reinforce rather than destroy one another. The strategy here is to make full use of the strengths obtainable by emphasizing the points of agreement.

For instance, by referring to the earlier discussion of patterns of response to organizational needs, one may suggest how this strategy of reinforcement will unfold. The demand for accountability or responsibility can be translated into an internalized acceptance of responsibility by individual professional staff members. By this is meant not merely a verbalization but actual transfer of accountability from the administrator to the professional. In a school organization, then, this would mean that each teacher stands on his own two feet insofar as his responsibility to the public is concerned.

If the administrator stands in place of the public, then the administrator is obliged to see to it that the teacher does in fact account for his actions. Where the public, that is the parent, is able to make direct demands, the administrator steps aside and allows the teacher

to stand or fall. This behavior implies that the teacher really does have the skill required to do the job; it also implies that the job will have been defined in a limited and realistic way. However, the line of reasoning seems fairly clear; if the teacher is to have professional freedom, full responsibility for his professional activity must accompany the freedom. The reinforcement occurs because the professional's willingness to accept responsibility for his own actions coincides with organizational demands for accountability.

If one considers another organizational need, namely, the need for equity or justice, the reinforcement principle becomes even more acceptable. Surely when one is dealing with individual persons and stressing the importance of meeting their special needs, one is being as equitable as possible. If the organizational response is identifiable as "impersonality", then it is this response which is out of phase with the logical basis for demand. Impersonality is perhaps a common response to the demand for the appearance of justice, while the professional's stress upon individualized treatment is a much more relevant response.

Similar ways in which professional behavior reinforces basic organizational needs could be suggested for at least some of the other patterns of response. The preceding brief arguments may illustrate the essence of this particular strategy.

THE ADMINISTRATOR'S ROLE

Upon this cursory examination of conflict areas and strategies for their resolution, a fairly useful analysis of administrator behavior may be based. This analysis takes account of the general problem area indicated by the title of this paper, in that it recognizes that using professional talent calls for some unique skills on the part of the educational administrator. The problem is not peculiar to educational administrators; but it is potentially as acute in this setting as in any other professionally staffed organization. The advantage held by educational administrators is that the problem is being identified before it becomes full blown.

If one adopts the reinforcement strategy which seems the most tenable and is surely the most useful one, the administrator's role can be described in fairly specific terms. The administrator's major contribution is as an interpretor of the logical demands of the organization. He is the one who translates the requirements into operational terms which reinforce rather than interfere with professional attitudes and behaviors. Looked at in this way, the role of the administrator is a dynamic one in that he must take the given requirements and operationalize them for professional staff members. He becomes, as is so often the case in administration, a special kind of middleman between the abstract organizational goals and the real world of professional behavior. The strategy which he adopts and from which his tactical, day to day, behavior will flow will reflect the kind of assumption he makes about the organizational–professional conflict. He may not even be aware that the possibility of conflict exists; but his behavior can be classified as exemplifying one or another of the strategies described in this paper. To some extent his behavior will be based on the analysis of the various factors discussed here; in part, his values will determine his choice of alternative lines of behavior; in the final analysis, his personality and the situation in which he acts will contribute much to his behavioral patterns. This is where the logic of the present analysis will begin to break down; but as far as it goes, this kind of analysis may improve the contribution made by the rational, predictable sources of administrator behavior.

CONCLUSION

In summary, the argument presented here is that in a school organization there are two different systems of behavior or two different ways of responding to organizational needs. One of these is best exemplified by the bureaucratic model of formal organization; the other may be viewed through the analytical framework developed by Corwin and implicit in the literature dealing with professionalisms. Between these two sets of responses there is at least the possibility for conflict. Assumptions about the nature and degree of this conflict range from a "no real conflict" to a "necessary conflict" point of view. Implicit in each type of assumption is a general reaction or strategy for administrators. As the person who can exert great influence upon the operational specification or organizational needs, the administrator plays a key role in resolving the conflict.

While admitting that administration is still far from being an exact science, the main point which this paper is intended to make is that systematic analysis and predictions of the probabilities associated with organizational behavior will enhance the performance of the school administrator.

REFERENCES

[1] Ronald G. Corwin, "Professional Persons in Public Organizations," *Educational Administration Quarterly.* 1:3 (Autumn, 1965), pp. 1–22.

[2] *Ibid.* p. 7.

[3] N. P. Hrynyk, N. Robinson, Ph.D. research now in progress, University of Alberta.

[4] D. A. MacKay, "An Empirical Study of Bureaucratic Dimensions and Their Relation to Other Characteristics of School Organization." Unpublished Ph.D. Dissertation, University of Alberta, 1964.

[5] Studies in progress at University of Alberta, Ontario Institue for Studies in Education, and Syracuse University.

[6] MacKay. *op. cit.*

19.

RELATION OF BUREAUCRATIZATION TO SENSE OF POWER AMONG TEACHERS

GERALD H. MOELLER
W. W. CHARTERS

The present investigation concentrated on the feelings of powerlessness among classroom teachers in the social organization of the school as those feelings derived from the school's bureaucratic structure.

Although powerlessness has usually been studied in the larger societal context, this investigation, like Pearlin's[1] and Clark's,[2] narrowed the context to a particular organization. Such narrowing gives rise to several problems about the concept of powerlessness, defined by Seeman as a person's "expectancy . . . that his own behavior cannot determine the occurrence of the outcomes, or reinforcements, he seeks."[3]

INTRODUCTION

Source of "sense of power"

One issue is the extent to which a person's sense of powerlessness in the organizational context is a generalized attitude derived from his early socializing experiences or elsewhere and brought by him to the organizational setting. Treatment of the concepts of alienation and powerlessness in the literature imply that these are highly pervasive attitudes. Dean[4]

From Gerald H. Moeller and W. W. Charters, "Relation of Bureaucratization to Sense of Power among Teachers," *Administrative Science Quarterly*, 10:444–465, 1966. Reprinted by permission.

reported substantial correlations between measures of powerlessness, normlessness, and social isolation on a sample of residents in a Midwestern city, while Douvan and Walker[5] believed they had traced sense of effectiveness in public affairs to fundamental personality attributes:

> The fact that the sense of effectiveness has been shown to be in many people part of a general way of looking at the world—that governmental affairs become a vehicle for the expression of a personal orientation—suggests that whatever external factors enter as determinants of this attitude are at least to some extent mediated through a screen of stable personality characteristics.[6]

Shipton and Belisle,[7] too, regarded the feelings of local inefficacy which they found among school patrons to stem from a more basic phenomenon; they suggested that powerlessness reflected "some generalized feelings of futility and dissatisfaction which are projected upon either local government or public education in general."[8] The present study, on the other hand, assumed that powerlessness, or "sense of power" as it is termed here, is in some degree situationally specific—that it would vary with the bureaucratic character of the teacher's work setting. Clearly, tenability of the assumption must be examined closely in the data.

A second issue, especially salient in a study of teaching personnel, is the particular realms of organizational life in which powerlessness is experienced. In his study of the mental hospital, Pearlin[9] measured the nurse's feeling of powerlessness principally over her immediate work situation. Clark's[10] study of members of a farm cooperative, on the other hand, measured their feelings of powerlessness to control major organizational policies. In the case of teachers, a sense of power may be examined with regard to affairs of the classroom or with regard to affairs of the school. Teachers in today's schools typically are accorded a great deal of autonomy in their classrooms, an autonomy protected by their physical insulation from observability and fortified by strong professional norms. With respect to school policies, however, teachers traditionally have lacked power. Subordinated to administrators, school boards, and vocal citizens, largely unorganized for (and even unsympathetic to) collective action on their own behalf, teachers frequently have been prey to arbitrary manipulations of their conditions of work. In consequence, a teacher might well feel fully in command of the classroom learning process, but feel essentially powerless to control his fate in the larger organizational setting. This study measured sense of power from the standpoint of the ability of the teachers to influence the larger organizational forces that importantly shape their destiny.

A final issue is the relationship between feelings of powerlessness and the objective situation of power. In a sense, this is the other side of the coin of the first issue—concerning alienation as a generalized attitude—but it draws attention to a different problem. If a measure of sense of power were nothing more than a report on a person's location in a power structure, the concept would have little significance. A psychological feeling of power or powerlessness must carry implications which transcend the fact of power position. Indeed, it is precisely the far-reaching implications of the concept which most of the published studies of alienation have documented.[11] At the same time, the studies consistently indicate that experienced powerlessness is not independent of objective circumstances. Campbell, Gurin, and Miller,[12] for example, showed that males had a higher sense of political efficacy than females, and persons with higher incomes, more extensive educational training, and higher social status felt greater power with respect to public affairs than less advantaged people. A subjective sense of power, then, must be rooted in both situational determinants and personal responses, as Douvan and Walker[13] emphasized. In this study, "sense of power" scores reflected variations in teachers' access to the decision-making arena, to

some extent, thereby providing evidence on construct validity of the measure.

The organizational structure of the school provides the arena where teachers' orientations to power and the realities of power meet. This structure may be described in terms of the degree of bureaucracy exhibited. The bureaucratic model describes organizations designed to accomplish large administrative tasks by systematically coordinating the work of many individuals. The bureaucratic organization, according to Blau,[14] includes a definite division of labor, a hierarchy of authority with carefully prescribed reponsibilities, a system of rules or policy, impersonality in the interaction of its members, employment based on technical qualifications, and efficiency from a technical standpoint. These aspects of bureaucracy are the basis of the analysis of the organizational structure of the school systems studied.

Hypothesis and design

The primary hypothesis of the study was that teachers in highly bureaucratized school systems would have a much lower "sense of power" than teachers in less bureaucratic systems. The hypothesis assumed that the teacher, constrained by rules and regulations in whose establishment he had but a small voice, would respond to the impersonality, the magnitude, and the complexity of the bureaucratic system with a distinct feeling of impotence to control events which would affect his interests. The teacher in the small, structurally simple system, on the other hand, was expected to feel less ineffectual.

A second hypothesis was introduced to demonstrate the situational specificity of teachers' sense of power. If sense of power derives from exposure to the particular organizational setting in which teachers work rather than from previous experience in the society at large or from other sources, then it should follow that the difference between sense of power among teachers in highly bureaucratic school systems and less bureaucratic systems would increase with the length of exposure to their respective environments.

To test the hypotheses, 20 school systems employing from 37 to 700 full-time classroom teachers were selected from the St. Louis metropolitan area exclusive of the city of St. Louis itself.[15] The systems were rated by panels of schoolmen in such a way that scores of degree of bureaucratization were available for each. For most of the statistical analyses, the systems were categorized on the basis of the scores as highly bureaucratic and less bureaucratic. Superintendents of the systems were visited by the research staff for authorization to contact teachers, who, once approval was given, were randomly selected from faculty rosters. Twenty elementary school and twenty secondary school teachers were chosen, whenever faculty size permitted. They were given a questionnaire, which included measures of sense of power, and obtained information on length of service in the school and a number of other variables. By follow-up procedures, the final return rate reached 88 percent of all teachers sampled, or 692 responses, of which 30 had to be discarded for lack of sufficient data and other reasons.

The primary analysis compared the sense of power scores of teachers in systems varying in the degree of bureaucratization. Although the school systems were alike in several gross features—for example, all were public systems with twelve grades—it was necessary to conceptualize and measure a number of additional features of the environments and of the teachers which could affect sense of power and render spurious the relationship expected between bureaucratization and sense of power. Most of the statistical analyses for testing the principal hypothesis involved only teachers who had been teaching in the particular school system four years or longer. This limitation was based on the assumption that issues of power with respect to school system affairs become salient only after teachers had come to terms with the procedures and problems of classroom instruction.

METHOD

Measure of sense of power

Sense of power was conceived as a continuum. At one end are teachers who feel unlimited in the degree to which they can affect school system policy, and at the other end are those who feel totally powerless to influence its direction in any way. A set of Likert-form questionnaire items was prepared, tested on a pilot group of 100 classroom teachers, and subjected to a Guttman scale analysis. Six items with marginal distributions well distributed over a range between 0.2 and 0.8 and with low error counts were selected for the final measure. These six items constituting the sense of power scale are:

In the school system where I work, a teacher like myself . . .

a. Believes he has some control over what textbooks will be used in the classrooms.
b. Feels he does not know what is going on in the upper levels of administration.
c. Never has a chance to work on school committees which make important decisions for the school system.
d. Considers that he has little to say over what teachers will work with him on his job.
e. Usually can find ways to get system-wide policies changed if he feels strongly enough about them.
f. Feels he has little to say about important system-wide policies relating to teaching.

Teachers responded to each item by choosing "strongly agree," "agree," "maybe and maybe not," "disagree," or "strongly disagree."

For the purpose of scoring, responses to each item were dichotomized: a "disagree" or "strongly disagree" response was assigned a positive value and one of the other three alternatives a negative value. (In Items a and e the procedure was reversed; "agree" and "strongly agree" alternatives had the positive value.)

Later, using the responses of the teachers in the main study, scale analysis was again conducted to determine whether unidimensionality could be cross-validated. The six items were scaled in the same order as before and gave a coefficient of reproducibility of 0.93, when chance reproducibility would have given 0.85.

Measure of bureaucratization

Development of a measure of the degree of bureaucratization among public school systems was hindered by the fact that American schools are typically highly bureaucratic organizations, governed by a complex body of law, and characterized by an elaborate division of labor and formal structure of administrative authority. Teachers are certified for their jobs on criteria of technical competence and usually are promoted on the basis of seniority. Consequently, distinctions drawn among school systems must necessarily be within a relatively narrow range on a continuum of bureaucratization.[16]

Using an eight-item forced-choice instrument, based on Blau's characterization of bureaucracy, a group of persons with first-hand knowledge of school systems in the area made judgments which provided the data for ordering the twenty systems on a scale of bureaucratization. The method of scaling followed, in general, the procedures outlined by Riley, Riley, and Toby for object scales based upon collective responses.[17] Each of the twenty systems was rated by three, four, or five judges. If a majority of judges chose the bureaucratic alternative on a given item when rating a school, a positive entry was made in the scaling matrix; otherwise a negative entry was made. In this way a single set of ratings over the eight items was obtained for each system based upon the majority response of the system's judges. A Guttman scale analysis was performed, but with reference to the objects of the ratings, the school systems.

The scaling procedure arranged the pairs of items from most to least bureaucratic, as shown in Table 19–1. The bureaucratic and nonbureaucratic alternatives are listed separately in the table. In the forms used by judges, however, the alternatives were intermixed and the pairs of items were listed in a different order.

The limited number of objects (school systems) used in the scale analysis makes the coefficient of reproducibility meaningless, but interrater reliability, following the analysis of variance design proposed by Ebel when several raters are used,[18] was computed to be 0.47. This statistic, however, underestimates the interrater correlation, since it does not permit the removal of between-rater variance.

A parallel scale analysis was followed with the same data to determine the bureaucratic bias of the various judges. A school system might achieve a high score by having as its judges persons who were inclined to see a great deal of bureaucracy in any school they rated. The subject scale of bureaucracy[19] (in which judges rather than school systems were ranked) indicated that systematic differences existed among judges in their inclinations to choose the bureaucratic alternative in rating school systems. Cross-tabulations of subject and object scores, however, showed the correlation, as estimated by the contingency coefficient, to be essentially zero; therefore school system scores on bureaucratization appeared to be independent of the bureaucratic bias of the judges who rated them.

The scale analyses of bureaucracy ratings violated one of the principal assumptions underlying the method—that there be sufficient cases to afford stability to the scale patterns—but they were pursued as an alternative to an even more arbitrary procedure, the construction of a simple index. Only a study conducted on a far larger sample of ratings could verify the unidimensionality which was assumed for this measure.

TABLE 19–1   FORCED-CHOICE MEASURES OF BUREAUCRATIZATION OF SCHOOL SYSTEMS WITH SCALE WEIGHTS

Bureaucratic alternative	Nonbureaucratic alternative	Scale weight
A uniform course of study is developed or specified for the system, and teachers are expected to follow it.	If there is a course of study recommended in the system, teachers may depart from it or alter it to suit their own tastes.	8
The superintendent or school board members are likely to communicate with their employees only through established channels.	The superintendent or school board members are likely to talk directly to any person in their employ about school business.	7
Uniform procedures are set up for hiring and dismissing teachers and are applied in all cases.	Procedures for hiring or dismissing teachers depend upon the circumstances and may vary from one case to another.	6
It is next to impossible for administrators or nonteaching personnel to lose their jobs unless they violate a specific regulation regarding their job performance.	Administrators and nonteaching personnel may be dismissed for a variety of reasons other than incompetency in performing their job.	5
Decisions tend to be made by administrators on the basis of established, written school policies.	Decisions tend to be made by administrators on the merits of issues as they arise, without reliance on established policy.	4
The job of each member of the school system is clearly defined, and he knows exactly where his responsibility begins and where it ends.	In defining his job, each member of the school system is likely to "play by ear" and fill in where needed.	3
Each member in the school system is directly responsible to someone higher in authority for his work.	Little emphasis is placed on laying out the lines of authority in the system.	2
A standard policy determines where on a salary schedule the new teacher will be placed.	Starting salaries and other conditions of employment for new teachers vary from one case to another, depending on how badly the system needs them.	1

Control variables

A number of attributes of school systems, of individual teachers, and of teachers' positions within school systems were also measured, so that they could be introduced as controls in the study. The following variables, suspected of affecting the sense of power of teachers, were singled out as especially relevant.

1. *Climate of repressive authority.* The investigators believed that feelings of powerlessness could be generated in the relatively nonbureaucratized systems under a superintendent

whose leadership style was coercive and oppressive. Consequently, a rough measure of teachers' perceptions of the repressiveness of the administrative climate was developed and used to control for this factor. Four items were selected from the Leadership Behavior Description Questionnaire,[20] asking teachers to describe the frequency with which their superintendent—"Rules teachers with an iron hand," "Speaks to teachers in a manner not to be questioned," "Refuses to explain his actions to teachers," and "Acts without consulting his teachers." A simple index was contrived by weighting the frequency categories and summing teacher responses over the school system.

2. *Teachers in positions of responsibility.* Teachers who hold positions of substantial responsibility in the system might well manifest higher scores on sense of power than their colleagues without such assignments. This variable would have a spurious influence on the results if, in addition, positions of responsibility were more widely distributed among teachers in the less bureaucratic systems. The difference in sense of power between the school systems created thereby could be mistakenly attributed to the more pervasive environmental influence under investigation. Items on the teacher questionnaire asked about extra-classroom responsibilities, and responses were coded according to their significance in the school's power structure.

3. *Relations with school officials.* Even in the absence of formal positions of responsibility, teachers might have personal access to school board members, superintendents, and other officials by virtue of extra-school friendship ties which could enhance their feelings of power. Such informal avenues to policymakers almost certainly would be more common in the less bureaucratic systems, typical of small towns or rural communities, and this advantage would render spurious any relationship observed between degree of bureaucratization and teachers' sense of power. An index of particularistic relations was obtained through the teacher questionnaire by responses indi-

cating a visiting relationship and/or a first-name relationship between the teacher and school officers.

4. *Length of service.* Although the investigators intended to limit the study principally to teachers of relatively long tenure in the schools—four years or more—it seemed important to exercise even closer control over length of service. Teachers who remain in the systems for extensive periods of time should find themselves favorably situated in the informal if not the formal power structure. Seniority is a significant fact in most American public schools, bringing not only higher salaries but rights and privileges and usually greater responsibility in policy decisions. It is highly probable that older teachers have served under several sets of school officers, or if not, that they are known intimately by the officials and parents in the community. Length of service was expected to operate in two ways to affect sense of power: first, to enhance directly teachers' feelings of capability to influence affairs of the school, and second to expose the teachers longer to the diffuse influence of the organizational environment, increasing the difference between those in the highly bureaucratic systems and those in the less bureaucratic systems with respect to sense of power.

5. *Sex, social class, and teaching level.* Teachers' sex and social class (measured by father's occupation) were introduced as controls since, as noted earlier, they are known to correlate with alienation. Teaching level was examined because of the evidence that elementary and secondary teachers constitute markedly different populations.[21]

Role of teachers' organizations

A final factor, not strictly a control variable, which entered into the analysis was evidence about teachers' organizations in the various school systems. One consequence of teachers' position in the power hierarchy of the school is the emergence of associations through which they seek to redress the power imbalance. Bureaucratization of the school may well lead to feelings of powerlessness among teachers, but it may also lead to the development of groups which effectively restore the sense of power. The hypothesized differences in sense of power could be obscured by such a counter-vailing force.

Evidence was obtained, therefore, on the existence and nature of associations to which the teacher could turn to reverse an unfavor-able administrative decision. Teacher responses indicated the availability of three types of association: (1) local groups affiliated with the National Education Association, (2) "teacher welfare committees," members of which usu-ally are chosen by popular vote of classroom teachers in a particular school system, and (3) labor union locals affiliated with the American Federation of Teachers. Following Lieberman,[22] the investigators assumed the most effective association in providing redress of power for teachers would be the teachers' union, the least effective the local professional association of the N.E.A., with the welfare committees falling between the other two. The investigators hypothesized that the more highly bureaucratized systems would have the more effective teachers' associations and, where they did not, the sense of power among the teach-ers would be inordinately low.

RESULTS

Control variables

The relationship between teachers' sense of power and the control variables generally fol-lowed expectations.

1. *Climate of repressive authority.* The cli-mate of repressive authority, measured by teacher responses to a four-item description of the superintendent's leadership style, was found to be related to sense of power. School systems characterized by an arbitrary, oppres-sive style of administration (high mean scores on repressive authority) also tended to be those in which teachers' mean scores on sense

of power were low. Contrary to expectation, repressive authority was as common in the highly bureaucratic as in the less bureaucratic schools.

2. *Teachers in positions of responsibility.* These showed significantly higher scores in sense of power than teachers without such responsibilities, but highly bureaucratic and less bureaucratic systems did not differ in the proportions of their staffs occupying responsible positions.

3. *Relations with school officials.* Teachers reporting relations of friendship with school officials also scored higher on sense of power than those lacking personal contacts; in this case, however, particularistic relationships with school officials were reported considerably more frequently in the less bureaucratic than in the highly bureaucratic systems, and it was clear that this variable would have to be intro-duced as a control.

4. *Length of teachers' service.* This variable was found to be closely related to sense of power. Moreover, systems differed greatly in the proportion of high-seniority teachers in their faculties, with the highly bureaucratic systems having more teachers of long service. Length of service, therefore, had to be con-trolled so that its effects would not obscure the expected difference between the two orga-nizational types.

5. *Sex, social class, and teaching level.* Males felt a greater sense of power than females, a finding in accord with other studies; and elementary school teachers felt a greater sense of power than secondary school teachers. A cross-tabulation of sex and teaching level revealed one subgroup with a strikingly high sense of power—the male elementary school teacher (although male elementary teachers were very few in number). The two types of systems did not differ, however, in the propor-tions of either males or elementary school teachers on their staffs. Also in accord with previous studies, social class origin was found to be directly associated with sense of power; teachers from professional homes were highest and those with labor origins lowest, while the

business-managerial and the clerical-white collar groups fell in this order in between. Teachers from farm families, surprisingly, were second highest in their feelings of sense of power. Since highly bureaucratic systems drew more heavily from the upper social class levels and less heavily from farm origins for their staffs than the less bureaucratic systems, this variable, too, had to be controlled in tests of the principal hypothesis.

In brief, all of the control variables measured in this study were significantly related to teachers' sense of power. The only variables to which a difference between highly and less bureaucratic systems might be attributed, however, were particularistic relations, length of service, and social class. There was a disproportionate distribution between the two types of school system on these variables, but an equal distribution on the other variables. (Analyses, nevertheless, were carried out with all control variables in an attempt to discover interaction effects with bureaucratization.)

Primary hypothesis

With respect to the primary hypothesis, analyses demonstrated a significant difference between types of systems in sense of power, but in a direction opposite to that hypothesized. Teachers in highly bureaucratic systems had a significantly higher, not lower, sense of power than those in less bureaucratic systems. A rank correlation between degree of bureaucratization and sense of power means over the twenty systems was 0.40 ($p < 0.05$).[23] Furthermore, the greater sense of power in highly bureaucratic schools was not affected by the introduction of statistical controls on the three variables requiring it. The means in Table 19–2 show, for example, that teachers in the highly bureaucratic systems exceeded teachers in the less bureaucratic systems at every level of length of service, as was true for social class and for particularistic relations with school officials. In all cases the main effect of bureaucratization was statistically significant

well beyond the 0.01 level (see Table 19–3). Thus, the principal hypothesis was unequivocally refuted.

In exploring effects of the other control variables on scores of sense of power, positions of extra-classroom responsibility revealed a significant interaction with bureaucratization. This variable was related to teachers' sense of power only in the highly bureaucratic systems; it had no effect on sense of power in the less bureaucratic schools.

The climate of repressive authority failed to reveal an anticipated interaction with bureaucratization. In highly bureaucratic administrations where reliance is placed upon rationality and impersonal structures to achieve organizational objectives, the investigators expected that repressive authority would only rarely be reported; and if it were reported, the personal style of a single administrative official would have little effect upon sense of power. Neither prediction was supported by the findings. As already noted, climates of repressive authority were reported as often in the highly bureaucratic as in the less bureaucratic systems, and the impact of administrative style on sense of power scores was observed in both types of schools. Apparently, rationality in bureaucratic organization does not preclude the use of restrictive and coercive measures. As Gouldner has noted,[24] bureaucracies may be punishment-centered, using compulsion and sanctions; or bureaucracies may be representative, using human relations techniques, information feedback, and education to attain compliance with organizational objectives.

Secondary hypothesis

In spite of the lack of confirmation of the principal hypothesis, it is still reasonable to examine the second hypothesis and ask whether the difference in sense of power between teachers in highly bureaucratic and less bureaucratic systems was induced by exposure to the organizational environment or whether it was due to some differential in the

**TABLE 19–2   TEACHERS' SENSE OF POWER IN HIGHLY
BUREAUCRATIC AND LESS BUREAUCRATIC SCHOOL SYSTEMS WITH
LENGTH OF SERVICE, SOCIAL CLASS ORIGINS, AND
PARTICULARISTIC RELATIONS CONTROLLED**

Control variables	Mean sense of power	
	Highly bureaucratic	Less bureaucratic
Length of service (years):	N = 329	N = 317
1	3.76	2.61
2–3	2.48	2.33
4–5	2.79	2.18
6–7	2.63	2.41
8–9	3.20	2.63
10–19	3.48	2.71
20 and over	3.61	3.04
Mean	3.14	2.51
Social class origin:	N = 328	N = 313
Professional	3.29	2.81
Business, managerial	3.15	2.41
Clerical, white collar	3.32	2.25
Labor	2.75	2.21
Farm	3.23	2.83
Mean	3.15	2.50
Particularistic relations*:	N = 220	N = 178
Visiting relation	3.73	2.65
First-name basis, no visits	2.91	2.20
No visits, no first-name basis	3.03	2.61
Mean	3.19	2.56

* Data for teachers with 4 or more years of service.

selection of teachers. On the assumption that a feeling of sense of power was the result of the situation, it was hypothesized that the longer persons are exposed to the two environments the more their scores of sense of power would diverge. The plots of scores of sense of power among teachers with varying lengths of service in the two types of system displayed in Figure 19–1 (based upon the means in Table 19–2) provide a rough test of the hypothesis. The test is limited, of course, by the fact that the data are cross-sectional rather than longitudinal. It is clear that the difference in sense of power does not become magnified with length of exposure to the contrasting environments. Especially noteworthy is the fact that in their first year of teaching respondents in the two types of systems differed as much in sense of power as any other tenure group. A t test showed this difference to be statistically significant beyond the 0.05 level. These data were obtained after the first-year respondents had been teaching for five months, and it is possible that the scores of teachers in the two types of systems would have been more similar had they been measured earlier in the year. On the other hand, new teachers normally are so engrossed in coping with problems of classroom teaching in their first few years that they probably have little inclination to consider their position with respect to the school system.

Since the difference between highly bureaucratic and less bureaucratic systems did not

TABLE 19–3   ANALYSES OF VARIANCE OF SENSE OF POWER SCORES
FOR BUREAUCRATIZATION BY LENGTH OF SERVICE, SOCIAL
CLASS ORIGINS, AND PARTICULARISTIC RELATIONS

Source	Sum of squares	df	Mean square	F
Length of service:				
Bureaucracy	2.05	1	2.05	26.93**
Length of service	1.50	6	0.25	3.29**
Among lengths of service	1.33	5	0.26	3.57**
First year vs. other service	0.16	1	0.16	2.24
Bureaucracy × service	0.75	6	0.12	1.64
Error		634	0.07	
Social class origin:				
Bureaucracy	1.02	1	1.02	20.51**
Social class	0.46	4	0.12	2.40*
Bureaucracy × class	0.13	4	0.03	0.57
Error		604	0.05	
Particularistic relations:				
Bureaucracy	0.81	1	0.81	26.26**
Particularistic relations	0.41	2	0.20	6.55**
Bureaucracy × particularistic relations	0.11	2	0.06	1.77
Error		392	0.03	

* $p < 0.05$.
** $p < 0.01$.
Note: Numerals beyond the second decimal place used in the calculations are omitted in the table. Since subclass frequencies are unequal, the approximation procedure recommended by Walker and Lev was followed; see Helen M. Walker and Joseph Lev, Statistical Inference (New York: Holt, Rinehart, and Winston, 1953), pp. 381–382.

increase with longer exposure to the system (longer tenure), the higher scores in sense of power in highly bureaucratic systems may be a function of the tendency of these systems to recruit teachers with initially greater feeling of power. The basis of differential selectivity is not clear even after the investigators conducted further analyses on the first-year teachers alone. There were attributes measured in this study which distinguished beginning teachers in highly bureaucratic systems from beginners in the less bureaucratic systems and which, simultaneously, related to their scores on sense of power. Examined were such variables as sex, prior teaching experience, size of the building unit in which teachers worked, teaching level, social-class origins, home-town teaching, as well as positions of responsibility, repressive authority, particularism, and the like. In no instance however, did the difference between first-year teachers in the two types of systems disappear when they were equated on these variables.

Role of teachers' organizations

Remaining to be considered is the role of the teachers' organizations in affecting sense of power. Earlier it was proposed that the emergence of a strong association of classroom teachers could offset the feelings of powerlessness among teaching staffs in the highly bureaucratic school systems. None of the available evidence, however, supports this conjecture. First, what the investigators considered on a priori grounds to be the most effective association in enhancing teachers' sense of power—the teachers' union—was found to be the least effective. Highest scores on sense of

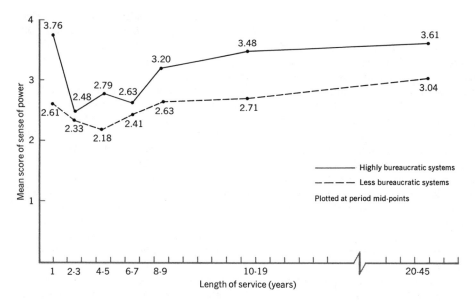

Figure 19–1. Mean scores of sense of power by length of service in highly bureaucratic and less bureaucratic systems.

power were associated with the existence of teacher welfare committees, next highest with the professional associations. Furthermore, such organizations, did not appear to be the result of a high degree of bureaucratization. Five of the ten less bureaucratic systems and six of the ten highly bureaucratic systems had either a union or welfare committee. (All but one of the twenty systems had NEA-affiliated professional associations.) Finally, considering only the highly bureaucratic schools, scores of sense of power clearly were not higher in the systems with a welfare committee or union than in systems where these supposedly powerful organizations were absent (see Table 19–4). The over-riding influence of the bureaucratization variable is obvious irrespective of the teachers' associations.

TABLE 19–4   SENSE OF POWER MEANS IN HIGHLY BUREAUCRATIC
AND LESS BUREAUCRATIC SCHOOL SYSTEMS AS RELATED TO
TYPES OF TEACHERS' ORGANIZATIONS

	Highly bureaucratic		Less bureaucratic	
*Type of organization**	*Sense of power*	*N*	*Sense of power*	*N*
Union	2.65	1	2.19	1
Welfare committee	3.25	5	2.89	4
Local professional only	3.34	4	2.40	5

* Nineteen of the 20 school systems had local professional associations affiliated with the National Education Association. The one exception, a highly bureaucratic system, had a labor-affiliated union instead. With that exception, existence of a union or welfare committee in a system is in addition to the presence of a local professional association.

DISCUSSION

Bureaucratization of school systems in this study was assumed to vary over a narrow band of a unidimensional continuum. While results of the scale analyses of the bureaucratization measure were not inconsistent with the assumption of unidimensionality, the number of cases were insufficient for the scale analyses to test it. Certain of Udy's[25] data challenge the assumption, although he dealt with a far broader spectrum of organizations than modern American school systems. Several anomalies in the relation of bureaucratization and size of schools are worth noting. The largest school system of all, with nearly 700 teachers and an administrative and clerical staff of 160 persons, was one of the three lowest on the measure of bureaucratization. It had the same position as a system with 38 teachers and an administrative-clerical staff of 7 and another system with 74 teachers and 18 administrators and clerks. Two small, quasi-rural systems had bureaucratization scores above the median. The rank correlation between degree of bureaucratization and school system size was a modest 0.43. Patently, the measure of bureaucratization used in the present study demands further examination in a larger sample of systems in which objective indicators of bureaucratization are also employed.[26]

What of the finding that teachers' sense of power was greater, contrary to expectations, in the highly bureaucratic than in the less bureaucratic schools? It clearly challenges the conception of the nature of bureaucratic organizations with which the investigators began the study.[27] But the various analyses also bring into question the assumption that the difference is traceable to the character of the organizational environment in which the teachers perform their work. Taking all the analyses into consideration, the evidence on the situational specificity of teachers' sense of power is mixed. On the one hand, it may be that teachers in the highly bureaucratic systems bring a strong sense of power into the schools at the time of their employment, although the personal attributes associated with the selectivity remain obscure in the present data. Differences in scores of sense of power were as great among first-year teachers as for any group of longer service.

On the other hand, the remarkable drop in sense of power in the second through the seventh year of teaching, observable in Figure 19–1 for both types of systems, suggests that perhaps some specific organizational phenomenon operates across school systems to eliminate those with a high sense of power at the end of the first year of teaching. It is difficult to attribute this striking pattern of findings to forces which are not associated with the organizational setting, but longitudinal data are required to clarify the issue.[28] Still other evidence supports the proposition of situational specificity. When the superintendent produced a climate of repressive authority, sense of power was low; when the climate was less restrictive, sense of power was higher. When teachers engaged in a visiting relationship with school officials, their sense of power was higher than when they did not. And when teachers were in positions of responsibility, their sense of power scores responded correspondingly, albeit only in the highly bureaucratic systems. Thus, it seems that feelings of power are sensitive to some organizational circumstances.

That scores of sense of power were related to teachers' extraclassroom positions of responsibility only in the highly bureaucratic systems suggests that these positions of responsibility did not constitute avenues to power in the less bureaucratic systems. Perhaps the greater visibility of the teacher in the smaller less bureaucratic school reduced the importance of the formal committee structure as a source of influence with respect to educational policies. The informal road to influence, at least as captured in the measure of particularistic relations with school officials, may have made the extra-classroom position of responsibilities less important sources of influence. This speculation is based upon the assumption that the scores of sense of power reflect in part the objective circumstances of power in the organization.

In sum, teachers' feelings of power to influence school system policies appear to be affected by variables lying within the teachers themselves and in the organizational structure of the school systems. The initial hypothesis on the impact of a diffuse bureaucratic ethos upon sense of power was not upheld, but several specified attributes of organizational structure were shown to enhance or depress the scores of sense of power. In some degree, teachers' feelings of power seem to reflect their objective positions of power within the schools' social system. In some degree, too, feelings of power may reflect more general attitudes associated with the teachers' sex, social-class origins, and still unspecified attributes which served to differentiate teachers selected for employment in the highly bureaucratic from those in the less bureaucratic school systems.

NOTES

[1] Leonard I. Pearlin, Alienation from Work: A Study of Nursing Personnel, *American Sociological Review*, 27 (June 1962), 314–326.

[2] John P. Clark, Measuring Alienation within a Social System, *American Sociological Review*, 24 (December 1959), 849–852.

[3] Melvin Seeman, On the Meaning of Alienation, *American Sociological Review*, 24 (December 1959), 783–791.

[4] Dwight G. Dean, Alienation: Its Meaning and Measurement, *American Sociological Review*, 26 (October 1961), 753–758.

[5] Elizabeth Douvan and Alan M. Walker, *The Sense of Effectiveness in Public Affairs* (Psychological Monographs, 1956, 70, No. 22 (Whole No. 429).

[6] *Ibid.*, p. 19.

[7] James M. Shipton and Eugene L. Belisle, Who Criticizes the Public Schools, *Phi Delta Kappan*, 37 (April 1956), 303–307.

[8] *Ibid.*, p. 307.

[9] Pearlin, *op. cit.*

[10] Clark, *op. cit.*

[11] In a letter to the editor, C. J. Browning, M. F. Farmer, H. D. Kirk, and G. D. Mitchell proposed that powerlessness is the first of a series of stages leading to global alienation; see *American Sociological Review*, 26 (October 1961), 780–781.

[12] Angus Campbell, Gerald Gurin, and Warren E. Miller, *The Voter Decides* (Evanston, Ill.: Row-Peterson, 1954).

[13] Douvan and Walker, *op. cit.*

[14] Peter M. Blau, *Bureaucracy in Modern Society* (New York: Random House, 1956).

[15] Details of the study, of which this article is a partial summary, are given in Gerald H. Moeller, *The Relationship Between Bureaucracy in School System Organization and Teachers' Sense of Power*, unpublished Ed.D. dissertation, Washington University, 1962. This study was part of a larger project, Project No. 929, U. S. Office of Education, Cooperative Research Program, "Teacher Perceptions of Administrator Behavior," in which W. W. Charters, Jr., was the principal investigator.

[16] For this reason, a measure such as Udy's, which covers a far wider band on the continuum was not suitable. See Stanley Udy, Jr., "Bureau-

cratic" Elements in Organizations: Some Research Findings, *American Sociological Review*, 23 (August 1958), 415–418.

[17] Matilda W. Riley, John W. Riley, Jr., and Jackson Toby, *Sociological Studies in Scale Analysis* (New Brunswick, N.J.: Rutgers University, 1954), ch. v.

[18] R. L. Ebel, Estimation of the Reliability of Ratings, *Psychometrika*, 16 (December 1951), 407–424.

[19] Again a collective scale was used; judges were scored positive or negative on each item according to the proportion of school systems to which they attributed the "bureaucratic" alternative.

[20] Andrew W. Halpin, *Leadership Behavior of School Superintendents* (School-Community Development Study Monograph No. 4, Columbus, Ohio: Ohio State University, 1957).

[21] See, for example, David G. Ryans, *Characteristics of Teachers: Their Description, Comparison and Appraisal* (Washington, D.C.: American Council on Education, 1960).

[22] Myron Lieberman, *Education as a Profession* (Englewood Cliffs, N.J.: Prentice-Hall, 1956), pp. 281–296.

[23] A plot of sense of power means against the score indicating degree of bureaucratization for each school showed the relationship to be essentially linear.

[24] Alvin W. Gouldner, "Organizational Analysis," in Robert K. Merton and Leonard S. Cottrell, Jr., *Sociology Today* (New York: Basic Books, 1959), p. 403.

[25] Stanley U. Udy, Jr., "Bureaucracy" and "Rationality" in Weber's Organization Theory: An Empirical Study, *American Sociological Review*, 24 (December 1959), 791–795.

[26] For the development of objective indicators of the complexity of work structures in public school systems, see Roland Keene, *Operational Freedom in Complex Organizations*, unpublished Ed.D. dissertation, Washington University, 1962, ch. ii.

[27] Implications of the findings for the conception of bureaucracy were elaborated by the senior author in the principal report; see Moeller, *op. cit.*, ch. iv. An abbreviated consideration of the implications appeared in Moeller, Bureaucracy and Teachers' Sense of Power, *Administrator's Notebook*, 9 (November 1962), p. 4.

[28] Longitudinal data have recently become available. By identifying which of Moeller's first-year teachers remained to teach in their school systems in the second year, Charters demonstrated that selective resignations could not account for the apparent drop in sense of power. W. W. Charters, Jr., Sense of Power and Length of Service among Public School Teachers: Some Further Analyses, unpublished paper, December, 1964. A dissertation by James A. Hopson is nearing completion at Washington University, which fails to confirm the unusually high sense of power scores among new groups of first-year teachers but which shows a substantial decline in scores of Moeller's first-year teachers when re-measured after four years in their systems. Hopson's data also replicate the sense of power differences by level of bureaucratization.

20.

FACTORS WHICH AFFECT SATISFACTION AND DISSATISFACTION OF TEACHERS

THOMAS J. SERGIOVANNI

Satisfaction and dissatisfaction of teachers has long been an area of intense interest to researchers in school personnel management. In a recent review of industrial and education job satisfaction research Robinson[1] notes that over 40 per cent of the studies reviewed relate to teachers and their satisfaction or morale. However, the voluminous research in the field to date appears to be lacking in conceptual perspective and may, in fact, be misleading.

An assumption basic to the literature in this area is that factors which account for job satisfaction of teachers and factors which account for job dissatisfaction of teachers are arranged on a conceptual continuum (Fig. 20–1). Thus, a factor identified as a source of dissatisfaction is also likely to be a potential satisfier. The administrative prescription based on this assumption is that if a factor accounting for dissatisfaction is altered or eliminated, job satisfaction will result. Or, failure to maintain a satisfaction condition will result in teacher dissatisfaction.

The Herzberg study

The impetus for the research reported here comes from the work of Frederick Herzberg,

From Thomas J. Sergiovanni, "Factors Which Affect Satisfaction and Dissatisfaction of Teachers," *The Journal of Educational Administration* (University of New England), 5:66–82, 1967. Published by the University of Queensland Press. Reprinted with permission.

Bernard Mausner, and Barbara Snyderman.[2] In a review of industrial motivation studies Herzberg observed that a difference in the primacy of work factors appeared depending upon whether the investigator was searching for factors which led to job satisfaction or factors which led to job dissatisfaction.[3] This observation led to the concept that some factors in the work situation were "satisfiers" and other factors were "dissatisfiers." Herzberg hypothesized that some factors were satisfiers when present but not dissatisfiers when absent; other factors were dissatisfiers, but when eliminated as dissatisfiers did not result in positive motivation (Fig. 20–2).

Herzberg's research with accountants and engineers[4] tends to confirm the existence of the satisfier and dissatisfier phenomenon. Herzberg found that five factors (achievement, recognition, work itself, responsibility and advancement) tended to affect job attitudes in only a positive direction. The absence of these factors did not necessarily result in job dissatisfaction. The eleven remaining factors, if not present, led to employee dissatisfaction. The absence of these factors tended not to lead to employee satisfaction. Herzberg observed that job factors which resulted in satisfaction were directly related to the work itself. Job factors which resulted in dissatisfaction tended to be related to the environment of work. The factors in their two sub-categories are as follows.

Satisfiers
(found in work itself)

1. Achievement
2. Recognition
3. Work itself
4. Responsibility
5. Advancement

Dissatisfiers
(found in the environment of work)

1. Salary
2. Possibility of growth
3. Interpersonal relations (subordinates)
4. Status

Figure 20–1. The continuum assumption.

5. Interpersonal relations (superiors)
6. Interpersonal relations (peers)
7. Supervision—technical
8. Company policy and administration
9. Working conditions
10. Personal life
11. Job security

Though arrived at empirically, the Herzberg findings appear to be consistent with the motivational theory proposed by Maslow.[5] Maslow hypothesized a hierarchy into which needs arranged themselves in order of their appearance. The Maslow hierarchy of needs, from lowest order (most prepotent) to highest order (least basic or prepotent), is as follows: physiological needs, security needs, social needs, esteem needs, and the need for self actualization. Needs that are at or near the top of the hierarchy, assuming that lower order needs are met, will tend to be the focus of an individual's attention. As long as lower order needs are satisfied, they cease to motivate the individual; in our society the physiological and security needs are well met for most people, thus they seldom motivate behavior.

Herzberg identified two levels of needs for his subjects; "hygienic" needs (which tend to focus on the dissatisfaction factors identified in his study) and satisfaction needs (which tend to focus on the satisfaction factors identified). According to Herzberg if "hygienic" needs are not met, the individual is unhappy. Provision for "hygienic" needs, however, does not ensure increased motivation. The satisfaction needs have motivational potential but depend upon reasonable satiation of "hygienic" needs before they become operative.[6]

Herzberg's findings have important implications for educational administration and supervision. They suggest that much of present practice in personnel administration may be directed at controlling the hygienic conditions which have, at best, limited motivating power for professional teachers.

THE PROBLEM

The writer undertook a study to determine whether or not the factors reported by teachers would distribute themselves into mutually ex-

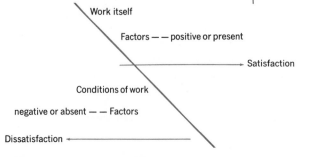

Figure 20–2. Herzberg hypothesis: satisfaction factors and dissatisfaction factors are mutually exclusive.

clusive satisfaction and dissatisfaction categories. Further, if the satisfaction-dissatisfaction phenomenon existed for teachers, would the factors resulting in satisfaction be concerned with the work itself, and would the factors resulting in dissatisfaction be concerned with the environment of work?

The following questions were raised:

1. Is there one set of factors which tends to satisfy teachers and another set which tends to dissatisfy teachers? Or are these factors better described as being arranged on a continuum with each being a potential satisfier and dissatisfier?
2. Will the distribution of factors vary for subpopulations of teachers? (Subgroups included: (1) male teachers v. female teachers, (2) tenure teachers v. nontenure teachers, (3) elementary school teachers v. secondary school teachers.)

METHODOLOGY

The overall design of this study followed, with some additions and modifications, the design developed and used by Herzberg. Respondents were asked to report incidents judged by them to be representative of their job feelings. Each incident or sequence consisted of three phases: (1) the respondent's attitudes expressed in terms of high job feelings and low job feelings, (2) the first-level and second-level factors[7] which accounted for these attitudes, (3) the effects of these attitudes and factors as reported by respondents. Through content analysis the factors which accounted for the expressed attitudes were sorted into the categories developed, defined, and used by Herzberg in the original study. The effects were sorted and categorized in the same manner.

The population and sample

The population for this study consisted of teachers in school districts in Monroe County, New York (the City of Rochester was not included in the sample population). The districts ranged from semi-rural to suburban in orientation and in size from a teaching staff of 36 to a teaching staff of 528. The total sample population consisted of 3,382 teachers.

One hundred and twenty-seven respondents were selected at random from the 3,682 teachers who comprised the study population. The sample was drawn from lists furnished by each of the participating school districts. Administrators, guidance counselors, department chairmen not involved in actual teaching, librarians, supervisors, and other nonteaching personnel were not included in the sample. Seventy-one of the 127 teachers agreed to participate.

The sample included 30 male teachers and 41 female teachers. Elementary school positions were held by 37 respondents and junior high or senior high school positions were held by 34 respondents. Thirty-seven of the 71 respondents held tenure appointments. Respondents ranged in age from 21 years to 64 years with the average age being 37 and the median age being 32. Years of teaching experience ranged from three months to 36 years with the average experience being nine years and the median experience being seven years.

The interview

The interview outline and interviewing procedure used in this study was a direct adoption of the Herzberg format. Respondents were told that they could start with either a time when they had felt unusually high or good about their job or a time when they had felt unusually low or bad about their job. After the first unusual sequence each respondent was asked to give another. If he had previously given a high story, he was then asked for a low. The same procedure was followed for most recent high feelings and most recent low feelings.

The objective events, the actual stories, which were reported by respondents as being the source of high or low feelings about their jobs were coded as first-level factors. The second-level factors were categories which constituted respondents' feelings as a result of the objective stories they had related and the attitudes they had identified. The analysis of second level factors came primarily from respondents' answers to two questions: "Can you tell me more precisely why you felt the way you did?" and "What did these events mean to you?" One respondent related a story involving a merit salary increase as a source of good feelings about his job. When asked why he felt the way he did, he replied, "It meant that the administration or whoever was responsible for the increase felt that I was doing a good job." The first-level factor in this sequence was coded as salary. This was the objective occurrence. The second-level factor in this sequence, however, was coded as recognition. The respondent perceived the merit increase as a source of recognition.

Respondents were limited to four specific sequences: an unusual high attitude sequence, an unusual low attitude sequence, a most recent high attitude sequence, and a most recent low attitude sequence. Two hundred and eighty-four sequences were collected for the study. The statistical analysis was based on the number of sequences rather than the number of respondents. Focusing on sequences was consistent with the method used by Herzberg.

Analysis of the interviews

The technique of content analysis was used in coding each sequence. Herzberg suggests two basic approaches to content analysis. The first is an a priori approach in which the analysis is based upon a predetermined categorical scheme. The second approach extracts the categories from the raw data itself. Herzberg chose the a posteriori approach which produced categories specifically related to the data collected in his study. Herzberg noted, however, that the resulting categorical scheme developed through the a posteriori approach was not very different from that which could have been derived from an analysis of the literature.[8]

The scheme used for content analysis in this study was a direct adoption of the categories developed and used by Herzberg, and so represents an a priori approach, but one based on empirical evidence.

Coding procedure

The next step in the analysis of the interviews required that the factors contained in the high and low attitude stories of respondents be identified and coded into the categorical scheme. Further, since several factors could appear in a given story, the factor which contributed most to the expressed feeling was to be isolated for subsequent analysis. Each sequence was coded in terms of expressed attitude (high or low), sequence type (unusual or recent), and level (first and second).

Sequences were coded, independently, by three of five judges. A total of 284 sequences were coded for the study. Coding decisions were classified as unanimous choice, majority choice, or consensus choice. First-level coding choices of judges for each of the first 160 sequences included 87 unanimous decisions, 69 majority decisions, and 4 consensus decisions. For the second-level factors there were 96 unanimous decisions and 64 majority decisions. Three-way disagreements did not occur for the second-level factors.

Figure 20–3 summarizes the basic features of the content analysis.

THE ANALYSIS OF RESULTS

The results of the study are presented in two sections. The first reports the results relating to the mutual exclusiveness of factors for the total sample. This section includes an analysis of the first-level and second-level factors which appeared in high attitude sequences and an analysis of the first-level and second-level factors which appeared in low attitude sequences.

The second section includes a summary of the difference in responses for male teachers as compared with female teachers, tenure

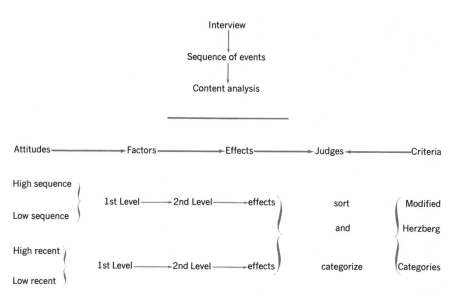

Figure 20–3. Basic design features of the content analysis.

teachers as compared with nontenure teachers, and for elementary as compared with secondary teachers.

HIGH ATTITUDE SEQUENCES CONTRASTED WITH LOW ATTITUDE SEQUENCES

Table 20–1 includes the percentages and values of chi-squared for the frequency with which first-level factors appeared in high attitude sequences as compared with low attitude sequences for the total group.

Sixty-nine per cent of the sequences which accounted for high job attitudes included the first-level factors achievement, recognition, and work itself. Responsibility appeared in seven per cent of the high attitude sequences. Advancement did not appear in the 142 high attitude stories.

First-level factors six through 16 (the environment of work factors) appeared in 24 per cent of the high attitude sequences. The major contributors to the 24 per cent were possibility of growth (6%), and interpersonal relations with subordinates (7%). Personal life, status, and security did not appear in the high attitude sequences.

Interpersonal relations (subordinates), interpersonal relations (peers), supervision technical and school policy and administration appeared in 58 per cent of the low attitude sequences. Achievement, recognition, work itself, responsibility and advancement accounted for 21 per cent of the incidence of factors which appeared in the lows. Status did not appear as a first-level factor in low attitude sequences.

The first-level factors which appeared more often in high attitude sequences were achievement*, recognition*, work itself, responsibility*, and possibility of growth. The first level factors which appeared more often in low attitude sequences were advancement, salary, interpersonal relations (subordinates)*, interpersonal relations (superior), interpersonal relations (peers)*, supervision technical*, school

* Difference between Highs and Lows is significant. Minimum P = .05.

TABLE 20–1   PERCENTAGES AND VALUES OF CHI SQUARED FOR THE
FREQUENCY WITH WHICH EACH FIRST-LEVEL FACTOR APPEARED IN
HIGH ATTITUDE SEQUENCES AS CONTRASTED WITH LOW ATTITUDE
SEQUENCES FOR THE TOTAL GROUP

Factor	High	Low	Chi squared	P
	+ NS = 142	NS = 142		
1. Achievement	30*	9	10.500	.01
2. Recognition	28*	2	30.139	.001
3. Work itself	11	8	.346	
4. Responsibility	7*	1	5.818	.05
5. Advancement	0	1		
6. Salary	2	3		
7. Possibility of growth	6	2	1.454	
8. Interpersonal relations (subordinates)	7	20*	7.605	.01
9. Interpersonal relations (superiors)	3	4	.900	
10. Interpersonal relations (peers)	1	15*	14.086	.001
11. Supervision—technical	1	10*	8.470	.01
12. School policy and administration	2	13*	10.227	.01
13. Working conditions	2	6	2.083	
14. Personal life	0	5*	5.142	.05
15. Status	0	0		
16. Security	0	1		

+ NS in this table and in Table 20–2 refers to number of sequences.
Percentages in this table and in Table 20–2 are approximate but do not vary more than
.0075.
* Difference between Highs and Lows is significant. Chi squared value required for
significance at the .05 level is 3.841.

policy and administration*, working conditions, personal life*, and security.

The percentages and values of chi-squared for the frequency with which second-level factors appeared in high attitude and low attitude sequences are reported in Table 20–2.

Achievement, which appeared in 50 per cent of the sequences, was the dominant second-level factor for the highs. Recognition appeared in 21 per cent of the sequences involving high job feelings. The remaining factors appeared in 29 per cent of the high attitude sequences. The major contributors to the 29 per cent were work itself (6%) and possible growth (6%). The second-level factors advancement, status, salary and fairness did not appear in high attitude sequences.

For second-level low attitude sequences feel-ings of unfairness, with 32 per cent, was the dominant factor. Feelings of guilt and inade-quacy, security, and work itself appeared in 31 per cent of the low sequences. Recognition with seven per cent and lack of achievement with 13 per cent were other contributors to low job feelings. The remaining six factors ap-peared in 15 per cent of the low sequences. The factor advancement did not appear in the lows.

The second-level factors which appeared more often in high attitude sequences were recognition*, achievement*, and possible growth. The second-level factors which ap-peared more often in low attitude sequences were work itself, status*, security, feelings of unfairness*, feelings of guilt and inadequacy, and salary.

* Difference between Highs and Lows is significant. Minimum P = .05.

Summary

The results presented in the first section demonstrate that many of the factors which accounted for high job feelings of teachers and many of the factors which accounted for low job feelings of teachers were mutually exclusive.

The first-level factors which appeared significantly as highs (as contrasted with lows) were recognition, achievement, and responsibility. The first-level factors which appeared significantly as lows (as contrasted with highs) were interpersonal relations (subordinates), interpersonal relations (peers), supervision—technical, school policy and administration, and personal life.

Achievement and recognition were the second-level factors which appeared significantly as highs. Feelings of unfairness and low status were the only second-level factors which appeared significantly as lows.

Subgroup differences

The analysis of results relating to the second question raised in this study strongly suggests that subgroups of teachers tend not to differ in their responses to sources of high and low job feelings. Significant differences were found in only three of 168 possibilities.

Men teachers tended *not* to respond differently from women teachers to sources of high and low job attitudes. No significant exception to this tendency was found.

Tenure teachers and nontenure teachers tended *not* to differ in their responses to sources of high and low job feelings. Three significant exceptions to this tendency were found:

1. The first-level factor interpersonal relations (superior) appeared as a source of low job feelings for tenure teachers in four per cent of the 142 low attitude sequences. This factor did not appear as a source of low job feelings for nontenure teachers.
2. Eleven per cent of the low attitude sequences involved nontenure teachers citing the first-level factor interpersonal relations (peers) as a source of low job attitudes. This was in contrast to four per cent for tenure teachers.
3. Security, a second-level factor, appeared in 11 per cent of the low attitude sequences. Nine of the 11 per cent were cited by nontenure teachers.

Elementary school teachers and secondary

TABLE 20–2   PERCENTAGES AND VALUES OF CHI SQUARED FOR THE FREQUENCY WITH WHICH EACH SECOND-LEVEL FACTOR APPEARED IN HIGH ATTITUDE SEQUENCES AS CONTRASTED WITH LOW ATTITUDE SEQUENCES FOR THE TOTAL GROUP

Factor	High	Low	Chi squared	P
	NS = 142	NS = 142		
1. Recognition	21*	7	9.025	.01
2. Achievement	50*	13	26.677	.001
3. Work itself	6	9	.190	
4. Advancement	0	0		
5. Responsibility	4	4		
6. Group feelings	3	3		
7. Possible growth	6	3	1.230	
8. Status	0	5*	5.1428	.05
9. Security	5	11	1.565	
10. Fairness-unfairness	0	32*	43.022	.001
11. Pride, guilt, inadequacy	5	11	2.782	
12. Salary	0	2		

* Difference between Highs and Lows is significant. Chi squared value required for significance at the .05 level is 3.841.

school teachers tended *not* to differ in their responses to sources of high job attitudes and low job attitudes. No significant exception to this tendency was found.

DISCUSSION

The polarity of factors

The results of this study indicated that achievement, recognition, and responsibility were factors which contributed predominantly to teacher job satisfaction. Interpersonal relations (subordinates), interpersonal relations (peers), supervision—technical, school policy and administration, personal life, and fairness-unfairness were factors which contributed predominantly to teacher job dissatisfaction. The remaining factors appeared to be bi-polar, possessing the potential to contribute to both satisfaction and dissatisfaction (many of the factors did not appear with sufficient frequency to test adequately for polarity).

The satisfaction factors

The three dominant factors which appeared in high attitude sequences were achievement, recognition and responsibility. Achievement accounted for nearly one out of three first-level high attitude sequences and for one out of two second-level high attitude sequences. In view of the predominance of the factor achievement, it is interesting to note that most of the teacher achievement-centered stories involved less concrete evidence of actual success and more sensing and feeling by teachers that students had been reached and were presumably affected in some positive way.

This noticeable lack of concrete success reinforces Lortie's notion of psychic gratification as a reward base for teachers. Lortie[9] argues that societal rewards (salary, prestige, and power) are, in general, not perceived by teachers as being in abundance. Thus, teachers tend to focus on psychic gratification as a primary source of reward in their work. One of the major sources of psychic gratification, ac-

cording to Lortie, is the interaction that the teacher has with individual students and classes where the teacher perceives that something has happened. The teacher senses or believes that, as a result of his activity, a change has taken place in the student or class. Lortie cites the terms "I reached them," "It went today," as being common expressions used by teachers to describe this phenomenon.

This psychic gratification, which is characterized by a task-oriented interaction with some perceived measurable result, was most typical of many of the success stories related by teachers.

Recognition appeared three times as often in high sequences as in low sequences. Sources of recognition for teachers varied. Teachers talked about feedback from principals, supervisors, parents, students, and fellow teachers. Recognition took the form of letters, oral statements, gifts, incentives, and committee appointments.

The need for recognition, the overt bolstering of self-esteem, appears to be important to teachers. The absence of recognition tends not to affect low job attitudes of teachers.

Responsibility, although significantly found to be a high, appeared in only seven per cent of the high attitude sequences. This percentage is small when one considers that teachers do assume a considerable amount of responsibility. As the classroom door closes behind the teacher, it is implied that she assumes responsibility for her own work. This responsibility is limited, however, and falls within the framework of the rules and regulation of the school, school district, and school board. Further limits are imposed by the state legislature and our society at large. Whatever responsibility a teacher assumes, in terms of what to teach, falls within the framework of the prescribed curriculum.

Perhaps even more interesting than the appearance of achievement, recognition and responsibility as positive polar factors was the absence of advancement and work itself. These factors did appear as satisfiers in Herzberg's study.

The factor advancement was not mentioned by teachers in high attitude stories. Teaching offers little opportunity for concrete advancement (change in status or position) and in fact any particular teaching assignment could be considered as a terminal position. Whatever potential the factor advancement has as a satisfier appears to be lost for teachers under our present system. Capitalizing on this factor, as a potential source of satisfaction, implies providing overt opportunities for advancement within the ranks of teachers.[10]

Work itself appeared as a bi-polar factor in the study. Although the factor appeared more frequently in teacher high attitude stories, it also appeared as a frequent source of low job feelings. It appears that the job of teacher (although potentially able to provide unlimited opportunity for creative and varied work) requires considerable attention to maintenance type activity. Routine or maintenance tasks range from attendance and scheduling details, daily health checks, study hall assignments, and lunch duty to blowing noses and pouring young scholars into snow suits. The work itself factor, although found to be rich in satisfaction potential, was frequently cited as a source of dissatisfaction for teachers.

The dissatisfaction factors

Perhaps of greatest interest among the dissatisfiers was the factor interpersonal relations (subordinates), which appeared in 20 per cent of the low attitude sequences and in seven per cent of the high attitude sequences.

It seems appropriate to assume that since students are the very crux of a teacher's work, they should account for many of the successes and good feelings that teachers have. Indeed, this is so. The students were the raw material for the achievement successes and acts of recognition which teachers perceived as sources of great satisfaction. Establishing an appropriate relationship with students appears to be critical. Once established, the teacher can capitalize on this relationship in pursuit of work-centered or job itself satisfaction. It appears that a happy relationship with students is not in itself potent enough to be a source of job satisfaction. A poor relationship with students, however, can be a source of considerable teacher dissatisfaction.

Responses of subgroups tend not to differ

A most interesting finding of the study was that subgroups of teachers—tenure and non-tenure, male and female, elementary and secondary—tended not to differ in their responses to sources of job satisfaction and dissatisfaction. There were only three exceptions, out of 168 possibilities, to this tendency. All three involved tenure and nontenure teachers.

One interpretation of this finding is that the satisfaction and dissatisfaction factors identified in this study apply to teachers irrespective of their sex, teaching level or tenure status.

CONCLUSION

This study provides support for the hypothesis that satisfiers and dissatisfiers tend to be mutually exclusive. Further, it was found that factors which accounted for high attitudes of teachers were related to the work itself and factors which accounted for low attitudes of teachers were related to the conditions or environment of work.

Relative to other activities, teachers derive the most satisfaction from work-centered activity. This finding was reflected in the predominance of achievement, recognition and responsibility as sources of teacher job satisfaction. The low attitude sequences, however, revealed factors which were not in themselves work-centered; rather, they focused on the conditions and people which surround the actual work.

Can we conclude that as long as a teacher experiences personal success, and is recognized for this success, the conditions of work need not be considered? It may be possible (although unlikely) for a teacher, who is immersed in an unsatisfactory work environment, to experience personal success and thus achieve considerable job satisfaction. An environment relatively free from sources of dissatisfaction, however, will tend to increase or enhance the appearance of factors which are direct contributors to job satisfaction.

Herzberg refers to the dissatisfaction factors as "hygienic." In describing these factors, Herzberg states:

They act in a manner analogous to the principles of medical hygiene. Hygiene operates to remove health hazards from the environment of man. It is not a curative; it is, rather, a preventive.[11]

The "hygienic" factors, according to Herzberg, are essential in preventing dissatisfaction, in making work tolerable. Herzberg describes the satisfaction factors as motivators. These are the job-centered, the task-oriented factors which permit the individual to satisfy his need for self actualization in his work.

The dissatisfaction factors identified for teachers tend to focus on conditions and circumstances which teachers expect to be maintained at acceptable levels. It seems reasonable that teachers should expect fair and adequate supervision, supportive school policies and administrative directives, friendly interpersonal relationships and pleasant working conditions. However, the satisfaction factors focus directly on conditions and circumstances that are not givens, which do not come with the job. These factors constitute rewards that must be earned through performance of the job. The reinforcement potential of the satisfiers is dependent upon a teacher's individual performance.

What then are the implications of the study for administrative behavior? The findings suggest that the present emphasis on "teacher-centered" behavior (supportive supervision, interpersonal relations, effective communications, and group effectiveness) is an important prescription for effective administrative behavior. The "teacher-centered" approach, however, is limited in that it tends to concentrate on the elimination of dissatisfaction factors and thus does not contribute directly to teacher job satisfaction.

"Task-oriented" behavior (organizing and planning work, implementing goal achievement) emerges as an important and direct contributor to teacher job satisfaction. Such behavior, on the part of the administrator, would include increasing the opportunities for teachers to experience personal and professional success. Basic to this undertaking is the proposition that administrators will permit and encourage teachers to (1) exercise more autonomy in making decisions (intensifying collaborative efforts and consultative management would be a good start), (2) increase individual responsibility in developing and implementing teaching programs, and (3) develop professional skills. These variables will serve to increase individual identification with the task.[12] Task identification appears to be a prerequisite for focusing on achievements as a means to personal and professional success and subsequent job satisfaction.

A corollary to personal success is recognition for such success. Although recognition was not found to be as potent as actual success, it was perceived by teachers as a measure of success. Capitalizing on recognition, as a satisfier for teachers, implies that dispensing of recognition should be as closely associated with successful teacher task-oriented behavior as possible.

Finally, effective administrative behavior would not exclude or ignore the sources of job dissatisfaction. Supervisory behavior, interpersonal relationships, and other factors relating to the conditions of work are necessary components in promoting an environment which will enhance job itself satisfaction for teachers. Teachers whose energies are taxed in coping with sources of job dissatisfaction will tend not to be vigorous and dynamic pursuers of work-centered satisfaction.

An inherent assumption, in the discussion above, has been that job satisfiers are reinforcers of behavior and motivators of performance. Considerable evidence has been accumulated which disputes the claim that a satisfied worker is more productive than a dissatisfied one. However, when satisfaction is dependent upon performance in work, satisfaction and productivity are related.[13]

The satisfaction factors identified for teachers cannot be separated from performance and, in fact, are dependent upon performance. It was successful performance which accounted for the high attitudes expressed in achievement-centered stories. Performance was also the basis for recognition-centered sequences. If performance is rewarded in terms of intrinsic personal success and extrinsic recognition for success, it will tend to be repeated.

SUMMARY

The assumption that factors which tend to satisfy teachers and factors which tend to dissatisfy teachers are arranged on a conceptual continuum tends *not* to be supported by this study. Factors which appeared as sources of high job feelings for teachers tended to differ from factors which appeared as sources of low job feelings. Further, the satisfaction factors tended to focus on the work itself, and the dissatisfaction factors tended to focus on the conditions of work.

It was concluded that the elimination of the dissatisfiers would tend not to result in job satisfaction. However, it does not appear likely that one can experience work satisfaction *without* the elimination or tempering of the dissatisfiers. Deriving satisfaction from work-centered activity assumes that one's energies and efforts are not taxed or depleted by unsatisfactory conditions of work. The point is not whether satisfiers are more crucial than dissatisfiers, or *vice versa*, but rather the dependence of the satisfiers on the elimination or tempering of the dissatisfiers.

REFERENCES

[1] Robinson, Alan, Ralph Conners and Ann Robinson. "Job Satisfaction Researches of 1963." *Personnel and Guidance Journal.* XLIII, 1964. p. 361.

[2] Herzberg, Frederick, Bernard Mausner, and Barbara Snyderman. *The Motivation to Work.* New York. John Wiley and Sons. 1959.

[3] Herzberg, Frederick, Bernard Mausner, Richard Peterson and Dora Capewell: *Job Attitudes: Review of Research and Opinion.* Pittsburgh. Psychological Service of Pittsburgh. 1957.

[4] Herzberg, *The Motivation to Work.*

[5] Maslow, A. H. *Motivation and Personality.* New York. Harper & Brothers. 1954.

[6] Herzberg, *The Motivation to Work.* pp. 113–119.

[7] Herzberg differentiated between the objective events, the actual stories, reported by respondents and the subsequent perceptions of respondents of what the objective events meant to them. The actual stories were the basis for the first-level factors and the "interpretation" of the stories by respondents comprised the second-level factors. First-level factors are listed in Table 20–1 and second-level factors are listed in Table 20–2.

[8] Herzberg, *The Motivation to Work.* p. 38.

[9] Lortie, Dan, "The Changing Role of Teachers as a Result of Such Innovations as Television, Programmed Instruction, and Team Teaching." Richard Lonsdale and Carl Steinhoff (eds.). *The Administrative Analysis of Selected Educational Innovations.* Report of the First Interuniversity Conference for School Administrators. Syracuse University, 1964.

[10] Schools frequently contain an informal promotion system for teachers. Advancement within the informal promotion system may include movement to another grade level, being assigned "quality" students, receiving equipment and facility priorities, and moving to a better school within the district. This informal promotion system was not described in teacher high attitude sequences but did appear in low attitude sequences. Judges coded these low attitude sequences into the factor categories working conditions or school policy and administration.

[11] Herzberg. *The Motivation to Work.* p. 113.

[12] March, John and Herbert Simon. *Organizations.* New York. John Wiley and Sons. 1958. p. 77.

[13] Bass, Bernard. *Organizational Psychology.* Boston. Allyn and Bacon, Inc. 1965. p. 38.

21.

SOME NOTES ON POWER-EQUALIZATION

GEORGE STRAUSS

THE PERSONALITY-VERSUS-ORGANIZATION HYPOTHESIS

Over the years, out of the contributions of individuals such as Argyris[1], Hertzberg,[2] Maier,[3] Maslow,[4] and McGregor[5] has come a consistent view of human motivation in industry.[6] With due credit to Chris Argyris, I would like to call it the "personality versus organization" hypothesis. I will state this hypothesis briefly first and then criticize it.

1. Human behavior in regard to work is motivated by a hierarchy of needs, in ascending order: physical, safety, social, egoistic, and self-actualization. By "hierarchy" is meant that a higher, less basic need does not provide motivation unless all lower, more basic needs are satisfied, and that, once a basic need is satisfied, it no longer motivates.

Physical needs are the most fundamental, but once a reasonable (satisficing, as Simon would put it) level of physical-need satisfaction is obtained (largely through pay), individuals become relatively more concerned with other needs. First they seek to satisfy their security needs (through seniority, fringe benefits, and so forth). When these, too, are reasonably satisfied, social needs (friendship, group support, and so forth) take first priority. And so forth. Thus, for example, hungry men have little interest in whether or not they belong to strong social groups; relatively well-off

From Harold J. Leavitt (ed.), *The Social Science of Organizations*, Prentice-Hall, Inc., Englewood Cliffs, N.J., 1963, pp. 45–59.

individuals are more anxious for good human relations.

Only when most of the less pressing needs are satisfied will individuals turn to the ultimate form of satisfaction, self-actualization, which is described by Maslow[7] as "the desire to become more and more what one is, to become everything that one is capable of becoming. . . . A musician must make music, an artist must paint, a poet must write, if he is to be ultimately happy. What a man *can* be, he *must* be." (p. 372.)

2. Healthy individuals desire to mature, to satisfy increasingly higher levels of needs. This, in practice, means that they want more and more opportunity to form strong social groups, to be independent, creative, to exercise autonomy and discretion, and to develop and express their unique personality with freedom.

3. The organization, on the other hand, seeks to program individual behavior and reduce discretion. It demands conformity, obedience, dependence and immature behavior. The assembly-line worker, the engineer, and the executive are all subject to strong pressures to behave in a programmed, conformist fashion.[8] As a consequence, many individuals feel alienated from their work.

4. Subordinates react to these pressures in a number of ways, most of which are dysfunctional to the organization. Individuals may fight back through union activity, sabotage, output restriction, and other forms of rational or irrational (aggressive) behavior. Or they may withdraw and engage in regression, sublimation, childish behavior, or failure to contribute creative ideas or to produce more than a minimum amount of work. In any case, employees struggle not to conform (at least at first). To keep these employees in line, management must impose still more restrictions and force still more immature behavior. Thus, a vicious cycle begins.

5. Management pressures often lead to excessive competition and splintering of work groups and the consequent loss of cooperation and social satisfaction. Or work groups

may become even stronger, but their norms may now be anti-management, those of protecting individuals against pressures from above.

6. A subtle management, which provides high wages, liberal employee benefits, "hygienic," "decent" supervision, and not too much pressure to work, may well induce employees to *think* they are happy and not *dissatisfied*.[9] But they are not (or should not be) truly *satisfied*; they are apathetic and have settled for a low level of aspiration. They do as little work as they can get away with and still hold their job. This is an unhealthy situation which is wasteful both to the individual and to the organization.

7. There seem to be some differences in emphasis among authorities as to whether the behavior of the typical subordinate under these circumstances will be rational (reality-oriented) or irrational (frustration-oriented). In any case, organizational pressures, particularly being subjected to programmed work, may lead to serious personality disturbances and mental illness.[10] Thus, traditional organizational techniques not only prevent the organization from operating at maximum efficiency, but, in terms of their impact on individual adjustment, they are also very expensive to society as a whole.

8. The only healthy solution is for management to adopt policies which promote intrinsic job satisfaction, individual development, and creativity, according to which people will willingly and voluntarily work toward organizational objectives because they enjoy their work and feel that it is important to do a good job.[11] More specifically, management should promote job enlargement, general supervision, strong cohesive work groups, and decentralization. In a nutshell, management should adopt "power-equalization techniques."

CRITICISM

The above is, in a sense, a hypothesis as to human behavior in organizations. But it is more than a coldly objective hypothesis: it is a pre-

scription for management behavior, and implicit in it are strong value judgments.[12] With its strong emphasis on individual dignity, creative freedom, and self-development, this hypothesis bears all the earmarks of its academic origin.

Professors place high value on autonomy, inner direction, and the quest for maximum self-development. As much as any other group in society, their existence is work-oriented; for them, creative achievement is an end in itself and requires no further justification. Most professors are strongly convinced of the righteousness of their Protestant ethic of hard work and see little incongruity in imposing it upon the less fortunate.

And yet there are many misguided individuals (perhaps the bulk of the population) who do not share the professor's values and would not be happy in the professor's job. Further, the technical requirements of many lines of work are very different from those of academia. Academic work is best accomplished by those with academic values, but it is questionable whether these values are equally functional in other lines of work—where creativity is not required to get the job done, but only the ability to follow orders.

In the pages which follow, I shall seek to re-evaluate the personality-versus-organization hypothesis. I shall suggest, first, that it contains many debatable value judgments, and, second, that it ignores what Harold Leavitt has called "organizational economics." I shall conclude that a broad range of people do not seek self-actualization on the job—and that this may be a fortunate thing because it might be prohibitively expensive to redesign some jobs to permit self-actualization.

VALUE JUDGMENTS

It seems to me that the hypothesis, as often stated, overemphasizes (1) the uniqueness of the personality-organization conflict to large-scale industry, (2) the universality of the desire to achieve self-actualization, and (3) the importance of the job (as opposed to the community or the home) as a source of need satisfaction. Thus, too little attention is given to economic motivation.[13]

The uniqueness of the problem

At least some authors seem to over-dramatize the personality-organization conflict as something unique to large-scale organization (particularly to mass-production industry). But this conflict is merely one aspect of what has been variously characterized as the conflict between individual and society, individual and environment, desire and reality, id and superego. "Thus the formal organization . . . is not truly the real villain; rather any kind of organized activity, from the most democratic to the most authoritarian contains within itself the necessary conditions for conflict."[14]

Similarly, the impact of the industrial revolution on work satisfaction can be overemphasized. Much is made of "alienation" (dictionary meaning: turning away) from work. Comparisons are constantly made between the old-time craftsman who did the entire job and the mass-production worker of today. But I doubt whether the medieval serf or the Egyptian slave enjoyed much sense of autonomy or creativity (although one might perhaps argue that he had more of a sense of identification and less of a feeling of anomie than does his better-fed modern counterpart). Perhaps there is less job satisfaction today than there was 100 years ago. Obviously, there are no objective ways of measuring this, but my surmise is that the "turning away" has been less dramatic than some have suggested. There have been boring, programmed jobs throughout history.

Others are as skeptical as I am regarding the theory of increased alienation. In his conclusion to a survey of job-satisfaction studies, Robert Blauner[15] questions "the prevailing thesis that most workers in modern society are alienated and estranged. There is a remarkable consistency in the findings that the vast majority of workers, in virtually all occupations and industries, are moderately or highly satisfied, rather than dissatisfied with their jobs. . . . The real character of the [pre-mass production] craftsman's work has been romanticized by the prevalent tendency to idealize the past. . . ." (pp. 352–353). And J. A. C. Brown[16] asserts "that in modern society there is far greater scope of skill and craftsmanship than in any previous society, and that far more people are in a position to use such skills" (p. 207).

The universality of the desire for self-actualization

The basic hypothesis implies a strong moral judgment that people should want freedom and self-actualization,[17] that it is somehow morally wrong for people to be lazy, unproductive, and uncreative. It seems to me that the hypothesis overemphasizes individuals' desire for freedom and underemphasizes their desire for security. It can even be argued that some of the personality-versus-organization writing has a fairly antisocial, even nihilistic flavor; it seems to emphasize individual freedom and self-development as the all-important values. Yet "mature" behavior does not mean freedom from all restrictions; it means successful adjustment to them.

As Erich Fromm has suggested, most people do not want complete freedom. They want to know the limits within which they can act (and this is true both on and off the job). To put it another way: most people are willing to tolerate and may even be anxious for a few areas of their life which are unpredictable and exciting, but they insist that, in a majority of areas, events occur as expected. The research scientist, for example, may relish the novelty and uncertainty of laboratory work, but he insists that his secretary be always on call, that his technician give predictable responses, and that his car start with complete regularity.

True, some people seek much broader limits than do others, and some are not too upset if the limits are fuzzy. However, there are many who feel most comfortable if they work in a highly defined situation. For them, freedom is a burden; they want firm, secure leadership.

And there are many more who, if not fully happy with programmed work, find it rather easy to accommodate themselves to it.

Argyris, for example, might reply that such individuals are immature personalities who have adjusted to organizational restrictions by becoming apathetic and dependent. Were the organizational environment healthy, these individuals would react differently. But in many cases, the restrictions which made these people this way occurred in childhood or are present in the culture. Such individuals may be "too far gone" to react well to power equalization, and their attitude is not likely to be changed short of intensive psychotherapy. Indeed, many people may have internalized and made part of their self-concept a low level of aspiration regarding their on-the-job responsibilities and their ability to handle these. What psychologists call the *theory of dissonance* suggests that sudden attempts to increase their sense of autonomy and self-determination might be quite disturbing.

Impressive evidence of the need for self-actualization is provided by the preliminary results of the mental health studies, which suggest that poor mental health is correlated with holding low-skilled jobs. And yet the evidence is still not complete. Apparently, not everyone suffers equally from unskilled work, and some adjust more easily than others. (Perhaps these studies will help us to improve the prediction process, so that we can do a better job of selecting and even training people for this kind of work.)

Further, it is far from clear whether this lower mental health is caused primarily by the intrinsic nature of unskilled work or by the fact that such work pays poorly and has low status both off and on the job.[18] In so far as mental disturbances are caused by economic and social pressures at home, higher wages may be a better solution than improved human relations on the job or a rearrangement of work assignments.

A hasty glance at the research in this field, as summarized in two reviews (Kasl and French[19]; Vroom and Maier[20]; see also Guerin, et al.[21]), makes it abundantly clear that un-

skilled workers are not the only ones to suffer from poor mental health. Depending on which study one looks at or what mental health index is used, one can conclude that executives, clerical personnel, sales-people, and lower-level supervisors *all* suffer from below-average mental health. The evidence makes one sympathize with the old Quaker, "All the world is queer save me and thee; and sometimes I think thee is a little queer."

The job as the primary source of satisfaction

There is an additional value judgment in the basic hypothesis that the *job* should be a primary form of need satisfaction for everyone (as it is for professors). But the central focus of many peoples' lives is not the job (which is merely a "way of getting a living"), but the home or the community. Many people find a full measure of challenge, creativity, and autonomy in raising a family, pursuing a hobby or taking part in community affairs. As Robert Dubin[22] puts it:

> Work, for probably a majority of workers, and even extending into the ranks of management, may represent an institutional setting that is not the central life interest of the participants. The consequence of this is that while participating in work a general attitude of apathy and indifference prevails. . . . Thus, the industrial worker does not feel imposed upon by the tyranny of Organizations, company, or union (p. 161).[23]

In my own interviewing experience in factories, I often ran across women who repeated variants of, "I like this job because it gets me away from all the kids and pressures at home." One girl even told me, "The job is good because it gives me a chance to think about God." Such individuals may feel little need for power equalization.

In any case, as Kerr, Dunlap, Harbison, and Myers[24] predict, work, in the future, will doubtless be increasingly programmed and will provide fewer and fewer opportunities for creativity and discretion on the job. On the other hand, the hours will grow shorter and there will be a "new bohemianism" off the job. All this suggests the irreverent notion that *perhaps* the best use of our resources is to accelerate automation, shorten the work week just as fast as possible, forget about on-the-job satisfactions, and concentrate our energies on making leisure more meaningful.

Underemphasis on economic rewards

Since the hypothesis over-emphasizes the job as a source of need satisfaction, it also under-emphasizes the role of money as means of motivation. The hypothesis says that, once employees obtain a satisficing level of economic reward, they go on to other needs and, presumably, are less concerned with money. However, the level of reward which is *satisficing* can rise rapidly over time. Further, money is a means of satisfying higher needs, too—ego, safety, and, for some, even self-actualization needs, for example, the individual who (perhaps misguidedly) seeks to live his life off the job engaging in "creative" consumption. True, employees expect much better physical, psychological, and social conditions on the job today than they did fifty years ago. But they also expect more money. There is little evidence that money has ceased to be a prime motivator.

"ORGANIZATIONAL ECONOMICS"

Perhaps the most fundamental criticisms of the personality-organization hypothesis is that it ignores (or at least misapplies) "organizational economics"; that is, it fails to balance carefully the costs and gains of power equalization. To be sure, most power-equalization advocates point out the hidden costs of autocracy: apathetic and resentful employees, turnover, absenteeism, sabotage, resistance to change, and all the rest. Traditional forms of supervision may be expensive in terms of the lost motivation and energy which might have been turned to organizational ends; they are even more expensive in terms of mental health. Yet some

writers, in their moments of wilder enthusiasm, tend to overestimate the gain to be derived from eliminating autocracy and to underestimate the costs of power equalization.

The gains from eliminating autocracy

Carried to excess, anxiety and aggression are undoubtedly harmful to both the organization and the individual. But many psychological studies suggest that dissatisfaction and anxiety (and even aggression, depending on how it is defined) spur individuals to work harder—particularly in simple, highly programmed tasks. Autocratic, work-oriented bosses very often get out high production; on occasion, their subordinates even develop high morale and cohesive work groups.[25]

Still, beyond certain limits, dissatisfaction, anxiety, and aggression are not in the organization's interests. There is much more doubt about apathy and conformity. It is often argued that an apathetic worker who is subject to "hygienic" supervision will only work enough so as not to get fired, that he will never exercise creativity or imagination or put out an outstanding performance.

On many jobs, however, management has no use for outstanding performance. What is outstanding performance on the part of an assembly-line worker? That he works faster than the line? That he shows creativity and imagination on the job? Management wants none of these. *Adequate* performance is all that can be used on the assembly line and probably on a growing number (I know no figures) of other jobs in our society. Here the conformist, dependent worker may well be the best.[26] As Leavitt and Whisler put it, "The issue of morale versus productivity that now worries us may pale as programming moves in. The morale of programmed personnel may be of less central concern because less (or at least a different sort of) productivity will be demanded of them."[27]

Even at the management level, there may be an increasing need for conforming, unimaginative types of "organization men" if Leavitt and Whisler's prediction comes true that "jobs at today's middle-management levels will become highly structured. Much more of the work will be programmed, i.e., covered by sets of operating rules governing the day-to-day decisions that are made."[28] Despite the *organization man*, it might be argued that nonconformity will be useful to the organization only in increasingly limited doses.

The costs of power-equalization

On the other hand, power-equalization can be quite costly to the organization. To make general supervision or participative management work, many of the old-line autocratic supervisors must be retrained or replaced; this is an expensive process which may result in the demoralization or elimination of the organization's most technically competent individuals. Since it is extremely difficult to develop internalized motivation on many routine jobs, once the traditional, external sanctions (monetary rewards, fear of discharge, and so forth) are removed, *net* motivation may fall on balance. And it is fairly meaningless to talk of permitting exercise of discretion to assembly-line workers or girls on a punch-card operation; the very nature of the technology requires that all essential decisions be centrally programmed.

"But if the nature of the job makes power-equalization techniques impractical," some may argue, "change the nature of the job." Rensis Likert puts this well:

> To be highly motivated, each member of the organization must feel that the organization's objectives are of significance and that his own particular task contributes in an indispensable manner to the organization's achievement of its objectives. He should see his role as difficult, important, and meaningful. This is necessary if the individual is to achieve and maintain a sense of personal worth and importance. *When jobs do not meet this specification they should be reorganized so that they do* [p. 103, my emphasis].[29]

True, there are many opportunities to re-design jobs and work-flows[30] so as to increase various forms of job satisfaction such as autonomy and achievement. But whether such changes should be made is a matter for organizational economics.

In many instances these changes, when accompanied by appropriate forms of supervision and proper selection of personnel, may result in substantial increases of productivity. (Purely technological losses in efficiency may be more than offset by increased motivation, less work-flow friction, and so forth.) Obviously, in such instances organizational economics would dictate that the changes should be introduced.

But there are other areas where technological changes can be made only at a substantial cost in terms of productivity—and the impact of automation and information technology seems to be increasing the number of jobs where this may be true. Should we scrap the advances of technology in these areas in order to foster good human relations? Or should we say, "Thank God for the number of people who have made an apparent adjustment to routine jobs. Would that there were more." Perhaps—as has been suggested earlier—it would be best to devote our resources to ever-shortening the work week and helping people to enjoy their leisure more fully.

There seems to be considerable evidence that a relatively stable situation can exist in which workers perform relatively routine, programmed jobs under hygienic supervision.[31] Although these workers may not be satisfied (in the Hertzberg sense) and may be immature, apathetic, and dependent (in the Argyris sense), they are not actively dissatisfied, they do not feel a need for additional responsibility and they seek meaning in life from their home and community rather than from their jobs. To be sure, these individuals are maximizing neither their productive efforts nor their possible job satisfaction. But both management and employees find the situation satisficing (in the Simon sense). Barring sudden change, it is stable. It may well be the best we are likely to get in many situations without costly changes in technology, child upbringing, and so forth.

THE PERSONALITY-ORGANIZATION HYPOTHESIS SUMMARIZED

My concern in this section has been with the personality-versus-organization hypothesis. I have tried to demonstrate:

1. Although many individuals find relatively little satisfaction in their work, this may not be as much of a deprivation as the hypothesis would suggest, since many of these same individuals center their lives off the job and find most of their satisfactions in the community and the home. With these individuals, power-equalization may not liberate much energy.
2. Individuals are not motivated solely to obtain autonomy, self-actualization, and so forth. With various degrees of emphasis, individuals also want security and to know what is expected of them. Power-equalization may certainly stir up a good deal of anxiety among those who are not prepared for it, and at least some individuals may be reluctant to assume the responsibility that it throws upon them.
3. Power-equalization techniques are not too meaningful when management needs no more than an "adequate" level of production, as is often the case when work is highly programmed. Under such circumstances, the costs entailed by modification in job design and supervisory techniques may be greater than the gains obtained from increased motivation to work.

All of the above does not mean either that the personality-organization hypothesis is meaningless or that power-equalization techniques are not useful. Quite the contrary. What it does mean is that many individuals can accommodate themselves to the demands of the organization without too much psychological loss, and for them the personality-organization conflict is not particularly frustrating. Similarly, in many circumstances the gains to the organization from power equalization may be moderate and more than offset by its costs.

For other individuals (for example, scientists working in large companies), the personality-organization conflict may be felt quite acutely. For the most part, these are the very individuals whose work cannot be programmed and from whom management wants more than merely "adequate" production.

All this re-emphasizes the often-made point that no single style of leadership can be universally appropriate. The techniques which work on the assembly line will almost certainly fail with research scientists. Indeed, it is fair to predict that, over time, the differences among supervisory styles may increase. Perhaps, in the future, we shall have at one extreme research scientists and others doing creative work who will be putting in a 40-hour or longer work week under conditions of relative power-equalization. At the other extreme may be those who submit to close supervision on highly programmed jobs, but for only 20 hours or so. Shades of *Brave New World*: the alphas and the gammas!

NOTES

[1] Chris Argyris, *Personality and Organization*. New York: Harper & Row, Publishers, 1957.

[2] Frederick Hertzberg, Bernard Mausner, and Barbara Snyderman, *The Motivation to Work*. New York: John Wiley & Sons, 1960.

[3] Norman R. F. Maier, *Psychology in Industry*. Boston: Houghton Mifflin Company, 1955, 2nd ed.

[4] A. H. Maslow, *Motivation and Personality*. New York: Harper & Row, Publishers, 1954.

[5] Douglas McGregor, *The Human Side of Enterprise*. New York: McGraw-Hill Book Co., 1960.

[6] For an excellent summary of this hypothesis and its application, see James V. Clark, "Motivation and Work Groups: A Tentative View," *Human Organization*, v. 19, (Winter, 1960–61) pp. 119–208. Somewhat the same position is taken by Robert K. Merton, *Social Theory and Social Structure*. Glencoe, Ill.: The Free Press, 1957, and Philip Selznick, *TVA and the Grass Roots*, Berkley: University of California Press, 1949; both suggest that organizational attempts to obtain conformity lead to unanticipated consequences, such as lack of innovation and even rebellion.

[7] Maslow, A. H., "A Theory of Human Motivation," *Psychological Review*, 50, (July, 1943), p. 372.

[8] These three groups are discussed in Charles R. Walker and Robert H. Guest, *The Man on the Assembly Line*, Cambridge: Harvard University Press, 1952; Herbert Shepard, "Nine Dilemmas in Industrial Research," *Administrative Science Quarterly*, 1, (Fall, 1960), pp. 245–259; and Wm. H. Whyte, Jr., *The Organization Man*, New York: Simon and Schuster, 1946.

[9] Frederick Herzberg, Bernard Mausner, and Barbara Snyderman, *The Motivation to Work*. New York: John Wiley & Sons, 1959, distinguish between dissatisfiers (basically, the absence of "hygienic" factors such as good "supervision, interpersonal relations, physical working conditions, salary, company policies, and administrative practices, benefits, and job security") (p. 113) and motivators (basically, challenge, autonomy, and interesting work). Similar conclusions are reached by Gerald Guerin, Joseph Vernoff, and Sheila Feld, *Americans View Their Mental Health*, New York: Basic Books, Inc., 1960. The Herzberg, Mausner, Snyderman analysis is criticized by Victor Vroom, Norman R. F. Maier, "Industrial Social Psychology," *Annual Review of Psychology*, Paul Farnsworth, ed., 12 (Palo Alto: Annual Review, 1960).

[10] Recent evidence suggests that unskilled workers are significantly more likely to suffer from personality disturbances and psychosomatic illnesses than are skilled workers, and that these differences become manifest only after the individuals take up their work. (In other words, once individuals land in unskilled jobs, they tend to become more maladjusted.) Cf. Arthur Kornhauser, "Mental Health of Factory Workers: A Detroit Study," *Human Organization*, 21 (Spring, 1962), pp. 43–46, and John French, Robert L. Kahn, and Floyd C. Mann, eds., "Work, Health, and Satisfaction," *Journal of Social Issues*, 18 (July, 1962).

[11] Perhaps the most general statement of this position is McGregor's Theory Y. Cf. Douglas McGregor, *The Human Side of Enterprise*. New York: McGraw-Hill Book Company, 1960.

[12] There seems to be a certain amount of confusion as to whether prescriptions for power-equalization are written from the point of view of organizational efficiency or that of mental health (and possibly the degree of confusion has increased since the primary source of research funds in this area has shifted from the military to the National Institute of Mental Health). There are those who claim that what is good for the individual will, in the long run, be good for the organization, and vice versa. Regardless, it is useful to keep one's criteria explicit.

[13] I must confess that many of these criticisms apply to my own writing.

[14] Warren G. Bennis, "Leadership Theory and Administrative Behavior," *Administrative Science Quarterly*, 4 (December, 1959), p. 281. Ironically, some of those most concerned with the tyranny of the organization would substitute for it the tyranny of the participative group.

[15] Robert Blauner, "Work Satisfaction and Industrial Trends in Modern

Society." In Walter Galenson and Seymour Martin Lipset, *Labor and Trade Unionism*. New York: John Wiley & Sons, 1960.

[16] J. A. C. Brown, *The Social Psychology of Industry*. Baltimore: English Pelican edition, 1954.

[17] Though the concept of self-actualization is insightful, I tend to agree with Bennis (1959) that it "is, at best, an ill-defined concept . . . [and that] self-actualized man seems to be more myth than reality" (p. 279).

[18] Both the Wayne State and the Michigan studies emphasize that no single factor explains the relationship. Kornhauser (1962) concludes: "Both on rational grounds and from empirical evidence, I see no reason to think that it is useful to single out one or a few of the job-related characteristics as distinctly important . . . If we are to understand why mental health is poorer in less skilled, more routine factory jobs, we must look at the entire pattern of work and life conditions of people in these occupations—not just at single variables." (p. 46).

[19] Stanislov V. Kasl and John R. P. French, Jr., "The Effects of Occupational Status on Physical and Mental Health," *Journal of Social Issues*, 18 (July, 1962), pp. 67–89.

[20] Victor Vroom and Norman R. F. Maier, "Industrial Social Psychology," *Annual Review of Psychology*, Paul Farnsworth, ed. 12 (Palo Alto: Annual Review, 1960).

[21] Guerin, *et al., op. cit.*

[22] Robert Dubin, "Industrial Research and the Discipline of Sociology," in *Proceedings of the 11th Annual Meeting*. Madison: Industrial Relations Research Association, 1959, p. 161.

[23] A. H. Maslow, *Motivation and Personality*. New York: Harper & Row, Publishers, 1954, himself suggests that self-actualization can be obtained off the job, as "an ideal mother [or] . . . athletically" (p. 373), Dubin's point may also be exaggerated. I would guess that for the most part those who participate actively (seek self-actualization) off the job also seek to participate actively on the job, a "an ideal mother [or] . . . athletically" (p. 373). Dubin's point may be community and at home.

[24] Clark Kerr, John T. Dunlap, Frederick H. Harbison, and Charles A. Myers, *Industrialism and Industrial Man: The Problems of Labor and Management*. Cambridge: Harvard University Press, 1960.

[25] For a list of the conditions under which "authoritarian leadership might be as effective as its alternatives," see Harold W. Wilensky, "Human Relations in the Work-place," in *Research in Human Industrial Relations*, 12, Apensberg, *et al.*, eds., New York: Harper & Row, Publishers, 1957, pp. 25–50. Interestingly, the personality-organization hypothesis is strongly influenced by Freud. Yet Freud postulated that "productive work is partially a function of the expression of hostility to the leader" (Bennis, p. 292).

[26] William J. Goode and Irving Fowler, "Incentive Factors in a Low-Morale Plant," *American Sociological Review*, 14 (October, 1949), pp. 619–624.

[27] Harold J. Leavitt and Thomas Whisler, "Management in the 1980's," *Harvard Business Review*, 36 (November, 1958), p. 46.

[28] Leavitt and Whisler, p. 41.

[29] Rensis Likert, *New Patterns of Management*. New York: McGraw-Hill Book Company, 1961, p. 103.

[30] Louis E. Davis and Richard Werling, "Job Design Factors," *Occupational Psychology*, 34 (April, 1960), pp. 109–132.

[31] Chris Argyris, *Understanding Organizational Behavior*. Homewood: Dorsey Press, Inc., 1960, ch. 5.

22.

THE POLITICAL COMMUNITY AND THE FUTURE OF WELFARE (SOCIAL SELF-MANAGEMENT)

EUGEN PUSIC

If we do not find a way, and soon, to adapt politically to the decisive increase in both productivity and destructiveness, any discussion of human welfare is irrelevant. The choice we have to make is, unhappily, as simple as that. I say unhappily, because we all find it extremely difficult to face the implications of circumstances that are really and radically new.[1] Always, however, at crucial turns in history, some momentous change in the external or internal situation has had to be compensated by a decisive breakthrough in the pattern of our thinking and functioning. It looks as if the next great inventions might have to come in the political field in order to neutralize the dangerous combination of new technological development and old ways of thinking and feeling about man in society.

I

Life in society, as far as we can see through history, seems to have been determined by two basic and complementary facts: the necessity of co-operation and the inevitability of conflict.[2]

In the history of ideas the emotionally intensive experience of conflict attracted earlier and wider attention than did the equally obvious concept of co-operation. In the early re-

ligious systems conflict is already projected into the realm of the transcendental, into the never-ending struggle of good and evil. On a higher level of religious development the metaphysical representations are retroprojected[3] into society: what are the implications of this all-embracing war between light and darkness for practical human action? Sometimes conflict is given a positive value as an expression of solidarity of the faithful and a method of spreading the faith. In other instances, conflict is transferred to the intra-personal field. Man has to combat evil in himself in order to be counted on the winning side of the metaphysical battle, or for more disinterested reasons of personal spiritual improvement.

Co-operation was given more systematic thought only when the development of economic productivity made co-ordination of human effort one of its most obvious prerequisites. The growth of commerce and industry and the concomitant need for public peace and security, which alone could satisfy the requirement of "laissez faire, laissez passer," found expression in corresponding ideologies of co-operation, in theories of natural law and of social contract. The assumed primaeval, chaotic state of "bellum omnium erga omnes" gave place to a state of "prestabilized" harmony within the framework of supposedly aprioristic rules.

In the history of institutions, however, in the reality of their social life and whatever the current ideologies of the time, people have always had to cope with the simultaneous tasks of finding the most appropriate method of co-operating with each other and the most effective means of fighting against each other. These two aims were sometimes fused into one overriding objective: to work together in order to survive in conflict.

For a long time the possibilities of co-operation were defined by the scope of the human eye and the power of the human voice, and were limited essentially to the face-to-face group. As with organic forms, however, the range of adaptability of institutional structures is not unlimited. The increased division of labour and the accelerated rate of change have put increasing strain on the face-to-face group. The ever-more detailed specialization of tasks has called for additional precision in the determination of behaviour. On the other hand, a more rapid succession of shifts in the social situation has intensified the requirements of elasticity, of a speedier response to change. These two tendencies have exerted a heavier and heavier pressure on the existing institutional structure. Reaching the end of its capacity for adaptation the primary group has developed pseudo-solutions of considerable interest. Behaviour patterns prescribed in the most minute detail, as in marriage ceremonies or in commercial transactions, are evidence of the attempt to find an answer to the problems imposed by the advance of the division of labour. What was won in precision, however, was lost in elasticity. The initially rational definition of individual tasks lost its meaning with the changing situation, but the behaviour, learned through repetition of the same situation in the group and reinforced by a battery of social and magic sanctions, persisted as formalized ceremonial conduct. It still yielded the social benefit of generating feelings of solidarity and security, but these advantages had to be measured against the growing handicaps to practical and efficient action.

A second contradiction in the crisis of the face-to-face structure was the opposition between the requirement for greater differentiation in social relationships and at the same time greater stability in human relations. It was evident that with trade, with migration, with colonization, it was practically useless to think of all people in black and white patterns. There were in-between relationships which could be quite profitable. One would trade with people not of one's own group, and at the same time establish quite friendly relationships. It would obviously be beneficial if this kind of relationship could be made more stable—if it did not have to be conducted under the always existing risk that any such relationship could immediately turn into open hostility.

This double challenge—detailed allocation of tasks and speedy adjustment to the changing environment, and greater differentiation in human relationships and greater stability in them—was beyond the structural possibilities of the face-to-face group. In order to find an answer a new institution was necessary, and in time a new institution was evolved: organization, one of the most remarkable social inventions of man. Organization is an instrument for achieving consciously chosen goals. It relates ends to the means necessary for achieving them by setting up a stable structure of relationships among people at work. It makes possible the planning of on-going activities, the devising of detailed programmes and blueprints for action. This is achieved by dividing the over-all task into smaller and simpler parts and by subdividing these parts until individual operations are defined to the last movement, where necessary. The lines traced in the course of this process constitute the network for the co-ordination of the total planned activity and its orientation towards the established goal. At the same time the whole system can be changed with an ease and speed difficult to imagine under earlier conditions. From the most general goal to the most specific element of action, everything can be subjected to scrutiny, analysed, compared and changed in the same way in which it was introduced in the first place, by explicit arrangement. Organization is a powerful new instrument for co-operation towards the satisfaction of human needs.

Human needs, however, have to be satisfied under conditions of scarcity of resources and within human society—conditions which define conflict as a situation where the needs of an individual or a group can be satisfied only at the expense of the needs of another individual or group.[4] There are several possible answers to a situation of conflict: one party dominates the others and satisfies its needs without regard to anyone else's needs; one or several parties abandon their original aims and reorient their wants towards other objectives; the conflicting parties reach a compromise where everyone gets some satisfaction but nobody fully realizes his original goals.

Each of these methods, in the course of social development, evolves its corresponding set of institutions. Domination is socially stabilized through power; reorientation is expressed through the great systems of religious thought and aesthetic creation; and compromise is regulated through the institution of contract, through systems of rules and through the judicial process.

The original methods employed within this institutional framework are determined by the type of structure available for social action generally. Power is based on actual physical violence or on the immediate threat of it; religious communion is achieved through direct charismatic experience; the institutions of compromise function in face-to-face contact only.

In conflict, as well as in co-operation, the coming of organization marks an epoch. The field of action of the different institutions is decisively widened, the methods are transformed, their mutual relationships are altered. Power develops the continuity, the territorial links and the relative permanence we associate with the more modern notion of political power;[5] religious movements consolidate into organizations of churches with a considerably widened span of influence; contracts and rule systems become independent of the physical presence of the affected parties. At the same time power becomes less dependent on the immediate use of violence; religious experience loses some of its emotional pitch as charisma becomes gradually bureaucratized; and the area of compromise is widened in an increasingly rational atmosphere. In the mutual relations among the different institutional systems political power comes to occupy a central place. As power-systems become larger and more stable, the traditional systems of reorientation, such as religion, lose some of their former conflict-solving capacity and are relegated to the inner councils of the individual—if the corresponding church-organizations do not in turn develop

some form of political power—while institutions of compromise are integrated into the political power system and become, at least in principle, dependent on it.

II

Organizations are groups of people who in one of their social roles are bound by specific sets of rules to apply given resources in order to achieve prescribed ends by performing one of the activities into which the overall task is divided and by submitting to coordination for the most efficient achievement of the general goal. The simultaneous presence of the opposite tendencies in organization—division and fusion—is the principal source of its achievements and also the ultimate cause of its demise. There can be no doubt that today organization as an institution is facing a crisis. It seems that organization has completed its circle and in its turn has reached the limits of its capacity to adapt to changed circumstances. The crisis of organization is brought about by its role in human co-operation as well as by its place in human conflict.

As indicated earlier, the tension between the need for precision and the requirement of elasticity was too great for the face-to-face group. In the same way a new antithesis between the drive towards specialization and the necessity to co-ordinate is developing into a force likely to destroy the traditional structure of organization.

The process of differentiation of labour tends, within organizations, to take two different forms. One, implied in the organizational process itself, consists in the division of complex tasks into progressively more detailed and less complex action-elements. The result of this "crumbling"[6] of work is the production line, the conveyer belt, the standardized simple action prescribed to the last detail of time and motion, and fitted into larger schemes independently of the will or even the knowledge of the individual worker. The advantages of precision and of simplicity have to be paid for by a loss of meaningfulness, by the deadening effect on the relation between man and his work.

The other form which the differentiation of labour takes is that of professional specialization. There are activities which cannot be usefully broken up into simpler elements. They are based on a systematic knowledge of more complex relationships among natural or social phenomena and on the learning of more intricate skills. Here the differentiation of labour proceeds through a progressive narrowing of the range of concern, a reduction of the field of interest, while the action-processes themselves within the smaller field remain intact. A cardiologist, for instance, does not perform simpler functions than a general practitioner, nor is a specialist of international law less qualified than a general lawyer.

In organizations the differentiation of labour develops both ways, up to a point. Comparatively early in the development of the division of labour the standardization of individual operations implicit in the first method—that is of breaking up an activity into simpler components—suggested the transfer of these well defined movements to machines. But in very recent times developments based on cybernetics and information theory have made possible the construction of large-scale chains of action where the standardized elements are performed without human intervention. The development of automation spells an end to the first method of differentiation of human labour in organizations by dividing the work-process. Whatever can be standardized can, in principle, be transferred to machines. This increases considerably the importance of the other method, the differentiation of labour by professional specialization.[7]

Professional specialization leaves the specialist in possession of the necessary knowledge and skill to perform complex and meaningful activities. He is much less in danger of being separated from the meaning of his work and, therefore, much more independent. He knows his work and does not need to wait for others to assign tasks to him. Still the work of the individual specialist has to be coordinated and integrated into larger contexts. An individual physician in a hospital, a social worker in an agency, a scientist in a laboratory, a teacher in a school, an administrator in an office can make their full contribution only as their work is brought into rational relationships with the work of others. The very independence of their individual activities, however, makes co-ordination both more necessary and more difficult. The classical school of administrative science early became aware that the span of control—the number of people to be co-ordinated by one superior—was in inverse proportion to the professional level of the work co-ordinated.

The methods of co-ordination practiced within the traditional structure of organization seem to be ill adapted to the task of tying together the work of professional specialists. The work of individuals is co-ordinated within an organization by a hierarchy of superiors who are responsible for the allocation of work tasks to those below them as well as for the control and necessary correction of their work performances. With the increasing complexity of organizations and of the work done by their individual members the hierarchical method of co-ordination requires more and more of everybody's time. The flow of directives down the line and of reports up the line becomes more abundant. More time is spent in meetings and other forms of face-to-face contact. More writing and reading for purposes of co-ordination have to be done at all levels. Administrative procedures become more involved, formalities more numerous as the organizational system tries to counteract the centrifugal tendencies of specialization. This increase of co-ordinating activities, however, has to find its place within the fixed time-budget at the disposal of the organization. Co-ordination can ultimately expand only at the expense of the main activity, which is the initial social reason for the existence of the system. More co-ordination means less health work, less social welfare services, less education, less research by the respective organizations. The point of diminishing returns can be clearly seen: it is the moment when the balance between co-ordination and basic activity becomes so unfavourable that organization will no longer be the socially most economical method of human co-operation.

Also, the method of co-ordination prevailing in organizations is based on the assumption that the existing inequalities among individuals as to their respective possibilities of contributing to the common goal are, on the whole, correctly expressed through the existing hierarchy. Individuals at lower levels perform simpler tasks and have, therefore, to know less than those at higher levels who instruct and control them and who should possess greater insight into the more complex interrelationships between the more elementary contributions of their inferiors. With the possibility of eliminating these simpler tasks altogether by transferring them to machines and with increasing professional specialization, this assumption no longer holds. Those members of the organization who are directly performing its basic activity, and who are therefore at the bottom of the traditional hierarchical pyramid, have really to be the most knowledgeable and skilful. What wonder that they adjust less and less easily to the traditional method of co-ordination which is based on the assumption that the higher echelons of the hierarchy are manned by people who are necessarily wiser and whose contribution is more valuable than that of their inferiors. This new situation is finally irreconcilable with the organizational relationship of subordination and super-ordination.

In its other aspect as well, its place in human conflict, organization is approaching the point of crisis. Organization implies a substantial increase in the efficiency of power. Through organization, power becomes impersonal and can exert a greater pressure on the individual who most fears what he cannot grasp and know: he tends to respond by aggressive and hostile attitudes to power-in-organization which presents the blank facade of anonymity to his hostility. Through organization, also, power

gains a stability and continuity, an independence from the turnover of its personnel never before imagined. To human ambition organization offers the prize of power without necessarily requiring the Alcibiadic[8] talents of moving people, which imply at least a minimum of empathetic identification of the leader with the led. Power based on huge organizational systems develops a gravitational pull strong enough to draw into its orbit existing interests over a wide field. The rulers rule; the growing bureaucracy derives its living and its sense of personal value from its position; more and more people feel somehow protected by power, dependent on it, or simply fear change more than the status quo, having carved, by thousands of small adjustments, a nook for themselves. Organization makes power at the same time more all-pervading and more remote, more intermingled with everyone's interests and more independent of them. Techniques developed in order to control power of a different magnitude become manifestly inadequate.

The crucial new element in power based on organizational systems is not only its increase in quantity and stability, but the phenomenon of displacement of goals. Every organization develops a kind of staying power expressed in the loyalty of its members, in their readiness to find new tasks for it when the original purpose has been exhausted, in their commitment to values implicit in what the organization has set them to do. This loyalty, however, is to the organization more than to any other value. The existence and growth of the organization become a goal in their own right—a goal which commands, more and more, the emotions and the motivations of people working for the organization, and dominates, by its importance and appeal, the original aims for the pursuit of which the organization was created. As long as these aims justify the development of the organization and contribute to its prosperity they are maintained and used in order to legitimate the organization's activities. When they no longer perform this function they are discarded and other aims are put in their place. The organization is important, not the aims. The existence and growth of the organization are becoming its institutional goal, in contrast to the functional goals which its creators had in mind. This institutional goal tends, in the long run, to dominate and to displace also the individual objectives that the organization's members might have at any time and to subordinate their strivings, sociologically as well as psychologically, to the "reason of State" of the organization.

This displacement of individual goals and interests by the institutional goal of the organization increases with the size of the organization, in order to reach a practically inescapable level of intensity in the large organizational systems which are the basis of political power. The reason of State, the cause of the preservation and the agrrandizement of the power system as such—whatever the form in which this cause is rationalized—becomes the supreme law not only for members of the organization, but also for the political rulers and even for their opponents, the "loyal opposition." A situation may then arise when mere "bystanders," the ruled, people who apparently have everything to lose by the complete subordination of their interests to the State, are drawn into the magnetic field of the system and its institutional goals. The climate created by the endless echoing process of reinforcement of emotions similar to physical induction, makes it possible to impose the existential goals of the organizational system not only against the interests that the system was supposed to serve in the first place, but sometimes also against the manifest, basic interests of all the people concerned. And, most dangerous of all, the intrinsic purposes of different large power systems are by definition opposed to each other. While it is conceivably possible, with an increase of resources, to satisfy a multiplicity of material interests formerly conflicting in a situation of scarcity, rival power goals admit, logically, of no simultaneous satisfaction.[9]

To summarize the argument: no sooner did organizations come to dominate the institutional scene than they entered an epoch of crisis resulting from the conflict in their internal structure between specialized service and the growing need for co-ordination in large organizational systems. This tension became intensified by the parallel tensions between the independence of the professionals and the presumptions of the hierarchy. Moreover there was in the social role of the organization the increasing difficulty of controlling political power based on organizations, as well as the danger inherent in the opposition between the institutional goals of different power systems.

III

The present situation, where we have to look for a solution to the institutional crisis of our society, is affected in two important ways by technological development.

The one, and most pressing, new factor is the present level of destructiveness of weapons. Conflicts which would involve their use (i.e., conflicts between large political power systems) have to be avoided. The obvious solution is the establishment of a world community. Before this can be attempted, however, it will probably be necessary to relax gradually the structural base of the big concentrations of power as well as to modify their emotional and ideological superstructures. A process of deconcentration will have to be devised which does not aim at the utopian goal of preorganizational simplicity but is able to reconcile the increasing interrelatedness of people and their activities with an expanding multiplicity of goals, orientations, and interests.

The other important technological factor is the accelerating increase in productivity. Estimates may differ as to the moment when we have reached, or shall reach, the level of productivity where it becomes possible to satisfy the basic material needs of all inhabitants of this planet. The reality of want and poverty in which the majority of the earth's population are still living today may label as impractical all discussions of this possibility. Still the fact remains that, technologically, the possibility is within our reach. The traditionally fundamental source of conflicts among people, competing claims for scarce resources, would then play a considerably reduced role.[10] The consequence would probably be a phenomenon which we are already witnessing today in its beginnings, the dispersion of interests.[11] What I mean by the dispersion of interests is that people participate in a greater number of various interest groups than before while the hierarchical ordering among their different interests becomes less clear and less well determined. Their various interests associate them with various, and only sometimes partially overlapping, interest groups, so that it is more unlikely that large numbers of people will become polarized into large classes based upon opposing interests.

Both technological factors point in the same direction and two general conclusions can be drawn immediately about the forms of institutional transformation that must necessarily take place.

The new structures will have to be, in a way, looser and more unified at the same time. They will have to give greater scope to the individual, to his creativity, to the independence of his specialized professional contribution, to the multitude of existing interests. They will have to isolate conflicts instead of reinforcing them to the highest emotional pitch. They will have to diffuse power into a network of mutual influence instead of concentrating it. Instead of facilitating goal-displacement they will have to counteract it. At the same time, these new institutional structures will have to simplify large-scale planning, to reflect the growing interrelatedness of human activity, in order to prevent an uncontrolled increase in social entropy.[12]

In the institutional system that must now be evolved, the process of the realization of interests will have to be integrated with the handling of interest conflicts. What we identify today as the service aspect and the political aspect of organizational systems will have to be understood as two sides of the same coin.[13] Assuming a growing dispersion of interests it would, perhaps, be more appropriate to speak of diverging rather than of conflicting interests.

This new social process which might tentatively be called the process of social self-management, will have to be carried by a new institutional structure. The process of social self-management will have to provide the means to integrate the activities of individuals aimed at the realization of socially accepted interests under conditions of diverging individual interest positions, with the maximum social efficiency compatible with respect for the autonomy of the individual contribution. Whether we shall call the institutional structure designed for this process an "organization" or invent another name for it is a matter of personal preference. But what points can be indicated to sketch, at least in outline, the emerging structure?

If the nature of the process is to be reflected in the structure, then the institutions of social self-management will have to be constructed around opposite focal points. The first pair of these points might be the individual and the work team. The important difference from organization as we know it today is a shift in accent. The starting point in organizational structuring is the overall objective. This is divided and subdivided until each individual can be assigned his function, as it were from above; and in the course of action everything is again oriented to and measured by the general goal. Organization by its very structure pushes its members into purely instrumental roles.

The new structure starts from the individual specialist who is supposed to know his function by diagnosing given situations in the light of his knowledge and applying his skill to them without any assignment from outside. This basic element of the individual contribution is then integrated into progressively wider patterns, the basic unit of integration being the work team. The work team does not detract in any way from the professional autonomy of each of its members, but it gives to each individual activity its social meaning. In tackling the situation of a family in trouble, for instance, or planning the rehabilitation of a decaying neighbourhood, the work team will be composed of social workers, sociologists, psychologists, psychiatrists, public health specialists, lawyers, town planners, architects, and possibly others. The contribution of each is independent because his very profession is independent, and it cannot be overruled except by technical argument on its own professional ground.[14] At the same time, the socially indicated objective—to help the family, to rehabilitate the neighbourhood—can be reached only by integrated action. There are situations where there can be no action at all without a team. Surgical operations or the acting of a play are obvious illustrations. The integration of the individual professional specialist into the team has to be based on his own free acceptance and has to respect the conditions imposed by his expertise. The co-ordination by hierarchical decree or by the order of a superior is unacceptable on sound logical grounds as well as for psychological reasons. It is meaningless to give anybody the responsibility of giving orders to specialists outside his own field. Within the same field, things have to be decided by technical argument on the basis of the actual accountability for the result.

We can already point to examples of this process taken from fields where professional specialization already prevails. In order to make this situation general the process of transferring standardized, routine operations in factory and office from people to machines will have to progress much beyond the point reached at present. Only when the professional specialist becomes the prevailing type of worker, and the menial worker performing simple repetitive operations the exception, can be rigid normative structure of most of our organizational systems be replaced by the freer atmosphere of the work team. But even when the dominance of the norm is succeeded by the "hypothetical imperative" of the technical rule, there will be considerable areas left for normative regulation.

In the field of human relations especially, the internationalization of the norms of professional ethics and the development of other appropriate attitudes will be another prerequisite for the functioning of the individual in the work group. The successful integration then promises to be, among other things, a better solution of the problem of the opposite drives towards new experience and towards security than anything that is possible under present circumstances. In the freedom of their professional work, people ought to find a better outlet for their tendencies towards achievement than in the discipline of the organization, while the equality of the working group might be more favourable to security than the competition for hierarchical advancement.

The work group, however, is only the basic unit of a much wider process of integration. With ascending levels two complexes of problems are likely to grow more intricate: the heterogeneous character of the work and the divergence of interests. With the multiplication of the number of work teams in a system an increase in the variety of functions is to be expected. New auxiliary and secondary functions become necessary simply because of the expansion of the network. Traditionally, these secondary and auxiliary functions are the background of the co-ordinating activity of the hierarchy in organizations. In the new structures they will have to become the task of specific work teams who will service, on a basis of equality, a number of other professional teams. For example, no consequences as to the subordination of superordination of the different individuals or groups would necessarily follow from the fact that a team is engaged in testing or examining personnel for other teams, or that it is constructing and implementing a system of salaries, or keeping a number of accounts. Even today there is no reason why an executive officer of a university or an administrator of a hospital should be hierarchically superior or inferior to the different functional specialists working in the institution. By their very function the work teams performing secondary auxiliary functions for other teams will come to represent for them a sort of contact point, a platform for wider integration on a basis of service and not of hierarchical command.

Still, decisions will have to be taken, decisions on higher levels of integration affecting a substantial number of individuals and work teams and involving, to a greater or lesser degree, their diverging interests. The logic of the system requires that the interested individuals be associated, in one way or another, with decisions affecting their interests. The functional contact points between the work teams will have to be supplemented by a system of collective bodies with changing membership and very elastic rules of procedures which will have to be convened at various levels whenever a decision about indeterminate alternatives involving interests—i.e., not a purely technical decision—has to be taken. The membership in each instance will depend on the content of the decision, giving voice or fair representation to the individuals or the work teams whose interests are touched. The functioning of a hospital board or of a faculty meeting are rudimentary examples of what these interest-decision-making bodies might be. The general application of this method will require, besides much greater elasticity in composition and procedure, the invention of a process of selection by which the handling of most divergencies of interests will be kept as near their source as possible and only those will be filtered to higher levels of integration where this more costly alternative might be worthwhile from a social point of view.

The relationship between the work groups serving as contact points for other teams and the collective bodies responsible for interest decisions should be purely functional, i.e., exist when necessary, as long as necessary, and to the extent required in a specific case, instead of the actual permanent ties of organization. This also applies to the relations between each of the two structural elements and the individuals and teams involved in their activities. All these relations have to be seen as much more fluid than the present organizational rigidities.

This leads to the third pair of problems posed by the new institutional structure: what about the interests of people affected by the activities of the professional teams, as users or consumers, and not as members of other work teams? And how is the looseness of the relationships among work teams, contact points, and decision-making bodies to be reconciled with the requirement of a more dependable prediction of human behaviour in social situations?

The obvious answer to the first question is to include the representatives of the consumers in the decision-making bodies. As consumers they are vitally interested in the "product" of the work teams concerned, in the quality of their work, but not primarily interested in the personal or institutional goals of the teams and their members. The consumers, then, are theoretically in an ideal position to voice constructive criticism of the professionals in the teams. They are clearly well-intentioned with regard to the function and able to see and to point out quickly dysfunctions. At the same time their presence could function as a diluting and sedative agent on the intensity of conflict brought before the collective bodies by the interested members of the work teams. Finally they would act as an additional factor of integration counteracting possible technocratic tendencies and clannishness on the part of the professionals.

On the other hand, the participation of the consumers in the decision-making bodies, besides involving a number of puzzling issues of recruitment and representation, might run counter to the tendency towards the differentiation of work and the dispersion of interests. If brought to its logical conclusion, the principle of representation of consumers would involve every individual in all the activities from which he derives a benefit, directly or indirectly. That is manifestly impossible and irreconcilable with present levels of technological development. The basic interest of each individual is that the multitude of services and activities necessary for the satisfaction of his needs should function normally and satisfactorily without his intervention. That means that consumer representation can be only an auxiliary or temporary device, and that the basic mechanism of integration has to be found elsewhere.

My first question was how to ensure the participation of consumers in the decision-making process. In the light of my analysis, this question now converges upon my second question: how to combine a minimum of intervention with a maximum of predictability of behaviour? The conditions for the creation of some kind of automatic regulation of behaviour in society have been considered before by utopian and by more practical thinkers. The efforts to set up "steering situations," to discover "laws of the situation"[15] are not without precedent. The imposition of negative sanctions, requiring a power relationship, can be dispensed with where the infraction of rules is followed by the loss of benefits independently from any sanctioning activity. The rules of exogamy (marrying outside one's own group), for instance, were probably most effectively "enforced" by the prospect of the offender's going without dowry and missing the opportunity to establish friendly relations with another clan. The market economy, as compared with a slave-holder or a feudal economy, has a "built-in" system of sanctions, and demands the intervention of power, in principle, only in order to guarantee the rules of the game. The public service systems, such as social security, health, education, and others, can impose a rather elaborate and sometimes vexing system of rules on their consumers simply by the threat of withholding their services or benefits. There are, therefore, no essential difficulties in establishing such services organizationally outside the system of governmental administration, which is actually done, particularly for social security, in a number of countries. Here again the intervention of power becomes necessary the moment when consumers do not want to "consume"—e.g., in order to enforce school attendance—or when the service, instead of giving, is asking for something—e.g., collecting fees or premiums. The relative number of public services of that type seems to be on the increase. Manifest danger from disobeying regulations, danger for the transgressor stemming from the situation created by disobedience, obviates enforcement in a majority of cases. It is well known, for instance, how difficult it is to enforce traffic regulation below a given level of density of traffic, while beyond that level people will tend to conform to the commands given by automatic traffic lights.[16]

Even the idea of "creative conflict" was institutionally anticipated in practical attempts at large-scale regulation, as in the mechanism of the separation of powers. In order to avoid the overriding social influence that a large system of political power necessarily has, the attempt was made to partition power. Its various attributes were vested in different carriers—legislative assemblies, courts, executives—at least in part independent of each other. Conflicts among them were not only anticipated but regarded as the main method by which they might check each other and achieve a balance of power diminishing, to an extent, their cumulative influence in the social universe.

The relationship between interest decisions and technical decisions is basically affected by the introduction of planning. The logic of planning calls for such long chains of interconnected decisions that interests can be expressed only on the most general levels and at crucial points. All other decisions are determined by previous choices to such an extent that their technical determining factors can be comparatively little affected by interests. Besides, the network of possible consequences grows so complex that it becomes increasingly difficult for the persons involved to foresee the consequences of alternative modes of behaviour. Planning, in a way, transfers the solving of interest conflicts to an earlier point in time before they have had the opportunity to reach dangerous levels of intensity.

With the dispersion of interests the old calculus of lost opportunities, used at one time to discredit the psychological credibility of the *homo oeconomicus*, could reappear in a possibly more realistic form. More and more interest conflicts may become intra-personal instead of inter-personal. The individual deciding to pursue one of his many interests through the collective bodies for the regulation of interest-conflicts will have to balance very carefully the maximum benefit obtainable from this course of action against the loss of opportunity to follow at the same time a multitude of other interests. This appraisal might contribute significantly to the limitation of conflicts introduced into the solving-mechanisms and burdening the collective decision-making bodies.[17] On the other hand, this internalization of conflict does not mean necessarily an intensification of internal conflict in the individual. Different interests which are in conflict simply by having different subjects might well find, in one individual, an ordered scale of individual preference assigning to each of them rank and precedence.

Around the three levels of constructive points already identified, the new structures will have to be built according to general principles somewhat like the following. The starting point would have to be, not the common task, which is then subdivided into more elementary action elements, but the other way around—the expertise of the individual specialist. For example, if we plan to dig a ditch with a number of people employed, we will normally keep in mind the totality of the task—where we want the ditch to go, how deep it is to be, etc.—and assign to each of the men a task according to this common plan. It is unnecessary that each of the men should know what we are trying to do, why we are digging a ditch, how long and how deep it finally is going to be; everybody knows exactly what he has to do, and that is enough. But if we take a surgical team at a surgical operation, this method does not hold. We do not have an idea of a total operation which is then to be divided into action tasks. On the contrary, each of the specialists in the surgical operation has to have his own judgment and to behave according to his own judgment, and the whole undertaking can function only if nobody has to tell each specialist what to do, only on condition that each member of the team, through his expertise and through analysing the situation before him on the operating table, knows exactly what to do.

The second characteristic change in the new situation would be the unity between administrative and political processes, in the widest sense of the term. This is a rather far-reaching change if one thinks of the implications. For example, if a faculty of a school in the university today has a meeting to decide on the curriculum, here it is very difficult to separate administration from policy-making. The people who are to decide on the curriculum will also implement it, which is usually considered administration. Their experience from their past implementation will influence their own policy decisions. Institutions like faculties, hospitals, research institutions, etc. are already foreshadowing the future general types of co-operative action.

So far, I have identified a number of changing patterns of human behaviour in the institutional situation. I have suggested that we must recognize and put to constructive use a number of pairs of contrasting and potentially conflicting roles. First, the autonomy of the individual in his work as contrasted with the equality of members in the work team. Second, the parallel functioning of professionals and administrators without hierarchical relationships as contrasted with collective bodies for the regulation of conflicts. Third, the representation in the decision-making process of all the interests at risk as contrasted with attempts at the development of self-regulation and self-regulating situations. All of these phenomena are embodied in a number of institutional examples that exist today. The critical task for the future seems to me, however, to be to investigate their mutual interconnections, to trace these interrelationships as they merge into a balanced system of social relations, and, in particular, to examine their implications for human well-being.

NOTES

[1] One of the typical defence mechanisms against an unfathomable reality is "to face the situation squarely," to try to calculate the number of the dead and to imagine the next technical tasks of those still alive. It seems

redundant to point out to those who write "On Thermonuclear War" and similar "hard headed" studies the many unwarranted assumptions they make in the technical field. Their main omission seems to be not to take sufficiently into account the unstabilizing social and psychological effects of a traumatic experience of that order of magnitude.

Another reaction is to project the present into a still uncertain future. So Raymond Aron: "L'économie s'efface avec la rareté. L'abondance laisserait subsister des problèmes d'organization, non des calculs économiques. De même, la guerre cesserait d'être un instrument de la politique le jour où elle entraînerait le suicide commun de belligérants. La capacité de production industrielle rend quelque actualité à l'utopie de l'abondance, la capacité destructrice des armes ranime les rêves de paix éternelle" (*Paix et Guerre entre les nations* [Paris: Calman-Levy, 1962], p. 30).

[2] The complementarity of co-operation and conflict as basic principles of social life seems to be presently accepted even by the most pronounced theoreticians of a harmonious view of society. Cf., Talcott Parsons, "Die jüngsten Entwicklungen in der strukturell-funktionalen Theorie," *Kölner Zeitschrift für Soziologie und Sozialpsychologie*, no. 1, 1964, pp. 30–49. It would seem easy to make the additional step of understanding "homeostatic" processes in society as complementary to social change.

[3] The mechanisms of projection and retroprojection have been studied in detail by Ernst Topitsch, *Vom Ursprung und Ende der Metaphysik* (Wien: Springer Verlag, 1958).

[4] Needs, and therefore conflicts, are not limited, of course, to material necessities. They range all the way to Coser's "non-realistic" conflicts generated by the need to release tensions (L. Coser, *The Functions of Social Conflict* [Glencoe, Ill.: The Free Press, 1956], p. 156).

[5] The characteristic of legitimacy of power, made popular through Max Weber, pertains to a different point of view: the motivation why people obey. That some of his subjects are prepared to obey a monarch in exile does not yet invest him with political power.

[6] According to the expression by Georges Friedmann "l'émiettement du travail" made popular through his book *La travail en miettes: spécialisation et loisirs* (Paris: Gallimard, 1956).

[7] At least in one of the aspects of their role Gouldner's ideal-types of "cosmopolitans" and "locals" are related to the difference between professional specialization and the fragmentation of the work-process. Gouldner does not seem, at least in his original formulations, to have taken into account the probable influence of automation on the relationship between his two types (cf., A. W. Gouldner, "Cosmopolitans and Locals: Toward an Analysis of Latent Social Roles," *Administrative Service Quarterly*, no. 3, 1957; no. 4, 1958).

[8] The reference is to the imagined conversation between Socrates and Alcibiades in B. de Jouvenel, *The Pure Theory of Politics* (Cambridge: at the Clarendon Press, 1963).

[9] "If the purpose of States were the wealth, health, intelligence or happiness of their citizens, there would be no incompatibility; but since these, singly and collectively, are thought less important than national power, the purposes of different States conflict, and cannot be furthered by amalgamation" (B. Russell, *Power—A New Social Analysis* [London: George Allen and Unwin, 1938], pp. 179–80).

[10] Barring development which can be prevented by rational action, such as "the population explosion."

[11] The term "interest" is used in the meaning "situation permitting the maximization of a socially accepted value in relation to an individual or to a group of individuals." The purely subjective aspect of interest—the motivational orientation independent from the real-world situation—is called subjective interest. An interest group is a group of people who are in the same objective interest-situation. "Conflict of interests" denotes a situation where the maximization of a value for an individual or group of individuals is possible only at the expense of another individual or group.

[12] Students of the problem at present seem to be primarily preoccupied with the loosening of organizational structures. The tenets about the span of control are turned upside down by the suggestion to increase the span in order to prevent the managers from managing too much. Cf., W. F. Whyte, "Human Relations—A Progress Report" in A. Etzioni, ed., *Complex Organizations* (New York: Holt, Rinehart & Winston, 1961), p. 111. D. Katz feels that "we must be able to tolerate the ambiguity of a loose organization with wide margins of tolerance with respect to meeting role requirements" ("Human Relationships and Organizational Behavior" in S. Malick and E. H. Van Ness, *Concepts and Issues in Administrative Behavior* [New Jersey: Prentice Hall, 1962], p. 173). Even direct contradictions and unrealistic requirements in role definition are justified as "creative disorder" and its stimulating effects pointed out (A. G. Frank, "Goal Ambiguity and Conflicting Standards: An Approach to the Study of Organizations," *Human Organization*, vol. 17, no. 4).

[13] Here as well, usually that side of the picture is pointed out which is new. Conflict is seen as the essence of the functioning of complex organizations (cf. M. Dalton, *Men Who Manage—Fusions of Feeling and Theory in Administration* [New York-London: J. Wiley-Chapman & Hall, 1959]) and a constructive role in organizational change ascribed to it (cf., L. Coser, *op. cit.*, p. 154).

[14] On the other hand, the dispersion of interests counteracts the possible tendency towards narrow-mindedness and one-sidedness inherent in an increasingly detailed professional specialization.

[15] The expression "steering situation" is derived from the terminology of cybernetics; the term "law of the situation" belongs to Mary Parker Follett (cf., H. C. Metcalf and L. Urwick, *Dynamic Administration, The Collected Papers of Mary Parker Follett* [New York: Harper, 1942]).

[16] On situations of this kind B. de Jouvenel bases his "law of conservative exclusion" and his argument for the social usefulness of power. It seems, however, that these are precisely the examples where people will have the least difficulty of finding ways to "eliminate conflicting signals" without the intervention of power (cf., B. de Jouvenel, *op. cit.*, p. 111).

[17] It is interesting that in a socialist economic system as well deliberate planning seems to be supplemented by processes independent from active intervention. Nemčinov defines planning as the "harmonious co-ordination of the economic principle of conscious control of social production—in accordance with the known objective laws of economic development—with the cybernetic principle of the automatic, autoregulatory and autoorganizing flow of the economic process" (V. S. Nemčinov, *Ekonomiko-matematičeskije metodi i modeli* [Moskva: Izdatelstvo socialno-ekonomičeskoj literaturi, 1962], p. 52).

PART FOUR

THE INTERACTION- INFLUENCE SYSTEM

The interaction-influence system consists of those patterns of administrative behavior and dimensions of the administrative process which interact with the dynamics of organization and people as the school attempts to pursue its goals and influence its environment. The nine papers which compose this section were chosen from five areas: leadership, decision making, group processes, change, and systems of values. Each of these areas is an essential and interdependent component of school administration. These components are in a large sense the means by which organizations achieve their goals. As such, they permeate and stimulate the interchange which exists between individuals and organizations.

Part 4 begins with a consideration of leadership behavior. In the first article, "How Leaders Behave," Halpin brings together materials which appeared in four of his previous articles on leadership. Included in this paper is the pioneering aircraft-commander study as well as Halpin's now-classic investigation of the leadership behavior of school superintendents.

The study of leadership has relied heavily on the identification and use of two dimensions of leadership behavior: concern for job and concern for people. This two-theme convention is evidenced by the development of such concepts as task effectiveness and interaction effectiveness, goal achievement and group maintenance, concern for production and concern for people, production-centered and employee-centered, and, recently, system orientation and person orientation. Halpin found that individuals who exhibited desirable leader behavior achieved high scores on both initiating structure (a task dimension) and consideration (a person dimension) as measured by the Leadership Behavior Description Questionnaire. This pattern of research has found wide use in the study of the leadership phenomenon in school administration.

Gibb identifies two leadership patterns, the "defensive" and the "participative," in his paper, "Dynamics of Leadership." He proposes a schema based on the leader's concept of self, as opposed to external foci such as task or people, as a basis for classifying and understanding styles of leader behavior. He argues that the prevalence of a given style orientation will depend largely upon the administrator's feelings of openness and self-adequacy.

Much attention has been given to the concept of decision making as a critical component of administrative theory and process (see, for example, Griffiths' paper, "Administration as Decision-making," which appears in Part 2). Academic decision makers advocate, through their writings, a rational decision-making model based largely on the problem-solving strategy popularized for educators by John Dewey. This is a model which describes what ought to be but which often neglects the incompleteness and complexity of real decision problems. Actual decision makers, on the other hand, focus on relatively narrow areas and yield too easily to the "necessity of immediacy" in solving problems. This often results in premature abortion of search activities and mediocre organizational performance.

Lindblom's paper, "The Science of Muddling Through," provides a contrast to rational decision-making models without yielding entirely to intuitive approaches of the fire-fighting tradition. He compares a theory based on strategy (the root method) with an intuitive model based on successive limited comparisons (the branch method).

Schelling's article, "An Essay on Bargaining," provides school administrators with a timely and insightful view of the nature of the bargaining environment and the substance of the bargaining act. The circumstances usually associated with decision making in professional negotiations (crisis, testing, bluffing, chance, and ritual) are remarkably similar to those associated with typical box games. This similarity is exploited by Schelling as he illustrates his arguments by presenting a bargaining game.

The next paper, which deals with group behavior and interaction patterns, focuses on the matter and energy of organizational life. The emergence of group structures and patterns of communications is a natural part of organizational development. They emerge as a result of a favorable organizational environment or in spite of a hostile environment; in support of the administrative and supervisory staff or in opposition to this staff; to facilitate school purposes or to retard, frustrate, or sabotage such efforts. Much like the proverbial two-edged sword, group life and patterns of communications have the potential to help or hinder the administrative process. "The Nature of Highly Effective Groups" represents a chapter of the same name from Likert's award-winning book, *New Patterns of Management*. Professor Likert proposes that highly effective work groups (those characterized by cohesion, interaction facility, and high commitment to organizational goals) are the crucial building blocks of an effective organization.

Survival for most organizations as they enter the next decade depends largely on their adaptability. Schools are no exception. As the demands of society increase and as the uncertainties of the future become more apparent, schools will need to increase their effectiveness in providing each client with a school experience which will be socially, emotionally, and intellectually enriching to him. The rapid progress being made in understanding human behavior, developments in the social sciences and in educational technology, and expansions in the curriculum fields are all indicative of the urgent need for adaptive school organizations.

The process of change, strategies for change, and models of change have become the foci of study for many scholars interested in educational administration. Although this frame of reference is important, it is limited by frequent neglect of a host of interrelated conditions which compose the complex organization. The three papers which follow give attention to organizational susceptibility to change, rather than the process of change, as they attempt to map those conditions and characteristics which comprise the innovative organization.

Griffiths uses systems theory as a model to propose a theory of administrative change in "Administrative Theory and Change in Organizations." The theory is illustrated through a series of propositions concerning stimulants of change, homeostasis, and resistance to change. "Planned Change and Organizational Health: Figure and Ground" by Miles suggests that organizational adaptiveness is only one of several characteristics of organizational health. Further, since the various components of organizational health are interdependent (Miles identifies at least ten), the promotion of change requires attention to all of them.

Thompson's vivid description of "The Innovative Organization" illustrates and summarizes those characteristics which provide organizations with a high capacity to innovate. The implementation of Thompson's suggestions will require an enormous commitment from those who seek increases in organizational adaptability as they attempt to renovate prevailing assumptions, beliefs, structures, attitudes, habits, and traditions which characterize schools today.

In an original essay for this book, Smith appraises contemporary organizational settings from the perspective of the humanist. Displaying a comprehensive grasp of administrative and organizational literature, Smith charts the development of organizational thought from the scientific management approach through the human relations period up to the present structuralist theories. Contrasting the classical figure of Achilles, who represents the Western high point of human nobility, with the pathetic Mr. K. of Kafka's penetrating indictment of impersonal bureaucracy, the author points to two possibilities for modern man. With the humanistic goal of education clearly established, administrators within the school are cautioned to recognize that although schools resemble other modern organizations, the inextricably humanistic purpose of the school demands that administrators give priority to those processes which further this purpose. While the other essays of this book would not deny such humanistic concern, it seems fitting that a book of this nature should conclude with this perspective highlighted, for it is through such a vision that attention to operational processes of the school as an organization becomes a distinctly human enterprise.

23.

HOW LEADERS BEHAVE
ANDREW W. HALPIN

We will greatly increase our understanding of leadership phenomena if we abandon the notion of leadership as a trait, and concentrate instead upon an analysis of "the behavior of leaders."[1]

The idea of leadership has been used in a variety of ways, most commonly in referring to the "leader" as an outstanding member of a class. Thus radio and TV commercials proclaim that a certain brand of cigarettes is the leading one, and that a new movie star is the leader of the current covey of actresses. Because of our American predilection for bigness, in no matter what sphere, the leader in this sense refers to the most popular product—or more specifically, to that item with the greatest sales-market potential. Similarly in education, we often confuse leadership with sheer bigness. But this use of the term applies equally to either things or people, and fails to take into account the central psychological characteristic of leader behavior: that this is the behavior of a leader functioning vis-à-vis members of a group in an endeavor to facilitate the solution of group problems. The behavior of the leader and the behavior of group members are inextricably interwoven, and the behavior of both is determined to a great degree by formal requirements imposed by the institution of which the group is a part. For example, Mary Noel, fourth-grade teacher, is the formally designated leader of the children in her class. How she behaves as a leader is influenced by the behavior of the children (which includes

From Andrew W. Halpin, *Theory and Research in Administration*, The MacMillan Company, New York, 1966, pp. 81–130. Copyright © 1966 by The MacMillan Company. Reprinted by permission.

their expectations of how a teacher *should* behave as a leader). Moreover, her behavior is conditioned by the policies and regulations, both written and unwritten, of the particular school system in which she is employed. As a result of the year which they spend with her, the children in Mary's class are expected to show certain minimum changes in behavior, especially in respect to scholastic achievement and skill in interpersonal relations. The accomplishment of these objectives is the salient group problem to which Mary must contribute her solution, and it is presumed that her contribution will be greater than that of any other group member in her fourth-grade class. This, of course, is why she was employed.

In accepting her assignment as teacher of the fourth grade, Mary assumes a role as leader of this group. This, however, tells us absolutely nothing about the effectiveness of her performance in this role—that is, how effectively she contributes to the solution of group problems. What, then, are we to mean by leadership? The assumption of a leader's role? The effectiveness with which this role is performed? Or the capacity of the individual to perform this role effectively? These cause a further question to arise: By what criteria are we to judge effectiveness? For research on leader behavior shows that effectiveness in respect to Criterion X is not necessarily correlated with effectiveness in regard to Criterion Y. For example, the behavior of a leader who is effective in maintaining high morale and good human relations within the group is not necessarily effective in accomplishing high production and goal-achievement.

This dilemma of definition emerges from the fact that we have incorporated into the term "leadership" both descriptive and evaluative components, and have thus burdened this single word (and the concept it represents) with two connotations: one refers to a role and the behavior of a person in this role, and the other is an evaluation of the individual's performance in the role. We have compounded this confusion even more by conceptualizing leadership as an essentially innate capacity of the individual manifested with equal facility, regardless of the situation in which the leader finds himself. Yet Stogdill[2] has shown that the trait approach to leadership, as it has been used in most studies reported in the literature, has yielded negligible, and often contradictory, results. Sanford has aptly summarized the situation:

> From all these studies of the leader we can conclude, with reasonable certainty, that:
> (a) there are either no general leadership traits or, if they do exist, they are not to be described in any of our familiar psychological or common-sense terms,
> (b) in a specific situation, leaders do have traits which set them apart from followers, but *what* traits set *what* leaders apart from *what* followers will vary from situation to situation.[3]

In short, the behavior of leaders varies widely from one leadership situation to another. In this connection, Hemphill,[4] in an elaborate and careful study of approximately 500 assorted groups, has demonstrated empirically that variance in leader behavior is significantly associated with situational variance. For example, let us consider the size of the group as a situational determinative. Hemphill has analyzed in detail the relation between the leader's behavior and the size of the group and has concluded that, as compared with small groups, large groups make more and different demands upon the leader. In general, the leader in a large group tends to be impersonal and is inclined to enforce rules and regulations firmly and impartially. In smaller groups, the leader plays a more personal role. He is more willing (and perhaps also more able) to make exceptions to rules and to treat each group member as an individual. Stated baldly, the evidence from these studies means that it is possible for Mary to function effectively as a leader in the fourth-grade class of *East* Clambake Elementary School, and yet operate quite ineffectively as a leader in the fourth-grade class of *West* Clambake Elementary School. In brief, much depends on the situation.

However, we do not want to overemphasize the determinative effects of a given situation on a given leader. The question never is one of whether the results of a leader's efforts are determined *either* by the situation *or* by specific behaviors of the leader. Rather must we phrase our question in a different form: how much of the variance in group productivity is associated with variance in Situational Variable *A*? With variance in Situational Variable *B*? How much of the variance in productivity is associated with variance in, for example, the Consideration of the leaders? With variance in the leader's skill in Initiating Structure in his interaction among group members?

We can understand the current status of leadership research better if we will first stop to analyze briefly the way in which knowledge is accumulated in any scientific area.

Historically, in most disciplines one discovers a tendency for new movements or emphases to arise in revolt against the orthodoxies of a given period. These new movements later tend to crystalize into the orthodoxies of the next period, and fresh countermovements arise in turn. The final position we reach is usually one on middle ground between the original orthodoxy and the first reaction against it. Zig-zag movements of this kind are not uncommon in the progress of science. Leadership research is currently in the process of following this same developmental course. Early research was marked by a search for traits of leadership that would discriminate between leaders and nonleaders. The situational emphasis which has characterized research during the past decade arose as a protest against the earlier trait approach, but in some respects this present emphasis may have been carried to excess. To say that leader behavior is determined exclusively by situational factors is to deny to the leader freedom of choice and determination. This violates common sense and experience. Even now, within research circles, a gradual but growing counterreaction is taking shape—a drawing away from the extreme situational position, with increasing recognition that the truth probably lies in an area of middle ground.

But now in appraising the trait approach

anew, we will have the advantage of a fresh perspective. In the next decade, research workers may be less avid in seizing upon convenient phenotypic data as pertinent variables and may be more willing to explore the relevance of genotypic variables that are not as readily discernible as "givens."[5] In short, in the past we have tended to examine essentially peripheral traits and attributes. Although we have been guided by intuition about possible relationships between these attributes of leaders and other leadership phenomena, we have operated, for the most part, without the benefit of sufficient empirical information about leadership phenomena that would enable us to sharpen our definitions of the variables involved. Herein lies a major benefit of the period of situationally-oriented leadership research: this research has suggested new ways of constituting the more crucial variables that pertain to the individual as a leader. Eventually, it may be possible to define a few variables of genotypic order that will prove predictive of leader behavior in a variety of situations. For example, McClelland's[6] series of studies on the achievement motive may throw new light on leadership behavior. Thus Hemphill and his co-workers[7] have conducted a series of experiments on small groups in order to determine the relationship between (1) "need achievement and need affiliation," and (2) the frequency with which group members attempt leadership acts. With the accumulation of a fund of experimental evidence in this area, the new theories of leadership that are generated probably will incorporate ideas which, at least superficially, will resemble those that characterized the original trait approach. The difference in conceptual sophistication is likely, however, to be no less profound than that between pre-Einsteinian and post-Einsteinian physics. All this, of course, rests with the future. The point is made at this juncture simply to underscore one salient feature of good research strategy—that it is sometimes wise to move backwards (or at least in a direction that appears to be backwards) in order to insure greater and more sure-footed strides into the future.

These, then, are the reasons why we prefer at this time to think in terms of leader behavior rather than leadership. Our concept of leader behavior sidesteps a few important issues. It limits us, for instance, to dealing with formal organizations, and focuses attention exclusively upon the "head men" within these organizations. Furthermore, the whole question of the distribution of leadership acts among members of the group is avoided. Nor are our formulations readily adaptable to certain aspects of leadership phenomena that can be observed within informal community groups. Our only defense of such limitations is that we have had to start somewhere. We chose to start with the officially designated leaders of formal organizations. This was an heuristic decision. As more information is gathered and as we gradually begin to build a systematic conceptual framework within which additional hypotheses about leader behavior can be tested, we shall undoubtedly test these hypotheses in informal as well as formal organizations, and with group members other than those officially designated as leaders. The fact that we have not explored these other leadership phenomena implies no skepticism of their importance but is simply an admission that we have not yet found the time and the opportunity (and the funds) to investigate these equally challenging areas.

What, then, do we gain by shifting our emphasis from leadership to the analysis of the behavior of leaders? There are two major methodological advantages. In the first place, we can deal directly with observable phenomena and need make no a priori assumptions about the identity or structure of whatever capacities may or may not undergird these phenomena. Secondly, this formulation keeps at the forefront of our thinking the importance of differentiating between the *description* of how leaders behave and the *evaluation* of the effectiveness of their behavior in respect to specified performance criteria.

DIMENSIONS OF LEADER BEHAVIOR

Evaluations of leadership, on the one hand, can be obtained readily enough by means of various rating schedules. On the other, the measurement of a group's description of its leader's behavior is a less commonly used procedure. Because we can never measure *all* the behavior of an individual, any measurement procedure we adopt must entail some form of selection. We have chosen to measure two specific dimensions of leader behavior: "Initiating Structure" and "Consideration." You will recall that Initiating Structure refers to the leader's behavior in delineating the relationship between himself and members of the work-group, and in endeavoring to establish well-defined patterns of organization, channels of communication, and methods of procedure. Consideration refers to behavior indicative of friendship, mutual trust, respect, and warmth in the relationship between the leader and the members of his staff.

It is important to note that this concept of Consideration does not include what can be best described as merely "spray-gun consideration." The latter behavior is typified by the PTA smile, and by the oily affability dispensed by administrators at faculty picnics and office parties. Promiscuous Consideration defeats its purpose by its very promiscuity. Genuine Consideration must be focused upon the individual recipient and must be tuned to his requirements at a particular time and place.

There is nothing especially novel about these two dimensions of leader behavior. The principles embodied in the concepts of Initiating Structure and Consideration probably have always been used by effective leaders in guiding their bahavior with group members, while the concepts themselves, with different labels perhaps, have been invoked frequently by philosophers and social scientists to explain leadership phenomena. Practical men know that the leader must lead—must initate action and get things done. But because he must accomplish his purposes through other people, and without jeopardizing the intactness or integrity of the group, the skilled executive knows that he also must maintain good "human relations" if he is to succeed in furthering the purposes of the group. In short, if a leader—

whether he be a school superintendent, an aircraft commander, or a business executive—is to be successful, he must contribute to both major group objectives of *goal achievement* and *group maintenance*. In Barnard's terms,[8] he must facilitate cooperative group action that is both *effective* and *efficient*. According to the constructs that we have formulated, this means that the leader should be strong in Initiating Structure and should also show high Consideration for the members of his work-group.

These two kinds of behavior are relatively independent but not necessarily incompatible. Cartwright and Zander, for example, have observed:

> Any given behavior in a group may have significance both for goal achievement and for maintenance. Both may be served simultaneously by the actions of a member, or one may be served at the expense of the other. Thus, a member who helps a group to work cooperatively on a difficult problem may quite inadvertently also help to develop solidarity. In another group, however, an eager member may spur the group on in such a way that frictions develop among the members, and even though the goal is achieved efficiently,[9] the continued existence of the group is seriously endangered.[10]

To measure leader behavior and leadership ideology, we have used a Leader Behavior Description Questionnaire[11] devised by the Personnel Research Board at The Ohio State University. Hemphill and Coons[12] constructed the original form of this questionnaire, and Halpin and Winer,[13] in reporting the development of an Air Force adaptation of this instrument, identified Initiating Structure and Consideration as two fundamental dimensions of leader behavior. These dimensions were identified on the basis of a factor analysis of the responses of 300 crew members who described the leader behavior of their 52 aircraft commanders. Initiating Structure and Consideration accounted for approximately 34 and 50 per cent, respectively, of the common variance.

On the basis of the factor analysis, keys

were constructed for these two dimensions of leadership behavior. The original Consideration key of 28 items has an estimated reliability (corrected by the Spearman-Brown formula) of .94. The corresponding estimate for the 29-item Initiating Structure key is .76. In the later, published form of the LBDQ there are only 15 items on each of the keys. The estimated reliabilities are .93 and .86, respectively.

By measuring the behavior of leaders on the Initiating Structure and the Consideration dimensions, we can determine by objective and reliable means how specific leaders differ in leadership style, and whether these differences are related significantly to independent criteria of the leader's effectiveness and efficiency. In sum, the Leader Behavior Description Questionnaire offers a means of defining these leader behavior dimensions *operationally*,[14] making it possible for us to submit to empirical test additional specific hypotheses about leader and group behavior.

The LBDQ is composed of a series of short, descriptive statements of ways in which leaders may behave. The members of a leader's group indicate the frequency with which he engages in each form of behavior by checking one of five adverbs: always, often, occasionally, seldom, or never. Each of the keys to the dimensions contains 15 items, and each item is scored on a scale from 4 to 0. Consequently, the theoretical range of scores on each dimension is from 0 to 60. The 15 items which define each dimension follow:

Initiating structure

1. He makes his attitudes clear to the staff.
2. He tries out his new ideas with the staff.
3. He rules with an iron hand.*
4. He criticizes poor work.
5. He speaks in a manner not to be questioned.
6. He assigns staff members to particular tasks.
7. He works without a plan.*
8. He maintains definite standards of performance.
9. He emphasizes the meeting of deadlines.
10. He encourages the use of uniform procedures.
11. He makes sure that his part in the organization is understood by all members.
12. He asks that staff members follow standard rules and regulations.
13. He lets staff members know what is expected of them.
14. He sees to it that staff members are working up to capacity.
15. He sees to it that the work of staff members is coordinated.

Consideration

1. He does personal favors for staff members.
2. He does little things to make it pleasant to be a member of the staff.
3. He is easy to understand.
4. He finds time to listen to staff members.
5. He keeps to himself.*
6. He looks out for the personal welfare of individual staff members.
7. He refuses to explain his actions.*
8. He acts without consulting the staff.*
9. He is slow to accept new ideas.*
10. He treats all staff members as his equals.
11. He is willing to make changes.
12. He is friendly and approachable.
13. He makes staff members feel at ease when talking with them.
14. He puts suggestions made by the staff into operation.
15. He gets staff approval on important matters before going ahead.

The form on which the group members describe their leader's behavior is referred to as the "LBDQ-Real, Staff." With modified instructions, this same instrument may be used to measure the leader's own leadership ideology. On this form each item is worded to indicate how a leader *should* behave, and the leaders answer the questionnaire accordingly. This form is designated as the "LBDQ-Ideal, Self."[15]

* Scored negatively.

Similarly, we may ask the staff members to describe how they believe the leader *should* behave. Such scores are termed "LBDQ-Ideal, Staff."

Although group members differ in their perception of the leader's behavior, analyses of variance in which the "between group" variance and the "within group" variance on these dimension scores were compared for several independent samples of leaders have yielded F ratios all significant at the .01 level of confidence. The leader's behavior therefore can be described most succinctly by assigning to him, for each dimension, the mean of the LBDQ-Real scores by which his group members have described him. The correlations between these Consideration and Initiating Structure scores range between 0.38 and 0.45.

The LBDQ can be adapted readily to different group requirements without altering the meaning of the items. For example, with Air Force personnel the term "crew" is used; with educational administrators, "staff" is substituted for "crew." Similarly, for industrial and other situations, minor changes in wording can be made in each item according to the nature of the groups with which the questionnaire is used.

Again, the leader behavior dimensions of Initiating Structure and Consideration are not to be conceived as traits of leadership. They simply describe the behavior of a leader as he operates in a given situation. Nothing in the research completed to date with the LBDQ contradicts this position. The questionnaire measures the leader's behavior in a specified situation—for example, as the commander of an aircrew, or as an administrator in a public school—but does not purport to measure an intrinsic capacity for leadership. But whether individuals tend to employ the same style of leader behavior in different situations is an empirical question that remains to be answered.[16] However, certain organizational climates can coerce the man to change his leadership style simply to save his job, at no matter what cost in his loss of human dignity.

RESEARCH ON LEADER BEHAVIOR

With this background on the theoretical predilections that provided the impetus for The Ohio State Leadership Studies,[17] we now are ready to examine the substantive findings of a group of these studies in which the LBDQ was used.

Most of the developmental work on the Leader Behavior Description Questionnaire was done in a series of studies of aircraft commanders. Related studies have also been conducted in industry and education. Since the industrial studies were concerned primarily with training, they are not directly pertinent to our present purposes. In this section, therefore, we shall first summarize five of the Air Force studies and one educational study; we then will describe in detail the findings of two other educational studies.

Air crew studies

1. LBDQ scores were obtained on 52 B-29 commanders during training in the fall of 1950, and 33 of these commanders were subsequently rated on their combat performance in flying over Korea during the summer of 1951.[18] Twenty-nine of these 33 commanders were described again on the LBDQ by their combat crews. For 27 of the crews, a Crew Satisfaction Index was computed on the basis of the member's answer to the question: "If you could make up a crew from among the crew members in your squadron, whom would you choose for each position?" The ratio between the number of nominations in incumbent commander received and the number of nominations made for the aircraft commander position was used as an index of the crew's satisfaction with the incumbent's leadership. The LBDQ scores in training were correlated with this index and with superiors' ratings of the commanders' combat performance. Similarly, the LBDQ scores in the Far East Air Force were correlated with both the index and the ratings. Finally, in each situation—training and

combat—partial correlations were computed for the relationship between each dimension and the ratings (or index) with the effect of the other dimension partialled out.

In both the training and combat situations, a trend was found toward negative correlations between the superiors' ratings and the Consideration scores, and positive correlations between these ratings and the Initiating Structure scores. Conversely, the correlations between the Crew Satisfaction Index and the Consideration scores were positive and high. The partial correlations served to accentuate this trend, which was more pronounced in combat than in training. Thus superiors and subordinates are inclined to evaluate oppositely the contribution of the leader behavior dimensions to the effectiveness of leadership. This difference in evaluation would appear to confront the leader with conflicting role expectations.

2. Eighty-seven B-29 aircraft commanders, flying combat missions over Korea, were the subjects of a study with a design similar to the one reported above.[19] The commanders were rated by their superiors on seven characteristics (for example, "effectiveness in working with others," "attitude and motivation," "over-all effectiveness") and by their crews on three characteristics: "confidence and proficiency," "friendship and cooperation," and "morale." Furthermore, as in the earlier study, a Crew Satisfaction Index was computed. The Consideration and the Initiating Structure scores were correlated with the ratings by superiors and by crew members, and with the Crew Satisfaction Index.

The ratings by superiors yielded significant correlations with the Initiating Structure scores, whereas none of the corresponding Consideration correlations was significant. The crew ratings, including the Index, correlated significantly with both leader behavior dimensions but tended to be higher for the Consideration scores. Two of the Consideration correlations in particular should be noted: .75 with the Crew Satisfaction Index and .84 with the crew

ratings of the commanders on "friendship and cooperation." Both correlations differ significantly from the corresponding correlations of .47 and .51 (in themselves significant at the .01 level) with the Initiating Structure scores.

One further hypothesis was tested in this study: that the commanders rated highest by their superiors would score above the mean on both leader behavior dimensions whereas those commanders rated lowest by their superiors would score below the mean on both dimensions. The commanders had been rated on "over-all effectiveness in combat." Two groups of commanders were identified: 13 men in the upper 15 per cent of this rating distribution and 12 in the lower 15 per cent. For each group taken separately, the Consideration and the Initiating Structure scores were plotted into the four quadrants defined by co-ordinates corresponding to the means of the two leader behavior dimensions. These two scatter-plots were then collapsed to construct the 2×2 classification presented in Figure 23–1.

The probability of occurrence of frequencies (Figure 23–1) as deviant from the null hypothesis frequencies—or of greater deviance—is less that 3 in 100. This means that commanders who score above the average on both leader behavior dimensions are evaluated by their superiors as high in over-all effectiveness, whereas those who score below the average on both dimensions are likely to be rated low in effectiveness. In short, the successful leader is the man who furthers both group maintenance and group achievement.

3. The members of 52 newly assembled B-29 crews at Combat Crew Training School described their commanders on the Leader Behavior Description Questionnaire and rated each other and the crews as units on such items as "crew morale," "friendship," "proficiency," and "willingness to go into combat with each other." These measures of crew attitudes were obtained twice—at the beginning of the training period and toward the end of training. An average period of 10 days intervened between two administrations of the

	Below mean on both consideration and initiating structure	Above mean on both consideration and initiating structure
Upper 15 percent on over-all effectiveness	1	8
Lower 15 percent on over-all effectiveness	6	4

Figure 23–1. Number of commanders in high and low groups on rating of over-all effectiveness scoring above and below the mean on both leader behavior dimensions. (From Andrew W. Halpin, "Studies in Aircrew Composition: III," The Combat Leader Behavior of B–29 Aircraft Commanders, HFORL Memo. No. TN–54–7. Washington, D.C.: Human Factors Operations Research Laboratory, Bolling Air Force Base, September 1953, p. 15.)

questionnaire. Correlations were computed between *changes in attitude* and the Initiating Structure and Consideration scores on the Leader Behavior Description Questionnaire.[20] It was found that the members of crews whose commanders were described as high on Consideration tended to increase their ratings of each other on such attitude items as "mutual confidence," and "willingness to go into combat together," and that the members of crews whose commanders were described as high on Initiating Structure tended to increase their ratings of each other on "friendship" and "Confidence." It was concluded that during this initial period of crew assembly the members of crews whose commanders scored high on both Consideration and Initiating Structure tended to develop more favorable crew attitudes than the members of those crews led by commanders who scored low on both leader behavior dimensions. These findings indicate the influence of leadership style upon early group-learning experience.

4. Rush[21] has reported the relationship between the Leader Behavior Description Questionnaire scores of B-29 and B-50 aircraft commanders and "group dimension" measures of air crews drawn from three independent samples: Combat Crew Training School, Combat Crew Standardization School, and Far East Air Force:

> For each sample, crew means on the five dimensions of the Crew Dimension Questionnaire (CDQ)[22] were correlated with mean scores for the two LBDQ dimensions. Results were highly consistent across samples and appeared meaningful in terms of the definitions of the various dimensions. Perhaps the best way to summarize the results of this analysis is to discuss the correlations for each of the CDQ dimensions as follows:
>
> *Control*—Scores on this dimension were negatively related to Consideration in all three samples, while the correlations with Initiating Structure were not significant. *One possible interpretation of these results is that when crew members perceive the AC [that is, the aircraft commander] as a controlling agent, they construe his behavior as not considerate.*
>
> *Intimacy*—Initiating Structure was not significantly related to this dimension but Consideration showed significant positive correlations. Crews which describe themselves as more intimate tend to judge their AC's as being more considerate.
>
> *Harmony*—Scores on this dimension correlated positively with Consideration while the correlations with Initiating Structure were not significant. This would seem to point to

the influence of leader behavior in establishing certain interpersonal relationships among crew members. The amount of effort he spends in organizing crew relations and defining the roles of crew members doesn't seem to make much difference in the harmony of the crew. However, the *way* in which he goes about his duties does appear to be a factor in the development of compatible relationships.

Procedural Clarity—This characteristic of crews, which refers to the way procedures and duties are defined for each crew member, was related to Initiating Structure in a positive direction. Correlations with Consideration were not significant. Thus the *manner* in which the leader acts toward crew members does not appear significant in establishing a well-defined set of relationships among crew members. But the frequency with which he engages in acts construed as Initiating Structure is related to the clarity of duties and functions in the crew.

Stratification—Scores on this dimension were highly related to Consideration in a negative direction, while correlations with Initiating Structure were not significant. In other words, crews which describe their leader as relatively less considerate tend to be characterized by greater awareness of status hierarchies within their crew.

In general, these results point to the interaction between group dimensions and leader behavior. It seems clear that if we are to understand the psychological characteristics of crews, we must deal not only with *what* the AC does, but also *how* he does it. In air crews, the actions of the AC may set the style, so to speak, for the interpersonal relations of crew members.[23]

5. In a study of 132 B-29 and B-50 commanders, a comparison was made between commanders' ideologies of leadership behavior and their crews' descriptions of their actual behavior in relation to the two leader behavior dimensions.[24] The ideology scores were computed from the commanders' own responses to the LBDQ-Ideal. In expressing their leadership ideology, the commanders clearly recognized the desirability of scoring high on both dimensions of leader behavior, but the correspondence between their statements of how they should behave and their behavior as described by their crews was negligible. In the case of the Initiating Structure dimension, the correlation did not differ significantly from zero. Although the corresponding correlation of .14 for the Consideration dimension was significant at the .05 level of confidence, this represented only a low degree of association. The moderate reliability of the Initiating Structure and Consideration scales, and the fact that the distributions are not entirely normal, probably contribute to the low magnitude of the correlations obtained. *Nevertheless, the evidence suggests that the aircraft commander's knowledge of how he should behave as a leader has little bearing upon how he is perceived as behaving by the members of his crew.*

Educational study

So much for the Air Force studies; now let us examine an important early study by Hemphill, using the LBDQ in education.[25]

The members of 18 departments in a liberal arts college described their department heads and indicated on the LBDQ-Ideal how they believed a department head should behave.[26] They also ranked the five departments in the college that had the general reputation on the campus of being best led or best administered and the five departments that were least well led or least well administered. In making these rankings, each respondent excluded his own department. The correlations between the reputation scores and the LBDQ-Real scores were .36 for Consideration and .48 for Initiating Structure, with .47 required for significance at the .05 level. When discrepancy scores—measuring the absolute difference between the Real and the Ideal scores on each of the leader behavior dimensions—were correlated with the reputation scores, the obtained coefficients, − .52 and − .55, respectively, were both statistically significant. The greater the departure of the actual behavior of the department head (on either leader behavior dimension) from the norm of how ideal behavior on this dimension was conceived by the members of his department, the poorer was the administrative reputation of the department.

A cutting score of 41 on Consideration and 36 on Initiating Structure for the split on one co-ordinate, and the median reputation score for the split on the other, were used to distribute the 18 cases into quadrants as illustrated in Table 23–1.

The import of these data is clear: the departments with high reputation are those whose chairmen score high on *both* leader behavior dimensions.

It is appropriate at this point to summarize five principal findings of this series of leader behavior studies.

1. The evidence indicates that Initiating Structure and Consideration are fundamental dimensions of leader behavior, and that the Leader Behavior Description Questionnaire provides a practical and useful technique for measuring the behavior of leaders on these two dimensions.

2. Effective leader behavior is associated with high performance on both dimensions. The aircraft commanders rated highest by their superiors on "over-all effectiveness in combat" are alike in being men who (a) define the role which they expect each member of the work-group to assume, and delineate patterns of organization and ways of getting the job done, and (b) establish a relationship of mutual trust and respect between the group members and themselves.

3. There is, however, some tendency for superiors and subordinates to evaluate oppositely the contribution of the leader behavior dimensions to the effectiveness of leadership. Superiors are more concerned with the Initiating Structure aspects of the leader's behavior, whereas subordinates are more concerned with (or "interested in") the Consideration the leader extends to them as group members. This difference in group attitude appears to impose upon the leader some measure of conflicting role-expectations.

4. Changes in the attitudes of group members toward each other, and group characteristics such as harmony, intimacy, and procedural clarity, are significantly associated with the leadership style of the leader. High Initiating Structure combined with high Consideration is associated with favorable group attitudes and with favorable changes in group attitude.

5. There is only a slight positive relationship between the way leaders *believe* they should behave and the way in which their group members *describe* them as behaving. *For this reason, those engaged in leadership training programs should be especially wary of accepting*

TABLE 23–1   THE RELATIONSHIP BETWEEN THE REPUTATION ACHIEVED BY COLLEGE DEPARTMENTS AND THE CONSIDERATION AND INITIATING STRUCTURE SCORES OF DEPARTMENT CHAIRMEN TAKEN CONJUNCTIVELY (N = 18)

Chairman's leadership	Number of Chairmen	
	Below median reputation	Above median reputation
Score of 41 or larger on Consideration and a score of 36 or more on Initiating Structure	1	8
Score of less than 41 on Consideration or less than 36 on Initiating Structure	8	1

Source: After John K. Hemphill, "Leadership Behavior Associated with the Administrative Reputation of College Departments," The Journal of Educational Psychology, 46, No. 7, November 1955, p. 396. *Reprinted by permission of the publisher.*

trainees' statements of how they should behave as evidence of parallel changes in their
actual behavior.

We have seen that the most effective leaders
are those who score high on *both* dimensions
of leader behavior. These dimensions may be
diagrammed according to the scheme in Figure
23–2; the ordinates are defined by the aver-
ages of the respective dimensions, and the four
quadrants are designated by Roman numerals.

The leaders described in Quadrant I are
evaluated as highly effective, whereas those in
Quadrant III, whose behavior is ordinarily accompanied by group chaos, are characterized
as most ineffective. The leaders in Quadrant
IV are the martinets and the "cold fish" so
intent upon getting a job done that they forget
they are dealing with human beings, not with
cogs in a machine. The individuals described
in Quadrant II are also ineffective leaders. They
may ooze with the milk of human kindness, but
this contributes little to effective performance
unless their Consideration behavior is accompanied by a necessary minimum of Initiating
Structure behavior.

Educational administrators and aircraft commanders

Having presented this background material on
the LBDQ, we will now discuss two studies that
deal directly with school superintendents. The
first of these two compares superintendents
and aircraft commanders.[27]

It is presumed that every leader, irrespective
of the institutional setting within which he operates, engages to some extent in both forms
of leader behavior—Initiating Structure and
Consideration. Consequently, in comparing
groups of leaders from different institutional
settings we should expect to find some degree
of overlap in leadership behavior. But where
the institutional settings differ markedly—as in
the case of public education and the Air
Force—we also should expect to discover significant difference between groups of leaders
drawn from two such settings. The leaders
whom we have studied—educational administrators and aircraft commanders—function
within institutional settings that traditionally
would appear to emphasize different aspects of
leader behavior. On the basis of predicated differences between these two settings, the following hypothesis was formulated: that educational administrators will demonstrate, in both
leader behavior and leadership ideology, more
Consideration and less Initiation of Structure
than aircraft commanders. Accordingly, the
purpose of this study is to determine whether
these two groups of leaders differ significantly
in their leadership ideology and their leadership style.

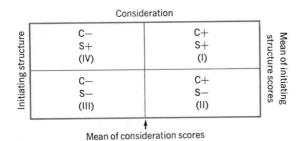

*Figure 23–2. A quadrant scheme for describing leaders' be-
havior on the Initiating Structure and Consideration dimensions. (From Andrew W. Halpin, "The Superintendent's Effectiveness as a Leader,"* Administrator's Notebook, 7, *No. 2,
October 1958.)*

The sample was composed of two groups of subjects: 64 educational administrators and 132 aircraft commanders.

The 64 educational administrators were drawn from two sources. Thirteen of the group were participants in an interdisciplinary graduate seminar on "Leadership for Educational Administrators"[28] conducted during the Winter Quarter, 1954, and sponsored by the School-Community Development Study at The Ohio State University. Eight of the 13 members were principals; the others, local superintendents and supervisors. The remaining 51 members of this sample were all superintendents of Ohio schools studied during the spring of 1954. Sixty-two of the sample were men, and two were women. These 64 administrators answered the LBDQ-Ideal, and also were described on the LBDQ-Real by 428 members of their respective staffs. The LBDQ-Real and the LBDQ-Ideal were administered by members of a research team with the guarantee that the anonymity of each respondent would be protected. On the average, 6.7 descriptions ($\sigma = .8$) were secured for each administrator.

The 132 aircraft commanders were in charge of B-29 and B-50 crews. The two aircraft are essentially similar, with an eleven-man crew on the B-29 and a ten-man crew on the B-50. Seventy-six of the commanders were studied in the Far East Air Force at the time they were flying combat missions over Korea.[29] The other 56 were members of select Strategic Air Command crews undergoing evaluation in this country.[30] These two groups of commanders did not differ significantly either in leadership ideology or in leader behavior as measured here, and hence have been combined into a single sample. The 132 commanders answered the LBDQ-Ideal and were described on the LBDQ-Real by 1099 members of their respective crews. On the average, 8.3 descriptions ($\sigma = 1.6$) were secured for each commander.

For the combined sample, the primary data consist of the responses of 196 group leaders to the LBDQ-Ideal and descriptions of these leaders on the LBDQ-Real by the 1527 members of their respective groups.

The 1723 LBDQ's were scored on the Consideration and Initiating Structure dimensions. The leader's own scores on the Ideal form were used to represent his ideology in respect to the two dimensions. With the LBDQ-Real, it was appropriate to determine first how well group members agreed in describing their respective leaders. Accordingly, for each sample and separately by dimension, between-group versus within-group analyses of variance were made. The F ratio was significant at the .01 level of confidence in each instance. The extent of agreement among group members in describing their leaders may be expressed by the unbiased correlation ratio (epsilon). These ratios for the Consideration dimension are .49 and .61 for the administrators and commanders, respectively. The corresponding ratios for Initiating Structure are .49 and .44. For the LBDQ-Real, group-mean Initiating Structure scores were therefore used as indices of the leader's behavior on these dimensions.

For each leader, and on each dimension, one score (the LBDQ-Ideal) expresses his own ideology, and another (the LBDQ-Real) describes his behavior as perceived by the members of his own group. The comparisons of the leadership ideology and leader behavior of the administrators and the commanders have been made exclusively in terms of group differences, and have been analyzed in two ways: first, by t ratios of the mean difference between the number of leaders from each group who scored either above or below the mean of the pooled samples on each (and both) of the dimensions; secondly, the differences in leadership styles have also been analyzed according to number and per cent of cases in each sample that fall into the quadrants listed in Table 23–4.

Table 23–2 presents a comparison of the mean LBDQ-Real and the mean LBDQ-Ideal scores of the educational administrators and the aircraft commanders.

In Table 23–3 are listed, by sample, the correlations between the leader behavior dimension scores on the LBDQ-Real and the LBDQ-Ideal, and the correlations between the

TABLE 23–2   LEADER BEHAVIOR DESCRIPTION QUESTIONNAIRE
(REAL AND IDEAL) MEANS, STANDARD DEVIATIONS, AND *t* RATIOS
OF MEAN DIFFERENCES, FOR EDUCATIONAL ADMINISTRATORS AND
AIRCRAFT COMMANDERS

	Real				*Ideal*				*t*(Ideal-Real)*	
	Considera-tion		*Initiating structure*		*Considera-tion*		*Initiating structure*		*Considera-tion*	*Initiating structure*
	Mean	*σ*	*Mean*	*σ*	*Mean*	*σ*	*Mean*	*σ*		
Educational administrators (N = 64)	44.7	6.0	37.9	4.4	52.4	3.9	43.8	6.4	8.95	7.28
Aircraft commanders (N = 132)	39.7	8.0	40.9	4.9	48.7	5.3	51.0	4.6	11.69	18.50
t* (EA—AC)	4.38		−4.11		4.93		−8.97			

* All reported t's are significant at the .001 level of confidence.
Source: From Andrew W. Halpin, "The Leader Behavior and Leadership Ideology of
Educational Administrators and Aircraft Commanders," Harvard Educational Review,
25, Winter 1955, p. 24.

Real and the Ideal scores on each dimension.

The findings in Table 23–2 support the hypothesis that leaders who function within these two different institutional settings exhibit differences in their leadership ideology and differences in their style of leadership behavior. Specifically, the administrators, in both leadership ideology and leader behavior as measured by the LBDQ, show more Consideration and less Initiation of Structure than the commanders. These differences are all significant at the .001 level of confidence.

The leaders in both samples indicate that they should show more Consideration and greater Initiation of Structure than their group members perceive them as doing. These differences, too, are significant at the .001 level of confidence. The differences between the two samples on the Ideal are in the same direction as those on the Real, so that the pattern of Ideal means corresponds to the pattern of Real means.

But this similarity in pattern of group means does not imply a necessary relationship between how individual leaders behave and how they believe they should behave. It has been noted previously that a leader's beliefs about

his leadership behavior are not highly associated with his leadership behavior as described by his own group members. In general, this is confirmed by the present findings (two top rows of Table 23–3).

The commanders, both on the LBDQ-Real and on the LBDQ-Ideal, show significant correlations between the Consideration and the Initiating Structure scores, whereas the administrators do not. Although the interdimension correlations do not differ significantly in the case of the Ideal, the difference between the interdimension correlations on the LBDQ-Real is statistically significant. This indicates that the administrators, to a greater extent than the commanders, treat the two dimensions as if they were independent.

The differences between the leadership styles of the administrators and the commanders may be analyzed also according to the number and per cent of cases in each sample that fall into each of four quadrants: (1) "above the mean on Consideration" and "above the mean on Initiating Structure," (2) "below the mean on Consideration" and "below the mean on Initiating Structure," (3) "above the mean on Consideration" but "below the mean on

TABLE 23–3 PRODUCT-MOMENT CORRELATIONS BETWEEN LEADER BEHAVIOR DESCRIPTION QUESTIONNAIRE REAL AND IDEAL SCORES FOR EDUCATIONAL ADMINISTRATORS AND AIRCRAFT COMMANDERS, AND BETWEEN CONSIDERATION AND INITIATING STRUCTURE SCORES ON THE REAL AND ON THE IDEAL

	Educational administrators (N = 64)	*Aircraft commanders (N = 132)*	*t*
Consideration—Real, Consideration—Ideal	.09	.17*	.53
Initiating Structure—Real, Initiating Structure—Ideal	.34**	.14	1.37
Consideration—Real, Initiating Structure—Real	.13	.45**	2.28*
Consideration—Ideal, Initiating Structure—Ideal	.22	.29**	.48

**Significant at the .05 level of confidence.*
*** Significant at the .01 level of confidence.*
Source: From Andrew W. Halpin, "The Leader Behavior and Leadership Ideology of Educational Administrators and Aircraft Commanders," Harvard Educational Review, *25, Winter 1955, p. 24.*

Initiating Structure," and (4) "above the mean on Initiating Structure" but "below the mean on Consideration." The two means are based upon the pooled samples of administrators and commanders and may be constructed as coordinates which define these four quadrants. For the LBDQ-Real, the number and per cent of cases in each sample that fall into each quadrant are presented in Figure 23–3.

Earlier findings with aircraft commanders have suggested that the most effective leaders are those represented in the upper right quadrant, and the least effective those in the lower left quadrant. The leaders represented in the other two quadrants may be conceived as falling within a middle range of effectiveness. In the one instance, represented by those leaders in the lower right quadrant, there is a tendency to show sufficient Consideration but not enough Initiation of Structure; in the other, the con-

Initiating structure	Consideration: Below mean			Consideration: Above mean		
Above mean	EA	5	(7.8%)	EA	21	(32.8%)
	AC	37	(28.0%)	AC	57	(43.2%)
Below mean	EA	8	(12.5%)	EA	30	(46.9%)
	AC	29	(22.0%)	AC	9	(6.8%)

Mean = 39.9

Mean = 4.14

Figure 23–3. Number and percent of educational administrators (N=64) and aircraft commanders (N=132) with LBDQ-Real Scores above and below the mean on Initiating Structure and Consideration. (From Andrew W. Halpin, "The Leader Behavior and Leadership Ideology of Educational Administrators and Aircraft Commanders," Harvard Educational Review, *25, Winter 1955, p. 25.)*

verse holds—the leaders are strong in Initiating Structure but fail to show enough Consideration for the members of the group.

The statistical significance of the difference between the number of administrators and the number of commanders who scored in each quadrant was determined by the chi-squared test. The χ^2 values and corresponding p values are presented in Table 23.4.

At the .05 level of confidence, the two groups of leaders do not differ significantly in respect to either the number of highly effective or highly ineffective leaders. It should be noted, however, that the χ^2 value in the upper right quadrant (3.80) does approach the value required (3.84) for significance at the .05 level of confidence. This suggests that according to the posited criterion of effectiveness the commanders show a greater tendency toward effective leadership than is demonstrated by the administrators.

The principal differences between the two groups of leaders are found in the off-quadrants. Those leaders among the administrators who score in neither the highly effective nor the highly ineffective quadrant tend to cluster in the lower right quadrant, and are characterized by high Consideration but low Initiation of Structure. Conversely, those leaders among the commanders who score in neither the highly

effective nor the highly ineffective quadrant tend to cluster in the upper left quadrant, and are characterized by high Initiation of Structure and low Consideration. In both instances, the differences are highly significant. In short, these findings suggest that the leaders in these two groups who are not effective differ systematically in the nature of their shortcomings. *The aircraft commanders are inclined to show less Consideration than is desirable, whereas the educational administrators tend to be remiss is not initiating sufficient structure.*

A similar analysis was made for the LBDQ-Ideal scores. The number and per cent of administrators and commanders who score in each quadrant are given in Figure 23–4; and the χ^2 and the corresponding p values for tests of the significance of the difference between the incidence of cases in each group are listed by quadrant in Table 23–5.

The administrators and the commanders differ significantly in their leadership ideology. The most pronounced difference occurs in the lower right quadrant of Figure 23–4 in which are found the scores of 61.0 per cent of the administrators but of only 7.6 per cent of the commanders. Conversely, in the other off quadrant (low Consideration and high Initiation of Structure) are found the scores of 37.1 per cent of the commanders but of only 7.8 per

TABLE 23–4 χ^2 AND p VALUES FOR DIFFERENCE BETWEEN THE NUMBER OF EDUCATIONAL ADMINISTRATORS AND THE NUMBER OF AIRCRAFT COMMANDERS WHOSE LBDQ-REAL SCORES FALL IN EACH QUADRANT

Quadrant	χ^2	p^*
Above mean on both Initiating Structure and Consideration	3.80	> .05
Below mean on both Initiating Structure and Consideration	2.54	> .05
Above mean on Consideration but below mean on Initiating Structure	43.61	< .001
Above mean on Initiating Structure but below mean on Consideration	10.43	< .01

* With 1 df, require 3.84 at p = .05, 6.64 at p = .01, and 10.83 at p = .001.
Source: From Andrew W. Halpin, "The Leader Behavior and Leadership Ideology of Educational Administrators and Aircraft Commanders," Harvard Educational Review, 25, Winter 1955, p. 26.

	Consideration					
	Below mean			Above mean		
Initiating structure — Above mean	EA	5	(7.8%)	EA	10	(15.6%)
	AC	49	(37.1%)	AC	47	(35.6%)
Initiating structure — Below mean	EA	10	(15.6%)	EA	39	(61.0%)
	AC	26	(19.7%)	AC	10	(7.6%)

Mean = 48.6

Mean = 49.9

Figure 23–4. Number and percent of educational administrators (N=64) and aircraft commanders (N=132) with LBDQ-Ideal Scores above and below the mean on Initiating Structure and Consideration. (From Andrew W. Halpin, "The Leader Behavior and Leadership Ideology of Educational Administrators and Aircraft Commanders," Harvard Educational Review, 25, Winter 1955, p. 27.)

cent of the administrators. The probability of obtaining differences of this magnitude by chance alone is less than .001.

Finally, instead of comparing the two groups of leaders by this quadrant method we may simply note the per cent of each group that scores above the mean of both samples on each leader behavior dimension, both Real and Ideal. The juxtaposition of the data for this purpose, as given in Table 23–6, highlights the fact that an essentially similar pattern of differences between the administrators

and the commanders obtains in respect to both the LBDQ-Real and the LBDQ-Ideal.

The findings support the basic hypothesis that educational administrators differ from aircraft commanders in both leadership ideology and leadership style. The administrators tend to show greater Consideration and less Initiating of Structure than the commanders. These differences are presumably associated with differences between the institutional settings within which the two groups of leaders operate.

Since the concept of institutional setting

TABLE 23–5 χ^2 AND p VALUES FOR DIFFERENCE BETWEEN THE NUMBER OF EDUCATIONAL ADMINISTRATORS AND THE NUMBER OF AIRCRAFT COMMANDERS WHOSE LBDQ-IDEAL SCORES FALL IN EACH QUADRANT

Quadrant	χ^2	p^*
Above mean on both Initiating Structure *and* Consideration	8.32	< .01
Below mean on both Initiating Structure *and* Consideration	.50	> .05
Above mean on Consideration *but* below mean on Initiating Structure	65.46	< .001
Above mean on Initiating Structure *but* below mean on Consideration	18.46	< .001

* With 1 df, require 3.84 at p = .05, 6.64 at p = .01, and 10.83 at p = .001.

Source: From Andrew W. Halpin, "The Leader Behavior and Leadership Ideology of Educational Administrators and Aircraft Commanders," Harvard Educational Review, 25, Winter 1955, p. 27.

TABLE 23–6   PER CENT OF EDUCATIONAL ADMINISTRATORS AND OF
AIRCRAFT COMMANDERS WHO SCORE ABOVE THE COMBINED MEANS
OF BOTH GROUPS ON INITIATING STRUCTURE AND
CONSIDERATION, REAL AND IDEAL

		Educational administrators	Aircraft commanders	χ^2	p^*
Initiating	Real	40.6	71.2	17.03	$< .001$
Structure	Ideal	23.4	72.7	42.45	$< .001$
Consideration	Real	79.7	50.0	15.80	$< .001$
	Ideal	76.6	43.2	19.37	$< .001$

* With 1 df, *require* 10.83 *at* p = .001.

Source: From Andrew W. Halpin, "The Leader Behavior and Leadership Ideology of Educational Administrators and Aircraft Commanders," Harvard Educational Review, *25, Winter 1955, p. 27.*

possesses a certain heuristic value, further comparative studies of leaders drawn from different institutional settings should increase our understanding of leadership behavior. These studies need not be confined to the American culture, for cross-cultural studies of leadership afford an equally important area for investigation. For example, are the present findings about the leader behavior of educational administrators peculiar to American educators; or is the same leadership style characteristic of school administrators in Germany or in England? But in spite of its heuristic value, the concept of institutional setting is limited by its lack of specificity. To know that different institutional settings foster different leadership styles is important, but we also need to know what specific factors in each setting are associated with these differences. Therefore, it would be preferable to study various specific conditions of group operation that are imposed upon both the leader and his group. Some conditions are clearly a function of the institutional setting; others are defined by the mission of the group; and others are determined by local mores and regulations, and by temporal exigencies. It should be possible, however, to isolate particular conditions of group operation and determine their relationship to different leadership styles. For example, what is the relationship between the specificity with

which a group goal has been defined and the way the leader behaves? What effect does the visibility of group products have on the leader's behavior? The speed with which the leader and the group receive feedback information on these products? In education—where goals ordinarily are broadly defined, where the responsibility for their accomplishment is diffused, where the products of group effort are not readily visible, and where considerable time often elapses before the leader and the group receive feedback on the success of the group's efforts —do these conditions prompt the administrator to stress Consideration more than the Initiation of Structure? The limitations in the design of this study permit only speculation about these questions. They deserve, however, further careful investigation.

It has been noted that the leader's belief in how he should behave is not strongly associated with how his group members describe his behavior. In examining the pattern of the four correlations in the two top rows of Table 23–3, we note, however, that the Real *versus* Ideal correlations are significant for the commanders on Consideration, and for the administrators on Initiating Structure. Although these correlations are low, they suggest an interesting speculation. In public education where a high value is placed upon Consideration, and Initiating Structure is not a dominant theme of the institutional mores, we find a significant relationship between the Real and the Ideal scores on Initiating Structure. Conversely, in the Air Force where a high value is placed upon Initiating Structure behavior, and Consideration is not a major theme of the institution, we find a significant relationship between the Real and Ideal scores on Consideration. *In both institutional settings the relationship between the Real and the Ideal scores tends to be greater for that aspect of leadership behavior which is least supported by the institutional mores.* This suggests that the leader's belief in how he should behave is reflected in his behavior—as perceived by his own group members—most clearly in respect to that aspect of leadership behavior which is *least* endorsed by the institutional norms. Whether this is due to a closer parallel between the leader's ideology and his actual behavior on this score, or whether it is due instead to a closer relationship between his ideology and the discrimination with which the group members perceive his leader behavior, is a question for further research. In either event, the implications for leadership training programs are provocative, for if this finding is corroborated by other cross-institutional studies of leader behavior, then we should expect to find that changes in an individual's leadership ideology will be reflected in his leader behavior principally in those aspects of behavior that are least endorsed by the norms of the specific institution within which he functions.

The leader behavior of the school superintendent

The preceding series of studies provided the chief impetus for the next investigation of 50 Ohio school superintendents.[31] Although the findings of earlier investigations had indicated that effective leaders are those whose performance is high both in Initiating Structure and Consideration, we are not directly concerned in this effort with *evaluating* the superintendents. Our objective is simpler and, in one sense,

more fundamental: to determine the relationship between the superintendent's own perception of how he behaves on the Initiating Structure and Consideration dimensions, as contrasted with the board and staff perception; and, furthermore, to discover the corresponding relationship between his, the board's, and the staff's beliefs concerning how he *should* behave as a leader. This, of course, implies several additional questions. To what extent do board members agree in their descriptions of the superintendent's leader behavior? Is there greater agreement about how he *should* behave than about how he *does* behave? These are the major questions that we shall examine in this study.

The superintendent, as the officially designated leader in charge of the school organization, is confronted by two major sets of responsibilities. He is responsible to the board of education, but he also must be responsive to the members of his own professional staff. Both reference groups, the board and the staff, impose upon him expectations of how he should behave as a leader. When these expectations are essentially similar, he probably encounters no difficulty in orienting his behavior to them. But to the extent that they are incompatible, he is placed in a position of potential role-conflict. How should he behave as the leader? Should he respond principally to the expectations of his board or to those of his staff? Or should he "be his own man" and persist in his own style of leadership irrespective of what either board or staff may wish? These practical questions plague most school administrators and are of equal concern to those responsible for their pre-service and in-service training.

This investigation is closely related to the whole question of evaluating the performance of school superintendents. Objective measures of the superintendent's job performance or of the effectiveness of his leadership are extremely rare, for the development of such measures is a sorely neglected area of research. Evaluations of the superintendent's job performance customarily take the form of subjective ratings of his effectiveness. These ratings are seldom made with the help of a well-constructed rating schedule that elicits evaluations of his performance in specified areas of his job; instead, they usually entail little more than global judgments of whether the superintendent's performance is "good" or "bad." This is not the place to explore the ramifications of the criterion problem in educational administration. But one troublesome question must be raised: If we discover an appreciable lack of relationship between the descriptions of the superintendent's behavior given by his board members and by his staff, and also find that the agreement among board members about how the superintendent behaves is far less than perfect, with what degree of confidence can we then accept, as a dependable criterion of the superintendent's performance, an evaluation of his behavior given by a single board member?

Accurate and judicious evaluation of an individual's performance admittedly involves a more complex process than a straightforward description of what he does—of how he behaves. A valid criterion of ideal behavior should provide the foundation for whatever evaluation is made of the effectiveness of the behavior of a particular individual. Hence, to such extent that a given rater's information about how a person does behave is unreliable, his evaluation of the effectiveness of that behavior is suspect. In short, if board members do not possess sufficient information about how the superintendent actually behaves to permit them to describe his behavior consistently among themselves and in reasonable agreement with the consensus of staff members, then a serious question can be raised about using board members' evaluations of the superintendent as the *sole* criterion of how effectively he performs his job. There is need for empirical research designed to explore this aspect of the criterion problem. Obviously, the present investigation provides no final answer on this score. Nevertheless, we shall examine the findings in terms of the question: What are the implications of these results for improving our present methods of evaluating the job performance of superintendents?

This study of the leadership behavior of 50 Ohio school superintendents deals again with the same dimensions of leader behavior: Initiating Structure and Consideration. The superintendents' behavior in respect to these two dimensions of behavior has been measured with the LBDQ-Real on which the staff and board respondents and the superintendents themselves indicate the frequency with which the superintendent engages in specific forms of leader behavior. The leadership ideology of the members of these same three respondent groups was measured by having each respondent indicate on the LBDQ-Ideal how he believed an Ideal superintendent *should* behave. The items on the LBDQ-Real and the LBDQ-Ideal are identical.

The LBDQ's were administered in each community by a member of the research team. The meetings with the staff and the board were held separately but not necessarily on the same day. Each team member assured the participants that the anonymity of their answers would be protected. Although the general purpose of the study was explained to all participants, *no reference whatsoever was made to the concepts of Initiating Structure and Consideration as dimensions of leader behavior.*

The raw data consisted of the responses on 1274 questionnaires divided equally between LBDQ-Real and LBDQ-Ideal. Each questionnaire was scored on the Initiating Structure and Consideration dimensions. The LBDQ-Self scores, both Real and Ideal, were secured directly from the superintendents themselves. Each of the fifty superintendents received an Initiating Structure score and a Consideration score that expressed his description of his own behavior in respect to these two dimensions. Similarly, his two LBDQ-Ideal scores indicated what he believed his behavior should be on these dimensions. The staff scores were obtained by having seven members of each superintendent's staff (that is, members of the work-group that reported directly to him) describe his leader behavior. The average of the seven scores by which his staff members described his Initiating Structure behavior was designated as his LBDQ-Real staff score on Initiating Structure. Likewise, an LBDQ-Real staff Consideration score was computed for each superintendent. The corresponding LBDQ-Ideal staff scores were determined in the same way. Scores for the boards' descriptions of the superintendents' behavior (LBDQ-Real, board) and scores that expressed their leadership ideology (LBDQ-Ideal, board) were computed by an analogous procedure. On the average, five board-member descriptions were obtained for each superintendent.

By this procedure the responses from the 1274 questionnaires were reduced to 600 scores, with 12 scores for each of the 50 superintendents:

1.	LBDQ-Real, Self	Initiating Structure
2.	LBDQ-Real, Self	Consideration
3.	LBDQ-Real, Staff	Initiating Structure
4.	LBDQ-Real, Staff	Consideration
5.	LBDQ-Real, Board	Initiating Structure
6.	LBDQ-Real, Board	Consideration
7.	LBDQ-Ideal, Self	Initiating Structure
8.	LBDQ-Ideal, Self	Consideration
9.	LBDQ-Ideal, Staff	Initiating Structure
10.	LBDQ-Ideal, Staff	Consideration
11.	LBDQ-Ideal, Board	Initiating Structure
12.	LBDQ-Ideal, Board	Consideration

The data were then analyzed in respect to these 12 scores. The findings can be summarized as follows:

1. On each leader behavior dimension, the staff respondents tend to agree in the description of their respective superintendents. Likewise, the board respondents tend to agree in the description of their respective superintendents. *Although the staff and the board members each agree among themselves as a group in their description of the superintendent's leadership behavior, the two groups do not agree with each other.* Thus knowledge of the superintendent's leadership behavior as perceived by his board does not permit us to predict with greater than chance accuracy how

these same aspects of the superintendent's behavior will be perceived by the members of his immediate staff. Hence, if we intend to use descriptions of the superintendent's leadership behavior as a criterion of performance, we need to take into full account the source of the description. It is evident that such descriptions should be secured from both board and staff. Neither source by itself provides a complete description of the superintendent's behavior. We conclude from these findings that the superintendents tend to adopt different behavioral roles in dealing with the members of staff and board groups.

2. Although the boards, on the whole, show statistically significant agreement among their members in their descriptions of their superintendents' leadership behavior, this agreement is far from perfect. The unbiased correlation ratio is .52 for Initiating Structure and .63 for Consideration. This finding raises a provocative question: if board member agreement in describing the leadership behavior of superintendents is no greater than these correlations indicate, then how much confidence can we place in an evaluation of the superintendents' effectiveness based upon board members' ratings? The same argument applies to staff member descriptions of the superintendent's behavior. Here again, the unbiased correlation ratio (.44 for each dimension), though statistically significant, reflects far less than perfect agreement.

3. In respect to Consideration, consistency in the superintendent's role behavior in dealing with the several members of his board shows only a chance association with the consistency the superintendent displays in dealing with several members of his staff. In short, the superintendent may reveal a consistent "front" of Consideration to all members of his board, but it does not follow from this that he displays a similarly consistent "front" of Consideration to all members of his staff.

4. *In respect to Consideration, the superintendents do not see themselves as either their staffs or boards see them.* The staffs see the superintendents as showing less Consideration than they are described as showing either by

the boards or by the superintendents themselves.

5. There is significant but low correlation (.44) between the superintendents' self-descriptions and the staff members' descriptions of their Initiating Structure behavior.

6. The boards describe the superintendents as Initiating Structure to a greater extent than they are perceived as doing by either the staffs or the superintendents themselves.

7. *On both dimensions, the board descriptions show only chance relationship with both the staff and the self descriptions.* The boards tend to describe the superintendents as higher on both Consideration and Initiating Structure than they are described by the staffs and in this sense show greater inclination than the staffs to view their superintendents as effective leaders. This suggests that the superintendents "play up to the boards"—behave, in fact, more effectively as leaders in dealing with their boards than in working with their own staffs. Even though the superintendent may possess good leadership skills as evidenced in his relationship with his board, he seems inclined to "let down a little" in his dealings with his staff.

8. The boards do not differ significantly from school to school in their expectation of how the superintendent should behave on either dimension.

9. There are significant differences between boards and staffs in the extent of their agreement about how the superintendent should behave on Consideration. But in respect to Initiating Structure, the within-group agreement for boards and for staffs is approximately the same for all staffs and all boards.

10. The staffs do not differ significantly from school to school in their expectation of how much Consideration the superintendent should show, but there is a slight difference in their expectation of how much Structure he should Initiate.

11. For the most part, staff and board conceptions of how an Ideal superintendent should behave do not differ from school to school. These conceptions constitute general norms of how staffs, boards, and superintendents believe a superintendent should behave. All three groups of respondents characterize an Ideal superintendent as one who scores high on both Consideration and Initiating Structure.

12. The superintendents set for themselves higher standards of Consideration than either the staffs or the boards set for them. *The boards, in fact, expect the superintendents to show greater Consideration to their staffs than the staffs themselves posit as Ideal.*

13. The boards believe that a superintendent should be very strong in Initiating Structure. The superintendents themselves and the staffs both believe that the superintendents should Initiate far less Structure than the boards expect. The staffs, in turn, prefer less Structure than the superintendents believe they should Initiate.

14. The perceived leadership behavior of the fifty superintendents differs significantly from the ideal behavior of a superintendent as conceived by all three respondent groups. Whereas only 19 superintendents are described by their staffs in the "high-high" quadrant (Figure 23–1), 48 out of 50 of these staffs believe that this quadrant characterizes the leadership behavior of an Ideal superintendent. Conversely, though eight of the superintendents are described in the "low-low" quadrant, the staffs unanimously agree that an Ideal superintendent would *not* behave in this fashion. Similar differences between the Real and the Ideal distributions by quadrant occur for both other respondent groups.

15. An analysis was made of the number of superintendents classified in the two quadrants on the main diagonal according to the descriptions of their behavior given by both their boards and their staffs. Eleven of the 50 superintendents (22 percent of the sample) were described as effective leaders by both their staffs and their boards—that is, were described as scoring high on both Consideration and Initiating Structure. On the other hand, only two of the 50 superintendents were described by both their staffs and their boards as ineffective leaders—that is, low on both dimensions. This quadrant analysis technique

provides a useful way of evaluating the leadership effectiveness of superintendents and appears especially applicable in those instances where the description of the superintendent's leadership behavior by *both* his staff and his board indicates that he can be classified in either the "high-high" or the "low-low" quadrants.

The leadership ideology of board and staff members, and of the superintendents themselves, is essentially the same. Effective or desirable leadership behavior is characterized by high scores on both Initiating Structure and Consideration. Conversely, ineffective or undesirable leadership behavior is marked by low scores on both dimensions. These findings on the leadership ideology of superintendents, staff members, and board members agree with the results of the earlier Air Force study in which it was found that aircraft commanders rated effective both by superiors and crew score high on both leader behavior dimensions. These results are also consistent with Hemphill's finding that college departments with a campus reputation for being well administered are directed by chairmen who score high on both leader behavior dimensions. In short, the effective leader is one who delineates clearly the relationship between himself and the members of the group, and establishes well-defined patterns of organization, channels of communication, and way of getting the job done. At the same time, his behavior reflects friendship, mutual trust, respect, and warmth in the relationships between himself and the members of the group.

The findings indicate that the superintendents differentiate their role behavior. In dealing with their boards they tend to be effective as leaders, but they are inclined to be less effective in working with their staffs. Even when superintendents possess sufficient skill to be highly effective as leaders, they often "let down" a little in dealing with their staffs. Here it is important to note that the superintendent has less frequent direct contacts with his board than with his staff. This affords him more time for planning the strategy of his behavior in working with the board. Because the board is in a stronger power position than the staff, the superintendent evidently puts this time to good use. In his relationship with his staff, on the other hand, the superintendent is frequently forced to meet exigencies, with the result that he may not have sufficient time to apply to each new problem his full potentiality for leadership.

It is difficult, but not impossible, to overcome the pressure of events. To avoid being crowded by time, many executives delegate to associates a large share of authority and responsibility. This transfer of authority is in itself, of course, an essential aspect of Initiating Structure in the interaction of group members. Hence the present findings confirm our subjective impression that far too many superintendents allow their principal responsibilities to become obscured by trivia, with the result that they abdicate their leadership role and allow themselves to degenerate into mere functionaries. Routine and perfunctory activities have a specious attractiveness because they often allay anxieties that are inherent in the superintendent's leadership role. But we must avoid the mistake of confusing sheer routine activity with the productivity and creativity required for effective leadership.

The superintendent's tendency to play different roles with board and staff is revealed by the lack of relationship between the board and staff descriptions of the superintendent's leader behavior. Although the members of each of these two reference groups show statistically significant agreement in their perceptions of the superintendent's behavior, the agreement is far from perfect. This finding has important implications for research on the effectiveness of the superintendent's job performance. The salient implication concerns the use of board member ratings as the criterion of leadership effectiveness. Our findings have provided two cogent arguments against this practice. First, we have noted that the board members show considerably less than perfect agreement in simply *describing* how the superintendent behaves, a finding which casts serious doubt upon how much board member agreement we can expect to find among independent *evaluations* of the superintendent's leadership effectiveness. This criticism applies especially to global judgments made without the benefit of a carefully constructed rating schedule of known reliability. Second, in evaluating the superintendent, we must take into account information from all relevant reference groups. When the descriptions of the superintendent's behavior emanating from two relevant reference groups such as the board and staff are not significantly correlated, it is all the more imperative that data from *both* sources be examined as potential criteria. In the present study, we have not exhausted the reference groups that can furnish independent and pertinent criterion information on the superintendent's performance. We have confined our inquiry to reference groups focal to the superintendent's efforts in the internal administration of the schools. Similar studies could be developed to examine the superintendent's behavior in external administration—that is, in community and public relations activities.

Our findings point up the need for a multiple-criteria approach to the study of the leadership effectiveness of school superintendents. This means that we must first establish several independent, objective criteria of the superintendent's effectiveness and then determine the relationship between (1) these criteria and selected predictor variables and (2) the criteria themselves. Predictor variables can be posited readily enough. What we lack are dependable, *objective* criteria of effective school administration. Criteria, by definition, entail value-judgments. For this reason, whenever we are confronted by several criteria that do not have a high correlation with each other, a further value-judgment may be required to rank the relevance of the separate criteria. The responsibility for a judgment of this kind should rest with the board of education as the official body representing the community in matters of public education. The social scientist, as a scientist, is not required to make these value-decisions, but he can make an equally important, and perhaps even more fundamental, contribution. He can demonstrate to what extent the various criteria proposed are dependable and whether they are in any way incompatible with each other. He can show, for example, that Leadership Style A is effective in terms of Criterion A, and Leadership Style B is effective in respect to Criterion B. He may also note, however, that Leadership Styles A and B are incompatible, perhaps even antithetical. For instance, the superintendent who must spend a lot of time "politicking" in the community in order to put through a salary raise for his teachers may be forced to spend so little time with his teachers that they characterize his behavior as low in consideration. If the board or the staff should insist that the superintendent be active in securing better salaries for teachers (Criterion A), and also that he be perceived by his staff as Considerate (Criterion B), then the superintendent may be faced by a real dilemma. For if he is to be perceived as considerate by the staff he must devote time to personal interaction with individual staff members. If this same time is demanded for community contacts to gain support for a salary increase for teachers, the superintendent has to make a choice. There are only 24 hours in a day, and the superintendent, like every executive, must choose how he can best allocate the time at his disposal. Under such circumstances as these, if the board demands that the superintendent satisfy both Criterion A and Criterion B, they may impose upon him an intolerable burden of role-conflict. On this point Seeman[32] has provided an illuminating discussion of role-conflict and ambivalence in the leadership behavior of school superintendents. As we have said, the choice of the criteria of effective administration is a prerogative of the local community, but it should be an informed choice in which conflicting or incompatible demands upon the administrator are clearly recognized as such. It is here that research can make a trenchant contribution by furnishing dependable, objective data that will permit communities to make wiser and better-informed decisions in establishing criteria for evaluating the performance of their school superintendents.

The fact that the superintendents play a different role with their boards from that which they assume with their staffs does not necessarily imply that they are confronted by role-conflict. Some administrators undoubtedly compartmentalize their behavior, and in so doing minimize the likelihood of role-conflict. Others, however, may find themselves torn by what they perceive as differential expectations imposed upon them by board and staff. In the present study we have not attempted to explore the dynamics of the superintendent's behavior in the matter of role differentiation. To do this would require a clinical, case-study approach similar to that employed by Seeman.[33] As he has clearly demonstrated, this is an important area for further research in educational administration, and one in which the methods of the present study can be used in conjunction with straightforward case-study techniques.

Until such time as we are sure of the ultimate criteria we seek, we may be wise to settle for "intermediate" criteria that have strong presumptive evidence in their favor. The LBDQ-Real scores may be construed as an intermediate criterion of this kind. Inasmuch as we lack suitable objective criteria of the effectiveness of school executives at this time, we may assume tentatively that the relationship between leader behavior dimension scores and effectiveness which has been found in the Air Force and in higher education studies we have cited applies with equal force to school superintendents. Our present findings on leadership ideology support this assumption. *If we are willing to accept it, then we may use LBDQ-Real scores secured from board and staff as an intermediate criterion for evaluating the effectiveness of the superintendent's behavior.* Obviously it is a rough measure, but it does provide a first approach to the objective appraisal of leadership effectiveness. We would suggest that those who are interested in

experimenting with this approach use the quadrant analysis technique that we have described.

Although the three respondent groups of the present study all agree on the Ideal, the behavior of this sample of 50 superintendents—as described by the boards, the staffs, and the superintendents themselves—falls significantly short of the ideal. This discrepancy should not necessarily be conceived as an indictment of these superintendents; for ideals, by definition, are objectives difficult to attain. It is heartening to find that approximately one-fifth of the superintendents in the sample approach the ideal in the eyes of their boards *and* staffs. At the opposite end of the scale, only 4 per cent of these superintendents are categorized, both by their boards and staffs, as ineffective leaders.

In what way do the superintendents tend to fall short of the Ideal? On the one hand, these administrators demonstrate good leader behavior in their high Consideration for members of their staffs; on the other, they fail to Initiate Structure to as great an extent as is probably desirable. As a group, they appear somewhat disinclined to Initiate Structure in their interaction with group members. One may speculate about possible reasons for this. In some of our discussions with administrators we have encountered a tendency to view Consideration and Initiating Structure as incompatible forms of leader behavior. Some administrators act as if they were forced to emphasize one form of behavior at the expense of the other. Yet the correlation between the LBDQ-Real dimension scores for this sample is .23 (not significant) for the staff descriptions and .61 (significant at the .01 level) for board descriptions. Hence there is nothing negative or antithetical in this interdimensional relationship.[34] The fact that the interdimension correlation for the board's descriptions is higher than the corresponding correlation for staff descriptions suggests that the superintendents can stress both dimensions of behavior when they believe that this is sufficiently worth their effort—especially in dealing with members of the board.

Why, then, the apparent disinclination to place similar stress upon both aspects of behavior in dealing with the staff? This reluctance may be a reflection of some of the current emphasis in education upon "human relations." The human relations approach and the burgeoning interest in group dynamics have developed in part as a protest against reactionary and even authoritarian leadership styles that have prevailed in far too many school situations. But in our enthusiasm for the new approach, have we perhaps swung the pendulum too far?

In applying the human relations approach it is important that we do not overlook the responsibility imposed upon every official leader by the institutional realities of the formal organization of which he is a part. The official leader has a responsibility and, in fact, a contractual obligation to accomplish a specified mission, and certain aspects of this mission may be beyond the purview of decision by the immediate work group. It therefore is imperative for us to re-examine our ideas about the proper balance between human relations— that is, Consideration—and Initiating Structure behavior within formal organization, and to become more critical about applying generalizations adduced from experience with informal groups to groups embedded within formal hierarchical organizations. Some principles may apply to both kinds of groups, but there is insufficient research evidence to permit us to assume a priori that leadership styles that succeed in informal, autonomous groups will be equally effective in formally organized workgroups.

The swing of the pendulum seems also to be associated with a tendency to judge the Initiation of Structure as being nondemocratic. This point of view is ill-founded, for there is no necesssary negative relationship between democratic leadership and the Initiation of Structure. In fact, it is our impression—and here we are speculating—that what ordinarily is referred to as democratic administration or democratic leadership is precisely what we have defined "operationally" as leadership behavior char-

acterized by high Initiation of Structure and high Consideration. This we have evaluated as effective leadership. Where the Initiation of Structure is weak, however, it is doubtful that there exists sufficient leadership—whether democratic or nondemocratic—to be dignified by the name. Democratic leadership is highly desirable, but, for a leader's behavior to earn this description, it is not sufficient for the leader to be democratic—he must also demonstrate definite acts of leadership.

Having diagnosed the superintendent's leadership skills, what can we do to help him improve these skills? It is regrettable that there is no pat answer; we must read the notes as well as we can and let our own psychological insights suggest the tune. Role-playing can help, and professional counseling can accomplish a great deal. Practice in situational analysis and case-study methods are often useful. But the training task is formidable; nor are we always sure that the training methods achieve what was intended in the first place. Yet the situation is not entirely hopeless; on the basis of present knowledge, we can avoid several false starts. For example a glib prescription for men low on Consideration is to "give them a course on Consideration." I do not believe this will work, for we cannot make men more considerate by teaching them these skills directly; the necessary changes need to be induced through a therapeutic relationship.

Industrial consultant organizations have devised ingenious ways for improving executive skills; these methods often include a professional counseling relationship between the executive and the consultant. It may be time for us to examine similar possibilities in education—and this does not mean that we must install a psychoanalyst's couch in each superintendent's office! Furthermore, we are at a point where we can start some important basic research on better training procedures for school administrators. Increasingly, however, we have learned that how-to-do-it recipes are not enough; that we shall have to pay greater attention to administrative theory.[35]

The LBDQ technique provides one method

for evaluating certain aspects of the superintendent's effectiveness as a leader. The project on effectiveness criteria for elementary principals has developed important techniques for evaluating principals.[36] Several additional evaluation procedures are being devised at other universities. The question now is whether school administrators do, in fact, want to have their own effectiveness evaluated.

Our findings have clear implications for the training of educational administrators to the extent that we can describe those forms of leadership behavior which the board, the staff members, and the superintendents themselves consider most desirable, and which also are the most effective. Furthermore, we can specify the character of the role differentiation used by the superintendents vis-à-vis their boards and their staffs. But at this point, about all that we can say to the trainee or to the superintendent in service is, "This is how we believe you should behave." The chief shortcoming to be found with this is that exhortation is a notoriously poor training method. Little is accomplished by merely telling trainees how they should behave; we must also establish conditions in the training situation itself that will be conducive to behavioral change in the desired direction. Training in administrative skill involves many subtleties and is a complex process. We cannot inoculate a trainee with high Consideration and high skill in Initiating Structure in the same way that we inoculate a child with the virus of the Salk vaccine. The required leadership skills must be learned, and, as with all learning, ample opportunity for practice must be provided.

In leadership training we must examine our assumptions very cautiously. It has been theorized, for example, that human relations training will increase the Consideration that trainees show their work-group members. But Fleishman,[37] in a study for the International Harvester Company, has demonstrated that the success of human relations training depends upon a variety of factors, not the least of which is the "social climate" in which the trainee

functions in performing his job. An orthodox human relations training program can, under some circumstances, not only fail to achieve its stated purpose, but even boomerang upon its initiators by instilling in trainees apathetic, and often negative, attitudes toward human relations objectives. In short, we cannot assume on faith that the training we conduct will achieve the purposes we have in mind. Nor can we measure the effectiveness of training by the good intentions our trainees profess. The ultimate test of the success or failure of training lies in the changes that take place in the trainees' behavior.

Evidence from this inquiry and findings from an earlier Air Force study show that the leader's description of his own leadership behavior and his concept of what his behavior should be have little relationship to others' perceptions of his behavior that others have. In the case of the superintendents, this is especially true in respect to Consideration. For this reason we must be extremely wary about using statements made by the trainees as an index of the success of training. What a man says about himself is not the most dependable measure of changes that have assertedly taken place in his behavior. On the other hand, changes which his direct associates perceive in his behavior would appear to constitute a suitable index of the results of training. Our present evidence indicates that the LBDQ-Real is well adapted to this purpose and can provide a reliable gauge of the superintendent's leadership behavior in respect to the Initiating Structure and Consideration dimensions. It should be possible to conduct training experiments in which the difference between the LBDQ pre-training scores and the LBDQ post-training scores is used as an indicator of change by which we can evaluate the effectiveness of the training program. This technique, however, cannot be used for pre-service training of school administrators because a dependable pre-training LBDQ measure is unobtainable. But for the in-service training of men currently employed as administrators, such a method of evaluating training should prove quite valuable. It can even provide a means for comparing the relative effectiveness of various training procedures.

SUMMARY

The evidence from these inquiries shows that effective leadership is characterized by high Initiation of Structure and high Consideration. These two dimensions of leader behavior represent fundamental and pertinent aspects of leadership skill. The LBDQ-Real provides an objective and reliable method of describing the leader's behavior on these two dimensions. It should be possible to train leaders in the skills that compose these dimensions, but the methods for accomplishing this training have yet to be developed. We have noted two practical applications of the present approach: (1) the use of LBDQ-Real scores as an intermediate criterion of the leadership effectiveness of superintendents and (2) the use of differences between pre-training and post-training LBDQ-Real scores as an index of changes in behavior attributable to specific training programs.

The dimensions of leadership behavior we have delineated obviously do not exhaust the field. It would be fatuous to imply that these dimensions constitute *the* criterion of leadership effectiveness. They do not. However, they probably do represent *a* criterion that should be taken into account in evaluating the leadership skills of superintendents. Ours is only one approach to the study of the leader's behavior. Other investigators will, in turn, supplement our findings, and will take into account additional variables which we were not ready to include in the present series of studies.

NOTES

[1] In this chapter I have drawn heavily upon material from four earlier publications: (a) *The Leadership Behavior of School Superintendents* (Columbus, Ohio: College of Education, The Ohio State University, 1956); 2nd ed. (Chicago: Midwest Administration Center, University of Chicago, 1959); (b) "The Leader Behavior and Leadership Ideology of Educational Administrators and Aircraft Commanders," *Harvard Educational Review*, 25 (Winter 1955), pp. 18–32; (c) "The Behavior of Leaders," *Educational Leadership*, 14, No. 3 (December 1956), pp. 172–176; and (d) "The Superintendent's Effectiveness as a Leader," *Administrator's Notebook*, 7, No. 2 (October 1958). I gratefully acknowledge the publishers' permission to republish the material here.

[2] Ralph M. Stogdill, "Personal Factors Associated with Leadership: A Survey of the Literature," *Journal of Psychology*, 25, No. 25 (1948), pp. 35–71.

[3] Fillmore H. Sanford, "Research on Military Leadership," in John C. Flanagan (ed.), *Psychology in the World Emergency* (Pittsburgh; University of Pittsburgh Press, 1952), p. 51.

[4] John K. Hemphill, *Situational Factors in Leadership*, Bureau of Educational Research Monograph No. 32 (Columbus, Ohio: Bureau of Educational Research, The Ohio State University, 1949).

[5] The distinction between a phenotypic and a genotypic research approach is described in Ch. 1 of Kurt Lewin, *Dynamic Theory of Personality* (New York: McGraw-Hill Book Co., 1935).

[6] David C. McClelland *et al.*, *The Achievement Motive* (New York: Appleton-Century-Crofts, 1953).

[7] John K. Hemphill *et al., Leadership Acts I: An Investigation of the Relation Between Possession of Task Relevant Information and Attempts to Lead* (Columbus, Ohio: The Ohio State University Research Foundation, 1954).

For a detailed discussion of Hemphill's theory of leadership, see John K. Hemphill, "Administration as Problem-solving," in Andrew W. Halpin (ed.), *Administrative Theory in Education* (Chicago: Midwest Administration Center, University of Chicago, 1958), pp. 89–118.

[8] Chester I. Barnard, *The Functions of the Executive* (Cambridge, Mass.: Harvard University Press, 1938).

[9] In Barnard's terminology, this would read "effectively" rather than "efficiently."

[10] Dorwin Cartwright and Alvin Zander (eds.), *Group Dynamics: Research and Theory*, 2nd ed. (Evanston, Ill.: Row, Peterson & Company, 1960), p. 496.

[11] Published by the Bureau of Business Research, The Ohio State University, Columbus 10, Ohio. This questionnaire may not be used, either as a whole or in part, without permission.

[12] John K. Hemphill and Alvin E. Coons, *Leader Behavior Description* (Columbus, Ohio: Personnel Research Board, The Ohio State University, 1950).

[13] Andrew W. Halpin and B. James Winer, *The Leadership Behavior of the Airplane Commander*, Technical Report III prepared for Human Resources Research Laboratory, Department of the Air Force under Contracts AF 33 (038)-10105 & AF 18 (600)-27 (Columbus, Ohio: The Ohio State University Research Foundation, 1952), mimeo.

[14] This refers to operational definitions in science as described by Percy W. Bridgman, *The Logic of Modern Physics* (New York: The Macmillan Company, 1927), especially Ch. 1.

[15] The reliability estimates for the LBDQ-Ideal are lower than for the LBDQ-Real. Thus, for the LBDQ-Ideal-Self, the reliabilities are only .66 for Consideration and .69 for Initiating Structure.

[16] Some studies suggest that the leader does take a good share of his own style with him from job to job. See Edwin F. Harris and Edwin A. Fleishman, "Human Relations Training and the Stability of Leadership Patterns," *Journal of Applied Psychology*, 39 (1955), pp. 20–25; and Ralph M. Stogdill *et al., A Predictive Study of Administrative Work Patterns*, Research Monograph No. 85 (Columbus, Ohio: Bureau of Business Research, 1956), p. 35.

[17] The Ohio State Leadership Studies were initiated and directed by Dr. Carroll L. Shartle.

[18] Andrew W. Halpin, "The Leadership Behavior and Combat Performance of Airplane Commanders," *Journal of Abnormal and Social Psychology*, 49 (January 1954), pp. 19–22.

[19] Andrew W. Halpin, "Studies in Aircrew Composition: III," *The Combat Leader Behavior of B-29 Aircraft Commanders*, HFORL Memo. No. TN-54–7 (Washington, D.C.: Human Factors Operations Research Laboratory, Bolling Air Force Base, September 1953).

[20] Charlotte A. Christner and John K. Hemphill, "Leader Behavior of B–29 Commanders and Changes in Crew Members' Attitudes Toward the Crew," *Sociometry*, 18 (February 1955), pp. 82–87.

[21] Carl H. Rush, Jr., *Group Dimensions of Aircrews* (Columbus, Ohio:

Personnel Research Board, The Ohio State University Research Foundation, 1953).

[22] Crew Dimension Questionnaire, adapted from the Group Dimension Questionnaire described by John K. Hemphill and Charles M. Westie, "The Measurement of Group Dimensions," *Journal of Psychology*, 29, No. 29 (1950), pp. 325–342.

[23] Rush, *Group Dimensions of Aircrews*, pp. 132–136. Italics mine.

[24] Andrew W. Halpin, "The Leadership Ideology of Aircraft Commanders," *Journal of Applied Psychology*, 39 (April 1955), pp. 82–84.

[25] John K. Hemphill, "Leadership Behavior Associated with the Administrative Reputation of College Departments," *The Journal of Educational Psychology*, 46, No. 7 (November 1955), pp. 385–401.

[26] Note that this use of the LBDQ-Ideal differs from that employed in the last study cited where the leader himself stated how he *should* behave. In Hemphill's study the "Ideal" is used with the group members who state how they believe the leader *should* behave.

[27] Andrew W. Halpin, "The Leader Behavior and Leadership Ideology of Educational Administrators and Aircraft Commanders," *Harvard Educational Review*, 25 (Winter 1955), pp. 18–32.

[28] See Roald F. Campbell, "The Interdepartmental Seminar for School Administrators," *Graduate School Record* (Columbus, Ohio: The Ohio State University, 1954), 7, No. 9, pp. 4–6.

[29] Dr. John K. Hemphill and Lt. Col. Fred E. Holdrege, as members of a Human Resources Research Laboratories team, collected these data as one part of a larger study conducted in the Far East Air Force during the summer of 1951.

[30] Data collected at MacDill Air Force Base, Tampa, Florida, during 1951.

[31] Andrew W. Halpin, *The Leadership Behavior of School Superintendents* (Columbus, Ohio: College of Education, The Ohio State University, 1956).

[32] Melvin Seeman, "Role Conflict and Ambivalence in Leadership," *American Sociological Review*, 18 (August 1953), pp. 373–380.

[33] Melvin Seeman, *Social Status and Leadership: The Case of the School Executive* (Columbus, Ohio: Bureau of Educational Research and Service, The Ohio State University, 1960).

[34] Similarly, for crew descriptions of the leader behavior of 249 aircraft commanders, an interdimension correlation of 0.38 was found.

[35] See, for example, Andrew W. Halpin (ed.), *Administrative Theory in Education*.

[36] John K. Hemphill, Daniel E. Griffiths, and Norman Frederiksen, *Administrative Performance and Personality* (New York: Teachers College, Bureau of Publications, Columbia University, 1962).

[37] Edwin A. Fleishman, *"Leadership Climate" and Supervisory Behavior* (Columbus, Ohio: Personnel Research Board, The Ohio State University, 1951), lithoprinted.

24.

DYNAMICS OF LEADERSHIP

JACK R. GIBB

People must be led. People perform best under leaders who are creative, imaginative, and aggressive—under leaders who lead. It is the responsibility of the leader to marshall the forces of the organization, to stimulate effort, to capture the imagination, to inspire people, to coordinate efforts, and to serve as a model of sustained effort.

The leader should keep an appropriate social distance, show no favorites, control his emotions, command respect, and be objective and fair. He must know what he is doing and where he wants to go. He must set clear goals for himself and for the group or institution, and then communicate these goals well to all members of the organization. He must listen for advice and counsel before making decisions. But it is his responsibility to make decisions and to set up mechanisms for seeing that the decisions are implemented. After weighing the facts and seeking expert counsel, he must make policy and rules, set reasonable boundaries, and see that these are administered with justice and wisdom, even compassion.

The leader should reward good performance and learn effective ways of showing appreciation. He must be equally ready to give negative criticism where warranted and to appraise performance frequently, fairly, and unequivocally. He must command strong discipline, not only because people respect a strong leader, but because strength and firmness communicate care and concern. Good leadership requires

From *In Search of Leaders*, American Association for Higher Education, N.E.A., Washington, D.C., 1967, pp. 55–66. Reprinted by permission.

good fellowshop. People tend to follow good leaders. Leaders are born. Methods of election and selection are thus very important. Finding the right chairman or president is the critical variable in the success of a program or an institution. The quality of an organization is often judged by the perceived quality of the leadership.

The above is an oversimplified statement of one view of leadership theory and practice. A similarly oversimplified statement of an alternative viewpoint follows below.

People grow, produce, and learn best when they set their own goals, choose activities that they see as related to these goals, and have a wide range of freedom of choice in all parts of their lives. Under most conditions persons are highly motivated, like to take responsibilities, can be trusted to put out a great deal of effort toward organizational goals, are creative and imaginative, and tend to want to cooperate with others.

Leadership is only one of several significant variables in the life of the group or the institution. Leaders *can* be helpful and often are. The most effective leader is one who acts as a catalyst, a consultant, and a resource to the group. His job is to help the group to grow, to emerge, and to become more free. He serves the group best when he is a whole person, is direct, real, open, spontaneous, permissive, emotional, and highly personal. The leader at his best is an effective member. He acts in such a way as to facilitate group strength, individual responsibility, diversity, nonconformity, and aggressiveness. The leader is thus not necessary to the group and quickly becomes replaceable, dispensable, and independent. The good leader tends not to lead. He permits, feels, acts, relates, fights, talks—acts human as do other members of the group and the institution. The leader is present, available, and with the group *as a person*, not as a role.

We find many shades and variations of each of these two oversimplified statements of the theory and practice of leadership in our society. Several years of consulting and research in representative organizations make it very clear to me that attitudes toward leadership tend to cluster around these two poles. This bifurcation has analogues in current educational theory, politics, religion, philosophy, and administration.

The first view, described variously as authoritarian, paternalistic, or conservative, I classify as defensive because dynamically the view defends the administrator against his own fears and distrusts and against perceived or anticipated attack from the outside.

This authoritarian or defensive view is particularly appropriate to some viable aspects of the culture we live in to organizational forms inherited from the medieval church and military; to a life of vertical hierarchy, prescribed role responsibilities, and delegated authority; to a highly competitive economic and educational system; to the current dominant values of efficiency, excellence, producitivity, task performance, and perfectionism; to the impersonality, alienation, loneliness, impotence, and indifference in our people; to a world of automation, programming, data processing, and engineering; to a forensic, persuasive, public relations, and marketing mode of interpersonal commerce; to a world continually at war, threatened by war, or preparing for war; in short, to a world of machines. It is not accidental that all around the country when administrators administer the ultimate forensic weapon in arguing against participative forms of leadership they say, "But it would never work in the military or on the production line." Actually, research indicates that this point is probably not true, but in any event the image of the leaders of our educational and governmental institutions using as a reference point for administrative theory the demands of the military organization and the production line is at least disconcerting.

It seems to me equally clear that defensive leadership is highly inappropriate and perhaps even fundamentally dissonant with another viable side of the world we live in: with education for growth, intimacy, authenticity, humanness, and creativity; with the Judeo-Christian ethics of love, honesty, intimacy, faith, cheekturning, and brotherhood; with a climate for research, inquiry, scholarship, contemplation, and learning; with cooperation, group planning, team building, and various successful forms of group effort; with the new emerging models of industrial organization and manufacturing productivity; with what might be thought of as the behavioral science approach to organizational productivity and organizational change; with the world of ambiguity, feeling, conflict, sorrow, creativity, and diversity; with many new and exciting developments in education, architecture, the creative arts, economics, management, and all phases of modern life; in short, with the world of human beings, with people.

I have deliberately drawn sharp and oversimplified distinctions in a problem area which is very complex and legitimately polemic. It is essential today that those who are administratively responsible for the colleges and universities of America see clearly this conflict and its implications for all facets of American life. It is my observation that much of the dysfunctional disturbance that the papers report daily from the college campuses is created as unintended but inevitable effects of defensive leadership practices among administrators of American colleges.

Let us look at the dynamics of defensive leadership. The major dynamic of the defensive model is fear and distrust. Observations indicate that people who have mild or more serious fears tend to do several things: distrust the people being led; filter the data that are given to the followers and develop strategies for such filtering and programming of data dissemination; attempt to control and manipulate the motivations of the followers; and attempt to control their behavior. The incidence and degree of low trust, strategic, persuasional, and controlling behavior varies directly with the amount of fear. Most of us who are leaders or are placed in leadership roles have varying degrees of fear about our own adequacy, how we are seen by others, the effectiveness of our leadership strategies, the effects of rebellion, the anxieties about insubordination and other unfollowerlike behavior. I guess that our major fear has to do with anxiety about being followed!

The behavior of leaders tends to camouflage, perhaps even to themselves, the underlying fears which support the strategic, manipulative, and controlling behavior. For images of fear on assuming leadership roles one has but to think of the new teacher in the schoolroom, the new mother bringing back her first baby from the hospital, the new lieutenant guiding a patrol into action, or the newly appointed administrative official handling a student riot. The fears that we all have are quelled and softened by various adaptive, self-deceptive, and façade-building mechanisms for presenting ourselves to ourselves and to others.

Some educational leaders are today more fearful than ever. In reaction to student strikes, riots, demonstrations, and protests, as well as to the more normal vicissitudes of campus life, college and university leaders utilize defensive practices that generate unintended byproducts of fear, distrust, hostility, and counter-defensive behavior. The classical models of leadership are time and again proved to be ineffective. Why does defensive leadership arise and persist among educational leaders?

A reciprocal or circular process seems to be operating. Normal fears of life are exacerbated by the ambiguity, high control, and threat of the group or organization. However necessary this ambiguity and control is thought to be, it serves to create fears and hostilities which in turn call forth still more restrictive ambiguity and controlling behavior. This reciprocal fear-distrust cycle sustains the defensive behavior of leadership. The fears accompany and reinforce feelings of inadequacy and self-rejection in leaders and other members of the group or organization.

But the fears, hostilities, and distrusts are so successfully camouflaged in the social defenses that the casual observer might well think the above description of educational life to be strangely out of touch with reality as he sees it. Certainly it is not the conscious intent of educational leaders to create such a state of affairs.

Why is it then that we get in the university so many unintended effects? These unintended effects seem to result from a kind of self-fulfilling prophecy: low-trust, high-fear theories, when put into practice, actually generate distrust and fears that not only confirm the assumptions underlying the theories, but also provide emotional support and strong motivation to continue the low-trust, high-fear behavior. An interactive and self-preserving cycle is thus set in motion, supported in depth by latent fear-distrusts and by rationalized theories which appear to be confirmed. Leadership behavior, thus supported, is exceedingly difficult to change.

Behind the façade of paternalism, politeness, one-big-happy-family-living, heartiness, and the accompanying soft-sell influence and velvet-glove control lie defensive relationships that pervade the colleges. Defensive leadership is characterized by low trust, data distortion, persuasion, and high control. These four aspects of defensive leadership are parallel to four basic dimensions of all group or social behavior: the feeling climate, the flow of data within the system, the formation of goals, and the emergence of control.

The key to defensive leadership is a state of low trust. The defensive leader assumes that the average person cannot be trusted, he is essentially lazy and irresponsible, action must be taken to inspire and motivate him, and he requires supervision and control. The defensive leader can counteract his feelings of inferiority by assuming that his subordinates are less than they actually are; and he can service his hostile feelings by keeping the subordinate in demeaning, dependent, and inferior roles in relation to himself and to leadership as a class.

The defensive leader or administrator rationalizes the service of his needs by developing formal or informal leader theories which both justify and camouflage his fears and hostilities. An essential step in theory and in practice is to manipulate the flow of information and communication within the organization. Information sent down from the top is often deliberately "corrected" to increase morale, to allay fears, to put the best administrative foot forward, and to justify administrative action. "Correction" is achieved by consciously or unconsciously filtering and distorting information to present a good image, to encourage positive thinking, or to build loyalty.

Strategies are devised to improve the administrative image: a worker's name is remembered to make him feel good; a birthday file is kept to demonstrate that the administrator feels the subordinate is important enough to warrant a birthday card. The "good" administrator is especially careful to smile acceptingly at those members of the "family" team towards whom he has temporary or sustained feelings of animosity. Interpersonal cues are thus manipulated and distorted to present a facade of warmth, friendliness, or cohesiveness.

The defensive leader is continually challenged to create new prods, rewards, and gimmicks as the old ones become ineffective. Thus the responsibility for sustaining motivations is thrust upon the administrator or teacher rather than upon the student. The inherent impetus to derive self-satisfaction and self-respect through accomplishment for its own sake becomes atrophied and lost. Self-satisfaction becomes dysfunctional as an incentive system.

The person who is being motivated by others through extrinsic rewards tends either to resist being influenced or to come under the control of the rewarder. He is motivated, not to achieve something, but to gain the approval of the teacher or administrator, to hunt for his satisfactions in status, grade, and social approval rather than to look for his satisfactions *within*, in terms of self-respect, self-approval, and the achievement of personal goals.

Thus the roots of dependence and apathy lie in the reward system, for the person who learns to find his values from without is always at the mercy of other persuaders—teachers, companions, demagogues, groups, or other sources of approval and authority. He becomes dependent, passive, and susceptible to all sorts of external controls.

The reward system may in others foster resistance and rebellion, resentment, cynicism, and a variety of negative and competitive feelings. People who work under competition learn to be competitive, and the extrinsic rewards do not satisfy the deep needs for self-satisfaction and self-respect which are gained by achieving our personal goals as unique individuals.

Both dependency and resistance require controls, and the defensive leader expends a considerable amount of energy devising a variety of controls both for the people and for the processes of the enterprise. The more fearful and anxious he is, the more he feels caught in recurring emergencies and the greater is his need to control. Regulations are put on car-parking, coffee-break duration, channels of reporting, library schedules, methods of work, habits of dress, use of safety devices, more and more complex filing systems, rigid report systems—until all aspects of living in the organization are controlled.

The conscious and official reasons given for the controls usually relate to organization and productive efficiency, but the underlying impulses often spring from, or are reinforced by, the leader's personal needs for rigid order or needs to demonstrate his superiority and strength, express hostility, exercise power, justify his position ("What else would I do if I didn't plan these controls?"), reinforce hierarchy, force people to be orderly or conforming, and keep them in line.

Control systems become functionally autonomous—traditional and conventional elements of the organizational system—and often outlive any practical utility. Indeed, people seem to sense that many regulations actually serve personal needs for punishment or power and bear little relation to the actual needs of the organization itself. In looking at organizations we have often found that many controls are universally violated in the system by common consent. In fact, there is clear indication—and often conscious awareness—that some controls are so dysfunctional that if everyone obeyed them the system would come to a grinding halt.

These defensive techniques of leadership produce certain predictable results. Fear and distrust beget fear and distrust. People who are distrustful tend to see untrustworthy behavior in others. If the relationship between an administrator and his subordinate is basically one of distrust, almost any action on either's part is perceived by the other as untrustworthy. Thus a cycle is created which nurtures self-corroborating leadership hypotheses.

This cycle is well illustrated in connection with communications. Any restriction of the flow of information and any closed strategy arouses energy devoted to circumventing the strategy and fosters counter-strategies that are at least as imaginative and often more effective than the original inducing strategy. A familiar example is the strategy of countering the top brass by distorting the upward-flowing data: feelings of hostility are camouflaged by deferential politeness; reports are "fixed up"; records are doctored or "cooked" to fit administrative goals and directives. Such attempts are augmented by emergency and threat; the greater the fear and distrust, the greater the circumvention, counter-strategy, and counter-distortion.

Defensive leaders use various forms of persuasion to motivate subordinates towards the organization's goals, but often the results are either apathy and passivity or frenetic conformity. Persuasion is a form of control and begets resistance, which may take many subtle forms. Open and aggressive cold war between teachers and administrators, for instance, is an obvious form. More common—and less easy to deal with—is passive, often unconscious resistance such as apathy, apparent obtuseness, dependent demands for further and more minute instructions, bumbling, wheel-spinning, and a whole variety of inefficiences that reduce creative work.

As we have seen, tight control leads to some form of dependency and its accompanying hostility; it may vary from the yes man's de-

ference and conformity to the no man's rebellion against even the most reasonable and normal requests and rules. Deference and rebellion are cut from the same cloth. When unnecessary and arbitrary controls are imposed, or when normal controls are seen as unnecessary or abritary, as is the case when there is fear and distrust, then almost all members of the hierarchy become concerned with their feelings about authority. Most of us are ambivalent toward authority figures, and these mixed feelings are augmented in periods of stress and fear. In tightly controlled, disciplining, and disciplined organizations members demand clarity in rules and in boundary demarcations. But rules can never be made completely clear in practical work situations; boundaries are always permeable and inadequately defined. Thus the demands for further clarification are endless, and controls lead to further controls.

We see how the cycle is set up: hostility and its inevitable counterpart, fear, are increased by the distrust, distortion, persuasion-reward, and control systems of defensive leadership; and the continuing cycle is *reinforced* at all stages, for as fear breeds distrust, distrust is rationalized and structured into theories which sanction distrustful leadership practices. The practices reinforce distrust; now the theorist is justified, and latent motivation to continue the cycle is itself reinforced.

Defensive leadership theories and practices permeate our society. We find them in the home, in school, and in the church, as well as in business organizations. Let us see, for instance, how the child-rearing patterns of our culture fit the picture described above. There are so many frightening things in the world that can harm helpless children. The fearful person can, with little effort, find a variety of frightening aspects in the environment of the child—anything from matches and electric outlets to busy roads and unacceptable playmates. Anxiety makes it easy to exaggerate the number of people ready to kidnap and even rape one's child; the fears of the parent embellish natural dangers and provide nourishment and comforting rationalization for defensive practices.

Communications must be managed for the good of the child. Because he might be worried or upset, emotional and financial discord must be camouflaged and a façade of security and serenity maintained. Children are inexperienced and immature, therefore they cannot be trusted to do things on their own. Moreover, since the natural interests of the child are likely to be frivolous, demeaning, or harmful, he should be carefully guided and persuaded to do what is right—to select appropriate playmates, read good books, and generally adopt goals set by the parental culture or aspirations. To protect the child from ubiquitous dangers and to set his feet on the proper path, parents readily learn to use bribes, praise, and deprivation as tools of coercion. And because children are initially dependent and helpless, it is easy for the fearful parent to prolong the period of dependency.

Schools reinforce these patterns. They receive children whose dependency has been created by defensive parental techniques, and they maintain the dependency by continuing these practices. Having been distrusted, children continue to be untrustworthy. The insecure teacher finds it necessary to maintain a protective façade; she rationalizes her behavior by making a number of low-trust, tight-control assumptions about the children under her tutelage. She builds a changing repertoire of tricks to keep them busy, orderly, neat, attentive, and—she hopes—motivated. Impressed by the awesome culture heritage she is charged to transmit, she feels it imperative that she instill in her pupils the goals, ideals, and rules of the culture. As bodies of knowledge become increasingly standardized, pressures towards indoctrination increase. By codifying rules, regulations, and standards, the teachers build internal control systems—in the classroom, and hopefully, in the children themselves. As part of the informal curriculum, children are taught façade-building; they are encouraged to put the best foot forward, to be polite, to be decorous, and to adopt the essentially hypocritical social graces of the dominant middle class.

What is the alternative to defensive leadership? This is not as easy to specify. The key to emergent leadership centers in a high degree of trust and confidence in people. Leaders who trust their colleagues and subordinates and have confidence in them tend to be open and frank, to be permissive in goal setting, and to be noncontrolling in personal style and leadership policy. People with a great deal of self-acceptance and personal security do trust others, do make trust assumptions about their motives and behavior. The self-adequate person tends to assume that others are also adequate and, other things being equal, that they will be responsible, loyal, appropriately work-oriented when work is to be performed, and adequate to carry out jobs that are commensurate with their levels of experience and growth.

Just as we saw that distrust arises from fear and hostility, so we can see that people with little fear and minimal needs to be hostile are ready to trust others. Of course, there is some risk in trusting others, in being open and freedom-giving.

People naturally tend to share their feelings and concerns with those whom they trust, and this is true at the simplest and most direct level of interpersonal relationships as well as at more complex levels of organizational communication. Thus a high-trust system may institute open planning meetings and evaluation meetings; public criteria for promotion; easily available information on salaries, cost figures, and budgets; and easy access to material in the files. There is comparatively little concern with public relations, with the corporate or family image, or with communications programs. Communication in such a system is a *process* rather than a program.

The participative leader is permissive in his relations with subordinates, for he assumes that as people grow they learn to assess their own aptitudes, discover their deep-lying interests, and develop their basic potentials.

Therefore he gives his subordinates every opportunity to maximize self-determination and self-assessment, to verbalize their goals, to try new jobs or enlarge the scope of the work they are doing, and he trusts them to make mature judgments about job assignments. Where he is dealing with a work-team or a group, he lets the group make decisions about job allotments and work assignments.

This process of allowing people to be responsible for their own destinies, for setting their own targets, assessing their own development needs, searching out resources to aid in job accomplishment, and participating in setting organizational objectives is basic to high-trust leadership. Instead of using conventional defensive-leadership techniques of skilled persuasion to induce acceptance of leadership goals, the high-trust administration participates in cooperative determination of goals and in cooperative definition of production and staff problems. He knows that goal-formation is a significant skill that must be learned, and that to develop such skill students and adults must exercise a variety of opportunities to make decisions, explore goals, and experiment with many kinds of activities.

The participative administrator joins in creating a climate in which he has no need to impose controls. He knows that in a healthy group controls emerge from group processes as the need is perceived. Then controls are mediated by group or organization objectives and by such relevant data as deadlines and target dates. People or groups who have set their own objectives and have clearly stated their own goals build internal tension-systems which maintain goal orientation and create appropriate boundaries.

Formal and written rules about such things as work space, library use, and stockroom neatness are less and less necessary when people are engaged in a common task with others whose feelings and perceptions they freely share; when there is trust and mutuality, people are inclined to respect the rights and concerns of fellow members. This principle applies to large and small systems alike——in either, the participative administrator reduces as far as practicable all formal controls evidenced by rules, regulations, written memoranda, signs, formal job specification sheets, rigid lines of responsibility and authority, and the like.

The effects of participative leading are diametrically contrary to those of defensive leading. Love begets love. Respect begets respect. Trust produces trust. People who are trusted tend to trust themselves and to trust those in positions of responsibility. Moreover, the feeling that one is trusted encourages exploration, diversity, and innovation, for the person spends little time and energy trying to prove himself. His time and energy are freed to define and solve problems, accomplish work, and create new dimensions of his job. A fearful person uses a great deal of energy in defending himself against present or anticipated threat or attack; a confident and self-assured person can direct his energy towards goals that are significant to him as a person.

Again, openness begets openness. In the long run, at least, one who freely shares data, whether of feelings or of figures, reduces fear and distrust in himself and in others. Defensive administrators build massive communication programs, not to disseminate objective information but to mold attitudes, create favorable and appropriate images, and influence people. Such persuasional and distortive communication produces resistance. Direct and open flow of information, on the other hand, serves to create an atmosphere which encourages people to share information with those above as well as with those below.

In general, openness and information giving improves the decision-making process, for experience in giving information and expressing feelings enhances consensus; and the more nearly a group can reach consensus on operational issues, the higher the quality of the decision and the greater the group's commitment to the program.

Moreover, participative goal-formation optimizes self-determination and self-assessment. Intrinsic motivations become increasingly relevant and powerful. People explore their own capacities and interests, and try to find or create work for themselves that is satisfying and fulfilling. They enlarge their own jobs, asking for more responsibility and more creative and interesting work. Such work is fulfilling to the person, and extrinsic rewards are secondary to satisfaction in accomplishing the task. Administrators find that people like to work; they "own" their jobs and feel great loyalty and responsibility toward the common goals of the group. People feel little need to escape from the work situation, and the "thank goodness it's Friday" clubs become less enticing. Concerns over salary and merit increases are symptomatic of defensive-leading pressures.

Participative administration creates interdependence and diminishes the problem of authority. For instance, work is allocated by consensus—people assess their abilities and select or create appropriate tasks. Where there is interdependence, conflict and disagreement are openly expressed and can thus be resolved and integrated into productive work. Where people feel they are working together for a common goal, the organization of work can be flexible, diverse, and informal, with a minimum of written job boundaries and rigid role requirements. Channels of communication are free, open, and spontaneous.

The attainment of emergent leadership on the college campus is a developmental task of awesome proportion. If the above analysis of the leadership problem has some validity, then it is clear where some responsibilities lie.

These concepts particularly are a challenge to the university. The Ohio State studies, particularly, showed how far behind even the military and industry the university administration is in achieving some kind of more participative and less authoritarian administrative relationships. The headlines today are filled with conflicts. The university is in many ways more susceptible to the pressures which produce fear than is industry, government, or business. The university is at one and the same time vulnerable to attacks from public opinion and also historically inviolate. The products of the university are highly intangible, and it is diffi-

cult to apply vigorous controls to the product and to tell if the university is successful in the same way that a business or even the military is with its hard criteria for productivity, profit, or victory. Thus highly vulnerable, the university has preserved a historical isolation from social pressures; and administrative behavior is often strangely medieval and out of touch with the vigorous demands of democratic growth. The university, strangely, is sometimes a citadel for autocratic administrative behavior.

I should say a word about the implications of this model for ethical behavior. In abstract, this model of leadership specifies a theory of ethics. That behavior is more ethical when it is most trusting, most open, most self-determining, and most interdependent. Thus one would look in the university setting for unethical or moral behavior in the areas of distrust, strategic filtering of feelings and ideas (honesty), manipulative abridgement of self-determination, and dependency-producing or rebellion-producing high control behavior.

It seems to me that joint, interdependent, and shared planning is the central concept of the kind of participative, consultative leadership that we are considering. Planning, to be moral, in this framework, to be efficient, and to be growth-producing must be organic to the institution, involve to an optimal degree all of the participants, and must be done interdependently. It is easy to find illustrations on the university campus of buildings in architectural styles that are unrelated to experimental learning theory, fund-raising methods that are planned by a special group of people who are usually collecting funds in ways that would be anathema to other members of the college community, athletic programs that arise from financial need rather than from educational policy, personnel practices that are inherited unabashedly from business institutions that have aims that are incommensurate with university goals, and many other illustrations where planning is a fragmentary, emergency process engaged in by small groups of people who are often out of touch with the university as a community.

Our assumption is that the blocks to innovation and creativity are fear, poor communication, imposition of motivations, and the dependency-rebellion syndrome of forces. People are innovative and creative. The administration of innovation involves freeing the creativity that is always present. The administrative problem of innovation is to remove fear and increase trust, to remove strategic and distortional blocks to open communication, to remove the tight controls on behavior that tend to channel creative efforts into circumvention, counter-strategy, and organizational survival rather than into innovative and creative problem-solving.

Valid, direct, and open communication among all segments of the organic institution is a central process of effective leadership in the model we are examining. Effective leadership grows with communication in depth. Effective leadership is hampered by all forces which inhibit or restrain communication in depth. If emergent or participative leadership were prevalent on the campus, communication programs would become less and less necessary. Defensive administration breeds the conditions that require an increasing escalation of massive communication programs to hopefully alleviate the conditions produced by the defensive leadership.

We are attempting to *become* as a people and as culture. We are in the process of discovering and creating models of interdependent, high trust, self-determining, and open behavior. We are trying to create an interdependent, achieving, free, becoming culture. This has never before been done in the world, and the strains of transition are awesome and somewhat frightening. But for those of us who are dedicated to the university as a way of life, the challenge to the college and university administrator and leader is clear. The challenge is there. The road is unclear. The goal is at one and the same time the preservation of certain concepts we hold dear and the achievement of a more free, a more open, a more self-determining, and a more human environment for learning and growth.

25.

THE SCIENCE OF MUDDLING THROUGH

CHARLES E. LINDBLOM

Suppose an administrator is given responsibility for formulating policy with respect to inflation. He might start by trying to list all related values in order of importance, e.g., full employment, reasonable business profit, protection of small savings, prevention of a stock market crash. Then all possible policy outcomes could be rated as more or less efficient in attaining a maximum of these values. This would of course require a prodigious inquiry into values held by members of society and an equally prodigious set of calculations on how much of each value is equal to how much of each other value. He could then proceed to outline all possible policy alternatives. In a third step, he would undertake systematic comparison of his multitude of alternatives to determine which attains the greatest amount of values.

In comparing policies, he would take advantage of any theory available that generalized about classes of policies. In considering inflation, for example, he would compare all policies in the light of the theory of prices. Since no alternatives are beyond his investigation, he would consider strict central control and the abolition of all prices and markets on the one hand and elimination of all public controls with reliance completely on the free market on the other, both in the light of whatever theoretical generalizations he could find on such hypothetical economies.

From Charles E. Lindblom, "The Science of Muddling Through," *Public Administration Review*, 19:79–88, 1959. Reprinted by permission of the American Society for Public Administration.

Finally, he would try to make the choice that would in fact maximize his values.

An alternative line of attack would be to set as his principal objective, either explicitly or without conscious thought, the relatively simple goal of keeping prices level. This objective might be compromised or complicated by only a few other goals, such as full employment. He would in fact disregard most other social values as beyond his present interest, and he would for the moment not even attempt to rank the few values that he regarded as immediately relevant. Were he pressed, he would quickly admit that he was ignoring many related values and many possible important consequences of his policies.

As a second step, he would outline those relatively few policy alternatives that occurred to him. He would then compare them. In comparing his limited number of alternatives, most of them familiar from past controversies, he would not ordinarily find a body of theory precise enough to carry him through a comparison of their respective consequences. Instead he would rely heavily on the record of past experience with small policy steps to predict the consequences of similar steps extended into the future.

Moreover, he would find that the policy alternatives combined objectives or values in different ways. For example, one policy might offer price level stability at the cost of some risk of unemployment; another might offer less price stability but also less risk of unemployment. Hence, the next step in his approach—the final selection—would combine into one the choice among values and the choice among instruments for reaching values. It would not, as in the first method of policy-making, approximate a more mechanical process of choosing the means that best satisfied goals that were previously clarified and ranked. Because practitioners of the second approach expect to achieve their goals only partially, they would expect to repeat endlessly the sequence just described, as conditions and aspirations changed and as accuracy of prediction improved.

BY ROOT OR BY BRANCH

For complex problems, the first of these two approaches is of course impossible. Although such an approach can be described, it cannot be practiced except for relatively simple problems and even then only in a somewhat modified form. It assumes intellectual capacities and sources of information that men simply do not possess, and it is even more absurd as an approach to policy when the time and money that can be allocated to a policy problem is limited, as is always the case. Of particular importance to public administrators is the fact that public agencies are in effect usually instructed not to practice the first method. That is to say, their prescribed functions and constraints—the politically or legally possible —restrict their attention to relatively few values and relatively few alternative policies among the countless alternatives that might be imagined. It is the second method that is practiced.

Curiously, however, the literatures of decision-making, policy formulation, planning, and public administration formalize the first approach rather than the second, leaving public administrators who handle complex decisions in the position of practicing what few preach. For emphasis I run some risk of overstatement. True enough, the literature is well aware of limits on man's capacities and of the inevitability that policies will be approached in some such style as the second. But attempts to formalize rational policy formulation—to lay out explicitly the necessary steps in the process—usually describe the first approach and not the second.[1]

The common tendency to describe policy formulation even for complex problems as though it followed the first approach has been strengthened by the attention given to, and successes enjoyed by, operations research, statistical decision theory, and systems analysis. The hallmarks of these procedures, typical of the first approach, are clarity of objective, explicitness of evaluation, a high degree of comprehensiveness of overview, and wherever possible, quantification of values for mathematical analysis. But these advanced procedures remain largely the appropriate techniques of relatively small-scale problem-solving where the total number of variables to be considered is small and value problems restricted. Charles Hitch, head of the Economics Division of RAND Corporation, one of the leading centers for application of these techniques, has written:

> I would make the empirical generalization from my experience at RAND and elsewhere that operations research is the art of suboptimizing, i.e., of solving some lower-level problems, and that difficulties increase and our special competence diminishes by an order of magnitude with every level of decision making we attempt to ascend. The sort of simple explicit model which operations researchers are so proficient in using can certainly reflect most of the significant factors influencing traffic control on the George Washington Bridge, but the proportion of the relevant reality which we can represent by any such model or models in studying, say, a major foreign-policy decision, appears to be almost trivial.[2]

Accordingly, I propose in this paper to clarify and formalize the second method, much neglected in the literature. This might be described as the method of *successive limited comparisons*. I will contrast it with the first approach, which might be called the rational-comprehensive method.[3] More impressionistically and briefly—and therefore generally used in this article—they could be characterized as the branch method and root method, the former continually building out from the current situation, step-by-step and by small degrees; the latter starting from fundamentals anew each time, building on the past only as experience is embodied in a theory, and always prepared to start completely from the ground up.

Let us put the characteristics of the two methods side by side in simplest terms.

Rational-comprehensive (root)	Successive limited comparisons (branch)
1a. Clarification of values or objectives distinct from and usually prerequisite to empirical analysis of alternative policies.	1b. Selection of value goals and empirical analysis of the needed action are not distinct from one another but are closely intertwined.
2a. Policy-formulation is therefore approached through means-end analysis: First the ends are isolated, then the means to achieve them are sought.	2b. Since means and ends are not distinct, means-end analysis is often inappropriate or limited.
3a. The test of a "good" policy is that it can be shown to be the most appropriate means to desired ends.	3b. The test of a "good" policy is typically that various analysts find themselves directly agreeing on a policy (without their agreeing that it is the most appropriate means to an agreed objective).
4a. Analysis is comprehensive; every important relevant factor is taken into account.	4b. Analysis is drastically limited: i) Important possible outcomes are neglected. ii) Important alternative potential policies are neglected. iii) Important affected values are neglected.
5a. Theory is often heavily relied upon.	5b. A succession of comparisons greatly reduces or eliminates reliance on theory.

Assuming that the root method is familiar and understandable, we proceed directly to clarification of its alternative by contrast. In explaining the second, we shall be describing how most administrators do in fact approach complex questions, for the root method, the "best" way as a blueprint or model, is in fact not workable for complex policy questions, and administrators are forced to use the method of successive limited comparisons.

INTERTWINING EVALUATION AND EMPIRICAL ANALYSIS (1b)

The quickest way to understand how values are handled in the method of successive limited comparisons is to see how the root method often breaks down in its handling of values or objectives. The idea that values should be clarified, and in advance of the examination of alternative policies, is appealing. But what happens when we attempt it for complex social problems? The first difficulty is that on many critical values or objectives, citizens disagree, congressmen disagree, and public administrators disagree. Even where a fairly specific objective is prescribed for the administrator, there remains considerable room for disagreement on sub-objectives. Consider, for example, the conflict with respect to locating public housing, described in Meyerson and Banfield's study of the Chicago Housing Authority[4]—disagreement which occurred despite the clear objective of providing a certain number of public housing units in the city. Similarly conflicting are objectives in highway location, traffic control, minimum wage administration, development of tourist facilities in national parks, or insect control.

Administrators cannot escape these conflicts by ascertaining the majority's preference, for preferences have not been registered on most issues; indeed, there often *are* no preferences in the absence of public discussion sufficient to bring an issue to the attention of the electorate. Furthermore, there is a question of whether intensity of feeling should be considered as well as the number of persons preferring each alternative. By the impossibility of doing otherwise, administrators often are reduced to deciding policy without clarifying objectives first.

Even when an administrator resolves to follow his own values as a criterion for decisions, he often will not know how to rank them when they conflict with one another, as they usually do. Suppose, for example, that an administrator must relocate tenants living in tenements scheduled for destruction. One objective is to empty the buildings fairly promptly, another is to find suitable accommodation for persons displaced, another is to avoid friction with residents in other areas in which a large influx would be unwelcome, another is to deal with all concerned through persuasion if possible, and so on.

How does one state even to himself the relative importance of these partially conflicting values? A simple ranking of them is not enough; one needs ideally to know how much of one value is worth sacrificing for some of another value. The answer is that typically the administrator chooses—and must choose—directly among policies in which these values are combined in different ways. He cannot first clarify his values and then choose among policies.

A more subtle third point underlies both the first two. Social objectives do not always have the same relative values. One objective may be highly prized in one circumstance, another in another circumstance. If, for example, an ad-

ministrator values highly both the dispatch with which his agency can carry through its projects *and* good public relations, it matters little which of the two possibly conflicting values he favors in some abstract or general sense. Policy questions arise in forms which put to administrators such a question as: Given the degree to which we are or are not already achieving the values of dispatch and the values of good public relations, is it worth sacrificing a little speed for a happier clientele, or is it better to risk offending the clientele so that we can get on with our work? The answer to such a question varies with circumstances.

The value problem is, as the example shows, always a problem of adjustments at a margin. But there is no practicable way to state marginal objectives or values except in terms of particular policies. That one value is preferred to another in one decision situation does not mean that it will be preferred in another decision situation in which it can be had only at great sacrifice of another value. Attempts to rank or order values in general and abstract terms so that they do not shift from decision to decision end up by ignoring the relevant marginal preferences. The significance of this third point thus goes very far. Even if all administrators had at hand an agreed set of values, objectives, and constraints, and an agreed ranking of these values, objectives, and constraints, their marginal values in actual choice situations would be impossible to formulate.

Unable consequently to formulate the relevant values first and then choose among policies to achieve them, administrators must choose directly among alternative policies that offer different marginal combinations of values. Somewhat paradoxically, the only practicable way to disclose one's relevant marginal values even to oneself is to describe the policy one chooses to achieve them. Except roughly and vaguely, I know of no way to describe—or even to understand—what my relative evaluations are for, say, freedom and security, speed and accuracy in governmental decisions, or low taxes and better schools than to describe my preferences among specific policy choices that might be made between the alternatives in each of the pairs.

In summary, two aspects of the process by which values are actually handled can be distinguished. The first is clear: evaluation and empirical analysis are intertwined; that is, one chooses among values and among policies at one and the same time. Put a little more elaborately, one simultaneously chooses a policy to attain certain objectives and chooses the objectives themselves. The second aspect is related but distinct: the administrator focuses his attention on marginal or incremental values. Whether he is aware of it or not, he does not find general formulations of objectives very helpful and in fact makes specific marginal or incremental comparisons. Two policies, X and Y, confront him. Both promise the same degree of attainment of objectives *a, b, c, d,* and *e.* But X promises him somewhat more of *f* than does Y, while Y promises him somewhat more of *g* than does X. In choosing between them, he is in fact offered the alternative of a marginal or incremental amount of *f* at the expense of a marginal or incremental amount of *g.* The only values that are relevant to his choice are these increments by which the two policies differ; and, when he finally chooses between the two marginal values, he does so by making a choice between policies.[5]

As to whether the attempt to clarify objectives in advance of policy selection is more or less rational than the close intertwining of marginal evaluation and empirical analysis, the principal difference established is that for complex problems the first is impossible and irrelevant, and the second is both possible and relevant. The second is possible because the administrator need not try to analyze any values except the values by which alternative policies differ and need not be concerned with them except as they differ marginally. His need for information on values or objectives is drastically reduced as compared with the root method; and his capacity for grasping, com-

prehending, and relating values to one another is not strained beyond the breaking point.

RELATIONS BETWEEN MEANS AND ENDS (2b)

Decision-making is ordinarily formalized as a means-ends relationship: means are conceived to be evaluated and chosen in the light of ends finally selected independently of and prior to the choice of means. This is the means-ends relationship of the root method. But it follows from all that has just been said that such a means-ends relationship is possible only to the extent that values are agreed upon, are reconcilable, and are stable at the margin. Typically, therefore, such a means-ends relationship is absent from the branch method, where means and ends are simultaneously chosen.

Yet any departure from the means-ends relationship of the root method will strike some readers as inconceivable. For it will appear to them that only in such a relationship is it possible to determine whether one policy choice is better or worse than another. How can an administrator know whether he has made a wise or foolish decision if he is without prior values or objectives by which to judge his decisions? The answer to this question calls up the third distinctive difference between root and branch methods: how to decide the best policy.

THE TEST OF "GOOD" POLICY (3b)

In the root method, a decision is "correct," "good," or "rational" if it can be shown to attain some specified objective, where the objective can be specified without simply describing the decision itself. Where objectives are defined only through the marginal or incremental approach to values described above, it is still sometimes possible to test whether a policy does in fact attain the desired objectives; but a precise statement of the objectives takes the form of a description of the policy chosen or some alternative to it. To show that a policy is mistaken one cannot offer an abstract argument that important objectives are not achieved; one must instead argue that another policy is more to be preferred.

So far, the departure from customary ways of looking at problem-solving is not troublesome, for many administrators will be quick to agree that the most effective discussion of the correctness of policy does take the form of comparison with other policies that might have been chosen. But what of the situation in which administrators cannot agree on values or objectives, either abstractly or in marginal terms? What then is the test of "good" policy? For the root method, there is no test. Agreement on objectives failing, there is no standard of "correctness." For the method of successive limited comparisons, the test is agreement on policy itself, which remains possible even when agreement on values is not.

It has been suggested that continuing agreement in Congress on the desirability of extending old age insurance stems from liberal desires to strengthen the welfare programs of the federal government and from conservative desires to reduce union demands for private pension plans. If so, this is an excellent demonstration of the ease with which individuals of different ideologies often can agree on concrete policy. Labor mediators report a similar phenomenon: the contestants cannot agree on criteria for settling their disputes but can agree on specific proposals. Similarly, when one administrator's objective turns out to be another's means, they often can agree on policy.

Agreement on policy thus becomes the only practicable test of the policy's correctness. And for one administrator to seek to win the other over to agreement on ends as well would accomplish nothing and create quite unnecessary controversy.

If agreement directly on policy as a test for "best" policy seems a poor substitute for test-ing the policy against its objectives, it ought to be remembered that objectives themselves have no ultimate validity other than they are agreed upon. Hence agreement is the test of "best" policy in both methods. But where the root method requires agreement on what elements in the decision constitute objectives and on which of these objectives should be sought, the branch method falls back on agreement wherever it can be found.

In an important sense, therefore, it is not irrational for an administrator to defend a policy as good without being able to specify what it is good for.

NON-COMPREHENSIVE ANALYSIS (4b)

Ideally, rational-comprehensive analysis leaves out nothing important. But it is impossible to take everything important into consideration unless "important" is so narrowly defined that analysis is in fact quite limited. Limits on human intellectual capacities and on available information set definite limits to man's capacity to be comprehensive. In actual fact, therefore, no one can practice the rational-comprehensive method for really complex problems, and every administrator faced with a sufficiently complex problem must find ways drastically to simplify.

An administrator assisting in the formulation of agricultural economic policy cannot in the first place be competent on all possible policies. He cannot even comprehend one policy entirely. In planning a soil bank program, he cannot successfully anticipate the impact of higher or lower farm income on, say, urbanization—the possible consequent loosening of family ties, possible consequent eventual need for revisions in social security and further implications for tax problems arising out of new federal responsibilities for social security and municipal responsibilities for urban services. Nor, to follow another line of repercussions, can he work through the soil bank program's effects on prices for agricultural products in foreign markets and consequent implications for foreign relations, including those arising out of economic rivalry between the United States and the U.S.S.R.

In the method of successive limited comparisons, simplification is systematically achieved in two principal ways. First, it is achieved through limitation of policy comparisons to those policies that differ in relatively small degree from policies presently in effect. Such a limitation immediately reduces the number of alternatives to be investigated and also drastically simplifies the character of the investigation of each. For it is not necessary to undertake fundamental inquiry into an alternative and its consequences; it is necessary only to study those respects in which the proposed alternative and its consequences differ from the status quo. The empirical comparison of marginal differences among alternative policies that differ only marginally is, of course, a counterpart of the incremental or marginal comparison of values discussed above.[6]

Relevance as well as realism

It is a matter of common observation that in Western democracies public administrators and policy analysts in general do largely limit their analyses to incremental or marginal differences in policies that are chosen to differ only incrementally. They do not do so, however, solely because they desperately need some way to simplify their problems; they also do so in order to be relevant. Democracies change their policies almost entirely through incremental adjustments. Policy does not move in leaps and bounds.

The incremental character of political change in the United States has often been remarked. The two major political parties agree on fundamentals; they offer alternative policies to the voters only on relatively small points of difference. Both parties favor full employment, but they define it somewhat differently; both favor the development of water power resources, but in slightly different ways; and both favor unemployment compensation, but not the same

level of benefits. Similarly, shifts of policy within a party take place largely through a series of relatively small changes, as can be seen in their only gradual acceptance of the idea of governmental responsibility for support of the unemployed, a change in party positions beginning in the early 30's and culminating in a sense in the Employment Act of 1946.

Party behavior is in turn rooted in public attitudes, and political theorists cannot conceive of democracy's surviving in the United States in the absence of fundamental agreement on potentially disruptive issues, with consequent limitation of policy debates to relatively small differences in policy.

Since the policies ignored by the administrator are politically impossible and so irrelevant, the simplification of analysis achieved by concentrating on policies that differ only incrementally is not a capricious kind of simplification. In addition, it can be argued that, given the limits on knowledge within which policy-makers are confined, simplifying by limiting the focus to small variations from present policy makes the most of available knowledge. Because policies being considered are like present and past policies, the administrator can obtain information and claim some insight. Non-incremental policy proposals are therefore typically not only politically irrelevant but also unpredictable in their consequences.

The second method of simplification of analysis is the practice of ignoring important possible consequences of possible policies, as well as the values attached to the neglected consequences. If this appears to disclose a shocking shortcoming of successive limited comparisons, it can be replied that, even if the exclusions are random, policies may nevertheless be more intelligently formulated than through futile attempts to achieve a comprehensiveness beyond human capacity. Actually, however, the exclusions, seeming arbitrary or random from one point of view, need be neither.

Achieving a degree of comprehensiveness

Suppose that each value neglected by one policy-making agency were a major concern of at least one other agency. In that case, a helpful division of labor would be achieved, and no agency need find its task beyond its capacities. The shortcomings of such a system would be that one agency might destroy a value either before another agency could be activated to safeguard it or in spite of another agency's efforts. But the possibility that important values may be lost is present in any form of organization, even where agencies attempt to comprehend in planning more than is humanly possible.

The virtue of such a hypothetical division of labor is that every important interest or value has its watchdog. And these watchdogs can protect the interests in their jurisdiction in two quite different ways: first, by redressing damages done by other agencies; and, second, by anticipating and heading off injury before it occurs.

In a society like that of the United States in which individuals are free to combine to pursue almost any possible common interest they might have and in which government agencies are sensitive to the pressures of these groups, the system described is approximated. Almost every interest has its watchdog. Without claiming that every interest has a sufficiently powerful watchdog, it can be argued that our system often can assure a more comprehensive regard for the values of the whole society than any attempt at intellectual comprehensiveness.

In the United States, for example, no part of government attempts a comprehensive overview of policy on income distribution. A policy nevertheless evolves, and one responding to a wide variety of interests. A process of mutual adjustment among farm groups, labor unions, municipalities and school boards, tax authorities, and government agencies with responsibilities in the fields of housing, health, highways, national parks, fire, and police accomplishes a distribution of income in which particular income problems neglected at one point in the decision processes become central at another point.

Mutual adjustment is more pervasive than the explicit forms it takes in negotiation between groups; it persists through the mutual impacts of groups upon each other even where they are not in communication. For all the imperfections and latent dangers in this ubiquitous process of mutual adjustment, it will often accomplish an adaptation of policies to a wider range of interests than could be done by one group centrally.

Note, too, how the incremental pattern of policy-making fits with the multiple pressure pattern. For when decisions are only incremental—closely related to known policies, it is easier for one group to anticipate the kind of moves another might make and easier too for it to make correction for injury already accomplished.[7]

Even partisanship and narrowness, to use pejorative terms, will sometimes be assets to rational decision-making, for they can doubly insure that what one agency neglects, another will not; they specialize personnel to distinct points of view. The claim is valid that effective rational coordination of the federal administration, if possible to achieve at all, would require an agreed set of values[8]—if "rational" is defined as the practice of the root method of decision-making. But a high degree of administrative coordination occurs as each agency adjusts its policies to the concerns of the other agencies in the process of fragmented decision-making I have just described.

For all the apparent shortcomings of the incremental approach to policy alternatives with its arbitrary exclusion coupled with fragmentation, when compared to the root method, the branch method often looks far superior. In the root method, the inevitable exclusion of factors is accidental, unsystematic, and not defensible by any argument so far developed, while in the branch method the exclusions are deliberate, systematic, and defensible. Ideally, of course, the root method does not exclude; in practice it must.

Nor does the branch method necessarily

neglect long-run considerations and objectives. It is clear that important values must be omitted in considering policy, and sometimes the only way long-run objectives can be given adequate attention is through the neglect of short-run considerations. But the values omitted can be either long-run or short-run.

SUCCESSION OF COMPARISONS (5b)

The final distinctive element in the branch method is that the comparisons, together with the policy choice, proceed in a chronological series. Policy is not made once and for all; it is made and re-made endlessly. Policy-making is a process of successive approximation to some desired objectives in which what is desired itself continues to change under reconsideration.

Making policy is at best a very rough process. Neither social scientists, nor politicians, nor public administrators yet know enough about the social world to avoid repeated error in predicting the consequences of policy moves. A wise policy-maker consequently expects that his policies will achieve only part of what he hopes and at the same time will produce unanticipated consequences he would have preferred to avoid. If he proceeds through a *succession* of incremental changes, he avoids serious lasting mistakes in several ways.

In the first place, past sequences of policy steps have given him knowledge about the probable consequences of further similar steps. Second, he need not attempt big jumps toward his goals that would require predictions beyond his or anyone else's knowledge, because he never expects his policy to be a final resolution of a problem. His decision is only one step, one that if successful can quickly be followed by another. Third, he is in effect able to test his previous predictions as he moves on to each further step. Lastly, he often can remedy a past error fairly quickly—more quickly than if policy proceeded through more distinct steps widely spaced in time.

Compare this comparative analysis of incre-

mental changes with the aspiration to employ theory in the root method. Man cannot think without classifying, without subsuming one experience under a more general category of experiences. The attempt to push categorization as far as possible and to find general propositions which can be applied to specific situations is what I refer to with the word "theory." Where root analysis often leans heavily on theory in this sense, the branch method does not.

The assumption of root analysis is that theory is the most systematic and economical way to bring relevant knowledge to bear on a specific problem. Granting the assumption, an unhappy fact is that we do not have adequate theory to apply to problems in any policy area, although theory is more adequate in some areas—monetary policy, for example—than in others. Comparative analysis, as in the branch method, is sometimes a systematic alternative to theory.

Suppose an administrator must choose among a small group of policies that differ only incrementally from each other and from present policy. He might aspire to "understand" each of the alternatives—for example, to know all the consequences of each aspect of each policy. If so, he would indeed require theory. In fact, however, he would usually decide that, *for policy-making purposes*, he need know, as explained above, only the consequences of each of those aspects of the policies in which they differed from one another. For this much more modest aspiration, he requires no theory (although it might be helpful, if available), for he can proceed to isolate probable differences by examining the differences in consequences associated with past differences in policies, a feasible program because he can take his observations from a long sequence of incremental changes.

For example, without a more comprehensive social theory about juvenile delinquency than scholars have yet produced, one cannot possibly understand the ways in which a variety of public policies—say on education, housing, recreation, employment, race relations, and policing—might encourage or discourage delinquency. And one needs such an understanding if he undertakes the comprehensive overview of the problem prescribed in the models of the root method. If, however, one merely wants to mobilize knowledge sufficient to assist in a choice among a small group of similar policies—alternative policies on juvenile court procedures, for example—he can do so by comparative analysis of the results of similar past policy moves.

THEORISTS AND PRACTITIONERS

This difference explains—in some cases at least—why the administrator often feels that the outside expert or academic problem-solver is sometimes not helpful and why they in turn often urge more theory on him. And it explains why an administrator often feels more confident when "flying by the seat of his pants" than when following the advice of theorists. Theorists often ask the administrator to go the long way round to the solution of his problems, in effect ask him to follow the best canons of the scientific method, when the administrator knows that the best available theory will work less well than more modest incremental comparisons. Theorists do not realize that the administrator is often in fact practicing a systematic method. It would be foolish to push this explanation too far, for sometimes practical decision-makers are pursuing neither a theoretical approach nor successive comparisons, nor any other systematic method.

It may be worth emphasizing that theory is sometimes of extremely limited helpfulness in policy-making for at least two rather different reasons. It is greedy for facts; it can be constructed only through a great collection of observations. And it is typically insufficiently precise for application to a policy process that moves through small changes. In contrast, the comparative method both economizes on the need for facts and directs the analyst's attention to just those facts that are relevant to the fine choices faced by the decision-maker.

With respect to precision of theory, economic theory serves as an example. It predicts that an economy without money or prices would in certain specified ways misallocate resources, but this finding pertains to an alternative far removed from the kind of policies on which administrators need help. On the other hand, it is not precise enough to predict the consequences of policies restricting business mergers, and this is the kind of issue on which the administrators need help. Only in relatively restricted areas does economic theory achieve sufficient precision to go far in resolving policy questions; its helpfulness in policy-making is always so limited that it requires supplementation through comparative analysis.

SUCCESSIVE COMPARISON AS A SYSTEM

Successive limited comparisons is, then, indeed a method or system; it is not a failure of method for which administrators ought to apologize. None the less, its imperfections, which have not been explored in this paper, are many. For example, the method is without a built-in safeguard for all relevant values, and it also may lead the decision-maker to overlook excellent policies for no other reason than that they are not suggested by the chain of successive policy steps leading up to the present. Hence, it ought to be said that under this method, as well as under some of the most sophisticated variants of the root method—operations research, for example—policies will continue to be as foolish as they are wise.

Why then bother to describe the method in all the above detail? Because it is in fact a common method of policy formulation, and is, for complex problems, the principal reliance of administrators as well as of other policy analysts.[9] And because it will be superior to any other decision-making method available for complex problems in many circumstances, certainly superior to a futile attempt at superhuman comprehensiveness. The reaction of the public administrator to the exposition of method doubtless will be less a discovery of a new method than a better acquaintance with an old. But by becoming more conscious of their practice of this method, administrators might practice it with more skill and know when to extend or constrict its use. (That they sometimes practice it effectively and sometimes not may explain the extremes of opinion on "muddling through," which is both praised as a highly sophisticated form of problem-solving and denounced as no method at all. For I suspect that in so far as there is a system in what is known as "muddling through," this method is it.)

One of the noteworthy incidental consequences of clarification of the method is the light it throws on the suspicion an administrator sometimes entertains that a consultant or adviser is not speaking relevantly and responsibly when in fact by all ordinary objective evidence he is. The trouble lies in the fact that most of us approach policy problems within a framework given by our view of a chain of successive policy choices made up to the present. One's thinking about appropriate policies with respect, say, to urban traffic control is greatly influenced by one's knowledge of the incremental steps taken up to the present. An administrator enjoys an intimate knowledge of his past sequences that "outsiders" do not share, and his thinking and that of the "outsider" will consequently be different in ways that may puzzle both. Both may appear to be talking intelligently, yet each may find the other unsatisfactory. The relevance of the policy chain of succession is even more clear when an American tries to discuss, say, antitrust policy with a Swiss, for the chains of policy in the two countries are strikingly different and the two individuals consequently have organized their knowledge in quite different ways.

If this phenomenon is a barrier to communication, an understanding of it promises an enrichment of intellectual interaction in policy formulation. Once the source of difference is understood, it will sometimes be stimulating for an administrator to seek out a policy analyst whose recent experience is with a policy chain different from his own.

This raises again a question only briefly discussed above on the merits of like-mindedness among government administrators. While much of organization theory argues the virtues of common values and agreed organizational objectives, for complex problems in which the root method is inapplicable, agencies will want among their own personnel two types of diversification: administrators whose thinking is organized by reference to policy chains other than those familiar to most members of the organization and, even more commonly, administrators whose professional or personal values or interests create diversity of view (perhaps coming from different specialties, social classes, geographical areas) so that, even within a single agency, decision-making can be fragmented and parts of the agency can serve as watchdogs for other parts.

NOTES

[1] James G. March and Herbert A. Simon similarly characterize the literature. They also take some important steps, as have Simon's recent articles, to describe a less heroic model of policy-making. See *Organizations* (John Wiley and Sons, 1958), p. 137.

[2] "Operations Research and National Planning—A Dissent," 5 *Operations Research* 718 (October, 1957). Hitch's dissent is from particular points made in the article to which his paper is a reply; his claim that operations research is for low-level problems is widely accepted.

For examples of the kind of problems to which operations research is applied, see C. W. Churchman, R. L. Ackoff and E. L. Arnoff, *Introduction to Operations Research* (John Wiley and Sons, 1957); and J. F. McCloskey and J. M. Coppinger (eds.), *Operations Research for Management,* Vol. II, (The Johns Hopkins Press, 1956).

[3] I am assuming that administrators often make policy and advise in the making of policy and am treating decision-making and policy-making as synonymous for purposes of this paper.

[4] Martin Meyerson and Edward C. Banfield, *Politics, Planning and the Public Interest* (The Free Press, 1955).

[5] The line of argument is, of course, an extension of the theory of market choice, especially the theory of consumer choice, to public policy choices.

[6] A more precise definition of incremental policies and a discussion of whether a change that appears "small" to one observer might be seen differently by another is to be found in my "Policy Analysis," 48 *American Economic Review* 298 (June, 1958).

[7] The link between the practice of the method of successive limited comparisons and mutual adjustment of interests in a highly fragmented decision-making process adds a new facet to pluralist theories of government and administration.

[8] Herbert Simon, Donald W. Smithburg, and Victor A. Thompson, *Public Administration* (Alfred A. Knopf, 1950), p. 434.

[9] Elsewhere I have explored this same method of policy formulation as practiced by academic analysts of policy ("Policy Analysis," 48 *American Economic Review* 298 [June, 1958]). Although it has been here presented as a method for public administrators, it is no less necessary to analysts more removed from immediate policy questions, despite their tendencies to describe their own analytical efforts as though they were the rational-comprehensive method with an especially heavy use of theory. Similarly, this same method is inevitably resorted to in personal problem-solving, where means and ends are sometimes impossible to separate, where aspirations or objectives undergo constant development, and where drastic simplification of the complexity of the real world is urgent if problems are to be solved in the time that can be given to them. To an economist accustomed to dealing with the marginal or incremental concept in market processes, the central idea in the method is that both evaluation and empirical analysis are incremental. Accordingly I have referred to the method elsewhere as "the incremental method."

26.

AN ESSAY ON BARGAINING

THOMAS C. SCHELLING

This paper presents a tactical approach to the analysis of bargaining. The subject includes both explicit bargaining and the tacit kind in which adversaries watch and interpret each other's behavior, each aware that his own actions are being interpreted and anticipated, each acting with a view to the expectations that he creates. In economics the subject covers wage negotiations, tariff negotiations, competition where competitors are few, settlements out of court, and the real estate agent and his customer. Outside economics it ranges from the threat of massive retaliation to taking the right of way from a taxi.

Our concern will *not* be with the part of bargaining that consists of exploring for mutually profitable adjustments, and that might be called the "efficiency" aspect of bargaining. For example, can an insurance firm save money, and make a client happier, by offering a cash settlement rather than repairing the client's car; can an employer save money by granting a voluntary wage increase to employees who agree to take a substantial part of their wages in merchandise? Instead, we shall be concerned with what might be called the "distributional" aspect of bargaining: the situations in which more for one means less for the other. When the business is finally sold to the one interested buyer, what price does it go for? When two dynamite trucks

From Thomas C. Schelling, "An Essay on Bargaining," *The American Economic Review*, 46:281–306, 1956. Reprinted by permission of the American Economic Association. This article appeared later in his book, *The Strategy of Conflict*, Howard University Press, Cambridge, Mass., 1960.

meet on a road wide enough for one, who backs up?

These are situations that ultimately involve an element of pure bargaining—bargaining in which each party is guided mainly by his expectations of what the other will accept. But with each guided by expectations and knowing that the other is too, expectations become compounded. A bargain is struck when somebody makes a final, sufficient concession. Why does he concede? Because he thinks the other will not. "I must concede because he won't. He won't because he thinks I will. He thinks I will because he thinks I think he thinks so. . . ." There is some range of alternative outcomes in which any point is better for both sides than no agreement at all. To insist on any such point is pure bargaining, since one always *would* take less rather than reach no agreement at all, and since one always *can* recede if retreat proves necessary to agreement. Yet if both parties are aware of the limits to this range, *any* outcome is a point from which at least one party would have been willing to retreat and the other knows it! There is no resting place.

There is, however, an outcome; and if we cannot find it in the logic of the situation we may find it in the tactics employed. The purpose of this essay is to call attention to an important class of tactics, of a kind that is peculiarly appropriate to the logic of indeterminate situations. The essence of these tactics is some voluntary but irreversible sacrifice of freedom of choice. They rest on the paradox that the power to constrain an adversary may depend on the power to bind oneself; that, in bargaining, weakness is often strength, freedom may be freedom to capitulate, and to burn bridges behind one may suffice to undo an opponent.

I. BARGAINING POWER: THE POWER TO BIND ONESELF

"Bargaining power," "bargaining strength," "bargaining skill" suggest that the advantage goes to the powerful, the strong, or the skillful. It does, of course, if those qualities are defined to mean only that negotiations are won by those who win. But if the terms imply that it is an advantage to be more intelligent or more skilled in debate, or to have more financial resources, more physical strength, more military potency, or more ability to withstand losses, then the term does a disservice. These qualities are by no means universal advantages in bargaining situations; they often have a contrary value.

The sophisticated negotiator may find it difficult to seem as obstinate as a truly obstinate man. If a man knocks at a door and says that he will stab himself on the porch unless given $10, he is more likely to get the $10 if his eyes are bloodshot. The threat of mutual destruction cannot be used to deter an adversary who is too unintelligent to comprehend it or too weak to enforce his will on those he represents. The government that cannot control its balance of payments, or collect taxes, or muster the political unity to defend itself, may enjoy assistance that would be denied it if it could control its own resources. And, to cite an example familiar from economic theory, "price leadership" in oligopoly may be an unprofitable distinction evaded by the small firms and assumed perforce by the large one.

Bargaining power has also been described as the power to fool and bluff, "the ability to set the best price for yourself and fool the other man into thinking this was your maximum offer."[1] Fooling and bluffing are certainly involved; but there are two kinds of fooling. One is deceiving about the facts; a buyer may lie about his income or misrepresent the size of his family. The other is purely tactical. Suppose each knows everything about the other, and each knows what the other knows. What is there to fool about? The buyer may say that, though he'd really pay up to twenty and the seller knows it, he is firmly resolved as a tactical matter not to budge above sixteen. If the seller capitulates, was he fooled? Or was he convinced of the truth? Or did the buyer really not know what he would do next if the tactic

failed? If the buyer really "feels" himself firmly resolved, and bases his resolve on the conviction that the seller will capitulate, and the seller does, the buyer may say afterwards that he was "not fooling." Whatever has occurred, it is not adequately conveyed by the notions of bluffing and fooling.

How does one person make another believe something? The answer depends importantly on the factual question, "Is it true?" It is easier to prove the truth of something that is true than of something false. To prove the truth about our health we can call on a reputable doctor; to prove the truth about our costs or income we may let the person look at books that have been audited by a reputable firm or the Bureau of Internal Revenue. But to persuade him of something false we may have no such convincing evidence.

When one wishes to presuade someone that he would not pay more than $16,000 for a house that is really worth $20,000 to him, what can he do to take advantage of the usually superior credibility of the truth over a false assertion? Answer: make it true. How can a buyer make it true? If he likes the house because it is near his business he might move his business, persuading the seller that the house is really now worth only $16,000 to him. This would be unprofitable; he is no better off than if he had paid the higher price.

But suppose the buyer could make an irrevocable and enforceable bet with some third party, duly recorded and certified, according to which he would pay for the house no more than $16,000, or forfeit $5,000. The seller has lost; the buyer need simply present the truth. Unless the seller is enraged and withholds the house in sheer spite, the situation has been rigged against him; the "objective" situation— the buyer's true incentive—has been voluntarily, conspicuously, and irreversibly changed. The seller can take it or leave it. This example demonstrates that if the buyer can accept an irrevocable commitment, in a way that is unambiguously visible to the seller, he can squeeze the range of indeterminacy down to the point most favorable to him. It also suggests, by its artificiality, that the tactic is one that may or may not be available; whether the buyer can find an effective device for commiting himself may depend on who he is, who the seller is, where they live, and a number of legal and institutional arrangements (including, in our artificial example, whether bets are legally enforceable).

If both men live in a culture where "cross my heart" is universally accepted as potent, all the buyer has to do is allege that he will pay no more than $16,000, using this invocation of penalty, and he wins—or at least he wins if the seller does not beat him to it by shouting "$19,000, cross my heart." If the buyer is an agent authorized by a board of directors to buy at $16,000 but not a cent more, and the directors cannot constitutionally meet again for several months and the buyer cannot exceed his authority, and if all this can be made known to the seller, then the buyer "wins"—if, again, the seller has not tied himself up with a commitment to $19,000. Or if the buyer can assert that he will pay no more than $16,000 so firmly that he would suffer intolerable loss of personal prestige or bargaining reputation by paying more, and if the fact of his paying more would necessarily be known, and if the seller appreciates all this, then a loud declaration by itself may provide the commitment. The device, of course, is a needless surrender of flexibility unless it can be made fully evident and understandable to the seller.

Incidentally, some of the more contractual kinds of commitments are not as effective as they at first seem. In the example of the self-inflicted penalty through the bet, it remains possible for the seller to seek out the third party and offer a modest sum in consideration of the latter's releasing the buyer from the bet, threatening to sell the house for $16,000 if the release is not forthcoming. The effect of the bet—as of most such contractual commitments—is to shift the locus and personnel of the negotiation, in the hope that the third party will be less available for negotiation or less subject to an incentive to concede. To put it differently, a *contractual* commitment is usually

the assumption of a contingent "transfer cost," not a "real cost"; and if all interested parties can be brought into the negotiation the range of indeterminacy remains as it was. But if the third party were available only at substantial transportation cost, to that extent a truly irrevocable commitment would have been assumed. (If bets were made with a number of people, the "real costs" of bringing them into the negotiation might be made prohibitive.)[2]

The most interesting parts of our topic concern whether and how commitments can be taken; but it is worth-while to consider briefly a model in which practical problems are absent—a world in which absolute commitments are freely available. Consider a culture in which "cross my heart" is universally recognized as absolutely binding. Any offer accompanied by this invocation is a final offer, and is so recognized. If each party knows the other's true reservation price, the object is to be first with a firm offer. Complete responsibility for the outcome then rests with the other, who can take it or leave it as he chooses (and who chooses to take it). Bargaining is all over; the commitment (*i.e.*, the first offer) wins.

Interpose some communication difficulty. They must bargain by letter; the invocation becomes effective when signed but cannot be known to the other until its arrival. Now when one party writes such a letter the other may already have signed his own, or may yet do so before the letter of the first arrives. There is then no sale; both are bound to incompatible positions. Each must now recognize this possibility of stalemate, and take into account the likelihood that the other already has, or will have, signed his own commitment.

An asymmetry in communication may well favor the one who is (and is known to be) unavailable for the receipt of messages, for he is the one who cannot be deterred from his own commitment by receipt of the other's. (On the other hand, if the one who cannot communicate can feign ignorance of his own inability, the other too may be deterred from his own commitment by fear of the first's unwitting commitment.) If the commitments depend not just on words but on special forms or ceremonies, ignorance of the other party's commitment ceremonies may be an advantage if the ignorance is fully appreciated, since it makes the other aware that only his own restraint can avert stalemate.

Suppose only part of the population belongs to the cult in which "cross my heart" is (or is believed to be) absolutely binding. If everyone knows (and is known to know) everyone else's affiliation, those belonging to this particular cult have the advantage. They can commit themselves, the others cannot. If the buyer says "$16,000, cross my heart" his offer is final; if the seller says "$19,000" he is (and is known to be) only "bargaining."

If each does not know the other's true reservation price there is an initial stage in which each tries to discover the other's and misrepresent his own, as in ordinary bargaining. But the process of discovery and revelation becomes quickly merged with the process of creating and discovering commitments; the commitments permanently change, for all practical purposes, the "true" reservation prices. If one party has, and the other has not, the belief in a binding ceremony, the latter pursues the "ordinary" bargaining technique of *asserting* his reservation price, while the former proceeds to *make* his.

The foregoing discussion has tried to suggest both the plausibility and the logic of self-commitment. Some examples may suggest the relevance of the tactic, although an observer can seldom distinguish with confidence the consciously logical, the intuitive, or the inadvertent, use of a visible tactic. First, it has not been uncommon for union officials to stir up excitement and determination on the part of the membership during or prior to a wage negotiation. If the union is going to insist on $2 and expects the management to counter with $1.60, an effort is made to persuade the membership not only that the management could pay $2 but even perhaps that the negotiators themselves are incompetent if they fail to obtain close to $2. The purpose—or, rather,

a plausible purpose suggested by our analysis—is to make clear to the management that the negotiators could not accept less than $2 *even if they wished to* because they no longer control the members or because they would lose their own positions if they tried. In other words, the negotiators reduce the scope of their own authority, and confront the management with the threat of a strike that the union itself cannot avert, even though it was the union's own action that eliminated its power to prevent the strike.

Something similar occurs when the United States government negotiates with other governments on, say, the uses to which foreign assistance will be put, or tariff reduction. If the executive branch is free to negotiate the best arrangement it can, it may be unable to make any position stick and may end by conceding controversial points because its partners know, or believe obstinately, that the United States would rather concede than terminate the negotiations. But if the executive branch negotiates under legislative authority, with its position constrained by law, and it is evident that Congress will not be reconvened to change the law within the necessary time period, then the executive branch has a firm position that is visible to its negotiating partners.

When national representatives go to international negotiations knowing that there is a wide range of potential agreement within which the outcome will depend on bargaining, they seem often to create a bargaining position by public statements, statements calculated to arouse a public opinion that permits no concessions to be made. If a binding public opinion can be cultivated, and made evident to the other side, the initial position can thereby be made visibly "final."

These examples have certain characteristics in common. First, they clearly depend not only on incurring a commitment but on communicating it persuasively to the other party. Second, it is by no means easy to establish the commitment, nor is it entirely clear to either of the parties concerned just how strong the commitment is. Third, similar activity may be available to the parties on both sides. Fourth, the possibility of commitment, though perhaps available to both sides, is by no means equally available; the ability of a democratic government to get itself tied by public opinion may be different from the ability of a totalitarian government to incur such a commitment. Fifth, they all run the risk of establishing an immovable position that goes beyond the ability of the other to concede, and thereby provoke the likelihood of stalemate or breakdown.

II. INSTITUTIONAL AND STRUCTURAL CHARACTERISTICS OF THE NEGOTIATION

Some institutional and structural characteristics of bargaining situations may make the commitment tactic easy or difficult to use, or make it more available to one party than the other, or affect the likelihood of simultaneous commitment or stalemate.

Use of a bargaining agent

The use of a bargaining agent affects the power of commitment in at least two ways. First, the agent may be given instructions that are difficult or impossible to change, such instructions (and their inflexibility) being visible to the opposite party. The principle applies in distinguishing the legislative from the executive branch, or the management from the board of directors, as well as to a messenger-carried offer when the bargaining process has a time limit and the principal has interposed sufficient distance between himself and his messenger to make further communication evidently impossible before the time runs out.

Second, an "agent" may be brought in as a principal in his own right, with an incentive structure of his own that differs from his principal's. This device is involved in automobile insurance; the private citizen, in settling out of court, cannot threaten suit as effectively as the insurance company since the latter is

more conspicuously obliged to carry out such threats to maintain its own reputation for subsequent accidents.[3]

Secrecy vs. publicity

A potent means of commitment, and sometimes the only means, is the pledge of one's reputation. If national representatives can arrange to be charged with appeasement for every small concession, they place concession visibly beyond their own reach. If a union with other plants to deal with can arrange to make any retreat dramatically visible, it places its bargaining reputation in jeopardy and thereby becomes visibly incapable of serious compromise. (The same convenient jeopardy is the basis for the universally exploited defense, "If I did it for you I'd have to do it for everyone else.") But to commit in this fashion publicity is required. Both the initial offer and the final outcome would have to be known; and if secrecy surrounds either point, or if the outcome is inherently not observable, the device is unavailable. If one party has a "public" and the other has not, the latter may try to neutralize his disadvantage by excluding the relevant public; or if both parties fear the potentialities for stalemate in the simultaneous use of this tactic, they may try to enforce an agreement on secrecy.

Intersecting negotiations

If a union is simultaneously engaged, or will shortly be engaged, in many negotiations while the management has no other plants and deals with no other unions, the management cannot convincingly stake its bargaining reputation while the union can. The advantage goes to the party that can persuasively point to an array of other negotiations in which its own position would be prejudiced if it made a concession in this one. (The "reputation value" of the bargain may be less related to the outcome than to the firmness with which some initial bargaining position is adhered to.) Defense against this tactic may involve, among other things, both misinterpretation of the other party's position and an effort to make the eventual outcome incommensurable with the initial positions. If the subjects under negotiation can be enlarged in the process of negotiation, or the wage figure replaced by fringe benefits that cannot be reduced to a wage equivalent, an "out" is provided to the party that has committed itself; and the availability of this "out" weakens the commitment itself, to the disadvantage of the committed party.

Continuous negotiations

A special case of interrelated negotiations occurs when the same two parties are to negotiate other topics, simultaneously or in the future. The logic of this case is more subtle; to persuade the other that one cannot afford to recede, one says in effect, "If I conceded to you here, you would revise your estimate of me in our other negotiations; to protect my reputation with you I must stand firm." The second party is simultaneously the "third party" to whom one's bargaining reputation can be pledged. This situation occurs in the threat of local resistance to local aggression. The party threatening achieves its commitment, and hence the credibility of its threat, not by referring to what it would gain from carrying out the threat in this particular instance but by pointing to the long-run value of a fulfilled threat in enhancing the credibility of future threats.

The restrictive agenda

When there are two objects to negotiate, the decision to negotiate them simultaneously or in separate forums or at separate times is by no means neutral to the outcome, particularly when there is a latent extortionate threat that can be exploited only if it can be attached to some more ordinary, legitimate, bargaining situation. The protection against extortion depends on refusal, unavailability, or inability, to negotiate. But if the object of the extortionate threat can be brought onto the agenda with the other topic, the latent threat becomes effective.

Tariff bargaining is an example. If reciprocal tariffs on cheese and automobiles are to be negotiated, one party may alter the outcome by threatening a purely punitive change in some other tariff. But if the bargaining representatives of the threatened party are confined to the cheese-automobile agenda, and have no instructions that permit them even to take cognizance of other commodities, or if there are ground rules that forbid mention of other tariffs while cheese and automobiles remain unsettled, this extortionate weapon must await another opportunity. If the threat that would be brought to the conference table is one that cannot stand publicity, publicity itself may prevent its effective communication.

The possibility of compensation

As Fellner has pointed out, agreement may be dependent on some means of redistributing costs or gains.[4] If duopolists, for example, divide markets in a way that maximizes their combined profits, some initial accrual of profits is thereby determined; any other division of the profits requires that one firm be able to compensate the other. If the fact of compensation would be evidence of illegal collusion, or if the motive for compensation would be misunderstood by the stockholders, or if the two do not sufficiently trust each other, some less optimum level of *joint* profits may be required in order that the initial accrual of profits to the two firms be in closer accordance with an agreed division of gains between them.

When agreement must be reached on something that is inherently a one-man act, any division of the cost depends on compensation. The "agenda" assumes particular importance in these cases, since a principal means of compensation is a concession on some other object. If two simultaneous negotiations can be brought into a contingent relationship with each other, a means of compensation is available. If they are kept separate, each remains an indivisible object.

It may be to the advantage of one party to keep a bargain isolated, and to the other to joint it to some second bargain. If there are two projects, each with a cost of three, and each with a value of two to A and a value of four to B, and each is inherently a "one-man" project in its execution, and if compensation is institutionally impossible, B will be forced to pay the entire cost of each as long as the two projects are kept separate. He cannot usefully threaten nonperformance, since A has no incentive to carry out either project by himself. But if B can link the projects together, offering to carry out one while A carries out the other, and can effectively threaten to abandon both unless A carries out one of them, A is left an option with a gain of four and a cost of three, which he takes, and B cuts his cost in half.

An important limitation of economic problems, as prototypes of bargaining situations, is that they tend disproportionately to involve divisible objects and compensable activities. If a drainage ditch in the back of one house will protect both houses; and if it costs $1,000 and is worth $800 to each home-owner; neither would undertake it separately, but we nevertheless usually assume that they will get together and see that this project worth $1,600 to the two of them gets carried out. But if it costs 10 hours a week to be scoutmaster, and each considers it worth 8 hours of his time to have a scout troop but one man must do the whole job, it is far from certain that the neighbors will reach a deal according to which one puts 10 hours on the job and the other pays him cash or does 5 hours' gardening for him. When two cars meet on a narrow road, the ensuing deadlock is aggravated by the absence of a custom of bidding to pay for the right of way. Parliamentary deadlocks occur when logrolling is impracticable. Measures that require unanimous agreement can often be initiated only if several are bundled together.[5]

The mechanics of negotiation

A number of other characteristics deserve mention, although we shall not work out their im-plications. Is there a penalty on the conveyance of false information? Is there a penalty on called bluffs, *i.e.*, can one put forth an offer and withdraw it after it has been accepted? Is there a penalty on hiring an agent who pretends to be an interested party and makes insincere offers, simply to test the position of the other party? Can all interested parties be recognized? Is there a time limit on the bargaining? Does the bargaining take the particular structure of an auction, a Dutch auction, a sealed bid system, or some other formal arrangement? Is there a *status quo*, so that unavailability for negotiation can win the *status quo* for the party that prefers it? Is renegotiation possible in case of stalemate? What are the costs of stalemate? Can compliance with the agreement be observed? What, in general, are the means of communication, and are any of them susceptible of being put out of order by one party or the other? If there are several items to negotiate, are they negotiated in one comprehensive negotiation, separately in a particular order so that each piece is finished before the next is taken up, or simultaneously through different agents or under different rules.

The importance of many of these structural questions becomes evident when one reflects on parliamentary technique. Rules that permit a president to veto an appropriation bill only in its entirety, or that require each amendment to be voted before the original act is voted on, or a priority system accorded to different kinds of motions, substantially alter the incentives that are brought to bear on each action. One who might be pressured into choosing second best is relieved of his vulnerability if he can vote earlier to eliminate that possibility, thereby leaving only first and third choices about which his preference is known to be so strong that no threat will be made.

Principles and precedents

To be convincing, commitments usually have to be qualitative rather than quantitative, and to rest on some rationale. It may be difficult to conceive of a really firm commitment to $2.07½; why not $2.02¼? The numerical scale is too continuous to provide good resting places, except at nice round numbers like $2.00. But a commitment to the *principle* of "profit sharing," "cost-of-living increases," or any other basis for a numerical calculation that comes out at $2.07½, may provide a foothold for a commitment. Furthermore, one may create something of a commitment by putting the principles and precedents themselves in jeopardy. If in the past one has successfully maintained the principle of, say, nonrecognition of governments imposed by force, and elects to nail his demands to that principle in the present negotiation, he not only adduces precedent behind his claim but risks the principle itself. Having pledged it, he may persuade his adversary that he would accept stalemate rather than capitulate and discredit the principle.

Casuistry

If one reaches the point where concession is advisable, he has to recognize two effects: it puts him closer to his opponent's position, and it affects his opponent's estimate of his firmness. Concession not only may be construed as capitulation, it may mark a prior commitment as a fraud, and make the adversary skeptical of any new pretense at commitment. One, therefore, needs an "excuse" for accommodating his opponent, preferably a rationalized reinterpretation of the original commitment, one that is persuasive to the adversary himself.

More interesting is the use of casuistry to release an opponent from a commitment. If one can demonstrate to an opponent that the latter is not committed, or that he has miscalculated his commitment, one may in fact undo or revise the opponent's commitment. Or if one can confuse the opponent's commitment, so that his constituents or principals or audience cannot exactly identify compliance with the commitment—show that "productivity" is ambiguous, or that "proportionate contributions" has several meanings—one may undo

it or lower its value. In these cases it is to the opponent's disadvantage that this commitment be successfully refuted by argument. But when the opponent has resolved to make a moderate concession one may help him by proving that he *can* make a moderate concession consistent with his former position, and that if he does there are no grounds for believing it to reflect on his original principles. One must seek, in other words, a rationalization by which to deny himself too great a reward from his opponent's concession, otherwise the concession will not be made.[6]

III. THE THREAT

When one threatens to fight if attacked or to cut his price if his competitor does, the threat is no more than a communication of one's own incentives, designed to impress on the other the automatic consequences of his act. And, incidentally, if it succeeds in deterring, it benefits both parties.

But more than communication is involved when one threatens an act that he would have no incentive to perform but that is designed to deter through its promise of mutual harm. To threaten massive retaliation against small encroachments is of this nature, as is the threat to bump a car that does not yield the right of way or to call a costly strike if the wage rate is not raised a few cents. The distinctive feature of this threat is that the threatener has no incentive to carry it out either before the event or after. He does have an incentive to bind himself to fulfill the threat, if he thinks the threat may be successful, because the threat and not its fulfillment gains the end; and fulfillment is not required if the threat succeeds. The more certain the contingent fulfillment is, the less likely is actual fulfillment. But the threat's efficacy depends on the credulity of the other party, and the threat is ineffectual unless the threatener can rearrange or display his own incentives so as to demonstrate that he would, *ex post*, have an incentive to carry it out.[7]

We are back again at the commitment. How can one commit himself in advance to an act that he would in fact prefer not to carry out in the event, in order that his commitment may deter the other party? One can of course bluff, to persuade the other falsely that the costs or damages to the threatener would be minor or negative. More interesting, the one making the threat may pretend that he himself erroneously believes his own costs to be small, and therefore would mistakenly go ahead and fulfill the threat. Or perhaps he can pretend a revenge motivation so strong as to overcome the prospect of self-damage; but this option is probably most readily available to the truly revengeful. Otherwise he must find a way to commit himself.

One may try to stake his reputation on fulfillment, in a manner that impresses the threatened person. One may even stake his reputation *with the threatened person himself*, on grounds that it would be worth the costs and pains to give a lesson to the latter if he fails to heed the threat. Or one may try to arrange a legal commitment, perhaps through contracting with a third party.[8] Or if one can turn the whole business over to an agent whose salary (or business reputation) depends on carrying out the threat but who is unalterably relieved of any responsibility for the further costs, one may shift the incentive.

The commitment problem is nicely illustrated by the legal doctrine of the "last clear chance" which recognizes that, in the events that led up to an accident, there was some point at which the accident became inevitable as a result of prior actions, and that the abilities of the two parties to prevent it may not have expired at the same time. In bargaining, the commitment is a device to leave the last clear chance to decide the outcome with the other party, in a manner that he fully appreciates; it is to relinquish further initiative, having rigged the incentives so that the other party must choose in one's favor. If one driver speeds up so that he cannot stop, and the other realizes it, the latter has to yield. A legislative rider at the end of a session leaves the President the last

clear chance to pass the bill. This doctrine helps to understand some of those cases in which bargaining "strength" inheres in what is weakness by other standards. When a person— or a country—has lost the power to help himself, or the power to avert mutual damage, the other interested party has no choice but to assume the cost or responsibility. "Coercive deficiency" is the term Arthur Smithies uses to describe the tactic of deliberately exhausting one's annual budgetary allowance so early in the year that the need for more funds is irresistibly urgent.[9]

A related tactic is maneuvering into a *status quo* from which one can be dislodged only by an overt act, an act that precipitates mutual damage because the maneuvering party has relinquished the power to retreat. If one carries explosives visibly on his person, in a manner that makes destruction obviously inevitable for himself and for any assailant, he may deter assault much more than if he retained any control over the explosives. If one commits a token force of troops that would be unable to escape, the commitment to full resistance is increased. Walter Lippmann has used the analogy of the plate glass window that helps to protect a jewelry store: anyone can break it easily enough, but not without creating an uproar.

Similar techniques may be available to the one threatened. His best defense, of course, is to carry out the act before the threat is made; in that case there is neither incentive nor commitment for retaliation. If he cannot hasten the act itself, he may commit himself to it; if the person to be threatened is already committed, the one who would threaten cannot deter with his threat, he can only make certain the mutually disastrous consequences that he threatens.[10] If the person to be threatened can arrange before the threat is made to share the risk with others (as suggested by the insurance solution to the right-of-way problem mentioned earlier) he may become so visibly unsusceptible to the threat as to dissuade the threatener. Or if by any other means he can either change or misrepresent his own incentives, to make it appear that he would gain in spite of threat fulfillment (or perhaps only that he thinks he would), the threatener may have to give up the threat as costly and fruitless; or if one can misrepresent himself as either unable to comprehend a threat, or too obstinate to heed it, he may deter the threat itself. Best of all may be *genuine* ignorance, obstinacy, or simple disbelief, since it may be more convincing to the prospective threatener; but of course if it fails to presuade him and he commits himself to the threat, both sides lose. Finally, both the threat and the commitment have to be communicated; if the threatened person can be unavailable for messages, or can destroy the communication channels, even though he does so in an obvious effort to avert threat, he may deter the threat itself.[11] But the time to show disbelief or obstinacy is before the threat is made, *i.e.*, before the commitment is taken, not just before the threat is fulfilled; it does no good to be incredulous, or out of town, when the messenger arrives with the committed threat.

In threat situations, as in ordinary bargaining, commitments are not altogether clear; each party cannot exactly estimate the costs and values to the other side of the two related actions involved in the threat; the process of commitment may be a progressive one, the commitments acquiring their firmness by a sequence of actions. Communication is often neither entirely impossible nor entirely reliable; while certain evidence of one's commitment can be communicated directly, other evidence must travel by newspaper or hearsay, or be demonstrated by actions. In these cases the unhappy possibility of both acts occurring, as a result of simultaneous commitment, is increased. Furthermore, the recognition of this possibility of simultaneous commitment becomes itself a deterrent to the taking of commitments.[12]

In case a threat is made and fails to deter, there is a second stage prior to fulfillment in which *both* parties have an interest in undoing the commitment. The purpose of the threat is gone, its deterrence value is zero, and only the commitment exists to motivate fulfillment.

This feature has, of course, an analogy with stalemate in ordinary bargaining, stalemate resulting from both parties getting committed to incompatible positions, or one party mistakenly committting himself to a position that the other truly would not accept. If there appears a possibility of undoing the commitment, *both* parties have an interest in doing so. How to undo it is a matter on which their interests diverge, since different ways of undoing it lead to different outcomes. Furthermore, "undoing" does not mean neglecting the commitment regardless of reputation; "undoing," if the commitment of reputation was real, means disconnecting the threat from one's reputation, perhaps one's own reputation with the threatened person himself. It is therefore a subtle and tenuous situation in which, though both have an interest in undoing the commitment, they may be quite unable to collaborate in undoing it.

Special care may be needed in defining the threat, both the act that is threatened against and the counter act that is threatened. The difficulty arises from the fact, just noted, that once the former has been done the incentive to perform the latter has disappeared. The credibility of the threat before the act depends on how visible to the threatened party is the ability of the threatening party to rationalize his way out of his commitment once it has failed its purpose. Any loopholes the threatening party leaves himself, if they are visible to the threatened party, weaken the visible commitment and hence reduce the credibility of the threat.

It is essential, therefore, for maximum credibility to leave as little room as possible for judgment or discretion in carrying out the threat. If one is committed to punish a certain type of behavior when it reaches certain limits, but the limits are not carefully and objectively defined, the party threatened will realize that when the time comes to decide whether the threat must be enforced or not, his interest and that of the threatening party will coincide in an attempt to avoid the mutually unpleasant consequences.

In order to make a threat precise, so that its

terms are visible both to the threatened party and to any third parties whose reaction to the whole affair is of value to the adversaries, it may be necessary to introduce some arbitrary elements. The threat must involve overt acts rather than intentions; it must be attached to the visible deeds, not invisible ones; it may have to attach itself to certain ancillary actions that are of no consequence in themselves to the threatening party. It may, for example, have to put a penalty on the carrying of weapons rather than their use; on suspicious behavior rather than observed misdemeanors; on proximity to a crime rather than the crime itself. And, finally, the act of punishment must be one whose effect or influence is clearly discernible.[13]

In order that one be able to pledge his reputation behind a threat, there must be continuity between the present and subsequent issues that will arise. This need for continuity suggests a means of making the original threat more effective; if it can be decomposed into a series of consecutive smaller threats, there is an opportunity to demonstrate on the first few transgressions that the threat will be carried out on the rest. Even the first few become more plausible, since there is a more obvious incentive to fulfill them as a "lesson."

This principle is perhaps most relevant to acts that are inherently a matter of degree. In foreign aid programs the overt act of terminating assistance may be so obviously painful to both sides as not to be taken seriously by the recipient, but if each small misuse of funds is to be accompanied by a small reduction in assistance, never so large as to leave the recipient helpless nor to provoke a diplomatic breach, the willingness to carry it out will receive more credulity; or, if it does not at first, a few lessons may be persuasive without too much damage.[14]

The threatening party may not, of course, be able to divide the act into steps. (Both the act to be deterred and the punishment must be divisible.) But the principle at least suggests the unwisdom of defining aggression, or transgression, in terms of some critical degree or amount that will be deemed intolerable. When the act to be deterred is inherently a sequence of steps whose cumulative effect is what matters, a threat geared to the increments may be more credible than one that must be carried either all at once or not at all when some particular point has been reached. It may even be impossible to define a "critical point" with sufficient clarity to be persuasive.

To make the threatened acts divisible, the acts themselves may have to be modified. Parts of an act that cannot be decomposed may have to be left out; ancillary acts that go with the event, though of no interest in themselves, may be objects to which a threat can effectively be attached. For example, actions that are only preparatory to the main act, and by themselves do no damage, may be susceptible of chronological division and thus be effective objects of the threat. The man who would kick a dog should be threatened with modest punishment for each step toward the dog, even though his proximity is of no interest in itself.

Similar to decomposing a threat into a series is starting a threat with a punitive act that grows in severity with the passage of time. Where a threat of death by violence might not be credited, cutting off the food supply might bring submission. For moral or public relations purposes, this device may in fact leave the "last clear chance" to the other, whose demise is then blamed on his stubbornness if the threat fails. But in any case the threatener gets his overt act out of the way while it is still preliminary and minor, rather than letting it stand as a final, dreadful, and visible obstacle to his resolution. And if the suffering party is the only one in a position to know, from moment to moment, how near to catastrophe they have progressed, his is the last clear chance in a real sense. Furthermore, the threatener may be embarrassed by his adversary's collapse but not by his discomfort; and the device may therefore transform a dangerous once-for-all threat into a less costly continuous one. Tenants are less easily removed by threat of forcible eviction than by simply shutting off the utilities.[15]

A piecemeal approach may also be used by the threatened person. If he cannot obviate the threat by hastening the entire act, he may hasten some initial stage that clearly commits him to eventual completion. Or, if his act is divisible while the threatener's retaliation comes only in the large economy size, performing it as a series of increments may deny the threatener the dramatic overt act that would trigger his response.

IV. THE PROMISE

Among the legal privileges of corporations, two that are mentioned in textbooks are the right to sue and the "right" to be sued. Who wants to be sued! But the right to be sued is the power to make a promise: to borrow money, to enter a contract, to do business with someone who might be damaged. If suit does arise the "right" seems a liability in retrospect; beforehand it was a prerequisite to doing business.

In brief, the right to be sued is the power to accept a commitment. In the commitments discussed up to this point, it was essential that one's adversary (or "partner," however we wish to describe him) not have the power to release one from the commitment; the commitment was, in effect, to some third party, real or fictitious. The promise is a commitment to the second party in the bargain, and is required whenever the final action of one or of each is outside the other's control. It is required whenever an agreement leaves any incentive to cheat.[16]

This need for promises is more than incidental; it has an institutional importance of its own. It is not always easy to make a convincing, self-binding, promise. Both the kidnapper who would like to release his prisoner, and the prisoner, may search desperately for a way to commit the latter against informing on the captor, without finding one. If the victim has committed an act whose disclosure could lead to blackmail, he may confess it; if not, he might commit one in the presence of his captor, to create the bond that will ensure his silence. But these extreme possibilities illus-

trate how difficult, as well as important, it may be to assume a promise. If the law will not enforce price agreements; or if the union is unable to obligate itself to a no-strike pledge; or if a contractor has no assets to pay damages if he loses a suit, and the law will not imprison debtors; or if there is no "audience" to which one can pledge his reputation; it may not be possible to strike a bargain, or at least the same bargain that would otherwise be struck.

Bargaining may have to concern itself with an "incentive" system as well as the division of gains. Oligopolists may lobby for a "fair-trade" law; or exchange shares or stocks. An agreement to stay out of each other's market may require an agreement to redesign the products to be unsuitable in each other's area. Two countries that wish to agree not to make military use of an island may have to destroy the usefulness of the island itself. (In effect, a "third-party commitment" has to be assumed when an effective "second-party commitment" cannot be devised.)[17]

Fulfillment is not always observable. If one sells his vote in a secret election, or a government agrees to recommend an act to its parliament, or an employee agrees not to steal from inventory, or a teacher agrees to keep his political opinions out of class, or a country agrees to stimulate exports "as much as possible," there is no reliable way to observe or measure compliance. The observable outcome is subject to a number of influences, only one of which is covered by the agreement. The bargain may therefore have to be expressed in terms of something observable, even though what is observable is not the intended object of the bargain. One may have to pay the bribed voter if the election is won, not on how he voted; to pay a salesman a commission on sales, rather than on skill and effort; to reward policemen according to statistics on crime rather than on attention to duty; or to punish all employees for the transgressions of one. And where performance is a matter of degree, the bargain may have to define arbitrary limits distinguishing performance from nonperformance; a specified loss of inventory treated as evidence of theft; a specified increase in exports considered an "adequate" effort; specified samples of performance taken as representative of total performance.[18]

The tactic of decomposition applies to promises as well as to threats. What makes many agreements enforceable is only the recognition of future opportunities for agreement that will be eliminated if mutual trust is not created and maintained, and whose value outweighs the momentary gain from cheating in the present instance. Each party must be confident that the other will not jeopardize future opportunities by destroying trust at the outset. This confidence does not always exist; and one of the purposes of piecemeal bargains is to cultivate the necessary mutual expectations. Neither may be willing to trust the other's prudence (or the other's confidence in the first's prudence, etc.) on a large issue. But if a number of preparatory bargains can be struck on a small scale, each may be willing to risk a small investment to create a tradition of trust. The purpose is to let each party demonstrate that he appreciates the need for trust and that he knows the other does too. So if a major issue has to be negotiated, it may be necessary to seek out and negotiate some minor items for "practice," to establish the necessary confidence in each other's awareness of the long-term value of good faith.

Even if the future will bring no recurrence, it may be possible to create the equivalence of continuity by dividing the bargaining issue into consecutive parts. If each party agrees to send a million dollars to the Red Cross on condition the other does, each may be tempted to cheat if the other contributes first, and each one's anticipation of the other's cheating will inhibit agreement. But if the contribution is divided into consecutive small contributions, each can try the other's good faith for a small price. Furthermore, since each can keep the other on short tether to the finish, no one ever need risk more than one small contribution at a time. Finally, this change in the incentive structure itself takes most of the risk out of the

initial contribution; the value of established trust is made obviously visible to both.

Preparatory bargains serve another purpose. Bargaining can only occur when at least one party takes initiative in proposing a bargain. A deterrent to initiative is the information it yields, or may seem to yield, about one's eagerness. But if each has visible reason to expect the other to meet him half way, because of a history of successful bargaining, that very history provides protection against the inference of overeagerness.[19]

V. AN ILLUSTRATVE GAME

Various bargaining situations involving commitments, threats, pormises, and communication problems, can be illustrated by variants of a game in which each of two persons has a pair of alternatives from which to choose. North chooses either A or α; East chooses either B or β. Each person's gain depends on the choices of both. Each of the four possible combined choices, AB, $A\beta$, αB, or $\alpha\beta$, yields a particular gain or loss for North and a particular gain or loss for East. No compensation is payable between North and East. In general, each person's preference may depend on the choice the other makes.

Each such game can be quantitatively represented in a two dimensional graph, with North's gain measured vertically and East's horizontally, and the values of the four combined choices denoted by points labeled AB, $A\beta$, $\alpha\beta$, and αB. In spite of the simplicity of the game there is actually a large number of qualitatively different variants, depending not only on the relative positions of the four points in the plane but also on the "rules" about order of moves, possibility of communication, availability of means of commitment, enforceability of promises, and whether two or more games between two persons can be joined together. The variations can be multiplied almost without limit by selecting different hypotheses about what each player knows or guesses about the "values" of the four outcomes for the other player, and what he guesses the other party guesses about himself. For convenience we assume here that the eight "values" are obvious in an obvious way to both persons. And, just as we have ruled out compensation, we rule out also threats of actions that lie outside the game. A very small sample of such games is presented.

Figure 26–1 represents an "ordinary" bargaining situation if we adopt the rule that North and East must reach explicit agreement before they choose. $A\beta$ and αB can be thought of as alternative agreements that they may reach, while AB and αB, with zero values for both persons, can be interpreted as the bargaining equivalent of "no sale." Whoever can first commit himself wins. If North can commit himself to A he will secure $A\beta$, since he leaves East a choice between $A\beta$ and AB and the former is obviously East's choice under the circumstances. If East could have committed himself first to B, however, North would have been restricted to a choice of αB or no agreement (i.e., of αB or AB) and would have agreed to αB. As a matter of fact, first commitment is a kind of "first move"; and in a game with the same numbers but with moves in turn, first move would be an advantage. If, by mistake, both parties get committed, North to A and East to B, they lock themselves in stalemate at AB.

Figure 26–2 illustrates a deterrent threat if we interpret AB as the *status quo*, with North planning a shift to α (leading to αB) and East threatening a shift to β (resulting in $\alpha\beta$) if he does. If North moves first, East can only lose by moving to β, and similarly if North can commit himself to α before East can make his threat; but if East can effectively threaten the mutually undesirable $\alpha\beta$, he leaves North only a choice of $\alpha\beta$ or AB and North chooses the latter. Note that it is not sufficient for East to commit his *choice* in advance, as it was in Figure 1; he must commit himself to a *conditional* choice, B or β depending on whether North chooses A or α. If East committed his choice he would obtain only the advantage of "first move"; and in the present game, if moves were in turn, North would win at αB regardless of who moved first. (East would choose B rather than β, to leave North a choice of αB or AB rather than of $\alpha\beta$ or $A\beta$; and North would take αB. North, with first move, would choose α rather than A, leaving East $\alpha\beta$ or αB rather than $A\beta$ or AB; East would take αB.)

Figure 26–3 illustrates the promise. Whoever goes first, or even if moves are simul-

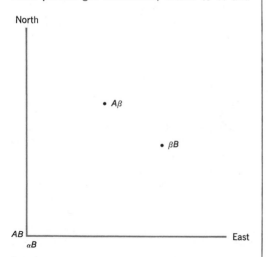

Figure 26–1.

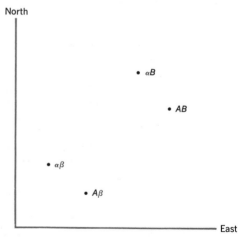

Figure 26–2.

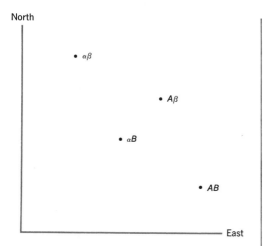

Figure 26–3.

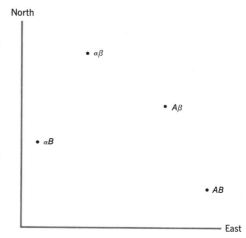

Figure 26–4.

taneous, αB is a "minimax"; either can achieve it by himself, and neither can threaten the other with anything worse. Both would, however, prefer $A\beta$ to αB; but to reach $A\beta$ they must trust each other or be able to make enforceable promises. Whoever goes first, the other has an incentive to cheat; if North chooses A, East can take AB, and if East chooses β first, North can choose $\alpha\beta$. If moves are simultaneous each has an incentive to cheat, and each may expect the other to cheat; and either deliberate cheating, or self-protection against the other's incentive to cheat, indicates choices of α and B. At least one party must be able to commit himself to abstention; then the other can move first. If both must move simultaneously, both must be able to make enforceable promises.

Figure 26–4 is the same as Figure 26–3 except that αB has been moved leftward. Here, in the absence of communication, North wins at $\alpha\beta$ regardless of whether he or East moves first or moves are simultaneous. If, however, East can communicate a conditional commitment, he can force North to choose A and an outcome of $A\beta$. But this commitment is something more than either a promise or a threat; it is both a promise and a threat. He must threaten αB if North chooses α; and he must

promise "not AB" if North chooses A. The threat alone will not induce North to avoid α; αB is better than AB for North, and AB is what he gets with A if East is free to choose B. East must commit himself to do, either α or A, the opposite of what he would do if he were not committed: abstention from AB or immolation at αB.

Finally, Figures 26–5 and 26–6 show two games that separately contain nothing of interest but together make possible an extortionate threat. Figure 26–5 has a minimax solution at αB; either can achieve αB, neither can enforce anything better, no collaboration is possible, no threat can be made. Figure 26–6, though contrasting with Figure 26–5 in the identity of interest between the two parties, is similarly devoid of any need for collaboration or communication or any possible threat to exploit. With or without communication, with or without an order of moves, the outcome is at AB.

But suppose the two games are simultaneously up for decision, and the same two parties are involved in both. If either party can commit himself to a threat he may improve his position. East, for example, could threaten to choose β rather than B in game 6, unless North chose A rather than α in game 5; alternatively, North could threaten α in game 6 un-

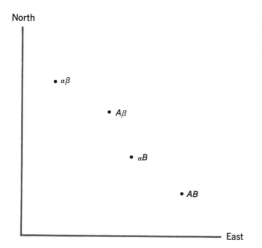

Figure 26–5.

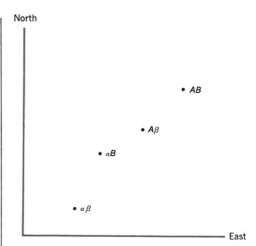

Figure 26–6.

less East chose β in game 5. Assuming the intervals large enough in game 6, and the threat persuasively committed and communicated, the threatener gains in game 5 at no cost in game 6. Because his threat succeeds he does not carry it out; so he gets AB in 6 as well as his preferred choice in game 5. To express this result differently, game 6 supplies what was ruled out earlier, namely the threat of an act "outside the game." From the point of view of game 5, game 6 is an extraneous act, and East might as well threaten to burn North's house down if he does not choose A in 5. But such purely extortionate threats are not always easy to make; they often require an occasion, an object, and a means of communication, and additionally often suffer from illegality, immorality, or resistance out of sheer stubbornness. The joining of two negotiations on the same agenda may thus succeed where a purely gratuitous threat would be impracticable.

If North cannot commit himself to a threat, and consequently desires only to prevent a threat by East, it is in his interest that communication be impossible; or, if communication occurs, it is in his interest that the two games not be placed on the same agenda; or, if he cannot prevent their being discussed to-

gether by East, it is in his interest to turn each game over to a different agent whose compensation depends only on the outcome of his own game. If North can force game 6 to be played first, and is unable to commit himself in response to a threat, the threat is obviated. If he can commit his choice in game 5 before the threat is made, he is safe. But if he can commit himself in game 5, and game 6 is to be played first, East could threaten to choose β in game 6 unless North assumed a prior commitment to A in game 5; in this case North's ability to commit himself is a disadvantage, since it permits him to be forced into "playing" game 5 ahead of 6.

Incidentally, dropping AB vertically in Figure 26–2 to below the level $\alpha\beta$ would illustrate an important principle, namely, that moving one point in a manner "unfavorable" to North may actually improve the outcome for him. The threat that kept him from winning in Figure 26–2 depends on the comparative attractiveness of AB over $\alpha\beta$ for North; of AB is made worse for him than $\alpha\beta$ he becomes immune to the threat, which then is not made, and he wins at $\alpha\beta$. This is an abstract analogy of the principle that, in bargaining, weakness may be strength.

NOTES

¹ J. N. Morgan, "Bilateral Monopoly and the Competitive Output," *Quart. Jour. Econ.*, Aug. 1949, LXIII, 376, n.6.

² Perhaps the "ideal" solution to the bilateral monopoly problem is as follows. One member of the pair shifts his marginal cost curve so that joint profits are now zero at the output at which joint profits originally would have been maximized. He does this through an irrevocable sale-leaseback arrangement; he sells a royalty contract to some third party for a lump sum, the royalties so related to his output that joint costs exceed joint revenue at all other outputs. He cannot now afford to produce at any price or output except that price and output at which the entire original joint profits accrue to him; the other member of the bilateral monopoly sees the contract, appreciates the situation, and accepts his true minimum profits. The "winner" really gains the entire original profit via the lump sum for which he sold royalty rights; this profit does not affect his incentives because it is independent of what he produces. The third party pays the lump sum (minus a small discount for inducement) because he knows that the second party will have to capitulate and that therefore he will in fact get his contingent royalty. The hitch is that the royalty-rights buyer must not be available to the "losing member"; otherwise the latter can force him to renounce his royalty claim by threatening not to reach a bargain, thus restoring the original marginal cost situation. But we may imagine the development of institutions that specialize in royalty purchases, whose ultimate success depends on a reputation for never renegotiating, and whose incentives can thus not be appealed to in any single negotiation.

³ The formal solution to the right-of-way problem in automobile traffic may be that the winner is the one who first becomes fully and visibly insured against all contingencies; since he then has no incentive to avoid accident, the other must yield and knows it. (The latter cannot counter in kind; no company will insure him now that the first is insured.) More seriously, the pooling of strike funds among unions reduces the visible incentive on each individual union to avoid a strike. As in the bilateral monopoly solution suggested earlier, there is a transfer of interest to a third party with a resulting visible shift in one's own incentive structure.

⁴ W. Fellner, *Competition Among the Few* (New York, 1949), pp. 34–35, 191–97, 231–32, 234.

⁵ Inclusion of a provision on the Saar in the "Paris Agreements" that ended the occupation of Western Germany may have reflected either this principle or the one in the preceding paragraph.

⁶ In many textbook problems, such as bilateral monopoly between firms, the ends of the bargaining range are points of zero profits for one or the other party; and to settle for one's minimum position is no better than no settlement at all. But apart from certain buying and selling situations there are commonly limits on the range of acceptable outcomes, and the least favorable outcome that one is free to accept may be substantially superior to stalemate. In these cases one's overriding purpose may be to forestall any misguided commitment by the other party. If the truth is more demonstrable than a false position, a conservative initial position is indicated, as it is if any withdrawal from an initial "advanced" position would discredit any subsequent attempt to convey the truth. Actually, though a

person does not commonly invite penalties on his own behavior, the existence of an enforceable penalty on falsehood would be of assistance; if one can demonstrate, for example, his cost or income position by showing his income tax return, the penalties on fraud may enhance the value of this evidence.

Even the "pure" bilateral monopoly case becomes somewhat of this nature if the bargaining is conducted by agents or employees whose rewards are more dependent on *whether* agreement is reached than on how favorable the terms of the agreement are.

[7] Incidentally, the deterrent threat has some interesting quantitative characteristics, reflecting the general asymmetry between rewards and punishments. It is not necessary, for example, that the threat promise more damage to the party threatened than to the party carrying it out. The threat to smash an old car with a new one may succeed if believed, or to sue expensively for small damages, or to start a price war. Also, as far as the power to deter is concerned, there is no such thing as "too large" a threat; if it is large enough to succeed, it is not carried out anyway. A threat is only "too large" if its very size interferes with its credibility. Atomic destruction for small misdemeanors, like expensive incarceration for overtime parking, would be superfluous but not exhorbitant unless the threatened person considered it too awful to be real and ignored it.

[8] Mutual defense treaties among strong and weak nations might best be viewed in this light, *i.e.*, not as undertaken to reassure the small nations nor in exchange for a *quid pro quo*, but rather as a device for surrendering an embarrassing freedom of choice.

[9] A. Smithies, *The Budgetary Process in the United States* (New York, 1955), pp. 40, 56. One solution is the short tether of an apportionment process. See also T. C. Schelling, "American Foreign Assistance," *World Politics*, July 1955, VII, 609–25, regarding the same principle in foreign aid allocations.

[10] The system of supplying the police with traffic tickets that are numbered and incapable of erasures makes it possible for the officer, by writing in the license number of the car before speaking to the driver, to preclude the latter's threat. Some trucks carry signs that say, "Alarm and lock system not subject to the driver's control." The time lock on bank vaults serves much the same purpose, as does the mandatory secret ballot in elections. So does starting an invasion with a small advance force that, though too small and premature to win the objective, attaches too much "face" to the enterprise to permit withdrawal: the larger force can then be readied without fear of inviting a purely deterrent threat. At Yale the faculty is protected by a rule that denies instructors the power to change a course grade once it has been recorded.

[11] The racketeer cannot sell protection if he cannot find his customer at home; nor can the kidnapper expect any ransom if he cannot communicate with friends or relatives. Thus, as a perhaps impractical suggestion, a law that required the immediate confinement of all interested friends and relatives when a kidnapping occurred might make the prospects for ransom unprofitably dim. The rotation of watchmen and policemen, or their assignment in random pairs, not only limits their exploitation of bribes but protects them from threats.

[12] It is a remarkable institutional fact that there is no simple, universal way for persons or nations to assume commitments of the kind we have been discussing. There are numerous ways they can try, but most of them

are quite ambiguous, unsure, or only occasionally available. In the "cross-my-heart" society adverted to earlier, bargaining theory would reduce itself to game strategy and the mechanics of communication; but in most of the contemporary world the topic is mainly an empirical and institutional one of who can commit, how, and with what assurance of appreciation by the other side.

13 During 1950, the Economic Cooperation Administration declared its intention to reward Marshall Plan countries that followed especially sound policies, and to penalize those that did not, through the device of larger or smaller aid allotments. But since the base figures had not been determined, and since their determination would ultimately involve judgment rather than formulas, there would be no way afterwards to see whether in fact the additions and subtractions were made, and the plan suffered from implausibility.

14 Perhaps the common requirement for amortization of loans at frequent intervals, rather than in a lump sum at the end of the loan period, reflects an analogous principle, as does the custom of giving frequent examinations in a college course to avoid letting a student's failure hinge exclusively on a single grading decision after the course is finished.

15 This seems to be the tactic that avoided an explosion and induced de Gaulle's forces to vacate a province they had occupied in Northern Italy in June 1945, after they had announced that any effort of their allies to dislodge them would be treated as a hostile act. See Harry S. Truman, *Year of Decisions* (New York, 1955), pp. 239–42; and Winston S. Churchill, *Triumph and Tragedy*, Vol. VI of *The Second World War* (Boston, 1953), pp. 566–68.

16 The threat may seem to be a promise if the pledge behind it is only one's reputation with his adversary; but it is not a promise from which the second party can unilaterally release the threatener, since he cannot convincingly dissociate his own future estimate of the threatener from the latter's performance.

17 In an earlier age, hostages were exchanged.

18 Inability to assume an enforceable promise, like inability to perform the activity demanded, may protect one from an extortionate threat. The mandatory secret ballot is a nuisance to the voter who would like to sell his vote, but protection to the one who would fear coercion.

19 Perhaps two adversaries who look forward to some large negotiated settlement would do well to keep avenues open for negotiation of minor issues. If, for example, the number of loose ends in dispute between East and West should narrow down so much that nothing remains to be negotiated but the "ultimate issue" (some final, permanent disposition of all territories and armaments) the possibility of even opening negotiations on the latter might be jeopardized. Or if the minor issues are not disposed of, but become so attached to the "big" issue that willingness to negotiate on them would be construed as overeagerness on the whole settlement, the possibility of preparatory bargains might disappear.

27.

THE NATURE OF HIGHLY EFFECTIVE GROUPS

RENSIS LIKERT

The form of organization which will make the greatest use of human capacity consists of highly effective work groups linked together in an overlapping pattern by other similarly effective groups. The highly effective work group is, consequently, an important component of the newer theory of management. It will be important to understand both its nature and its performance characteristics. We shall examine these in this chapter, but first a few words about groups in general.

Although we have stressed the great potential power of the group for building effective organizations, it is important to emphasize that this does *not* say that all groups and all committees are highly effective or are committed to desirable goals. Groups as groups can vary from poor to excellent. They can have desirable values and goals, or their objectives can be most destructive. They can accomplish much that is good, or they can do great harm. There is nothing *implicitly* good or bad, weak or strong, about a group.

The nature of the group determines the character of its impact upon the development of its members. The values of the group, the stability of these values, the group atmosphere, and the nature of the conformity demanded by the group determine whether a group is likely to have a positive or negative impact upon the growth and behavior of its members. If the

values of the group are seen by the society as having merit, if the group is stable in its adherence to these values, and if the atmosphere of the group is warm, supportive, and full of understanding, the group's influence on the development of its members will be positive. A hostile atmosphere and socially undesirable or unstable values produce a negative impact upon the members' growth and behavior.

Loyalty to a group produces pressures toward conformity. A group may demand conformity to the idea of supporting, encouraging, and giving recognition for individual creativity, or it may value rigidity of behavior with seriously narrowing and dwarfing consequences. This latter kind of pressure for conformity keeps the members from growing and robs the group of original ideas. Many writers have pointed to these deleterious effects of conformity. They often overlook the capacity of groups to stimulate individual creativeness by placing a high value on imaginative and original contributions by their members. As Pelz's findings demonstrate, groups can contribute significantly to creativity by providing the stimulation of diverse points of view within a supportive atmosphere which encourages each individual member to pursue new and unorthodox concepts.

Some business executives are highly critical of groups—or committees—and the inability of committees to accomplish a great deal. Their criticisms are often well warranted. In many instances, committees are wasteful of time and unable to reach decisions. Sometimes the decisions, when reached, are mediocre. Moreover, some members of management at various hierarchical levels use committees as escape mechanisms—as a way to avoid the responsibility for a decision.

The surprising thing about committees is not that many or most are ineffective, but that they accomplish as much as they do when, relatively speaking, we know so little about how to use them. There has been a lack of systematic study of ways to make committees effective. Far more is known about time-and-motion study, cost accounting, and similar aspects of management than is known about groups and group processes. Moreover, in spite of the demonstrated potentiality of groups, far less research is being devoted to learning the role of groups and group processes and how to make the most effective use of them in an organization than to most management practices. We know appreciably less about how to make groups and committees effective than we know about most matters of managing.

We do know that groups can be powerful. The newer theory takes this into account and tries to make constructive use of the group's potential strength for developing and mobilizing human resources.

In this and other chapters the use of the term "group" may give the impression that groups have the capacity to behave in ways other than through the behavior of their members. Thus, such expressions appear as the "group's goals," "the group decides," or the "group motivates." In many instances, these expressions are used to avoid endless repetition of the words, "the members of the group." In other instances, something more is meant. Thus, in speaking of "group values," the intent is to refer to those values which have been established by the group through a group-decision process involving consensus. Once a decision has been reached by consensus, there are strong motivational forces, developed within each individual as a result of his membership in the group and his relationship to the other members, to be guided by that decision. In this sense, the group has goals and values and makes decisions. It has properties which may not be present, as such, in any one individual. A group may be divided in opinion, for example, although this may not be true of any one member. Dorwin Cartwright puts it this way: "The relation between the individual members and the group is analogous to the distinction made in mathematics between the properties of a set of elements and the properties of the elements within a set. Every set is composed of elements, but sets have properties which are not identical with the properties of the elements of the set."

THE HIGHLY EFFECTIVE WORK GROUP

Much of the discussion of groups in this chapter will be in terms of an ideal organizational model which the work groups in an organization can approach as they develop skill in group processes. This model group, of course, is always part of a large organization. The description of its nature and performance characteristics is based on evidence from a variety of sources. Particularly important are the observational and experimental studies of small groups such as those conducted by the Research Center for Group Dynamics (Cartwright & Zander;[1] Hare et al.;[2] Institute for Social Research, 1956;[3] Institute for Social Research, 1960;[4] Thibaut & Kelley [5]). Extensive use is made of data from studies of large-scale organizations. Another important source is the material from the National Training Laboratories (Foundation for Research on Human Behavior;[6] National Training Laboratories, 1953;[7] National Training Laboratories, 1960;[8] Stock & Thelen [9]). The NTL has focused on training in sensitivity to the reactions of others and in skills to perform the leadership and membership roles in groups.

In addition to drawing upon the above sources, the description of the ideal model is derived from theory. Some of the statements about the model for which there is little or limited experimental or observational data have been derived directly from the basic drive to achieve and maintain a sense of importance and personal worth. At several points in this chapter the author has gone appreciably beyond available specific research findings. The author feels, however, that the generalizations which are emerging based on research in organizations and on small groups, youth, and family life, personality development, consumer behavior, human motivation, and related fields lend strong support to the general theory and the derivations contained in this book.

It has been necessary to go beyond the data in order to spell out at this time in some detail the general pattern of the more complex but more effective form of organization being created by the higher-producing managers. The author hopes that the theory and model proposed will stimulate a substantial increase in basic and developmental research and that they will be tested and sharpened by that research.

The body of knowledge about small groups, while sufficiently large to make possible this description of the ideal model, is still relatively limited. Without question, as the importance of the work group as the basic building block of organizations becomes recognized, there will be a great increase in the research on groups and our knowledge about them. The over-all pattern of the model described here will be improved and clarified by such research. Our understanding of how to develop and use groups effectively will also be greatly advanced.

The following description of the ideal model defines what we mean by a *highly effective group*. The definition involves reference to several different variables. Each of them can be thought of as a continuum, i.e., as a characteristic which can vary from low to high, from unfavorable to favorable. For example, a group can vary from one in which there is hostility among the members to one in which the attitudes are warm and friendly. The ideal model is at the favorable end of each variable.

THE NATURE OF HIGHLY EFFECTIVE WORK GROUPS

The highly effective group, as we shall define it, is always conceived as being a part of a larger organization. A substantial proportion of persons in a company are members of more than one work group, especially when both line and staff are considered. As a consequence, in such groups there are always linking functions to be performed and relationships to other groups to be maintained. Our highly effective group is not an isolated entity.

All the persons in a company also belong to groups and organizations outside of the company. For most persons, membership in several groups both within and outside the company is the rule rather than the exception. This means, of course, that no single group, even the highly effective work group, dominates the life of any member. Each member of the organization feels pressures from membership in several different groups and is not influenced solely by loyalty to any one group.

Since the different groups to which a person belongs are apt to have somewhat different and often inconsistent goals and values, corresponding conflicts and pressures are created within him. To minimize these conflicts and tensions, the individual seeks to influence the values and goals of each of the different groups to which he belongs and which are important to him so as to minimize the inconsistencies and conflicts in values and goals. In striving for this reconciliation, he is likely to press for the acceptance of those values most important to him.

The properties and performance characteristics of the ideal highly effective group are as follows:

1. The members are skilled in all the various leadership and membership roles and functions required for interaction between leaders and members and between members and other members.

2. The group has been in existence sufficiently long to have developed a well-established, relaxed working relationship among all its members.

3. The members of the group are attracted to it and are loyal to its members, including the leader.

4. The members and leaders have a high degree of confidence and trust in each other.

5. The values and goals of the group are a satisfactory integration and expression of the relevant values and needs of its members. They have helped shape these values and goals and are satisfied with them.

6. In so far as members of the group are performing linking functions they endeavor to have the values and goals of the groups which they link in harmony, one with the other.

7. The more important a value seems to the group, the greater the likelihood that the individual member will accept it.

8. The members of the group are highly motivated to abide by the major values and to achieve the important goals of the group. Each member will do all that he reasonably can— and at times all in his power—to help the group achieve its central objectives. He expects every other member to do the same. This high motivation springs, in part, from the basic motive to achieve and maintain a sense of personal worth and importance. Being valued by a group whose values he shares, and deriving a sense of significance and importance from this relationship, leads each member to do this best. He is eager not to let the other members down. He strives hard to do what he believes is expected of him.

9. All the interaction, problem-solving, decision-making activities of the group occur in a supportive atmosphere. Suggestions, comments, ideas, information, criticisms are all offered with a helpful orientation. Similarly, these contributions are received in the same spirit. Respect is shown for the point of view of others both in the way contributions are made and in the way they are received.

There are real and important differences of opinion, but the focus is on arriving at sound solutions and not on exacerbating and aggravating the conflict. Ego forces deriving from the desire to achieve and maintain a sense of personal worth and importance are channeled into constructive efforts. Care is taken not to let these ego forces disrupt important group tasks, such as problem-solving. Thus, for example, a statement of the problem, a condition which any solution must meet, a suggested solution or an item of relevant fact are all treated as from the group as a whole. Care is taken so that one statement of the problem is not John's and another Bill's. A suggested solution is not referred to as Tom's and another as Dick's. All the material contributed is treated as *ours*: "One of our proposed solutions is A, another is B." In all situations involving actual or potential differences or conflict among the members of the group, procedures are used to separate the ego of each member from his contribution. In this way, ego forces do not stimulate conflict between members. Instead, they are channeled into supporting the activities and efforts of the group.

The group atmosphere is sufficiently supportive for the members to be able to accept readily any criticism which is offered and to make the most constructive use of it. The criticisms may deal with any relevant topic such as operational problems, decisions, supervisory problems, interpersonal relationships, or group processes, but whatever their content, the member feels sufficiently secure in the supportive atmosphere of the group to be able to accept, test, examine, and benefit from the criticism offered. Also, he is able to be frank and candid, irrespective of the content of the discussion: technical, managerial, factual, cognitive, or emotional. The supportive atmosphere of the group, with the feeling of security it provides, contributes to a cooperative relationship between the members. And this cooperation itself contributes to and reinforces the supportive atmosphere.

10. The superior of each work group exerts a major influence in establishing the tone and atmosphere of that work group by his leadership principles and practices. In the highly effective group, consequently, the leader adheres to those principles of leadership which create a supportive atmosphere in the group and a cooperative rather than a competitive relationship among the members. For example, he shares information fully with the group and creates an atmosphere where the members are stimulated to behave similarly.

11. The group is eager to help each member develop to his full potential. It sees, for example, that relevant technical knowledge and training in interpersonal and group skills are made available to each member.

12. Each member accepts willingly and without resentment the goals and expectations that he and his group establish for themselves. The anxieties, fears, and emotional stresses produced by direct pressure for high performance

from a boss in a hierarchical situation is not present. Groups seem capable of setting high performance goals for the group as a whole and for each member. These goals are high enough to stimulate each member to do his best, but not so high as to create anxieties or fear of failure. In an effective group, each person can exert sufficient influence on the decisions of the group to prevent the group from setting unattainable goals for any member while setting high goals for all. The goals are adapted to the member's capacity to perform.

13. The leader and the members believe that each group member can accomplish "the impossible." These expectations stretch each member to the maximum and accelerate his growth. When necessary, the group tempers the expectation level so that the member is not broken by a feeling of failure or rejection.

14. When necessary or advisable, other members of the group will give a member the help he needs to accomplish successfully the goals set for him. Mutual help is a characteristic of highly effective groups.

15. The supportive atmosphere of the highly effective group stimulates creativity. The group does not demand narrow conformity as do the work groups under authoritarian leaders. No one has to "yes the boss," nor is he rewarded for such an attempt. The group attaches high value to new, creative approaches and solutions to its problems and to the problems of the organization of which it is a part. The motivation to be creative is high when one's work group prizes creativity.

16. The group knows the value of "constructive" conformity and knows when to use it and for what purposes. Although it does not permit conformity to affect adversely the creative efforts of its members, it does expect conformity on mechanical and administrative matters to save the time of members and to facilitate the group's activities. The group agrees, for example, on administrative forms and procedures, and once they have been established, it expects its members to abide by them until there is good reason to change them.

17. There is strong motivation on the part of each member to communicate fully and frankly to the group all the information which is relevant and of value to the group's activity. This stems directly from the member's desire to be valued by the group and to get the job done. The more important to the group a member feels an item of information to be, the greater is his motivation to communicate it.

18. There is high motivation in the group to use the communication process so that it best serves the interests and goals of the group. Every item which a member feels is important, but which for some reason is being ignored, will be repeated until it receives the attention that it deserves. Members strive also to avoid communicating unimportant information so as not to waste the group's time.

19. Just as there is high motivation to communicate, there is correspondingly strong motivation to receive communications. Each member is genuinely interested in any information on any relevant matter that any member of the group can provide. This information is welcomed and trusted as being honestly and sincerely given. Members do not look "behind" the information item and attempt to interpret it in ways opposite to its purported intent. This interest of group members in information items and the treatment of such items as valid reinforces the motivation to communicate.

20. In the highly effective group, there are strong motivations to try to influence other members as well as to be receptive to influence by them. This applies to all the group's activities: technical matters, methods, organizational problems, interpersonal relationships, and group processes.

21. The group processes of the highly effective group enable the members to exert more influence on the leader and to communicate far more information to him, including suggestions as to what needs to be done and how he could do his job better, than is possible in a man-to-man relationship. By "tossing the ball" back and forth among its members, a group can communicate information to the leader which no single person on a man-to-man basis dare do. As a consequence, the boss receives all the information that the group possesses to help him perform his job effectively.

22. The ability of the members of a group to influence each other contributes to the flexibility and adaptability of the group. Ideas, goals, and attitudes do not become frozen if members are able to influence each other continuously.

Although the group is eager to examine any new ideas and methods which will help it do its job better and is willing to be influenced by its members, it is not easily shifted or swayed. Any change is undertaken only after rigorous examination of the evidence. This stability in the group's activities is due to the steadying influence of the common goals and values held by the group members.

23. In the highly effective group, individual members feel secure in making decisions which seem appropriate to them because the goals and philosophy of operation are clearly understood by each member and provide him with a solid base for his decisions. This unleashes initiative and pushes decisions down while still maintaining a coordinated and directed effort.

24. The leader of a highly effective group is selected carefully. His leadership ability is so evident that he would probably emerge as a leader in any unstructured situation. To increase the likelihood that persons of high leadership competence are selected, the organization is likely to use peer nominations and related methods in selecting group leaders.

An important aspect of the highly effective group is its extensive use of the principle of supportive relationships. An examination of the above material reveals that virtually every statement involves an application of this principle.

LEADERSHIP FUNCTIONS

Several different characteristics of highly effective groups have been briefly examined. The role of the leader in these groups is, as we have suggested, particularly important. Certain leadership functions can be shared with group members; others can be performed only by the designated leader. In an organization, for example, the leader of a unit is the person who has primary responsibility for linking his work group to the rest of the organization. Other members of the group may help perform the linking function by serving as linking pins in overlapping groups other than that provided by the line organization, but the major linking is necessarily through the line organization. The leader has full responsibility for the group's performance and for seeing that his group meets the demands and expectations placed upon it by the rest of the organization of which it is a part. Other members of the group may share this responsibility at times, but the leader can never avoid full responsibility for the adequate performance of his group.

Although the leader has full responsibility, he does not try to make all the decisions. He develops his group into a unit which, with his participation, makes better decisions than he can make alone. He helps the group develop efficient communication and influence processes which provide it with better information, more technical knowledge, more facts, and more experience for decision-making purposes than the leader alone can marshal.

Through group decision-making each member feels fully identified with each decision and highly motivated to execute it fully. The overall performance of the group, as a consequence, is even better than the excellent quality of the decisions.

The leader knows that at times decisions must be made rapidly and cannot wait for group processes. He anticipates these emergencies and establishes procedures with his group for handling them so that action can be taken rapidly with group support.

The leader feels primarily responsible for establishing and maintaining at all times a thoroughly supportive atmosphere in the group. He encourages other members to share this responsibility, but never loses sight of the fact that as the leader of a work group which is part of a larger organization his behavior is likely to set the tone.

Although the leader accepts the responsibility associated with his role of leader of a group which is part of a larger organization, he seeks to minimize the influence of his hierarchical position. He is aware that trying to get results by "pulling rank" affects adversely the effectiveness of his group and his relationship to it. Thus, he endeavors to deemphasize status. He does this in a variety of ways that fit his personality and methods of leading, as for example by:

Listening well and patiently

Not being impatient with the progress being made by the group, particularly on difficult problems

Accepting more blame than may be warranted for any failure or mistake

Giving the group members ample opportunity to express their thoughts without being constrained by the leader pressing his own views

Being careful never to impose a decision upon the group

Putting his contributions often in the form of questions or stating them speculatively

Arranging for others to help perform leadership functions which enhance their status

The leader strengthens the group and group processes by seeing that all problems *which involve the group* are dealt with by the group. He never handles such problems outside of the group nor with individual members of the group. While the leader is careful to see that all matters which involve and affect the whole group are handled by the whole group, he is equally alert not to undertake in a group-meeting agenda items or tasks which do not concern the group. Matters concerning one individual member and only that member are, of course, handled individually. Matters involving only a subgroup are handled by that subgroup. The total group is kept informed, however, of any subgroup action.

The leader fully reflects and effectively represents the views, goals, values, and decisions of his group in those other groups where he is performing the function of linking his group to the rest of the organization. He brings to the group of which he is the leader the views,

goals, and decisions of those other groups. In this way, he provides a linkage whereby communication and the exercise of influence can be performed in both directions.

The leader has adequate competence to handle the technical problems faced by his group, or he sees that access to this technical knowledge is fully provided. This may involve bringing in, as needed, technical or resource persons. Or he may arrange to have technical training given to one or more members of his group so that the group can have available the necessary technical know-how when the group discusses a problem and arrives at a decision.

The leader is what might be called "group-centered," in a sense comparable with the "employee-centered" supervisor. He endeavors to build and maintain in his group a keen sense of responsibility for achieving its own goals and meeting its obligations to the larger organization.

The leader helps to provide the group with the stimulation arising from a restless dissatisfaction. He discourages complacency and passive acceptance of the present. He helps the members to become aware of new possibilities, more important values, and more significant goals.

The leader is an important source of enthusiasm for the significance of the mission and goals of the group. He sees that the tasks of the group are important and significant and difficult enough to be challenging.

As an over-all guide to his leadership behavior, the leader understands and uses with sensitivity and skill the principle of supportive relationships.

Many of these leadership functions, such as the linking function, can be performed only by the designated leader. This makes clear the great importance of selecting competent persons for leadership positions.

ROLES OF MEMBERSHIP AND LEADERSHIP

In the highly effective group, many functions are performed either by the leader or by the members, depending upon the situation or the requirements of the moment. The leader and members, as part of their roles in the group, establish and maintain an atmosphere and relationships which enable the communication, influence, decision-making, and similar processes of the group to be performed effectively. This means not only creating positive conditions, such as a supportive atmosphere, but also eliminating any negative or blocking factors. Thus, for example, groups sometimes have to deal with members who are insensitive, who are hostile, who talk too much, or who otherwise behave in ways adversely affecting the capacity of the group to function. In handling such a problem, the group makes the member aware of his deficiency, but does this in a sensitive and considerate manner and in a way to assist the member to function more effectively in the group. The members of most ordinary groups stop listening to a member who expresses himself in a fuzzy or confused manner. In a highly effective group, the members feed back their reaction to the person involved with suggestions and assistance on how to make his contributions clear, important, and of the kind to which all will want to listen. Friendly assistance and coaching can help a member overcome excessive talking or help him to learn to think and express himself more clearly.

Benne and Sheats (10) have prepared a description of the different roles played in well-functioning groups. These roles may at times be performed by one or more group members, at other times by the leader. The list, while prepared on the basis of roles in discussion and problem-solving groups, is useful in considering the functions to be performed in any work group which is part of a larger organization.

The following material is taken from the Benne and Sheats article (pp. 42–45) with slight modifications. Group roles are classified into two broad categories:

1. *Group task roles.* These roles are related to the task which the group is deciding to undertake or has undertaken. They are directly concerned with the group effort in the selection and definition of a common problem and in the solution of that problem.

2. *Group building and maintenance roles.* These roles concern the functioning of the group as a group. They deal with the group's efforts to strengthen, regulate, and perpetuate the group as a group.

Group task roles

The following analysis assumes that the task of the group is to select, define, and solve common problems. The roles are identified in relation to functions of facilitation and coordination of group problem-solving activities. Each member may, of course, enact more than one role in any given unit of participation and a wide range of roles in successive participations. Any or all of these roles may be performed, at times, by the group "leader" as well as by various members.

A. *Initiating-contributing:* suggesting or proposing to the group new ideas or a changed way of regarding the group problem or goal. The novelty proposed may take the form of suggestions of a new group goal or a new definition of the problem. It may take the form of a suggested solution or some way of handling a difficulty that the group has encountered. Or it may take the form of a proposed new procedure for the group, a new way of organizing the group for the task ahead.

B. *Information seeking:* asking for clarification of suggestions made in terms of their factual adequacy, for authoritative information and facts pertinent to the problems being discussed.

C. *Opinion seeking:* seeking information not primarily on the facts of the case, but for a clarification of the values pertinent to what the group is undertaking or of values involved in a suggestion made or in alternative suggestions.

D. *Information giving:* offering facts or generalizations which are "authoritative" or involve presenting an experience pertinent to the group problem.

E. *Opinion giving:* stating beliefs or opinions pertinent to a suggestion made or to alternative suggestions. The emphasis is on the proposal of what should become the group's view of pertinent values, not primarily upon relevant facts or information.

F. *Elaborating:* spelling out suggestions in terms of examples or developed meanings, offering a rationale for suggestions previously made, and trying to deduce how an idea or suggestion would work out if adopted by the group.

G. *Coordinating:* showing or clarifying the relationships among various ideas and suggestions, trying to pull ideas and suggestions together or trying to coordinate the activities of various members or sub-groups.

H. *Orienting:* defining the position of the group with respect to its goals by summarizing what has occurred, departures from agreed upon directions or goals are pointed to, or questions are raised about the direction the group discussion is taking.

I. *Evaluating:* subjecting the accomplishment of the group to some standard or set of standards of group functioning in the context of the group task. Thus, it may involve evaluating or questioning the "practicality," the "logic," or the "procedure" of a suggestion or of some unit of group discussion.

J. *Energizing:* prodding the group to action or decision, attempting to stimulate or arouse the group to "greater" activity or to activity of a "higher quality."

K. *Assisting on procedure:* expediting group movement by doing things for the group—performing routine tasks, e.g., distributing materials, or manipulating objects for the group, e.g., rearranging the seating or running the recording machine, etc.

L. *Recording:* writing down suggestions, making a record of group decisions, or writing down the product of discussion. The recorder role is the "group memory."

Group building and maintenance roles

Here the analysis of member-functions is oriented to those activities which build group loyalty and increase the motivation and capacity of the group for candid and effective interaction and problem-solving. One or more members or the leader may perform each of these roles.

A. *Encouraging:* praising, showing interest in, agreeing with, and accepting the contributions of others; indicating warmth and solidarity in one's attitudes toward other group members, listening attentively and seriously to the contributions of group members, giving these contributions full and adequate consideration even though one may not fully agree with them; conveying to the others a feeling that—"that which you are about to say is of importance to me."

B. *Harmonizing:* mediating the differences between other members, attempting to reconcile disagreements, relieving tension in conflict situations through jesting or pouring oil on troubled waters, etc.

C. *Compromising:* operating from within a conflict in which one's ideas or position is involved. In this role one may offer a compromise by yielding status, admitting error, by discipling oneself to maintain group harmony, or by "coming half-way" in moving along with the group.

D. *Gate-keeping and expediting:* attempting to keep communication channels open by encouraging or facilitating the participation of others or by proposing regulation of the flow of communication.

E. *Setting standards or ideals:* expressing standards for the group or applying standards in evaluating the quality of group processes.

F. *Observing:* keeping records of various aspects of group process and feeding such data with proposed interpretations into the group's evaluation of its own procedures. The contribution of the person performing this role is usually best received or most fittingly received by the group when this particular role has been performed by this person at the request of the group and when the report to the group avoids expressing value judgments, approval, or disapproval.

G. *Following:* going along with the group, more or less passively accepting the ideas of others, serving as an audience in group discussion and decision.

The *group task roles* all deal with the intellectual aspects of the group's work. These roles are performed by members of the group during the problem-solving process, which usually involves such steps as:

1. Defining the problem
2. Listing the conditions or criteria which any satisfactory solution to the problem should meet
3. Listing possible alternative solutions
4. Obtaining the facts which bear on each possible solution
5. Evaluating the suggested solutions in terms of the conditions which a satisfactory solution should meet
6. Eliminating undesirable solutions and selecting the most desirable solution

The *group building and maintenance roles* are, as the label suggests, concerned with the emotional life of the group. These roles deal with the group's attractiveness to its members, its warmth and supportiveness, its motivation and capacity to handle intellectual problems without bias and emotion, and its capacity to function as a "mature" group.

The membership roles proposed by Benne and Sheats, while they are not definitive or complete, nevertheless point to the many complex functions performed in groups and dealt with by leader and members. The members of a highly effective group handle these roles with sensitivity and skill, and they see that the emotional life of the group contributes to the performance of the group's tasks rather than interfering with them.[11]

The highly effective group does not hesitate, for example, to look at and deal with friction between its members. By openly putting such problems on the table and sincerely examining them, they can be dealt with constructively. An effective group does not have values which frown upon criticism or which prevent bringing friction between members into the open. As a consequence, it does not put the lid on these emotional pressures, causing them to simmer below the surface and be a constant source of disruption to the performance of group tasks. The intellectual functions of any group can be performed without bias and disruption only when the internal emotional tensions and conflicts have been removed from the life of the group. Differences in ideas are stimulating and contribute to creativity, but emotional conflict immobilizes a group.

Group building and maintenance functions and group task functions are interdependent processes. In order to tackle difficult problems, to solve them creatively, and to achieve high performance, a group must be at a high level of group maintenance. Success in task processes, fortunately, also contributes to the maintenance of the group and to its emotional life, including its attraction to members and its supportive atmosphere.

In the midst of struggling with a very difficult task, a group occasionally may be faced with group maintenance problems. At such times, it may be necessary for the group to stop its intellectual activity and in one way or another to look at and deal with the disruptive emotional stresses. After this has been done, the group can then go forward with greater unity and will be more likely to solve its group task constructively.

The leader and the members in the highly effective group know that the building and maintenance of the group as well as the carrying out of tasks need to be done well. They are highly skilled in performing each of the different membership and leadership roles required. Each member feels responsible for assuming whatever role is necessary to keep the group operating in an efficient manner. In performing these required roles, the member may carry them out by himself or in cooperation with other group members. Each exercises initiative as called for by the situation. The group has a high capacity to mobilize fully all the skills and abilities of its members and focus these resources efficiently on the jobs to be done.

The larger the work group, the greater the difficulty in building it into a highly effective group. Seashore[12] found that group cohesiveness, i.e., attraction of the members to the group, decreased steadily as work groups increased in size. This finding is supported also by other data (Indik;[13] Reavans [14]).

To facilitate building work groups to high levels of effectiveness it will be desirable, consequently, to keep the groups as small as possible. This requirement, however, must be balanced against other demands on the organization, such as keeping the number of organizational levels to a minimum. This suggests the desirability of running tests and computing the relative efficiences and costs of different-sized work groups. It is probable also that the optimum size for a group will vary with the kind of work the group is doing.

The highly effective group as described in this chapter, it will be recalled, is an "ideal model." It may sound completely unattainable. This does not appear to be the case. There is impressive evidence supporting the view that this ideal can be approximated, if not fully reached, in actual operations in any organization. This evidence is provided by the highest-producing managers and supervisors in American industry and government. If the measure-

ments of their work groups and the reports of their work-group members are at all accurate, some of these managers have built and are operating work groups strikingly similar to our ideal model.

This chapter started by observing that groups can have constructive or destructive goals and can achieve these goals fully or partially, that there is nothing inherently good or bad about groups. If we reflect on the nature and functional characteristics of the highly effective group, however, some qualification of our initial comments may be warranted. In the highly effective group, the members can and do exercise substantial amounts of influence on the group's values and goals. As a consequence, these goals reflect the long-range as well as the short-range needs, desires, and values of its members. If we assume that the long-range desires and values will reflect, on the average, some of the more important long-range values and goals of the total society, we can draw some inferences about the highly effective group. These groups will, in terms of probability, reflect the constructive values and goals of their society. They are likely to be strong groups seeking "good" goals.

NOTES

[1] D. Cartwright, and A. Zander (eds.), *Group Dynamics: Research and Theory*, 2nd ed. (Evanston, Ill.: Row, Peterson, 1960).

[2] P. Hare, E. F. Borgatta, and R. F. Bales, *Small Groups* (New York: Knopf, 1955).

[3] Institute for Social Research, *Publications: 1946–1956* (Ann Arbor, Mich.: Author, 1956).

[4] Institute for Social Research, *Publications: Sept. 1956-Jan. 1960* (Ann Arbor, Mich.: Author, 1960).

[5] J. W. Thibaut, and H. H. Kelley, *The Social Psychology of Groups* (New York: Wiley, 1959).

[6] Foundation for Research on Human Behavior, *An Action Research Program for Organization Improvement* (Ann Arbor, Mich.: Author, 1960).

[7] National Training Laboratories, *Explorations in Human Relations Training* (Washington: National Education Association, 1953).

[8] National Training Laboratories, *An Annotated Bibliography of Research, 1947–1960* (Washington: National Education Association, 1960).

[9] D. Stock, and H. A. Thelen, *Emotional Dynamics and Group Culture* (Washington: National Training Laboratories NEA, 1958).

[10] K. D. Benne, and P. Sheats, "Functional Roles of Group Members," *Journal of Social Issues*, (Spring, 1948), vol. 4, no. 2, pp. 42–45.

[11] Although the Benne and Sheat list does not define each category unambiguously, it is useful in helping a group analyze and improve its processes. Another list has been prepared by Bales (1950) which has relatively precise definitions. The Bales list will be of interest to those who wish to do research on group processes or who wish to observe and analyze them systematically. Cf. R. F. Bales, *Interaction Process Analysis: A Method for the Study of Small Groups* (Reading, Mass.: Addison-Wesley, 1950).

[12] S. E. Seashore, *Group Cohesiveness in the Industrial Work Group* (Ann Arbor, Mich.: Institute for Social Research, 1954).

[13] B. P. Indik, "Organization Size and Member Participation," unpublished doctoral dissertation, University of Michigan, 1961.

[14] R. W. Reavans, *Operational Research and Personnel Management*, part II (London: Institute of Personnel Management, 1959).

28.

ADMINISTRATIVE THEORY AND CHANGE IN ORGANIZATIONS

DANIEL E. GRIFFITHS

The observer of social organizations is forced to the conclusion that organizations are *not* characterized by change. Indeed, when organizations are viewed over a long period of time, their outstanding characteristic appears to be stability, rather than change. A social organization is the structural mechanism employed by a society to achieve one or more of its commonly accepted goals. Since the goals do not change noticeably and each organization's activities are rather clearly demarcated, any particular organization comes into existence with a great deal of built-in stability. This stability is so great as to constitute a powerful resistance to change.[1] On the other hand, it is clear that organizations *do* change. In many the increments of change are small, but in others change is so radical as to cause the disappearance of the original organization and the appearance of a new one.

The Roman Catholic Church is an excellent example of a highly stable organization, existing in the same form over a long period of time. Its organizational goals have varied but little since its inception, yet it has changed. The changes have generally been small and well spaced, and have tended to vary internal procedures or policies necessary to defend the Church against an unfriendly environment. Radical changes, on the other hand, are illustrated by governmental revolutions. The over-

From Matthew B. Miles, ed., *Innovations in Education*, Teachers College Press, New York, 1964, pp. 425–436. © 1964, Teachers College, Columbia University. Reprinted with the permission of the publisher.

throw of the Tsarist regime in Russia and the eventual rule of the Bolshevists point up the fact that an organization (the governing body) can change to such a degree that it is completely replaced.

It should be noted in both these cases that the stimulus for change came from *outside* the organization. It would not be a far-fetched presumption to state that the hierarchies of the Catholic Church and of the Tsarist government alike would have much preferred to go on as they had been going.

There are few empirical measures of the initiation of change in organizations. However, the one most familiar to the writer substantiates the basic assumption of this paper. A measure called *Organizational Change* was developed as part of the scoring procedure in a study of the administrative performance of elementary school principals in a simulated school.[2] The average score (highest possible, 70) was 5.88; standard deviation, 2.92; and odd-even reliability, .61. The observer of change must reconcile himself to study of the infrequent, not the frequent, in organizational life.

This paper attempts to state a theory of administrative change which will, at least in part, account for some of the commonly made observations concerning change in organizations. Space limitations prevent a full description of detailed observations of change in organizations. The questions to which the theory is addressed are: (1) Under what conditions does change occur? (2) Under what conditions is change least apt to occur?

DEFINITIONS: ORGANIZATION, ADMINISTRATION, CHANGE

It is necessary to say what is meant by the terms *organization, administration,* and *change.*

First of all, only *formal* organization is being considered; this term is construed to mean an ensemble of individuals who perform distinct but interrelated and coordinated functions, in order that one or more tasks may be completed. Thus we have the public school, the army, the governmental bureau, the business company. In each type of organization, the task is more or less clearly understood and approved by the public. It is obvious that organizations are, at least to some extent, a consequence of division of labor in society. It follows that any one organization functions as part of a larger social system.[3]

What Kaufman[4] has to say about organizations is also acceptable as contributing to a definition of the concept:

> The term *organization* will refer to all sets of human beings who exhibit the following five properties . . . :
> 1. Some criterion or set of criteria by which *members* may be distinguished from non-members (i.e., demarcation of boundaries, though not necessarily territorial boundaries);
> 2. Some method of *replenishment* of materials used up by the members (also, for long-lived organizations, some methods of *replacing personnel* lost by the organization through death, departure, disablement, or other factors);
> 3. *Elicitation of effort* of some kind by individual members of the organization;
> 4. *Coordination* of individual activities— that is to say, some blending of the methods of eliciting effort and the methods of inhibiting activity such that the timing and character of each member's activities facilitate, or at least do not impede, the activities of other members.
> 5. Some pattern of *distribution* of materials and messages among the members, and perhaps of movement of people as well.

In summary, a formal *organization* comprises a number of people who perform a task sanctioned by the society in which it functions. The members of the organization are visible as such to the public, work together, and have methods of replenishing the organization with both materials and members.

The term *administration* is used to designate the process (cycle of events) engaged in by all the members of the formal organization to direct and control the activities of the members of the organization. Though all members participate in "administration," there is of course differential distribution of influence within the organization. Those members who are officially charged with the functions of administration are called *administrators*.[5]

It is assumed that educational organizations do not differ in essential characteristics from any other type of formal organization. When one uses definitions such as those employed above, it is difficult to imagine what the differences could be.

The word *change* is used to mean an alteration in the structure of the organization, in any of its processes, or in its goals or purposes. The revision of a rule, the introduction of a new procedure, or the revision of the purposes or direction of the organization are all subsumed under the concept of change. There are different degrees of change; a variation in a teacher's lunchroom assignment might be considered a minor change, and the reconstituting of a public school system to include a junior college might be considered a major change.

THE MODEL: SYSTEM THEORY

The model employed in building this theory of administrative change is system theory as discussed by Hearn.[6] Although Hearn's ideas are based upon those of Miller[7] and other system theorists, his careful work is a definite improvement over that of his predecessors.

Systems

A *system* may be simply defined as a complex of elements in mutual interaction. This construct has been used in almost every area of science for a long period of time. Allport[8] offered a more comprehensive definition:

> . . . any recognizably delimited aggregate of dynamic elements that are in some way interconnected and interdependent and that continue to operate together according to certain laws and in such a way as to produce some characteristic total effect. A sys-

tem, in other words, is something that is concerned with some kind of activity and preserves a kind of integration and unity; and a particular system can be recognized as distinct from other systems to which, however, it may be dynamically related. Systems may be complex; they may be made up of interdependent sub-systems, each of which, though less autonomous than the entire aggregate, is nevertheless fairly distinguishable in operation.

A more succinct definition is that of Hall and Fagen[9]: "A system is a set of objects together with relationships between the objects and between their attributes."

All systems except the smallest have *subsystems*, and all but the largest have *suprasystems* which are their environments.

Systems may be *open* or *closed*. An open system is related to and makes exchanges with its environment, while a closed system is not related to and does not make exchanges with its environment. Further, a closed system is characterized by an increase in entropy, while open systems tend toward a steady state.

Open systems

Open systems, of course, have the properties of systems in general, but also have certain characteristics which distinguish them from closed systems.[10]

1. Open systems exchange matter, energy, and information with their environment; that is, they have *inputs* and *outputs*.

2. Open systems tend to maintain themselves in *steady states*. A steady state occurs when a constant ratio is maintained among the components of the system, given a continuous input to the system. A burning candle is often used as an example of a steady state. Upon being lighted the flame is small, but it rapidly grows to its normal size and maintains the size as long as the candle and its environment exist.

3. Open systems are *self-regulating*. In the illustration above, a sudden draft will cause the flame to flicker, but with the cessation of the draft the flame regains its normal characteristics.

4. Open systems display *equifinality*; that is, identical results can be obtained from different initial conditions. Hearn points out that equifinality in the human being (an open system) is illustrated by the case of two babies, one born prematurely, the other at full term. The babies may look very different at birth, and may be in different stages of development, but within a few months the differences will have disappeared. Even though the initial states may differ, human beings generally achieve the same stages of development.

5. Open systems maintain their steady states, in part, through the *dynamic interplay of sub-systems operating as functional processes*. This means that the various parts of the system function without persistent conflicts that can be neither resolved nor regulated.

6. Open systems maintain their steady states through *feedback* processes. The concept of feedback as used in system theory is more elaborate than its normal usage implies. The reader is referred to Hearn[11] for a full discussion. In general, feedback refers to that portion of the output of a system which is fed back to the input and affects succeeding outputs, and to the property of being able to adjust future conduct by reference to past performance.

7. Open systems display *progressive segregation*.[12] This process occurs when the system divides into a hierarchical order of subordinate systems, which gain a certain independence of each other.

Hearn[13] summarizes the properties of *open* or *organismic systems* in this manner:

> There is a dynamic interplay among the essential functional sub-processes or sub-systems in the organismic system which enables it to maintain itself in a homeostatic steady state. Assuming a sufficient input of material from its environment, the organism develops toward a characteristic state despite initial conditions (equifinality). All of this is accomplished through an automatic self-regulatory process.

A THEORY OF ADMINISTRATIVE CHANGE

It is proposed that system theory serve as a model for a theory of administrative change. As indicated above, any open system has supra-systems and sub-systems. Let an organization be considered as an open system, comprised of human interactions, that maintains a definite boundary. Further, consider administration as an open sub-system, and the environment as a supra-system. The administration sub-system is located at the point of tangency of the three systems, as in Figure 28–1.

Infrequency of change

The above model for a theory of administrative change would lead one to hypothesize that change would be relatively infrequent. Open systems maintain themselves in steady states (a constant ratio is maintained among the components of the system), whereas change calls for the establishment of new ratios among the components of the system. One could also argue on purely logical grounds that society establishes organizations, or sanctions their establishment, to accomplish rather specific purposes. It is, in part, this original sanction that gives organizations their characteristic steady state.

Conditions aiding change

Although it is infrequent, change does occur in organizations; at times the change is radical. Under what conditions might change be expected to occur?

Several characteristics of open systems were discussed in the presentation of the model. Some of these have relevance here: input–output, steady state, self-regulation, interplay of sub-systems, feedback, and progressive segregation. An examination of these characteristics leads to several ideas about organizational change.

Since the tendency of organizations is to maintain a steady state, the major impetus for change comes from outside rather than

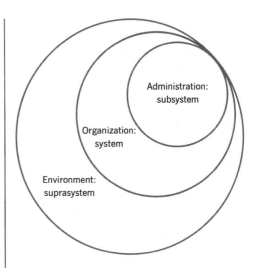

Figure 28–1.

inside an organization. Since organizations are open systems, they have a self-regulating characteristic which causes them to revert to the original state following a minor change made to meet demands of the supra-system.

Many organizations bring in outsiders as administrators, believing that change for the better will result. This apparently works in many cases, and the proposed theory can accommodate this observation. All organizations exhibit some form of progressive segregation or hierarchical order. The order makes it possible for change to occur from the top down but practically impossible for it to occur from the bottom up.

These ideas and others are now formulated as a series of propositions.

PROPOSITION 1. The major impetus for change in organizations is from the outside.

Discussion. It is speculated that when change in an organization does occur, the initiative for the change is from outside the system— that is, from the supra-system. In the study of elementary school principals mentioned above, it was found that those who scored relatively higher on *Organizational Change* were not aggressive leaders as such, but administrators with a tendency to make changes in the organization to please outsiders and superiors, or to comply with suggestions of subordinates.[14] The correlation between the *Organizational Change* score and response to outsiders was somewhat higher than the correlation between the *Organizational Change* score and response to subordinates. The nature of changes made in response to outsiders and insiders was not determined in this study, but it could be hypothesized that changes made in response to insiders will be concerned with clarification of rules and internal procedures, while those made in response to outsiders will be concerned with *new* rules and procedures, and possibly with changes in purpose and direction of the organization. It appears that administrators who initiate change are influenced more by those outside the system than by those inside.

Practical administrators are well aware of this proposition. The use of consultants, evaluation teams, citizens' committees, and professional organizations to bring change to an organization suggests a clear recognition on the part of administrators that an organization is more apt to change in response to an external force than to an internal force.

PROPOSITION 2. The degree and duration of change is directly proportional to the intensity of the stimulus from the supra-system.

Discussion. As an illustration of the proposition (but not, of course, as proof of it), it has been noted that the rate of instructional innovation in New York State public schools more than doubled within fifteen months of the launching of the Soviet Sputnik I; this increase was maintained through 1961.[15]

In order that this proposition be tested, it will be necessary to establish ways of measuring degree of change and intensity of stimulus. Duration is simply a matter of time. If the suggested measurements could be made, the proposition could be tested in all of its ramifications.

PROPOSITION 3. Change in an organization is more probable if the successor to the chief administrator is from outside the organization, than if he is from inside the organization.

Discussion. The model specifies feedback as a characteristic of open systems. Feedback tends to maintain the system in a steady state. The administrator who comes from outside does not receive feedback from his actions, since well-established channels for feedback to him do not exist. When an insider is appointed to the top post in an organization, the feedback channels which have been established over the years function to keep him operating in the steady state.

An outsider may bring change into an organization out of sheer ignorance. Not knowing the system, he will function in terms of a system which he *does* know. Being without ties in the system, he will not receive the feedback that would keep an insider from initiating procedures and policies differing from those in use.

The insider will also keep the sub-systems functioning without conflicts, since he knows how these sub-systems function to maintain the steady state. The outsider may upset the functioning of the sub-systems, through either ignorance or design. Not knowing how sub-systems function, he can inadvertently throw them into conflict through orders or expectations not customarily held for these systems. On the other hand, he may introduce conflict among the sub-systems, by purposefully changing their functions. This will, of course, upset the steady state and may in time create a state more to the liking of the chief administrator. The notion of controlled conflict as a method of change in an organization may have a sound theoretical base.

In a study of school superintendents, Carlson[16] found that those appointed from inside the system tend to act in such a way as to maintain the system, while those appointed from outside tend to be innovators.

PROPOSITION 4. "Living systems respond to continuously increasing stress first by a lag in response, then by an over-compensatory response, and finally by catastrophic collapse of the system."[17]

Discussion. What happens to a system subjected to constantly increasing stress? Miller has formulated the above proposition, which appears to have much relevance to education. As public education is attacked (for example, on the teaching of reading), it responds by proclaiming a strong defense. The schools claim that they have been teaching reading well. In those districts where the defense was not strong enough and the attack grew even stronger, the schools responded by changing their methods of teaching reading. The proposition has not been tested fully, because at this point the stress has always been lifted.

Revolutionary changes occur when the prediction of this proposition is carried through to completion. The collapse of the old system is followed by the establishment of a new system.

Conditions inhibiting change

Many of the characteristics of organizations are such that they make the initiation of change difficult. When organizations are viewed in terms of the system-theory model these characteristics appear very clearly.

PROPOSITION 5.   The number of innovations is inversely proportional to the tenure of the chief administrator.

Discussion. The longer an administrator stays in a position, the less likely he is to introduce change. The model indicates some reasons for this. All of the processes which bring about the steady state have been given time to operate. Feedback channels have become fully established. Progressive segregation has set in; the sub-systems have become structured and have gained relative independence. Change is thus more difficult, because the frequency of interaction between sub-systems is decreased, and the chances for effective communication are diminished.

PROPOSITION 6.   The more hierarchical the structure of an organization, the less the possibility of change.

Discussion. The system-theory model points out that a characteristic of open systems is progressive segregation, and this occurs as the system divides into a hierarchical order of subordinate systems which gain a degree of independence of each other. The more hierarchical the sub-systems become, the more independent the sub-systems, and the more difficult it is to introduce change.

PROPOSITION 7.   When change in an organization does occur, it will tend to occur from the top down, not from the bottom up.

Discussion. Using the same reasoning as in Proposition 6, a hierarchical order would enable change to occur from the top down, but the relative independence of the sub-systems would tend to slow down the rate of change. The structure makes change from the bottom up very difficult; one would expect little if any change to be introduced in this way.

PROPOSITION 8.   The more functional the dynamic interplay of sub-systems, the less the change in an organization.

Discussion. As a system operates, the sub-systems develop methods of interacting in which conflict is at a minimum. Each of the sub-systems has a function to perform, and each does so in such a manner as to allow it to maintain a high degree of harmony with the others. Each says to the others, in effect, "If you don't rock the boat, I won't." Change is practically synonymous with conflict, since it means that the arrangements the sub-systems have worked out no longer hold. Sub-systems resist conflict, and in the same manner resist change.

SUMMARY

Using system theory as a model, this paper develops a set of propositions concerning change in organizations. The propositions are restated briefly in the following paragraphs.

Change in organizations will be expedited by the appointment of outsiders rather than insiders as chief administrators. Such administrators will introduce change either because they do not know the system, or because they have a different concept of how the system should function. Most changes result as responses to the demands of the supra-system. The magnitude and duration of change is directly proportional to the intensity of the stimulus from outside. Revolutionary change occurs when a system is placed under continuous, unrelenting stress which is maintained in spite of overcompensating responses, and which results in the collapse of the system and its replacement by a new system.

Change is impeded by the hierarchical nature of organizations. The hierarchical structure makes innovation from the bottom virtually impossible, and the independence of the subsystems isolates them from innovative activity. The functional nature of the activities of each sub-system generates conflict-reducing behavior which, again, is counter to change-inducing behavior. Further, the longer the tenure of the chief administrator, the fewer the changes.

NOTES

[1] See Presthus, R. *The organizational society*, (New York: Knopf, 1962), especially Chapters 1 and 2, for an analysis of the way in which system forces prevent change in organizations.

[2] Hemphill, J., Griffiths, D. E., & Frederiksen, N. *Administrative performance and personality*, (New York: Bureau of Publications, Teachers College, Columbia University, 1962), Esp. Chap. 8.

[3] Griffiths, D. E. *Administrative theory*, (New York: Appleton-Century-Crofts, 1959), p 77.

[4] Kaufman, H. Why organizations behave as they do: an outline of a theory. In *Papers presented at an interdisciplinary seminar on administrative theory*, (Austin: University of Texas, 1961), p. 39.

[5] Griffiths, *op. cit.*

[6] Hearn, G. *Theory building in social work*, (Toronto: University of Toronto Press, 1958).

[7] Miller, J. G. "Toward a general theory for the behavioral sciences," *Amer. Psychol.*, (1955, *10*), 513–531.

[8] Allport, F. H. *Theories of perception and the concept of structure*, (New York: Wiley, 1955), p. 469.

[9] Hall, A. D., & Fagen, R. E. General systems. In L. von Bertalanffy & A. Rapoport (Eds.), *Yearbook of the Society for the Advancement of General Systems Theory*, (Ann Arbor: Braun-Brumfield, 1956), p. 18.

[10] Hearn, *op. cit.*

[11] *Ibid.*

[12] von Bertalanffy, L., "An outline of general systems theory," *Brit. Jour. Philos. Sci.*, (1950, *1*), 148.

[13] Hearn, *op. cit.*, pp. 48–49.

[14] Hemphill *et. al.*, *op. cit.*

[15] Brickell, H. M. *Commissioner's 1961 catalog of educational change*, (Albany, New York: State Education Department, 1961), p. 27.

[16] Carlson, R. O., "Succession and performance among school superintendents," *Admin. Sci. Quart.* (1961, *6*), 210–227.

[17] Miller, *op. cit.*, p. 525.

29.

PLANNED CHANGE AND ORGANIZATIONAL HEALTH: FIGURE AND GROUND

MATTHEW B. MILES

Any observer of the applied behavioral sciences today would have to note a remarkable interest in the entire problem of planned change. Scientists and practitioners alike are concerned with the stages of planned change in groups, organizations, and communities; with the question of how change processes can be managed in a meaningful sense of that word; and with the characteristics of the "change agent," that miraculous middleman between What Science Has Proved and What We Are Up Against.

There is a growing literature, in journals as diverse as *Applied Anthropology* and *Petroleum Refiner*; there have already been thoughtful attempts to collect this literature, and to conceptualize the problems involved.[1,2] All this is gratifying to beleaguered school administrators—and to everyone who, following Kurt Lewin's most frequently-quoted dictum, believes that "there is nothing so practical as a good theory."

Yet it seems to me that there is an important, but often-overlooked aspect of what is being said and done about planned change: the notion that any particular planned change effort is deeply conditioned by the state of the system in which it takes place. For example, properties of the organization such as communication adequacy, and the distribution of influence have a powerful effect on the speed and durability of adoption of any particular

From *Change Processes in the Public Schools*, Center for the Advanced Study of Educational Administration, Oregon University, 1965, pp. 11–34. Reprinted by permission.

innovation, from *English 2600* to data processing of teacher marks. To use an image from Gestalt psychology, specific planned change attempts have most typically been "in figure," occupying the focus of attention, while the organization itself has remained the "ground."

I believe this emphasis is both practically and theoretically unfortunate. It is time for us to recognize that successful efforts at planned change must take as a primary target the improvement of *organization health*—the school system's ability not only to function effectively, but to develop and grow into a more fully-functioning system.

Perhaps I can illustrate my assertion that organization properties have often been treated peripherally, or left to sit as background phenomena. If you have examined the literature on the diffusion of innovations, perhaps with the aid of Everett Rogers' excellent compendium[3] you will notice that a good deal of attention is paid to the individual innovator, to when he adopts the innovation, and why. But the literature remains nearly silent on the organizational setting in which innovation takes place. I suspect this has several antecedents.

For one thing, the typical adopter in most rural sociological studies is an individual farmer rather than a collectivity such as an organization. The farmer's role in the community setting turns out to be important, but aside from studies on "traditional" versus "modern" community norms, the influence of the larger social setting tends to be underplayed.

Paul Mort did, on the other hand, make extensive studies of innovation by organizations—school districts.[4] But Mort, far from being even an amateur sociologist, appeared almost aggressively ignorant of available knowledge about the functioning of organizations and communities. His "common sense" categories and demographic indices give us no inkling of what was really going on in the districts who supplied him with data.

Even Dick Carlson's study[5] of the adoption of modern math by school superintendents suffers a bit, I think, from a kind of "great man" tendency; the internal dynamics of the school system are seen as less important than characteristics of the local superintendent, such as his position in the reference group of administrators in the region. His data are compelling, but I suspect they would have been even more powerful had he gone into more depth on the dynamics of the local setting.

From the anthropological side, I think it fair to say that there has been an over-emphasis on the properties of a particular innovation itself, its diffusion across systems, and its integration within systems—without a corresponding degree of interest in the dynamics and functioning of the receiving organization as such. Art Gallaher[6] has thoughtfully discussed power structure in innovation-receiving systems, the actual prestige of advocates of the innovation, and other matters influencing how (or if) an innovation will be integrated into the local organization. But even here, I think the analysis is overfocused on the "thinginess" of the particular innovation, taking the local system itself as a kind of unmodifiable ground against which the innovation shows up in stark figure.

One more example. The currently widespread emphasis on the importance of "dissemination of research findings," and even the recent effort of the U.S. Office to provide development and demonstration centers, likewise avoid the problem. They share the popular view that the *content* or demonstrated efficacy of a particular educational innovation, as such, is the crucial thing in determining whether or not it will be adopted and used effectively. As you can gather, I am taking a decidedly processual view here: organization dynamics are the focus of attention.

I hope I have not misrepresented the views of my colleagues. It would please me to be corrected, in fact. What I do want to counter in this paper is a set of assumptions (by scientists or practitioners) that organization properties—from decision-making methods to interpersonal climate—are simply "there," that they are relatively invariant, and cannot (or should not) themselves be made the subject of planned change efforts.

More generally, the position being taken is this. It seems likely that the state of health of an educational organization can tell us more than anything else about the probable success of any particular change effort. Economy of effort would suggest that we should look at the state of an organization's health as such, and try to improve it—in preference to struggling with a series of more or less inspired shortrun change efforts as ends in themselves.

To analogize with persons for a minute: the neurotic who struggles through one unavailing search for "something new" after another will never be genuinely productive until he faces and works through fundamental problems of his own functioning. Genuine productiveness—in organizations as in persons—rests on a clear sense of identity, on adequate connection with reality, on a lively problem-solving stance, and on many other things, to which I would like to turn in a moment. Here I only wish to leave you with the root notion that attention to organization health ought to be priority one for any administrator seriously concerned with innovativeness in today's educational environment.

In the remainder of this paper, I should like, first, to deal with some problems in the very concept of health, both generally and as applied to organizations. The next section reviews the conception of "organization" employed in the rest of the paper, and outlines some dimensions of organization health as I see them. All this is rather general, and I should then like to turn to some discussion of the special properties of *educational* organizations, as such, and what their particular ways of departing from optimum organization health seem to be. Lastly, as an applied behavioral scientist, I would be remiss if I did not discuss some representative technologies for inducing organization health, and suggest some principles underlying them.

Most of this paper is frankly speculative, though it is informed by a good deal of current work in the applied behavioral sciences—and even, now and then, by some contact with phenomena such as superintendents, principals, teachers and children. All of the notions in the paper need vigorous discussion and testing.

SOME PROBLEMS IN THE CONCEPT OF "HEALTH"

The historical, common-sense notion of health is that it represents absence of illness, disease, suffering, wrongness in an organism. If not arrested, a serious "sickness" may lead to irreversible changes, such as organ impairment, atrophy or death. But beginning (to my knowledge) with the interesting British work in preventive medicine dubbed the "Peckham Experiment," there has been more and more medical concern with the notion of positive well-being or optimal functioning. That is, disease-freeness, in and of itself, does not guarantee that an organism will in fact be coping with life's adventures with a sense of *élan*, and growing while it does so.

This conception of positive health—in many ways a sneaky, vague notion—has also been receiving more and more attention in the mental health literature.[7] And there is increasing interest in the fields of psychotherapy and human relations training with the notion of "self-actualization." Both "positive health" and "self-actualization" imply a considerable gap between sheer disease-freeness, and something that might be called the fully functioning human being. This is an attractive idea; it is consistent with much of our common sense experience, and it caters to the American notion of the (nearly) infinitely-improvable man.

But even if something like "positive health" or "self-actualization" can be said to exist— and Maslow's case studies[8] are instructive and plausible in this respect—there are some traps and difficulties in applying such concepts to organization functioning. One, of course, is the tendency to go "over-organismic," reifying the organization into some kind of gigantic person, or least organism. This, of course, leads into the hoary disputation about whether systems larger than that of the individual person are "real,"[9] a totally unprofitable byway which I do not propose to enter at the moment.

Another danger is that the notion of health implies "sickness"; school administrators are having enough difficulty as it is without being accused of being at the helm of pathological vessels on the stormy seas of innovation. The very image of "sickness" itself diverts attention away from the notion of positive growth and development, implying that only correction of some negative or painful state is required.

Finally, there are the risks involved in any discussion involving "ideal types"—distortion of reality, or blindness to large portions of it, and a prevalence of normative, preachment-type statement-making about any particular organization (or, more usually, *all* organizations).

All these objections have some validity; I do not propose to eradicate them here, only to bring them to awareness, so they do not hamper the subsequent discussion unduly. In brief, the intellectual risks of an "organization health" approach seem to me far outweighed by the advantages. A reasonably clear conception of organization health would seem to be an important prerequisite to a wide range of activities involving organizations: research of any meaningful sort; attempts to improve the organization as a place to live, work, and learn; and—not least—the day-to-day operations of any particular organization, such as your own school system.[10]

ORGANIZATIONS: THEIR NATURE

Formal definitions show that the author of the paper has paid his debt to "the literature"; they may sometimes even help in de-limiting the sphere of discussion. "Organization" is here treated as a special case of the more general concept "system," more particularly "open system." The latter is defined as:

A bounded collection of interdependent parts, devoted to the accomplishment of some goal or goals, with the parts maintained in a steady state in relation to each other and the environment by means of (1) standard modes of operation, and (2) feedback from the environment about the consequences of system actions.[11]

Argyris[12] poses a broadly similar definition: "(1) a plurality of parts, [which] (2) maintaining themselves through their interrelatedness and, (3) achieving specific objective(s), (4) while accomplishing (2) and (3) adapt to the external environment thereby (5) maintaining their interrelated state of parts."

Either of these definitions would apply to a system such as a candle flame, an air-conditioning unit, or a school district. For our purposes, it is perhaps sufficient to say that the above definitions, in the special case of the "organization," are expected to apply to social systems larger than a face-to-face group, and with a reasonable degree of goal specification (this latter to exclude larger systems, such as communities and nations).

Somewhat more specifically, reference to Figure 29–1 will indicate the notion "educational organization" used as a backdrop for this paper. Notice that the usual hierarchical arrangement is absent, since the "parts" are not seen as persons or work groups, but as social-psychological components of the system which cross-cut persons and groups. The figure indicates that the organization exists in an environment from which it receives inputs (money, personnel, and children) and to which it releases outputs in terms of goal achievement, and morale and learning motivation of the clients in the organization (children). Between the input and the output, to paraphrase T. S. Eliot, falls the shadow of a number of other components. The inhabitants of an educational organization must have reasonably clear perceptions of the goal or goals to which the system is devoted; these in turn affect role specifications and performance of the inhabitants. Systems of reward and penalty regulate role performance, as do the norms governing the style of interpersonal transactions in the system. The arrows in the diagram are intended to indicate directions of influence between parts of the system, as well as to suggest that a variety of feedback loops exist which serve to maintain the system in a reasonably steady state.

If all goes well, desired system outputs are achieved. But this is not all: above and beyond the network of parts and their functioning, we can conceive of a set of system "health" characteristics, which have to do with the continued adequacy and viability of the organization's coping. More of this below. Here it is perhaps sufficient to sketch out the schematic model, and point out that it assumes nothing about the specific kinds of structures—planful or emergent—appearing in any particular system. The model will presumably fit a classical pyramidal scheme, as well as a number of more or less radical variants from this (e.g., those suggested by Argyris).[13]

ORGANIZATION HEALTH

Our present thinking about organization health is that it can be seen as a set of fairly durable *second-order* system properties, which tend to transcend short-run effectiveness. A healthy organization in this sense not only survives in its environment, but continues to cope adequately over the long haul, and continuously develops and extends its surviving and coping abilities. Short-run operations on any particular day may be effective or ineffective, but continued survival, adequate coping, and growth are taking place.

A *steadily* ineffective organization would presumably not be healthy; on balance, "health" implies a summation of effective short-run coping. But notice that an organization *may* cope effectively in the short run (as for example by a speed-up or a harsh cost-cutting drive), but at the cost of longer-run variables, such as those noted below. The classic example, of course, is an efficiency drive which cuts short-run costs and results in long-run labor dissatisfaction and high turnover.

To illustrate in more detail what is meant by "second-order property," here is a list of ten dimensions of organization health that seem plausible to me. Many of them are drawn by heuristic analogy from the behavior of persons or small groups; this does *not* mean, of course, that organizations necessarily are precisely homologous to persons or groups—only that

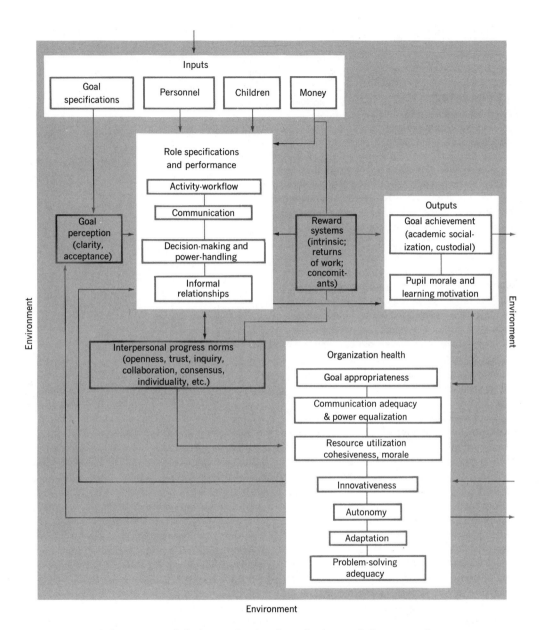

Figure 29–1. Schematic model of organization functioning and change environment.

thinking in this way may get us somewhere on what, it must be admitted, is a very complex problem indeed. Here then are ten dimensions. They are not, of course, mutually exclusive, and interact with each other vigorously within any particular organization. Both Jahoda[14] and Argyris[15] have commented on the importance of a multiple-criterion approach to the assessment of health, given the present state of our knowledge and the fact, as a college roommate of mine once remarked with blinding insight, "You know, everything is really connected to everything else."

The first three dimensions are relatively "tasky," in that they deal with organizational goals, the transmission of messages, and the way in which decisions are made.

1. *Goal focus.* In a healthy organization, the goal (or more usually goals) of the system would be reasonably clear to the system members, and reasonably well accepted by them.[16] This clarity and acceptance, however, should be seen as a necessary but insufficient condition for organization health. The goals must also be *achievable* with existing or available resources, and be *appropriate*—more or less congruent with the demands of the environment. The last feature may be most critical. Switching back to the person level for a moment, consider the obsessive patient who sets the clear, accepted, achievable goal for himself of washing his hands 250 times a day. The question remains: is this an appropriate goal in light of what else there is to do in life?

2. *Communication adequacy.* Since organizations are not simultaneous face-to-face systems like small groups, the movement of information within them becomes crucial. This dimension of organization health implies that there is relatively distortion-free communication "vertically," "horizontally," and across the boundary of the system to and from the surrounding environment. That is, information travels reasonably well—just as the healthy person "knows himself" with a minimum level of repression, distortion, etc. In the healthy organization, there is good and prompt sensing of internal strains; there are enough data about problems of the system to insure that a good diagnosis of system difficulties can be made. People have the information they need, and have gotten it without exerting undue efforts, such as those involved in moseying up to the superintendent's secretary, reading the local newspaper, or calling excessive numbers of special meetings.

3. *Optimal power equalization.* In a healthy organization the distribution of influence is relatively equitable. Subordinates (if there is a formal authority chart) can influence upward, and even more important—as Likert[17] has demonstrated—they perceive that their boss can do likewise with *his* boss. In such an organization, inter-group struggles for power would not be bitter, though inter-group conflict, (as in every human system known to man) would undoubtedly be present. The basic stance of persons in such an organization, as they look up, sideways and down, is that of collaboration rather than explicit or implicit coercion. The units of the organization (persons in roles, work groups, etc.) would stand in an interdependent relationship to each other, with rather less emphasis on the ability of a "master" part to control the entire operation. The exertion of influence in a healthy organization would presumably rest on the competence of the influencer *vis-à-vis* the issue at hand, his stake in the outcome, and the amount of knowledge or data he has—rather than on his organizational position, personal charisma, or other factors with little direct relevance to the problem at hand.

These then are three "task-centered" dimensions of organization health. A second group of three dimensions deals essentially with the internal state of the system, and its inhabitants' "maintenance" needs. These are resource utilization, cohesiveness, and morale.

4. *Resource utilization.* We say of a healthy person, such as a second-grader, that he is "working up to his potential." To put this another way, the classroom system is evoking a contribution from him at an appropriate and goal-directed level of tension. At the organization level, "health" would imply that the system's inputs, particularly the personnel, are used effectively. The overall coordination is such that people are neither overloaded nor idling. There is a minimal sense of strain, generally speaking (in the sense that trying to do something with a weak or inappropriate structure puts strain on that structure). In the

healthy organization, people may be working very hard indeed, but they feel that they are not working against themselves, or against the organization. The fit between people's own dispositions and the role demands of the system is good. Beyond this, people feel reasonably "self-actualized"; they not only "feel good" in their jobs, but they have a genuine sense of learning, growing, and delveloping as persons in the process of making their organizational contribution.

5. *Cohesiveness.* We think of a healthy person as one who has a clear sense of identity; he knows who he is, underneath all the specific goals he sets for himself. Beyond this, he *likes himself*; his stance toward life does not require self-derogation, even when there are aspects of his behavior which are unlovely or ineffective. By analogy at the organization level, system health would imply that the organization knows "who it is." Its members feel attracted to membership in the organization. They want to stay with it, be influenced by it, and exert their own influence in the collaborative style suggested above.

6. *Morale.* The history of this concept in the social-psychological literature is so appalling that I hesitate to introduce it at all. The implied notion is one of well-being or satisfaction. Satisfaction is not enough for health, of course; a person may report feelings of well-being and satisfaction in his life, while successfully denying deep-lying hostilities, anxieties, and conflicts. Yet it still seems useful to evoke, at the organization level, the idea of morale: a summated set of individual sentiments, centering around feelings of well-being, satisfaction, and pleasure, as opposed to feelings of discomfort, unwished-for strain and dissatisfaction. In an *unhealthy* system, life might be perceived rosily as "good," or as unabashedly bad; in a healthy organization it is hard to entertain the idea that the dominant personal response of organization members would be anything else than one of well-being.

Finally, there are four more dimensions of organization health, which deal with growth and changefulness: the notions of innovativeness, autonomy, adaptation *vis-à-vis* the environment, and problem-solving adequacy.

7. *Innovativeness.* A healthy system would tend to invent new procedures, move toward new goals, produce new kinds of products, diversify itself, and become more rather than less differentiated over time. In a sense, such a system could be said to grow, develop, and change, rather than remaining routinized, and standard. The analogue here is to the self-renewing properties of a Picasso; or to Schachtel's[18] "activity" orientation (curious, exploring) as contrasted with "embeddedness" orientation (tension-reducing, protective) in persons.[19]

8. *Autonomy.* The healthy person acts "from his own center outward." Seen in a training or therapy group, for example, such a person appears nearly free of the need to submit dependently to authority figures, *and* from the need to rebel and destroy symbolic fathers of any kind. A healthy organization, similarly, would not respond passively to demands from the outside, feeling itself the tool of the environment, and it would not respond destructively or rebelliously to perceived demands either. It would tend to have a kind of independence from the environment, in the same sense that the healthy person, while he has transactions with others, does not treat their responses as *determinative* of his own behavior.

9. *Adaptation.* The notions of autonomy and innovativeness are both connected with the idea that a healthy person, group, or organization is in realistic, effective contact with the surroundings. When environmental demands and organization resources do not match, a problem-solving, re-structuring approach evolves in which *both* the environment and the organization become different in some respect. More adequate, continued coping of the organization, as a result of changes in the local system, the relevant portions of the environment, or more usually both, occurs. And such a system has sufficient stability and stress tolerance to manage the difficulties which occur during the adaptation process. Perhaps inherent in this notion is that the system's

ability to bring about corrective change in itself is faster than the change cycle in the surrounding environment. Explanations for the disappearance of dinosaurs vary, but it is quite clear that in some way this criterion was not met.

10. *Problem-solving adequacy.* Finally, any healthy organism—even one as theoretically impervious to fallibility as a computer—*always* has problems, strains, difficulties, and instances of ineffective coping. The issue is not the presence or absence of problems, therefore, but the *manner* in which the person, group, or organization copes with problems. Argyris[20] has suggested that in an effective system, problems are solved with minimal energy; they stay solved; and the problem-solving mechanisms used are not weakened, but maintained or strengthened. An adequate organization, then, has well-developed structures and procedures for sensing the existence of problems, for inventing possible solutions, for deciding on the solutions, for implementing them, and for evaluating their effectiveness. Such an organization would conceive of its own operations (whether directed outward to goal achievement, inward to maintenance, or inward-outward to problems of adaptation) as being *controllable*. We would see active coping with problems, rather than passive withdrawing, compulsive responses, scapegoating, or denial.

Here then are ten dimensions of a healthy organization,[21] stated abstractly, even vaguely in many instances. They must, of course, be operationalized into meaningful indicators of organization functioning; the staff of our project is currently into this with more than a little trepidation, but with keen interest to see whether these ways of viewing the health of a system prove to have a reasonable amount of empirical steam behind them.

THE SPECIAL CASE OF EDUCATIONAL ORGANIZATIONS

These dimensions can presumably be applied to any type of organization. Much of the theory

and empirical data on which they are based was generated in industrial organizations in which "organization improvement" programs have become more and more widespread in the last few years. (See, for example, Bennis.)[22] We need, however, to determine the special properties of *educational* systems (if any) which pre-dispose them to particular types of ill health. It is also necessary to examine whether the technologies of organization improvement which have proved successful industrially need adaption in certain directions before they are likely to be efficacious in schools. If this is not done, we might well expect a recrudescence of the unfortunate enthusiasm of schoolmen for Taylorism and "scientific management" which occurred in the first decades of this century. (See the excellent treatment of this appalling subject in Callahan & Button.)[23]

In our own time, it has taken a good deal of agitation by people like Dan Griffiths to get school administrators and professors of education to accept the possibility that the school is in fact an organization, and as such shares certain properties with all other organizations, and that administrative theory, if well developed in any field of human endeavor, could apply to the school business. This is quite correct. However, emphasis on the commonality of all types of organizations has tended to obscure the fact that educational systems have special properties which condition the propositions of organization theory in reasonably predictable ways. What, then, are some of these properties?

1. *Goal ambiguity.* For many different reasons, it has seemed difficult to specify the output of educational organizations very precisely. Some of this is realistic: change in human beings is going on, with presumably cumulative effects over a long period of time. But part of this output measurement difficulty also seems to be a form of organization defense or protection against criticism from the surrounding environment (see below).

Whatever the reasons, supposed "unmeasurability" of organizational output (hence, of the effectiveness of particular role occupants) seems a fairly durable feature of educational organizations as we know them today.

In addition, certain goals of the school (such as "academic learning") are often given primacy in public pronouncements while others (for example, the socialization of achievement motivation and appropriate *Gesellschaftlich* behavior for the incoming denizens of an industrial society) are treated as background phenomena. Still others (such as keeping the kids off the streets and out of Mother's way—call it custodial care) are usually taboo as legitimate goal statements.[24]

It is possible, of course, that school system goals are not all that unmeasurable and ambiguous. In some exploratory interviewing we have been doing in two suburban school systems, teachers and principals, almost without exception, denied that "it is difficult to know when you are doing a good job"[25] and denied that "disagreement over the goals of the school" was present. We intend to pursue this further, because our hunch is that such protestations of agreement reflect defensive solutions to the actual problems of goal ambiguity and goal disagreement, which do in fact exist.

I believe that this ambiguity and pseudo-consensus around school output measurement encourages the institutionalization of ossification of teaching procedures. If it cannot really be determined whether one course of action leads to more output than another, then why stop lecturing? There is a further consequence (stemming particularly from the unacknowledged but powerful custodial function of the school): highly rigid time and personnel allocations in most American schools. Hall passes, the forty-seven-minute period, and the difficulty some teachers have in finding time to go to the toilet are all examples. It is interesting that the increasing use of computers for class scheduling has not, to my knowledge, exploited the enormous potential of information-processing machines for making a *more* rather than less flexible learning environment. In any event, I wish only to make the point that goal ambiguity and procedural rigidity may very well turn out to be closely connected.

2. *Input variability.* Another, possibly unique, property of educational organizations is a very wide variation in input from the environment, particularly in relation to children and personnel. Since the school is defined in America as publicly responsible, it must accept children of a very wide range of ability and motivation to carry out its activities (this holds true, of course, for custodial and socialization goals as well as academic learning goals). The current stress on programs for the "culturally deprived" only serves to divert attention from the fact that the American schools seem never to have been able to cope effectively with children from lower socioeconomic levels.[26]

This is no place to review in any detail the problem of variability in teacher performance, but here again it is important to note that the range of intellectual ability, interpersonal skill and knowledge of subject matter among teachers is probably at least as great as that among pupils. This variability causes considerable stress in educational organizations, and develops the need to provide teaching personnel with methods and procedures which are (in effect) teacher-proof. Wayland (1964) has reviewed this problem as a function of the enormous historical expansion of the scope of American education; he suggests that the teacher's role is now essentially that of a bureaucratic functionary, all protestations of "professionalism" to the contrary.

3. *Role performance invisibility.* Classrooms are in effect the production departments of the educational enterprise; in them teachers teach. Yet, this role performance is relatively invisible to status equals or superiors. Children can observe, usually very acutely, the quality of a teacher's execution of her role, but they are not allowed to comment on this, and have few (if any) sanctions to bring to bear. Thus, rewards in the teaching profession seem relatively detached from others' estimates of one's performance; the average teacher, as Lortie[27] has pointed out, gains most satisfaction from intrinsic properties of the role behavior involved. Teaching thus becomes a craft-like occupation, rather than a profession, and substitute criteria for teaching effectiveness, such as "how interested the kids are" begin to appear

and are used vigorously. Perhaps this is what our teachers meant when they said it was not difficult to know when they were doing a good job.

4. *Low interdependence.* A further characteristic of educational organizations, when compared with thing-producing systems, seems to be a relatively low interdependence of parts. Teacher A's failure to teach anything to her minions affects the job-relevant behavior of teacher B very little—except in a rather diffuse, blaming sense, as when junior high-school teachers devoutly declare their belief that basic skills are not present in newly-arrived seventh graders.

This low interdependence has several consequences. First, it tends to reinforce the pyramidal "man-to-man" style of supervision which Likert[28] and others have shown to be inimical to organization effectiveness. In the case of teachers of young children, it tends to promote a kind of infantilism and boredom; in many teachers, as suggested by a recent study[29] the peak of productive contribution tends to be in the twenties, with distancing from students and potential routinization starting in the mid-thirties. The reported stresses and strains in most accounts of team teaching—an attempt to increase interdependence in educational organizations—are mute testimony to the strength with which "separatist" norms have become institutionalized in the American public school.[30]

High interdependence is not without its difficulties, of course. As Golembiewski[31] has pointed out, the classical division of industrial organizations into specialized departments tends to promote hostility, competitiveness, and disjunction between the authority system and other aspects of the organization such as communication patterns, friendship relationships, and work flow. He suggests an alternative organization model involving the existence of "product divisions," each of which contains in it all the specialties necessary to undertake an operation such as buying materials for, producing and marketing a washing machine. Schools are organized in a product division manner, in effect. But Golembiewski's analy-

sis—this is crucial—depends on the existence of simple, rapidly-available output measures, so that the performance of a product division can be monitored. As we have seen, the absence of such measures—and more fundamentally, the belief that they can never be produced—is a serious barrier to the effectiveness of educational organizations.

5. *Vulnerability.* The American public school, even more than other public organizations, is subject to control, criticism, and a wide variety of "legitimate" demands from the surrounding environment: everyone is a stockholder. Any public organization tends to generate this type of relationship with systems and persons outside its boundary. But a people-processing organization such as the school is dealing with extremely valuable property—children—who return to their parents each night with more or less accurate news of how they have been treated. Thus, in the special kind of organization termed a school, almost any role occupant—board member, superintendent, principal, staff specialist, or teacher can be criticized by parents or citizens at large. To the system inhabitants, the organization skin seems extremely thin. Many kinds of ingenious defenses are adopted to solve this problem—policies about visiting the classroom, brain-washing of new board members by the superintendent and the old members (cf. Sieber, in press),[33] buffer devices such as the PTA, and so on. Yet, the fact remains that a consumer who doesn't like the octane rating of his gasoline cannot go to the refinery and criticize the operation of a cat-cracker—but a parent who feels conflicted about her child's reading ability can be pretty violent with the first grade teacher. (I might comment that this vulnerability seems most sharp when viewed from the inside. Many parents apparently feel that the school is impregnable, and that they must not raise complaints, rock the boat, etc.)

In any event, this state of affairs represents, I believe, a serious failure of adaptation skills of schools as organizations, and tends to reduce school system autonomy sharply. In recent years, I have met only one school superintendent who told me he was going ahead actively (and successfully) with curriculum and organization changes to which a majority of his community were opposed. As it turned out, he was an old private school man.

6. *Lay-professional control problems.* Public schools are governed by laymen, most of whom have not been inside a school for twenty years prior to their succession to the board. As a result, they often agree tacitly or explicitly on a division of labor with the superintendent and his staff (the policy—procedure distinction developed by Brickell and Davies is one such example). But even where the board is "well trained" and leaves the execution of policy to the superintendent, notice that the question of *educational policy* determination still remains a moot one.

And there are internal lay-professional problems as well. In many respects, the principal of an elementary or high school, in terms of expert knowledge, may find himself far behind the capabilities of particular teachers on his staff—and is in this sense a layman as well. The problems of organizations with high proportions of professionals have been studied vigorously (ex: hospitals, and research organizations); I only wish to indicate here that the fruits of such study so far have found little application in schools.[33]

7. *Low technological investment.* Lastly, it seems very clear that the amount of technology per worker in schools is relatively low. From 60% to 75% of a local school system's budget ordinarily goes to salary, with a fraction for equipment and materials. Even if we count buildings as "technological investment," the picture is rather different from that in most industries. This has consequences: social transactions, rather than socio-technical transactions, come to be the major mode of organization production. Because of this, it is possible that education, as James Finn has suggested, has never made it out of the folk culture stage. And we are back once again to goal ambiguity and its problems.

These, then, strike me as special strains, ways in which educational organizations as such and the public school in particular depart from the generalized model of organization health outlined earlier. In sum, I would suggest that, in terms of the dimensions above, the major difficulties to be expected in most public schools would center around goal focus, (as a consequence of goal ambiguity), difficulties in communication adequacy and power equalization stemming from low interdependence; and perhaps most centrally, failures in innovativeness, autonomy, adaptation, and problem-solving adequacy, because of vulnerability and lay-professional conflict.

Interestingly enough, I do not see any clear reason for believing that internal "maintenance problems" (such as those involved in effective resource utilization, cohesiveness, and morale) are sharp points of strain in most school systems; it may very well be that low interdependence, plus orientation to a professional reference group, carry with them a willingness to "settle for less" than the optimum in these areas.

THE INDUCTION OF ORGANIZATION HEALTH

The particular degree of health of any local school system, given a multiple-criterion approach such as that suggested here, undoubtedly varies from time to time. A question of considerable interest is: what can be done to induce a greater degree of organization health in any particular system? By now a fair amount of experience exists, drawn from the interesting blend of consultation and research in which an increasing number of behavioral scientists now find themselves involved, primarily with industrial organizations. These methods can perhaps most usefully be considered as *interventions* in the on-going life of a system; this term implies an action which interferes with or reorients processes—either pathological or normal—ordinarily occurring in the system. A teacher's intervention in a child's problem-solving serves to reorient his thinking; perhaps more importantly, it can aid the child to mobilize his own energies more effectively. Thus the usual aim of an intervention is to start internal change processes going in the system at hand, rather than only causing an immediate change.

Below are described six interventions aimed at improving organization health.[34] In some cases, plausible statements can be made about which dimensions of health are most typically influenced by a particular intervention. For the most part, however, we do not really know; it is exactly the function of our research project to discover how these are likely to work in educational organizations. In conclusion, some common principles underlying the six interventions are discussed.

1. *Team training.* In this approach, the members of an intact work group (for example, the superintendent and his central office personnel) meet for a period of several days away from their offices, with consultant help. They examine their own effectiveness as a problem solving team, the role of each member in the group and how it affects the group and the person himself, and the operations of the group in relation to its organizational environment. This problem-solving may be based on fairly careful prior data collection from individuals as to their views on the current problems of the system; these data are summarized and form the beginning of the group's agenda. Occasionally, exercises and theoretical material on group and organization functioning may be supplied by the outside consultant.

Under these circumstances, the members of the group usually improve in their abilities to express feelings directly, and to listen to—and understand—each other. Communication adequacy is thus considerably increased. The members also deal with internal conflicts in the team, and learn to solve problems more effectively as a unit, thus presumably increasing their ability to meet the demands placed upon them by other parts of the system. Over a period of time, beginning with the top decision-making group of the system, this intervention may be repeated with other groups as well. Industrial programs of this sort have been described by Argyris[35] and Blake and Mouton.[36]

2. *Survey feedback.* In this approach, data bearing on attitudes, opinions, and beliefs of members of a system are collected via questionnaire. An external researcher summarizes the data for the organization as a whole, and for each of a number of relevant work groups. Each work group, under the guidance of its own superior, and perhaps with consultant help, examines its own summarized data, in comparison with those for the organization as a whole. The group makes plans for change stemming from these discussions and carries them out. The focus of this intervention is on many or all of the work groups within a total setting. The aim is to free up communication, leading to goal clarification and problem-solving work. The relative objectification involved in looking at data helps to reduce feelings of being misunderstood and isolated, and makes problems more susceptible to solution, rather than retaining them as a focus for blaming, scapegoating, griping and so on. For an account of survey feedback procedure, see Mann;[37] Gage[39] has tried a similar approach effectively with student-to-teacher feedback, and is now studying teacher-to-principal feedback.

3. *Role workshop.* Sometimes called the "horizontal slice" meeting, this intervention involves all the people in a particular role (for example, elementary principal). They fill out research instruments dealing with role expectations which various others hold for them, the fit between their own wishes and these expectations, their actual role performance, etc. These data are summarized, and form the vehicle for a series of activities (discussion, role practice, decision-making exercises, problem-solving and so on) at a workshop attended by all the people in the role. The main focus here is on role clarity, effectiveness, and improved fit between the person and the role. By sharing common role problems, people occupying the role may develop alternative solutions which result in better performance of that role and more "self-actualized" operation in general.

4. *"Target setting" and supporting activities.* In this approach, periodic meetings are held between a superior and each of his subordinates, separately. In a school system, this might involve the superintendent and his staff

members, or a principal and his teachers. The work of each subordinate is reviewed in relation to organizational and personal goals, and the superior and subordinate agree collaboratively on new targets for the subordinate's work and personal development. These "targets" are in turn reviewed after some work time (usually six months or so) has elapsed. During that period, other activities such as role meetings, consultation, self-operated data collection, academic courses, and workshops, may be engaged in by the subordinate to develop needed skills and understandings as he works toward the collaboratively-set goals. The focus of attention here is the working relationship between superior and subordinate, and the degree to which they are together able to help the subordinate grow and develop on the job. Improved trust, feelings of support, better and more satisfying role performance, and more open communication usually result. Zander[39] has reviewed thoroughly the problems and values of performance appraisal, including commentary on the target-setting approach.

5. *Organizational diagnosis and problem-solving.* This intervention involves a residential meeting of members of an intact work group, usually at the top of the organization (or in small organizations, up to size 40–50, the entire work force). They meet for several days to identify problems facing the system, and the reasons for the existence of these; to invent possible solutions; to decide on needed system changes; and to plan implementation of these through regular channels and newly-constructed ones. It differs from team training as described above in that relatively less attention is given to team relationships and interpersonal effectiveness as such, and more to system problems in the large. The main focus of attention is on the organization and its current functioning. The improvement of problem-solving activity and communication adequacy are typical results. For an account of two such meetings conducted with an industrial organization, see Zand, Miles, and Lytle (forthcoming).[40]

6. *Organizational experiment.* In this approach, a major organizational variable of interest is changed *directly*,[41] by agreement of the responsible administrators, and needed implementation efforts. One such approach is described vividly by Morse and Reimer[42]: in several divisions of a large organization, the level of decision-making was moved radically downward, thus giving more autonomy to subordinates; in several other divisions the level of decision-making was moved up; and in several divisions no change was made. Such an approach requires the careful collection of pre-post data, and the use of control groups in order to test the consequences of the change. The halo of "experiment" is an aid to acceptance, since the arrangement is seen as not only temporary, but scientific, and responsibly managed. Such an approach ordinarily includes a feedback stage, in which the results are examined carefully and implications for the continuing functioning of the organization drawn.

These, then, are six possible approaches to the induction of organization health. Certain common threads appear to flow through all of them.

1. *Self-study.* These approaches reject the "technocratic" change model involving the recommendations of a detached expert, and actively involve the system itself in what might be called organizational introspection. The same holds true for approaches involving group self-study for various teams in the organization, and personal introspection and re-examination by role occupants.

In common with the action research movement in education, these approaches also carry the assumption that an operant stance on the part of the organization is both theoretically and practically preferable to the problems involved in dependence on outsiders for system change.

2. *Relational emphasis.* These approaches do not conceive of the organization as a collection of jobs with isolated persons in them, but as a network of groups and role relationships; it is the functioning of these groups and relationships, as such, which requires examination and self-operated, experimental alteration. The aim is not to ferret out and change the "atti-

tude" of old-fogey Principal A, but to focus on the relationships and group settings in which Principal A's attitudes are evoked.

3. *Increased data flow.* These approaches all involve the heightening or intensification of communication, especially vertically, but also diagonally and horizontally. New feedback loops are often built in to the existing system. The use of status-equalizing devices such as intensive residential meetings also encourages fuller and freer flow of information through channels which may have been blocked or have always carried distorted messages.

4. *Norms as a change target.* By focusing on groups and relationships, and increasing data flow, these approaches have the effect of altering existing norms which regulate interpersonal transactions in the organization. If, for example, a work group where the norms are "play it close to the vest, and don't disagree with the boss" engages in a team training session, it is quite likely—since all group members have participated in the experience—that norms such as "be open about your feelings whether or not they tally with the boss' wishes" will develop. These approaches thus have a strong culture-changing component, based on intensive, data-based interaction with others.[43]

5. *Temporary-system approach.* But norm-changing is by definition very difficult under the usual pressures of day-to-day operation in the organization. "Business as usual" has to prevail. Most of the interventions described involve the use of residential meetings, which constitute a detached, "cultural island" approach to organizational introspection and self-cerrection. They are in effect temporary systems,[44] where new norms can develop, and where, given the suspension of the usual pressures, meaningful changes can be made in the structure and functioning of the permanent system.

6. *Expert facilitation.* All of these interventions also include the presence of a semi-detached consultant figure, whose main functions are to facilitate, provoke, and support the efforts of the system to understand itself, free up communication and engage in more adequate problem-solving behavior. The outsider role, however, is seen as impermanent; it is only associated with the system during the actual period of the intervention itself. If the intervention is successful, the organization itself continues the self-corrective processes which have been begun by the intervention.

Whether or not these interventions, drawn from work with thing-producing organizations, can be used plausibly with people-processing organizations such as schools is an interesting question, to which my colleagues and I are beginning to gather some answers. Our impulse at the moment is to believe that the answer will be affirmative. With the assistance of two or three school systems, we expect to have some empirical data on intervention results in about two years, an eventuality to which we look forward with a good deal of pleasure.

IN CONCLUSION

It might be useful to point out in conclusion that the position taken in this paper is *not* that an organization must necessarily be brought to a state of perfect health before it can engage in any meaningful short-run innovative projects at all. Rather, we feel it is quite likely that the very act of carrying out small scale projects in planned change can undoubtedly strengthen the health of an educational organization—but only if *direct attention is paid concurrently to the state of the organization.* The basic innovative project, we believe, must be one of organization development itself.

NOTES

[1] Lippitt, R., Watson, J. and Westley, B. *The Dynamics of Planned Change,* (New York: Harcourt, Brace, 1958).

[2] Bennis, W. G., Benne, K. D., and Chin, R. *The Planning of Change:*

Readings in the Applied Behavioral Sciences, (New York: Holt, Rinehart and Winston, 1961).

[3] Rogers, E. M. *Diffusion of Innovations*, (New York: Free Press, 1962).

[4] Ross, D. H. (Ed.) *Administration for Adaptability*, (New York: Metropolitan School Study Council, 1958).

[5] Carlson, R. O. "School Superintendents and the Adoption of Modern Math: A Social Structure Profile." In M. B. Miles (Ed.), *Innovation in Education*, (New York: Bureau of Publications, Teachers College, Columbia University), pp. 329–342.

[6] Gallaher, A. "The Role of the Advocate and Directed Change." Paper presented at the Symposium on Identifying Techniques and Principles for Gaining Acceptance of Research Results of Use of Mass Media in Education, (Lincoln, Nebraska: November 24–27, 1963).

[7] Jahoda, M. *Current Concepts of Positive Mental Health*, (New York: Basic Books, 1958).

[8] Maslow, A. "Self-actualizing People: A Study of Psychological Health." In W. Wolff (Ed.), *Personality Symposium*, (New York: Grune and Stratton, 1950). Pp. 11–34.

[9] Warriner, C. J. "Groups are Real: A Reaffirmation," *American Sociological Review*, (1956, *21*), 549–554.

[10] For additional comments on the importance of the concept of organization health, see Bennis, W. G. "Towards a 'Truly' Scientific Management: The Concept of Organization Health." In A. Rapaport (Ed.), *General Systems*, (Yearbook of the Society for the Advancement of General Systems Theory, Ann Arbor, Michigan: 1962).

[11] Miles, M. B. *Innovation in Education*, (New York: Bureau of Publications, Teachers College, Columbia University, 1964), p. 13.

[12] Argyris, C. *Integrating the Individual and the Organization*, (New York: Wiley, 1964), p. 120.

[13] *Ibid.*

[14] Jahoda, *op. cit.*

[15] Argyris, *op. cit.*

[16] Note that the question of actual goal achievement as such is here conceived of as separate, analytically speaking, from the question of organization health. Argyris has suggested that organization effectiveness, a concept resembling the health notion, resides in the organization's ability to (1) achieve goals, (2) maintain itself internally, (3) engage in adaptation processes with the environment—and to accomplish these three "core activities" at a constant or increasing level of effectiveness, given the same or decreasing increments in energy input (Argyris, 1964, p. 123). This three-way scheme is also used in the present discussion.

[17] Likert, R. *New Patterns of Management*, (New York: McGraw-Hill, 1961).

[18] Schachtel, E. G. *Metamorphosis*, (New York: Basic Books, 1959).

[19] Clark has suggested that organization health resides primarily in the continuous possibility of *both* kinds of orientation: toward change and development, and for stability and maintenance. This dual possibility should be realized, he suggests, at the personal, group, inter-group, and total organizational levels.

Clark, J. V. "A Healthy Organization," (Los Angeles, California: Institute of Industrial Relations, University of California, 1962).

[20] Argyris, *op. cit.*

[21] Little has been said here about the actual form of the organization

which is most likely to meet these criteria of organizational health at some optimal level. Some applied work in organization change (Argyris, 1964; Bennis, 1962) suggests that strongly pyramidal organizations designed around strict division of labor, accountability, limited span of control, etc., are uniquely *ill*-fitted to the demands of survival in today's world. Argyris (1964) has suggested a number of alternatives to the pyramidal model, (such as the use of temporary "product teams" with power base on functional contribution rather than position) which he feels are not only more likely to lead in the direction of organization health but respect the "essential properties" of organizations as open systems. Empirical data on this question are not numerous; however, work with communication nets in small simulated organizations has suggested that relatively loose, power-equalized, full-communication models of organization are much more effective than traditional models when the environment is shifting and changing. This finding also appeared in a study of Scottish electronic firms by Burns and Stalker.

Burns, T. and Stalker, G. M. *The Management of Innovation*, (London: Tavistock Publications, 1961).

See also Likert, *op. cit.*

[22] Bennis, W. G. "A New Role for the Behavioral Sciences: Effecting Organizational Change," *Administrative Science Quarterly*, (1963, 8, 2), 125–165; and Bennis, W. G. "Theory and Method in Applying Behavioral Science to Planned Organizational Change," (Cambridge: Alfred P. Sloan School of Management, M.I.T., 1964). Mimeographed.

[23] Callahan, R. E. and Button, H. W. "Historical Change of the Role of the Man in the Organization, 1865–1950." In D. E. Griffiths (Ed.), *Behavioral Science and Educational Administration*, Sixty-third Yearbook (Part II), National Society for the Study of Education, (Chicago: University of Chicago Press, 1964).

[24] If you doubt for a minute that custodial care is an important goal of the American public school, try this "Gedanken-experiment." Which would be the most effective form of teacher strike: (a) for teachers to stay home; (b) for teachers to come to school, but teach the children nothing?

[25] This is a remarkable assertion, in light of the encyclopedic (and to me gloomily inconclusive) research findings on teacher effectiveness. See Gage, N. L., (Ed.), *Handbook of Research on Teaching*, (Chicago: Rand McNally, 1963).

[26] See, for example, the really staggering data on reading retardation and advancement as a function of social class in Barton, A. H. and Wilder, D. E. "Research and Practice in the Teaching of Reading: A Progress Report." In M. B. Miles (Ed.), *Innovation in Education*, (New York: Bureau of Publications, Teachers College, Columbia University, 1964), pp. 361–398.

[27] Lortie, D. C. "Craftsmen and Colleagueship, A Frame for the Investigation of Work Values Among Public School Teachers." Paper read at American Sociological Association meetings, 1961.

[28] Likert, *op. cit.*

[29] Peterson, W. A. "Age, Teacher's Role, and the Institutional Setting." In B. J. Biddle and W. J. Ellena (Eds.), *Contemporary Research on Teacher Effectiveness*, (New York: Holt, Rinehart and Winston, 1964), pp. 264–315.

[30] Lortie's (1961) comments on a three-part norm system are relevant here: He comments on the teacher as subscribing to the following beliefs: a) the teacher should be free of interference in his teaching; b) other

teachers should be considered and treated as equals (in spite of the fact that they obviously differ in interests and skill); c) teachers should act in a friendly manner toward one another in informal contacts. Note that these norms reinforce each other in such a way as to inhibit effective, interdependent work.

[31] Golembiewski, R. "Authority as a Problem in Overlays." *Administrative Science Quarterly*, (1964, *9*, 1), 23–49.

[32] Sieber, S. D. "The School Board as an Agency of Legitimation." *Sociology of Education*, in press. Bureau of Applied Social Research Reprint No. A-404, Columbia University.

[33] It is interesting to note that the greatest inroads of applied behavioral science seem to have been in research-based organizations, in areas such as aerospace, electronics, and petroleum refining. Why this has not happened in schools (and universities!) is an interesting question. It may very well be that a knowledge-*spreading* organization (such as a school) operates rather differently from a knowledge-*making* one (such as a research group).

[34] See Bennis (1963, 1964) for a thorough review of alternative approaches being used.

[35] Argyris C. *Interpersonal Competence and Organizational Effectiveness*, (Homewood, Ill.: Dorsey Press, 1962).

[36] Blake, R. R., Blansfield, M. G., and Mouton, J. S. "How Executive Team Training Can Help You," *Journal American Society of Training Directors*, (1962, *16*, 1), 3–11.

[37] Mann, F. C. "Studying and Creating Change." In W. G. Bennis, K. D. Benne, and R. Chin, *The Planning of Change: Readings in the Applied Behavioral Sciences*, (New York: Holt, Rinehart and Winston, 1961), pp. 605–615.

[38] Gage, N. L. "A Method for 'Improving' Teacher Behavior," *Journal of Teacher Education*, (1963, *14*, 3), 261–266.

[39] Zander, A. (Ed.) *Performance Appraisals: Effects on Employees and Their Performance*, (Ann Arbor, Michigan: Foundation for Research on Human Behavior, 1963).

[40] Zand, D., Miles, M. B., and Lytle, W. O. Jr. "Organizational Improvement Through Use of a Temporary Problem-Solving System." In D. E. Zand and P. C. Buhanan, (Eds.), *Organization Development: Theory and Practice*. Forthcoming.

[41] I am reminded of Hollis Caswell's classic remark when asked in 1943 how the newly-formed Horace Mann-Lincoln Institute would proceed in its program of school experimentation: "We'll change the curriculum by changing it."

[42] Morse, N. and Reimer, E. "The Experimental Change of a Major Organizational Variable," *Journal of Abnormal and Social Psychology*, (1956, 52), 120–129.

[43] In retrospect, the crucial role of norms in the maintenance of organizational health has probably been underplayed in this paper. In our research, we are planning to collect data on norms such as those regulating interpersonal authenticity and awareness, trust, objectivity, collaboration, altruistic concern, consensual decision-making, innovativeness, and creativity. Most of these are directly co-ordinated to the dimensions of organizational health reviewed above.

[44] Miles, M. B. "On Temporary Systems." In M. B. Miles (Ed.), *Innovation in Education*, (New York: Bureau of Publications, Teachers College, Columbia University, 1964), pp. 437–492.

30.

THE INNOVATIVE ORGANIZATION

VICTOR A. THOMPSON

In this section we try to bring together or summarize all the scattered suggestions of the preceding sections into a composite picture of an organization with a high capacity to innovate. First we shall consider briefly the qualities and conditions needed and then the structures or structural changes which we think will facilitate or create the required qualities and conditions.

First, resources are needed for innovation—uncommitted and relatively nonspecified resources. This means uncommitted money, time, skills, and goodwill. In the case of human resources it means upgraded work and workers. There is an optimum between the underutilized desk worker and the superficial dilettante. This optimum is reached by the person who has developed himself thoroughly in some area, about to the limits of his capacities, so that he has that richness of experience and self-confidence upon which creativity thrives. Roughly speaking, the optimum is reached by the worker whom we call a professional.

Furthermore, the use of a complex technology requires the administration of "technical generalists," or professionals. A technology is incorporated into an organization through individuals. To incorporate it through overspecification or task specialization[1] puts an enormous burden on coordination. Furthermore, coordinating the elements of a technology is part of the technology itself, as the current technical emphasis on systems design, sys-

Abridged from Victor Thompson, "Increasing the Innovative Capacity of Organizations," University of Illinois, Urbana. (Mimeographed.) Used by permission of the author.

tems engineering, etc., testify. The technology deals not only with simple relationships, but with the relationships between relationships as well. Hence, coordination is not a different, nontechnical process, such as management, but the very heart of the complex technology itself. There must be some who have mastered the technology if it is to be incorporated, as opposed to being rediscovered. A general overspecification of work makes it impossible to incorporate complex technologies. And although production interests may be well served by employing a few technical professionals to coordinate the many overspecified workers, the innovative potential of the technology can hardly be realized in this way.

The innovative organization will provide or allow that diversity of inputs, or variety of experience and stimulation, needed for the creative generation of ideas. Long periods of pre-entry professional training (formal, informal, or both) will provide individuals with the needed internal richness of experience and self-confidence. Wide diffusion of ideas within the organization, including diffusion of problems and suggested solutions, will provide the external variety and richness of experience required. There should also be a diffusion of uncertainty, so that the whole organization is stimulated to search, rather than just a few professional researchers. Involving larger parts of the organization in the search process also increases chances of acceptance and implementation.[2] This broad diffusion, in turn, will depend upon ease and freedom of communication and a low level of parochialism.

A particular kind of relationship between personal and organizational goals is needed. The organization man's complete commitment to the organization will not promote innovation, as we have seen. But neither will complete alienation from the organization. The organization's welfare should not be a matter of complete disinterest. The creative person's internal commitment to search needs to be harmonized with the organization's goals in some way. The ideal situation would seem to be one in which individuals perceive the organization as an avenue for professional growth. The interest in professional growth provides the rising aspiration level needed to stimulate search beyond the first-found satisfactory solution, and the perception of the organization as a vehicle for professional growth harnesses this powerful motivation to the interests of the organization in a partial fusion of goals, personal and organizational.[3] Thus, the innovative organization will have smaller than usual proportions of fully dedicated upwardly mobile individuals and of the alienated. Neither identity nor alienation is optimal.

These considerations suggest a deemphasis on the usual extrinsic organizational rewards of income, power, and status. Internal satisfactions from the search process, professional growth, and the esteem of knowledgeable peers—these are the rewards most conducive to innovation. Benign intellectual competition, rather than malignant status and power competition, is needed. For these reasons, creative work, the process of search and discovery, needs to be highly visible to respected peers. It is hardly reasonable to expect this widespread dedication to creative work if improved positional status continues to be defined as success, and status striving, therefore, as the principal sign of personal worth. But reduction of the importance of status striving is extremely important in another way. Status striving is inescapably associated with personal insecurity,[4] and personal insecurity is hardly compatible with creativity. What is needed is a certain level of problem insecurity and challenge, but also a high level of personal security.[5]

It would seem that the creative atmosphere is an indulgent one, free from external pressure. A person is not likely to be very creative with the sword hanging over his head. Furthermore, he is unlikely to be creative if too much hangs on a successful outcome of his search activities. He will have strong personal needs to accept the first satisfactory solution whether or not it seems novel or the best possible. Thus, he needs indulgency with regard to time and resources and particularly with regard to

organizational evaluations of his activities. He needs freedom to innovate. He also needs considerable, but not complete autonomy and self-direction, and a large voice in deciding at what he will work.[6] It does not seem that a production-control—oriented organization can permit much creativity.

All this adds up to saying that the innovative organization will be much more professional than most existing ones. Work will be much less determined by production-oriented planners on the Smith's pins model and more determined by the extended periods of preentry training. The desk classes will decline in number and importance. There will be a great increase in interorganizational mobility and a corresponding decline in organizational chauvinism. The concept of organizations as organic entities with some claim to survive will tend to be replaced by the concept of organizations as opportunities for professional growth. The professional is just as interested as anyone else in "getting ahead," but he is likely to interpret it differently. He is just as interested as anyone else in income, but not at the expense of his professional standing. He seeks these extrinsic rewards through professional growth. It has been well said that he changes his jobs to pursue his interests rather than his interests to pursue his job. In the innovative organization, professional orientations and loyalties will predominate over organizational or bureaucratic ones. Esteem striving will tend to replace status striving. There will be less control by superiors and more by self and peers. Power and influence will be much more broadly dispersed.

The dispersal of power is important. Concentrated power is a substitute for imaginative coping with problems. When power meets power, problem solving is necessarily called into play. The power of unions has undoubtedly stimulated managerial innovations.[7] Power is important in human affairs. What is to be avoided is its concentration. Dispersed power, paradoxically, can make resources more readily available to support innovative projects because it makes possible a larger number and variety of subcoalitions. It expands the number and kinds of possible supporters and sponsors.

Above, we have listed a number of qualities and conditions of the innovative organization. Now let us take a look at some of the structural variables. The innovative organization will be characterized by structural looseness generally. It will not be concerned with narrow, nonduplicating, nonoverlapping definitions of duties and responsibilities. Job descriptions will be of the professional type rather than the duties type. Communications will be freed and legitimate in all directions. Assignment and resource decisions will be much more decentralized than at present. Incidentally, if currently expressed hopes of automating and programming the intellectual phases of organizational activity (decision making) by means of the new science of management decision are realized, it would seem that increased organizational innovation can be forgotten. In the completely programmed organization, innovation can occur only in the design phase. Thereafter, it will be a closed society. Computer logic strongly impels in this direction. This situation needs careful watching by everyone.

The innovative organization will not be so highly stratified as are existing ones. This result is implied in the freeing of communication. The decline in the importance of the extrinsic rewards of position and status and the growth of interest in professional esteem would bring this about anyway. Salary scales will be adjusted accordingly and will no longer reflect chiefly awesome status differences. Subordinates will frequently earn more than superiors, as market conditions and creative capacity dictate.

Group processes will be more, and more openly, used than at present. We have already noted the importance of the group in the generation and acceptance of new ideas. The freer communication system, the broader work assignments, the carelessness about overlap and duplication, the lessened emphasis upon authority—all will work in the direction of a greater amount of interpersonal communica-

tion and multiple-group membership. Multiple-group membership will facilitate innovation in several ways. First, it will increase the amount and diversity of input of ideas and stimulations. Second, it will act as a discipline of the hierarchical veto, already much weakened by lessened emphasis on authority and the extrinsic rewards of power and status, and the reevaluation of the relative importance of managerial and nonmanagerial roles. When a new idea is known, and even supported, by groupings beyond the authority grouping, it is a good deal harder to kill (veto). An individual will have many possible sources of support. Multigroup membership helps to overcome the absence of a formal appeal by providing an informal appeal to a free constituency of peers. In fact, any broadening of communications and alliances attacks the monocratic structure, dependent as it is on a superior's monopoly of information and external contact.

Procedural devices to discipline the veto power, such as requiring that all proposals be passed on with comments and recommendations, cannot work well in the monocratic structure. A superior whose recommendations were frequently disregarded would feel that his career was in jeopardy. If he makes any recommendation at all, he will be wise to recommend a veto. This is only to say that the process of acceptance of new ideas needs personal security just as much as the process of generation. To increase the acceptance of innovation, the greatest weight should be given to the recommendations of the group closest to the point of generation because it will know most about the proposal, and groups are "riskier" than individuals.

In an atmosphere which encourages and legitimizes multiple group membership, the malignant peer competition of the authority grouping (of fellow subordinates) will no longer exercise the powerful constraints against "showing up" others by introducing new ideas.[8] The greater ease of acquiring group memberships and the greater legitimacy of groups will reduce the risk of innovation to the individual.

Responsibility for new, hence risky, ideas can be shared as also can the onus of promoting them. Wide participation in the generation process will greatly facilitate acceptance and implementation.

Present methods of departmentalization, of assigning missions to subunits, encourage parochialism with its great resistance to new ideas from "outside." Actually, we do not assign goals, but jurisdictions—rights over areas of continuing activities. A departmental unit, once established, assumes immortality. (For example, with 98 percent of the farms electrified, the Rural Electrification Administration is still in business.) It is not a group of interdependent skills brought together to carry out some project, but a conference of sovereignty. At the simple unit level (superior and subordinates), it is often, but not always, an aggregative grouping—a number of people with the same skills doing the same thing. "Like activities should be in the same place." Lacking the stimulation of different skills, views, and perspectives, and the rewards of project completion and success, such groupings are likely to pin their hopes on extrinsic rewards and seek them through the organizational political system. Assuming that any enthusiasm and interest are generated at all, they are more likely to be spent in playing politics than in creating.

Other simple units, even though not composed of aggregations of people doing the same thing, are very often composed of overspecified desk classes carrying out some continuing program, say, getting out the house organ, or managing the budget, or recruiting, or keeping stores. In such an integrative grouping there may be more interpersonal stimulation, but overspecification—the sheer subprofessional simplicity of the jobs—prevents the diversity and richness required for anything but very minor innovations. Furthermore, the loyalty and attachment of the desk classes to their hypostatized programs make them generally conservative and resistant to new ideas.

The aggregative grouping has neither interdependence nor goal. Group innovation is therefore impossible. Individual innovation in the interest of the organization is hardly likely, unless the organization offers rewards for it. Sometimes organizations reward individual innovative suggestions through suggestion-box systems. Such systems are rarely, if ever, successful. As far as aggregative units are concerned, the lack of input diversity to these discrete, noninteracting individuals, especially if the units are composed of overspecified desk workers, prevents any important innovative insights. For integrative units, suggestion boxes are frequently disruptive because the true authorship of the suggestion is likely to be in dispute, and the group will often feel that the idea should have been presented to it rather than individually presented for an award.[9]

In the innovative organization, departmentalization must be so contrived as to keep parochialism to a minimum. It would seem that some overlapping and duplication, some vagueness about jurisdictions, would make a good deal of communication necessary. People would have to define and redefine their responsibilities continually, case after case. They would have to probe and seek for help. New problems could not with certainty be rejected as ultra vires.[10]

The simple unit would better be an integrative grouping of various kinds of professionals and subprofessionals engaged upon an integrative task requiring a high degree of technical interdependence and group problem solving. Or else the simple unit should be merely a housekeeping unit. Project teams could be drawn from such units. Ideally, individuals would have projects rather than continuing assignments. If project organization is not feasible, individuals should be rotated occasionally. Even if continuing assignments, or jurisdictions, seem to be technically necessary, organization units can probably convert a large part of their activities into successive projects, or have a number of projects going on at the same time, so that individuals can be constantly renewing themselves in new and challenging problems and experiencing a maximum input of diverse stimulations and ideas. It might even be possible for individual and unit jurisdictions and responsibilities to be exchanged occasionally.

If formal structures could be sufficiently loosened, it might be possible for organizations and units to restructure themselves continually in light of the problem at hand, as Carlson's Raiders were alleged to have done during World War II. Thus, for generating ideas, for planning and problem solving, the organization or unit would "unstructure" itself into a freely communicating body of equals. When it came time for implementation, requiring a higher degree of coordination of action (as opposed to stimulation of novel or correct ideas), the organization could then restructure itself into the more usual hirearchical form, tightening up its lines somewhat.

Empirical evidence that different kinds of structure are optimal for different kinds of problems is quite compelling.[11] Almost equally compelling is the evidence that leadership role assignments need to be changed as the situation changes.[12] Bureaucratic rigidity makes such rational structural alterations all but impossible. We cannot escape the conclusion that our current organization structures are *not* the most rational adaptations for *some* kinds of problem solving at the very least. Although it is true that experimental groups have been successfully restructured from bureaucratic to collegial by means of verbal redefinitions of roles along lines perceived to be more appropriate to the task at hand,[13] such restructuring is probably impossible in real-life, "traditionated" organizations as presently constituted. Ritual restructuring, as in office Christmas parties, is infrequent, short-lived, and aimed at reestablishing some modicum of organizational solidarity threatened by repressed and smoldering hostility.[14] In fact, the hostility derives from the inability of the organization to restructure along task-appropriate lines and from the tensions generated by the large elements of dramaturgy required for task performance within task-inappropriate structures.

The abandonment of the use of hierarchical positions as prizes or rewards, however, and the decline in the importance of extrinsic rewards generally, would render organizational structure much more amenable to instrumental manipulation. The personal appropriation of administrative resources (such as position and authority), so completely universal in modern bureaucratic organizations and so reminiscent of primitive agrarian cultures, could decline considerably.[15]

If it should prove impossible for organizations to acquire a degree of flexibility sufficient to allow them to structure and restructure themselves in light of the problem at hand, it would be better from the standpoint of innovation for them to remain permanently loose in the interest of generating new ideas and to suffer from stumbling and fumbling in the attempt to coordinate action for the purpose of carrying them out. After all, thought and action cannot be sharply distinguished, and a good deal of creativity and problem solving occur during implementation.[16] The thinking is tested and completed during this phase; the details are then worked out. In fact, the suggestion for successive alterations of structure may be like the origins of bicameralism in early Germanic tribes, who are alleged to have debated each issue twice—once drunk and once sober.

Integrative departmentalization, combined with freedom of communication, interunit projects, and lessened subunit chauvinism, will create extra departmental professional ties and interests. All these things will increase the diversity and richness of inputs and increase their diffusion, thereby stimulating creativity. Intellectual competition is more likely to be provided by this broader milieu. It is more likely to be the generating area than is the smaller authority grouping or the large organization.

We need to think in terms of innovative areas rather than formal departments, in terms of the conditions for generating new and good ideas rather than of jurisdictions. In the innovative organization, innovation will not be assigned to an isolated or segregated jurisdiction such as R&D or research. The innovative contributions of everyone, including the man at the machine, are needed. Characteristically, the innovative area will be larger than the formal unit and smaller than the organization. Resource control should be sufficiently decentralized so that appropriate resource accumulation through subcoalition is possible within the innovative area. In effect, the formal structure—the distribution of jurisdictions—should be just a skeleton upon which to fall back should an arbitrary decision be needed.

It might be well to say a word about the physical aspect of organizations. The architecture and furnishings of today's bureaucratic organizations seem to be departing further and further from the needs of the innovative organization as we have defined them above. The majestic, quiet halls and closed, windowless office doors are not designed to encourage communication. They fill a potential communicator with fear. "Will I be disturbing him?" he wonders. It is doubtful that deep blue rugs have anything to do with discovery and invention. We all remember where the first atomic chain reaction took place. Modern bureaucratic architecture and furnishings seem to reflect an increased concern with the extrinsic reward system. We seem to be in the midst of a new primitivism; the means of administration seem to be increasingly appropriated by the officials. An easily frightened person might expect to see the sale and inheritance of offices reestablished any day.[17]

A less alarming interpretation of these neosacral phenomena is possible, however. They may reflect a desperate attempt by the monocratic organization to attract innovative technical and scientific talent. With "success" available to only a few and the organization increasingly dependent upon large numbers of highly trained professionals and subprofessionals, it is hoped that richness of surroundings will do what an archaic reward system cannot do. The competition for talent is keen. And for those dependent upon positional status symbols for self-evaluation, the decreasing visibility of a generalized social-stratification system increases the importance of visibility in a localized system of stratification.

The purchase of motivation with extrinsic rewards is becoming more and more costly, and innovation cannot be purchased in this way at all. What is needed is both much less expensive and much more costly—the devaluation of authority and positional status and the recognized official sharing of power and influence.

Although such speculations are highly inconclusive, we wonder whether more and more people are not becoming concerned with what the psychologist Maslow calls the highest need—self-actualization—and are not, therefore, finding the excessive concern with ego needs somewhat childish or even unhealthy. Recent research on job satisfaction certainly suggests that this is so. Could it be that our basic reward system, our very concept of success, is oriented to the needs of the psychologically ill?[18]

Associated with all of these structural changes there will need to be many changes in administrative practices. We shall mention only a few of the most obvious ones. Evaluations of performance in the innovative organization will probably have to be peer group evaluations. In fact, the whole question of evaluations in relation to innovation needs much more thought and research. In management theory, the term "supervision" probably refers to continuous evaluation of the activities of subordinates and the feedback to them of the results of this evaluation. Continuous feedback of evaluations of search activities probably encourages premature termination of search and the quest for justifications rather than better or novel solutions. Whereas the rapid feedback of success or failure of proposed solutions is probably needed, the more ego-involved evaluations of the quality or value of the work are probably better delayed until the individual is emotionally disengaged from the project, and he should probably be protected from some evaluations entirely. In the latter category we would include data tending to show that the problem is insoluble or that some secondary consequences of a solution might be unusually pernicious. One wonders if the scientists who made the atom bomb possible would have been able to find the needed solutions if their postwar frame of mind had dominated them during the search period.

It would seem that the present common practice of annual performance ratings by superiors would have to be dropped. Many people believe that this practice is hostile to production interests as well as to interest in innovation.[19] It is clearly inconsistent with increasing professionalism. Professional standing is not determined by a hierarchical superior. Rather than a single system of ranks, with corresponding salaries, there will be a multiple ranking system and multiple salary scales. The managerial or hierarchical ranking system will be only one among many. Presumably, it will not carry the highest ranks. The American public has for a long time ranked several occupations above management.[20]

Job descriptions and classifications will have to accommodate an increasing proportion of professionals. The duties and responsibilities approach to job descriptions was designed for a desk class age.[21] It does not accommodate professional work easily. What does an engineer do? He does engineering work. Of course, if his job has been overspecified, following Smith's admonition, it might be possible to list his duties and responsibilities—"designs tool handles for superior's review and approval." In the innovative organization, however, he will do "creative engineering."

Peer evaluations will become more important in recruitment and placement, and it is possible that a kind of election process will be used to fill authority positions. At any rate, the wishes of subordinates will probably be considered a good deal more than is present practice. One would expect considerable modification in procedures relating to secrecy and loyalty. The innovative organization will be more indulgent with regard to patents, publications, etc. The relationship between visibility and professional growth will require this, and

increased interorganizational mobility will enforce it. Present fringe benefit devices that tend to restrict mobility will have to be altered.

Above we mentioned that administrative innovation tends to lag behind technical innovation. In general, administrative innovation requires the same conditions and structures, but there are some special considerations which should be mentioned. Professionalization in this area also requires the elimination of overspecified resources. The unskilled administrative worker should go along with his blue-collar counterpart. Many administrative technologies are poorly accredited and some are perhaps phony—pseudoskills in handling some more or less complex procedure. All we need to do is change the procedure and these "skills" will no longer be needed. It is not clear that the rapid expansion of administrative overhead in recent years has contributed to productivity, suggesting that some of this expansion may not have been technically justified, but rather that it represents organizational slack made possible by increased productivity due to other causes.[22]

Administrative activities should be dispersed and decentralized down to the level of the innovative area. This will allow administrative personnel also to become part of integrative problem-solving groups rather than resentful onlookers sharpshooting from the outside.[23] The innovative organization is innovative throughout, ont only in certain segregated jurisdictions. The innovative insights of the engineer, the research scientist, the machine tender, the administrative expert—all are needed. Perhaps part of administrative work could be decentralized down to the individual level so that everyone would have to do a few things for himself. If responsibilities and jurisdictions are occasionally exchanged, as suggested above, administrative responsibilities should be included in such exchanges. To paraphrase a famous expression, administrative work is too important to be left entirely to administrators.

Resistance to suggestions of this kind will be especially strong in the production-control–

oriented monocratic organization. However, the reevaluation of the relative importance of managerial and nonmanagerial activities and the declining emphasis on extrinsic rewards, both implied in increasing professionalization of organizations, will reduce this resistance. The "need to control" is an almost inevitable psychological product of the structured field which the modern bureaucratic organization constitutes. If we alter that field, we alter the product.

Our emphasis on the need for free resources, time, indulgency with regard to controls, decentralization, etc., suggests on the surface that the innovative organization will be a costly one. Maybe we cannot afford a high level of innovation. However, we do not have the knowledge to reach this conclusion. We just do not know. We do not know the value of the novel ideas, processes, and products which might be produced by the innovative organization, and we do not know that our present methods of costing and control are the best approach to achieving low-cost production. Likert's arguments that present methods of cost reduction are superficial and actually increase costs in the long run by impairing the health of the social organism are impressive.[24] It would seem that the overspecification of work would automatically create the need for a costly administrative overhead apparatus to plan, schedule, coordinate, and control so that all the overspecified parts are kept fully meshed and fully occupied. The problem is like the one of keeping inventory costs down when a very large number of items must be kept in inventory.

We cannot say that the organizational structure we have been outlining will be either more or less costly, more or less beneficial to society, but it will be more innovative. We also suspect that it may be a fair projection of the organization of the future.

Although we have come close to saying it, we have not actually said that the innovative organization must be formally pluralistic. At the informal level all organizations are pluralistic. They are coalitions.[25] Formally, however, our bureaucratic organizations are monocratic. What we propose is that greater recognition and legitimacy be given to many of the informal pluralistic aspects of these organizations. Large elements should be left open and undetermined, including aspects of the goal structure. Decision models that limit search to the means for reaching sacred and predetermined goals were more appropriate to an era of information scarcity. Under conditions of information affluence such as exist today, we need to find new goals and values if we are to put all our information to work. It is said that American industry is sixty to a hundred years behind American technology.[26] Models which attempt to fix goals and maximally specify or program all means for reaching them are dangerous to innovation. Closed systems cannot innovate, even though they contain the authority to alter themselves. Whether such authority will be used innovatively depends upon the accidents of personality and placement, upon who gets into the veto system. We are interested in innovative organizations rather than innovative individuals, and such organizations will be more pluralistic and open than our standard bureaucracies.

We have argued that the dynamics of more professionalized organizations will achieve this result. With this emphasis, certain problems of professionalism come into focus as limiting factors: professional jealousy and arrogance toward other specialties, resistance to new specialties, difficulties of interdisciplinary cooperation and communication. Some of these problems can be approached through professional education. Everyone should be taught about the problems and requirements of cooperation in a complex world, not just students of administration. Everyone, not just managers, needs to know how to get along in large, complex organizations.[27] Other problems of professional differentiation will be mitigated with further rationalizing of rewards in modern organizations. Awareness of interdependence is growing, and interdisciplinary cooperation is becoming increasingly successful. (Nowhere is this better illustrated than in many business administration or industrial relations schools and departments.) Integrative organizational arrangements can do much, and anything else that facilitates interdisciplinary communication and problem solving can be effective also.

Some caveats with regard to increasing professional differentiation (elsewhere we have called it "personal specialization") are based on confusion. It is said that professional specialists have debilities, such as "trained incapacity" or "tunnel vision," and that, therefore, we ought to be turning out "generalists."[28] However, specialization is a fact, not a proposal. It occurs in a free society because of the felt needs of individuals as they face the problems of modern life. Furthermore, we all have "trained incapacity" and "tunnel vision," because we are all specialists—that is, we are all either specialists or ignoramuses. The generalist is a figment of the imagination, although we all occasionally fill generalist roles (that is, we participate in problem solving in subject areas about which we are largely ignorant). The exclusive association of debilities like "trained incapacity" and "tunnel vision" with doctors, lawyers, engineers, and scientists is based upon a profound confusion.

Our population is rapidly being upgraded. We should look forward to a not distant time when a majority of the people in organizations will be college graduates. This great equalizing of abilities within organizations will have enormous effects upon all aspects of organizational experience. Most of these people will not be denied "success"; they will simply redefine it. Power, status, and other extrinsic rewards will be more equalized. More dignified treatment will be demanded and, we expect, given. The role relations of superior and subordinate will be altered beyond recognition. These and many more changes will alter the organization in a direction which approaches the requirements of the innovative organization. All these changes are now going on. It is likely that organizations are becoming more innovative.[29]

NOTES

[1] Victor Thompson, *Modern Organization* (New York: Alfred A. Knopf, Inc., 1961), chap. 3.

[2] The arguments for dispersing science throughout the federal administration rather than concentrating all science-supporting activities in a single national agency like the National Science Foundation are also the arguments for dispersing R&D rather than segregating it in a single unit of an organization. "We need to see that it [science] is infused into the program of every department and every bureau," as Don Price said. To which we add, "and every division and every branch," etc. See his *Government and Science* (New York: New York University Press, 1954), p. 63 and chap. II in general. The Chicago Board of Education recently established the position of Assistant Superintendent for Integration. But of course integrationists want integrative thinking throughout the School Board organization—not just in a Department of Integration—even as Mr. Price urged scientific thinking throughout the federal government—not just in a Department of Science. This "pin-pointing of responsibility" is a typical amateur reaction to organization problems. It is not based on hard knowledge of organizational phenomena.

[3] Peter M. Blau and W. Richard Scott, *Formal Organizations* (San Francisco: Chandler Publishing Company, 1962), pp. 60–74.

[4] See Rollo May, *The Meaning of Anxiety* (New York: The Ronald Press Company, 1950), esp. pp. 181–189, and A. H. Maslow, *Motivation and Personality* (New York: Harper and Brothers, 1954), chap. 5.

[5] The importance of this combination of problem challenge plus personal self-confidence is extensively documented in David C. McClelland, *The Achieving Society* (Princeton, N.J.: D. Van Nostrand Company, Inc., 1961).

[6] A fairly large part of the literature is summarized in Morris I. Stein and Shirley J. Heinze, *Creativity and the Individual* (Glencoe, Ill.: The Free Press, 1960). The relation between scientific productivity and freedom is documented in R. W. Gerard, *Mirror to Physiology: A Self-survey of Physiological Science* (Washington: American Physiological Society, 1958), and D. C. Pelz, "Motivation of the Engineering and Research Specialist", *General Management Series*, American Management Association, no. 186, 1957, pp. 25–46.

[7] See Eric Hoffer, *The Ordeal of Change* (New York: Harper and Row, Publishers, 1964), pp. 81–82, and Seymour Melman, *Decision-making and Productivity* (Oxford, England: Basil Blackwell & Mott, Ltd., 1958).

[8] William H. Whyte, *The Organization Man* (Garden City, N.Y.: Anchor Books, Doubleday and Company, Inc., 1957).

[9] Norman J. Powell, *Personnel Administration in Government* (Englewood Cliffs, N.J.: Prentice-Hall, Inc., 1956), pp. 438–444. Powell believes that suggestion-box systems are better than no communication with rank and file at all. Because of disputed authorship of suggestions, the TVA decided to give only group (noncash) awards.

[10] Tom Burns and G. M. Stalker, *The Management of Innovation* (London: Tavistock Publications, 1959). See also Gordon and Becker, *op. cit.*

[11] Some of this evidence is reviewed in Blau and Scott, *op. cit.*, chap. 5.

[12] The evidence is reviewed in Cecil A. Gibb, "Leadership," in Gardner Lindzey, ed., *Handbook of Social Phychology* (Reading, Mass.: Addison-Wesley Publishing Company, Inc., 1954), vol. II, pp. 877–917. See also the leadership studies included in Dorwin Cartwright and Alvin Zander, eds., *Group Dynamics*, 2d ed. (Evanston, Ill.: Row, Peterson and Company, 1962), part 5.

[13] Andre L. Delbecq, "Leadership in Business Decision Conferences" (unpublished Ph.D. dissertation, Indiana University, Bloomington, 1963).

[14] See Irving Goffman, "Characteristics of Total Institutions," in Maurice R. Stein, Arthur J. Vidich, and David Manning White, eds., *Identity and Anxiety* (Glencoe, Ill.: The Free Press, 1960), pp. 449–479.

[15] Any sacrifice of organizational goals in the interests of individuals or groups within the organization represents the personal appropriation of administrative resources. Cyert and March define organizations in terms of personal appropriation of administrative resources, that is, as coalitions. See Richard M. Cyert and James G. March, *A Behavioral Theory of the Firm* (Englewood Cliffs, N.J.: Prentice-Hall, Inc., 1963), pp. 27–28.

For various forms in which this ancient administrative phenomenon survives, see Victor A. Thompson, "Bureaucracy in a Democracy," in Roscoe Martin, ed., *Public Administration and Democracy* (Syracuse, N.Y.: Syracuse University Press, forthcoming).

[16] See Victor A. Thompson, "Administrative Objectives for Development Administration", *Administrative Science Quarterly*, vol. 9, no. 1 (June, 1964), pp. 91–108.

[17] For the best statement of the differences between early and modern administrative behavior, see Fred W. Riggs, "Agraria and Industria: Toward a Typology of Comparative Administration," in William J. Siffin, ed.,

Toward the Comparative Study of Public Administration (Bloomington: Indiana University Press, 1959), pp. 23–116.

[18] M. Scott Meyers, "The Management of Motivation to Work," (unpublished report on a motivation research project at Texas Instrument Company.) See also Frederick Herzberg, Bernard Mausner, and Barbara Snyderman, *The Motivation to Work* (New York: John Wiley and Sons, Inc., 1959).

[19] See *Efficiency Rating Systems for Federal Employees, Hearings before the Subcommittee of the Committee on Post Office and Civil Service on S. Res. 105*, 80th Cong., 2d Sess., (1948). Powell says, "Some personnel men are edging close to the position that the service rating is a useless tool. In the opinion of the writer that position is well taken," *op. cit.*, p. 390.

[20] See Maphaus Smith, "An Empirical Scale of the Prestige Status of Occupations," *American Sociological Review*, April, 1963; Delbert C. Miller and William H. Form, *Industrial Sociology* (New York: Harper and Brothers, 1951), pp. 367–369; Alex Inkeles and Peter H. Rossi, "National Comparisons of Occupational Prestige," in Seymour Martin Lipset and Neil J. Smelser, eds., *Sociology: The Progress of a Decade* (Englewood Cliffs, N.J.: Prentice-Hall, Inc., 1961), pp. 506–516; and National Opinion Research Center, "Jobs and Occupations: A Popular Evaluation," in Reinhard Bendix and Seymour Martin Lipset, *Class, Status and Power* (Glencoe, Ill.: The Free Press, 1953).

[21] Classification "science" developed in a desk class age and assumes overspecified jobs, *i.e.*, task specialization. It also stresses physical rather than mental programs, another sign of its backward orientation since the development of knowledge moves ever away from physical programs to more and more mental ones. For example, note the following instruction on the Baltimore Civil Service Commission position classification questionnaire: "Under item 11 describe the specific kinds of work you do, using a separate sentence for each physical or mental activity required to accomplish your work. . . . Start each sentence with the pronoun 'I' followed immediately by an action verb in the present tense." A reply which stated "I think" or "I create" would be regarded as facetious.

The "duties" approach, task specialization, rejects personal specialization and hence professionalism. It is based on the concept of labor as a commodity. Personal specialization (professionalism) is based on the new concept of investment in human capital. [See Gary S. Becker, *Human Capital* (New York: Columbia University Press, 1964).] The cost of this capital stays the same even though it is underutilized. We need to know the social cost of the underutilization. The only way to know this is to require the user to pay the full price (cost) of human capital—*e.g.*, professional salaries—regardless of how it is being used (what the professional is asked to do). If a doctor is used as a janitor he should still be paid a doctor's salary. The hostility of position classification to this point of view should be obvious. To it, the human being has no capital value. It is as though the value of a hammer changed from moment to moment depending upon what it was being used for.

[22] See Seymour Melman, "The Rise of Administrative Overhead in the Manufacturing Industries of the United States, 1899–1947," *Oxford Economic Papers*, vol. 3, (1951), and *Dynamic Factors in Industrial Productivity* (Oxford, England: Basil Blackwell & Mott, Ltd., 1956). Blau and Scott conclude that "it remains a moot question whether or under which

conditions an enlarged administrative machinery contributes to productive efficiency," *op. cit.*, p. 214.

23 Victor A. Thompson, *The Regulatory Process in OPA Rationing* (New York: King's Crown Press, 1950), pp. 286–292.

24 Rensis Likert. "Motivation and Increased Productivity," *Management Record*, vol. 18, no. 4 (April, 1956), p. 128.

25 Cyert and March, *op. cit.*

26 From a paper by Joseph Harrington, Jr. presented to the Joint Economic Committee. See *New Views on Automation*, Joint Economic Committee, 86th Cong., 2d Sess., 1960, p. 44.

27 "It is not a question of a gap between the humanistic and the scientific-technological cultures [as Sir Charles Snow said]. . . . It is, rather a matter of creating and establishing a third culture, a culture of deeper civil understanding. . . . It is . . . not an integration of the humanistic and natural science cultures of which [we] stand in need but an integration of the professional and the civil culture." Edward Shils, "Demagogues and Cadres in the Political Development of the New States," in Lucien Pye, ed., *Communication and Political Development* (Princeton, N.J.: Princeton University Press, 1963), p. 76.

28 This position seems to be especially associated with traditionally educated political scientists and others in the humanities. See for example, Herber Kaufman's review of *Modern Organization* in the *Administrative Science Quarterly*, March, 1962. On the contrary, empirical studies show that the specialized professional-turned-administrator adjust to his new role easily enough. "The scientist manages well the transition from researcher to administrator." Lewis C. Mainzer, "The Scientist As Public Administrator," *The Western Political Quarterly*, vol. XVI, no. 4 (December, 1963). After all, political scientists, historians, philosophers, and literature students are all highly specialized. About the only way to find a manager who is not a specialist is to find one with no education beyond high school. The question is not whether the education of the manager is to be specialized but whether it is to be relevant to any of the duties he will perform. The British say it should be irrelevant because a gentleman's education must be occupationally irrelevant. Traditionalists often follow the British on this point as they do on others (i.e., Parliamentary government, strong two-party system, etc.). There are signs that the British are becoming disillusioned with their "generalist", amateur administrators. See Robert Presthus, "Decline of the Generalist Myth," *Public Administration Review*, vol. 24, no. 4 (December, 1964), pp. 211–216, and "British Amateurs and American Experts: Bureaucratic Theory Undone", a paper prepared for the 1965 meetings of APSA in Washington, D.C., September 8–11.

29 Morris Janowitz discusses the growth of innovative capacity in military organization. Morris Janowitz, *The Professional Soldier* (Glencoe, Ill.: The Free Press, 1960).

31.

HUMAN VALUES, MODERN ORGANIZATIONS, AND EDUCATION

RALPH A. SMITH

The objectives must determine the organization or else the organization will determine the objectives. *Cardinal Principles of Secondary Education, 1918.*

This essay presents an appraisal of modern forms of organization and their effects on human behavior. "Appraisal" here means a kind of value analysis or value criticism. In particular it implies the clarification of the basic purpose patterns of organizations and the significance of such clarification for educational administration. If value analysis centers on the notion of *purpose*, it is because knowledge of purposes, or what may be called *telic* knowledge, yields a standard of achievement and thus criteria for judging success and failure. Telic knowledge is not factual or objective in the commonly accepted sense. Rather it is normative knowledge about the values and purposes which *ought* to govern a domain of thought and action, and hence implicitly it suggests some of the conditions required for realizing value in a domain. The propriety of calling an understanding of values "knowledge" will be discussed in the last part of this essay.[10,11]

The need for value studies of school organization is underscored by the realization that the juxtaposition of managerial and educational functions in the school setting tends toward the dominance of the coordinating and supervising elements and a consequent distrust of personal initiative and freedom. Indeed, there are grounds for concluding that the way in which we organize and operate our schools—

with their undue emphasis on chain of command, stifling bureaucracy, and excessive supervision—is anathema to the educative process.[20] Thus, if we pose to the schools what may be called the fundamental humanistic question—What measure of man does this situation propose?—the school's answer must be less than satisfactory; and the degree of the unsatisfactoriness of the answer is the extent to which schooling is dehumanizing. Before considering in more detail the nature of school organization and the type of value analysis relevant to it, it might be helpful to recall some of the principal tenets of the humanistic tradition, or of that attitude of mind known as *humanism*.[14,15,19] In an age of accelerating change, quickening obsolescence, and increasing mechanization, we are in danger of forgetting the sources and distinctive character of our guiding ideals.

The most obvious idea associated with humanism is concern with the individual in his secular estate. Humanism, however, expresses its concern with the individual in a special way: it is concerned with shaping and molding the individual in light of a consciously pursued ideal of human nature. Accordingly, it is the role of the community, and of education in general, to aim at the making of a higher type of person. Werner Jaeger emphasizes the point that humanism starts with the ideal and not with the private, subjective self, even though the quality and freedom of the individual in the state are its ultimate goal.[19] Humanism thus seeks to educate man into his true form, his real and genuine nature. As an aesthetic program it seeks nothing less than the creation of man as a work of art, and it is an active awareness of a standard by which to evaluate its artistry which distinguishes humanism's efforts. Now if an ideal of humanity which all are bound to imitate provides the model, *paideia*—a complex Greek idea connoting the values of civilization, culture, tradition, literature, and most of all, education—comprises the means by which the ideal is to be approached. What does humanism look like in the concrete? Moses Hadas relates an incident from the *Iliad* which illustrates the humanistic concern in generic form:

> The normal form of divine intervention, in Homer, is not by importing a miracle to change the normal course of nature but by causing an individual to operate at his highest capacity. So at the beginning of the *Iliad* when Achilles has half-drawn his sword to attack Agamemnon in open meeting, Athena appears to gaze into his eyes (it is important to notice that no man else saw her) and he bethinks himself that there are better ways for expressing his anger and returns his sword to its scabbard. Athena had not held his wrist; his action was his own.[15]

Hadas goes on to suggest that the highpoint in all of Western literature occurs when Achilles prevails over his own powerful impulses to abuse the body of Hector and returns it to Priam for proper burial.

If we like, we may see the superintending power of Athena and Achilles' response as one of the first expressions of a humane supervisory-client relationship which, in principle, is expressed whenever one person or group helps another to give appropriate form to his experience. This in brief is the essence of the Greek ideal of culture and education, what is classic about it. Man should always strive to achieve, but in so doing he must clothe his acts in appropriate form. Achilles falls from grace when he loses his style. Humanism thus emphasizes a cluster of interrelated ideas: the idea of man the measure, which implies an ideal of humanity; the aspiring toward that ideal, or the striving for excellence; and human limitation, imposed by the restrictions of external fate. The important point for this discussion is that humanism exhorts man "to operate at his highest capacity."

People in modern organizations are denied the wisdom and guidance of the gods. In their place we have created and elevated to high status a vast pantheon of managers and administrators and invested them with godlike controls. Does the school administrator in fulfilling his role of placing the organization of the school at the service of the educative process help individuals to operate at their highest capacities? Or does the school's bureaucratic structure impede this goal's attainment? Further, are the requirements of larger organizational forms in industry and government essential elements of school organization? If so, can the schools avoid being the mere projection of technical procedures which emerged in response to the distinctive needs of industrial growth and not predominantly educational goals? Do the purpose patterns of corporations and schools therefore imply different types of organization? Before a prognosis is made for the schools, it will be useful to consider empirical studies dealing with the purported purposes and effects of modern forms of organizations on human behavior primarily in the factory and office setting. An instance of imaginative literature will also be considered. The empirical writings will be subsumed under the labels of scientific management, human relations, and structuralism.[8] Franz Kafka's *The Castle* will provide the literary illustration.[2]

Scientific management, an influential movement in the earlier part of the century, viewed human transactions within industrial organizations from the standpoint of the formal organization and the managerial function and assumed no necessary incompatibility between the demands of organization and the needs of individuals. Conceiving motivation in basically economic terms, the personal fulfillment of workers was believed to be in direct proportion to the amount of their paychecks. Scientific management thus was conceived as creating devices which enabled workers to give expression to their economic drives. Tied to a theory of economic motivation was a conception of specialization and division of labor and a network of authority which extended from the centers of power and decision making at the top of the organizational pyramid to the bottom.

Scientific management was a powerful instrument in achieving the goals of the formal organization, and its emphasis on technical rationality in the achievement of greater efficiency can be discerned today in the use and application of systems analysis and operations research techniques in industry and government, and also in the development of engineering models for curriculum design and innovation in education. Its ideology and methods, moreover, were attractive to school administrators constantly under pressure from predominantly business-minded school boards.[5] Scientific management accordingly contributed a major if not altogether distinguished chapter to the history of educational administration.[6] It failed to account, however, as later theorists were to point out, for the actual complexities of men and organizations, and in fact it did not produce the economically contented worker in the smoothly running organization. The emphasis on technical rationality and the primacy of the formal organization encountered increasing opposition.

Recognizing the oversimplified view of human nature held by scientific management, human relations sought to meet a variety of human needs, especially those involving the more emotional, nonrational, and unplanned aspects of organizational life. In contrast to scientific management it focused on the informal rather than the formal elements of organization, and instead of trying to persuade workers to mesh their efforts and goals with the latter, it urged the formation of workers' social groups which stressed participation, communication, and leadership. If scientific management conjured up an image of a blueprint with precise specifications to be adhered to, human relations connoted a working society of friends and communal feeling. Human relations theorists hypothesized that new forms of social groupings and institutional arrangements caused by industrialism would destroy earlier forms of solidarity, and that what social change had set asunder, the place of employment should preserve and restore. The same notion appeared in Dewey's idea of the school as an embryonic community. Although different in many ways from scientific management, especially in tone, style, and basic perspective,

human relations was one with scientific management in holding to the noninevitability of conflict between worker satisfaction and organizational effectiveness. Human relations thus sought ways by which the emotional satisfactions of the worker could be maximized while at the same time his efforts contributed to the goals of the organization. Human relations, an influential movement in both business and education, is still a pervasive feature of the contemporary scene.

Both scientific management and human relations, however, failed to deal adequately with the elements of conflict and strain in modern organizations. It remained for an approach called structuralism to isolate and project these characteristics of stress. Structuralism is at once an ideological critique of earlier theories, especially of human relations, and a method of study and analysis which seeks to understand the functional interdependence of units within organizations and the relations of organizations to external forces. Structuralism further attempts to synthesize the chief strands of scientific management and human relations, trying to find a proper place for both the formal and the informal aspects of organizations. It has also spawned comparative studies of the ways in which organizations are more or less effective in achieving their goals, whatever they may be. Most pertinent to this discussion, however, is structuralism's recognition of inevitable conflict and its role in organizational life. It raises in a new context the question of whether or not the demands of organization are in basic conflict with the needs of individuals. Does the existence of such conflict intensify worker dissatisfaction?

Current studies and interpretations of modern organizations, such as those by Kenneth Galbraith,[9] continue to clarify the functional requirements of the so-called mature corporation, especially how the built-in technological imperatives of planning, specialization, coordination, capital input, and control of market demand affect a complex system of motivation, and also how the internal logic of the modern corporation inhibits commitment to nontechnological goals, such as aesthetic experience. However, new understanding of the nature of power and decision making prompts reconsideration of the problem of worker satisfaction. Especially the realization that power passes to those in the organization with specialized skills and knowledge—that its locus in other words is no longer exclusively the executive suite—has made it appear probable that work is becoming more interesting. It may thus be possible for workers not only to identify with the goals of the organization but also to achieve a sense of personal fulfillment in doing so. Although the extremes of mindless conformity and destructive striving connoted by such expressions as "organization man," "other-directedness," and "rat race" are real enough, they may not exhaust the catalog of human types and relationships in today's organizations.

The foregoing has considered modern organizations and their effects on human behavior from the point of view of the social sciences, but nowhere have alternatives to humane types of human associations been portrayed more vividly than in imaginative literature. Studies of the modern organization do not usually refer to the aesthetic insights of the artist, but if it is conceded that there is an aesthetic way of knowing phenomena,[4,16,25] then I think the reflections of organizational life in the arts are legitimate data and should not be overlooked.

In an examination of four contemporary novels, Kenneth D. Benne indicates how various writers characterize the nature of life within bureaucracies, and he takes the predicament of K. in Franz Kafka's The Castle as a classic negative example. K.'s career is described as consisting of continual efforts to find his way up through the graded ranks of the castle's bureaucracy to someone who can validate his role and status, but such efforts are persistently thwarted. Consequently, what is basically a limited vocational demand is transformed into a total demand, which perverts and distorts the full range of K.'s choices and acts. The castle's denial of his desperate

quest for identity renders his striving pathetic, and in the end K. is completely isolated from all human contact, his self sacrificed to the Moloch who lives in the castle. The fate of K. is thus a warning of what to avoid when designing and operating organizations. In this respect The Castle conveys a value judgment regarding a type of human predicament which is all the more convincing because of its persuasive form. Homer, it will be recalled, also made value judgments about the acts of men, but the "managerial hierarchy" of the Iliad preserved a humane element which on occasion enabled men to realize their inherent nobility. The bureaucracy of the castle, on the other hand, was indifferent to human worth and significance.

It is the convergence of the findings of modern social science and artistic criticism which presses the pessimistic conclusion that, as presently constituted and operated, all is not well with regard to human values in modern organizations. And yet it is the manner of operating modern organizations that is at issue and not the inevitability of dehumanization. Many of the striking characteristics of modern organizations—for example, an outmoded structure of authority and excessive supervision—are not essential ones. There are organizational units in modern society, such as research and development teams in industry and government, voluntary associations of many different types, and certain arrangements in higher education, which occasion collective effort in the pursuit of organizational objectives while granting degrees of personal fulfillment and achievement. The common complaints of those in the schools, however, suggest that the conditions which govern the foregoing types of association are not yet sufficiently operative in the schools.

Thus far the nature of modern organizations and their effects on human behavior have been examined from the vantage point of what at the beginning was called a value perspective. Accordingly, the discussion has centered on the human side of organizations, on whether or not modern organizations exact too high a human cost. As an ideal against which to assess life within organizations, some of the principle tenets of the humanistic tradition were recalled. In particular, it was asked if modern organizations help persons to operate at their highest capacity. The answers of scientific management, human relations, and structuralism were then considered, as well as an instance of imaginative literature. The generally pessimistic conclusion reached was qualified by new insights regarding the nature and locus of power and decision making in the modern corporation. A few more words about the nature of value inquiry and knowledge will now pick up the strand of the opening paragraph.

To urge that educational administration be sensitive to values and conceive them humanistically is empty exhortation without some indication of how values become functional in institutional arrangements. There is reason to believe that administration theorists, along with others involved in empirical inquiry, are uncertain about the appropriateness of value questions to their professional interests because of the traditional fact-value dichotomy. It is frequently held that matters of good and evil, of the "ought" of human action, are inaccessible to empirical treatment because they are held to be a priori, to be grasped only by an intuition properly attuned to The Good and hence are incapable of demonstration. Or it is thought that values are purely private and subjective, mere utterances of personal preference incapable of public verification.

Both positions are extreme and may be meliorated by a third which proposes that subjective, private values are only one kind of values. Reflection and observation reveal that many values are public, commonly held, and consequently potentially open to discussion and criticism. The possibility of values being objective becomes evident once it is conceded that a good need not be The Good, intrinsic and absolute, but may be a *telic* value, that is, good for some ongoing enterprise, or good in relation to a purpose.

Such a view presupposes that each domain of human activity, so long as it is purposive activity, has a distinctive telic structure, a pattern of purposes which can and should be subjected to methodical inquiry, clarification, and description. This investigation into purposes would presuppose great factual knowledge of the field in question, an understanding of the purposes and goals actually operating, as well as an awareness of a domain's unrealized value possibilities, that is, the values and purposes which ought to be insisted upon. The translation of purposes into procedures would require further relevant types of knowledge, but such translation would be more rational and justifiable because of prior value inquiries.

This conception of value inquiry is applicable to any domain of purposive activity. Two questions, however, remain. First of all, granted that value inquiry through empirical methods is a possibility, how much attention should it receive within a particular field? Secondly, granted that a telic pattern can be constructed for a domain and significance attached to whatever conduces to this telic structure, what justifies *that* structure? Fortunately neither question proves particularly troublesome when applied to educational administration. What needs to be kept in mind is the fact that the domain here being discussed is not autonomous; it is *educational* administration, a subfield of the larger domain of education and hence closely in harmony with the purposes of education. Education, moreover, is obviously and preeminently a value enterprise. Its outcomes are not properly construed as contributions to national defense or as measurable increases in the Gross National Product. Education is the process by which certain broad kinds of values—intellectual, moral, and aesthetic—become instrumental in the lives of individuals and society. Since values play so dominant a role in education, or ought to, it is only natural to expect value inquiry to play an important role in educational administration. Does value inquiry currently constitute an important part of the subdomain of educational administration?

The second question concerns the higher-order values which would lend justification to a telic structure descriptive of the value possibilities of educational administration. These justifying values, of course, are the values of education as such. The perennial debate over just what these values are—what education, in other words, is supposed to be all about—does not mean that value inquiry in educational subdomains is doomed to founder. For there is one educational value in our particular form of society which debate does not abrogate: concern with the sovereignty and dignity of the individual and commitment to the realization of his uniquely human capacities. This is to say that the dominant values of education are humanistic, and educational administration is accordingly enlisted in their service. Educational administration is thus justified by its success in promoting these human rather than distinctively organizational ends. I take it that this is what the authors of *Cardinal Principles* had in mind, and the growth of modern organizations makes their warning even more appropriate today than it was fifty years ago.

In concluding I am conscious of having stated a truism: that educational administration should serve education humanistically conceived. Does the educational administrator need to be told this? If not, why take up space reiterating the obvious? Perhaps one reason is that we cannot always tell when the assumptions, procedures, and logic of one domain are beginning to overlap and transform the business of another domain with a different purpose. The danger in this, of course, is that in adapting certain kinds of organizational methods and procedures, say from industry to education, the differences between the purposes and goals of industry and those of education will be sloughed over or insufficiently appreciated. The educational process will come to be seen, as it was in the earlier part of the century when scientific management held sway, as involving the coordination of staff, students, and materials in technical procedures, as so much input and output which can be readily identified, controlled, and measured. Such cautionary statements are not unwarranted. The language of science and the computer are already pervasive, and the increasing "humanization" of machines implies that the mechanical conception of a self-regulatory system guided by symbolic feedback is becoming a paradigm of human behavior.[1,11] The humanist points out that this is an anthropomorphic error and that men, not machines, provide the proper models for emulation. There is a tendency, in other words, to forget that education is a distinctive domain and not business, economics, politics, engineering, art, or science. Growth, for example, means something different in each of these domains. So perhaps it is not redundant after all to emphasize that domains are not reducible to each other, that while domain purposes may in certain respects overlap and while one domain usually has implications for another, the purposes of domains are not identical. But just what the purposes and goals of education are needs continuous clarification and articulation. This, I suppose, is the import of this essay.

REFERENCES

[1] Barzun, Jacques. *Science: The Glorious Entertainment.* New York: Harper and Row, 1964. Chap. 9.

[2] Benne, Kenneth D. "Man and Moloch." *Journal of Social Issues.* **20:** 97–115 (January 1964).

[3] Broudy, Harry S. "Conflicts in Values." In Ohm, R. E., and Monahan, W. C. (eds.). *Educational Administration: Philosophy in Action.* Norman: University of Oklahoma Press, 1965.

[4] Broudy, Harry S. "The Structure of Knowledge in the Arts." In Ralph

A. Smith (ed.). *Aesthetics and Criticism in Art Education*. Chicago: Rand McNally & Company, 1966.

[5] Callahan, Raymond E. *Education and the Cult of Efficiency*. Chicago: University of Chicago Press, 1962.

[6] Cremin, Lawrence A. *The Transformation of the School*. New York: Alfred A. Knopf, Inc., 1961. Chap. 6.

[7] Etzioni, Amitai (ed.). *Complex Organizations: A Sociological Reader*. New York: Holt, Rinehart and Winston, Inc., 1961.

[8] Etzioni, Amitai. *Modern Organizations*. Englewood Cliffs, N.J.: Prentice-Hall, Inc., 1964.

[9] Galbraith, John Kenneth. *The New Industrial State*. Boston: Houghton Mifflin Company, 1967.

[10] Gotshalk, D. W. *Patterns of Good and Evil*. Urbana: University of Illinois Press, 1963.

[11] Gotshalk, D. W. *Human Aims in Modern Perspective*. Yellow Springs, Ohio: Antioch Press, 1966.

[12] Gotshalk, D. W. "Aesthetic Education as a Domain." *Journal of Aesthetic Education*. 2:43–50 (January 1968).

[13] Griffiths, D. E., *Administrative Theory*. New York: Appleton-Century-Crofts, 1959.

[14] Hadas, Moses. *Humanism*. New York: Haper & Brothers, 1960.

[15] Hadas, Moses. "Humanism: The Continuing Ideal." *Jennings Scholar Lectures, 1965–66*. Cleveland, Ohio: The Educational Research Council of Greater Cleveland.

[16] Halpin, Andrew W. "Ways of Knowing." *Administrative Theory as a Guide to Action*. Chicago: University of Chicago Press, 1960.

[17] Halpin, Andrew W. "Muted Language." *School Review*. 68:85–104 (Spring 1960).

[18] Hanlon, James M. *Administration and Education*. Belmont, Calif.: Wadsworth Publishing Company, 1968.

[19] Jaeger, Werner. *Paideia: The Ideals of Greek Culture*. Three vols. New York: Oxford University Press, 1939, 1945. Introduction, vol. I.

[20] Kimball, Solon T., and McClellan, James E. *Education and New America*. New York: Random House, Inc., 1962. Chap. 9.

[21] McClellan, James E. "Theory in Educational Administration." *School Review*. 68:210–27 (Summer 1960).

[22] McDonald, G. E. "Is the School Administrator Capable of Receiving Guidance from Philosophy?" *Educational Administration and Supervision*. 42:35–67 (October 1956).

[23] Phenix, Philip H. *Philosophy of Education*. New York: Henry Holt and Company, Inc., 1958. Chap. 6.

[24] Smith, Philip G. *Philosophic-Mindedness in Educational Administration*. Columbus: Ohio State University, School of Education, 1956.

[25] Smith, Ralph A. "Aesthetic Criticism: The Method of Aesthetic Education." *Studies in Art Education*. 9:12–31. (Spring 1968).

[26] Walton, John. "The Theoretical Study of Educational Administration." *Harvard Educational Review*. 25:169–78 (Summer 1955).

[27] Walton, John. *Administration and Policy Making in Education*. Baltimore: Johns Hopkins Press, 1959.